We Are All Ourselves

"Why am I me?" The chills and sensations of first being conscious of myself being conscious of myself are still vivid in my memory. I was a ten year old child then, sitting alone in my parents' bedroom, touching my own solid consciousness and playing with it. I was stepping through the looking-glass seeing myself being myself seeing myself being myself . . . tasting infinity.

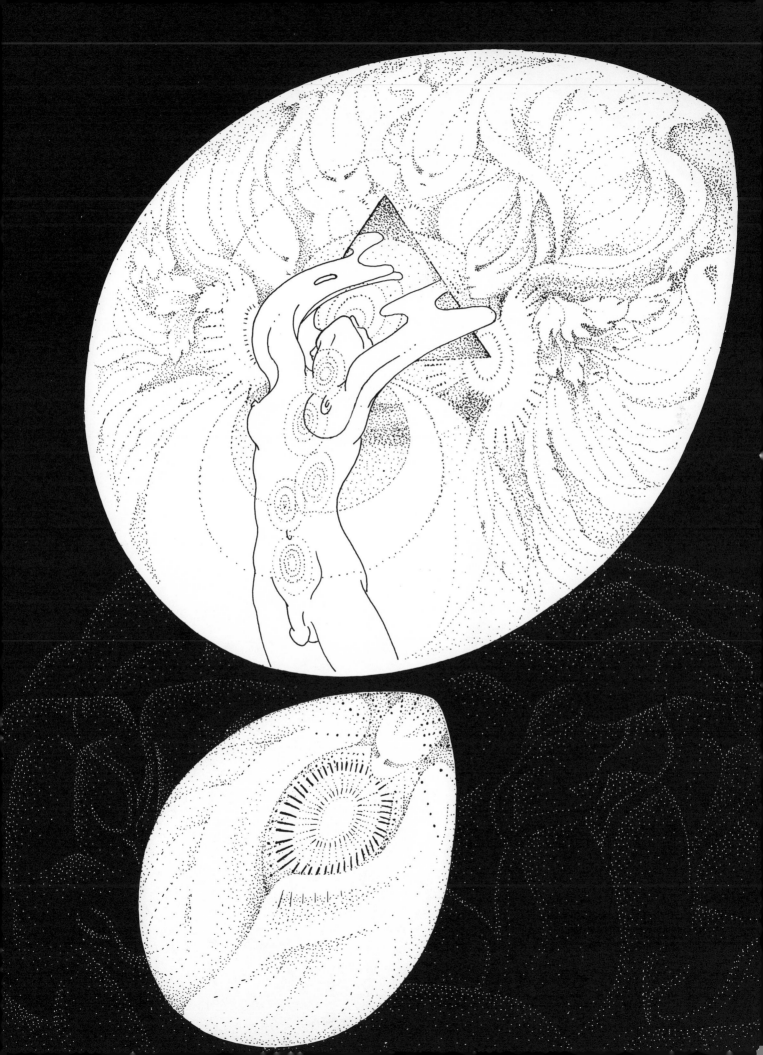

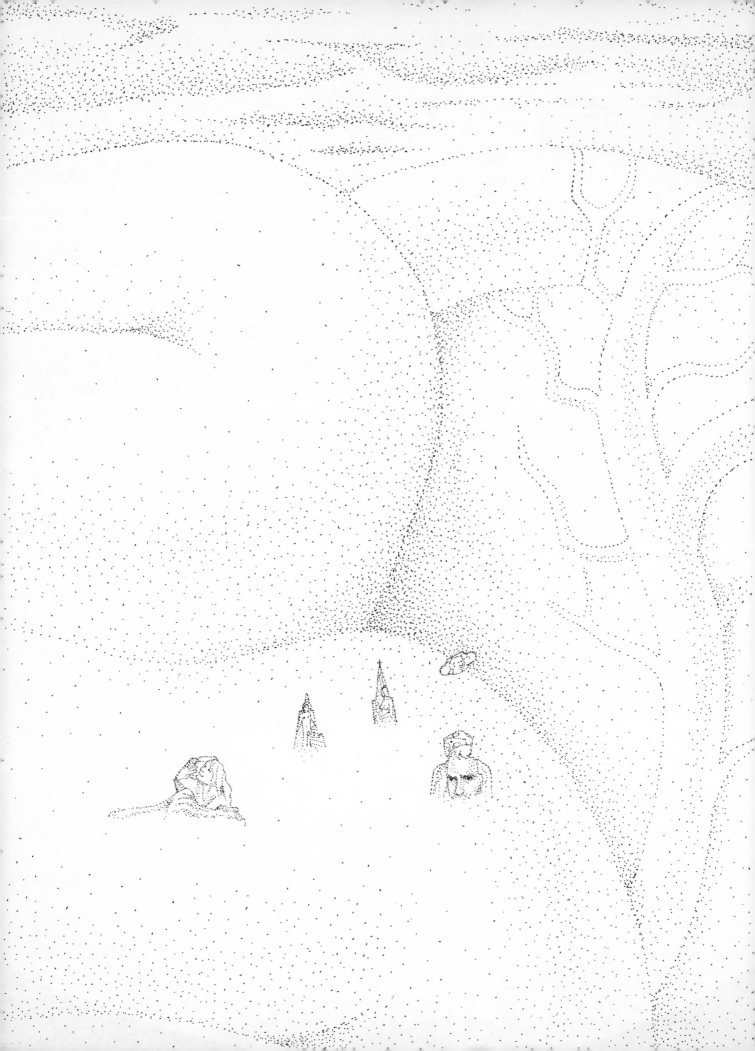

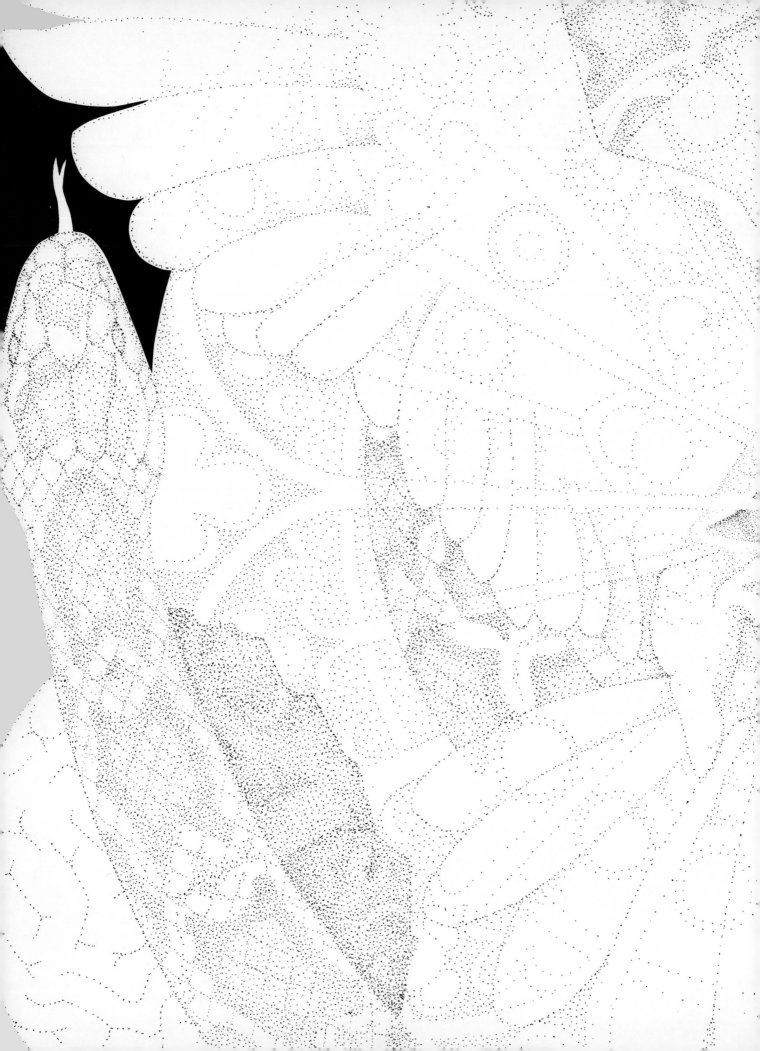

The
Roots

of Consciousness

Psychic Liberation through History, Science and Experience

Jeffrey Mishlove

A RANDOM HOUSE • BOOKWORKS BOOK

First printing, August 1975, 30,000 copies in paperback
Second printing, March 1977, 10,000 copies in paperback

Cover illustration from a painted sculpture by Vijali.*
Typeset by Vera Allen Composition Service, Castro Valley, California
    (special thanks to Vera, her staff and especially Betty)
Printed and bound under the supervision of Dean Ragland, Random House

This book is co-published by   Random House Inc.
                                  201 East 50th Street
                                  New York, N.Y. 10022

                          and   The Bookworks
                                  628 Vincente Avenue
                                  Berkeley, California 94707

Distributed in the United States by Random House and simultaneously published in
Canada by Random House of Canada Limited, Toronto.
Booksellers please order from Random House.

See page 336 for acknowledgment of permissions to quote published sources.

Library of Congress Cataloging in Publication Data

Mishlove, Jeffrey, 1946-
    The roots of consciousness.

    "A Random House/Bookworks book."
    Includes bibliographical references and index.
    1. Psychical research.   2. Occult sciences.
I. Title. [DNLM: 1. Consciousness.   2. Parapsychology.
3. Occultism. BF1031 M678r]
BF1031.M56   133   75-10311
ISBN 0-394-73115-8 pbk.

Manufactured in the United States of America.

*Readers interested in seeing showings of the new and powerful talent of Vijali should contact
P.O. Box 4334, Milpas Sta., Santa Barbara, California 93103 for appointment and information.

DEDICATION

This book only exists as a product of the entire community of beings who have inspired me and whose names can generally be found in the references or index. For *each* I have special feelings.

I would particularly like to acknowledge the participation of Sherry Hogue, whose artwork inside the cover introduces this book and whose love has been a source of delight and fulfillment; Don Gerrard, an unusual publisher of warmth, strength, and resource; James P. Driscoll, Saul-Paul Sirag, and Robert Morris—for their friendship and criticism; Sharon Stein, Maulsby Kimball, Marilee Kernis and Vigali Clark—artists; Henry Dakin, Thelma Moss, Alicia Saunders, Janelle Barlow, Rammurti Mishra, Professor James Harder. Mark and Elizabeth Kuder, David Hoffman, Adrian Boshier, Ray Stanford, Milan Ryzl, Earle Lane, Dr. Jule Eisenbud, Dr. Berthold Schwarz, Dr. Barnard Grad, Professor Ted Mann, Professor William Tiller, Charles Musés, J. B. Rhine, Bill Roll, Dr. Helmut Schmidt, Dr. A. R. G. Owen, *Psychic Magazine*, and the S. F. Theosophical Library for the generosity of their time and resources; Arthur M. Young and Jack Sarfatti, for their friendship and their written contributions. Radio stations KPFA-FM and KSAN-FM as well as the University of California have provided space for me to experiment creatively within an environment of recognition and support. I have also benefited from the practices, the philosophy and the examples of Maharishi Mahesh Yogi, Yogi Bhajan, Werner Erhard, and . . .

You, reading this book now, are the most important source of its creation. Your experience of The Roots of Consciousness within you creates the strongest link between higher intelligence and our mutual environment. This book is dedicated to The Roots of Consciousness which resonate between us all.

Contents

Color Illustrations

Guide to the color plates following page 254.

Plate One

Pranayama Energy Chart showing currents of life energy passing between the body and the cosmos as understood in pranayama yoga. This chart is designed for use as a focus during meditation. (Courtesy of Dr. Rammurti S. Mishra.)

Plate Two

Kundalini Chakra Poster showing the seven centers of psychic perception as depicted in ancient Hindu scriptures. These chakras are associated, but not identical, to the endocrine glands. (Courtesy of Dr. Rammurti S. Mishra.)

Plate Three

Tibetan Tanka depicting an ancient system of astrology. The universe is shown on the stomach of a tortoise. This system integrates the changing cycles of planetary fluctuation with the trigrams of the Chinese *I Ching* or Book of Changes which are shown in the lower left hand corner. (Courtesy of Dorje Ling, San Rafael, Ca.)

Plate Four

River of Light, a watercolor painting by Maulsby Kimball, former Director of the Anthroposophical Society in America, depicting the spiritual worlds as described by the Austrian seer Rudolf Steiner. (Courtesy of Maulsby Kimball.)

Plate Five

Seven layers of the human aura according to a theosophical manuscript published in 1896. Each layer is said to represent finer and finer particles of matter.

Plate Six

Upper-left: The astral body of an average man according to the clairvoyant vision of the Reverend C. W. Leadbeater, originally published in *Man, Visible and Invisible,* New York, 1903.

Upper-right: The astral body of a devotional type individual.

Lower-left: The astral body of a scientific type person.

Lower-right: The astral body of a developed man.

Plate Seven

The aura of the author as portrayed by Berkeley artist and psychic reader Rick Stevens. Three layers of the aura—the etheric, the psychological, and the spiritual—as well as the seven chakras, are shown. Each color and image may be interpreted symbolically.

Plate Eight

Upper-left: The seven chakras with astrological correlations according to the seventeenth century German mystic, Georges Johann Gichtel.

Upper-right: The Seven chakras with connecting cords or *nadis* as described by C. W. Leadbeater. (Courtesy of the Theosophical Publishing House, Adyar, India.)

Lower-left: The naval chakra as seen by Leadbeater. (Courtesy of the Theosophical Publishing House.)

Lower-right: The chakras and the nervous system according to Leadbeater. (Courtesy of the Theosophical Publishing House.)

Plate Nine

''Psychic surgery'' in the Phillipines. Such photographic evidence is insufficient for determining the genuineness of the phenomena. (Courtesy of George Meek and Mrs. Mark Kuder.)

Plate Ten

Firewalking rituals in Taiwan. (Courtesy of Janelle Barlow, Ph.D.)

Upper-right and left: From a ritual witnessed at Da Hsi in August 1971. These coals are red hot, although they may not appear so in daylight.

Center: Preparations for a ritual at Hsin Chuang in October 1971. On the table are ceremonial objects and a bottle of wine for the Taoist diety No-cha. The pile of hot coals is ankle deep and will require several steps to pass through.

Lower-left: Taoist priest in charge of the ritual.

Lower-right: Pile of hot coals with footprints in the evening after the ritual.

Plate Eleven

Kirlian photographs showing states of relaxation and arousal. (Courtesy of Dr. Thelma Moss, U.C.L.A. Center for the Health Sciences.)

Upper-left: Typical fingerpad of a relaxed subject.

Middle-left: Same fingerpad as above with subject in an emotionally aroused state.

Upper-middle: Normal elbow.

Center: Same elbow as above after an accidental shock.

Upper-right: Fingerpad of a subject before smoking marijuana.

Middle-right: Fingerpad of same subject as above during marijuana intoxication.

Lower-left: Fingerpad of a subject before taking alcohol.

Lower-middle: Fingerpad of same subject after nine ounces of bourbon.

Lower-right: Fingerpad of same subject after seventeen ounces of bourbon.

Plate Twelve

Kirlian photographs showing human interactions. (Courtesy of Thelma Moss, Ph.D.)

Upper-left: Baseline of index fingerpad of subject A—no bubbles.

Upper-right: Baseline of index fingerpad of subject B—with bubbles.

Middle-right: Index fingerpads of subjects A and B together, with bubbles on both.

Middle-left: Index fingertips of two subjects during sexual imagery.

Bottom: Index fingertips of two subjects—the subject on the right is visualizing pricking the subject on the left with a needle in the end of the finger.

Plate Thirteen

Kirlian photographs relating to health.

Upper-left: Fingerpad of healer before healing. (Courtesy of Thelma Moss, Ph.D.)

Upper-middle: Fingerpad of patient with chronic kidney disease before healing. (Courtesy of Thelma Moss, Ph.D.)

Middle-left: Fingerpad of healer after performing healing treatment. (Courtesy of Thelma Moss, Ph.D.)

Center: Kidney patient after psychic healing treatment. (Courtesy of Thelma Moss, Ph.D.)

Lower-left: Fingerpad of a healer in a relaxed state. (Courtesy of Mrs. Ethel De Loach.)

Lower-middle: Fingerpad of a healer while thinking of psychic healing. (Courtesy of Mrs. Ethel De Loach.)

Upper-right: Typical fingerpad of a tobacco smoking subject. (Courtesy of Earle Lane.)

Center-right: Typical fingerpad of a non-smoker. (Courtesy of Earle Lane.)

Lower-right: Fingerpad showing a flare associated with the acupuncture point, large-intestine one. (Courtesy of Earle Lane.)

Plate Fourteen

Miscellaneous Kirlian photographs.

Upper-left: Relaxed subject before inhaling nitrous-oxide. Taken with infra-red film. (Courtesy of Earle Lane.)

Second-left: Same subject after inhaling nitrous-oxide. (Courtesy of Earle Lane.)

Third-left: Leaf after being held for about five minutes by an individual with a "brown thumb." (Courtesy of Thelma Moss, Ph.D.)

Lower-left: Same leaf as above before "brown thumb" treatment. (Courtesy of Thelma Moss, Ph.D.)

Upper-middle: Fingerpad of an individual who appears to be aroused. This picture was made by manipulating the distance between the film backing and the electrode, as well as by adjusting finger-pressure on the film. (Courtesy of David Boyers and William Tiller, Stanford University.)

Second-middle: Same fingerpad as above with slightly different electrode placement. The individual is not in a different physiological state. (Courtesy of David Boyers and William Tiller.)

Upper-right: The three colors which generally appear on Kirlian photographs made on ektachrome film, produced by ultra-violet exposure on the front of the film (blue), front and back (white), and only back of the film (red). This suggests that all Kirlian coronas may be in the ultra-violet range. (Courtesy of David Boyers and William Tiller.)

Second-right: Kirlian image photographed from a camera several inches away from a transparent electrode showing only blue and white, in confirmation of the above theory. (Courtesy of David Boyers and William Tiller.)

Third-middle: Sex polarity in plants. The yellow discharge indicates the female section of a longitudinally cross-sectioned piece of *cattleya androgynophore.* (Courtesy of Thelma Moss, Ph.D.)

Lower-middle: Magnetic polarity. The red corners of the magnet indicate the south pole. (Courtesy of Earle Lane.)

Third-right: Barrier interaction between two fingers. The fingerpad on the left has totally disappeared, an effect generally associated with fatigue, anxiety, a trance-like state, or psychological subordination to the partner. The invisible field still has an effect on the other fingerpad, resulting in the "barrier." (Courtesy of Thelma Moss, Ph.D.)

Lower-right: Barrier interaction between the fingerpads of two individuals, perhaps suggesting emotional protectiveness. (Courtesy of Dr. Thelma Moss.)

Plate Fifteen

An enlargement of Ted Serios' color picture of the Denver Hilton Hotel. This is a "thoughtograph" taken while Dr. Jule Eisenbud, of the University of Colorado School of Medicine, held and triggered the model 100 Polaroid camera, which was pointed at the forehead of the psychic Serios. Eisenbud points out that the picture was taken while Serios was trying to produce an image of the Chicago Hilton ("I missed, damn it.") (Courtesy of Jule Eisenbud, M.D.)

Plate Sixteen

Unidentified objects photographed in Yungay, Peru, March 1967. The aura-like glow around the objects, particularly noticeable in the upper-right photograph, makes it unlikely that these images were fraudulently produced. Identical objects have been photographed independently in other parts of the world. (Courtesy of the Aerial Phenomena Research Organization Bulletin, January 1969.)

INTRODUCTION

We derived the name for *The Roots of Consciousness* from a statement by cosmologist Arthur M. Young who cautioned against seeking only the flowers of consciousness. Although flowers provide moments of pleasure and delight, they are soon forgotten after they wilt and die.

The flowers of consciousness are the exquisitely intriguing foliage blooming in psychology's borderland—*telepathy, clairvoyance, precognition, psychokinesis, astrology, astral projection, UFO's, mysticism,* and other *occult* hidden, psi, or inner phenomena. These things may seem strange or super-natural to western man's current ways of thinking—or even non-existent. However, it is our contention that they are not paranormal and therefore unreal or insignificant; indeed they are rooted in the essential core of our cosmic existence, in our cultural history, in our scientific knowledge, and in our social institutions.

For me, the exploration of consciousness really has its ori-gins in sparks of wonderment at my own existence which have recurred many times in different ways. These are the simplest experiences which underlie the science of consciousness—a newly emerging discipline which, like music, art, medicine or physical education, involves intense personal commitment as well as objective understanding.

When consciousness is approached, and its roots in bare existence experienced in this fashion, the flowers can receive sustenance from the entire mind and bear fruits in spiritual realization. This book is designed to satisfy all levels of your consciousness. Read it. Look at it. Close your eyes and taste it with your whole awareness.

One of the profoundest speculations on the origins of consciousness occurs in a hymn from the *Rig Veda*, written over 3,000 years ago, in which the sages search their hearts for the personal, social and cosmic origins of being:

Neither not being nor being was there at that time; there was no air-filled space nor was there sky which is beyond it. What enveloped all? Under whose protection? What was the unfathomable deep water?

Neither was death there, nor even immortality at that time; there was no distinguishing mark of day and night. That One breathed without wind in its own special manner. Other than It, indeed, and beyond, there did not exist anything whatsoever.

In the beginning there was darkness concealed in darkness; all this was an indistinguishable flood of water. That which, possessing life-force, was enclosed by the vacuum, the One, was born from the power of heat from its austerity.

Upon It rose up, in the beginning, desire, which was the mind's first seed. Having sought in their hearts, the wise ones discovered, through deliberation, the bond of being and non-being.

Right across was their dividing line extended. Did the below exist then, was there the above? There were the seed planters, there were the great forces of expansion. Below there was self-impulse, above active imparting.

Who knows it for certain; who can proclaim it here; namely, out of what it was born and wherefrom this creation issued? The gods appeared only later—after the creation of the world. Who knows, then, out of what it has evolved?

Wherefrom this creation has issued, whether He has made it or whether He has not—He who is the superintendent of this world in the highest heaven—He alone knows, or, perhaps, even He does not know.[1]

Imagine all the processes which connect us with the universe.

There is the unfathomably deep water, the *void*, the *absolute*, darkness concealed in darkness, the *unknown*, that which is beyond. From this, through the power of heat was born the *One*. About the unknown void little can be said, although we say that this void permeates everything—including the most solid-appearing objects. Regarding heat, the origin of the One, the science of physics can shed some light. Heat is transmitted by particle-waves called *photons* in the infra-red area of the electromagnetic spectrum. All electromagnetic interactions from radio waves and light to cosmic rays are mediated by photons. This idea perhaps correlates with other creation myths, including the version in *Genesis*, which states that light was the first manifestation from the void. Photons are the basic quantum unit of the action of electromagnetic radiation. They have no mass and no charge. They travel through space at 186,000 miles per second with no loss in energy until they collide with other particles. Imagine that you are a photon travelling through space at the speed of light! If you were to look at your watch, you would, according to the theory of relativity discover that time was standing still. Hence you could travel to the very edges of the known universe without aging a single day, although, to an observer on earth, it would take you three billion years to get there. Thus photons, tiny particle-waves with no mass, no charge, no time, neither matter nor anti-matter, but with a unit spin, constitute the basic quantum of action in physics. In some uncanny way, photons seem to describe the mythical Vedic One which was born out of the void of heat.

In the seventeenth century, the *principle of least action* was discovered to be true of light—and subsequently found to apply to almost all physical phenomena. This principle states that light always follows the path which gets it to its destination in the shortest possible time. To Leibnitz and some more contemporary scientists including Max Planck, this principle evidenced a higher intelligence in nature with a purpose and destiny—as if photons already knew which path to take! This principle has remained somewhat problematic to thinkers who do not want to admit *teleology* or purpose or consciousness into science.[2]

Although photons are said to obey the law of least action, they are also subject to Heisenberg's *principle of uncertainty* or indeterminacy. This means that it is impossible to predict the destination of any given photon, and has led physicists to describe these wave-particles as "packets of uncertainty." Any given uncertainty packet is theoretically located everywhere in the universe, with the probability densities being greater, perhaps, for some particular space-time coordinates. According to the *branching universe theory* in physics, everytime an observation is made, the universe branches in such a fashion that the potentialities which were not observed continue to exist and progress in other dimensions.[3] Imagine yourself existing everywhere in the universe at once—even places where no one sees you! This idea of unpredictability represents a breakdown of the nineteenth century notion of a mechanical determinism which governed all of nature—including human consciousness —and which separated consciousness from experience. Now scientists are beginning to see that the process of observation itself influences the universe. Thus the Uncertainty Principle has introduced the phenomena of perceptual consciousness as problematic in the context of current theories and physicists are beginning to search for a new understanding. I imagine that the day is drawing near when they will find the unifying principle both within themselves and in their laboratories.

Photons, like all known physical phenomena, pulsate or vibrate. Planck's law states that the photon's energy is directly proportional to the frequency of its vibration. The constant of proportionality between the energy of photons and the frequency of vibration is known as *Planck's constant*, or *h*, which is a very important unit in describing wholeness as well as indeterminacy in physics.

A photon, when it is annihilated, is able to create particles of matter and anti-matter which have both mass, charge, and time, such as *electrons* and *positrons*, or *protons* and *anti-protons*. It's tempting to suggest that these particles with their charges represent the principle of desire or attraction, which in the *Vedic* myth arose from the One.

Protons and electrons, of course, are attracted to each other and form the basic constituents of atoms and molecules. Electrons have a negative charge and protons, which are much heavier, have a positive charge. Positrons and anti-protons are particles of what is called anti-matter. In an atom of anti-matter, the light weight positrons orbit around a nucleus which contains negatively charged anti-protons. When particles of matter and anti-matter come into contact with each other, they are annihilated and photons are produced. Physicists suggest that particles of anti-matter move backwards through time. Imagine yourself moving through time like a movie played backwards!

As the extreme energy of the photons becomes somewhat solidified in the form of the mass of protons and electrons and their anti-matter counterparts, the amount of free energy which these particles possess is accordingly reduced. Also the amount of indeterminacy, or unpredictability of these particles, while still great, is less than the photon exhibits. According to Heisenberg's uncertainty principle, the product of uncertainty of the position and momentum of these particles is equal to or greater than Planck's constant, h. In other words, the more certain you are of the position of a particle, the less certain you can be of its momentum, and *vice-versa*

Of course, protons and electrons combine to form *atoms* which have even greater mass and less indeterminacy. There are 106 known different kinds of atoms whose identity is determined by the number of charged particles which have come together. These atoms compose the elements of the periodic table which combine chemically into *molocules* to form all of the substances which we experience in our day-to-day living. The indeterminacy atoms and molecules exhibit is limited to the amounts of energy which they can absorb and release and the times at which they release and absorb this energy, which is in the form of photons. This indeterminacy though very small is real. Consequently scientists no longer believe that atoms and molocules generally behave exactly like the predictable billiard balls of nineteenth century physics. The atoms and molecules of the universe combine to form the stars and the planets and newly discovered fantastic structures in outer-space whose origins and properties are still quite mysterious to us. The expansion of the universe, the nature of the black holes, and the nature of quasars all imply notions of time, space and matter that are quite foreign to the rules of classical Newtonian physics which sometimes seem to guide our daily reality. (More on Newton in the next chapter.)

The small amount of uncertainty which remains in molocules may play an important role in the curious growth properties polymers display. These long molecular chains—such as rubber, cellulose and nylon—seem to anticipate the growth of cellular life itself. Functional polymers such as proteins are the primary constituents of animal life; and the proteins actin and myosin, the primary ingredients of muscle tissue, exhibit properties of animal mobility. Perhaps the most important molecule of all is deoxyribosenucleic acid or DNA. These complex molecules contain in their double-helix structure all of the information necessary for living cells to grow and

FOOD VACUOLE

CONTRACTILE VACUOLE

NUCLEUS

ECTOPLASM

ENDOPLASM

CELL MEMBRANE

Unicellular Organism

function. Some scientists say that these molecules contain within their structure all of the information necessary for the complete development of an organism, such as the human being. This is still very doubtful; however a single DNA molecule can store much more information than is contained in this book. When cells divide, DNA molecules also divide in two and are able to reproduce themselves. DNA molecules are also able to transcribe the information which they contain onto other molecules of ribonucleic acid or RNA. Certain very complex molecules of DNA or RNA combined with protein, called viruses, actually seem to be alive and can reproduce themselves when they are inside of another living organism. However these viruses are quite inert in the free state.

Although science has not yet filled in all of the links in the process of evolution, one can sense a naturalness in the emergence of cellular life from a sea of complex molecules. Unicellular organisms probably constitute the majority of living creatures on earth. Microscopic structures within these cells, called organelles, perform the digestive, respiratory, metabolic and reproductive functions of the organism. While the cells are said to be alive, the *organelles* themselves are not, although this is perhaps questionable in the case of the virus.

When similar kinds of cells group together, *colonies* are formed—such as fungi or algae or sponges. Several different types of cells coming together lead to the formation of different *tissues* within each organism. In more complex creatures, these tissues have joined further into units called *organs*. The most complex organisms contain not only many tissues and organs, but groups of organs may also form one or more structural organizations called *organ systems*.

Ontogeny recapitulates phylogeny. This means that the growth of any individual organism, from conception, follows the same pattern of development as the evolution of that species. Thus when you were an embryo you passed through all the stages of growth in a nine month period, which led to man's three billion year evolution from a single-celled organism.

Beyond organisms of all kinds, higher levels of life may be distinguished in the form of social groupings such as *families*, *hives*, *tribes*, *societies*, *populations*, *species*, and local *communities*. The sum of all living communities represents the ecological system of the whole living world—which in turn interacts with the entire universe.

Human cultural history goes back about five thousand years; however the existence of the *homo sapiens* species can be traced back at least 500,000 years. Thus in some sense it can be said that humanity has evolved through qualitative changes of consciousness during the life of our species

Human beings exhibit free will, a phenomenon reminiscent of the unpredictability photons and sub-atomic wave-particles display. Perhaps, in fact, the highest manifestation consciousness can take lies in a realization of the total creative potential the photon possesses, returning now, with experience of diversity, to the Absolute from which it emerged long ago.

From the evolution of the universe which we have just briefly traced, there seems to emerge patterns, pulsations, vi-

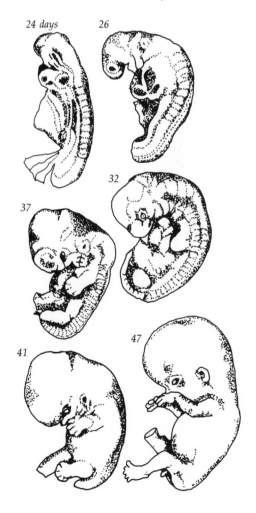

Stages in the Growth of a Human Foetus

24 days   26

32

37

41   47

brations and cycles. The loss of uncertainty, the entrapment of spirit in matter as we descend from the photon to the molecule, seems to be balanced by the increased freedom, the rise of matter into spirit, as we ascent through the plant, animal and human kingdoms. The orchestration of the universe is a most complex and subtle symphony. This book, this moment, is a small part of the harmony of the universe as it comes to understand itself. Imagine that!

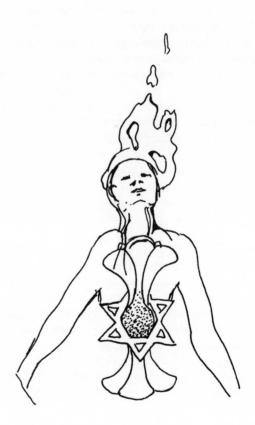

A BRIEF HISTORY OF THE
EXPLORATION OF CONSCIOUSNESS

I

A BRIEF HISTORY OF THE EXPLORATION OF CONSCIOUSNESS

Prehistoric Exploration of Consciousness

The peoples of prehistoric times and primitive cultures have laid the groundwork for modern consciousness exploration. Our knowledge of these groups comes from archeological or anthropological observation. In some cases, researchers have lived for long periods in the wilderness with primitive peoples. We will find that return to the wilderness has been used throughout history to explore the deeper layers of the psyche.

During a week of solitude in the Mt. Shasta National Forest, I experienced a type of consciousness while dancing naked, alone on a glacier, in which the boundaries of my civilized self evaporated and I became part of the ice and the mountain, the forest and the sky. Sherry, whose illustrations introducing this book reflect this mythological connection in a spatial, preverbal fashion, experienced this same awareness of fusion with nature while living alone for 6 months in a cave. Living in this way, we found ourselves becoming sensitive to a natural ebb and flow of rhythms, within ourselves, in nature, and in the sky. We were able to establish a direct awareness of the continuum of consciousness from sleep to waking that included dreams, hypnagogic states, and meditative states. The subtle effects different food substances have upon consciousness became more

3

apparent. Gradually we developed a keen sensitivity even to the alertness of animals.

A natural extension of this sensitivity includes feelings of spiritual presences and telepathic contact with nature, and there is a merging of this reality into the dream life in such a way that consciousness permeates and animates all existence.

The way of perceiving the world which emphasizes the existence of spirits, ghosts, and gods who interact with men and inhabit objects is called *animism*. Animism characterizes virtually all primitive and ancient cultures.[1] In many languages, the word for spirit is also the word for breath—that which leaves the body at death. Spirits could occupy the bodies of living men and animals causing either illness or insanity, but they often imparted higher wisdom. Psychic powers were ascribed to aid from such spirits. Also commonly found in primitive cultures is the correlative belief in a general spiritual force, or *mana*, which permeates all of nature.

A belief in or a sensitivity to life beyond death is indicated by numerous and varied types of ancient burials, beginning with the Mousterian culture in France some 80,000 years ago. Evidence from cave art, dating back at least 30,000 years, suggests caves were used for magical ritual purposes. In certain cases it must have been necessary to crawl for hours through the caves in order to reach the locale of the artwork and related artifacts. It may be that solitude inside such a cavern was an initiation technique used to explore the inner realms of being. Markings on antlers and bones indicate that man made notations of the phases of the moon as long as 30,000 years ago and suggest that the cave rituals and other cultural practices had a seasonal or periodical orientation.[2] It has recently been suggested by Dr. Charles Muses that prehistoric man may have been sensitive to different phases in the lunar cycle as special times for meditation.[3] The monumental Stonehenge, built in prehistoric England, which is oriented towards equinoxes, solstices and lunar eclipses during the equinox, suggests similar usage.[4]

The leader in such practices and rituals was a kind of medicine man-priest-healer-psychiatrist-teacher-prophet who is called a *shaman* by anthropologists. He was the earliest professional man. It was he who mediated between the inner life of the tribe and their external affairs. It was he who presided at all "rites of passage" such as births, puberty initiations, marriages, and deaths as well as all "rites of intensification" which attempted to strengthen man's relation with the powerful forces in times of crises such as famines, storms, and epidemics.

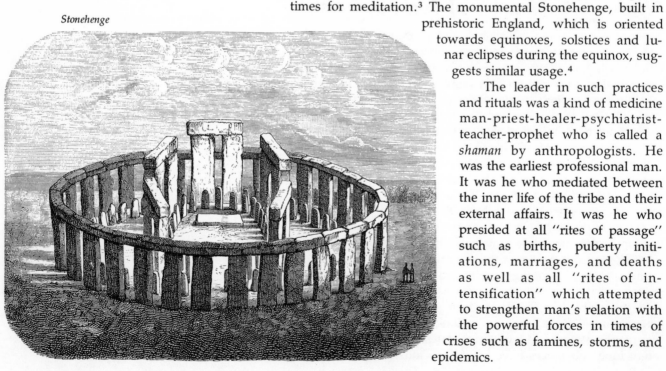

Stonehenge

4

Of course, the role of the shaman varied from culture to culture and with different circumstances. In some cultures shamanistic ideology and techniques dominated social interactions while in others they constituted a secondary phenomenon. The word shaman itself has a *Sanskrit* origin, and means ascetic.

The shaman's power essentially lies in mastering the techniques for inducing ecstacy through dreams, visions, and trances. *Ecstacy* in its original sense meant an altered state of consciousness with an awareness of the single emotion rapture. The shaman also must master the traditional mythology, genealogy, belief system and secret language of the tribe as well as its various healing methods. The youth who is called to be a shaman attracts attention through his love for solitude, desire to roam in the woods or in unfrequented places, visions, and spontaneous song-making. Sometimes he enters trance-like states which make him unconscious. These signs are regarded with pleasure and awe by his people who generally believe that his soul is being carried away by spirits to a place where he is instructed, sometimes by his shaman ancestors, in the secrets of the profession.

In some cultures the behavior of the prospective shaman is described in terms which to us seem to indicate psychopathology. However it is precisely because they succeed in curing themselves that these individuals become shamans. Often a crisis which borders on madness is provoked in the future shamans by the sudden announcement to others in the tribe that he has been chosen by the spirits for this profession. In other cases this *initiatory sickness* is induced through the use of drugs or fasting and other austerities. Regardless of the means, the symbolic pattern of death and rebirth common to all initiation rites will be reenacted.

The initiatory rituals peculiar to Siberian and central Asian shamanism include a ritual series of waking dreams. During this ritual Siberian shamans maintain that they "die" and lie inanimate for from three to seven days in a tent or other solitary place. Imagine having your body dismembered by demons or ancestral spirits; your bones cleaned, the flesh scraped off, the body fluids thrown away, and your eyes torn from their sockets, but set aside so that you may watch the entire procedure! It is only after such a purgative experience that the shaman can obtain the powers of shamanistic healing. Then he is given new flesh and the spirits instruct him in magical arts. He experiences the gods of the heavens; he learns to find the souls of sick men who have wandered or been carried by demons away from their bodies. He learns how to guide the soul of a dead man to its new abode; and he adds to his knowledge by regular association with higher beings.

The shaman is a man who can "die" and return to life many times. He knows how to orient himself in the unknown regions which he enters during his ecstasy. He learns to explore the new planes of existence his experiences disclose.[5]

In some cultures, such as the Senoi of Malaya, the shamanistic role is shared by most of the adults. The particular trait emphasized in this culture is the exploration and interpretation of dreams.

The Senoi live in an isolated rain forest in the Central Range of the Malay Peninsula. They claim to have lived for two or three centuries without violent crime, armed conflict, or mental and physical diseases. They attribute the alleged high degree of psychological integration and emotional maturity to the insight of their healers and teachers. Dream interpretation is a regular feature of their education and daily social intercourse. Tribal members are encouraged from a young age to reveal their inner lives through their dreams. Nothing is withheld. Sexual dreams, for instance, are encouraged to move through orgasm. The dreamer is expected to demand from his dream lover the poem, the song, the dance, the knowledge which will express the beauty of the dream love to the tribal group. Fearful dreams are thought of as opportunities for psychological integration of environmental stresses. A child who experiences the dream of falling will be given the following advice:

> The falling spirits love you. They are attracting you to their land, and you have but to relax and remain asleep in order to come to grips with them. When you meet them, you may be frightened of their terrific power, but go on. When you think you are dying in a dream, you are only receiving the powers of the other world, your own spiritual power which has been turned against you, and which now seeks to become one with you if you will accept it.[6]

In this way all the fearful elements in the dream become the allies of the dreamer. Dreams of falling soon change to joyful dreams of flying. Anytime a dreamer dreams about someone else in the tribe, they are sure to recollect the experience with that person when they awaken. The dream experiences are considered just as real and valid as the waking ones. Thus many social and personal problems are resolved in the dreams of the Senoi.[7]

Evidence suggests to us that ancient shamans possessed a very detailed knowledge about the use of a wide variety of mind-altering drugs. The earliest religious literature of India points to prehistoric use of a mythical, or at least undiscovered, drug called *soma* for inducing contact with nature's innermost forces. The primitive tribes of South America are known for their ritualistic use of drugs such as *yage*, *peyote*, and a number of others for the purpose of inducing ecstatic experiences. At times ecstacy is induced through drum rhythms and night-long dancing.[8]

There is also no reason to believe that ancient shamans did not engage in practices which could be considered the prototype of modern systems of yoga and meditation.

It was commonly thought that while in these various altered states of consciousness the shaman had the ability to diagnose diseases, see into the future, see objects at a great distance, walk over hot coals, and speak to the spirits of the dead.

Sir Arthur Grimble, who served as the British resident Commissioner for the Gilbert and Ellis Islands in the South Pacific, reports witnessing a scene in which a native shaman entered a dream state in order to "call porpoises." After a period of time he awoke from his sleep and announced to the tribe

6

that the porpoises were coming. The village of about 1000 individuals rushed down to the beach eagerly expecting a rare feast, and Grimble documents that he observed an entire flotilla of porpoises swim onto the beach, passively offering themselves to the natives:

> They were moving toward us in extended order with spaces of two or three yards between them, as far as the eye could reach. So slowly they came they seemed to be hung in a trance . . . It was as if their single wish was to get to the beach.[9]

Accounts of this type are all too common in the stories researchers and explorers bring back. However, a most promising line of research into the nature of such oddities has been taken up by at least one unusual young man. Adrian Boshier, of the Museums of Science and Man in Johannesburg, South Africa, uses an approach which combines living off the land in the African wilds while receiving initiations as a *sangoma* or witchdoctor with the objective work of a scientist studying other shamens. In his explorations, he has discovered 112 previously unknown prehistoric cave paintings whose ritual function and value has been preserved in the secret oral traditions of the witchdoctors whose friendship and trust he has cultivated. In the following passage, he discusses one such encounter:

> Upon arrival at a village some ten miles away, we were directed to one of the mud huts where we found the woman, Makosa, sitting on the floor amongst bones, dice and shells — her instruments of divination. Completely unperturbed by the arrival of our party, she did not even look up, but continued studying the rethrowing the bones. Eventually she spoke. ''One of you is here to ask me questions, he has a head full of questions, he is not a man of this land, but comes from over the big water.'' Then ignoring the others, she looked directly at me and asked, ''What do you want?'' I chided her and in the traditional manner told her to inquire this of her spirits. Again she picked up her bones, blew on them, and cast them down. She repeated this process three times, studying carefully the pattern between each throw. After some time she picked up a small knuckle bone and said that this bone represented me. It was the bone of the impala. The impala ram is an animal that lives with its herd most of the time, she told me, but periodically it leaves its group and goes off into the wilds by itself. It always returns to its herd, but again it must leave to wander alone. ''This is you,'' she said, ''you live with your people, but sometimes you go into the bush alone. . . . You go out to learn, living in the wild places, the mountain, the desert. . . . This is your life's work. What you learn is what the spirits are teaching you. This is the only way.''
>
> The old woman continued throwing the bones and revealing personal details concerning my life, which were absolutely accurate. . . . Such an existence taught me much about the country and its wildlife, but probing the customs and beliefs of the people proved to be a far more difficult and lengthy undertaking, for the historians and spiritual leaders of African society are the witchdoctors — people like Makosa who tell only so much, whose revelations are very limited to the uninitiated.[10]

During each of the ceremonies at which animals are sacrificed to the ancestral spirits each witchdoctor is possessed by those spirits who talk through them; thanking the host, praising the spirits, giving advice, etc. The woman in the right foreground is in the midst of this. Jackson, Transvaal, 1971. (Courtesy Adrian K. Boshier)

A sangoma of the Koni tribe, North Western Transvaal (1970) studying her bones (taula) of divination. Her patients look on as she studies the pattern of the bones, shakes the rattle in her hand and calls upon her ancestors to help her "see." The bones are composed of ivory tablets with symbols engraved upon them; seashells, knuckle bones, tortoise shells, seeds and coins. (Courtesy of Adrian K. Boshier)

Boshier and a few of the 40 witchdoctors that attended a recent initiation. Transvaal, January 1975. (Courtesy Adrian K. Boshier)

In this photo a female trainee (on right with bladders in hair) is divining the whereabouts of hidden objects to prove her powers. The sangoma on the left who is testing her is on that Boshier has been studying for some years. The bladders in the hair of the initiate have been taken from sacrificial animals and have been filled with the breath of her teacher, which in this case represents one of the main essences of life. Today this girl is being "reborn" as a sangoma. Present to witness the ceremony are a large number of experienced witchdoctors and members of her family. Unlike the sangoma in the previous photo she divines purely with the spirit and does not utilize bones. Swaziland 1972. (Courtesy Adrian K. Boshier)

This innate vision, with which primitive peoples are so familiar, is the heritage of all peoples and has been preserved, in various forms within all cultures.

Ancient Mesopotamia

In ancient Mesopotamia the art of divination received more intense, sustained interest than in any other known civilization. Reading omens was particularly important since every event was thought to have a personal meaning to the observer. This attitude was scientific in that it stressed minute observation and description of phenomena. However causality was not an important notion—all events were seen as communications from the divine.[11]

The Mesopotamians were masters in the arts of prescience, predicting the future from the livers and intestines of slaughtered animals, from fire and smoke, and from the brilliancy of precious stones; they fortold events from the murmuring of springs and from the shape of plants. Trees spoke to them, as did serpents, "wisest of all animals." Monstrous births of animals and of men were believed to be portents, and dreams always found skillful interpreters.

Atmospheric signs, rain, clouds, wind and lightening were interpreted as forbodings; the cracking of furniture and wooden panels foretold future events . . . Flies and other insects, as well as dogs, were the carriers of occult messages.[12]

Mesopotamia was noted throughout the ancient world for its magi—men and women for whom nothing was accidental. They also saw a unity in nature and harmony in the universe which bound together all objects and all events. The Assyrians made accurate observations of stellar movements and developed mathematical formulas to predict heavenly events. Omens were often interpreted through paranomastic relations —puns and plays on words—between the ominous portent and its consequence.

The idea is expressed in Mesopotamian literature, that the soul, or some part of it, moves out from the body of the sleeping person and actually visits the places and persons the dreamer "sees" in his sleep. Sometimes the god of dreams is said to carry the dreamer.

In times of crisis, ancient kings, priests, or heros would spend the night in the inner room of the sanctuary of a god. After due ritual preparation, the god would appear to the dreamer and give him a very clear and literal message which would require no further interpretation.

The Assyrian king, Assurbanipal 668-626 BC, recounts the following incident in an ancient dream-book:

The army saw the river Idid'e which was at that moment a raging torrent, and was afraid of crossing. But the goddess Ishtar who dwells in Arbela let my army have a dream in the midst of the night addressing them as follows: "I shall go in front of Assurbanipal, the king whom I have created myself." The army relied upon this dream and crossed safely the river Idid'e.

This dream seems to have been reported simultaneously by many sleepers.[13]

Babylonian Winged God Nisroch

Bad dreams dealing with sexual life or tabooed relationships were thought of as diseases caused by evil demons rising from the lower worlds to attack man. Their contents were rarely mentioned for fear of causing increased entanglements. One intriguing technique used to obviate the consequences of such a dream was a practice of telling the dream to a lump of clay which is then dissolved.

To ancient Sumeria, we owe the inventions of the wheel, writing, arithmetic and geometry, and money. The Sumerian's own legend, as recorded by the ancient historian Berosus around 400 BC, is that the arts of civilization were taught to the savage inhabitants of the fertile crescent region by an unknown creature who possessed superhuman intelligence.

> There appeared, coming out of the sea where it touches Babylonia, an intelligent creature that men called Oan[nès] or Oè[s], who had the face and limbs of a man and who used human speech, but was covered with what appeared to be the skin of a great fish, the head of which was lifted above his own like a strange headdress. Images are preserved of him to this day.
>
> This strange being, who took no human nourishment, would pass entire days in discussions, teaching men written language, the sciences, and the principles of arts and crafts, including city and temple construction, land survey and measurement, agriculture, and those arts which beautify life and constitute culture. But each night, beginning at sundown, this marvelous being would return to the sea and spend the night far beyond the shore. Finally he wrote a book on the origin of things and the principles of government which he left his students before his departure. The records add that during later reigns of the prediluvian kings other appearances of similar beings were witnessed.[14]

Ancient Egypt

In Egypt, life after death was thought to be a natural continuation of life on earth, and one senses another inner reality merging with their technology.

The shamanistic practices of earlier tribes became incorporated into the organized Egyptian national priesthood. However, the Egyptian religion is no longer practiced, and the ancient language is largely lost. The evidence which remains regarding the different cults and their practices and theologies is still shrouded in inpenetrable mystery. Yet, these people devoted themselves so intensely to their cult of the dead, that it is easy to imagine that many of their seer-priests actually did see the spirits of their departed.

The following testament comes from the pyramid of Unas, a Uth Dynasty king.

> The heavens drop water, the stars throb, the archers go round about, the bones of Akeru tremble, and those who are in bondage to them take to flight when they see Unas rise up as a soul, in the form of the god who liveth upon his fathers and who maketh food of his mothers. Unas is the lord of wisdom and his mother knoweth not his name . . . The ka's of Unas are behind him, the sole of his foot is beneath his feet, his gods are over him, his uraei are upon his brow, the serpent guides of Unas are in front of him and the spirit of the flame looketh

Judgment Scene from the Egyptian Book of the Dead. The heart of the dead person is being weighed against a feather.

upon his soul. The powers of Unas protect him: Unas is a bull in heaven, he directeth his steps where he will, he liveth upon the form which each god taketh upon himself, and he eateth the flesh of those who come to fill their bellies with the magical charms in the Lake of Fire.[15]

Is there any reason to believe that the geography of the "other world" should be any less complicated than geography here on terra firma?

Different Egyptian manuscripts delve in detail into the nature of those parts of man which live on after death. There is the sahu, or the spiritual body; the ka, or double which can separate from the physical body and travel at will. The ba is the principle of life which dwells in the ka, much like the heart of the physical body. The klu is the radiance of the being in eternal life, and sekhem is the form through which a man exists in heaven. In addition there is the ren or spitual name of a being.[16]

The Egyptial version of existence in the afterworld is somewhat obscure. In certain instances it seems that the Egyptians actually believed in a physical existence after death for which the departed required his worldly riches and sustenance. Other descriptions are embodied more in the realm of mythology so that the nature of the afterlife is deeply symbolized in the god-forms themselves.

The Egyptian concept of spiritual resurrection after death has a mythological basis in the story of Osiris—the lord of creation who was also a king of Egypt. At the height of his

Sahu

Ka

Ba

Khu

Sekhem

Ren

11

Osiris

reign, Osiris was murdered by his jealous enemy Set. His body was enclosed in a chest which was placed at the mouth of the Nile, but eventually recovered by Osiris's wife, Isis. Set however, finds it once more and dismembers it into fourteen pieces which he scatters throughout the land.

Isis searches for the pieces of Osiris's body and finds all of them except the phallus. At this point, Horus, the sun, the Hawk god, appears on the scene. As the god of the sun, he always existed. In fact the Hawk is probably the first living thing worshipped by the Egyptians, yet he is conceived by Isis from the dismembered body of Osiris—lacking the progenitive organ! The appearance of Horus represents the resurrection of Osiris. Filled with his father's spirit, he defeats Set in battle.

The battle between Horus and Set is re-enacted each day. You can watch this epic drama as it unfolds in the sky by getting up several hours before dawn and silently observing the sunrise.

The ancient Egyptians believed that as the Hawk arose from the dismembered body of Osiris, so would their awareness survive the bodily death.[17] However they also seemed to believe that proper funeral rites were necessary to attaining afterlife in heaven. It seems that we are dealing with mixed popular superstitions with higher philosophy and occult practice. In many ways the Egyptians seem to describe the afterlife as being quite physical and sensory—but perhaps this is a description of how real it was for them. This physical imagery is, perhaps, a poetical metaphor for the images which the ancient seers had of the afterlife.

Dream interpretation and divination were both practiced in Egypt and often associated with the temples of the different gods. One interesting tradition was the sleep temple of Imhotep where an art of healing known as *incubation* was practiced. It is known that Imhotep is the architect who designed the first known pyramid for the Pharoah Zosar around 2700 BC. He developed a reputation as a magician and healer and some 2000 years later came to be regarded as a god. Exactly how this deification occurred is uncertain. However, people with illnesses would go to his temple and sleep there. It is claimed that he appeared to them in their dreams and healed them. This tradition, which was carried on in the Greek temples with the healing God Aesclepius, implies at the very least a very practical understanding of hypnotic suggestion—if not actual spiritual healing.

Egyptial manuscripts reveal deep knowledge of trance induction procedures and hypnotic techniques. The techniques frequently involved staring into a lamp as indicated in the following passage translated from a papyrus text by Dr. Charles Muses:

> When you desire to make inquiry of the lamp, fill your eyes with the ointment aforesaid, and then say, "I pray thee [meaning the deific power ruling the day] to reveal thyself here tonight, speak with me and give me the answer truly concerning the questions I ask of thee." Pronouncing this spell over the lamp [while gazing at it], you will see a figure of a god standing behind the lamp and he will respond to your query. Or you may lie down on green reeds, having abstained from sexual communion, your head southward and your face looking north toward the lamp.[18]

The use of ointment is to prevent eye strain. It is more than likely that the "magic lamp" of Arabian tradition is derived from this Egyptian practice.

Another Egyptian test dating from over 3,000 years ago, called the Bent-rosh Stela describes the sufferings a princess endured in a profound experience described as "possession by a spirit." The ministrations of the local psychiatrist or "artist of the heart" were insufficient to relieve her suffering. However, an immediate cure was affected upon the arrival of a high priest of Thoth who brought with him a great stone statue of the healing moon-diety aspect of the god. His journey had taken nearly a year and a half.[19] These techniques were preserved by the priesthood and also passed through mystery cults associated with the pyramids and sphinx. Pythagoras, Plato and other Greek philosophers were said to have been initiated

Egyptian Sphinx

13

into these cults.[20] The name Alchemy is derived from the word Kamt or Qemt which is the word meaning the black mud of the Nile and the name which the ancient Egyptians gave to their own country. The tradition of Hermetic mysticism also claims an origin in the legendary Egyptian god-sage Hermes Trismagistus. Likewise, tarot cards claim an Egyptial origin. There is also today a rather extensive cult based on the alleged properties of the Egyptian pyramids.

Ancient India

Contemporary Hindu culture originated primarily with the Aryans who invaded India about 1500 BC bringing with them the Sanskrit language and the Vedic religion. However, for at least 1000 years prior to this invasion, there existed a culture in India about which we know very little.

The cities of the Indus river valley left no large monuments and although they did have a written language, it has not yet been translated. From some fragmentary evidence which does remain, scholars conclude that this early culture contained within it many elements which were later incorporated into the Hindu religion.[21]

The exploration of consciousness has developed to a remarkable degree in the Hindu culture. In fact, the sanskrit language has shown itself to be so precise in describing the subtleties of consciousness exploration that many sanskrit words and concepts have become commonplace in our own comtemporary culture. Consider for example the following terms:

Asanas: postures used to stimulate flow of life-force through the body and to aid meditation.

Atman: The human soul or spirit—the essence of the inner man.

Ahimsa: The doctrine of non-violence toward sentient beings.

Akasha: The ether; primordial substance which pervades the entire universe; the substratum of both mind and matter. All thoughts, feelings, or actions are recorded within it.

Brahman: Hindu god who represents the highest principle in the universe; the essence which permeates all existence. Brahman is the same as atman in the philosophy of the Upanishads.

Chakras: Organs of psychic perception. There are seven main chakras as listed below.

> *Sahasrara*: The highest subtle center of consciousness, the crown chakra, the thousand-petaled lotus, that which unites man with the infinite.

> *Ajna*: Situated between the eyebrows, it is sometimes called the third eye. This center forms the organ of psychic visualization or clairvoyance.

> *Visuddha*: Situated at the throat this chakra mediates vocal expression.

> *Anahata*: Situated in the cardiac region, this chakra mediates the emotions of love and devotion.

> *Manipura*: Located at the level of the solar plexus; this is the power chakra and mediates one's ability to control situations.

The Chakras

14

Svadistana: This chakra is situated in the genital area and is associated with the exchange of sexual energies.

Muladhara: Situated at the base of the spinal column between the anus and the genitals, this center is the seat of a psychic form of energy known as kundalini; it also mediates the survival needs of the organism.

Dharma: One's personal path in life, the fulfillment of which leads to a higher state of consciousness.

Dhyana: The focusing of attention on a particular spiritual idea in continuous meditation.

Guna: A Cosmic force or quality.

Ishwara: Personal manifestation of the supreme; the cosmic self; cosmic consciousness.

Karma: The principle by which all of our actions will effect our future circumstances, either in the present or in future lifetimes.

Kundalini: A psychic force which lays coiled like a serpent in the muladhara chakra. When this force is activated, either naturally or through yogic disciplines, it rises up the spine and activates each of the chakras.

Mantras: Syllables, inaudible or vocalized, which are repeated during meditation.

Maya: The illusions the physical world generates to ensnare our consciousness.

Moksha: The attainment of liberation from the worldly life.

Mandala: Images used to meditate upon.

Nirvana: The transcendental state which is beyond the possibility of full comprehension or expression by the ordinary being enmeshed in the concept of selfhood.

Nadis: Conduits of psychic energy throughout the body, woven like threads in a spider web.

Ojas: Energy developed by certain yogic practices which stimulates endocrine activity within the body.

Prana: Life energy which permeates the atmosphere, enters the human being through the breath, and can be directed by thought.

Pranayama: Yogic exercises for the regulation of the breath flow.

Samadhi: State of enlightenment of superconsciousness. The union of the individual consciousness with cosmic consciousness.

Sadhanas: Spiritual disciplines. Practical means for the attainment of a spiritual goal.

Samsara: The phenomena of the senses. Attachment to Samsara leads to further rebirth.

Siddhis: Psychic and other paranormal powers which are the fruits of yogic disciplines.

Soma: A plant, probably with psychedelic properties, that was prepared and used in ritual fashion to enable men to communicate with the gods.

Tantras: Books dealing with the worship of the female deities and specifying certain practices to attain liberation through sensuality, particularly through the heightened union of male and female energies.

Yoga: This is the sanskrit word meaning union and refers to various practices which are designed to attain a state of perfect union between the self and the infinite. [In English, which descends from the same proto-Indo-European language as Sanskrit, the word *yoke* is derived from the same root as *yoga*. Thus we can see the close linguistic connection between spiritual freedom and physical bondage.]

The *Yoga Sutras of Patanjali* prescribe a system of eight stages, or limb's for one's higher development. The first two limbs are known as *Yama* and *Niyama*. They involve a highly ethical and disciplined lifestyle—control, indifference, detachment, renunciation, charity, celibacy, vegetarianism, cleanliness, and non-violence. The third step involves the development and care of the body through the use of exercises and postures called *Asanas*. The fourth stage involves *Pranayama* breathing exercises. The next stage, *pratyahara*, involves meditation, by means of which one withdraws consciousness from the senses.

The fifth limb of yoga is called *Dharana* which means concentration. An object of contemplation is held fixedly in the mind; it must not be allowed to waver or change its form or color—as it will have a tendency to do. Often the yogi will concentrate on different *chakras* or focal points within the body. Self-analysis is used to observe breaks in concentration. Often he will carry a string of beads and one is pulled over the finger every time a break begins. The next stage of *Dhyana* occurs when the sense of separateness of the self from the object of concentration disappears and one experiences a union or oneness with that object. In the final stage, *Samadhi*, one experiences an absolute, ecstatic cosmic consciousness. This does not, as some suppose, entail a loss of individuality. "The drop is not poured into the Ocean; the Ocean is poured into the Drop." The self and the entire universe are simultaneously experienced.[22]

During the development of the yogi, the awakening activity of the *kundalini* arouses activity in the various *chakras* and one attains certain psychic abilities or *siddhis*. Many traditions warn against the desire for psychic abilities as another trap in the way of ultimate enlightenment. Other traditions of a tantric nature stress their development, but warn against their misuse.

In the past decades, Western scientists have barely begun to study the various abilities which some yogis have achieved. Body functions such as heartbeat, temperature, and brainwaves—which had been previously thought of as totally autonomic—have been shown to be under the conscious control of some—but certainly not all—yogis. This research has paved the way for the newly emerging science of consciousness which will be discussed in the next chapter.

Buddhism, which originated in India, reached a height of consciousness exploration in Tibet. All states of existence for the Tibetan Buddhists other than pure Nirvana are reflections of the limited illusion of self-consciousness. The *Tibetan book of the Dead*, is the major document within this tradition; it describes the passage of consciousness from death to rebirth. Existence is divided into six *bardos*, three of which are experienced from birth to death and three of which occur from death to rebirth. Yet, Buddhist philosophy teaches that birth and death are not phenomena which occur only once in a human life; they are part of an uninterrupted process. Every instant something within us dies and something is reborn. The different *bardos* represent the different aspects of this process in our own lives. All of these states are in flux.[23]

16

JUDGMENT OF THE SOUL AFTER DEATH
Good and bad deeds are weighed against each other.

Chikhai Bardo: the experience of the primary clear light and the secondary clear light at the moment of death.

Chonyd Bardo: the state of psychic consciousness. Experiencing lights, sounds and rays. Seeing the peaceful deities and then the wrathful deities.

Sidpa Bardo: visions of the world into which one's karma leads one to be born. Visions of males and females in sexual union. Feelings of attachment and repulsion. Choosing and entering the womb.

Bsam-gtan Bardo: the dream state.

Skye-gnas Bardo: the everyday waking consciousness of being born into the human world..

These bardo states refer to the mental processes of the soul during the periods of life and rebirth. Outside of one's own consciousness there still remains another reality to be explored. Entrance to this reality is attained by recognizing at any point that the images and apparitions of the bardo state are merely the projections of one's own consciousness.

> With every thought of fear or terror or awe
> for all apparitional appearances set aside
> May I recognize whatever visions appear as
> reflections of mine own consciousness
> May I not fear the bands of peaceful and wrathful
> deities, mine own thought-forms.[24]

In the Sidpa bardo, before rebirth, there occurs a judgment of the good and bad deeds of the soul of the dead.

> If thou neither prayest nor knowest how to meditate upon the Great Symbol nor upon any tutelary deity, the Good Genius, who was born simultaneously with thee, will come now and count out thy good deeds with white pebbles, and the Evil Genius, who was born simultaneously with thee, will come and count out thy evil deeds with black pebbles. Thereupon, thou wilt be greatly frightened, awed, and terrified, and wilt tremble; and thou wilt, attempt to tell lies, saying 'I have not committed any evil deed.'
> Then the Lord of Death will say, 'I will consult the Mirror of Karma.'
> So saying, he will look in the Mirror, wherein every good and evil act is vividly reflected. Lying will be of no avail.[25]

This situation very closely parallels the weighing of the heart described in the Egyptian Book of the Dead as well as the judgments appearing in later Greek and Christian traditions. It seems to reflect an archetypal reality which permeates the deep consciousness of many cultures, perhaps the ultimate symbol of meaning and order in the universe. Modern research is still attempting to investigate this reality, though perhaps with less sophistication than the Tibetans who claim to have developed ways to communicate with the departed spirit after death in order to aid in its passing through the *bardo* states.

Interestingly enough, the Tibetan Book of the Dead, has been used as a "constant companion" by Carl Jung whose psychological theories tend to unite scientific logic with mysticism. It was also used by Timothy Leary, Richard Alpert and Ralph Metzner as the basis for understanding the nature of the *Psychedelic Experience.*

18

The Bardo states are accessible to everyone. Yet there is a subtle process involved in attaining all higher states of consciousness—a kind of trying not to try—which is embodied most clearly in the life of Tibet's great saint, Milarepa, who never uttered a word that did not come out in song and poetry.[26] This delicacy of living is manifest also in Chinese Taoism.

Ancient China

Lao Tsu was born in China in 604 BC. He held a number of public offices during his long life and was the curator of the royal library in Loyang. As an old man he retired from government service and traveled on buffalo-back to the region of the Gobi desert. Because of a boundary warden's plea, the sage paused long enough to inscribe a short record of his teachings. Leaving this, he resumed his journey to an unknown destination and was seen no more. His small book, the *Tao Te Ching*, is one of the world's great religious classics. Within a matter of centuries, Lao Tsu was worshipped as a god and his masterpiece was engraved on stone at the Capital of every Chinese state.

Will it be possible to describe the *Way of the Tao* in this book? Though thousands of volumes have been written about it, "The Tao that can be put into words is not the eternal Tai." We can only try to outline and summarize. There is a perfect balance which lies within each individual, and following this balance requires neither cunning nor striving. A story is told of a wonderful cook who has used the same knife to cut meat for over 20 years without every having to sharpen his knife, because he spontaniously moved his blade through the meat precisely and without effort or hacking. This is how the Tao is expressed.

Like the yogis in India, the Taoists developed exercises which enabled them to gain conscious control over internal states. Disciplined breathing constituted one basis of these exercises. Meditation was also used in order to separate the spirit from the body and travel independently of it as well as to maintain an eternal calm in the midst of changing conditions.[27]

Associated with the philosophy of Taoism is the method of *acupuncture* healing and the *I Ching*.

The oldest book on the subject of acupuncture is the *Nei Jing* or Book of the Yellow Emperor, which dates back to 200 BC, but contains material which is much older. The theory of acupuncture is based on the circulation of a vital energy or life force called *Qi*, which means air or breath, through twelve meridians in the body. If it fails to flow properly, the organs of the body will suffer from an inbalance of energy. The Chinese discovered about 1000 points along the meridians which can be stimulated to restore the flow of Qi in the body.

Modern research has shed much light on the still enigmatic process of acupuncture. Electronic equipment is now used to locate the acupuncture points by measuring galvanic skin response. However, the ancient Chinese developed a direct

When one is so far advanced that every shadow and every echo has disappeared, so that one is entirely quiet and firm, this is refuge within the cave of energy, where all that is miraculous returns to its roots. One does not alter the place, but the place divides itself. This is incorporeal space where a thousand and ten thousand places are one place. One does not alter the time, but the time divides itself. This is immeasurable time when all the aeons are like a moment. (The Secret of the Golden Flower, trans. by Richard Wilhelm.)

sensitivity to these subtle currents which was very precise and which required no instrumental augmentation.

Qi energy was said to be the product of the two great forces of yin and yang which run through the entire universe. All phenomenal manifestation exists as a tension between these two principles, which operate on all levels.

Yin	*Yang*
feminine	masculine
negative	positive
moon	sun
darkness	light
yielding	aggressive
wetness	dryness
left side	right side
heart	fire
lungs	intestines
spleen	stomach
kidneys	bladder
liver	gall bladder
autumn	spring
winter	summer

The flow and play of yin and yang also influence human affairs. This process has been treated extensively in the *I ching*, or Book of Changes, which is one of the oldest books in the world. This book consists of sixty-four sections, each headed by a figure made up of six lines, broken or unbroken, called a hexagram. Each of these hexagrams represents a different stage in the eternal flux of yin and yang. These hexagrams are described in poetic and often enigmatic terms that can touch deep levels of the mind; however there have been commentaries written about each hexagram by Confucius and other sages which have related the cosmic fluxes to specific human situations. Thus the book has been used, over several millenium, as a book of divination, as a source of philosophical wisdom, and as a practical guide to ethical questions. One consults the oracle by an ostensibly random process of flipping coins or shuffling yarrow stalks.[28]

The results are often uncanny. For example when I asked the I Ching to comment about the nature of *The Roots of Consciousness* the following hexagrams were indicated by tossing coins:

Limitation   ☵☱   which changes to

Holding Together   ☵☷

The dominant imagery in these hexagrams is water, the primordial substance which is the basis of all subjective and objective existence in ancient myths (such as the Rig Veda creation myth quoted in the introduction). Water is symbolized by the upper trigram ☵ in both hexagrams.

20

In the first hexagram, water is symbolized above the lake ☱ . This is a symbol of limitation, as the lake will only hold so much water before it overflows. The commentaries of the text are:

A lake can contain only a definite amount of the infinite quantity of water; this is its peculiarity. In human life too the individual achieves significance through discrimination and the setting of limits. . . . Unlimited possibilities are not suited to man; if they existed, his life would only dissolve in the boundless. . . . The individual attains significance as a free spirit only by surrounding himself with these limitations and by determining for himself what his duty is.

In the commentaries, the text emphasizes that, as the water will find an outlet when the lake is full, there are also (psychic) channels leading from each person which transcend the limitations of his individuality. "Discretion is of prime importance in preparing the way to momentous things." There is a time for accumulating energy within oneself, and then, when the proper time comes, not hesitating to transcend one's previous limitations.

The second hexagram which follows depicts the waters ☵ above the earth ☷ . The commentary indicates that there is a natural tendency for the waters on the surface of the earth to flow together. Thus all of the rivers flow into the oceans. In human situations, the text states:

What is required is that we unite with others, in order that all may complement and aid one another through holding together.

To me these answers apply to the nature of consciousness itself, to the book which you are now reading, and to my experience of writing this book. In each sense, the answers provided by the *I Ching* seem to me to be meaningful and accurate.* Modern researchers have noted clinically and experimentally that when the book is treated with respect the hexagrams which turn up, supposedly at random, do seem more applicable than other hexagrams chosen as controls.[29,30]

The *I Ching* seems to be operating on a cosmic principle by which all events in the universe are related to each other. The same flux of yin and yang which allows for the interpretation of the human situation in the state of consciousness of the questioner is also expressed in the random falling of a coin. This idea, which has been labelled *synchronicity* by Carl Jung, is beginning to play an enormous role in the development of a new model of the universe. It underlies all so-called "coincidences."

Many of you reading this book now will be smiling at this point because of some uncanny incidents which led you to this moment. Give yourself a chance to pause and reflect on the synchronicities in your own existence . . . the synchronicity of your existence . . . the synchronicity of existence. . . .

---

*When you finish reading *The Roots of Consciousness*, you may wish to come back to these hexagrams once more and experiment with yourself to see if they will have a deeper meaning for you.

Apollo Pythias–Deity of the Oracle at Delphi

Ancient Greece

The first recorded controlled parapsychological experiment took place in ancient Greece during the sixth century BC. Greece was at that time famous for its oracles which were generally connected with the temples of the various gods. Generally these oracles operated through a priestess or medium who went into a trance or became possessed by the god of the oracle and uttered prophetic words which were then interpreted by the priests. Their enormous prestige and political influence was attested to by kings and generals who would consult with these oracles before making major decisions.

Herodotus, the Father of History, reports that the King of Lydia, Croesus, wishing to test the different oracles, sent messengers to those of Aba, Miletus, Dodona, Delphi, Amphiaraus, Trophonius, and Jupiter Ammon. His idea was by this means to choose the best of them to consult about his proposed campaign against the Persians. On the hundredth day after their departures all of the messengers were to simultaneously ask the oracles to tell them what Croesus was doing at that very moment. Accordingly, on the day appointed, when the emissaries had entered the temple of Delphi, even before they had time to utter their mandate, which had been kept secret, the priestess said in verse:

> I count the grains of sand on the ocean shore
> I measure the ocean's depths
> I hear the dumb man
> I likewise hear the man who keeps silence.
> My senses perceive an odor as when one cooks
>   together the flesh of the tortoise and the lamb.
> Brass is on the sides and beneath;
>   Brass also covers the top.

This reply was committed to writing and rushed back to Croesus who received the lines of the priestess with utmost veneration. On the appointed day he had sought for something impossible to guess: having caused a tortoise and lamb to be cut into pieces, he had had them cooked together in a brass pan upon which he had afterwards placed a lid of the same metal. The oracle of Amphiaraus also proved lucid in this experiment; others were less definite. The presents which Croesus sent to Delphi were of incalculable value. A detailed list may be found in Herodotus.[31]

Another important part of Greek culture at this time were the mystery cults, into which many Greek philosophers were initiated. These cults developed impressive rituals which involved fasting, purification, song and dance, the use of mythology and poetry. It is said that Greek drama developed from these rituals. Many authors have written about the enormous impact which these initiations have had upon their understanding—although the specific nature of the rituals has still remained a secret. Doubtless profound states of consciousness developed.

The rituals of the Eleusinian mysteries dealt with the myth of Persephone, the daughter of Ceres, who was abducted by

Pluto, Lord of the Underworld, who forced her to become his queen. Ceres entered the Underworld in search of her daughter and at her request Pluto agreed to allow Persephone to live in the upper world half of the year if she would stay with him in the darkness of Hades for the remaining half. Of this ritual, Manley Palmer Hall states:

It is probable that the Eleusinians realized that the soul left the body during sleep, or at least was made capable of leaving by the special training which undoubtedly they were in a position to give. Thus Persephone would remain as the queen of Pluto's realm during the waking hours, but would ascend to the spiritual worlds during periods of sleep. The initiate was taught how to intercede with Pluto to permit Persephone (the initiate's soul) to ascend from the darkness of his material nature into the light of understanding.

The fact that initiates maintained that they had conquered the fear of death leads one to surmise that these rituals—akin to the cave rituals of prehistoric man and the ritual uses made of the great pyramid in Egypt[32]—developed a state which we now call the out-of-body experience.

Out of this cultural milieu developed a philosophical tradition which was *hylozoistic*, conceiving of nature as animated or alive; *ontological*, inquiring into the very essence of things; and *monistic*, seeking to find a single principle to explain all phenomena.

The pythagorean brotherhood formed a direct link between the mystery school tradition and the development of Greek philosophy. Pythagoras is credited with inventing the Western musical scale and the theorem by which the length of the hypotenuse of a right triangle is derived. He also taught the doctrine of the transmigration of the soul through successive incarnations. His philosophy was looked upon as mystical since he stressed the harmonious development of the soul within man. Relationships between all things could be expressed by numbers which took on qualitative properties which were analogous to the qualitative differences found in musical harmonies. The Pythagorians devoted themselves to studying the countless peculiarities discoverable in numbers, and ascribed these to the universe at large. Numbers were thus seen as a principle which linked the symbolic properties of the mind with the mechanisms of the universe.

Pythagoras did not begin to teach until the age of forty. Until that time he studied in foreign countries with the resolution to submit to all of his teachers and make himself a master of their secret wisdom. We are told that the Egyptian priests with whom he studied were jealous of admitting a foreigner into their secrets. They baffled him as long as they could, sending him from one temple to another. However, Pythagoras endured until he was rewarded accordingly for his patience. Later on he was no less strict in dealing with his own disciples. During the novitiate period of five years, a vow of strict silence was required. Only then were disciples permitted to participate in intellectual discourse with the master.[33] Members of the Pythagorean brotherhood held their goods in common, made fidelity chief virtue and held that the best should rule.

Pythagoras

23

One of the most influential concepts which was developed by the Pythagoreans was the notion of the *harmony of the spheres,* which related the inner music of the mind to the progression of the planets through the heavens. The cosmic origin of man's soul was understood in the context of an astronomy which dealt with the Earth as a spherical planet orbiting the sun. In states of inspiration, man ascended to these celestial spheres.

Before the beginning of reflective thought, man feels, in various contexts, an involvement. He unconsciously arranges the multiplicity of phenomena into a restricted number of schemata. It is the business of reflection, when it begins, to raise these transitory insights into the realm of consciousness, to name them, and to assimilate them to one another. This is how the world becomes comprehensible. In myth and ritual man tries to make these realizations present and clear, to assure himself that, in spite of all confusion and all the immediate threats of his environment, everything is "in order" It is in such a prescientific conception of order that the idea of cosmic music has its roots; and number speculation springs from the same soil.

But relationships that usually have their effect unconsciously, or only enter consciousness as the result of slow and patient reflection, become immediate, overwhelming experiences in ecstasy. The soul that in ecstasy, or dream, or trance, travels to heaven, hears there the music of the universe, and its mysterious structure immediately becomes clear to him. The incomparable and supernatural sound is part of the same thing as the incomparable beauty and colorfulness of other worlds. If Pythagoras was something like a shaman, who in ecstasy made contact with worlds "beyond," then the tradition that he personally heard the heavenly music surely preserves something of truth.[34]

That Pythagoras was indeed a shaman is a credible notion. What is more debatable is his claim to godhood. He generally allowed his followers to believe that he was the Hyperborean Apollo and that he assumed a human form in order to invite men to approach him. On several occasions he was known to demonstrate his celestial origins by revealing a thigh made of gold. As the centuries passed even more wondrous phenomena were attributed to Pythagoras. What all biographers do agree about, however, is that he claimed to have full memory of the many forms which he had taken in past incarnations.

In contrast to Pythagoras, Democritus, the originator of atomic theory, was more concerned with the substance of the universe than with its form. He maintained that the soul is composed of the finest, roundest, most nimble and fiery atoms. These atoms cannot be seen visually, but can be perceived in thought. At death, Democritus maintained in a book called *Chirokmeta*, that soul molecules detach themselves from the corpse, thus giving rise to spectres. Through this theory, Democritus also attempted to explain dreams, prophetic visions, and the gods.

Democritus held that objects of all sorts, and especially people continually emitted what he termed *images*—particles on the atomic level that carried representations of the mental activities, thoughts, characters and emotions of the persons who originated them. 'And thus charged, they have the effect of living agents: by their impact they

24

could communicate and transmit to their recipients the opinions, thoughts, and impulses of their senders, when they reach their goal with the images intact and undistorted.' The images 'which leap out from persons in an excited and inflamed condition,' yield, owing to their high frequency and rapid transit, especially vivid and significant representations.[35]

Socrates, who himself was gifted with precognitive perception, attributed his abilities to the aid of a personal *daemon*, which then meant demigod and not (evil) demon. In the *Theagetes*, Plato makes Socrates say:

> By favour of the Gods, I have, since my childhood, been attended by a semi-divine being whose voice from time to time dissuades me from some undertaking, but never directs me what I am to do. You know Charmides the son of Glaucon. One day he told me that he intended to compete at the Nemean games. . . . I tried to turn Charmides from his design, telling him, 'While you were speaking, I heard the divine voice. . . . Go not to Nemea.' He would not listen. Well, you know he has fallen.

In his *Apology for Socrates*, Xenophon attributes to him these words:

> This prophetic voice has been heard by me throughout my life: it is certainly more trustworthy than omens from the flight or entrails of birds: I call it a God or daemon. I have told my friends the warnings I have received, and up to now the voice has never been wrong.

Socrates spoke freely about his experiences and his honesty was profoundly respected by all who knew him—in fact his life was a model of integrity which inspired many philosophers. Although he himself left no writings his teachings and personality are preserved through the works of Plato, the most influential of all philosophers. The Socratic injunction of *Know Thyself* provides a basic impulse for the work in this book.

A great concern for exploring consciousness is expressed in the works of Plato, who was a student of Socrates. Plato maintains that the world of ideas itself is just as real as the world of objects, and that it is through ideas that man attains consciousness of the absolute.

He compares our human condition to that of slaves enchained in a cave where one can only see the shadows of people and objects passing by outside. Eventually we come to accept these shadows as reality itself, while the source of the shadows is ignored. Such is our ignorance of the spiritual world in which our own ideas have their being.[36]

Plato also makes a distinction between mere augury which tries to comprehend the workings of god through a rational process, and genuine prophecy—such as that instanced by Socrates—which utilizes inner voices, out-of-body experiences, inspired states, dreams and trances.

Like Pythagoras, Plato admits the pre-existence of the *nous*, or divine soul of man, which chooses the existence for which it must incarnate. It survives the death of the body, and if it has not attained sufficient perfection to merit endless bliss, it must be subjected to new tests by reincarnating in order to attain further progress and perfection.

Plato

In the last chapter of his masterpiece, *The Republic*, Plato vividly describes a vision of life after death attained by a young man named Er who was wounded in battle and thought to be dead. While this story is clearly augmented by the moralistic philosophy and cosmological views prevalent in his culture, Plato's account carries a ring which echoes in the after-death mythology of many different visionaries, and was very likely derived from the lore of the mystery cults into which he was initiated.

After the souls of the dead had received a thousand years of reward or punishment for the deeds of their previous lives, they are brought to a place where they choose their next incarnations. Reincarnation is necessary for the development of consciousness in order to

. . . know what the effect of beauty is when combined with poverty or wealth in a particular soul, and what are the good and evil consequences of noble and humble birth, of private and public station, of strength and weakness, of cleverness and dullness, and of all the natural and acquired gifts of the soul.[37]

Plato teaches that before each incarnation, the soul enters into a forgetfulness of what has gone before. The purpose of human learning and philosophy is, then, to reawaken in the soul remembrance of the eternal, spiritual realm of pure forms and ideas.[38]

Plato's greatest student Aristotle is noted for having turned away from the inner world of spiritual ideals which Plato loved towards a philosophy which was more rational and scientific. Instead of describing the spiritual world as having greater reality then the physical, he describes an *entelechy* or vital force urging the organism toward self-fulfillment. He describes this urge as the ultimate and immortal reality of the body. Aristotle also recognized in the stars embodied deities, beings of superhuman intelligence.

The Neoplatonic school, centered in Alexandria, combined mystical elements found in Judaism with Greek philosophy. Philosophers within this tradition sought to explain the world as an emanation from a transcendent God who was both the source and goal of all being. Philo Judaeus (30 BC-50 AD) described a process of mediation between god and man, in which the Jewish notions of angels and demons was equated with the world-soul or realm of ideas of the Greeks. Philo advocated using forms of asceticism in order to free oneself from the grip of sensory reality and enter into communion with spiritual reality.

Similar doctrines were taught by Plotinus who insisted that union with god cannot be realized by thought even freed from the senses. This experience is possible only in a state of ecstacy in which the soul totally transcends its own thought, loses itself in the being of God and becomes one with divinity.

The way in which the neo-Platonists probed into the magical workings of nature is reflected in the following questions posed by the philosopher Porphery to his teacher Iamblichus:

> . . . granted that there are Gods. But I inquire what the peculiarities are of each of the more excellent genera, by which they are separated from each other; and whether we must say that the cause of the distinction between them is from their energies, or their passive motions, or from things that are consequent, or from their different arrangement with respect to bodies; as, for instance, from the arrangement of the Gods with reference to etherial, but of daemons to aerial, and of souls to terrestrial bodies? . . .

> I likewise ask concerning the mode of divination, what it is, and what the quality by which it is distinguished? . . .

> The ecstasy, also, of the reasoning power is the cause of divination, as is likewise the mania which happens in diseases, or mental aberration, or a sober and vigilant condition, or suffusions of the body, or the imaginations excited by diseases, or an ambiguous state of mind, such as that which takes place between a sober condition and ecstasy, or the imaginations artificially procured by enchantment. . . .

> What also is the meaning of those mystic narrations which say that a certain divinity is unfolded into the light from the mire, that he is seated above the lotus, that he sails in a ship, and that he changes his forms every hour, according to the signs of the zodiac? For thus they say he presents himself to view, and thus ignorantly adapt the peculiar passion of their own imagination to the God himself. But if these things are asserted symbolically, being symbols of the powers of this divinity, I request an interpretation of these symbols.[39]

Iamblichus

These questions were all directed toward the operation of certain theurgical (magical) rites designed to evoke the powers of the gods to aid the philosophers.

The neoplatonic philosophers did not consider themselves the originators of a new school of thought. Rather, they felt they were carrying on the tradition of Plato, However, they developed a more active mysticism than is found in Plato himself, a mysticism which was to carry a great influence on later hermeticists, alchemists, and kabbalists.

Ancient Rome

The Greeks and the Romans were fascinated with stories of the marvelous. Pliney the Elder asserts that he collected 20,000 theurgical incidents taken from the writings of a hundred different authors. Historians such as Herodotus, Tacitus, Suetonius, Plutarch, and Titus Livius relate many such incidents in the lives of prominent men.

Plutarch reports for example that Calpurnia, Caesar's fourth wife, dreamt on the eve of the fatal Ides of March, that she saw her husband's blood being spilled. A comet and also many other portents ominously forewarned of Caesar's death.

In 150 BC the Romans passed a law declaring that no important resolution could be adopted without consulting the augers.

Cicero, (l06-43 BC), known as Rome's greatest orator, wrote a book on *Divination* in which he discusses the evidence pro and con for the accuracy of predictions. He attempts to take an impartial philosophic stance to the evidence. Inquiring into the nature of fate, he asks what use predictions are if the foretold events cannot be changed. How does free will fit into this picture? Cicero implies that for some events fate and determinism rule while for other categories of events men exercise an amount of free will.

The use of puns in prophecy finds a striking illustration in a story related by Tacitus about Vespasian before he attained the throne of the Roman Empire. Disturbed by several miraculous healings which occurred in his presence, Vespasian had decided to consult the oracle.

Entering the temple, he ordered everyone to leave. Suddenly, while his attention was turned to the god, he noticed behind him one of the principle Egyptian priests named Basilides, whom he knew to be several days' journey from Alexandria, and ill in bed at the time. Leaving the temple he went out into the streets and enquired if Basilides had not been seen in the city; finally he sent horsemen to the place where this priest lived, and learned that at the time he saw him Basilides was eighty miles away. Then he was forced to admit that he had really been favored with a vision: the word Basilides (from a Greek word for king) meant that he would attain to empire.[40]

The great historial Plutarch (born 47 AD) held that the human soul had a natural faculty for divination and added that it must be exercised at favorable times and in favorable bodily states. He described the daemon of Socrates as an intelligent light which resonated with Socrates because of his inner light. Plutarch also viewed such spirits as the mediators between god and men.

The philosopher, statesman, and playwrite Seneca (4 BA-65 AD) saw the emerging scientific outlook as a plausible substitute for existing religions and as a basis for a moral philosophy. He accepted divination in all of its forms, but stressed the personal inner growth of the scientist:

Those secrets [of nature] open not promiscuously nor to every comer. They are remote of access, enshrined in the inner sanctuary.[41]

Pliny the Elder wrote his *Natural History* in 77 AD. It contains 37 books which investigate most of the ancient arts and sciences. In this work, Pliny posits a stance which is often found in the writings of scholars since his time. He brands the magi of his day fools and imposters. Yet nonetheless he also deems certain "magical" procedures *proved by experience*. He recognizes the importance of the right spirit in science and offers frequent advice on chastity, virginity, nudity and fasting. Sometimes he urges physicians to be totally silent. He also speaks about sympathies and antipathies between various material objects, and uses this idea as the basis for many medical treatments. He acknowledged that the positions of the sun and the moon were important for such treatments.

Ptolemy (110-151 AD) who lived in Alexandria during the neoplatonic era was the ablest mathematician and closest scientific observer of his day. He made important contributions to trigonometry and cartography and while his geocentric theory was proven erroneous, it was well substantiated on the basis of the existing scientific evidence and in fact held for over one thousand years. He also formulated the principle (later known as Occam's razor) that one should always use the simplest hypothesis which was consistent with the facts. He wrote 21 books on geography, mathematics and astronomy, as well as four on control of human life by the stars. These books, known as the *Tetrabiblos* have formed the substantial base of all Western astrology since his day, although few modern astrologers have ever read Ptolemy or understood the caution which he urges.

Ptolemy contends that a certain force is diffused from the heavens over all things on earth. Yet he recognized that most applications of astrology were still hypothetical. He also acknowledged that it was easier to predict events which effect large areas, whole peoples or cities, rather than individuals. But astrology was not to be rejected simply because it was difficult to do and only partially accurate any more than one would reject the art of navigation because ships are frequently wrecked.

One of the fathers of medicine, Galen, (born 129 AD) began to study philosophy but turned to medicine at the age of seventeen because of a dream his father had. He innovated many medical practices and left us about twenty volumes of medical treatises, averaging one thousand pages each. He was the first to recognize the physiological symptoms of emotional states, such as the quickening of the heart beat of those who are in love. He refused to accept supernatural influences in medicine and felt that all his remedies were shown by experiment and experience and were naturally understandable.

Galen recognized the value of using dreams for diagnosing illness as well as for predicting the future. He divined propensities toward various diseases from a person's horoscope and recognized critical days when the moon had an influence on illness and on the appropriate treatments. He accepted the doctrine of occult virtues in medicine which were the property of the substance as a whole and not any part of it which might be isolated. These virtues were discovered through contemplation on a given substance.

Appolonius of Tyana

Approximately 217 AD, Philostratus composed the *Life of Appolonius* at the request of the learned wife of the emperor Septimus Severus who possessed documents belonging to Damis. Philostratus used the will and epistles of Apollonius and also personally took the trouble to visit the cities and temples which Appolonius had frequented in his lifetime about a hundred years earlier.

Appolonius was a Pythagorian philosopher whose miracles in raising the dead and healing the sick have been compared to those Christ performed. During his travels he associated with the brahmins of India and also the Persian magi. In Rome he was arrested and tried before the emperor Domition for sorcery, because he had managed to predict the plague at Ephesus. He claimed that it was merely his moderate diet which kept his senses clear and enabled him to see the present and the future with an unclouded vision. Philostratus implied that

29

Appolonius managed to inexplicably vanish from the courtroom.

Appolonius believed that health and purity were a prerequisite for divination. His life was also guided by dreams; and he would interpret the dreams of others as well. He would not sacrifice animals, but he enlarged his divinatory powers during his sojourn among the Arab tribes, by learning to understand the language of animals and listen to the birds—for animals and birds seemed to predict the future. He would also observe smoke rising from burning incense.

His ability to detect and deal with demons is illustrated in the story of a lamia (which has become immortalized in a poem by Keats) or evil demon which he disposed of through his penetrating insight. In fact, he was held with such awe by his disciples that they believed him to be a daemon or demigod.

Ancient Hebrews and Early Christians

One encounters many instances of higher communication in the Bible. Dream interpretation is common. God speaks to men directly and also through angels and at times appears in burning bushes and whirlwinds. Prophets communicate with God. Joseph, for example, uses a silver cup like a crystal ball—for divination. Miracles of a wide variety abound in the works attributed to Moses. Of particular interest is the *ark of the covenant*, a device through which the God of the Hebrews spoke to his people.

Judaism was neither a nature religion of the type which focused primarily on the changing of seasons and ensuring fertility, nor was it primarily a religion of mystical union through contemplation. There were elements of natural and mystical religion in Judaism, but it was primarily a historical religion in which God interacted with and shaped the destiny of the Hebrew nation.

Nevertheless there are many instances in Judaism of prayer as an altered state of consciousness, of healing, glossolalia or speaking in tongues, revelry, fasting, retreating to the wilderness, and possibly the use of mind-altering drugs as annointing oils, as well as esoteric communities such as the Essenes and various schools of prophecy.[42] An important branch of Jewish mysticism was based on attaining the vision of the throne of god as described in the first chapter of the Book of Ezekial. The cabalistic tradition in Judaism is based on the ascent of consciousness through various stages to the ultimate vision of the throne of glory—and beyond all vision to union with God.[43]

In Christianity one finds similar trends. Jesus is noted for miracles—or psychic feats: healing the sick, raising the dead, walking on water, multiplying loaves and fishes.

This excerpt from an apocryphal gospel of Mark quoted in a letter from an early Church father, Clement of Alexandria provides a glimpse into the powerful consciousness Jesus possessed:

30

And they came into Bethany. And a certain woman whose brother had died was there. And, coming, she prostrated herself before Jesus and says to him, 'Son of David,/ have mercy on me.' But the disciples rebuked her. And Jesus, being angered, went off with her into the garden where the tomb was, and / straightaway a great cry was heard from the tomb. And going near, Jesus rolled away stone from the door of the tomb. And straightaway, going in where the youth was, he stretched forth his hand and raised him, seizing his hand. But the youth, looking upon him, loved him / began to beseech him that he might be with him. And going out of the tomb they came into the house of the youth, for he was rich. And after six days Jesus told him what to do and in the evening the youth comes to him, wearing a linen cloth over his naked body. And he remained with him that night, for / Jesus taught him the mystery of the kingdom of God.[44]

This passage suggests that Jesus administered some sort of nocturnal initiation ritual, reminiscent of the Greek and Egyptian mysteries. Clement, who lived in the second century, was instrumental in integrating these pagan mysteries into the framework of a Christian spiritual life. However the main message of Jesus is that of living a life of virtue, obeying certain precepts—particularly the gentle virtues of love and kindness, the virtues of the heart. The early Christians, until the time Christianity was accepted by the Roman emperor Constantine, were strictly pacifists.

The teachings of Jesus can be seen as a form of bhakti yoga —attainment through love and devotion to a master. By stating that the Kingdom of Heaven is within you, Jesus was relating spiritual salvation to psychological growth.

The early Christian monastics, particularly in Egypt, practiced a number of austerities such as fasting, solitude, self-mortification, celibacy, sitting on poles, sleep-deprivation, etc.[45] Theirs was a mystical philosophy of the inner vision of Christ, and often many varieties of demons came to tempt them from the purity of their path. Mystics such as St. Anthony, when confronted by tormenting demons, recognized them as intangible thoughtforms who could not do harm (very much in the tradition of the *Tibetan Book of the Dead*.) The desert became so crowded with solitary monks that they founded their own communities. These monastaries were a mystical source of the power of the Church for many centuries.

In fact, it was this practice of holy penitance which eventually led to the penitentiaries of our "modern" penal system. The first institutions of this sort were operated by the Catholic Church in Europe and by the Quakers in the United States.

St. Augustine (354-430 AD) described in his *City of God* a very vivid picture of the evolution of the soul through stages towards the heavenly kingdom. Like later church fathers, he proclaimed that while magic was real, it was the work of the devil and therefore evil. On the other hand, while he repudiated pagan magic, Augustine fervently believed in the protection which angels and guardian spirits would provide to Christians:

They watch over and guard us with great care and diligence in all places and at all hours, assisting, providing for our necessities with so-

The Temptation of St. Anthony.

licitudes; they intervene between us and Thee, O Lord, conveying to Thee our sighs and groans, and bringing down to us the dearest blessings of Thy grace. They walk with us in all our ways; they go in and out with us, attentively observing how we converse with piety in the midst of a perverse generation, with what ardour we seek Thy kingdom and its justice, and with what fear and awe we serve Thee. They assist us in our labours; they protect us in our rest; they encourage us in battle; they crown us in victories; they rejoice in us when we rejoice in Thee; and they compassionately attend us when we suffer or are afflicted for Thee.[46]

Augustine claimed to attain his knowledge through a series of contemplative glimpses of supramundane reality which set the tone of Christian mysticism since his time:

My mind withdrew its thoughts from experience, extracting itself from the contradictory throng of sensuous images, that it might find out what light was wherein it was bathed. . . . And thus with the flash on one hurried glance, it attained to the vision of *That Which Is*. And then at last I saw Thy invisible things understood by means of the things that are made, but I could not sustain my gaze: my weakness was dashed back, and I was relegated to my ordinary experience, bearing with me only a loving memory, and as it were the fragrance of those desirable meats on which as yet I was not able to feed.[47]

32

In his *Dialogues*, Gregory the Great, who was Pope of the Church from 590-604 AD, describes many marvelous wonders which he has learned about Italy's saintly men of Italy either by personal experience or through trustworthy witnesses. Talking to animals, raising the dead, and stopping avalanches were all recorded phenomena in his time.

Hermeticism, Alchemy, and Cabala*

The notion that man can discover the nature of god and the universe by looking within himself has been called The Perennial Philosophy by Aldous Huxley:

> *Philosophia perennis*—the phrase was coined by Leibnitz; but the thing—the metaphysic that recognizes a divine Reality substantial to the world of things and lives and minds; the psychology that finds in the soul something similar to, or even identical with, divine Reality; the ethic that places man's final end in the knowledge of the immanent and transcedent Ground of all being—the thing is immemorial and universal. Rudiments of the Perennial Philosophy may be found among the traditionary lore of primitive peoples in every region of the world, and in its fully developed form it has a place in every one of the higher religions. A version of this Highest Common Factor in all preceding and subsequent theologies was first committed to writing more than twenty-five centuries ago, and since that time the inexhaustible theme has been treated again and again, from the standpoint of every religious tradition and in all the principle languages of Asia and Europe.[48]

Almost invariably this view is set at odds with the dominant social institutions of any culture, although there have been notable exceptions. The imprisonment of Socrates, the crucifixion of Christ, and the later persecution of the gnostics by the Christian church are examples of this basic motif which will continue weaving in and out of the historical orchestration of consciousness exploration as we progress through the centuries.

One method of avoiding persecution for maintaining such heretical views was to publish one's ideas under a pseudonym. This technique has had added advantage of eliminating ego-involvement with one's ideas. Given the psychic interconnection of all individuals, it seemed wise not to be too possessive of any given teachings. Thus the writers of the *Corpus Hermetica* attributed their philosophy—which was simply the latest edition of the Perennial Philosophy—to a legendary figure named Hermes Trismegistus (which means thrice-great). This figure is associated with the god Thoth or Hermes who was alleged to have given the Egyptians their knowledge of the arts and sciences. The main dictum of the hermetic tradition is found in the *Emerald Tablet* which in essence states "As Above, So Below" meaning that man will find within himself the nature of the entire universe.[49]

Professor Wayne Shumaker, a modern historian of the occult sciences, uses the following analogy to place Hermeticism within the vast history of human understanding.

Hermes Trismegistus

---

*Also spelled Cabala, Kabalah, Kabbalah, Qabala, etc.

Again and again we are told the whole world is alive. "If therefore the world is always a living animal—was, and is, and will be—nothing in the world is mortal. Since every single part, such as it is, is always living and is in a world which is always one and is always a living animal, there is no place in the world for death"(Ascl. 29). When in our own day, C. S. Lewis's fictive character Ransom first traveled through space, the word "space," the reader is told, was a "a blasphemous libel for this empyrean ocean of radiance in which they swam. He could not call it 'dead'; he felt life pouring toward him from it every minute." The Hermetic universe was similarly vitalistic, permeated with life. So is the universe of the low savage, the *Naturmensch*; but long before the second and third centuries of our era the primitive belief had been rationalized.[50]

Cabala is the word for the Jewish mystical tradition which acknowledges the personal experience of the absolute. The tree of life diagram shows the ten emanations of god which are the attributes of both man and the universe. In later occult systems the tree of life was used as a philosophical basis for integrating the tarot cards with astrology as well as a guide for meditation and reveries. In these ecstatic states one progressed through a hierarchy of visions which lead to ultimate mystical union. One might say that the tree of life served as a very sophisticated map of the inner spaces through which consciousness progresses.[51]

Alchemy, which has its origins before the time of Christ in the neoplatonic schools of Alexandria as well as in ancient China, was the art of transmuting lead into gold. In many esoteric traditions this transmutation could only be accomplished when the individual had transformed his own consciousness into a state in which he could psychokinetically transform all matter. This involved the possession of the symbolic "philosopher's stone," which required the thorough exploration of the unconscious powers of the mind through

34

dreams and visions. It also involved—especially in China—strenuous forms of yoga and mental concentration to enable one to control the physiological processes of the body. Alchemy assumed the unity of the universe in a primordial substance. The great work of transmutation was done by reducing oneself (or any metal) to that primordial substance and then rebuilding it into any desired element.[52] In a future chapter we will find similar ideas being invoked to explain the physical under-pinnings of parapsychology.

Several actual instances of transmutation have been reported throughout history, some of them recorded by serious scientists and by rulers who could not easily be deceived. For example, John Friedrich Schweitzer or Helvetius, who was the physician to the Prince of Orange in the 17th Century, and an antagonist to the claims of the alchemists, writes that he was visited one day by a stranger who claimed to have produced the fabled philosopher's stone. Helvetius managed to extract a few particles from the stone by which he was able to change three drachmas of lead into gold. The news spread quickly and the case was investigated by the philosopher Spinoza who visited both Helvetius and the goldsmith who had tested the gold. Although Helvetius expressed criticism of certain of Spinoza's theories and the men were not on friendly terms with each other, Spinoza attested to the reality of this transmutation.[53, 54]

The most famous of the alchemists was Nicolas Flamel who lived in Paris during the fourteenth and early fifteenth centuries. Although his transmutation has not been confirmed by witnesses, its reality seems plausible since his wealth is known to have suddenly increased. He and his wife founded, and endowed with revenues, fourteen hospitals, three chapels, and seven churches in Paris—and claim to have accomplished about as much in Boulogne. His name has long been venerated by the French People.[55]

During the period known as the European dark ages (from 600 to 1200 AD) very little progress in the arts or sciences was noted. Even the alchemy which flourished was of a very pragmatic sort, as free from mysticism, from dreams and visions as it was from theoretical discussion. However, in Arab countries the arts, sciences and the exploration of consciousness all continued to flourish.

Arabic Countries

One of the greatest Arab occult scholars was Ya'kub ibn Sabbah al Kindi who died in 873 AD and is simply known as Alkindi. He translated the works of Aristotle and other Greeks into Arabic, and wrote books about philosophy, politics, mathematics, medicine, music, astronomy and astrology. He developed his own very detailed philosophy based on the concept of the radiation of forces or rays from everything in the world. Fire, color and sound were common examples of this radiation.

Alkindi was quite careful to distinguish between radiation which could be observed through the science of physics—due

to the action of objects upon one another by contact—and radiation of a more hidden interaction, over a distance, which sages perceive inwardly. Radiant interactions were for him the basis of astrology. Human imagination, was capable of forming concepts and then emitting rays which were able to affect exterior objects. Alkindi claimed that frequent experiments have proven the potency of words when uttered in exact accordance with the imagination and intention.

Favorable astrological conditions were capable of heightening these "magical" effects. Furthermore, the rays emitted by the human mind and voice became the more efficacious for moving matter if the speaker had his mind fixed upon the names of god or some powerful angel. Such an appeal to higher powers was not necessary however when the person was attuned to the harmony of nature (or in Chinese terms, the Tao). Alkindi also advocated the use of magical charms and words:

> The sages have proved by frequent experiments that figures and characters inscribed by the hand of man on various materials with intention and due solemnity of place and time and other circumstances have the effect of motion upon external objects.''[56]

He further recognized that man's psychic vision is heightened when the soul dismisses the senses and employs the formative or imaginative virtues of the mind. This happens naturally in sleep.

Unfortunately, the details of the experimental techniques of Alkindi and his associates have not been handed down. Nevertheless he does deserve credit as an important pioneer of psychical research.

One of the most sophisticated critics of psychic phenomena, a contemporary of Alkindi, was Costa ben Luca of Baalbek who wrote an important work on magic called *The Epistle concerning Incantations, Adjurations and Suspensions from the Neck*. In this document he strongly asserts that the state of one's consciousness will have an effect on their body. If a man believes that a magical ritual or incantation will help him, he will at least benefit by his own confidence. Similarly, if a person is afraid that magic is being used against him, he may fret himself into illness. Ben Luca did not accept the notion of the occult virtues of stars or demons but did admit that strange phenomena were possible and will one day be understood. He listed a number of ancient magical techniques and felt that these were useful in treating people who feel they were enchanted.[57]

Although both Alkindi and ben Luca lived in Arab countries and wrote in Arabic, neither of them were Moslems. Like Judaism and Christianity, Islam was essentially an historical religion with primary emphasis on the law. Yet within Islam the perennial philosophy was maintained by the Sufi mystics—who were often persecuted.

The Sufi tradition, which originated in Persia, involved singing, dancing and storytelling as techniques for exploring the inner mind. Many of the wonders described in the *Tales of the Arabian Nights* are of Sufi origin. Snake charming and fire-eating practices still exist as testimony to the faith and spiritual power of certain sufi mystics.

36

One well-known Sufi was the Sheikh Shahab-el-Din. Idries Shah relates the following story about him:

> It is related of him that he once asked the Sultan of Egypt to place his head in a vessel of water. Instantly the Sultan found himself transformed into a shipwrecked mariner, cast ashore in some totally unknown land.
>
> He was rescued by woodmen, entered the nearest town (vowing vengeance against the Sheikh whose magic had placed him in this plight) and started work there as a slave. After a number of years he gained his freedom, started a business, married and settled down. Eventually, becoming impoverished again, he became a free-lance porter, in an attempt to support his wife and seven children.
>
> One day, chancing to be by the seashore again, he dived into the water for a bath.
>
> Immediately he found himself back in the palace at Cairo, again the King, surrounded by courtiers, with the grave-faced Sheikh before him. The whole experience, though it had seemed like years, had taken only a few seconds.
>
> This application of the doctrine that "time has no meaning to the Sufi" is reflected in a famous instance of the life of Mohammed. It is related that the Prophet, when setting out on his miraculous 'Night Journey,' was taken by the angel Gabriel to Heaven, to Hell and to Jerusalem. After four-score and ten conferences with God, he returned to earth just in time to catch a pot of water that had been overturned when the angel took him away.[58]

The Sufis loved to tell such stories.

Medieval Exploration of Consciousness

Moses Maimonides (1135-1204), the greatest Jewish medieval philosopher, lived in Cairo although he was born in Spain. There he was the chief physician to the vizier of the Sultan. Continuing the allegorical method of Philo, and well-steeped in the Cabala, he attempted to reconcile Jewish thought with Greek Philosophy. He held that the celestial bodies were living, animated beings and that the heavenly spheres were conscious and free. In his *Guide to the Perplexed*, written in Arabic in 1190, he states that all philosophers are agreed that the inferior world, of earthly corruption and degeneration, is ruled by the natural virtues and influences of the more refined celestial spheres. He even felt that every human soul has its origin in the soul of the celestial sphere.

Maimonides believed in a human faculty of natural divination and that in some men "imagination and divination are so strong that they correctly forecast" the greater part of future events. Nevertheless he upholds human free will and man's responsibility for his own actions.

While he did believe in angels, he would not accept the existence of demons—saying that evil was mere privation. Alleged cases of possession by demons were diagnosed by him as simple melancholy. In accordance with Mosaic law, he accepted injunctions against the occult practices of idolotry and magic. Yet he maintained that any practices which were known to have a natural cause or were proved efficacious by experience, as in the use of medicinal charms, were permissible. This differentiation between demonic and natural magic was to be emphasized by scholars for several centuries.

Medieval culture reached its height in the thirteenth century. The monastic orders, which had maintained traditions of mystical contemplation for nearly a thousand years, by then had extended their work into the realm of learning. The papacy of this period functioned as a world government more effectively than at any time before or since. Petty wars among princes were reduced, and the church evinced greater tolerance for heretics and mystics. Gothic architecture gave expression to the deepest ideals of the perennial philosophy, describing the soul of man reaching for the stars and beyond to the very throne of god. In some cases hermetic and astrological symbolism gracing the art work inside cathedrals clearly indicated the preservation of the esoteric traditions among the designers of these great monuments to a spiritually-oriented culture.[59,60] Soon intellectual life thrived and universities were founded. The leading figure in thirteenth century learning was Albertus Magnus, a Dominican friar who was finally cannonized as a saint in 1931.

Albertus, who has left us eight books on physics, six on psychology, eight on astronomy, twenty-six on zoology, seven on botany, five on minerals, one on geography, and three on

38

life in general, was strongly influenced by Aristotle. Believing that god acts through natural causes in natural phenomena, he conducted experiments in the field of animal behavior and thus became an important forerunner of modern experimental science. He was known to have had miraculous visions since childhood.

He was also an ardent philosopher of magic and expressed a very positive attitude toward the magi of the Bible as "masters who philosophize about the universe and . . . search the future in stars." This view still persists in the Roman Catholic Church.

For Albertus, heaven and the stars are the mediums between the primal cause, or Aristotle's prime mover, and matter. All things produced in nature or in art are influenced by celestial virtues. Man is an *images mundo*, or image of the universe, similar in conception to the hermetic notion of man as a microcosm. His natural magic thus made use of nature and the stars. It included astrology to find a favored hour for beginning a comtemplated act, or an act of contemplation. And Albertus was clearly interested in the transmutation of metals as well as the use of psychic abilities to find metals within the earth. Towards this last end, he recommended employing potions to clog and stupify the senses, thereby producing visions. He also advocated dream interpretation, the use of herbs and magical stones, animal potions and images engraved on gems. When these practices did not work, Albertus maintained that the defects were not to be found in the science of natural magic but in the souls of those who abused it.[61]

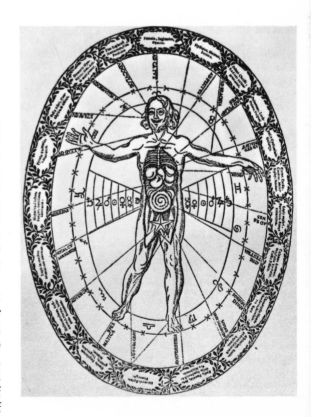

The fourteenth century produced many great European mystics, such as Meister Eckhart and Thomas a Kempis. Their doctrine—one tinged with elements of Kabbalah and hermeticism—is exemplified in a book of uncertain authorship called *The Cloud of Unknowing*. The essential experience which they encouraged was one of transcending experiential and intellectual knowledge to enter a kind of darkness, a cloud of unknowing, which then became illuminated by the love of god.[62]

39

Dante Allegheiri epitomizes the artistic evolution which signalled the end of the middle ages and the rise of the Italian Renaissance. His descriptions in the *Divine Comedy* of his own visions into the worlds of hell, purgatory, and paradise enjoy a paramount position in Western poetry. Yet there is a striking similarity in his work to the understanding of the afterworld one finds earlier in Egypt, Tibet, and Plato, as well as later in the visions of Emmanuel Swedenborg. Dante's familiarity with several systems of medieval mysticism leads us to believe that he used dream and reverie states as an inspirational source for his artwork. The following passage even suggests an out-of-body experience:

At the hour near morning when the swallow begins her plaintive songs, in remembrance, perhaps, of her ancient woes, and when our mind, more a pilgrim from the flesh and less held by thoughts, is in its visions almost prophetic, I seemed to see in a dream an eagle poised in the sky, with feathers of gold, with open wings and prepared to swoop. And I seemed to be in the place where his own people were left behind by Ganymede when he was caught up to the supreme conclave; . . .*[63]

Today we would have no difficulty in finding fault with the scientific methodology of even the greatest thinkers of these times, and there is little doubt that the professed magi of medieval and Renaissance times was often the gullible dupe of many superstitious fallacies. However magic was also the art of bringing divine life into physical manifestation. We can see throughout cultural history that the magi were artists who were able to infuse a delicately balanced state of consciousness into their lives and work—one which opens the intuition to the deepest levels of being and then exposes the insights attained to intellectual scrutiny and carefully controlled craftsmanship. It is precisely a process of this sort which underlies all genius. As history unfolds we shall cite other examples in which the development of this creative state of consciousness is clearly linked to esoteric or spiritual practices.

One of the most important metatheoretical assumptions of medieval times has been characterized aptly by Petirim Sorokin —the renowned head of the Department of Sociology at Harvard University.

Unlike our modern culture which offers a conglomeration of values, Sorokin saw medieval European culture as a unified system centering around the infinite, supersensory, omnipresent, omniscient reality known as God. The sensory world was merely considered a temporary "city of man" in which the Christian sought to render himself worthy to enter the City of God. Sorokin labels this type of culture ideational.[64]

These metatheoretical foundations were intimately linked to the social institutions of Medieval Europe, and changes in the broad world view of Western man are associated with the

---

*Ganymede was a Trojan boy of great beauty who was caught up by Jove's eagle and made a cupbearer to the gods.

processes of change which these institutions have undergone. Just as the ideational view of reality was the dominating principle around which medieval thought was organized, so the Christian Church, as guardian and defender of the faith, was the dominating institution around which all other institutions were integrated. Even the great states and nations of medieval Europe had sworn allegiance to the Church. Her sanctity penetrated the legal systems of nations and lent to them a moral authority which was unquestioned, except by heretical freethinkers, Jews, and Arabs—the bearers of the magical traditions.

Curiously one of the important mechanisms by which the Church maintained its sway over the superstitious medieval populace was through the use of magic. The Church maintained many monasteries and convents where "holy" men and women lived in small cells and spent their time in silent work, prayer, and penance. These individuals, conscious of sin within themselves, tried to live according to the ideals of Christian humility. Occasionally these monastic cells were used for

the purposes of punishing offenses of various sorts. This is one of the earliest known origins of our modern prisons:

> The penitant life of the cloistered, spent in small separate cells contiguous to a small workshop, in silence and prayers, was the genesis of the happy idea [of the penitentiary]. But these sainted men voluntarily treated themselves in this manner because they felt culpable in the eyes of God. However those who were guilty not only before God but before men as well could not be treated in like manner. Thus came the transformation of the prison into a school of corrective education which was to return the criminal to society when he had served the penalty, an entirely different man from the one who had entered the prison.[65]

Because of the life they led and the penances and mortifications they imposed on themselves, saints and holy men were believed to have an existence in the supersensual world of heaven and could be useful for relaying messages and prayers from the faithful to the diety. They were held in awe by the common people. Many cults developed which treated the saints like minor dieties—with both good and bad qualities—a hierarchical structure analogous to many polytheistic religions. Thus the myths of original sin and man's fall from paradise halfway to hell inspired emotions of guilt and fear which the Church recognized for which she handily offered Her own brand of salvation as an antidote.

So the Church utilized the penances of its clergy and the myths of its saints effectively to strengthen its moral authority. Men did not consider questioning the inequalities of the existing social order since they were divinely ordained for the purpose of tempering men's souls.[66] It is interesting to note that during the period from 800 to 1300 AD, the time the ideational codes of the Church held the greatest influence, the punishments imposed on offenders by the ecclesiastical authorities were milder than those of other periods.[67]

During the late Middle Ages, however, the authority of the Church began to lose ground. The rise of science and capitalism, the Protestant Reformation, political upheavals, the invention of printing and the spread of learning in popular languages, the rediscovery of classical literature, and other new social stirrings all threatened the security of the Church, which consequently became more repressive. The populace, intuitively sensing that the Church and Her rituals were becoming stale forms, outliving their own creativity, began to revive and adapt the remnants of surviving pagan and folk culture. This was done both as a protest, as in the Black Mass; and as a means to *reestablish contact with the creative psychic energy within*, as with the gnostics, cabbalists, astrologers, alchemists, and certain other mystics, wizards, and sorcerers. At the same time, the fathers of the Church were turning away from the contemplative and visionary tradition and towards the less passionate modes of philosophy, reason and dry scholasticism.

By the fifteenth century, the excesses of the Church heralded the decline of medieval culture. Peace within Europe had only been maintained by long and expensive crusades against the Moslems. Recent discoveries of explorers led to a questioning of established science and religion. Wandering

The Witch by Hans Weiditz from Petrarca's "Von der Artzney Beider Glück" (1532)

42

astrologers, transient alchemists, unlicensed medical practitioners and intellectual vagabonds were able to influence the ruling classes. They were popular with princes and patricians. Occultism now combined with a renewed skepticism of the church. Persecution for witchcraft and heresy were on the rise. People began to turn away Aristotelian logic, a resurgence of interest in Neo-Platonism. Scholars began to reject former theological views for a new humanism which attempted to recreate the "golden age" of ancient times. Natural and occult science, mathematics, medicine and classical studies offered a common meeting ground for individuals free from religious and political prejudices. A new spirit was born.[68]

One of the most remarkable documents of this period is a magical grimoire titled *The Book of the Sacred Magic of Abra-Melin, the Mage—As Delivered by Abraham the Jew Unto His Son Lamech*. Rich in its description of the magical spirit of the times and elegant in its exposition of an occult system, the grimoire is divided into three books allegedly written in 1458 by an aged occultist as a legacy to his son, Lamech.*

The first book describes the background and history of the author who, having been instructed in the Kaballah, eventually left home and travelled throughout Europe in search of greater wisdom. Abraham studied with many teachers, but was not satisfied with the depth of their understanding. For example, there was Rabbin Moses of Mayence:

> . . . in his Magic he did not in any way make use of the Wisdom of the Lord, but instead availed himself of certain arts and superstitions of infidel and idolatrous nations, in part derived from the Egyptians, together with images of the Medes and of the Persians, with herbs of the Arabians, together with the Power of the Stars and Constellations. . . . And in everything the spirits blinded him to such an extent, even while obeying him in some ridiculous and inconsequent matter, that he actually believed that his blindness and error were the Veritable Magic, and he therefore pushed no further his research into the True and Sacred Magic. . . .
> The Rabbin Moses persuaded me to be wise, while he himself, with words which neither he nor any other person understood, and with extravagant symbols made bells to sound, and while with execrable conjurations he made appear in glasses him who had committed a theft, and while he made a water causing an old man to appear young (and that only for the space of two hours and no longer).[69]

After ten years of wandering, Abraham finally encountered a teacher of the true wisdom in the form of Abra-Melin who lived as a hermit in the Egyptian desert. Abra-Melin accepted Abraham as a student, after satisfying himself as to the purity of his intentions, and instructed him in the sacred magic. Abraham then described the uses he puts his magic to in aiding the various princes and monarchs of Europe. The second two books describe an actual magical operation, the purpose of which was to invoke one's Holy Guardian Angel.

This invocation can not be accomplished without six months of preparatory purification and prayer, conducted in

*The alchemist, Nicolas Flamel, claimed to have learned his art from a rare manuscript also written by "Abraham the Jew."

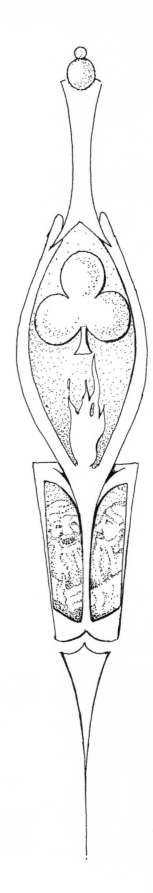

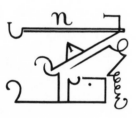

solitude. A number of magic squares for performing various magical feats are included in the third book—however their function is somewhat vague, as it is intended that detailed instruction will come directly from one's own Angel. According to this system of magic, after successfully invoking the angel, one then acquires dominion over all spirits and demons.

As for the art of invoking spirits, Cornelius Agrippa, a magus whose influence was considerable in his day, has left us the following description:

If you would call any evil Spirit to the Circle it first behooveth us to consider and to know his nature, to which of the planets he agreeth, and what offices are distributed to him from the planet.

This being known, let there be sought out a place fit and proper for his invocation, according to the nature of the planet, and the quality of the offices of the same Spirit, as near as the same may be done.

For example, if his power be over the sea, rivers or floods, then let a place be chosen on the shore, and so of the rest.

In like manner, let there be chosen a convenient time, both for the quality of the air—which should be serene, quiet and fitting for the spirits to assume bodies—and for the quality and nature of the planet, and so, too, of the Spirit: to wit, on his day, noting the time wherein he ruleth, whether it be fortunate or unfortunate, day or night, as the stars and Spirits do require.

These things being considered, let there be a circle framed at the place elected, as well as for the defense of the invocant as for the confirmation of the spirit. In the Circle itself there are to be written the general Divine names, and those things which do yield defense unto us; the Divine names which do rule the said planet, with the offices of the spirit himself; and the names, finally, of the good Spirits which bear rule and are able to bind and constrain the Spirit which we intend to call.

If we would further fortify our Circle, we may add characters and penticles to the work. So also, and within or without the Circle, we may frame an angular figure, inscribed with such numbers as are congruent among themselves to our work. Moreover, the operator is to be provided with lights, perfumes, unguents and medicines compounded according to the nature of the Planet and Spirit, which do partly agree with the Spirit, by reason of their natural and celestial virtue, and partly are exhibited to the Spirit for religious and superstitious worship.

The operator must also be furnished with holy and consecrated things, necessary as well for the defense of the invocant and his followers as to serve for bonds which shall bind and constrain the Spirits.

Such are holy papers, lamens, pictures, pentacles, swords, sceptres, garments of convenient matter and color, and things of like sort.

When all these are provided, the master and his fellows being in the Circle, and all those things which he useth, let him begin to pray with a loud voice and convenient gesture and countenance. Let him make an oration unto God, and afterwards entreat the good Spirits. If he will read any prayers, psalms or gospels for his defence, these should take the first place.

Thereafter, let him begin to invocate the Spirit which he desireth, with a gentle and loving enchantment to all the coasts of the world, commemorating his own authority and power, Let him then rest a little, looking about him to see if any Spirit do appear, which if he delay, let him repeat his invocation as before, until he hath done it three times.

If the Spirit be still pertinacious and will not appear, let him begin to conjure him with the Divine Power, but in such a way that all the conjurations and commemorations do agree with the nature and offices of the spirit himself.

Reiterate the same three times, from stronger to stronger, using objurations, contumelies, cursings, punishments, suspensions from his office and power and the like.

After all these courses are finished, again cease a little, and if any Spirit shall appear, let the invocant turn towards him, and receive him courteously and, ernestly entreating him, let him require his name. Then proceeding further, let him ask whatsoever he will.

But if in anything the Spirit shall show himself obstinate and lying, let him be bound by convenient conjurations, and if you still doubt of any lie, make outside the Circle, with the consecrated Sword, the figure of a triangle or pentacle, and compel the Spirit to enter it. If you would have any promise confirmed by oath, stretch the sword out of the Circle, and swear the Spirit by laying his hand upon the sword.

Then having obtained of the Spirit that which you desire, or being otherwise contented, license him to depart with courteous words, giving command unto him that he do no hurt.

If he will not depart, compel him by powerful conjurations and, if need require, expel him by exorcism and by making contrary fumigations.

When he is departed, go not out of the Circle, but stay, making prayer for your defense and conservation, and giving thanks unto God and the good angels. All these things being orderly performed, you may depart.

But if your hopes are frustrated, and no Spirit will appear, yet for this do not despair but, leaving the Circle, return again at other times, doing as before.[70]

Occult scholarship attempted to systematize everything from tastes, smells, colors, and body parts, to herbs, charms, spirits and dreams. It was an imaginative effort based primarily on introspection and reflection, but without proper standards of measurement and adequate means of correcting error. Nevertheless deep levels of the psyche were involved in this effort to condense esoteric knowledge into meaningful symbols. This in-depth study of the intuitive and emotional connections between consciousness and the external world has a built-in difficulty in that the exact conditions necessary to create subtle intuitions and visions do not readily repeat themselves.

Foremost among the occult scientists of his age was Phillipus Aureolus Theophrastus Bombastus von Hohenheim—otherwise known as Paracelsus. He was born in Switzerland in 1493 and spent his entire life wandering throughout Europe and acquiring a great reputation for medical ability, unorthodox views and a testy personality. For example, he was known to have publicly burned established medical texts. It is very difficult to distinguish his work from that of his students, interpreters, translators and editiors. Very little of his writing was published in his own lifetime and few of his original manuscripts survive today. His German writings were only noticed for their originality about twenty years after his death when scholars saw in him an alternative to stale medieval and latin learning.[71]

Today he is recognized as the first modern medical scientist, as the precursor of microchemistry, antisepsis, modern wound surgery, and homeopathy. He wrote the first comprehensive work on the causes, symptoms and treatment of syphilis. He proposed that epileptics should be treated as sick persons and not as lunatics possessed by demons. He studied bronchial illnesses in mining districts and was one of the first

A MAN OF MAGIC AND MEDICINE
Theophrastus Bombastus von Hohenheim, better known as Paracelsus, was the 16th Century Swiss physician who pioneered in the use of several modern medical techniques. Although he was also engrossed with the occult arts. Paracelsus is credited as the father of anesthesia; he wrote "Miners' Sickness," the first treatise on occupational diseases, and he insisted on cleanliness as a vital necessity for health.

people to recognize the connection between an industrial environment and certain types of disease. Notwithstanding this accurate scientific bent, his work is in close accord with the mystical alchemical tradition.

He wrote on furies in sleep, on ghosts appearing after death, on gnomes in mines and underground, of nymphs, pygmies, and magical salamanders. His world view was animistic. Invisible forces were always at work and the physician had to constantly be aware of this fourth dimension in which he was moving. He utilized various techniques for divination and astrology as well as magical amulets, talismans, and incantations. He believed in a vital force which radiated around every man like a luminous sphere and which could be made to act at a distance. He is also credited with the early use of what we now know as hypnotism. He believed that there was a star in each man.[72]

Another important occult scholar was John Dee (1527-1608) who was one of the most celebrated and remarkable men of the Elizabethan age. His world was half magical and half scientific; he was noted as a philosopher, mathematician, technologist, antiquarian, as well as a teacher and astrologer. He was the first Englishman to encourage the founding of a royal library. He personally owned the largest library in sixteenth century England, which contained over 4,000 volumes. He held a large influence over the intellectual life of his times. He wrote the preface for the first English translation of Euclid and is given credit for the revival of mathematical learning in rennaissance England.[73] According to Lynn Thorndike in the *History of Magic and Experimental Science:*

> For John Dee the world was a lyre from which a skillful player could draw new harmonies. Every thing and place in the world radiated force to all other parts and received rays from them. There were also relations of sympathy and antipathy between things. Species, both spiritual and natural, flowed off from objects with light or without it, impressing themselves not only on the sight but on the other senses, and especially coalescing in our imaginative spirit and working marvels in us. Moreover, the human soul and specific form of every thing has many more and more excellent virtues and operations than has the human body or the matter of the thing in question. Similarly the invisible rays of the planets or their secret influence surpass their sensible rays or light.

John Dee and Edmund Kelly evoking a spirit.

He maintained that these invisible influences could be made manifest through the art of crystal gazing, which involved entering into a trance-like consciousness. He conducted many experiments in which he claimed to be in contact with angels through the use of a medium.

Dee's philosophy was embodied in a work entitled *Hieroglyphic Monad Explained Mathematically, Cabalistically and Anagogically.* This book, which served as an important foundation of the Rosicrucian movement, attempted to synthesize and condense all of the then current mystical traditions within the symbolism which characterizes the planet Mercury.

Queen Elizabeth herself was very taken with Dee's ideas. She appointed him as her court philosopher and astrologer, and asked for personal instruction into the abstruse symbolic meanings of his book. Nevertheless he was still a very controversial figure because of his reputation as a conjurer. Dee lost favor with the court when James ascended to the throne.[74]

In Germany at the beginning of the 17th century, astrology itself was becoming very controversial. In 1610, the great astronomer Johannes Kepler published a work which attempted to intervene in a public conflict between a pastor who issued prognostications and a physician who had attacked astrology. The title was:

> A Warning to Sundry Theologians, Medical Men and Philosophers . . .that They, while very Properly Overthrowing Stargazing Superstition, do not Chuck out the Baby with the Bathwater and thereby Unwittingly Injure Their Profession.

Johannes Kepler

Kepler's reasoned attitude toward astrology was to try and determine precisely the extent and manner of the influence of the heavenly bodies upon the earth and its inhabitants. He was very concerned with revising and reforming the traditional rules of astrology in accordance with his own observations.

For example, he condemned the general run of astrological predictions, maintaining that only one in a hundred was accurate. He further argued that the division of the zodiac into twelve signs was also completely arbitrary and irrelevant. Nevertheless, he felt that these could be kept simply as a matter of convenience.

He emphasized the importance of the aspects, or angular relations between the different planets—in fact, he added several aspects of his own invention to those which astrologers traditionally used. In the next chapter we will note that modern experimental work in astrology has taken a similar position.

In 1619, Kepler published *Harmonice Mundi* in which he described the results of twenty years of astrological observations. He maintained that the degree of harmony of the rays descending from the heavenly bodies to the earth was a function of their angular relationships. He described the similarities between planetary aspects and musical consonance and the effects different configurations of the planets exerted on the emotional and mental lives of animals and humans. He also observed the weather's relationship to the planetary aspects. Of particular importance to him was the influence of the sun and the moon upon the earth. All bodily fluids waxed and waned with the moon, which was therefore very influential in the treatment of diseases. And he felt that the nature of planetary influences were revealed by their colors.

Kepler reaffirmed the importance of the positions of the planets at the moment of birth.

> In general there is no expedite and happy genesis unless the rays and qualities of the planets meet in apt, and indeed geometric, agreement.

He even thought that sons, particularly the first-born, were often born under horoscopes similar to their parents. This curious hypothesis is also born out by some current research which will be mentioned in the next chapter.

Kepler, of course, is best known to modern science for his laws of planetary motions and his support of the heliocentric theory of the solar system. He also felt that the sun itself was the soul of the whole universe, presiding over the movements of the stars, the regeneration of the elements, and the conservation of animals and plants.

To him the earth was like an animal, with "the twin faculty of attracting sea waters into the secret seats of concoction, and of expelling the vapors which have been thus concocted. By its perception of the celestial aspects it is stimulated and excited to excrete these vapors with a pleasure akin to that which an animal feels in the ejaculation of its semen. Man, too, is not merely a rational being but is endowed with a natural faculty like that of the earth for sensing celestial configurations, 'without discourse, without learning, without progress, without even being aware of it.'"[75]

Kepler developed his theories on the basis of explorations into the dimly lit archetypal regions of man's mind as surely as on his mathematical observations of the planetary motions. He was clearly a student in the tradition of earlier mystic-scientists such as Pythagoras and Paracelsus.[76]

This same fusion of world views is to be found in the teachings of the Rosicrucian movement, which caused quite a public stir in seventeenth century England, France, Italy and Germany. Only a limited number of men, most notably John Dee's student Robert Fludd, openly identified themselves as Rosicrucians. Most of the manifestos which caused a great uproar were published anonymously. Emphasizing earlier notions common to hermeticism, alchemy and the kabbalah, the Rosicrucian documents proclaimed the existence of a hidden brotherhood of scholars and explorers who were united in teaching the deepest mysteries of nature, free from religious and political prejudice.

The following excerpt is taken from the last paragraph of *Fame of the Fraternity of the Rosie Cross*—an early manifesto first printed in 1614 and translated into English by Thomas Vaughan in 1652:

> And although at this time we make no mention either of our names, or meetings, yet nevertheless every ones opinion shal assuredly come to our hands, in what language soever it be; nor any body shal fail, who so gives but his name to speak with some of us, either by word of mouth, or else if there be some lett in writing. And this we say for a truth, That wosoever shal earnestly, and from his heart, bear affection unto us, it shal be beneficial to him in goods, body and soul; but he that is false-hearted, or only greedy of riches, the same first of all shal not be able in any manner of wise to hurt us, but bring himself to utter ruine and destruction. Also our building (although one hundred thousand people had very near seen and beheld the same) shal for ever remain untouched, undestroyed, and hidden to the wicked world, *sub umbra alarum tuarum Jehova.**[77]

At this same time Sir Francis Bacon (1561-1626) in England was also calling for a brotherhood that would foster the "advance-

To Kepler the Earth was like an animal.

---

*"Under the shadow of thy wings, Jehova."

ment of learning". His effort ultimately lead to the founding of the Royal Society in 1660. During his association with King James in England, Bacon was careful never to publicly connect himself with the Rosicrucians or any other occult movements. However, in a work published after his death. *The New Atlantis*, he describes his own version of a utopian society, revealing his sympathies and possible connection with this movement, and the *Invisible College*.

In the following passage from *New Atlantis*, the governor of the invisible island of which Bacon writes, describes the pre-eminent reason for the greatness of his society:

It was the erection and institution of an order, or society, which we call Salomon's House; the noblest foundation, as we think, that was ever upon the earth, and the lantern of this kingdom. It is dedicated to the study of the works and creatures of God. Some think it beareth the founder's name a little corrupted, as if it should be Solamona's House. But the records write it as it is spoken. So as I take it to be

The Invisible College of The Rosicrucians

denominate of the king of the Hebrews, which is fameous with you, and no stranger to us; for we have some parts of his works which with you are lost; namely, that Natural History which he wrote of all plants, from the Cedar of Libanus to the moss that groweth out of the wall; and of all things that have life and motion. This maketh me think that our king finding himself to symbolize, in many things, with that king of the Hebrews (which lived many years before him) honoured him with the title of this foundation. And I am the rather induced to be of this opinion, for that I find in ancient records, this order or society is sometimes called Salomon's House, and sometimes the College of the Six Days' Works; whereby I am satisfied that our excellent king had learned from the Hebrews that God had created the world, and all that therein is, within six days: and therefore he instituted that house, for the finding out of the true nature of all things (whereby God ought have the more glory in the workmanship of them, and men the more fruit in the use of them), did give it also that second name. . . .[78]

The *Invisible College* was an important foundation of the Rosicrucian teaching. It was a building with wings, which existed nowhere and yet united the entire secret movement. The high initiates of this society, the R. C. Brothers, were said to be invisible and were able to teach their knowledge of a higher social and scientific order to worthy disciples who themselves became invisible. The symbolism of the invisible college is very complex and further complicated by the social furor which resulted from it. As adventurers and scholars desiring a new social order sought to make contact with the fabled R. C. Brothers, an increasing public outcry resulted in witchhunts and persecutions.[79]

In one sense, the invisible college refers to that type of teaching and inspiration which occurs to one in dreams. The following allegory, written in 1651 by Thomas Vaughan, is quite suggestive of this theory:

Magic Mountain

There is a mountain situated in the midst of the earth or center of the world, which is both small and great. It is soft, also above measure hard and stony. It is far off and near at hand, but by the providence of God invisible. In it are hidden the most ample treasures, which the world is not able to value. This mountain—by envy of the devil, who always opposes the glory of God and the happiness of man—is compassed about with very cruel beasts and ravening birds—which make the way thither both difficult and dangerous. And therefore until now—because the time is not yet come—the way thither could not be sought after nor found out. But now at last the way is to be found by those that are worthy—but nonetheless by every man's self-labor and endeavors.

To this mountain you shall go in a certain night—when it comes—most long and most dark, and see that you prepare yourself by prayer. Insist upon the way that leads to the Mountain, but ask not of any where the way lies. Only follow your Guide, who will offer himself to you and will meet you in the way. But you are not to know him. This Guide will bring you to the Mountain at midnight, when all things are silent and dark. It is necessary that you arm yourself with a resolute and heroic courage, lest you fear those things that will happen, and so fall back. You need no sword nor any other bodily weapons; only call upon God sincerely and heartily.

When you have discovered the Mountain the first miracle that will appear is this: A most vehement and very great wind will shake the Mountain and shatter the rocks to pieces. You will be encountered also by lions and dragons and other terrible beasts; but fear not any of these things. Be resolute and take heed that you turn not back, for your Guide—who brought you thither—will not suffer any evil to befall you. As for the treasure, it is not yet found, but it is very near.

50

After this wind will come an earthquake that will overthrow those things which the wind has left, and will make all flat. But be sure that you do not fall off. The earthquake being past there will follow a fire that will consume the earthly rubbish and disclose the treasure. But as yet you cannot see it.

After these things and near the daybreak there will be a great calm, and you will see the Day-star arise, the dawn will appear, and you will perceive a great treasure. The most important thing in it and the most perfect is a certain exalted Tincture, with which the world—if it served God and were worthy of such gifts—might be touched and turned into most pure gold.

This Tincture being used as your guide shall teach you will make you young when you are old, and you will perceive no disease in any part of your bodies. By means of this Tincture also you will find pearls of an excellence which cannot be imagined. But do not you arrogate anything to yourselves because of your present power, but be contented with what your Guide shall communicate to you. Praise God perpetually for this His gift, and have a special care that you do not use it for worldly pride, but employ it in such works as are contrary to the world. Use it rightly and enjoy it as if you had it not. Likewise live a temperate life and beware of all sin. Otherwise your Guide will forsake you and you will be deprived of this happiness. For know of a truth: whosoever abuses this Tincture and does not live exemplarly, purely and devoutly before men, will lose this benefit and scarcely any hope will be left of recovering it afterward.[80]

Descartes, who was certainly not an occult scholar or even a sympathizer, nevertheless attributed all of his philosophic ideas to images which appeared to him either in dreams or when he was in the hypnogogic state just before awakening.[81] In fact, he had to "prove his visibility" to keep from being associated with the invisible College. Certainly there was cause for public speculation about an actual college, perhaps diabolical, which dreamers visited in their sleep.

In another sense, the invisible college referred to an influential, though hidden, political, artistic, and scientific movement that included Francis Bacon and other notable Renaissance figures dedicated to the teachings of the perennial philosophy. For example there is evidence connecting Robert Boyle, who developed the laws relating the pressure of a gas at a fixed temperature to the inverse of its volume, with the college. Sir Isaac Newton also indicated an awareness of this movement.

Wilhelm Leibnitz

Deeply steeped in the occult lore of the Renaissance, the great philosopher and mathematician Gottfried Wilhelm Leibnitz (1646-1716) translated the inner-space studies of the astrologers, alchemists and rosicrucians into more refined mathematical and philosophical idioms. He was fascinated with John Dee's efforts to grasp the deep mechanisms of universal processes and condense them into symbols. It was his study of the use of hieroglyphs thoughout history that led him to the discovery of infintesimal calculus—which he foresaw would evolve into a universal language.[82]

Carrying on the Pythagorian-Platonic doctrine of universal harmony, Leibnitz developed an elegant grand philosophy based on the concept of an evolving unit of consciousness called the *monad*. Monads for Leibnitz are the most fundamental metaphysical points which have always existed and can never be destroyed.

Leibnitz felt that all matter is alive and animated throughout with monads. The monad is the principle of continuity between the physical and the psychological realms. The same principle which expresses itself within our minds is active in inanimate matter, in plants, and in animals. Thus the nature of the monad is best understood by studying the spiritual and psychic forces within ourselves.

Monads themselves vary in the amount of consciousness or clarity of their perceptions. Certain physical facts, such as the principle of least action, indicated to Leibnitz an intelligence within the most basic particles in creation. On the other hand, the findings of psychology have indicated that there are areas of the mind which are unconscious in their nature. In the lowest monads everything is obscure and confused, resembling sleep. While in man, consciousness attains a state of *apperception*—a reflexive knowledge of the self.

Every monad discovers its nature from within itself. It is not determined from without; there are no windows through which anything can enter; all of its experience already exists within each monad.

Both organisms and inorganic bodies are composed of monads, or centers of force, but the organism contains a central monad or "soul" which is the guiding principle of the other monads within its body. Inorganic bodies are not centralized in this way, but consist of a mere mass or aggregation of monads. The higher the organism, the more well-ordered will be its system of monads.

Every monad has the power to represent the entire universe within itself. It is a world in miniature, a microcosm, a "living mirror of the universe." Yet each monad has its own unique point of view, with its own characteristic degree of clarity. The higher the monad, the more distinctly it perceives and expresses the world; the monads with which it is most closely associated constitute its own body, and these it represents most clearly. Leibnitz states:

> Every body feels everything that occurs in the entire universe, so that anyone who sees all could read in each particular thing that which happens everywhere else and, besides all that has happened and will happen, perceiving in the present that which is remote in time and space.[83]

The monads form a graduated progressive series from the lowest to the highest. There is a continuous line of infinitesimal gradation from the dullest piece of inorganic matter to god, the monad of all other monads—just as the soul is the presiding monad over the other monads within the human body. There is a parallelism between mental and physical states here. The body is the material expression of the soul. However, while the body operates according to the deterministic laws of cause and effect, the soul acts according to the teleological principle of final causes towards its ultimate evolution. These two realms are in harmony with each other.

Another important philosopher of consciousness in this period was Bishop George Berkeley (1685-1753), after whom the City of Berkeley, California—where this book has been written

—was named. Berkeley was a strict idealist who tried to demonstrate that the only things which we ever experience are the perceptions, thoughts and feelings within our own minds. There is no need to ever assume that anything material exists whatsoever. The external world of physics is for all we know a figment of the imagination. Look about you. Everything which you see or sense in any way is simply a sensation in your minds. Is this a book you are reading? Did it take raw materials to produce? That was all somehow an illusion.

But, you will say, there must be some cause of the thoughts and sensations in our minds. For Berkeley this cause is one undivided active spirit which produces these effects upon our consciousness. Although we cannot perceive this spirit itself (any more than we could perceive such nonsense as matter) we still have some notion of it, some apprehension of the greater reality beyond us. You see, we all exist in the Mind of God. As the Hindus would say, this is all simply Shiva's dream.

Bishop George Berkeley

One of the more interesting characters that Shiva dreamt up was Sir Isaac Newton (1642-1727), generally regarded as one of the greatest scientists who ever lived. He discovered the binomial theorem, invented differential calculus, made the first calculations of the moon's attraction by the earth and described the laws of motion of classical mechanics, and formulated the theory of universal gravitation. He was very careful not to publish anything which was not firmly supported by experimental proofs or geometrical demonstrations—thus he exemplified and ushered in the Age of Reason.

However, if we look at Newton's own personal notes and diaries, over a million words in his own handwriting, a startlingly different picture of the man emerges. Sir Isaac Newton was an alchemist. He devoted himself to such endeavors as the transmutation of metals, the philosopher's stone, and the elixir of life. Lord Keynes describes this work in the Royal Society's *Newton Tercentenary Celebrations* of 1947:

> His deepest instincts were occult, esoteric, semantic—with a profound shrinking from the world . . . a wrapt, consecrated solitary, pursueing his studies by intense introspection, with a mental endurance perhaps never equalled.[84]

He attempted to discover the secrets of the universe in apocalyptic writings like the *Book of Revelations* or in occult interpretations of the measurements of Solomon's temple. But Lord Keynes even maintained that there was a magical quality to his scientific thought as well—that he solved a problem intuitively and dressed it up in logical proofs afterwards. Columbia University historian Lynn Thorndike feels one can safely go further than Lord Keynes and compares Newton's method of scientific discovery "to that of a medium coming out of a trance."[85]

Newton himself was astounded by the startling nature of his own theories.

> That gravity should be innate, inherent and essential to matter, so that one body may act upon another at a distance through a vacuum, without the mediation of anything else, by which their force and action may be conveyed to one another. . . .[86]

Sir Isaac Newton

Here he had framed a problem which has never been satisfactorily dealt with by scientists. Gravity is such a common effect that it is taken for granted nevertheless.

Newton used the term *ether* following Descartes to refer to a hypothetical substance which permeated the entire universe and was responsible for gravitation and electromagnetism as well as sensations and nervous stimuli. He felt that this ether itself was the living spirit, although he recognized that sufficient experimental proof did not exist in his own time.

It was only in the twentieth century that scientists actually discarded the concept of ether, although the term is still used pervasively in occult and spiritual circles. The elucidation of the field which unifies both psychical and physical phenomena is still one of the greatest challenges facing scientific research.

Newton normally spelled the word Nature with a capital and, like Kepler, regarded it as a Being or at least a wonderful mechanism second only to God. Newton described his conception of God as:

> Creator and governor of this mechanistic universe, who first created the fermental aether and its principles of action, and then assigned to a lesser power, Nature, the duty of forming and operating the perceptible mechanical universe.

Like most men at the close of the Seventeenth Century, Newton still believed in the existence of animal spirits in the human body. He described them as of an ethereal nature and subtle enough to flow through animal voices as freely as the magnetic effluvia flow through glass. For him, all animal motions resulted from this spirit flowing into the motor nerves and moving the muscles by inspiration.

His followers, however, emphasized his mechanistic view of the universe to the exclusion of his religious and alchemical views. In a sense, their action ushered in a controversy in psychical research which has existed ever since. Since Newton's time, all discoveries suggesting the presence of a spiritual force which transcended time or space were ironically considered to be a violation of Newton's Laws—even though Newton himself held these very beliefs!

Emanuel Swedenborg (1688-1772) the single individual who combined within himself the most intense spiritualistic exploration with the most sophisticated scientific expertise was born the son of a devout Swedish bishop whose family was ennobled by the King when he was thirty-one. Being the eldest son, Baron Emmanuel Swedenborg took a position in the Swedish House of Nobles.

During his long life Swedenborg published scientific papers on a wide variety of topics. They include soils and muds, stereometry, echoes, algebra and calculus, blast furnaces, astronomy, economics, magnetism, and hydrostatics. He founded the science of crystallography and was the first to formulate the nebular hypothesis of the creation of the universe. He spent many years exploring human anatomy and physiology and was the first to discover the functions of the ductless glands and the cerebellum.

Emanuel Swedenborg

In addition to mastering nine languages, he was an inventor and a craftsman. He built his own telescope and microscope. He designed a submarine, air pumps, musical instruments, a glider and mining equipment. Throughout his life he worked as a mining assessor in Sweden. He participated in the engineering of the world's largest drydock. He developed an ear trumpet, a fire extinguisher, and a steel rolling mill. He learned bookbinding, watchmaking, engraving, marble inlay, and other trades. At one point he engineered a military project for the King of Sweden which transported small battleships fourteen miles over mountains and through valleys. At the age of fifty-six, Swedenborg had mastered the known natural science of his day and stood at the brink of his great exploration of the inner worlds.

He began by surveying all that was understood by scholars in the area of psychology and published this in several volumes along with some observations of his own. Then he started writing down and interpreting his own dreams. He developed yoga-like practices of suspending his breathing and drawing his attention inward, thus enabling him to observe the subtle symbol-making processes of his mind. He carefully probed the hypnogogic state, the borderland between sleep and waking in which the mind forms its most fantastic imagery.

As he intensified this process he gradually began to sense the presence of other beings within his own inner states. Such a sensation is common to the hypnogogic state.[87] However for Swedenborg, these occasional glimpses into another world came to full fruition quite suddenly in April of 1744. From that time until his death, twenty-seven years later, he claimed to be in constant touch with the world of spirits. During his waking hours he regularly probed the vast regions of heaven and hell and engaged in long and detailed conversations with angels and spirits.

The following passages provide us with a typical example of Swedenborg's later thought:

OF THE SPEECH OF SPIRITS AND ANGELS

The discourse or speech of spirits conversing with me, was heard and perceived as distinctly by me as the discourse or speech of men; nay, when I have discoursed with them whilst I was also in company with men, I also observed, that as I heard the sound of man's voice in discourse, so I heard also the sound of the voice of spirits, each alike sonorous; insomuch that the spirits sometimes wondered that their discourse with me was not heard by others; for, in respect to hearing there was no difference at all between the voices of men and spirits. But as the influx into the internal organs of hearing is different from the influx of man's voice into the external organs, the discourse of the spirits was heard by none but myself, whose internal organs, by the divine mercy of the Lord, were open. Human speech or discourse is conveyed through the ear, by an external way, by the medium of the air; whereas the speech or discourse of spirits does not enter through the ear, nor by the medium of the air, but by an internal way, yet into the same organs of the head or brain. Hence the hearing in both cases is alike. . . .

The words which spirits utter, that is, which they excite or call forth out of a man's memory, and imagine to be their own, are well chosen and clear, full of meaning, distinctly pronounced, and applicable to the subject spoken of; and, what is surprising, they know how to choose expressions much better and more readily than the man himself; nay, as was shown above, they are acquainted with the various significations of words, which they apply instantaneously, without any premeditation; by reason, as just observed, that the ideas of their language flow only into those expressions which are best adapted to signify their meaning. The case, in this respect, is like that of a man who speaks without thinking at all about his words, but is intent only on their sense; when his thought falls readily, and spontaneously, into the proper expressions. It is the sense inwardly intended that calls forth the words. In such inward sense, but of a still more subtle and excellent nature, consists the speech of spirits, and by which man, although he is ignorant of it, has communication with them.

The speech of words, as just intimated, is the speech proper to man; and indeed, to his corporeal memory: but a speech consisting of ideas of thought is the speech proper to spirits; and, indeed, to the interior memory, which is the memory of spirits. It is not known to men that they possess this interior memory, because the memory of particular or material things, which is corporeal, is accounted every thing, and darkens that which is interior: when, nevertheless, without interior memory, which is proper to the spirit, man would not be able to think at all. From this interior memory I have frequently discoursed with spirits, thus in their proper tongue, that is, by ideas of thought. How universal and copious this language is may appear from this consideration, that every single expression contains an idea of great extent: for it is well known, that one idea of a word, may require many words to explain it, much more the idea of one thing; and still more the idea of several things which may be collected into one compound idea, appearing still as a simple idea. From these considerations may appear what is the natural speech of spirits amongst each other, and by what speech man is conjoined with spirits.[88]

It's tempting to think that Swedenborg went insane at this point. However he otherwise showed no signs of mental weakness. He continued to serve as a mining assessor, for instance, throughout his life. Yet, during this twenty-seven year period he wrote some 282 works in the above manner describing his inner explorations.

When asked how he could write so much, he casually answered that it was because an angel dictated to him. Numbers of people witnessed him speaking with invisible figures, yet he could always be interrupted in the midst of these states to deal with a visitor or a business matter.[89]

He described the world to which we all go after death like a number of different spheres representing various shades of light and happiness, each soul going to that for which his spiritual evolution has fitted him. The light of higher states seems painful and blinding to one who is not yet ready. These spheres resembled the earthly society which Swedenborg knew. His descriptions of life in the spheres are written with the careful mind of a scientist. He speaks of the architecture, the flowers and fruits, the science, the schools, the museums the libraries and the sports.

The great German philosopher Emmanuel Kant set about to examine the Swedenborg phenomena with an aim toward discrediting them. However Kant himself was at a loss to explain the well-reported incident in 1756, when Swedenborg, then in Gottenburg, clairvoyantly saw a fire raging three hundred miles away in Stockholm. This incident occurred in front of fifteen very distinguished observers.[90]

Due to the voluminous quantity of his erudite writings, Swedenborg's popularity has not been large among the general population. Often, his spiritual visions do seem to degenerate into arbitrary theological interpretations of scripture. After his death, the Church of the New Jerusalem was founded to preserve his teachings, which can be found in the encyclopediac *Heaven and Hell, The New Jerusalem* and the *Arcana Coelestia* as well as in several excellent biographies.

Swedenborg's thought was to exert a particular influence on two of Europe's great artistic geniuses, William Blake (1757-1827) and Johann Wolfgang von Goethe (1749-1832).

Perhaps more than any major artist, Blake's poetry and artwork give representation to the inner reality common to mystical philosophers and occult seers. Deep archetypal themes are expressed through the joyous power of Blake's own great imagination:

> Trembling I sit day and night, my
>   friends are astonish'd at me.
> Yet they forgive my wanderings. I rest
>   not from my great task!
> To open the Eternal Worlds, to open the
>   immortal Eyes
> Of Man inwards into the Worlds of Thought,
>   into Eternity
> Ever expanding into the Bosom of God, the
>   Human Imagination.
> O Saviour pour upon me thy Spirit of
>   meekness and love!
> Annihilate the Selfhood in me: be thou
>   all my life!
> Guide thou my hand, which trembles
>   exceedingly upon the rock of ages,
> While I write of the building of Golgonooza,
>   & of the terrors of Entuthon,
> Of Hand and Hyle & Cobon, of Kwantok, Peachey,
>   Brereton, Slayd & Hutton,
> Of the terrible sons & daughters of Albion
>   and their Generations.
>
>   *Jerusalem*, chapter 1

Goethe

Both Blake and Goethe also deeply felt the reality of Plato's World of Ideas as a presence inspiring their own artistic creations. Goethe, generally regarded as Germany's greatest poet and dramatist, actually spent many years of his life attempting to give scientific expression to his poetic insights.

His researches ranged through many fields: botany, animal morphology, physics, geology, and optics. He was recognized for a number of physiological discoveries including the intermaxillary bone and the vertebral theory of the skull in osteology. Goethe is also credited as a forerunner of Darwin's theory of organic development. However his greatest contribution to psychic development was his understanding that the archetypal impulses which motivated his poetry were the same primal Ideas which manifested elsewhere in the world of nature. Just as he was able to perceive these archetypes within his poetry, through the *perceptive power of thinking* he felt one could arrive in the same manner at a scientific understanding of the Ideas imminent in nature, the *Urphanomen*.

57

According to one of his biographers, Rudolph Steiner,* Goethe combined the vision of the mystic with the systematic searching of the scientist:

Primarily, two significant character traits come into consideration here. The first is the urge to reach the sources, the depth of all existence. In its ultimate foundation, it constitutes a belief in the Idea. the presentiment of a Something which is higher, better, inspired Goethe continuously. This might be called a deeply religious trait in his spirit. What so many people feel as an inner need to strip things of all that is sacred and drag them down to their own level Goethe did not feel. But he felt the opposite impulse, to sense some higher goal and to work his way up to that. In each endeavor he sought to gain possession of that aspect through which it could become sacred for him. . . .

This side of his nature is inseparably united with another. Goethe never seeks to approach this higher Being directly; he always seeks to draw near through nature. "The true is Godlike. It does not appear directly; we must divine it from its manifestations." Together with faith in the Idea, Goethe had another faith: that through reflection upon reality, we achieve the Idea. It never occurs to him to seek the Godhead elsewhere than in the works of nature, but he seeks everywhere to gain access to the divine aspect of nature's works . . .

Goethe approached reality with the conviction that everything is only a manifestation of Idea, which we achieve only when we have elevated sense experience into spiritual beholding.[91]

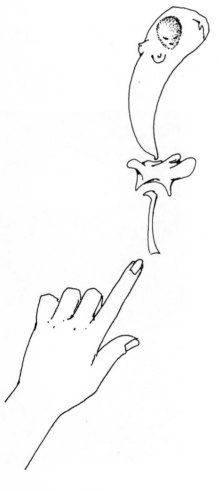

This notion, Goethe's greatest discovery, has generally been ignored by scientists since his time. While appreciating his other researches, they failed to grasp the importance of developing their own consciousness as the most delicate and powerful instrument with which to perceive the universe. Goethe, to obtain a clearer understanding of plantlife, would visualize at night before going to sleep the entire cycle of a plant's development through its various stages from seed to seed. With such methods he eventually came to see the enormous forces of nature at work in the simplest and most trivial of objects.

You can choose any object and imagine the entire natural history of that object passing through your mind while you concentrate on it or hold it in your hand. With practice you may reach a point which is beyond your own subjective inpressions; you will begin to visualize the inner workings of the *Urphanomen*. Parapsychologists have long recognized this process of perception in the form of *psychometry*, by which someone can intuit and then describe the past history of an object merely by coming into contact or proximity with it.

The following story about Goethe's own psychic sensitivity is related in *Phantasms of the Living*:

Wolfgang Goethe was walking one rainy summer evening with his friend K, returning from the Belvedere at Weimar. Suddenly the poet paused as if he saw someone and was about to speak to him. K noticed nothing. Suddenly Goethe exclaimed: "My God! If I were not sure that my friend Frederick is at this moment at Frankfort I should swear that it is he!" The next moment he burst out laughing. "But it is he—my friend Frederick. You at Weimar? But why are you dressed so

---

*Steiner himself was a great philosopher and esoteric teacher in his own right, whose anthroposophical movement was largely inspired by the life and works of Goethe.

—in your dressing gown, with your nightcap and my slippers here in the public road?" K, as I have just said, saw absolutely nothing and was alarmed, thinking that the poet had lost his wits. But Goethe, thinking only of what he saw, cried out again: "Frederick, what has become of you? My dear K, did you notice where that person went who came to meet us just now?" K, stupefied, did not answer. Then the poet, looking all around, said in a dreamy tone: "Yes, I understand . . . it is a vision. What can it mean though? Has my friend suddenly died? Was it his spirit?" Thereupon Goethe returned to the house and found Frederick there already. His hair stood on end. "Avaunt you phantom!" he exclaimed, pale as death. "But my friend," remonstrated Frederick, "is this the welcome that you give to your best friend?" "Ah, this time," exclaimed the poet, with such emotion, "it is not a spirit, it is a being of flesh and blood." The friends embraced warmly. Frederick explained that he had arrived at Goethe's lodging soaked by the rain, had dressed himself in the poet's dry clothing and, having fallen asleep in his chair, had dreamed that he had gone out to meet him and that Goethe had greeted him with the words: "You here! At Weimar? What! With your dressing gown, your nightcap and my slippers here on the public road?"

Ironically, it was in the eighteenth century, the Age of Reason, that the ancient and esoteric techniques of healing, trance induction, and consciousness alteration were reintroduced to the very forefront of public attention. Franz Anton Mesmer (1734-1815), a Vienese trained physician who held to the old astrological beliefs, initiated this new era of consciousness exploration.

At first Mesmer felt that the planets affected human beings through an influence resembling magnetism, and began treating patients by applying magnets to their bodies. Later he stopped using magnets and maintained that any curative influence emanated from the hands and nervous system of the healer. He believed that this influence, which he named *animal magnetism*, could be transmitted to objects held in or stroked by the hand. It could then be discharged to a patient through a suitable conductor. In 1778 he moved to Paris and attracted great notoriety with many patients and pupils among the wealthy classes.

In order to deal with the crowds of patients he attracted, he devised a wooden tub filled with water and iron filings, and containing many bottles of "magnetized water." Iron rods protruded from it which could be applied to diseased or damaged parts of his patients. Clothed in a magician's gown and wand, Mesmer himself moved among the company, making magnetic passes over his patients to a background of soft music and mysterious lighting. Many cures of various diseases were noted. Often they were preceded by convulsive movements and rapturous noises. Numbered among Mesmer's acquaintances, and possibly his patients, were Mozart and his family, King Louis XVI and his queen, Marie Antoinette, as well as Empress Maria Theresa of Austria.

In 1784, the French government appointed an official commission to investigate Mesmer. It was composed of several renowned scientists including Antoine Lavoisier, "the founder of modern chemistry" and Benjamin Franklin. They reported to the Academy of Sciences and the Royal Society of Medicine that the "magnetic fluid" was a myth. Although Mesmer's tech-

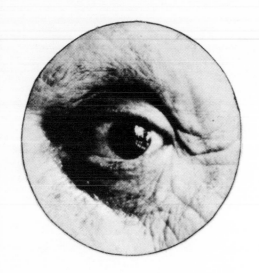

niques did give rise to certain psychophysiological states which might result in the curing of diseases, they agreed with the assumption that Mesmer played upon the imagination of his subjects. Primarily their report stressed the immorality of the healer making magnetic passes over the bodies of his female patients.[92]

Mesmer's reputation waned somewhat. He remained in Paris until 1789 when he fled the revolution. He never regarded himself as a fraud. From his writings there is evidence that he was aware his treatments held a greater significance than simply curing patients.[93]

The most influential of Mesmer's pupils, the Marquis De Puysegur, discovered that patients could be put by "Magnetization" into a sleep-like "somnambulistic" state in which cures could also be affected. Patients in this state showed themselves unusually responsive to the suggestions of the mesmerist, and could be made not only to perform actions, but also to feel emotions or to entertain delusory beliefs. Ordinary senses might be heightened, and other psychic sensitivities seemed to be induced. Of this state, Mesmer writes:

> The somnambulist may perceive the past and the future through an inner sense of his. . . . Man is in contact through his inner sense with the whole of nature and can always perceive the concatenation of cause and effect. . . . Past and future are only different relations of its different parts.[94]

Some patients would diagnose and prescribe for their own ailments, and sometimes they would do this for others using clairvoyance. Puysegur emphasized the importance of the will of the therapist as the directing influence behind the mesmerizing process and claimed the ability to put people into a trance telepathically. Ultimately his theories were no less influential than Mesmer's on the history and development of consciousness.

The following rules of magnetising, based on Puysegur's theories, were published in 1825 by Joseph Philippe Francois Deleuze:

> Cause your patient to sit down in the easiest position possible, and place yourself before him, on a seat a little more elevated, so that his knees may be between yours, and your feet by the side of his. Demand of him in the first place that he give himself up entirely, that he think of nothing, that he do not trouble himself by examining the effects which he experiences, that he banish all fear, and indulge hope, and that he be not disquieted or discouraged if the action of magnetism produces in him temporary pains.
> After you have brought yourself to a state of self-collectedness, take his thumbs between your two fingers, so that the inside of your thumbs may touch the inside of his. Remain in this situation five minutes, or until you perceive there is an equal degree of heat between your thumbs and his: that being done, you will withdraw your hands, removing them to the right and left, and waving them so that the interior surface be turned outwards, and raise them to his head; then place them upon his two shoulders, leaving them there about a minute; you will then draw them along the arm to the extremity of the fingers, touching lightly. You will repeat this pass* five or six times, always

---

*I employ here the word pass, which is common to all magnetizers: it signifies all the movements made by the hand in *passing* over the body, whether by slightly touching, or at a distance.

turning your hands and sweeping them off a little, before reascending: you will then place your hands upon the head, hold them there a moment, and bring them down before the face, at the distance of one or two inches, as far as the pit of the stomach: there you will let them remain about two minutes, passing the thumb along the pit of the stomach, and the other fingers down the sides. Then descend slowly along the body as far as the knees, or farther; and, if you can conveniently, as far as the ends of the feet. You may repeat the same processes during the greater part of the sitting. You may sometimes draw nearer to the patient so as to place your hands behind his shoulders, descending slowly along the spine, thence to the hips, and along the thighs as far as the knees, or to the feet. After the first passes you may dispense with putting your hands upon the head, and make the succeeding passes along the arms beginning at the shoulder: or along the body commencing at the stomach.

When you wish to put an end to the sitting, take care to draw towards the extremity of the hands, and towards the extremity of the feet, prolonging your passes beyond these extremities, and shaking your fingers each time. Finally, make several passes transversely before the face, and also before the breast, at the distance of three or four inches: these passes are made by presenting the two hands together and briskly drawing them from each other, as if to carry off the super-abundance of fluid with which the patient may be charged. You see that it is essential to magnetize, always descending from the head to the extremities, and never mounting from the extremities to the head. It is on this account that we turn the hands obliquely when they are raised again from the feet to the head. The descending passes are magnetic, that is, they are accompanied with the intention of magnetizing. The ascending movements are not. Many magnetizers shake their fingers slightly after each pass. This method, which is never injurious, is in certain cases advantageous, and for this reason it is good to get in the habit of doing it.

Although you may have at the close of the sitting taken care to spread the fluid over all the surface of the body, it is proper, in finishing, to make several passes along the legs from the knees to the end of the feet. . . .

This manner of magnetizing by longitudinal passes, directing the fluid from the head to the extremities, without fixing upon any part in preference to others, is called *magnetizing by the long pass*. . . . It is more or less proper in all cases, and it is requisite to employ it in the first sitting, when there is no special reason for using any other. The fluid is thus distributed into all the organs, and it accumulates naturally in those which have need of it. Besides the passes made at a short distance, others are made, just before finishing, at the distance of two or three feet. They generally produce a calm, refreshing and pleasurable sensation.

There is one more process by which it is very advantageous to terminate the sitting. It consists in placing one's self by the side of the patient, as he stands up, and, at the distance of a foot, making with both hands, one before the body and the other behind, seven or eight passes, commencing above the head and descending to the floor, along which the hands are spread apart. This process frees the head, re-establishes the equilibrium and imparts strength.

When the magnetizer acts upon the patient, they are said *to be in communication*, (rapport). That is to say, we mean by the word *communication*, a peculiar and induced condition, which causes the magnetizer to exert an influence upon the patient, there being between them a communication of the vital principle. . . . Ordinarily magnetism acts as well and even better in the interior of the body, at the distance of one or two inches, than by the touch. It is enough at the commencement of the sitting to take the thumbs a moment. Sometimes it is necessary to magnetize at the distance of several feet. Magnetism at a distance is more soothing, and some nervous persons cannot bear any other. . . .

It is by the ends of the fingers, and especially by the thumbs, that the fluid escapes with the most activity. For this reason it is, we take the thumbs of the patient in the first place, and hold them whenever we are at rest. . . .

The processes I have now indicated, are the most regular and advantageous for magnetism by the long pass, but it is far from being always proper, or even possible to employ them. When a man magnetizes a woman, even if it were his sister, it might not be proper to place himself before her in the manner described: and also when a patient is obliged to keep his bed, it would be impossible. . . .

Let us now consider the circumstances which point out particular processes.

When any one has a local pain, it is natural, after establishing a communication, to carry the magnetic action to the suffering part. It is not by passing the hands over the arms that we undertake to cure a sciatic; it is not by putting the hand upon the stomach that we can dissipate a pain in the knee. Here are some principles to guide us.

The magnetic fluid, when motion is given to it, draws along with it the blood, the humors and the cause of the complaint. For example, if . . . one has a pain in the shoulder, and the magnetizer makes passes from the shoulder to the end of the fingers, the pain will descend with the hand: it stops sometimes at the elbow, or at the wrist, and goes off by the hands, in which a slight perspiration is perceived. . . . [Magnetism seems to chase away and bear off with it what disturbs the equilibrium, and its action ceases when the equilibrium is restored.] It is useless to search out the causes of these facts, it is sufficient that experience has established them, for us to conduct ourselves accordingly, when we have no reason to do otherwise . . .

You may be assured that the motions you make externally, will operate sympathetically in the interior of the patient's body, wherever you have sent the fluid into it . . .

I think it important to combat an opinion which appears to me entirely erroneous, although it is maintained by men well versed in the knowledge of magnetism: viz. that the processes are in themselves *indifferent*; that they serve only to fix the attention, and that the will alone does all. . . .

The processes *are* nothing if they are not in unison with a determined intention. We may even say they are not the *cause* of the magnetic action; but it is indisputable that they are necessary for directing and concentrating and that they ought to be varied according to the end one has in view. . . . Each one might modify the processes according to his own views and practice; but not that he could omit them, or employ them in a manner contrary to the general rules. For example, various magnetizers act equally well by passes, more gentle or more rapid; by contact, or at a distance; by holding the hands to the same place, or by establishing currents. But it is absurd to believe one can cure chilblains on the feet, by placing the hands on the breast.

Persons who are not in the habit of magnetizing, think they ought to exert a great deal of force. For which purpose, they contract their muscles, and make efforts of attention and will. This method is . . . often injurious. When the will is calm and constant, and the attention sustained by the interest we take in the patient, the most salutary effects ensue, without our giving ourselves the least pain . . . A person ought not to fatigue himself by magnetic processes: he will experience fatigue enough from the loss of the vital fluid. . . .

It frequently happens that magnetism gradually re-establishes the harmony of the system without producing any sensation, and its influence is perceived only in the restoration of health. In that case you ought to continue zealously to follow the processes I have pointed out, without troubling yourself about the manner in which the magnetism acts, and without seeking for any apparent effect. . . .

There are patients in whom the influence of magnetism is displayed in two or three minutes; others, who do not feel it for a long time. There are some in whom the effects are constantly increasing; others, who experience at the first time all that they will experience in the course of a long treatment. . . .

The effects by which magnetism manifests its action are greatly varied . . . They change sometimes, in proportion to the change wrought in the malady.

I will now describe the effects which are most commonly exhibited.

The magnetized person perceives a heat escaping from the ends of your fingers, when you pass them at a little distance before the face, although your hands appear cold to him, if you touch him. He feels this heat through his clothes, in some parts, or in all parts of his body before which your hands pass. He often compares it to water moderately warm, flowing over him, and this sensation precedes your hand. His legs become numb, especially if you do not carry your hands as low as his feet; and this numbness ceases when, towards the close, you make passes along the legs to the toes, or below them. Sometimes instead of communicating heat, you communicate cold, sometimes also you produce heat upon one part of the body, and cold upon another. There is often induced a general warmth, and a perspiration more or less considerable. Pain is felt in the parts where the disease is seated. These pains change place, and descend.

Magnetism causes the eyes to be closed. They are shut in such a manner that the patient cannot open them; he feels a calm, a sensation of tranquil enjoyment; he grows drowsy, he sleeps; he wakes when spoken to, or else he wakes of himself at the end of a certain time, and finds himself refreshed. Sometimes he enters into somnambulism, in which state he hears the magnetizer and answers him without awaking . . . The state of somnambulism . . . does not take place except in a small number of cases . . .

Here I ought to observe, that the magnetic sleep is of itself essentially restorative. During this sleep, nature unassisted works a cure; and it is often sufficient to re-establish the equibilibrium, and cure nervous complaints.[95]

In 1825, Baron du Potet and Husson, a physician of the Paris Hospital and a member of the Academy of Medicine, made some remarkable experiments in which he telepathically induced somnambulism on an unaware subject. This report was quite controversial.[96]

In 1831 a second government report was issued which was much more favorable to the mesmerists.[97] Students of Mesmer were in practice throughout Europe and by that time most of the characteristic phenomena were well known. These included the following:

> Amnesia
> Acceptance of totally delusive beliefs
> Clairvoyance
> Heightened muscular power
> Impersonation with outstanding dramatic flair
> Improvement of skin complaints and warts
> Increased powers of memory
> Alleviation of neurotic states
> Anesthesia
> Sensory acuity
> Sensory hallucinations—in all senses
> Healing ability of self and others
> Stopping of bad habits
> Production of blisters and marks on the skin
> Suppression of physiological responses
> including those normally accompanying pain

The majority of those interested in mesmerism could be divided into two camps—those who believed in psychic phenomena and accepted some version of the magnetic fluid theory, and those who did not. James Braid (1795-1860) did the most to make mesmerism acceptable to the second group by changing the name to hypnotism and referring to the process strictly as a matter of "suggestion." Modern depth psychiatry and psychoanalysis stem from the use of hypnosis in treating clinical disorders, and the spiritualist movement—as well as the Christian Scientists—were also influenced by this practice.

The link between Mesmerism and spiritualism is most clearly evidenced by the researches of Baron Karl von Reichenbach, the German industrialist and chemist who discovered paraffin, creosote and several other organic compounds. During the 1840's, Reichenbach began a series of experiments with animal magnetism that was to engage his attention for several decades. He discovered that certain people, whom he called sensitives, were able to see a luminous glow around magnets and crystals, which he called the *odic force*. This *od* could be seen only in a darkened room. The north pole of a magnet radiated a bluish glow while the south pole was invariably in the yellow-red end of the spectrum.

The blue glow, which he called *od positive*, could be seen at the point end of a quartz crystal, and around the left side of the human body. The *od negative* yellow or red glow was seen at the base of quartz crystals and around the right side of the human body. Reichenbach also discovered that individuals who were able to perceive the od, which he himself was not, were easily somnambulized.

In 1856, Reichenbach stated that he experimented with 197 sensitives, fifty of whom were physicians, physicists, chemists, mathematicians, or philosophers. His subjects were of both sexes and included people of all social classes, including many of the nobility.

Reichenbach's researches were originally published in German in the prestigious *Annals of Chemistry* in 1845. In order to demonstrate that the odic luminosity was not simply a figment of the imagination or the result of a suggestion, Reichenbach arranged to take photographs of objects which had been charged with od—crystals, magnets, and fingertips. The photographs were taken under scientifically controlled conditions by Gunther, the photographer to the Royal Court in Berlin. These photographs, along with four short essays on "The laws of Odic Light" were submitted in 1861 to the *Annals of Physics and Chemistry*. The first was published (vol. 112, p. 459). However, the others failed to follow due to the displeasure which the first had aroused among certain Berlin physicists.[98] After this rebuff, Reichenbach continued his researches privately, using his concept of the *odic force* to explain many of the phenomena of spiritualism.

Until the middle of the nineteenth century, there was no recognized branch of experimental science whose domain of exploration was man's psyche. While there was generally a strong public interest in the researches of Mesmer and Reichenbach, there were no trained academicians or established professionals who were competent to research and judge extraordinary claims. Psychology was thought of as a branch of philosophy, until the pioneering research of Gustav Theodor Fechner (1801-1887) established psychology as an independent branch of science.

Fechner's formal training lay in medicine and physics. Like the acient shamans he showed a natural sensitivity to the subtle levels of his own inner world which he could not suppress. Writing under the pseudonym of Dr. Mises, he published a number of works both satirical and symbolic. His biographer, Dr. G. Stanley Hall, describes one of these books, written in 1825, entitled *Comparative Anatomy of the Angels:*

These are not symbolic, but real, living angels, which stand in the organic world a little higher than man, who is not the highest nor the most beautiful. Even the ass thinks his own type ideal. The human form is a strange aggregate of surfaces and curves, hollows and elevations. There are no flat surfaces and therefore curves and specifically the sphere are the ideal forms and these change (as, indeed, Plato had said). The parts of man's body are beautiful as they approach it, but the eyeball is most complete. It is the organ of light and in light angels live. Earth is not their fitting residence. They belong to higher bodies like the sun, the stars, or light. Just as the air is the element of the angels, who are simply free and independent eyes, all eye, or the eye-type in its highest and most beautiful development. Thus, what in man is a subordinate organ, in the angels is of independent worth. In animals the eyes look backward or sideward, whereas in man they look forward. But angels are single eyes. Their language is light and their tones are colors. The eye-language of love hints at the speech of angels, these creatures of the sun with their ethereal bodies. Their skin is merely connected vapors, like soap bubbles. Their transparent nature can take on colors. They change their form and expand and contract according to their feelings. They are attraction or repulsion, and with this goes the wonderful color play. They are organisms. They move by hovering and sweeping along. General gravitation, which relates all bodies, is their sense. They feel the farthest thing in the universe and the slightest change in it. They are, in short, living planets and, in fine, the planets are angels.*[99]

In his search for the archetypal form of angels, Fechner's work can be seen as in the scientific tradition of Goethe, his countryman, who attempted to reconcile science and poetry. In his perception of the earth and planets as living organisms, he is bearing witness to the ancient esoteric teachings. His cosmic speculations continue in a work called the *Book of Life After Death* which G. Stanley Hall describes thus:

How now do the dead live on? First and chiefly in us. Fechner takes his leading concept from the mystic way in which Christ lives in his followers, who are members of his body and branches of his vine. To this larger life of his in the Church, his earthly career is only a grain of mustard seed. Gloriously his soul has gone marching on. Just so the dead press in upon us, yearning to add their strength to ours, for thus they not merely live, but grow. New impulses and sudden insights in us are inspirations from them. Not only do the great and good dead influence and pervade us all the time, but we are exposed also to the bad. Many of them are always bad, and so if our will is weak and our personality unorganized, they may dominate us. Their visitation is insistent. They do not crave incarnation in the flesh, like Plato's spirits, but in our moral life, that therein they may be made perfect.

---

*This description is similar to what is found in the writing of modern seers, i.e., Geofrey Hodson, *Kingdom of the Gods.* Wheaton, Ill.: Theosophical Publishing House.

We all have in us sparks from the lives of Luther, Goethe, Napoleon, etc., who think and act in us "no longer restrained by the limitations of the body, but poured forth upon the world which in their lifetime they moulded, gladdened, swayed, and by their personality they now supply us with influences which we never discern as coming from them." Each great dead soul extends itself into many and unites them in a spiritual organism. Thus, the dead converse with each other in us. They also fight the good and bad in each other in us, causing strife in our souls. . . .

There is, however, a higher soul in which we and all things live, move, and have our being, and in which and only in which spirits are real. We are, in fact, what we have become. The brain is a kind of seed which decays that the soul may live. The individual soul may mount on the collective souls of the dead as a sparrow is carried up on an eagle's back to heights it never could attain, but, when there, can fly off and even a little higher. At death the soul seems to drop below a threshold and the spark of consciousness might be conceived to go out but for the fact that the soul is not projected into an empty world but into one where it incessantly meets varying resistances that keep personality above the point of submergence or any other extinction without appeal to the conservation of energy. Just as attention moves about from point to point within the body, so after death the soul moves around the world.[100]

One of the defining characteristics of Fechner's life is that he suffered a disease very much akin to the *initiatory sickness* known among shamans. In 1840 his eyesight began to fail him. Soon he could neither read nor write. He found that he could not eat or drink and he was unable to endure society. He lost all control over his thoughts or his attention. His dreams tormented him. His own state seemed to him like the condition of a puppet. By the end of 1843, people believed him to be incurably blind and completely insane. He spent months in solitude in a dark room; and at a level deep within himself he never lost hope. It was in this state, literally the dark night of his soul, that he felt that he was called upon by God to do extraordinary things which his sufferings had prepared him for. He recovered after this self-perception and soon discovered within himself even greater physical strength and psychic sensitivity. The whole world now revealed itself to him in a splendor and detail which exceeded his earlier visions. He resumed his academic work, no longer in physics but as a philosopher.

Fechner's first work after his recovery from illness was called *Nanna* or the *Soul Life of Plants*. In this work he revealed his conception of consciousness as applied to the plant kingdom:

If, indeed, we could invert things and set plants upon the throne of the earth and we become plants, we should be inclined to ask what these restless human bipeds are running about for and whether they have any use save to serve vegetable life. We, the plant people, would continue, remain in dignified rest in our own place, and need to do nothing save to spread out our roots and leaves in order to receive all divine gifts as our due tribute. Men live to prepare carbonic acid for our breath and die only that their decaying bodies may furnish us nitrogen. Men have to cultivate us in flowerpots and gardens, field and forest, and yet we consume them in the end. If we wish to send our bacterial army into their blood, we exterminate them, and, although they take a small part of our fruit and leaves, it is only to spread and

66

fertilize our seeds. Insects as far outnumber men as our leaves do insects, and yet even insects serve us as love messengers to bring the pollen of our blossoms to fertile corollas.

Plants participate in the cosmic soul life, and, indeed, have their own souls. They live, breathe, emit perfumes, bloom, propagate, and are beautiful, partly, surely, for their own sake. They must have a dim kind of feeling. Animals do not speak and yet we know that their feelings are much like ours. But plants respond with exquisite sensitiveness to their environment by changes in their organization and functions. Their psyche is not concentrated in a nervous system or brain, but diffused through all their parts. They do move their parts toward food, light, air, moisture, and who can say that consciousness cannot exist without a nervous system? Tones can be produced by either strings or reeds or vibrating columns of air, and psychic life may be as varied. Plants do not attend as we do and the consciousness attending the vegetative process may be blunt, but perhaps consciousness is more vital the wider its diffusion. They must feel discomfort when deprived of food, light, and air. They must have a sense of need and an inner compulsion toward satisfaction. Plants' souls are not miniature copes of human. It is an advantage that the soul is otherwise diffused among plants than in man, and perhaps that their responses are very slow . . . Surely, plants cannot be like blind eyes and deaf ears, but plant life is preparatory to a higher psychic life throughout nature.

The besouling of plants really rests upon the basal idea of psychic processes corresponding to physical processes; that the psychic is only the self-appearance of the material and the latter a form in which inner psychic processes can appear to others.[101]

This work led to some very cogent philosophical explorations into the nature of consciousness itself and from there to his pioneering experimental work in *psycho-physics:*

As to the origin of consciousness, we have a series of thresholds, upper and lower waves. The highest consciousness is God, who planned vaguely at first and is realizing his purpose in all the world processes, so that his plan progresses and becomes more definite and conscious. Thus, as Paracelsus and Jacob Bohme thought, God is growing in our experience, which, as it gives him character, also contributes to his consciousness and adds to his achievements. God comes to consciousness in us. . . .

Life and consciousness never arose, he said, but are original activities of the universe; they are two expressions of the same thing and differ only as a circle seen from within differs from one seen from without. From without all is manifold, from within all is unity, and both together constitute all there is. The soul is not punctual but is pervasive throughout all the body. Those processes immediately bound up with consciousness are *psycho-physic movements* and they are primordial and cosmogenic.[102]

The physical world operates under one law and we must assume that the spiritual world is no less so. There must be then, a priori, some exact mathematical relationship between the physical and the psychical, some law of concomitant variations, for all that is psychic is but the self-appearance of the physical; a material process runs parallel to every conscious process.[103]

In 1860, Fechner published a book, *Elemente der Psychophysik*, which is taken by many historians to mark the beginning of experimental psychology. The concepts which he used and the problems he defined have become the foundation of experimental work in sensory experience since his time. He developed the psychological measure known as the *just noticeable difference* (jnd) which is the smallest observable difference between two stimuli i.e. two different lights. He determined that the relationship between the intensity of a physical stimulus and the just noticable difference at that intensity is a logarithmic one. In other words, the difference in intensity between two very bright lights will have to be much greater than the difference in intensity of two very dim lights in order for a *jnd* to be perceived. Unlike the psychologists who followed in his footsteps, Fechner believed that he had discovered a relationship between the individual consciousness and the sublime universal soul. His students, such as Wilhelm Wundt, followed his experimental methods but lacked his imagination, his courage and his vision.

When the phenomena of spiritualism became popular in mid-nineteenth century Europe and America, Fechner sat with zeal at a number of séances. He was one of the few men of his age who, while not detecting trickery, had the depth of wisdom with which to incorporate but also transcend the sensationalism and trivia of the popular spiritualist impulse.

Spiritualism as a social movement apparently began in the small New York town of Hydesville in March of 1848, where several months earlier, the Fox family had taken over an old farmhouse about which the previous tenants had complained of strange noises. The Foxs' themselves soon noticed unusual rapping sounds which occurred in the night frightening the two younger daughters, Margaret and Kate, who then insisted on sleeping with their parents. On the fateful evening of March 31, the youngest daughter Kate playfully challenged the raps to repeat the snapping of her fingers. Her challenge was answered. Within hours many of the neighbors were brought over to the house to witness the uncanny demonstration.

By asking the sounds be repeated twice for a negative answer and only once for an affirmative, the people assembled were soon able to carry on a dialogue with the rapping—which had revealed itself to apparently be coming from a spirit source. One of the neighbors, Deusler, suggested naming the letters of the alphabet and having the spirit rap when they reached certain letters in order to spell out letters and sentences. In this way the spirit revealed himself to have been a travelling peddlar who was murdered in the house by a previous owner and buried in the cellar. Digging commenced, however a high water level prevented any immediate discoveries.

Meanwhile, hundreds of neighbors continued visiting the Fox house, day and night, listening to the spirit's rapping. They also formed an investigation committee to take testimony. The case was even studied by the Honorable Robert Dale Owen, a member of the U.S. Congress, and a founder of the Smithsonian Institute. In the summer of 1848, more digging unearthed human teeth, some fragments of bone and some human hair.

While the testimony is ambiguous, some neighbors reported that the raps continued in the Fox house even when family members were not present. However, it became apparent that this form of mediumship centered on the Fox sisters, though it soon spread to many other people as well.

The house in which spiritualism was reborn Hydesville, New York

Margaretta

Leah

Kate

Fifty-six years later in 1904, the gradual disintegration of one of the cellar walls of the Fox house exposed to veiw an entire human skeleton.

Other mediums, using the alphabet method, also claimed to be in contact with the spirits of the deceased. Their messages were generally not reliable however. It seems that for every apparently genuine medium there were many deluded or phony imitators.

During November 1849, the Spiritualists held their first public meeting in the largest hall available in Rochester, N. Y. Three different citizen's committees in Rochester were invited to investigate the Fox sisters. All three made favorable reports indicating that the sounds heard were not produced by ventriloquism or machinery. The public was outraged at these reports. A riot resulted and the girls had to be smuggled away from an angry crowd.

The Fox sisters made a career of their mediumship. They toured the country under the auspices of the showman, P. T. Barnum. While receiving the sympathetic attention of Horace Greeley, the editor of the New York Tribune, who later became a candidate for the U.S. presidency, the sisters remained a center of controversy. In 1871, Charles F. Livermore, a prominent

New York banker, sent Kate Fox to England in gratitude for the consolation he had received through her powers.[104] At that time she was examined by the physicist Sir William Crookes, who later received the Nobel prize for his discovery of thalium. Crookes published the following statement regarding this investigation:

> For several months I have enjoyed the almost unlimited opportunity of testing the various phenomena occurring in the presence of this lady, and I especially examined the phenomena of these sounds. With mediums, generally, it is necessary to sit for a formal *séance* before anything is heard; but in the case of Miss Fox it seems only necessary for her to place her hand on any substance for loud thuds to be heard in it, like a triple pulsation, sometimes loud enough to be heard several rooms off. In this manner I have heard them in a living tree—on a sheet of glass—on a stretched iron wire—on a stretched membrane—a tambourine—on the roof of a cab—and on the floor of a theatre. Moreover, actual contact is not always necessary; I have had these sounds proceeding from the floor, walls, &c, when the medium's hands and feet were held—when she was standing on a chair—when she was suspended in a swing from the ceiling—when she was enclosed in a wire cage—and when she had fallen fainting on a sofa. I have heard them on a glass hermonicon—I have felt them on my own shoulder and under my own hands. I have heard them on a sheet of paper, held between the fingers by a piece of thread passed through one corner. With a full knowledge of the numerous theories which have been started, chiefly in America, to explain these sounds, I have tested them in every way that I could devise, until there has been no escape from the conviction that they were true objective occurrences not produced by trickery or mechanical means.[105]

Sir William Crookes

The main argument used by skeptics to discredit the Fox sisters was that they created the rapping sounds themselves by cracking the bones in their toes and knuckles. This hypothesis, however, does not seem sufficient to explain the different kinds of sounds which appeared, their loudness, the fact that they often occurred in arpeggios and cadenzas, and the fact that they seemed to emanate from different places.

Nevertheless, in 1888, Margaret Fox made a public statement denouncing the spiritualists, claiming that she had made the noises by cracking her toes. Kate, who was with her at the time remained silent, as if in agreement. The following year, however, Margaret recanted, saying that she had fallen under the influence of people who were inimical to spiritualism and who had offered her money. Both sisters were alcoholics at this time. At no time in their careers were they actually detected in a fraudulent act.

Crookes also recorded an experience of *direct writing* with Ms. Fox:

> A luminous hand came down from the upper part of the room, and after hovering near me for a few seconds, took the pencil from my hand, rapidly wrote on a sheet of paper, threw the pencil down, and then rose up over our heads, gradually fading into darkness.[106]

From the ranks of the spiritualists investigations were also conducted, although along somewhat different lines than the experimental work of the scientists. The former attempted to describe the world according to the teachings of the spirits themselves. This theorization of spiritualism was mainly due to L. H. D. Rivail (1803-1869) a doctor of medicine who became celebrated under the pseudonym Allan Kardec.

Kardec's theories were simple enough: After death the soul becomes a spirit and seeks reincarnation, which, as Pythagoras taught, is the destiny of all human souls; spirits know the past, present, and future; sometimes they can materialize and act on matter. We should let ourselves be guided by good spirits, Kardec maintained, and refuse to listen to bad spirits.[107,108]

Kardec wrote many books which achieved enormous popularity in his own lifetime. His works also spread to Brazil, where he still has a huge following, and where postage stamps were recently issued in his honor.[109] His intellectual energy certainly deserves admiration. However, he built his theory on the untenable hypothesis that mediums, embodying a so-called spirit, are never mistaken, unless their utterances are prompted by evil spirits. This notion does not of course, take into account the possibilities of suggestion, multiple personality, or unconscious influences which were quickly developed as alternative hypotheses to outright fraud by skeptical scientific investigators such as Michael Faraday.

Many levels of the human personality clearly exist and are still generally unexplored and untapped. Yet a number of cases can be cited where even such explanations do not account for all the observed phenomena.

An outstanding example, and perhaps the greatest medium who has ever lived, was Daniel Douglas Home. He was born in 1833 near Edinburgh, in Scotland. However at an early age he went to New England to live with his aunt who adopted him. At the age of seventeen he had a vision of the death of his mother, which was soon verified. After that time the household was frequently disturbed with loud raps and moving furniture. Declaring that he had introduced the devil to the household, his aunt threw him out. He began living with his friends and giving séances for them.

Among those who were convinced of his abilities in this early period were Judge John Edmunds of the New York State Supreme Court and Robert Hare, an emeritus professor of chemistry at the University of Pennsylvania.

Home never accepted any payments for his séances. He exhibited religious reverence for the powers and knowledge which manifested through him along with a scientific curiosity to seek rational explanations. He did, however accept presents from his wealthy patrons. Napolean III of France provided for his only sister. Czar Alexander of Russia sponsored his marriage. He conducted séances with the Kings of Bavaria and Wurtemburg as well as William I of Germany and assorted nobility throughout Europe. Noted literata also consulted with him.

To Lord Bulwer Lytton's satisfaction, Home called up the spirit that influenced him to write his famous occult novel, *Zanoni*. He conducted a séance for Elizabeth Barrett Browning and her husband Robert. Although his wife protested, Robert Browning insisted that Home was a fraud and wrote a long poem called *Mr. Sludge, The Medium* describing an exposure

Allan Kardec

D. D. Home

which never took place. In fact, throughout his long career, Home was never caught in any verifiable deceptions.

In 1868, Home made experiments with Cromwell Varley, chief engineer of the Atlantic Cable Company and afterwards before members of the London Dialectical Society, who held fifty séances with him at which thirty persons were present. Their report, published in 1871, attested to the observation of sounds and vibrations, the movements of heavy objects not touched by any person, and well-executed pieces of music coming from instruments not manipulated by any visible agency, as well as the appearance of hands and faces, which did not belong to any tangible human beings, but which nevertheless seemed alive and mobile.[110] This report inspired Sir William Crookes to investigate Home for himself.

Crookes conducted two very ingenious experiments with Home in which he tested alterations in the weight of objects and the playing of tunes upon musical instruments under conditions rendering human contact with the keys impossible. For the first experiment, Crookes developed a simple apparatus which measured the changes in weight of a mahogany board.

One end of the board rested on a firm table, whilst the other end was supported by a spring balance hanging from a substantial tripod stand. The balance was fitted with a self-registering index, in such a manner that it would record the maximum weight indicated by the pointer. The apparatus was adjusted so that the mahogany board was horizontal, its foot resting flat on the support. In this position its weight was three pounds, as marked by the pointer of the balance.[111]

Crookes and eight other observers, including Sir William Huggins, a physicist and member of the Royal Society, observed Home lightly place his fingertips on the end of board and watched the register descend as low as nine pounds. Crookes notes that since Home's fingers did not cross the fulcrum, any tactile pressure he might have exerted would have been in opposition to the force which caused the other end of the board to move down (see illustration). This experiment was conducted many times. On some occasions, Home never even touched the board: he merely placed his hands three inches over it. In other experiments, Crookes used a recording device to make a permanent record of the fluctuations in the weight. This was done to confute the argument that he himself was a victim of hallucinations.

In order to test the stories about music being played on an instrument, Crookes designed a cage in which to place an accordian he purchased specifically for these experiments (see illustration). The cage would just slip under a table, allowing Home to grasp the instrument on the end opposite to the keys, between the thumb and the middle finger. Again many witnesses were present:

Mr. Home, still holding the accordian in the usual manner in the cage, his feet being held by those next him, and his other hand resting on the table, we heard distinct and separate notes sounded in succession, and then a simple air was played. As such a result could only have been produced by the various keys of the instrument being acted upon in harmonious succession, this was considered by those present to be a crucial experiment. But the sequel was still more striking, for Mr. Home then removed his hand altogether from the accordian, taking it quite out of the cage, and placed it in the hand of the person next to him. The instrument then continued to play, no person touching it and no hand being near it.[112]

Crookes submitted his experimental papers to the Royal Society in order to encourage a large-scale investigation of the phenomena, which he felt were caused by a psychic force. However, the secretary of the society rejected his papers and refused to witness his experiments.

Crookes also testified to having seen many other phenomena with Home, including levitation of Home's body, levitation of objects, handling of hot coals, luminous lights, and apparitions.

Home himself bitterly resented any fraud or deception. In his book, *Lights and Shadows of Spiritualism*, written in 1878, he takes an aggresive stance against phony mediums or even those who were unwilling to cooperate with scientists. Unlike most mediums, Home was always willing to be tested under well-lit and closely supervised conditions.[113]

Despite the rejection of his psychical research by the scientific establishment, Crookes asserted the validity of his work throughout his life. In 1913, he was elected president of the Royal Society, but unfortunately he had by then long since abandoned his experimental work with mediums and found it wise not to discuss his work often in public. The phenomena which Crookes reported have been beyond the experience of all researchers before or since his time. Often his experimental reports were inadequate by contemporary standards since he simply assumed that his own word was sufficient to establish general acceptance of a phenomenon. We cannot hastily conclude that Crookes was either deluded or duped, for he was at the height of his intellectual creativity at the time he conducted this research. In the words of his friend, Sir Oliver Lodge, "It is almost as difficult to resist the testimony as it is to accept the things testified." Crookes most amazing experiments were conducted with a medium named Florence Cook.

Cook's ability to materialize the forms of various spirits had caused quite a stir among spiritualists. The most notable spirit to appear identified herself as Katie King, the daughter, in a former life, of the buccaneer Henry Morgan.

The phenomena of spirit materialization had actually attracted public attention a few years earlier through a Mrs. Samuel Guppy, the protégée of Alfred Russell Wallace, a prominent spiritualist who was also noted as one of the discoverers with Darwin of the theory of evolution. Mrs. Guppy introduced into her work the use of a tightly sealed cabinet in which she was placed in order to build up sufficient "power" for the construction of a spirit form which could then stand the scrutiny of the light outside the cabinet. The cabinet also provided of course an ideal opportunity for subterfuge on the part of the medium, which was undoubtedly taken advantage of on many occasions, for rarely were any medium and her spirit seen together at the same time.

Florence Cook

Katie King

Crookes attended séances with Florence Cook for a period of over three years and studied her intensively for several months in a laboratory in his own home. He also made numerous observations of Katie King and took over forty photographs of her. On several occasions he had the opportunity of seeing both Florence and her spirit, Miss King, at the same time and even of photographing them together. Katie appeared quite solidly before the guests at the séance, sometimes staying and conversing with them for as long as two hours. Crookes even reports having embraced and kissed her. At other times she seems to have vanished instantaneously and soundlessly. It is difficult to believe that an accomplice could have continued such an intimate masquerade, in Crookes own home, for several months without detection. He gives several reasons why he feels Florence Cook could not have committed fraud.

During the last six months Miss Cook has been a frequent visitor at my house, remaining sometimes a week at a time. She brings nothing with her but a little handbag, not locked; during the day she is constantly in the presence of Mrs. Crookes, myself, or some other member of my family, and, not sleeping by herself, there is absolutely no opportunity for any preparation. . . . I prepare and arrange my library myself as the dark cabinet, and usually, after Miss Cook has been dining and conversing with us, and scarcely out of our sight for a minute, she walks direct into the cabinet, and I, at her request, lock its second door, and keep possession of the key all through the séance.[114]

Katie's height varies; in my house I have seen her six inches taller than Miss Cook. Last night, with bare feet and not "tip-toeing," she was four and a half inches taller than Miss Cook. Katie's neck was bare last night; the skin was perfectly smooth to touch and sight, whilst on Miss Cook's neck is a large blister, which under similar circumstances is distinctly visible and rough to the touch. Katie's complexion is very fair, while that of Miss Cook is very dark. Katie's fingers are much longer than Miss Cook's, and her face is also larger.[115]

Crookes also indicates that Miss Cook was willing to submit to any test which he wished to impose. Ironically enough, on two occasions, in 1872 and in 1880, individuals claimed to have exposed Florrie Cook fraudulently masquerading as her spirit.[116]

It's not unreasonable to suggest any of several contradictory hypotheses: (1) that Crookes himself may have been deluded or enchanted by Florence Cook or (2) that while Crookes himself did observe geniune phenomena, Cook sometimes lost her abilities and resorted to fraud, (3) that the alleged exposures were not genuine, or (4) that Crooke's accounts were fraudulent. Psychical phenomena have always had an ironic and paradoxical nature, and Crookes' experimental methodology was certainly not sufficient to answer all of the questions that one might like to ask. However, there was no reason then, nor is there now, to insist that these phenomena, if genuine, conform to our own, uninformed expectations.

It is so difficult to maintain that a man of Crookes' scientific caliber could have been taken in by cheap tricks, that some of his critics have assumed that he himself was in on the fraud. They claimed that Crookes had been involved in a love affair with Florence Cook, and that he testified to her phenomena in order to shield her reputation and hide his emotional entanglements with her. The arguments against this assertion are impressive. However even if it were so, other matters would remain quite unsolved. If Crookes was involved with Miss Cook, who was only fifteen years old at the time, this hypothesis cannot account for the phenomena he reported with both Home and Miss Fox. Nor does it begin to explain the research on the same phenomena reported by a number of other eminent scientists. Nevertheless, the accusation of experimenter fraud still continues to haunt psychical researchers, and will continue to do so as long as there are men who are psychologically blocked against accepting the mere possibility of psychic phenomena.

Another important medium in this period was the Reverend William Stainton Moses (1839-92), an Oxford graduate who was ordained as a minister in 1863. In 1872 Moses began to produce some physical phenomena along with automatic writing which seemed to contain evidence of thought transference. The phenomena he produced were not as convincing, however, as his own eloquent and sophisticated manner of speaking about them. On May 9, 1874, he discussed his own experiences with Edmund Gurney and F. W. H. Myers, two enquirers of high academic standing. Both of them were impressed with the respectability and seriousness of Moses' claims.

Soon after, Myers and Gurney formed an informal association for the investigation of spiritualistic phenomena. Into this group were drawn Henry Sidgewick, the eminent philosopher, and Arthur Balfour—who was later to become Prime Minister of England. For the next eight years, this group continued its investigation of mediums with mixed, and generally unimpressive results. The strongest evidence they obtained seemed not to favor the spiritualist hypothesis at all, but rather the theory of thought-transference or telepathy.

The notion of thought-transference was also intriguing to Sir William F. Barrett, a professor of physics at the Royal College of Science in Dublin, who had been conducting experiments which had attracted some notice. Barrett conceived of the idea of forming an organization of spiritualists, scientists, and scholars who would join forces in a dispassionate investigation of psychical phenomena. Myers, Gurney and Sidgewick attended a conference in London which Barrett had convened, and the Society for Psychical Research was created with Sidgewick, who had a reputation as an impartial scholar, accepting the first presidency.

The Society set up six working committees, each with a specific domain for exploration:

Rev. William Stainton Moses

1. An examination of the nature and extent of any influence which may be exerted by one mind upon another, apart from any generally recognized mode of perception.
2. The study of hypnotism, and the forms of so-called mesmeric trance, with its alleged insensibility to pain; clairvoyance and other allied phenomena.
3. A critical revision of Reichenbach's researches with certain organizations called "sensitive," and an inquiry whether such organizations possess any power of perception beyond a highly exalted sensibility of the recognized sensory organs.

75

4. A careful investigation of any reports, resting on strong testimony, regarding apparitions at the moment of death, or otherwise, or regarding disturbances in houses reputed to be haunted.

5. An inquiry into the various physical phenomena commonly called spiritualistic; with an attempt to discover their causes and general laws.

6. The collection and collation of existing materials bearing on the history of these subjects.[117]

The great American psychologist, William James, met Gurney in England in 1882 and immediately they struck up a close friendship. Later James also became a close friend of Myers. In 1884, Barrett toured the United States and succeeded in arousing the interest of American scholars in forming a similar society, which was established in 1885, and in which William James took an active role.

Working as honorary secretary of the S. P. R. and active on the literary committee, Edmund Gurney soon discovered that the largest single class of occurrences reported were what came to be labelled "crisis apparitions." This experience is one in which the figure or the voice of a living person who is experiencing a crisis—such as an accident or a death—is seen or heard.

Probably you or your friends have had such experiences, which are strangely confirmed by the news, later on, of the actual crisis.

Within one year of its organization, the S. P. R. had collected over 400 reports of such cases and in 1886, Gurney published a 1,300 page document entitled *Phantasms of the Living* in which 702 different apparition cases were analyzed. All of the evidence was obtained first-hand from the percipients and was generally backed by corroboratory testimony. Witnesses were also interviewed by S. P. R. members who appraised the value of all testimony.

Gurney described several categories of apparition cases. These are cases of spontaneous telepathy, which occur when the sender is undergoing some shock or strong emotion. For example a lady lying in bed may feel a pain in her mouth at the exact moment when her husband is accidently struck in the jaw. Then come cases where the percipient's experience is not an exact reproduction of the agent's experience, but is only founded upon it, the receiver building a detailed picture from his or her own mind. There are many cases of this type where a person about to arrive at a location is actually seen there by someone not expecting him before his arrival. It is very unlikely that the agent will have in his mind the image of himself as others see him. Finally Gurney refers to the cases in which the agent may be dead or dying while the phantom appears in quite normal behavior and clothing.

Gurney felt that these cases could be explained as hallucinations induced in the mind of the percipient by means of a telepathic message from the agent. What was harder to explain were collective apparitions in which several people independently perceive the identical phantom. There were also reciprocal cases whereby a person imagining himself to be at a distant scene is actually seen at that location by others. An example of such a case is reported on page 129.

Phantasms of the Living was soon criticized by the eminent American philosopher C. S. Pierce and several others on the grounds that the cases reported did not meet sufficient conditions to be acceptable as evidence. Most of these critical individuals simply did not read the entire book. Their criticisms focused on the weakest cases and overlooked certain cases which were very well documented in all regards. However, Gurney correctly felt that if only a few single cases were strongly evidential, the conclusions for crisis telepathy were inescapable. In the following passage he stresses the extent to which the skeptical arguments would have to be pushed in order to dismiss the entire bundle of data:

Not only have we to assume such an extent of forgetfulness and inaccurary, about simple and striking facts of the immediate past, as is totally unexampled in any other range of experience. Not only have we to assume that distressing or exciting news about another person produces a havoc in the memory which has never been noted in connection with stress or excitement in any other form. We must leave this merely general ground, and make suppositions as detailed as the evidence itself. We must suppose that some people have a way of dating their letters in indifference to the calendar, or making entries in their diaries on the wrong page and never discovering the error; and that whole families have been struck by the collective hallucination that one of their members had made a particular remark, the substance of which had never entered that members head; and that it is a recognized custom to write mournful letters about bereavements which have never occurred; . . .and that when a wife interrupts her husband's slumber with words of distress or alarm, it is only for fun, or a sudden morbid craving for underserved sympathy; and that when people assert that they were in sound health, in good spirits, and wide-awake, at a particular time which they had occassion to note, it is a safe conclusion that they were having a nightmare, or were the prostrate victims of nervous hypochondria. Every one of these improbabilities is, perhaps, in itself a possibility; but as the narratives drive us from one desperate expedient to another, when time after time we are compelled to own that deliberate falsification is less unlikely than the assumptions we are making, and then again when we submit the theory of deliberate falsification to the cumulative test, and see what is involved in the supposition that hundreds of persons of established character, known to us for the most part and unknown to one another, have simultaneously formed a plot to deceive us—there comes a point where reason rebels.[118]

Phantasms of the Living did not deal with apparitions of persons who had been dead for more than twelve hours. However, according to an article published by Mrs. Eleanor Sidgewick, the society had some 370 cases in its files "which believers of ghosts would be apt to attribute to agency of deceased human beings." While the majority of these cases might be dismissed as hallucinations, there were four types of cases which did seem to support the notion that some aspect of personality survives death.

1. Cases in which the apparition conveyed to the percipient accurate information which was previously unknown to him.

2. Cases in which the "ghost" seemed to be pursuing some well-defined objective. The spirit of Hamlet's father who makes

Hamlet swear to seek revenge for his murder is a famous literary example of this.

3. Cases in which the phantom bears a strong resemblance to a deceased person who is unknown to the percipient at the time of the manifestation. A case of this sort, incidently, recently made headlines in the *Berkeley Gazette,* as the phantom was observed in the Faculty Club of the University of California

4. Cases in which two or more people had independently seen similar apparitions: Into this category falls your typical haunting ghost or apparitions associated with a particular location. Often such phantoms are seen by individuals who are ignorant of previous sightings. These phantoms rarely seem to speak or take notice of humans, although voices and noises may be associated with them, and they are generally not seen for more than a minute before they vanish.[119]

Although members of the S. P. R. were never able to replicate the most striking of the physical phenomena which were reported by Sir William Crookes, their investigations of physical mediumship did yield some interesting results. Until the discovery of Eusapia Palladino by the S. P. R. in 1894, the most consistently studied physical phenomena was the slate writing of William Eglinton. Through his mediumship, Eglinton was said to cause writing to appear on a black slate which was generally held by both the medium and a sitter. Sometimes writing appeared on a closed and locked folding slate.

Occasionally sitters were privileged to witness the "book test." One person would take a book at random from a bookshelf; another would choose a page number, and another the number of a line. This information would be written on a slate and concealed from the medium. After a period of time, the appropriate line from the book would be found mysteriously written on the slate!

Quite a controversy arose within the Society over Eglinton's mediumship, for many members had witnessed his performances and were impressed. These people explicitly stated that they had closely watched the slate and the medium at the crucial times. However both Mrs. Sidgewick and Richard Hodgson were inclined to dismiss Eglinton's phenomena as sleight of hand. They suggested that the writing was executed beforehand and that Eglinton substituted a prepared slate while the attention of the sitters were distracted.

This situation was resolved somewhat through the efforts of a frail young man named S. J. Davey who was able, through conjuring, to reproduce most of Eglinton's successes. Witnesses at his séances were also willing to testify to his authenticity, although he later revealed all of his tricks. He was, nevertheless, unable to reproduce the "book test."

This period in the history of psychical research was marked by the exposure of many fraudulent mediums, much to the chagrin of their duped followers. The situation reached a point where many frustrated members of the S. P. R. maintained that any medium who manifested physical phenomena must automatically be using artifice.

In 1887 the following statement was issued in a report from a commission appointed to investigate spiritualism at the University of Pennsylvania:

> Again, at another séance, a woman, a visitor, led from the cabinet to me a Materialized Spirit, whom she introduced to me as 'her daughter, her dear darling daughter', while nothing could be clearer to me than the features of the medium in every line and lineament. Again and again, men have led round the circle the Materialized Spirits of their wives, and introduced them to each visitor in turn; fathers have taken round their daughters, and I have seen widows sob in the arms of their dead husbands. Testimony such as this staggers me. Have I been smitten with color blindness? Before me, as far as I can detect, stands the very medium herself, in shape, size, form and feature true to a line, and yet one after another, honest men and woman at my side, within ten minutes of each other, assert that she is the absolute counterpart of their nearest and dearest friends, nay that she *is* that friend.[120]

Another case is described where an emotional sitter actually kissed the handkerchief covered foot of the medium, claiming that it was her dead relation because it smelled exactly like her "dear dead body."[121]

The physical mediumship of Stainton Moses, the man who originally interested Gurney and Myers in psychical research, also remained an issue of controversy. The most crucial accounts of his levitations, materializations, musical sounds, and luminous lights came from his closest friends, whose testimony was therefore suspect. Only D. D. Home's phenomena seem to have been seen by a large number of disinterested witnesses under good conditions. It was difficult for the Victorian researchers to fault Moses, however, due to his high social standing and reputation. Moses' mediumship still remains an enigma.

Readers in our post-Watergate era will have no difficulty in imagining that individuals of prominent social standing are capable of deliberate deception. For psychical researchers this issue was already resolved early in the 1890s with the case of Mr. D. "a professional man of good social status and well-known amateur *savant* in the directions of philology, anthropology and ancient astronomy." Myers and Mrs. Sidgewick investigated him and were quite impressed with his abilities to levitate a table in good light. In fact they were planning to devote an issue of the Society's *Proceedings* to Mr. D's phenomena. Fortunately, one of Mr. D's accomplices came forth and revealed the source of the trickery, stating that Mr. D had simply wished to test the researcher's power of observation. Further cases of deception continued.

A most intriguing chapter in consciousness history involves the Theosophical Society, founded in 1875 by Madame Helena Petrovna Blavatsky (H.P.B. for short), a most notorious character.

Madame Blavatsky declared herself to be a *chela* or disciple of a brotherhood of spiritual adepts in Tibet whose members had acquired psychic powers beyond the reach of ordinary men. She asserted that they took a special interest in the Theosophical Society and all initiates of occult lore, being able to communicate intelligently with individuals by visiting them

H. P. Blavatsky

ALFRED RUSSELL WALLACE–
Co-author, with Darwin, of the
Theory of Evolution.

ANNIE BESANT–Fabian Socialist (and George Bernard
Shaw's lover) who headed the Theosophical Society after
the death of Blavatsky.

in a phantom or *astral* form. These beings were called the *Mahatmas* and are described as follows in Blavatsky's book *Isis Unveiled:*

> Travelers have met these adepts on the shores of the sacred Ganges, brushed against them on the silent ruins of Thebes, and in the mysterious deserted chambers of Luxor. Within the halls upon whose blue and golden vaults the wierd signs attract attention, but whose secret meaning is never penetrated by idle gazers, they have been seen, but seldom recognized. Historical memoirs have recorded their presence in the brilliantly illuminated salons of European aristocracy. They have been encountered again on the arid and desolate plains of the Great Sahara, or in the caves of Elephanta. They may be found everywhere, but they make themselves known only to those who have devoted their lives to unselfish study and are not likely to turn back.

According to William Q. Judge, a New York lawyer who was one of the co-founders of the Theosophical Society, such a Mahatma appeared to the first Theosophists when they held a meeting to frame their constitution. A "strangely foreign Hindoo," came before them, left a package and vanished. On opening the package they found the necessary forms of organization, rules, etc., which were adopted. The early history of the society was based largely on such miracles. Blavatsky's wonderworking and teaching attracted such notable students as Thomas Edison, Sir William Crookes, Alfred Russell Wallace, British Prime Minister William Gladstone, Alfred Tennyson, and later U.S. Vice-president Henry Wallace and Annie Besant.

After seeing the Society well established in New York, Madame Blavatsky moved to India. Marvelous phenomena of an occult nature were alleged to have taken place there at the Adyar headquarters. Mysterious, ghostly appearances of Mahatmas were seen, and messages were constantly received by supernatural means. One of the apartments, named the Occult Room in the headquarters, contained a sort of cupboard against the wall, known as the *Shrine*. Ghostly letters from the Mahatmas were received in this shrine, as well as sent. Skeptics were convinced and occult lodges spread rapidly. Madame Blavatsky and other Theosophists were interviewed in England by members of the S.P.R. who were favorably impressed.

At this point in 1884, a scandal broke out. Two members of Blavatsky's staff claimed that they had conspired with Madame, forging Mahatma letters and placing them in the shrine through a trap door. To back up their claim, they submitted private correspondences from H.P.B. Blavatsky countered with charges of her own. Leaders of the SPR considered the matter significant enough to send Richard Hodgson to India in order to personally investigate the matter. What followed was perhaps the most complicated and confused investigation in the history of psychical research.

Hodgson concluded that Madame Blavatsky was a phony —"one of the most accomplished, ingenious, and interesting imposters of history." His 200 page report attempted to reconstruct in detail all of the mechanisms by which she impersonated every sort of phenomena. He hired handwriting experts, for example, who determined that the Mahatma letters were really written in Madame's handwriting. Most of the evidence was of a circumstantial nature as the original shrine had been destroyed by the time Hodgson had arrived at Adyar.[122]

More recently, another researcher, Victor Endersby, has written a book challenging the Hodgson report point for point. Endersby cites independent testimony from handwriting experts who clearly disagree with those hired by Hodgson.[123] At this point, the case is still unsolved. The existence of the Mahatmas has not been disproved. All of the many allegations against the Theosophists are still controversial. Authorities differ on the authenticity of the material phenomena as well as the authenticity and legitimacy of the Theosophical teachings. Like many flamboyant psychics who were capable of producing genuine phenomena, Blavatsky's claims may have at times been fraudulent. A massive amount of detective work is required in such cases to tease out the genuine psychic manifestations from the host of unconscious projections and tricks.

Scholars have claimed that her voluminous writings were merely plagiarisms from dozens of other more academic works —and yet, she was not known to have a large library.[124] Her writings seemed to come automatically—according to her, at the dictation of the Mahatmas. An alternative hypothesis is that she was clairvoyantly transcribing other published works—a phenomena which has been observed in other cases.

In any case, the teachings of the Theosophists have had an enormous impact on western culture and for that reason are quoted several times in this book.

Eusaphia Palladino

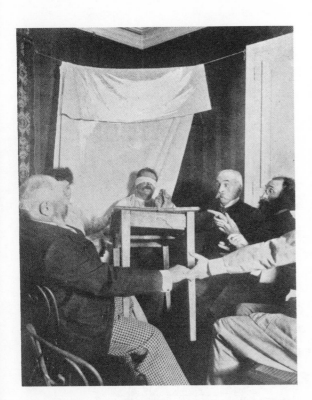

One of the most extraordinary physical mediums in the history of psychical research was Eusapia Palladino, a rough peasant woman from Naples. She came to the attention of the learned world through séances held with the eminent Italian sociologist Cesare Lombroso. These séances continued to be held in Italy until 1894 when the French physiologist Charles Richet invited her to his private island to attend séances with Frederick Myers and Sir Oliver Lodge as well as J. Ochorowicz, a Polish researcher.* It was Richet's belief that he would be able to prevent Eusapia from using props or accomplices while she was on the island. They witnessed most of the phenomena which had been previously reported: levitations, grasps, touches, lights, materializations, raps, curtains billowing, scents, and music. At all times the researchers were holding Eusapia's hands and feet.

The following excerpts are from the published account of one of these sessions:

Richet held both arms and one hand of E., while M. held both feet and her other arm. R. then felt a hand move over his head and rest on his mouth for some seconds, during which he spoke to us with his voice muffled. The round table now approached. R.'s head was stroked behind. . . . The round table continued to approach in violent jerks. . . . A small cigar box fell on our table, and a sound was heard in the air as of something rattling. . . . A covered wire of the electric battery came on to the table and wrapped itself around R.'s and E.'s heads, and was pulled till E. called out. . . . The accordian which was on the round table got on the floor somehow, and began to play single notes. Bellier [Richet's secretary] counted 26 of them and then ceased counting. While the accordian played, E's fingers made movements in the hands of both M. and L. in accord with the notes as if she was playing them with difficulty. . . . Eusapia being well held, Myers heard a noise on the round table at his side, and turning to look saw a white object detach itself from the table and move slowly through the clear space between his own and Eusapia's head. . . . Lodge now saw the object coming past Myer's head and settling on the table. It was the lamp-shade coming white side first. . . . The "chalet" [music box] which was on the round table now began to play, and then visibly approached, being seen by both Myers and Lodge coming through the air, and settled on our table against Myers chest. . . . During the latter half of the sitting, Eusapia had taken one of Myer's fingers and drawn some scrawls with it outside Richet's flannel jacket, which was buttoned up to his neck. Myers said, 'She is using me to write on you,' and it was thought no more of. But after the séance, when undressing, Richet found on his white shirt front, underneath both flannel jacket and high white waistcoat, a clear blue scrawl: and he came at once to bedrooms to show it.[125]

Myers, Lodge, and Richet were convinced of the genuineness of the phenomena which they reported and soon arranged for Eusapia to repeat her performance before SPR members in Cambridge. Again a number of phenomena were noted. Protuberances observed coming out of Eusapia's body and the billowing of curtains were particularly hard to explain away. However, at Hodgson's insistence the Cambridge group relaxed their controls over Eusapia's hands and feet to see if she would cheat if given an opportunity. Under these

---

*While generally acknowledged as the father of modern criminology, Lombroso's theories have been largely discredited. However, both Lodge and Richet were awarded the Nobel prize for their researches which have withstood the test of time.

conditions, Eusapia conducted several séances producing nothing but fraudulent phenomena, whereupon Hodgson insisted that none of her other phenomena could be trusted. Other investigators acknowledged that she would cheat if given a chance, but that nevertheless, under controlled conditions she did produce authentic phenomena.

The S. P. R. maintained a firm policy of rebuffing the phenomena of any mediums who have ever been found guilty of systematic fraud. Members were urged to ignore any future reports of experiments with Eusapia.

Reports concerning Eusapia, however, continued to flow in. In 1897, the noted French astronomer Camille Flammarion reported on a series of séances in which "spirit" impressions were made in wet putty. Flammarion gives us the following description of the event:

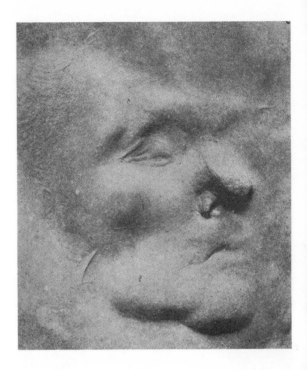

I sit at the right hand of Eusapia, *who rests her head upon my left shoulder*, and whose right hand I am holding. M. de Fontanay is at her left, and has taken great care not to let go of the other hand. The tray of putty, weighing nine pounds, has been placed upon a chair, twenty inches behind the curtain, consequently behind Eusapia. She cannot touch it without turning around, and we have her entirely in our power, our feet on hers. Now the chair upon which was the tray of putty has drawn aside the hangings, or portiéres, and moved forward to a point above the head of the medium, who remained seated and held down by us; moved itself also over our heads,—the chair to rest upon the head of my neighbor Mme. Blech, and the tray to rest softly in the hands of M. Blech, who is sitting at the end of the table. At this moment Eusapia rises, declaring that she sees upon the table another table and a bust, and cries out, "*E Fatto*" ("It is done"). It was not at this time, surely, that she would have been able to place her face upon the cake, for it was at the other end of the table. Nor was it before this, for it would have been necessary to take the chair in one hand and the cake with the other, and she did not stir from her place. The explanation, as can be seen, is very difficult indeed.
Let us admit, however, that the fact is so extraordinary that a doubt remains in our mind, because the medium rose from her chair almost at the critical moment. And yet her face was immediately kissed by Mme. Blech, who perceived no odor of the putty.[126]

Finally in 1909, the S. P. R. did publish a report of another series of séances with Eusapia which were conducted by a group of experimenters known for their exposure of other

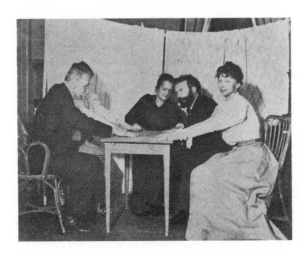

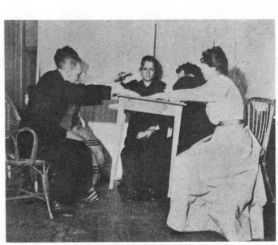

fraudulent mediums—the Hon. Everard Fielding, Hereward Carrington, and W. W. Baggally. They observed a number of levitations and materializations under good lighting conditions. These séances occurred in the middle room of a three room hotel suite which they had rented for the purpose in order to rule out the possibility of confederates. Their account is quite detailed and thorough, having been dictated minute by minute to a professional stenographer. They were favorably impressed with what they had observed. However, the following year Eusapia's abilities, whatever they were, seem to have faded and it was simply too late to conduct further research with her.

Another extraordinary physical medium whose ectoplasmic materializations were observed and photographed by many investigators was Marthe Béraud. Charles Richet describes the production of a phantom, called Bien Boa, under experimental conditions which he felt negated the possibility of theatrical props or accomplices:

BIEN BOA
(Courtesy Psychic Magazine.)

He seemed so much alive that, as we could hear his breathing, I took a flask of baryta water to see if his breath would show carbon dioxide. The experiment succeeded. I did not lose sight of the flask from the moment I put it into the hands of Bien Boa who seemed to float in the air on the left of the curtain at a height greater than Martha could have been even if standing up . . .
A comical incident occurred at this point. When we saw the baryta show white (which incidently shows that the light was good), we cried "Bravo." Bien Boa then vanished, but reappeared three times, opening and closing the curtain and bowing like an actor who receives applause.
However striking this was, another experiment seems to me even more evidential: Everything being arranged as usual. . . . after a long wait I saw close to me, in front of the curtain which had not been moved, a white vapour, hardly sixteen inches distant. It was like a white veil or handkerchief on the floor; it rose up still more, enlarged, and grew into a human form, a short bearded man dressed in a turban and white mantle, who moved, limping slightly, from right to left before the curtain. On coming close to General Noel, he sank down abruptly to the floor with a clicking noise like a falling skeleton, flattening out in front of the curtain. Three or four minutes later . . . he reappeared rising in a straight line from the floor, born from the floor, so to say, and falling back on it with the same clicking noise.
The only un-metapsychic explanation possible seemed to be a trap-door opening and shutting: but there was no trap-door, as I verified the next morning and as attested by the architect.
Several photographs were taken. . . . The softness and vaporous outline of the hands are curious; likewise the veil surrounding the phantom has indeterminate outlines. . . . A thick, black, artificial-looking beard covers the mouth and chin. . . . Bien Boa would seem to be a bust only floating in space in front of Marthe, whose bodice can be seen. Low down, between the curtain and Marthe's black skirt, there seem to be two small whitish rod-like supports to the phantom form.[127]

The most impressive evidence for ectoplasmic materializations comes from molds of "spirit hands" which have been made in paraffin. Richet reports his careful studies:

Geley and I took the precaution of introducing, unknown to any other person, a small quantity of cholesterin in the bath of melted paraffin wax placed before the medium during the séance. This

84

substance is insoluable in paraffin without discolouring it, but on adding sulphuric acid it takes a deep violet-red tint; so that we could be absolutely certain that any moulds obtained should be by the paraffin provided by ourselves . . .

During the séance the medium's hands were firmly held by Geley and myself on the right and on the left, so that he could not liberate either hand. A first mould was obtained of a child's hand, then a second of both hands, right and left; a third time of a child's foot. The creases in the skin and veins were visible on the plaster casts made from the moulds.

By reason of the narrowness of the wrist these moulds could not be obtained from living hands, for the whole hand would have to be withdrawn through the narrow opening at the wrist. Professional modellers secure their results by threads attached to the hand, which are pulled through the plaster. In the moulds here considered there was nothing of the sort; they were produced by a materialization followed by de-materialization, for this latter was necessary to disengage the hand from the paraffin "glove."[128]

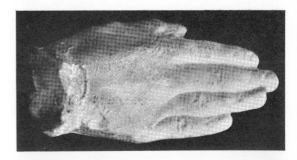

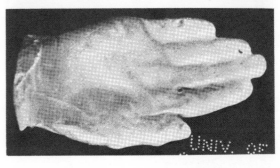

The plaster casts from these molds—including a cast of intertwining hands—are still available for inspection at the Metapsychic Institute in Paris. A physiologist of the first order, Richet sums up his research on ectoplasmic materialization as follows:

There is ample proof that experimental materialization (ectoplasmic) should take definite rank as a scientific fact. Assuredly we do not understand it. It is very absurd, if a truth can be absurd.

Spiritualists have blamed me for using this word "absurd"; and have not been able to understand that to admit the reality of these phenomena was to me an actual pain; but to ask a physiologist, a physicist, or a chemist to admit that a form that has circulation of the blood, warmth, and muscles, that exhales carbonic acid, has weight, speaks, and thinks, can issue from a human body is to ask of him an intellectual effort that is really painful.

Yes, it is absurd; but no matter—it is true.[129]

Most researchers who lacked firsthand experience still refused to accept the physical phenomena of mediumship. Too many fraudulent cases had been exposed for comfort. However, there was still a pronounced interest in the possibility of psychic thought transference. Kate Wingfield, a mental medium, met Frederick Myers in 1884. She produced automatic writing communications allegedly coming from deceased persons. Occasionally these writings included material which was considered evidential. She was also known for her ability to diagnose the illnesses of sitters at her séances with accuracy. She claimed to be able to see distant persons and scenes by staring into a crystal—a venerable technique since the times of John Dee. Later she was able to sustain this type of vision without the use of the crystal.

The problem with this type of mediumship was that the information coming spontaneously from the medium might have already been stored in the unconscious memory. What was needed to counter this objection was a medium who could consistently produce accurate information on demand and without advance notice. These criteria were amply satisfied by Mrs. Leonora E. Piper of Boston, Massachusetts. Her mediumship began spontaneously in 1884, on the occasion of going into a trance during the séance of another medium. At first her controlling spirits rather pretensiously claimed to be Bach and Longfellow. Then appeared a self-styled French doctor who gave the name of Phenuit and spoke in a gruff male voice full of Frenchisms, Negro patois, and vulgar Yankee slang, nevertheless offering successful diagnoses and prescriptions. Often the deceased relatives of the sitters would speak through Mrs. Piper at her séances.

In 1886 William James, the great American psychologist, anonymously attended one of her séances. He was sufficiently impressed with the information which she revealed to him that he sent some 25 other people, using pseudonyms, to her. Fifteen of these people reported back to James that they had received from her names and facts which it was improbable that she should know. In 1886, James issued a report to the SPR in which he made the following statement:

My own conviction is not evidence, but it seems fitting to record it. I am persuaded of the medium's honesty, and of the genuineness of her trance; and although at first disposed to think that the "hits" she made were either lucky coincidences, or the result of knowledge on her part of who the sitter was and of his or her family affairs, I now believe her to be in the possession of a power as yet unexplained.[130]

Despite his interest in Mrs. Piper, William James gave up the inquiry at this point. Having convinced himself of her validity, he chose to give his other work higher priority at that time. The following year, however, Richard Hodgson, who had gained a reputation as a skeptical researcher for his debunking of Madame Blavatsky, arrived in Boston to head the American branch of the SPR. He was astounded when Mrs. Piper was able to offer many details about his family in Australia. To check on her honesty, he even had her and her family shadowed for some weeks by detectives. James and Hodgson decided it would be wise to test Mrs. Piper in another environment, where she would have neither friends nor accomplices to aid her. Accordingly she was invited to England by the SPR organization there and set off in November of 1889.

The results with Mrs. Piper in England were mixed. On a good day she was able to produce a mass of detailed information about the sitters which generally left them dumbfounded. On a bad day, her control, Phenuit, would behave in a most obnoxious manner, keeping up a constant babble of false assertions and inane conversation, blatantly fishing for information, and generally provoking the sitters. On no occasions was it concluded that Phenuit was anything more than a secondary personality of Mrs. Piper's.

During one séance Mrs. Piper revealed to Sir Oliver Lodge a great deal of information regarding an uncle of his who had been dead for twenty years. Lodge sent an agent to inquire in the neighborhood where the uncle had lived. In three days he was unable to unearth as much information as Mrs. Piper had provided. All of her remarks were eventually verified by surviving relatives.

Leonora E. Piper

In 1890 Mrs. Piper returned to the United States where she worked very closely with Richard Hodgson who spent the next fifteen years investigating her mediumship.

Nandor Fodor gives us the following picture of Hodgson's research with Mrs. Piper:

His first report on the Piper phenomena was published in 1892. . . . In it no definite conclusions are announced. Yet, at this time Hodgson had obtained conclusive evidence. But it was of a private character and as he did not include the incident in question in his report, he did not consider it fair to point out its import. As told by Hereward Carrington in *The Story of Psychic Science,* Hodgson when still a young man in Australia had fallen in love with a girl and wished to marry her. Her parents objected on religious grounds. Hodgson left for England and never married. One day, in a sitting with Mrs. Piper, the girl suddenly communicated, informing Dr. Hodgson that she had died shortly before. This incident, the truth of which was verified, made a deep impression on his mind.[131]

At first Hodgson felt that Mrs. Piper's knowledge came to her telepathically. However, during a sitting in March of 1892 a new controlling spirit came who identified himself as a George Pellew, a prominent young man who had been killed a few weeks earlier and who was casually known to Hodgson. Five years previously he had had one anonymous sitting with Mrs. Piper. Pellew eventually replaced Phenuit as the main control, and as the intermediary between the sitters and the spirits of their deceased friends. This particular control was very realistic and seemed to Hodgson to be more than a mere secondary personality. He showed an intimate knowledge of the affairs of the actual George Pellew, by recognizing and commenting on objects that had belonged to him. Out of 150 sitters who had been introduced to him he recognized exactly those thirty people with whom the living Pellew had been acquainted. He even modified the topics and style of conversation with each of these friends, and showed a remarkable knowledge of their concerns. Very rarely did the Pellew personality slip up.

Mrs. Piper had never once in her career as a medium been detected in a dishonest action. Frank Podmore, the severest critic in the SPR, became convinced of the genuineness of her telepathic phenomena and, based on the Pellew material, the skeptical Richard Hodgson was inclined toward a spiritualistic position.

To credit spiritualism, he based his arguments for this position largely on the fact that a good amount of verified evidence which Pellew produced was unknown to anyone in the room at that time, and therefore could not have been picked up telepathically by any of the sitters.

In 1897, Hodgson published a report on Mrs. Piper in the *Proceedings of the Society for Psychical Research,* volume VIII which made the following definite statement:

At the present time I cannot profess to have any doubt that the chief communicators to whom I have referred in the foregoing pages are veritably the personages that they claim to be, and that they have survived the change that we call death, and that they have directly communicated with us whom we call living, through Mrs. Piper's entranced organism.

Dr. Richard Hodgson

Mrs. Sidgewick argued against this position, emphasizing the occasions which the personality of the control did seem to degenerate.

Eventually several other spirits seemed to take control over Mrs. Piper's mediumship including that of the departed Reverend Stainton Moses.

Many other phenomena were explored by the SPR during its early years. The major attempt to synthesize the great mass of date which had been gathered was undertaken by Frederick Myers and published in 1903 after his death in a work called *The Human Personality and Its Survival of Bodily Death*. Myers was widely read in all the fields of knowledge of his day. His work is a testimony to his wide-reaching and poetical mind and his deep interest in the work of the psychoanalysts. He was, in fact, the first writer to introduce the works of Freud to the British public, in 1893. His book is still regarded by many as the most important single work in the history of psychical research. Even those who do not accept his hypothesis of the survival of the soul are indebted to his explorations of the unconscious or *subliminal* regions of the personality.

Myers maintained that the human personality was composed of two active coherent streams of thoughts and feelings. Those lying above the ordinary threshold of consciousness were considered *supraliminal* while those which remain submerged beneath consciousness are *subliminal*. The evidence for the existence of this *subliminal* self derives from such phenomena as automatic writing, multiple personalities, dreams, and hypnosis. These phenomena all expose deeper layers of the personality which normally remain unseen. In many cases the deeper layers seem autonomous and

independent of the supraliminal self. For example, certain memories are uncovered through hypnosis and dreams which are normally inaccessible to the conscious mind. Or in the case of certain people of genius, complete works of art will emerge from dreams. Automatic writers can sometimes maintain two conversations at once, each unaware of the other one.

Myers examined all of these phenomena carefully and felt that they were part of a continuum which ranged from unusual personality manifestations to telepathic communications, travelling clairvoyance, possession by spirits, and actual survival of the subliminal layers of personality after the death of the body. He felt that each experience in this spectrum was integrally related to the other states of being. This insight was his deepest theoretical penetration into the roots of consciousness.

Myers begins his analysis by looking at the ways in which the personality was known to disintegrate. Insistent ideas, obsessing thoughts and forgotten terrors lead up to hysterical neuroses in which the subliminal mind takes over certain body functions from the supraliminal. Gradually these maladies merge with cases of multiple personalities. He notes that the subliminal personalities often represent an improvement over the normal conscious self, and suggests that:

> As the hysteric stands in relation to ordinary men, so do we ordinary men stand in relation to a not impossible ideal of sanity and integration.[128]

Thus from the disintegrated personality which reveals some of the negative aspects of the subliminal self, we move naturally to look at people of genius, which Myers defines as a state in which "some rivulet is drawn into supraliminal life from the undercurrent stream." He discusses mathematical prodigies and musicians whose works spring fully formed into their consciousness. Of particular interest is Robert Louis Stevenson who deliberately used his dream life in order to experiment with different dramatisations of his stories. Not mentioned by Myers, but certainly applicable here, would be the incredible inventions which entered the minds of Thomas Edison (himself a spiritualist) and Nicola Tesla, whose genius led him to develop alternating current and many modern electrical appliances. Myers does cite the poet Wordsworth as being particularly sensitive to this aspect of the creative process, which he describes in "The Prelude, or Growth of a Poet's Mind:"

F. W. H. Myers

> That awful power rose from the mind's abyss,
> Like an unfathomed vapor that enwraps,
> At once, some lonely traveller. I was lost;
> Halted without an effort to break through;
> But to my conscious soul I now can say—
> 'I recognize thy glory;' in such strength
> Of usurpation, when the light of sense
> Goes out, but with a flash that has revealed
> The invisible world, doth greatness make abode.[133]

In addition to people of genius, Myers includes saintly men and women whose lives have absorbed "strength and grace from an accessible and inexhaustible source."

From neurosis, genius and sainthood we move to a state of being which all individuals experience—sleep, which he describes as the abeyance of the supraliminal life and the liberation of the subliminal. The powers of visualization, for instance, are heightened during the *hypnogogic* state as one passes into sleep and in the *hypnopompic* state as the dream lingers into waking consciousness. Myer's also discerns the heightened powers of memory and reason which occur in some dreams, and further cases of clairvoyance and telepathy in dreams. And he cites cases of what seem to be "psychical invasion" in dreams by spirits of both living and departed persons. He concludes by suggesting that sleep is every man's gate to the "spiritual world."

Hypnosis is described as the experimental exploration of the sleep phase of man's personality. The unusual phenomena which occur in hypnosis are ascribed to the power of the subliminal self which is appealed to in such states. The subliminal self appears to enjoy greater control over the body than the supraliminal. Myers also points out the relationship of hypnosis to other phenomena such as faith healing, the miraculous cures at Lourdes, and the use of magical charms. He emphasizes the experimental work done in telepathic hypnotic induction at a distance as well as telepathy, clairvoyance and precognition observed in the hypnotized subject.

From hypnosis we move to visual and auditory hallucinations which psychical researchers have labelled *sensory automatism*. When hearing a sound or seeing a color or form carries with it an association of images from another sense, this process is within the brain and is termed *entencephalic*. The stages leading from such percepts to ordinary vision include *entoptic* impressions which are due to stimuli from the optic nerve or eye and after-images which are formed in the retina. Stages leading further inward from *entencephalic* vision include memory images, dreams, images of the imagination and hallucinations. Many hallucinations cited were shown to contain information which was later verified. Other hallucinations clearly seemed to hold positive benefits for the personality and were not associated in any way with disease. Crystal gazing is a possible positive use of the mind's ability to hallucinate. Other hallucinations include the phantasms of the living and the dead which we have already discussed.

From *sensory automatisms* we move to *motor automatisms* which includes automatic writing and speaking in tongues. Most of these phenomena can be attributed to the subliminal mind within the automatist's own brain. Other cases lead one to suspect telepathy and possible communication from deceased spirits. There are cases of automatic writing, for example, in which the handwriting of a deceased person is alleged. A further development of this would be possession by another personality other than the subliminal self. However, it is very difficult to distinguish cases of spirit possession from cases of multiple personality. The personal identity of such a spirit must be clearly distinguished by its memory and its character. Yet this is a phenomena which is common to all religious traditions and which has also been observed at least once, Myers feels, by SPR researchers. He notes that such possession does not appear to have an injurious effect on the medium.

The following case is listed by Myers as an incidence of multiple personality which strongly suggests the spiritualist hypothesis. It was originally published in the *Religio-Philosophical Journal* in 1879 and later in pamphlet form with the title "The Watseka Wonder," by E. W. Stevens. The editor of the journal, highly regarded as a skillful and honest investigator by Myers, spoke highly of Dr. Stevens and claimed to have taken great pains to "obtain full corroboration of the astounding facts" from competent witnesses. The case briefly is the alleged *possession* of thirteen year old Lurancy Vennum by the spirit of Mary Roff, a neighbor's daughter who had died at the age of eighteen when Lurancy was a child of about fifteen months.

Myers quotes the following statements of Dr. Stevens, putting his own abridgements in square brackets:

[Mary Lurancy Vennum, the "Watseka Wonder," was born April 16th, 1864, in Milford township, about seven miles from Watseka, Illinois. The family moved to Iowa in July 1864 (when Lurancy was about three months old), and returned to within eight miles from Watseka in October 1865 (three months after the death of Mary Roff). Lurancy was about a year and a half old. After two other moves in the neighbourhood, the family moved into Watseka on April 1st,

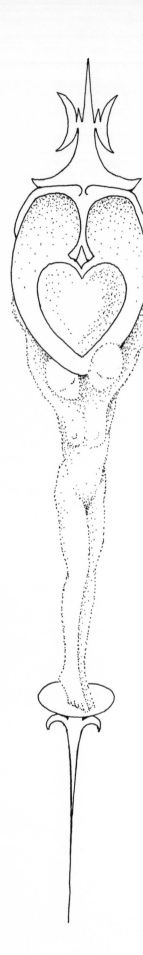

1871], locating about forty rods from the residence of A. B. Roff. They remained at this place during the summer. The only acquaintance ever had between the two families during the season was simply one brief call of Mrs. Roff, for a few minutes, on Mrs. Vennum, which call was never returned, and a formal speaking acquaintance between the two gentlemen. Since 1871 the Vennum family have lived entirely away from the vicinity of Mr. Roff's, and never nearer than now, on extreme opposite limits of the city.

"Rancy," as she is familiarly called, had never been sick, save a light run of measles in 1873.

[On July 11th, 1877, she had a sort of fit, and was unconscious for five hours. Next day the fit recurred, but while lying as if dead she described her sensations to her family, declaring that she could see heaven and the angels, and a little brother and sister and others who had died. The fits or trances, occasionally passing into ecstasy, when she claimed to be in heaven, occurred several times a day up to the end of January 1878; she was generally believed to be insane, and most friends of the family urged that she should be sent to an insane asylum.

At this stage Mr. and Mrs. Asa B. Roff, whose daughter, Mary Roff, as we shall see, had had periods of insanity, persuaded Mr. Vennum to allow him to bring Dr. E. W. Stevens of Janesville, Wisconsin, to investigate the case.]

On the afternoon of January 31st, 1878, the two gentlemen repaired to Mr. Vennum's residence, a little out of the city. Dr. Stevens, an entire stranger to the family, was introduced by Mr. Roff at four o'clock P.M.; no other persons present but the family. The girl sat near the stove, in a common chair, her elbows on her knees, her hands under her chin, feet curled up on the chair, eyes staring, looking every like an "old hag." . . . She refuses to be touched, even to shake hands, and was reticent and sullen with all save the doctor, with whom she entered freely into conversation giving her reasons for doing so; she said he was a spiritual doctor, and would understand her.

[She described herself first as an old woman named Katrina Hogan, and then as a young man named Willie Canning, and after some insane conversation had another fit, which Dr. Stevens relieved by hypnotising her. She then became calm, and said that she had been controlled by evil spirits. Dr. Stevens suggested that she should try to have a better control, and encouraged her to try and find one. She then mentioned the names of several deceased persons, saying there was one who wanted to come, named Mary Roff.

Mr. Roff being present, said: "That is my daughter; Mary Roff is my girl. Why, she has been in heaven twelve years. Yes, let her come, we'll be glad to have her come." Mr. Roff assured Lurancy that Mary was good and intelligent, and would help her all she could; stating further that Mary used to be subject to conditions like herself. Lurancy, after due deliberation and counsel with spirits, said that Mary would take the place of the former wild and unreasonable influence. Mr. Roff said to her, "Have your mother bring you to my house, and Mary will be likely to come along, and a mutual benefit may be derived from our former experience with Mary."

[On the following morning, Friday, February 1st, Mr. Vennum called at the office of Mr. Roff and informed him that the girl claimed to be Mary Roff, and wanted to go home. He said, "She seems like a child real homesick, wanting to see her pa and ma and her brothers."

Mary Roff was born in Indiana in October 1846. . . . Mary had had fits frequently from the age of six months, which gradually increased in violence. She had also had periods of despondency, in one of which, in July 1864, she cut her arm with a knife until she fainted. Five days of raving mania followed, after which she recognized no one, and seemed to lose all her natural senses, but when blindfolded could read and do everything as if she saw. After a few days she returned to her normal condition, but the fits became still worse, and she died in one of them in July 1865. Her mysterious illness had made her notorious in the neighbourhood during her life-time, and her alleged clairvoyant powers are said to have been carefully investigated "by all the prominent citizens of Watseka," including newspaper editors and clergymen.

It was in February 1878 that her supposed "control" of Lurancy began. The girl then became "mild, docile, polite, and timid, knowing none of the family, but constantly pleading to go home," and "only found contentment in going back to heaven, as she said, for short visits."]

About a week after she took control of the body, Mrs. A. B. Roff and her daughter, Mrs. Minerva Alter, Mary's sister, hearing of the remarkable change, went to see the girl. As they came in sight, far down the street, Mary, looking out of the window, exclaimed exultingly, "There comes my ma and sister Nervie!"—the name by which Mary used to call Mrs. Alter in girlhood. As they came into the house she caught them around their necks, wept and cried for joy, and seemed so happy to meet them. From this time on she seemed more homesick than before. At times she seemed almost frantic to go home.

On the 11th day of February, 1878, they sent the girl to Mr. Roff's, where she met her "pa and ma," and each member of the family, with the most gratifying expressions of love and affection, by words and embraces. On being asked how long she would stay, she said, "The angels will let me stay till some time in May;" . . .

The girl now in her new home seemed perfectly happy and content, knowing every person and everything that Mary knew when in her original body, twelve to twenty-five years ago, recognizing and calling by name those who were friends and neighbours of the family from 1852 to 1865, when Mary died, calling attention to scores, yes, hundreds of incidents that transpired during her natural life. During all the period of her sojourn at Mr. Roff's she had no knowledge of, and did not recognize any of Mr. Vennum's family, their friends or neighbours, yet Mr. and Mrs. Vennum and their children visited her and Mr. Roff's people, she being introduced to them as to any strangers. After frequent visits, and hearing them often and favourably spoken of, she learned to love them as acquaintances, and visited them with Mrs. Roff three times.

One day she met an old friend and neighbour of Mr. Roff's, who was a widow when Mary was a girl at home. Some years since the lady married a Mr. Wagoner, with whom she yet lives. But when she met Mrs. Wagoner she clasped her around the neck and said, "O Mary Lord, you look so very natural, and have changed the least of any one I have seen since I came back." Mrs. Lord was in some way related to the Vennum family, and lived close by them, but Mary could only call her by the name by which she knew her fifteen years ago, and could not seem to realize that she was married. Mrs. Lord lived just across the street from Mr. Roff's for several years, prior and up to within a few months of Mary's death; both being members of the same Methodist church, they were very intimate. . . .

One evening, in the latter part of March, Mr. Roff was sitting in the room waiting for tea, and reading the paper, Mary being out in the yard. He asked Mrs. Roff if she could find a certain velvet head-dress that Mary used to wear the last year before she died. If so, to lay it on the stand and say nothing about it, to see if Mary would recognize it. Mrs. Roff readily found and laid it on the stand. The girl soon came in, and immediately exclaimed as she approached the stand, "Oh, there is my head-dress I wore when my hair was short!" She then asked, "Ma, where is my box of letters? Have you got them yet?" Mrs. Roff replied, "Yes, Mary, I have some of them." She at once got the box with many letters in it. As Mary began to examine them she said, "Oh, ma, here is a collar I tatted! Ma, why did you not show to me my letters and things before?" The collar had been preserved among the relics of the lamented child as one of the beautiful things her fingers had wrought before Lurancy was born; and so Mary continually recognized every little thing and remembered every little incident of her girlhood. . . .

In conversation with the writer about her former life, she spoke of cutting her arm as hereinbefore stated, and asked if he ever saw where she did it. On receiving a negative answer, she proceeded to slip up her sleeve as if to exhibit the scar, but suddenly arrested the movement, as if by a sudden thought, and quickly siad, "Oh, this is not the arm; that one is in the ground," and proceeded to tell where it was buried, and how she saw it done, and who stood around, how they felt, &c., but she did not feel bad. I heard her tell Mr. Roff and the friends present, how she wrote to him a message some years ago through the hand of a medium, giving name, time, and place. Also of rapping and of spelling out a message by another medium, giving time, name, place, &c., &c. which the parents admitted to be all true. . . .

During her stay at Mr. Roff's her physical condition continually improved, being under the care and treatment of her supposed parents and the advice and help of her physician. She was ever obedient to the government and rules of the family, like a careful and wise child, always keeping in the company of some of the family, unless to go in to the nearest neighbours across the street. She was often invited and went with Mrs. Roff to visit the first families of the city, who soon became satisfied that the girl was not crazy, but a fine, well-mannered child.

As the time drew near for the restoration of Lurancy to her parents and home, Mary would sometimes seem to recede into the memory and manner of Lurancy for a little time, yet not enough to lose her identity or permit the manifestation of Lurancy's mind, but enough to show she was impressing her presence upon her own body.

[On May 19th, in the presence of Henry Vennum, Lurancy's brother, Mary left control for a time, and "Lurancy took full possession of her own body," recognizing Henry as her brother. The change of control occurred again when Mrs. Vennum came to see her the same day.]

On the morning of May 21st Mr. Roff writes as follows:—

"Mary is to leave the body of Rancy to-day, about eleven o'clock, so she says. She is bidding neighbours and friends good-bye. Rancy to return home all right to-day. Mary came from her room upstairs, where she was sleeping with Lottie, at ten o'clock last night, lay down by us, hugged and kissed us, and cried because she must bid us good-bye, telling us to give all her pictures, marbles, and cards, and twenty-five cents Mrs. Vennum had given her to Rancy, and had us promise to visit Rancy often."

[Mary arranged that her sister, Mrs. Alter, should come to the house to say good-bye to her, and that when Lurancy came at eleven o'clock she should take her to Mr. Roff's office, and he would go to Mr. Vennum's with her. There was some alternation of the control on the way, but the final return of the normal Lurancy Vennum took place before they reached Mr. Roff's office, and on arriving at her own home she recognized all the members of her own family as such, and was perfectly well and happy in her own surroundings. A few days later, on meeting Dr. Stevens, under whose care she had been at Mr. Roff's house, she had to be introduced to him as an entire stranger, and treated him as such. The next day she came to him spontaneously, saying Mary Roff had told her to come and meet him, and had made her feel he had been a very kind friend to her, and she gave him a long message purporting to be from Mary.[134]

In 1890, Dr. Richard Hodgson visited Watseka and interviewed many of the principle witnesses of this case. Their testimony was in agreement with Dr. Stevens' presentation. However, Hodgson was unable to get in touch with Lurancy Vennum herself. He draws the following conclusions to the case:

I have no doubt that the incidents occurred substantially as described in the narrative by Dr. Stevens, and in my view the only other interpretation of the case—besides the spiritistic—that seems at all plausible is that which has been put forward as the alternative to the

94

spiritistic theory to account for the trance-communications of Mrs. Piper and similar cases, viz., secondary personality with supernormal powers. It would be difficult to disprove this hypothesis in the case of the Watseka Wonder, owing to the comparative meagreness of the record and the probable abundance of "suggestion" in the environment, and any conclusion that we may reach would probably be determined largely by our convictions concerning other cases. My personal opinion is that the "Watseka Wonder" case belongs in the main manifestations to the spiritistic category.[135]

It is on the basis of this continuum of experiences that Myers asserts that the subliminal self is able to operate free from the brain in ways which modify both space and time as they appear to the supraliminal self. Just as the subliminal self is able to control physiological functions of the brain and body, as best exemplified through hypnotic experiments, so is it able to exert force on other physical objects accounting for levitations, materializations, spirit rapping, etc.

In 1897 and again on 1909, William James published papers summing up his impressions of the progress which psychical research had made. His comments, which are exerpted here, deal with the sociological as well as scientific impact of the SPR and represent a comprehensive, balanced sound scientific judgment on the research accomplished to the beginning of this century in America.

William James

WHAT PSYCHICAL RESEARCH HAS ACCOMPLISHED

"The great field for new discoveries," said a scientific friend to me the other day, "is always the unclassified residuum." Round about the accredited and orderly facts of every science there ever floats a sort of dust-cloud of exceptional observations, of occurrences minute and irregular and seldom met with, which it always proves more easy to ignore than to attend to. The ideal of every science is that of a closed and completed system of truth. The charm of most sciences to their more passive diciples consists in their appearing, in fact, to wear just this ideal form. Each one of our various *ologies* seems to offer a definite head of classification for every possible phenomenon of the sort which it professes to cover; and so far from free is most men's fancy, that, when a consistent and organized scheme of this sort has once been comprehended and assimilated, a different scheme is unimaginable. No alternative, whether to whole or parts, can any longer be conceived as possible. Phenomena unclassifiable within the system are therefore paradoxical absurdities, and must be held untrue. When, moreover, as so often happens, the reports of them are vague and indirect; when they come as mere marvels and oddities rather than as things of serious movement—one neglects or denies them with the best of scientific consciences. Only the born geniuses let themselves be worried and fascinated by these outstanding exceptions, and get no peace till they are brought within the fold. Your Galileos, Galvanis, Fresnels, Purkinjes, and Darwins are always getting confounded and troubled by insignificant things. Anyone will renovate his science who will steadily look after the irregular phenomena. And when the science is renewed, its new formulas often have more of the voice of the exceptions in them than of what were supposed to be the rules.

No part of the unclassified residuum has usually been treated with a more contemptuous scientific disregard than the mass of phenomena generally called *mystical*. Physiology will have nothing to do with them. Orthodox psychology turns its back upon them. Medicine sweeps them out; or, at most, when in an anecdotal vein, records a few of them as "effects of the imagination"—a phrase of mere dismissal, whose meaning, in this connection, it is impossible to make precise.

All the while, however, the phenomena are there, lying broadcast over the surface of history. No matter where you open its pages, you find things recorded under the name of divinations, inspirations, demoniacal possessions, apparitions, trances, ecstasies, miraculous healings and productions of disease, and occult powers possessed by peculiar individuals over persons and things in their neighborhood. We suppose that "mediumship" originated in Rochester, New York, and animal magnetism with Mesmer; but once look behind the pages of official history, in personal memoirs, legal documents, and popular narratives and books of anecdote, and you will find that there never was a time when these things were not reported just as abundantly as now. We college-bred gentry, who follow the stream of cosmopolitan culture exclusively, not infrequently stumble upon some old-established journal, or some voluminous native author, whose names are never heard of in *our* circle, but who number their readers by the quarter-million. It always gives us a little shock to find this mass of human beings not only living and ignoring us and all our gods, but actually reading and writing and cogitating without ever a thought of our canons and authorities. Well, a public no less large keeps and transmits from generation to generation the traditions and practices of the occult; but academic science cares as little for its beliefs and opinions as you, gentle reader, care for those of the readers of the *Waverley* and the *Fireside Companion*. To no one type of mind is it given to discern the totality of truth. Something escapes the best of us—not accidentally, but systematically, and because we have a twist. The scientific-academic mind and the feminine-mystical mind shy from each other's facts, just as they fly from each other's temper and spirit. Facts are there only for those who have a mental affinity with them. When once they are indisputably ascertained and admitted, the academic and critical minds are by far the best fitted ones to interpret and discuss them—for surely to pass from mystical to scientific speculations is like passing from lunacy to sanity; but on the other hand if there is anything which human history demonstrates, it is the extreme slowness with which the ordinary academic and critical mind acknowledges facts to exist which present themselves as wild facts, with no stall or pigeonhole, or as facts which threaten to break up the accepted system. In psychology, physiology, and medicine, wherever a debate between the mystics and the scientifics has been once for all decided, it is the mystics who have usually proved to be right about the facts, while the scientifics had the better of it in respect to the theories. The most recent and flagrant example of this is "animal magnetism," whose facts were stoutly dismissed as a pack of lies by academic medical science the world over, until the non-mystical theory of "hypnotic suggestion" was found for them—when they were admitted to be so excessively and dangerously common that special penal laws, forsooth, must be passed to keep all persons unequipped with medical diplomas from taking part in their production. Just so stigmatizations, invulnerabilities, instantaneous cures, inspired discourses, and demoniacal possessions, the records of which were shelved in our libraries but yesterday in the alcove headed "superstitions." now, under the brand-new title of "cases of hystero-epilepsy." are republished, reobserved, and reported with an even too credulous avidity.

Repugnant as the mystical style of philosophizing may be (especially when self- complacent), there is no sort of doubt that it goes with a gift for meeting with certain kinds of phenomenal experience. The writer of these pages has been forced in the past few years to this admission; and he now believes that he who will pay attention to facts of the sort dear to mystics, while reflecting upon them in academic-scientific ways, will be in the best possible position to help philosophy. It is a circumstance of good augury that certain scientifically trained minds in all countries seem drifting to the same conclusion. The Society for Psychical Research has been one means of bringing science and the occult together in England and America: and believing that this Society fulfills a function which, though limited, is destined

> In psychology, physiology, and medicine, wherever a debate between the mystics and the scientifics has been once for all decided, it is the mystics who have usually proved to be right about the facts, while the scientifics had the better of it in respect to the theories.

to be not unimportant in the organization of human knowledge, I am glad to give a brief account of it to the uninstructed reader

According to the newspaper and drawing-room myth, soft-headedness and idiotic credulity are the bond of sympathy in this Society, and general wonder-sickness its dynamic principle. A glance at the membership fails, however, to corroborate this view. The president is Professor Henry Sidgwick, known by his other deeds as the most incorrigibly and exasperatingly critical and skeptical mind in England. The hard-headed arthur Balfour is one vice-president, and the hard-headed Professor J. P. Langley, secretary of the Smithsonian Institution, is another. Such men as Professor Lodge, the eminent English physicist, and Professor Richet, the eminent French physiologist, are among the most active contributors to the Society's *Proceedings;* and through the catalogue of membership are sprinkled names honored throughout the world for their scientific capacity. In fact, were I asked to point to a scientific journal where hard-headedness and never-sleeping suspicion of sources of error might be seen in their full bloom, I think I should have to fall back on the *Proceedings of the Society for Psychical Research.* The common run of papers, say on physiological subjects, which one finds in other professional organs, are apt to show a far lower level of critical consciousness. Indeed, the rigorous canons of evidence applied a few years ago to testimony in the case of certain "mediums" led to the secession from the Society of a number of spiritualists. Messrs. Stainton Moses and A. R. Wallace, among others, thought that no experiences based on mere eyesight could ever have a chance to be admitted as true, if such an impossibly exacting standard of proof were insisted on in every case . . .

As a sort of weather bureau for accumulating reports of such meteoric phenomena as apparitions, the SPR has done an immense amount of work. As an experimenting body, it cannot be said to have completely fulfilled the hopes of its founders. But were there no experimental work at all, and were the SPR nothing but a weather bureau for catching sporadic apparitions, etc., in their freshness, I am disposed to think its function indispensable in the scientific organism. If any one of my readers, spurred by the thought that so much smoke must needs betoken fire, has ever looked into the existing literature of the supernatural for proof, he will know what I mean. This literature is enormous, but it is practically worthless for evidential purposes. Facts enough are cited, indeed; but the records of them are so fallible and imperfect that at most they lead to the opinion that it may be well to keep a window open upon that quarter in one's mind.

In the SPR's *Proceedings,* on the contrary, a different law prevails. Quality, and not mere quantity, is what has been mainly kept in mind. The witnesses, where possible, have in every reported case been cross-examined personally, the collateral facts have been looked up, and the story appears with its precise coefficient of evidential worth stamped on it, so that all may know just what its weight as proof may be. Outside of these *Proceedings,* I know of no systematic attempt to *weigh* the evidence for the supernatural. This makes the value of the volumes already published unique; and I firmly believe that as the years go on and the ground covered grows still wider, the *Proceedings* will more and more tend to supersede all other sources of information concerning phenomena traditionally deemed occult. Collections of this sort are usually best appreciated by the rising generation. The young anthropologists and psychologists who will soon have full occupancy of the stage will feel how great a scientific scandal it has been to leave a great mass of human experience to take its chances between vague tradition and credulity on the one hand and dogmatic denial at long range on the other, with no body of persons extant who are willing and competent to study the matter with both patience and rigor. If the Society lives long enough for the public to become familiar with its presence, so that any apparition, or house or person infested with unaccountable noises or disturbances of material objects, will as a matter of course be reported to its officers, we shall doubtless end by having a mass of

> . . . were I asked to point to a scientific journal where hard-headedness and never-sleeping suspicion of sources of error were in full bloom, I think I should have to fall back on the *Proceedings of the Society for Psychical Research.*

97

facts concrete enough to theorize upon. Its sustainers, therefore, should accustom themselves to the idea that its first duty is simply to exist from year to year and perform this recording function well, though no conclusive results of any sort emerge at first. All our learned societies have begun in some such modest way . . .

It is now time to cast a brief look upon the actual contents of these *Proceedings*. The first two years were largely taken up with experiments in thought-transference. The earliest lot of these were made with the daughters of a clergyman named Creery, and convinced Messrs. Balfour, Stewart, Barrett, Myers, and Gurney that the girls had an inexplicable power of guessing names and objects thought of by other persons. Two years later, Mrs. Sidgwick and Mr. Gurney, recommencing experiments with the same girls, detected them signaling to each other. It is true that for the most part the conditions of the earlier series had excluded signaling, and it is also possible that the cheating may have grafted itself on what was originally a genuine phenomenon. Yet Gurney was wise in abandoning the entire series to the skepticism of the reader. Many critics of the SPR seem out of all its labors to have heard only of this case. But there are experiments recorded with upwards of thirty other subjects. Three were experimented upon at great length during the first two years: one was Mr. G. A. Smith; the other two were young ladies in Liverpool in the employment of Mr. Malcolm Guthrie.

It is the opinion of all who took part in these latter experiments that sources of conscious and unconscious deception were sufficiently excluded, and that the large percentage of correct reproductions by the subjects of words, idagrams, and sensations occupying another persons' consciousness were entirely inexplicable as results of chance. The witnesses of these performances were in fact all so satisfied of the genuineness of the phenomena that "telepathy" has figured freely in the papers of the *Proceedings* and in Gurney's book on phantasms as a *vera causa* on which additional hypotheses might be built. No mere reader can be blamed, however, if he demand, for so revolutionary a belief, a more overwhelming bulk of testimony than has been supplied. Any day, of course, may bring in fresh experiments in successful picture-guessing. But meanwhile, and lacking that, we can only point out that the present data are strengthened in the flank, so to speak, by all observations that tend to corroborate the possibility of other kindred phenomena, such as telepathic impression, clairvoyance, or what is called "test-mediumship." The wider genus will naturally cover the narrower species with its credit.

Gurney's papers on hypnotism must be mentioned next. Some of them are less concerned with establishing new facts than with analyzing old ones. But omitting these, we find that in the line of pure observation Gurney claims to have ascertained in more than one subject the following phenomenon: The subject's hands are thrust through a blanket, which screens the operator from his eyes, and his mind is absorbed in conversation with a third person. The operator meanwhile points with his finger to one of the fingers of the subject, which finger alone responds to this silent selection by becoming stiff or anesthetic, as the case may be. The interpretation is difficult, but the phenomenon, which I have myself witnessed, seems authentic.

Another observation made by Gurney seems to prove the possibility of the subject's mind being directly influenced by the operator's. The hypnotized subject responds, or fails to respond, to questions asked by a third party according to the operator's silent permission or refusal. Of course, in these experiments all obvious sources of deception were excluded. But Gurney's most important contribution to our knowledge of hypnotism was his series of experiments on the automatic writing of subjects who had received post-hypnotic suggestions. For example, a subject during trance is told that he will poke the fire in six minutes after waking. On being waked he has no memory of the order, but while he is engaged in conversation his hand is placed on a planchette, which immediately writes the sentence, "P., you will poke the fire in six minutes." Experiments like this, which were repeated in great variety, seem to prove that below the upper consciousness the hypnotic consciousness persists, engrossed with the suggestion and able to express itself through the involuntarily moving hand . . .

The next topic worth mentioning in the *Proceedings* is the discussion of the physical phenomena of mediumship (slate-writing, furniture-moving, and so forth) by Mrs. Sidgwick, Mr. Hodgson, and "Mr. Davey." This, so far as it goes, is destructive of the claims of all the mediums examined. "Mr. Davey" himself produced fraudulent slate-writing of the highest order, while Mr. Hodgson, a "sitter" in his confidence, reviewed the written reports of the series of his other sitters—all of them intelligent persons—and showed that in every case they failed to see the essential features of what was done before their eyes. This Davey-Hodgson contribution is probably the most damaging document concerning eye-witnesses' evidence that has ever been produced. Another substantial bit of work based on personal observation is Mr. Hodgson's report on Madame Blavatsky's claims to physical mediumship. This is adverse to the lady's pretensions; and although some of Madame Blavatsky's friends make light of it, it is a stroke from which her reputation will not recover . . .

One of the most important experimental contributions to the *Proceedings* is the article of Miss X. on "Crystal Vision." Many persons who look fixedly into a crystal or other vaguely luminous surface fall into a kind of daze, and see visions. Miss X. has this susceptibility in a remarkable degree, and is, moreover, an unusually intelligent critic. She reports many visions which can only be described as apparently clairvoyant, and others which beautifully fill a vacant niche in our knowledge of subconscious mental operations. For example, looking into the crystal before breakfast one morning she reads in printed characters of the death of a lady of her acquaintance, the date and other circumstances all duly appearing in type. Startled by this, she looks at the *Times* of the previous day for verification, and there among the deaths are the identical words which she has seen. On the same page of the *Times* are other items which she remembers reading the day before; and the only explanation seems to be that her eyes then inattentively observed, so to speak, the death items, which forthwith fell into a special corner of her memory, and came out as a visual hallucination when the peculiar modification of consciousness induced by the crystal-gazing set in.

Passing from papers based on observation to papers based on narrative, we have a number of ghost stories, etc., sifted by Mrs. Sidgwick and discussed by Messrs. Myers and Podmore. They form the best ghost literature I know of from the point of view of emotional interest. As to the conclusions drawn, Mrs. Sidgwick is rigorously noncommittal, while Mr. Myers and Mr. Podmore show themselves respectively hospitable and inhospitable to the notion that such stories have a basis of objectivity dependent on the continued existence of the dead . . .

One's reaction on hearsay testimony is always determined by one's own experience. Most men who have once convinced themselves, by what seems to them a careful examination, that any one species of the supernatural exists, begin to relax their vigilance as to evidence, and throw the doors of their minds more or less wide open to the supernatural along its whole extent. To a mind that has thus made its *sulto mortale*, the minute work over insignificant cases of quiddling discussion of "evidential values" of which the Society's reports are full seem insufferably tedious. And it is so; few species of literature are more truly dull than reports of phantasms. Taken simply by themselves, as separate facts to stare at, they appear so devoid of meaning and sweep that, even were they certainly true, one would be tempted to leave them out of one's universe for being so idiotic. Every other sort of fact has some context and continuity with the rest of nature. These alone are contextless and discontinuous.

Hence I think that the sort of loathing—no milder word will do—which the very words "psychical research" and "psychical researcher" awaken in so many honest scientific breasts is not only natural, but in a sense praiseworthy. A man who is unable himself to conceive of any *orbit* for these mental meteors can only suppose that Messrs. Gurney, Myers, & Company's mood in dealing with them must be that of silly marveling at so many detached prodigies. And such prodigies! So science simply falls back on her general *non-possumus*; and most of the would-be critics of the *Proceedings* have been contended to oppose to the phenomena recorded the simple presumption that in some way or other the reports *must* be fallacious—for so far as the order of nature has been subjected to really scientific scrutiny, it always has been proved to run the other way. But the oftener one is forced to reject an alleged sort of fact by the use of this mere presumption, the weaker does the presumption itself get to be; and one might in course of time use up one's presumptive privileges in this way, even though one started (as our anti-telepathists do) with as good a case as the great induction of psychology that all our knowledge comes by the use of our eyes and ears and other senses. And we must remember also that this undermining of the strength of a presumption by reiterated report of facts to the contrary does not logically require that the facts in question should all be well proved. A lot of rumors in the air against a business man's credit, though they might all be vague, and no one of them amount to proof that he is unsound, would certainly weaken the *presumption* of his soundness. And all the more would they this effect if they formed what Gurney called a fagot and not a chain—this is, if they were independent of one another, and came from different quarters. Now, the evidence for telepathy, weak and strong, taken just as it comes, forms a fagot and not a chain. No one item cites the content of another item as part of its own proof. But taken together the items have a certain general consistency; there is a method in their madness, so to speak. So each of them adds presumptive value to the lot; and cumulatively, as no candid mind can fail to see, they subtract presumptive force from the orthodox belief that there can be nothing in anyone's intellect that has not come in through ordinary experiences of sense.

But it is a miserable thing for a question of truth to be confined to mere presumption and counter-presumption, with no decisive thunderbolt of fact to clear the baffling darkness. And, sooth to say, in talking so much of the merely presumption-weakening value of our records, I have myself been willfully taking the point of view of the so-called "rigorously scientific" disbeliever, and making an *ad hominem* plea. My own point of view is different. For me the thunderbolt *has* fallen, and the orthodox belief has not merely had its presumption weakened, but the truth itself of the belief is decisively overthrown. If I may employ the language of the professional logic-shop, a universal proposition can be made untrue by a particular instance. If you wish to upset the law that all crows are black, you must not seek to show that no crows are; it is enough if you prove one single crow to be white. My own white crow is Mrs. Piper. In the trances of this medium, I cannot resist the conviction that knowledge appears which she has never gained by the ordinary waking use of her eyes and ears and wits. What the source of this knowledge may be I know not, and have not the glimmer of an explanatory suggestion to make; but from admitting the fact of such knowledge I can see no escape. So when I turn to the rest of the evidence, ghosts and all, I cannot carry with me the irreversibly negative bias of the "rigorously scientific" mind, with its presumption as to what the true order of nature ought to be. I feel as if, though the evidence be flimsy in spots, it may nevertheless collectively carry heavy weight. The rigorously scientific mind may, in truth, easily overshoot the mark. Science means, first of all, a certain dispassionate method. To suppose that it means a certain set of results that one should pin one's faith upon and hug forever is sadly to mistake its genius, and degrades the scientific body to the status of a sect. . . .[136]

For twenty-five years I have been in touch with the literature of psychical research, and have had acquaintance with numerous "researchers." I have also spent a good many hours (though far fewer than I ought to have spent) in witnessing (or trying to witness) phenomena. Yet I am theoretically no "further" than I was at the beginning; and I confess that at times I have been tempted to believe that the

> For me the thunderbolt *has* fallen, and the orthodox belief has not merely had its presumption weakened, but the truth itself of the belief is decisively overthrown. . . . My own white crow is Mrs. Piper.

Creator has eternally intended this department of nature to remain *baffling*, to prompt our curiosities and hopes and suspicions all in equal measure, so that, although ghosts and clairvoyances, and raps and messages from spirits, are always seeming to exist and can never be fully explained away, they also can never be susceptible of full corroboration.

The peculiarity of the case is just that there are so many sources of possible deception in most of the observations that the whole lot of them *may* be worthless, and yet that in comparatively few cases can aught more fatal than this vague general possibility of error be pleaded against the record. Science meanwhile needs something more than bare possibilities to build upon; so your genuinely scientific inquirer —I don't mean your ignoramus "scientist"—has to remain unsatisfied. It is hard to believe, however, that the Creator has really put any big array of phenomena into the world merely to defy and mock our scientific tendencies; so my deeper belief is that we psychical researchers have been too precipitate with our hopes, and that we must expect to mark progress not by quarter-centuries, but by half-centuries or whole centuries. . . .

Not long after Darwin's *Origin of Species* appeared I was studying with that excellent anatomist and man, Jeffries Wyman, at Harvard. He was a convert, yet so far a half-hesitating one, to Darwin's views; but I heard him make a remark that applies well to the subject I now write about. When, he said, a theory gets propounded over and over again, coming up afresh after each time orthodox criticism has buried it, and each time seeming solider and harder to abolish, you may be sure that there is truth in it. Oken and Lamarck and Chambers had been triumphantly dispatched and buried, but here was Darwin making the very same heresy seem only more plausible. How often has "Science" killed off all spook philosophy, and laid ghosts and raps and "telepathy" away underground as so much popular delusion? Yet never before were these things offered us so voluminously, and never in such authentic-seeming shape or with such good credentials. The tide seems steadily to be rising, in spite of all the expedients of scientific orthodoxy. It is hard not to suspect that here may be something different from a mere chapter in human gullibility. It may be a genuine realm of natural phenomena.

Falsus in uno, falsus in omnibus, once a cheat, always a cheat, such as been the motto of the English psychical researchers in dealing with mediums. I am disposed to think that, as a matter of policy, it has been wise. Tactically it is far better to believe much too little than a little too much; and the exceptional credit attaching to the row of volumes of the SPR's *Proceedings* is due to the fixed intention of the editors to proceed very slowly. Better a little belief tied fast, better a small investment *salted down*, than a mass of comparative insecurity.

But, however wise as a policy the SPR's maxim may have been, as a test of truth I believe it to be almost irrelevant. In most things human the accusation of deliberate fraud and falsehood is grossly superficial. Man's character is too sophistically mixed for the alternative of "honest or dishonest" to be a sharp one. Scientific men themselves will cheat—at public lectures—rather than let experiments obey their well-known tendency towards failure. I have heard of a lecturer on physics who had taken over the apparatus of the previous incumbent, consulting him about a certain machine intended to show that, however the peripheral parts of it might be agitated, its center of gravity remained immovable. "It *will* wobble," he complained. "Well," said the predecessor, apologetically, "to tell the truth, whenever I used that machine I found it advisable to *drive a nail* through the center of gravity." I once saw a distinguished physiologist, now dead, cheat most shamelessly at a public lecture, at the expense of a poor rabbit, and all for the sake of being able to make a cheap joke about its being an "American rabbit"— for no other, he said, could survive such a wound as he pretended to have given it.

To compare small men with great, I have myself cheated shamelessly. In the early days of the Sanders Theater at Harvard, I once had charge of a heart on the physiology of which Professor Newell Martin

> **Scientific men themselves will cheat—at public lectures—rather than let experiments obey their well-known tendency towards failure. . . . I have myself cheated shamelessly.**

101

was giving a popular lecture. This heart, which belonged to a turtle, supported an index-straw which threw a moving shadow, greatly enlarged, upon the screen, while the heart pulsated. When certain nerves were stimulated, the lecturer said, the heart would act in certain ways which he described. But the poor heart was too far gone and, although it stopped duly when the nerve of arrest was excited, that was the final end of its life's tether. Presiding over the performance, I was terrified at the fiasco, and found myself suddenly acting like one of those military geniuses who on the field of battle convert disaster into victory. There was no time for deliberation; so, with my forefinger under a part of the straw that cast no shadow, I found myself impulsively and automatically imitating the rhythmical movements which my colleague had prophesied the heart would undergo. I kept the experiment from failing; and not only saved my colleague (and the turtle) from a humiliation that but for my presence of mind would have been their lot, but I established in the audience the true view of the subject. The lecturer was stating this; and the misconduct of one half-dead specimen of heart ought not to destroy the impression of his words. "There is no worse lie than a truth misunderstood," is a maxim which I have heard ascribed to a former venerated President of Harvard. The heart's failure would have been minunderstood by the audience and given the lie to the lecturer. It was hard enough to make them understand the subject anyhow; so that even now as I write in cold blood I am tempted to think that I acted quite correctly. I was acting for the *larger* truth, at any rate, however automatically, and my sense of this was probably what prevented the more pedantic and literal part of my conscience from checking the action of my sympathetic finger. To this day the memory of that critical emergency has made me feel charitable towards all mediums who make phenomena come in one way when they won't come easily in another. On the principles of the SPR, my conduct on that one occasion ought to discredit everything I ever do, everything, for example, I may write in this article—manifestly unjust conclusion.

Fraud, conscious or unconscious, seems ubiquitous throughout the range of physical phenomena of spiritism, and false pretense, prevarication, and fishing for clues are ubiquitous in the mental manifestations of mediums. If it be not everywhere fraud simulating reality, one is tempted to say, then the reality (if any reality there be) has the bad luck of being fated everywhere to simulate fraud. The suggestion of humbug seldom stops, and mixes itself with the best manifestations. Mrs. Piper's control, "Rector," is a most impressive personage, who discerns in an extraordinary degree his sitter's inner needs, and is capable of giving elevated counsel to fastidious and critical minds. Yet in many respects he is an arrant humbug—such he seems to me at least—pretending to a knowledge and power to which he has no title, nonplussed by contradiction, yielding to suggestion, and covering his tracks with plausible excuses. Now the non-"researching" mind looks upon such phenomena simply according to their face-pretension and never thinks of asking what they may signify below the surface. Since they profess for the most part to be revealers of spirit life, it is either as being absolutely that, or as being absolute frauds, that they are judged. The result is an inconceivably shallow state of public opinion on the subject. One set of persons, emotionally touched at hearing the names of their loved ones given, and consoled by assurances that they are "happy," accept the revelation, and consider spiritualism "beautiful." More hard-headed subjects, disgusted by the revelation's comtemptible contents, outraged by the fraud, and prejudiced beforehand against all "spirits," high or low, avert their minds from what they call such "rot" or "bosh" entirely. Thus do two opposite sentimentalisms divide opinion between them! A good expression of the "scientific" state of mind occurs in Huxley's *Life and Letters*:

"I regret," he writes, "that I am unable to accept the invitation of the Committee of the Dialectical Society. . . . I take no interest in the subject. The only case of 'Spiritualism' I have ever had the opportunity of examining into for myself was as gross an imposture as ever came

If it be not eveywhere fraud simulating reality . . . then the reality . . . has the bad luck of being fated . . . to simulate fraud.

under my notice. But supposing these phenomena to be genuine—they do not interest me. If anybody would endow me with the faculty of listening to the chatter of old women and curates in the nearest provincial town, I should decline the privilege, have better things to do. And if the folk in the spiritual world do not talk more wisely and sensibly than their friends report them to do, I put them in the same category. The only good that I can see in the demonstration of the 'Truth of Spiritualism' is to furnish an additional argument against suicide. Better live a crossing-sweeper, than die and be made to talk twaddle by a 'medium' hired at a guinea a *Seance*."[2]

Obviously the mind of the excellent Huxley has here but two whole-souled categories, namely revelation or imposture, to apperceive the case by. Sentimental reasons bar revelation out, for the messages, he thinks, are not romantic enough for that; fraud exists anyhow; therefore the whole thing is nothing but imposture. The odd point is that so few of those who talk in this way realize that they and the spiritists are using the same major premise and differing only in the minor. The major premise is: "Any spirit-revelation must be romantic." The minor of the spiritist is: "This *is* romantic"; that of the Huxleyan is: "This is dingy twaddle"—whence their opposite conclusions!

Meanwhile the first thing that anyone learns who attends seriously to these phenomena is that their causation is far too complex for our feelings about what is or is not romantic enough to be spiritual to throw any light upon it. The causal factors must be carefully dintinguished and traced through series, from their simplest to their strongest forms, before we can begin to understand the various resultants in which they issue . . .

Someone said to me a short time ago that after my twenty-five years of dabbling in "Psychics," it would be rather shameful were I unable to state any definite conclusions whatever as a consequence. I had to agree; so I now proceed to take up the challenge and express such convictions as have been engendered in me by that length of experience, be the same true or false ones. I may be dooming myself to the pit in the eyes of better-judging posterity; I may be raising myself to honor; I am willing to take the risk, for what I shall write is *my* truth, as I now see it.

I began this article by confessing myself baffled. I *am* baffled, as to spirit return, and as to many other special problems. I am also constantly baffled as to what to think of this or that particular story, for the sources of error in any one observation are seldom fully knowable. But weak sticks make strong faggots; and when the stories fall into consistent sorts that point each in a definite direction, one gets a sense of being in the presence of genuinely natural types of phenomena. As to there being such real natural types of phenomena ignored by orthodox science, I am not baffled at all, for I am fully convinced of it.

The first automatic writing I every saw was forty years ago. I unhesitatingly thought of it as deceit, although it contained vague elements of supernormal knowledge. Since then I have come to see in automatic writing one example of a department of human activity as vast as it is enigmatic. Every sort of person is liable to it, or to something equivalent to it; and whoever encourages it in himself finds himself personating someone else, either signing what he writes by fictitious name, or spelling out, by ouiji board or tabletops, messages from the departed. Our subconscious region seems as a rule, to be dominated either by a crazy "will to make-believe," or by some curious external force impelling us to personation. The first difference between the psychical researcher and the inexpert person is that the former realizes the commonness and typicality of the phenomenon here, while the latter, less informed, thinks it so rare as to be unworthy of attention. *I wish to go on record for the commonness.*

The next thing I wish to go on record for is *the presence*, in the midst of all the humbug, *of really supernormal knowledge.*. By this I mean knowledge that cannot be traced to the ordinary sources of information—the senses, namely, of the automatist. In really strong mediums this knowledge seems to be abundant, though it is usually spotty,

> . . . I wish to go on record for . . . *the presence*, **in the midst of all the humbug,** *of really supernormal knowledge.*

103

capricious, and unconnected. Really strong mediums are rarities; but when one starts with them and works downwards into less brilliant regions of the automatic life, one tends to interpret many slight but odd coincidences with truth as possibly rudimentary forms of this kind of knowledge.

The phenomena are enormously complex, especially if one includes in them such intellectual flights of mediumship as Swedenborg's, and if one tries in any way to work the physical phenomena in. That is why I personally am as yet neither a convinced believer in parasitic demons, nor a spiritist, nor a scientist, but still remain a psychical researcher waiting for more facts before concluding.

Out of my experience, such as it is (and it is limited enough), one fixed conclusion dogmatically emerges, and that is this, that we with our lives are like islands in the sea, or like trees in the forest. The maple and the pine may whisper to each other with their leaves, and Conanicut and Newport hear each other's foghorns. But the trees also commingle their roots in the darkness underground, and the islands also hang together through the ocean's bottom. Just so there is a continuum of cosmic consciousness, against which our several minds plunge as into a mother-sea or reservoir. Our "normal" consciousness is circumscribed for adaptation to our external earthly environment, but the fence is weak in spots, and fitful influences from beyond leak in, showing the otherwise unverifiable common connection. Not only psychic research, but metaphysical philosophy, and speculative biology are led in their own ways to look with favor on some such "panpsychic" view of the universe as this. Assuming this common reservoir of consciousness to exist, this bank upon which we all draw, and in which so many of earth's memories must in some way be stored, or mediums would not get at them as they do, the question is, What is its own structure? What is its inner topography? This question, first squarely formulated by Myers, deserves to be called "Myers's problem" by scientific men hereafter. What are the conditions of individuation or insulation in this mother-sea? To what tracts, to what active systems functioning separately in it, do personalities correspond? Are individual "spirits" constituted there? How numerous, and of how many hierarchic orders may these then be? How permanent? How transient? And how confluent with one another may they become? . . .[137]

SCIENTIFIC EXPLORATION

II

SCIENTIFIC EXPLORATION

Extra-Sensory Perception

Although many of you reading this book will have no personal doubt that extra-sensory perception is real, the effort to establish ESP as a scientific fact has been a continuous struggle. Many subjects whose demonstrations had originally convinced researchers from the SPR were later detected using bogus means to dupe these eminent scientists.[1] Fascinated by their few successes, researchers continued undaunted in the midst of failures, criticism, and detected frauds.

Between 1880 and 1940, 145 empirical ESP studies were published which used 77,796 subjects who made 4,918,186 single trial guesses. These experiments were mostly conducted by psychologists and other scientists. In 106 such studies, the authors arrived at results which exceeded chance expectations.[2]

Perhaps the most publicized early experiments were those published by Dr. J. B. Rhine in 1934 in a monograph entitled *Extra-Sensory Perception*, which summarized results from his experiments at Duke University beginning in 1927. Although this work was published by the relatively obscure Boston Society for Psychic Research, it was picked up in the popular press and had a large impact throughout the world. While earlier researches had been fruitful, they were generally neither as systematic nor as persistent as Dr. Rhine's studies.

107

Tarot cards can provide emotionally interesting targets for ESP testing.

These experiments used shuffled decks of Zener cards with five sets of five different symbols on them—a cross, a circle, a wavy line, a square and a star. This method reduced the problem of chance-expectation to a matter of exact calculations. Furthermore the cards were designed to be as emotionally neutral as possible to eliminate possible response biases caused by ideosyncratic preferences. However other studies have shown that emotionally laden targets can also work without impairing statistical analysis.

Rhine describes his early work with one of his more successful subjects, Hubert E. Pearce, a graduate divinity student:

The working conditions were these: observer and subject sat opposite each other at a table, on which lay about a dozen packs of the Zener cards and a record book. One of the packs would be handed to Pearce and he allowed to shuffle it. (He felt it gave more real "contact.") Then it was laid down and it was cut by the observer. Following this Pearce would, as a rule, pick up the pack, lift off the top card, keeping both the pack and the removed card face down, and after calling it, he would lay the card on the table, still face down. The observer would record the call. Either after five calls or after twenty-five calls—and we used both conditions generally about equally—the called cards would be turned over and checked off against the calls recorded in the book. The observer saw each card and checked each one personally, though the subject was asked to help in checking by laying off the cards as checked. There is no legerdemain by which an alert observer can be repeatedly deceived at this simple task in his own laboratory. (And, of course, we are not even dealing with amateur magicians.) For the next run another pack of cards would be taken up.[3]

The critical reader will find several faults with this experiment. First, as long as the subject is able to see or touch the backs or sides of the cards, there exists a channel of sensory leakage through which the subject might receive information about the face of the cards. Several critics reported that this was why they were able to obtain good scoring results. Secondly, there was no adequate safeguards against legerdemain. For example, what would prevent the subject from making small markings on the cards with his fingernails in order to identify the cards later on? It almost seems as if the optimism of the experimenter that this would not happen could mitigate against sufficiently careful observation. Furthermore, is it really possible for one experimenter to maintain sufficient concentration to insure that the subject does not cheat? Experience of other researchers has sadly shown that this is quite doubtful. Perhaps Rhine did utilize other safeguards. If so he could be fairly criticized for not adequately reporting his experimental conditions, although other experiments in his monograph were admittedly better controlled. Finally, there is no mention of any efforts to guard against recording errors on the part of the experimenter. One can hardly expect the cooperation of the subject, who may have a personal interest in the outcome, to be an adequate control against experimenter mistakes.

As Rhine's positive results gained more attention, arguments of this sort began to proliferate in the popular and scientific literature. It is much to Rhine's credit that he encouraged such criticism and modified his experiments accordingly. In 1940, Rhine, J. G. Pratt and their associates pub-

Drs. J. B. and Louisa E. Rhine (Courtesy Foundation for Research on the Nature of Man, Durham, North Carolina.)

lished a work, titled *Extra-Sensory Perception After Sixty Years*, which described the ways in which the ESP experiments had met the thirty-five different counter-hypotheses which had been published in the scientific and popular press.

The areas of criticism which Rhine and Pratt focused on in 1940 included the following: hypotheses related to improper statistical analysis of the results; hypotheses related to biased selection of experiments reported; hypotheses dealing with errors in the experimental records; hypotheses involving sensory leakage; hypotheses charging experimenter incompetence; and finally hypotheses of a general speculative character. In each case, Rhine and Pratt pointed to experimental evidence to counter the hypotheses.

Many prominent mathematicians in the field of probability who have made a detailed investigation have approved his techniques. In fact, in 1937 the American Institute of Statistical Mathematics issued a statement that Rhine's statistical procedures were not in the least faulty. In most experiments, both significant and chance results were reported and averaged into the data.

High scores due to inaccurate recording of results had been reduced to an insignificant level by double-blind techniques in

109

which both subject and experimenter notations were made without knowledge of the scores against which they were to be matched. Errors were further reduced by having two or more experimenters oversee the matching of scores. Furthermore, original experimental data had been saved and double checked for mistakes many times by investigators. Tampering with these original records was prevented by having several copies independently preserved.

Sensory cues were impossible in many tests of clairvoyance because the experimenter himself and all witnesses did not know the correct targets. In other tests, the cards were sealed in opaque envelopes, or an opaque screen prevented the subject from seeing the cards. Often the experimenter and the subject were in completely different rooms.

Those who charged the experimenters with incompetence failed to find any flaws in several experiments. In cases of inadequate reporting, Rhine indicates that further data was always supplied upon request. In several cases, experimenter fraud would have had to involve the active collusion on the part of several teams of two or more experimenters. Critics who claim that the results come only from the laboratories of those with a predisposition to believe in ESP were also ignoring at least six successful studies gathered from skeptical observers.

Other criticisms generally claimed that ESP could not exist because of certain philosophical assumptions about the nature of the universe or scientifically uninformed assumptions of what ESP would be like if it did exist. These assumptions are scarcely sufficient cause to dismiss the carefully observed experimental data.

Of the 145 experiments which had been reported in the sixty year period from 1880 to 1940, Rhine and Pratt were able to demonstrate that six different experimental studies of extrasensory perception were not amenable to explanation by any of the counter-hypotheses offered by critics of parapsychology.[4]

One of the more carefully controlled studies is the Pearce-Pratt series, which was carried out in 1933 with Dr. J. G. Pratt as agent and Hubert Pearce as subject. In these experiments, the agent and his subject were separated in different buildings over 100 yards apart. Pratt displaced the cards one by one from an ESP pack at an agreed time without turning them over. After going through the pack, Pratt then turned the cards over and recorded them. The guesses were recorded independently by Pearce. In order to eliminate the possibility of cheating, the precaution was taken that both placed their records in a sealed package which was handed to Rhine before the two lists were compared. Copies of these original records are still available for inspection. The total number of guesses was 1,850 of which one would expect one-fifth, or 370, to be correct by chance. The actual number of hits was 558. The probability that these results could have occurred by chance is much less than one in a hundred million.[5]

The combined probability of those experiments which met all objections critics raised proved absolutely astronomical. If one had conducted ESP experiments every minute throughout the entire history of the earth back to the days when it was a cloud of gas the probability of having encountered such high ESP results by chance, during that entire time would still be virtually negligible, less than one chance in billions.[6]

After the publication of *ESP After Sixty Years*, both the quality and quantity of criticism of ESP research declined. This is not to say, however, that parapsychology met with general acceptance in the United States or in other countries. The work of the parapsychologists was simply ignored by many universities and the major scientific publications. The public guardians were not then ready for ESP.

Finally in August, 1955, *Science* carried an editorial on ESP research by Dr. G. R. Price, a chemist from the University of Minnesota, which stated that scientists had to choose between accepting the reality of ESP or rejecting the evidence. Price had carefully studied the data and he frankly admitted that the best experiments could only be faulted by assuming deliberate fraud, or an abnormal mental condition, on the part of the scientists. Price felt that ESP, judged in the light of the accepted principles of modern science, would have to be classed as a miracle (this judgment, as we will point out later, is ill-founded). Rather than accept a miracle, he suggested accepting the position of the eighteenth-century philosopher, David Hume, who said that those who report miracles should be dismissed as liars.

Similar criticisms were published by Professor C. M. Hansel. Regarding the Pearce-Pratt experiment, he suggests that after Pratt had left him, Pearce departed from the University Library, followed Pratt to his office and looked through the fanlight of Pratt's door thus observing the target cards being recorded by Pratt.[7] While it is true that Hansel exposed the defect in the experimental design of having left Pearce alone in the library, the structure of Pratt's office would have made it impossible for Pearce to see the cards even if he had taken the great risk of staring through the fanlight of Dr. Pratt's door.[8] In subsequent experiments parapsychologists have eliminated such defects.

Official recognition of the experimental competency of parapsychologists did not come until December of 1969 when the American Academy for the Advancement of Science granted affiliate status to the researchers in the Parapsychological Association. Recent years have shown authoritative scientific voices displaying a new willingness to deal with the evidence for ESP. In the "letters" column of *Science* for January 28, 1972, there appeared a brief note from Dr. Price titled "Apology to Rhine and Soal," in which Price expressed his conviction that his original article was highly unfair to both Soal (a British mathematician and parapsychologist who also reported outstanding results) and Rhine.

Other criticisms relating to repeatability, fraud, statistical inferences, experimental design and interpretation of data have continued. In fact, the parapsychologists closely scrutinize each other's work and have been their own best critics. The experimental data has continued to improve throughout the

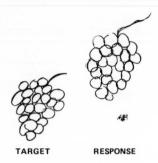

TARGET   RESPONSE

TARGET   *EPIDGE*

RESPONSE

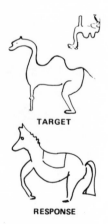

TARGET

RESPONSE

Some targets and responses from ESP tests with Uri Geller at Stanford Research Institute.

years. While many scientists still argue against the existence of ESP, the majority accept its reality or likelihood.* Many scientific journals have carried articles on ESP experiments.[9,10,11] One such article, published in *Nature,* in 1974 reported on experiments conducted by Dr. Harold Puthoff and Russell Targ at the Stanford Research Institute in Menlo Park, California. Their results, which covered studies taking place over an eighteen month period, described the following experiments:

In the experiments with [Uri] Geller, he was asked to reproduce 13 drawings over a week-long period while physically separated from his experimenters in a shielded room. Geller was not told who made any drawing, who selected it for him to reproduce or about its method of selection.

The researchers said that only after Geller's isolation—in a double-walled steel room that was acoustically, visually and electrically shielded from them—was a target picture randomly chosen and drawn. It was never discussed by the experimenters after being drawn or brought near Geller.

All but two of the experiments conducted with Geller were in the shielded room, with the drawings in adjacent rooms ranging from four meters to 475 meters from him. In other experiments, the drawings were made inside the shielded room with Geller in adjacent locations. Examples of drawings Geller was asked to reproduce included a firecracker, a cluster of grapes, a devil, a horse, the solar system, a tree and an envelope.

Two SRI researchers—not otherwise associated with this research—were given Geller's reproductions for judging on a "blind" basis. They matched the target data to the response data with no errors, a chance probability of better than one in a million per judgment. . . .

In another experiment with Geller, he was asked to "guess" the face of a die shaken in a closed steel box. The box was vigorously shaken by one of the experimenters and placed on a table. The position of the die was not known to the researchers.

Geller provided the correct answer eight times, the researchers said. The experiment was performed ten times but Geller declined to respond two times, saying his perception was not clear . . .**[12]

Encouraged with remote viewing experiments with earlier subjects, Targ and Puthoff reported on nine remote viewing experiments that were conducted with [Pat] Price as a subject. The SRI team chose natural sites in the San Francisco Bay Area on a double-blind basis, while Price, who remained at SRI in Menlo Park, California, was asked to describe the location and whatever activities were going on there. . . .

While one SRI experimenter was closeted with Price, a second experimenter would obtain a target location from an individual in SRI management not otherwise associated with the research. The targets—chosen from among 100 in the area—were clearly differentiated from each other and within 30 minutes driving time from SRI.

The team that had chosen the target proceeded to the location without communicating with the subject. The experimenter remaining behind with Price was not told of the location and questioned the subject, who described his impressions of the location on a tape recorder.

"To obtain a numerical evaluation of the accuracy of the remote viewing experiment, the experimental results were subjected to independent judging on a blind basis by five SRI scientist who were

*A survey published in *New Scientist,* on January 25, 1973, indicated that 25% of scientists polled considered paranormal phenomena "an established fact." Another 42% opted for "a likely possibility."

**Critics of this research maintained that Geller could have achieved his results through the use of complicated gimmicks such as trick dice or a hidden radio. These criticisms have been voiced and answered, quite adequately, in *The New Scientist.*

not otherwise associated with the research," the scientists said. "The judges were asked to match the nine locations, which they independently visited, against the typed manuscripts of the tape-recorded narratives of the remote viewer."

The panel of judges, by a plurality vote, correctly matched six of the nine descriptions and locations, Targ and Puthoff reported. The probability that this could have occurred by chance is one in a billion.

"Although Price's descriptions contain inaccuracies," Targ and Puthoff said, "the descriptions are sufficiently accurate to permit the judges to differentiate among the various targets to the degree indicated."

In a pilot study with six subjects, the scientists sought to determine whether brain wave recordings (EEGs) could be used as an indicator of information transfer between a subject and a remote flashing light. The study was based on the hypothesis that perception may take place below the level of personal awareness.

It was assumed that the application of a remote stimuli would result in responses similar to those of direct stimulation," said Targ and Puthoff. "For example, when normal subjects are stimulated with a flashing light their EEG typically shows a decrease in the amplitude of the resting rhythm and a driving of the brain waves at the frequency of the flashes.

"We hypothesized that if we stimulated one subject in this manner (a sender), the EEG of another subject in a remote room with no flash present (a receiver), might show changes in alpha activity, and possible EEG driving similar to that of the sender."*

The researchers reported they worked initially with six volunteer subjects but eventually concentrated on one subject who responded most dramatically. They then measured the subject's EEG for three days, gathering data from seven sets of 36 trials each with the subject, who was in an opaque, acoustically and electrically-shielded room seven meters from the sender.

Targ and Puthoff reported that while five subjects performed at chance levels, a sixth showed consistent and significant EEG changes associated with the presence of the remote stimuli under conditions of sensory shielding.

"We hypothesize that the protocol described here may prove to be useful as a screening procedure for latent remote perceptual ability in the general population," they said.

The researchers said that the channel through which information can be received about a remote location appears "imperfect," containing noise along with the signal. They said that while a signal-to-noise ratio cannot yet be determined, the channel nonetheless permits functioning at a useful level of information transfer.

Targ and Puthoff said the research constitutes "a first step" toward the goal of uncovering patterns of cause-effect relationships that lend themselves to analysis and hypothesis in the forms which are familiar in scientific study.[12]

ESP is generally divided into telepathy, ability to communicate with another mind extra-sensorily; clairvoyance, ability to perceive situations at a distance directly, without the mediation of another mind; and precognition, which is ESP across time into the future. There is still some controversy as to whether telepathy actually exists, or whether it is simply another form of clairvoyance. However, precognition, a most unusual ability in terms of our conventional notions of time and free will, is a rather well-established ESP phenomena. In fact precognition tests afford some of the best evidence for ESP, since sensory leakage from a target which has not yet been

TARGET

RESPONSE

---

*Research studies of this sort have been reported for many years in the Soviet Union.

113

determined is impossible. For example, in early studies with Hubert Pearce, the subject was able to guess what the order of cards in a pack *would be* after it was shuffled at the same high rate of scoring (up to 50% above chance levels) as in clairvoyance tests.

While many people tend to reject ESP because it seems to contradict the classical laws of science, precognition is even harder to swallow for exactly the opposite reason—it seems to imply a completely mechanical, predetermined universe. Ironically, it is this determinism which violates the sensibilities of twentieth-century science. In fact, precognition is very difficult to prove; although its alternatives are not exactly palatable.

For example in the precognitive card guessing studies, one might say that the subject psychokinetically caused the order of the cards to conform to his guesses. Or perhaps, more reasonably, the experimenter, using his clairvoyance subconsciously, determined the subject's guesses and shuffled the cards accordingly. Good precognitive experiments must rule out the possibility of contamination by other forms of psychic interaction. The methodological difficulty in distinguishing different types of extra-sensory transmission and reception had led researchers to use the more general term *psi*.

There is a good deal of evidence to warrant that precognition actually does occur—with all of its ramifications regarding time and free will. For instance, after a mine disaster in Wales, in which 144 people perished, researchers collected reports from individuals who claimed to have had premonitions of the event. Seventy-six reports were recieved. In twenty-four cases, the percipient had actually talked to another person about the premonition before the catastrophe. Twenty-five of the experiences were in dreams.[13]

Alan Vaughn
(*Courtesy* Psychic Magazine)

A study conducted by W. E. Cox indicates that precognition also operates on mass-awareness levels. Cox accumulated statistics on the numbers of passengers aboard 28 railroad trains which were involved in accidents. These figures were found to be significantly less than the number of passengers on the same trains one week before or a few days after the accident. People somehow avoided the accident-bound trains. There were also fewer passengers in damaged and derailed coaches than would have been expected according to the figures for non-accident days. Cox hypothesized that many potential passengers were aware of the oncoming tragedy, but not on a fully conscious level.[14,15] Another remarkable incident occurred in relationship to the assassination of Robert Kennedy on June 5, 1968. About two months before the assassination, Alan Vaughan, then in Germany studying synchronicity at the Freiburg University Institute for Border Areas of Psychology, began to develop a strong premonition that Kennedy would be assassinated. The event, he felt, was part of a complex archetypal pattern which he was tuned into, involving the killings of both JFK and Martin Luther King. Many coincidences and dreams began to support Vaughan's theory. On April 29 and again on May 28, Vaughan wrote letters to parapsychologists notifying them of his premonition and hoping that Kennedy

114

could be warned. His letter was received by Stanley Krippner at the Maimonides Hospital Medical Center on the morning of June 4.[16]

These events have forced psychic researchers to confront the ethical dilemmas of dealing with presumptive precognitive reports. Toward this end, a Central Premonitions Registry (Box 482, Times Square Station, New York, N.Y. 10036) and a Premonitions Registry Bureau (c/o KPFA-FM, 2207 Shattuck Ave., Berkeley, Ca. 94704) have been created for the purpose of screening potential premonitions. Perhaps if many people predict a similar event, or if an event is predicted by a psychic of tested reliability, proper notification will result in the prevention of disaster.

Ironically enough, at least three cases are on record regarding the accidental deaths of parapsychologists who did not heed the warnings of their psychic subjects.[17] Perhaps the subjects hadn't sufficiently demonstrated their reliability in the past.

Perhaps the most sophisticated tests for precognition were those designed by Dr. Helmut Schmidt at the Foundation for Research on the Nature of Man. Subjects in his experiments had to predict the lighting of one of four lamps which was determined by theoretically unpredictable, radio-active decay. Schmidt gives us the following description of his apparatus:

> The target generator consists of a radioactive source (strontium 90), a Geiger counter, and a four-step electronic switch controlling the four lamps [see illustration]. The strontium 90 delivers electrons randomly at the average rate of ten per second to the geiger counter. A high frequency pulse generator advances the switch rapidly through the four positions. When a gate between the Geiger counter and the four-step switch is opened, the next electron that reaches the Geiger counter stops the switch in one of its four positions (whichever one it happens to be in when the electron registers) and illuminates the lamp corresponding to that position.[18]

In precognition experiments, the subject makes his guess before the apparatus makes its random selection of a target. The results of these experiments were automatically recorded and the device was frequently subjected to tests of its true randomness. The instrument can also be modified for experiments in clairvoyance and psychokinesis. In all three modes of psi testing with the Schmidt device, significant results have consistently been obtained.[19,20,21] Many other studies also show precognition.

Probably the best experimental evidence for precognition comes from a study conducted by Nash in which subjects predicted the Dow-Jones stock market averages.[22]

Now that you've been exposed to a large body of evidence for the existence of extra-sensory perception, you're probably interested in finding out what clairvoyance, precognition and telepathy really are and how they work. Before describing the scanty but solid evidence obtained by scientists through research studies, it may be interesting to look at some of the explanations offered by occultists, mystics and psychics who have, or claim to have, direct experience in these matters.

A subject presses a button recording a guess on one of the automated testing devices developed by Helmut Schmidt. There is a probability of 1 in 4 that the subject will score correctly by chance alone. (Courtesy Foundation for Research on the Nature of Man.)

Dr. Rammurti S. Mishra

One of the most articulate modern spokesmen of the yogic tradition is Dr. Rammurti S. Mishra, who in addition to being a swami and spiritual teacher is also an endocrinologist, neurosurgeon, psychiatrist, and linguistic scholar.* In referring to the research of the parapsychologists, Dr. Mishra states:

Supernatural powers occupy the central place in psychic research. In Yoga, the central feature is *Nirvanam, Kaivalyam* [absolute liberation], where miracles and magical powers are regarded as obstacles in the path of Self-realization although they are by-products of *samadhi*, Cosmic Consciousness. Yogins themselves are reticent about these "miracles" although they are acquainted with them.

According to Yoga, the Self of man is omnipresent, omnipotent, and omniscient although such power is not fully manifested in an untrained mind. Individual mind is representative of Cosmic Mind, so it can communicate with any other individual mind or phenomenon anywhere, in any planet and solar system.

As in the principle of radioactivity all substances are radioactive, so all substances in the world are psycho-active. There is no substance on which mind cannot act and react. . . .

In the future, if basic laws concerning telepathy and clairvoyance are established, there will be a radical change in the science of psychology. Most theories in the West are built on non-admission of telepathy and clairvoyance. Yoga admits not only that such phenomena are possible but that they have been confirmed by experience of yogins in meditation. The system of Yoga admits individual mind and says that it is a manifestation of Cosmic Mind. Hence in purity of individual mind, there must be ability to communicate with all minds of the universe. Telepathy, clairvoyance, etc., are not the aim of Yoga practice. They are the by-products of this practice. Cosmic Consciousness and universal penetration are the inherent nature of mind. Individual mind does not feel its cosmic form because of impurities. It is only when these impurities have been removed that mind begins to feel cosmic penetration.[23]

This view which is similar to that suggested by William James in the preceding section, accords with the experimental inability to find physical structures or fields which can block ESP transmission. The relevant variables do indeed seem to be related to the consciousness of the individuals involved. Yet it seems quite ironic that ESP should be so pervasive and yet so uncommon.

The "spirit teachings" transmitted by an American housewife named Jane Roberts in *The Seth Material* suggest that there are actually psychic reasons for this paradoxical nature of ESP:

Your world is formed in faithful replica of your own thoughts. . . . Certain telepathic conditions exist that we call root assumptions, of which each individual is subconsciously aware. Using these, you form a physical environment cohesive enough so that there is general agreement as to objects and their placement and dimension. It is all hallucinatory in one respect, and yet is is your reality, and you must manipulate within it. The world in which your parents live existed first in thought. It existed once in the stuff of dreams, and they spawned their universe from this, and from this they made their world.**[24]

---

*Dr. Mishra has designed the images on color plates 1 and 2.

**This view parallels very strongly the sociological theory offered by Peter L. Berger and Thomas Luckman in a marvelous volume called *The Social Construction of Reality* N.Y., Anchor, 1967. .

Another perspective on this issue is offered by certain western traditions which relate the development of various psychic abilities to the unfolding of different centers of perception in the "astral," or emotional or desire body of the individual. The teachings of the California based Rosicrucian Fellowship provide some very explicit indications:

There are no organs in the desire body, as in the dense and vital bodies, but there are centers of perception, which, when active, appear as vortices, always remaining in the same relative position to the dense body, most of them about the head. In the majority of people they are mere eddies and are of no use as centers of perception. They may be awakened in all, however, but different methods produce different results.

In the involuntary clairvoyant developed along improper, negative lines, these vortices turn from right to left, or in the opposite direction to the hands of a clock—counter-clockwise.

In the desire body of the properly trained voluntary clairvoyant, they turn in the same direction as the hands of a clock—clockwise, glowing with exceeding splendor, far surpassing the brilliant luminosity of the ordinary desire body. These centers furnish him with means for perception of things in the Desire World and he sees, and investigates as he wills, while the person whose centers turn counter-clockwise is like a mirror, which reflects what passes before it. Such a person is incapable of reaching out for information.[25]

Other traditions have gone so far as to specify in some detail types of psychic abilities associated with the unfolding of particular centers in the higher bodies. Often these nodes are associated with the *chakras* of tantric yoga. The hypotheses of invisible bodies are, for the time being at least, difficult to verify. (Later in this chapter we'll explore further evidence which points toward the functioning of these "higher" bodies.)

There are now many questions about ESP which researchers are attempting to answer through scientific experimentation and observation, but even the early researchers were able to establish a few solid facts about the process. For example, no reliable relationship could be found between ESP scoring in the laboratory and such factors as sex, age, blindness, mental or physical illness, mediumship, or intelligence. Subjects seemed to score better in novel test situations and often when rewards or competition were involved. On the other hand, lengthy and formalized testing in which the subject was given no information regarding his scoring generally resulted in a decline of the subject's ESP ability. As mentioned before, no physical factors such as space and time have been found to have a limiting effect on ESP scoring. It was also quickly discovered that ESP is a rather erratic and unstable ability. While a subject may be able to direct his ESP to a particular target, very few tested subjects have ever shown the ability to activate their psychic abilities at will. The experimenter-subject relationship's great importance was quickly recognized.[26]

One of the strongest theories about the nature of ESP is one that was put forward by Frederick Myers when he associated psychic phenomena with the workings of the *subliminal self.* Myers, as mentioned in the last chapter, felt that the workings of the subliminal mind were most visible in such phenomena as dreams, trance states, hypnosis, and states of creative inspiration.

CURRENTS IN THE DESIRE BODY

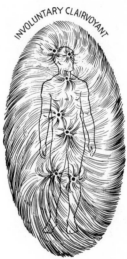

CURRENTS IN THE DESIRE BODY

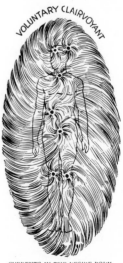

CURRENTS IN THE DESIRE BODY

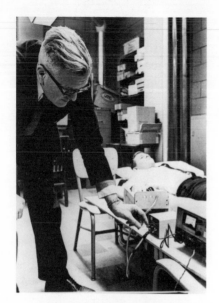

E. Douglas Dean conducting plethysmograph study. (Courtesy E. Douglas Dean.)

Stanley Krippner, Ph.D. former director of the Maimonides Hospital Division of Parapsychology and Psychophysics, past-president of the Association for Humanistic Psychology, and vice-president for the western hemisphere of the International Psychotronics Association, Krippner is also the editor of Psychoenergetics, *a new research journal. (Courtesy* Psychic Magazine).

This theory is supported by studies in which ESP signals are registered unconsciously by the body's physiological processes even when the subject is unaware of the message. For example, in a series of studies conducted by E. Douglas Dean, subjects were hooked up to a *Plethysmograph*. Sudden increases or decreases in blood volume, resulting from emotional responses, are measured by this instrument. A telepathic agent in another room then concentrated on different names, some of which were known to be emotionally significant to the subjects. The results indicated changes in the blood volume which significantly correlated with the emotionally laden target messages. This finding was confirmed in a second series of studies conducted by Dean and Dr. Carroll B. Nash at St. Joseph's College in Philadelphia. Most of the subjects were totally unaware of the changes in their blood supply which were responding to the target material.[27,28]

A similar study was conducted by Dr. Charles Tart in which subjects were hooked up to a plethysmograph, an electroencephalograph, and a device for measuring galvanic skin response. The agent in this experiment was periodically given a mild electric shock. The subjects did not know they were being tested for ESP, but rather were told to guess when a "subliminal stimulus" (sensory stimulation below the threshold of conscious awareness) was being directed to them. The subjects' hunches failed to correlate to this disguised target. However, their physiological measurements showed abrupt changes when the shocks were administered to the agent in another room.[29]

A large proportion of the reported cases of ESP occurred while the percipient was in such altered states of consciousness.

An important series of studies on the nature of ESP in dreams was carried out by a team of researchers at Maimonides Hospital in Brooklyn, New York. Using equipment which monitored brain waves and eye movements, the investigators could determine accurately when subjects were having dreams. By waking the subjects at these times they were then able to obtain immediate reports of the dream contents. Meanwhile, in another room, the telepathic senders were concentrating on target material which incorporated many different senses— pictures, sounds, objects all designed to create a particular impression.

Independent judges compared the similarity subject's responses displayed to a group of possible target choices and found considerable evidence for nocturnal telepathy and precognition (targets were not chosen until the following day) of the actual targets used.[23]*

In one especially significant experiment, telepathic transmission was obtained by having about 2,000 persons attending a Grateful Dead rock concert focus on a color slide

---

*Naturally these findings caused some scientists to timidly echo the speculations of Shakespeare that "we are the stuff that dreams are made of." This notion is actually beginning to take on some rather precise physical and mathematical coloring, as the alchemical and kaballistic traditions find renewal among scientists. See the chapter on the new physics in section three.

projection image and attempt to send it to the dream laboratory 45 miles away in Brooklyn. Many of these individuals were in altered states of consciousness from the music and the ingestion of psychedelic drugs. This test proved strikingly succesful.[31]

In one interesting set of experiments, subjects received a sort of brain stimulation known as "electrosleep" and were asked to rate the degree of change in their consciousness. Subjects who had reported greatly altered states of consciousness in these experiments also had higher ESP scores. The results have been tenuous and are sometimes disconfirmed. The mere fact that one's consciousness is not in the normal walking state is not sufficient to guarantee psychic ability.[32,33]

Numerous other studies have shown heightened ESP in states of physical relaxation or in trance and hypnotic states.[34,35,36,37] In fact, the use of hypnosis to produce high ESP scores is one of the most replicable experiments in parapsychology. A particularly notable series of experiments were described in 1910 by Emille Boirac, rector of the Dijon Academy in France, which produced what he described as an "externalization of sensitivity." When the hypnotist placed something in his mouth, the subject could describe it. If he pricked himself with a pin, the subject would feel the pain. The most striking experiments were those in which the subject was told to project his sensibility into a glass of water. If the water was pricked, the subject would react by a visible jerk or exclamation.[38] This phenomena has been repeated by the Finnish parapsychologist, Jarl Fahler.[39]

In a similar experiment performed by one of Boirac's associates, blisters were raised on the skin of a hypnotized subject, simply by pricking a photograph of the subject's hand.[40]

The Conductability of Psychic Force. The two glasses are connected by a copper wire. When the experimenter pinches the air-zone above the water-glass nearest him, or plunges his finger or pencil into it, the subject immediately reacts. This reaction disappears if the connection between the glasses is removed. These results may be shaped by the belief of systems of experimenter and subject.

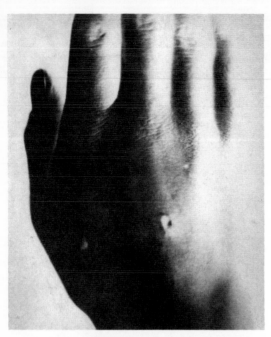

Exteriorization of the Sensitiveness. A photograph of the sensitive was taken and the negative (plate) was then held by her for a few moments. The experimenter, with a pin, scratched the hand in the plate. Instantly the sensitive ejaculated with pain and a small red spot appeared on the back of her hand. This rapidly grew into the blister shown in the above photograph.

Boirac, as well as Soviet investigators, have reported the ability to induce a hypnotic trance simply through telepathic concentration directed toward their subjects.[41,42]

In 1969, Charles Honorton and Stanley Krippner reviewed the experimental literature of studies designed to use hypnosis to induce ESP. Of nineteen experiments reported, only seven failed to produce significant results. Many of the studies produced astounding success. In a particularly important precognition study, conducted by Fahler and Osis with two hypnotized subjects, the task also included making *confidence calls*—predicting which guesses would be most accurate. The correlation of confidence call hits produced impressive results with a probability of 0.0000002.[43] Parapsychologists now frequently use the confidence call technique in order to improve ESP scores.

Many subjects seem to feel that by the "texture" of their mental impressions, they are able to separate an ESP impression from mere mental imagery.

In a recent study with an exceptional subject, Bill Delmore, confidence calls were made using a deck of ordinary playing cards as the target. The technique used was a "psychic shuffle" in which the experimenters randomly select a predetermined order which the subject must match by shuffling the target deck. In each of two shuffle series, with fifty-two cards in a series, Delmore made twenty-five confidence calls—all of which were completely correct. The probability of such success is only one in 52^{50}. Other studies with Delmore have also produced extraordinary results.[44]

Delmore does not seem to use an altered state of consciousness as a means of gaining psychic information. In fact, the research in altered states seems to point to other variables which are really more significant. For Delmore, a congenial atmosphere is important.

A very thoughtful approach toward understanding ESP was developed by Charles Honorton of the Miamonides group in Brooklyn. Honorton hypothesized that the reasons why high scoring did occur in altered states was that the normal, waking, supraliminal mind was less active at these times, thus there was less mental "noise" covering up the signals coming through the subliminal mind. To test this theory, he utilized a *ganzfeld* technique of covering the eyes of his subjects with halved ping pong balls so that the visual field was seen as solid white. A constant auditory environment was provided by either a white-noise generator or a tape of the seashore. Under these conditions, with a constant sensory input, non-sensory signals were expected to be easier to perceive. Subjects were put into this condition and asked to free-associate out loud while their responses were put on to magnetic tape. In another room, the telepathic sender chose, at random, a set of view-master slides to look at and try to send to the subject. After the experiment, the subject was asked to guess which of the view-master reels, of a group of four, had been the target. The subject's taped responses were also independently judged. The qualitative results of this experiment were often striking and statistical results also proved quite impressive.[45,46] The equipment for this experiment is inexpensive so readers of *The Roots of Consciousness* can use this technique to test their own psi talents. However, even with this un-sophisticated technique, some experimenters have been unable to achieve significant results.[47] This brings us to the important question of the role the experimenter plays in psychic research, or more generally speaking the role of individuals involved in psychic interactions.

For some time parapsychologists have been suggesting that the failure of some researchers to replicate their findings was due to attitudes and expectations, conscious or unconscious, which were communicated through subtle sensory or psychic channels to their subjects.[48] Recently Honorton reported on an experiment in which it was found that whether the experimenters smiled or not, and greeted their subjects in a cold or friendly manner had a noticeable effect on their subject's ESP scores.[49] Another recent study conducted at the University of Edinburgh in Scotland suggests that the attitude of the exerimenter regarding the existence of ESP correlates the results of that person's research.[50] Of course, effects of this sort have long been recognized in psychology, where they have been attributed to the desire of subjects to fulfill the expectations of the experimenters. Psychologists usually guard against this type of "artifact" by designing studies in which the subjects are kept unaware of the experimenter's hypotheses. However, the parapsychological experimenter effect actually has revolutionary implications for normal psychological research. The following study was reported by Professor Hans Kreitler and Dr. Shulamith Kreitler of the Department of Psychology at Tel Aviv University in Israel:

The first experiment dealt with the effect of ESP on the identification of letters projected as subliminal speed and illumination. The second experiment dealt with the effect of ESP on the direction of perceived autokinetic motion (i.e., of a stationary point of light in a dark room). The third experiment dealt with the effect of ESP on the occurrence of specific words and themes in the stories subjects tell to TAT (Thematic Apperception Test) cards.

In all these three experiments the subjects did not know that ESP communications were "sent" to them, the "senders" never met the subjects and "senders" were naive in the sense that they were not particularly interested in parapsychology, were unselected, and did not get any training for the experiments. The precautions undertaken against any sensory contact between "senders" and subjects were highly complex and included the spatial separation of "sender" and subject (they were in two different soundproof rooms with another room between them), the decentralization of information about the experiment among different people, strict randomization of all stimuli and sequences, the use of experimenters who were disbelievers in ESP, etc.

The results show that in every experiment there was a significant effect due to the ESP communication. . . . The effect . . . was particularly pronounced with regard to responses with an initially low probability of occurrence.[51]

Ironically, while scientists in many other fields question the reliability of experiments in parapsychology, it may well be that parapsychological effects underlie many controversial studies

Dr. Gertrude Schmeidler
(*Courtesy of* Psychic Magazine.)

in other areas of science which have proved difficult to repeat. For example physicists' attempts to measure gravity waves.

The conclusion that the attitude the experimenter takes can effect ESP scores also applies to ESP subject attitudes. Dr. Gertrude Schmeidler, of the City College of New York, divided her subjects into "sheep" who believed in ESP and "goats" who did not. Her studies, which were conducted over a nine year period and have since been replicated, showed an unquestionable difference between the "sheep" whose scores fell above chance expectation and "goats" who scored *below* chance levels. The phenomena of *psi missing* is thought to be a psychological effect in which psychic material is repressed from consciousness.[52,53]

A series of studies with high school students in India by B. K. Kanthamani and K. Ramakrishna Rao has given further insight into the personality traits associated with psi-hitters and psi-missers. The following adjectives summarize the results of their work.[54]

Positive ESP Scores	*Negative ESP Scores*
warm, sociable	tense
good-natured, easy going	excitable
assertive, self-assured	frustrated
tough	demanding
enthusiastic	impatient
talkative	dependent
cheerful	sensitive
quick, alert	timid
adventuresome, impulsive	threat-sensitive
emotional	shy
carefree	withdrawn
realistic, practical	submissive
relaxed	suspicious
composed	depression-prone

These particular traits are not suprising, in that a person who frustrates themselves in the course of their other affairs is quite likely to behave the same way with regard to psi. It is much harder to define the personality of someone who expresses no ESP ability and whose scores will always approximate chance. For example, many people who indicate a fair amount of spontaneous ESP experience, and even professional psychics (who I would assume have at least some ability) often do not score well in a laboratory. The nature of the test situation and the target material itself is likely to effect ESP scores. Some people prefer material which involves other human beings on a feeling level. Other subjects who do well with ESP cards show little psychic skill outside of the laboratory. The technical name for scoring well on some kind of targets and not on others is *the differential effect* and seems to follow a trend relating to emotional preferences, attitudes, and needs.

For example, in a test conducted by Jim Carpenter at the University of North Carolina, Chapel Hill, with male college students unknown to the subjects, some of the ESP cards had sexually arousing pictures drawn on them. The subjects showed a greater ability at guessing the ESP symbols on these cards than on the regular cards. In another study with a female patient in psychotherapy, an ESP test was given using words which were emotionally potent for her. Half of them were of a traumatic nature and half of them were of a pleasant nature. In this test, she showed psi-missing for the traumatic words and psi-hitting on the emotionally-positive targets. This test was conducted by Martin Johnson at Lund University in Sweden.

A question of great importance which is frequently asked is whether psychic ability can be developed in people. The notion that this is possible has been behind the training of many esoteric, occult, psychic, religious, shamanistic, meditative, spiritualistic, mystical, or mind-control organizations. The personal testimony of individuals who have been involved in such training programs is rather impressive. As of this writing, however, there are no laboratory tests which conclusively indicate that such ESP training programs have any greater effect than the known psi-conducive states of relaxation, hypnosis, etc.

The strongest claim for a successful, testable method of developing psychic talents goes to Dr. Milan Ryzl, a parapsychologist who defected to the United States from Czechoslovakia in 1967. Ryzl's technique involves the intensive use of deep hypnotic sessions almost daily for a period of several months. The purpose of these sessions is to instill confidence in his subjects that they do have ESP as well as to develop their ability to clearly visualize mental images. Once this stage is reached, Ryzl spends a great deal of time conducting simple ESP tests and giving his subjects immediate feedback so that they learn to associate certain mental states with accurate psychic information. Subjects are taught to reject any mental images which are fuzzy or unclear. This process continues until the subject is able to perceive clairvoyantly with great accuracy and detail. Then Ryzl attempts to wean the subject away from his own tutelage so that he or she can function

Milan Ryzl testing his star subject, Paul Stephanek. The target is inside a triple-sealed envelope. (Courtesy Dr. Milan Ryzl.)

123

independently. Ryzl, while still in Czechoslovakia, claimed to have used this technique with some 500 individuals, fifty of which achieved outstanding success.[55] Western researchers who travelled to Prague to personally investigate this phenomena, were able to test one of his better subjects, Pavel Stepanek. During a long period of experimental investigations, Stepanek proved to be one of the most successful subjects ever tested. More than twenty studies with him have now been published.[56]

What we still do not know is whether Stepanek always had this ESP ability or whether it developed as a result of Ryzl's training. There was a period of time during which Stepanek's scores did drop down to chance levels and then jumped up again after a hypnotic session with Ryzl. However, since he has been in the United States Ryzl has not published any studies which test ESP abilities both before and after his training. When I last spoke to him about this, he informed me that he was gathering data on a new procedure he has developed.[57]

Another effort to show ESP learning is through an automatic teaching machine developed by Russell Targ and David Hurt. Using modern electronic technology, the instrument is able to generate completely random targets which are displayed in a pictorial form after the subject has indicated his call. Correct scores are rewarded by the pleasant sounding tone of a bell. This simple setup provides immediate feedback to the subject and allows for accurate mechanical recording of scoring without an experimenter being present. Several experimental studies have shown a tendency for the scores of some subjects to improve after using such a machine. The highest scoring subjects in this test were individuals who had been engaged in yoga, meditation, or other similar relaxation disciplines.[58,59]

One of the most ingenious theories regarding the role of psi in everyday life was developed by Dr. Rex Stanford, who is currently teaching in the psychology department of St. John's University in Jamaica, New York. Stanford developed the concept of the psi-mediated instrumental response (PMIR) to explain non-intentional psychic experiences. For example, there is the story about a retired army colonel who found himself unconsciously getting off of the subway in New York at the wrong exit and then running into the very people he was intending to visit. Is it possible that his response of getting off the subway was triggered by ESP?

To test this hypothesis, experiments were designed to see if subjects would use ESP in a situation in which they would be rewarded for it, although they did not know they were being tested. In one such experiment, students in a psychology class were given an essay-type exam with the answers to half the questions sealed in opaque envelopes which were handed to them with the exam. They were told that the envelope contained carbon paper which would make copies of their answers. The experimenters thought that the students would use ESP as well as other means in order to do well on the examination. In fact, the students did better on the questions which were answered in the sealed envelopes. Furthermore, in a study

Dr. Rex Stanford
(*Courtesy* Psychic Magazine.)

where sealed answers were incorrect, the students did poorer on the corresponding questions. This study was conducted by Martin Johnson at Lund University in Sweden.

Another study has indicated that subjects who use the PMIR to avoid unpleasant situations and to encounter favorable situations, also score better than average on tests of conscious ESP.[60]

Stanford suggests that each person, or animal, is constantly using both ESP and regular senses to scan the environment for information which is relevant to its needs. The motivational arousal and focusing of conscious attention are important in the preparation of a setting within which the PMIR will occur. When a situation is psychically perceived which is relevant to a given need, the subliminal mind will trigger the readily available responses of the organism, in order to facilitate the satisfaction of that need. There need be no conscious awareness at the time that anything extraordinary is occurring.

Stanford does warn that in individuals with a negative self-image, a motivational conflict, or strong feelings of guilt, the PMIR may operate in a way which is detrimental to the person. Although the PMIR may operate more actively in individuals who are very flexible in their range of spontaneous responses, by utilizing unconscious timing mechanisms it can even overcome rigid behavioral patterns. If we carry this line of thought a little further it becomes reasonable to assume that all of the important coincidences in our lives were actually psi-mediated.

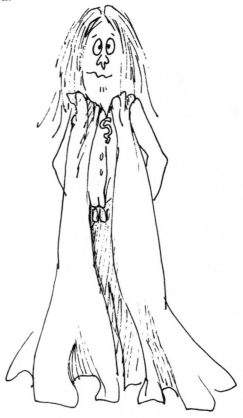

Out-Of-Body Experiences

Broadly speaking, we can define an astral projection, bilocation or out-of-body experience (OBE) as the sensation of observing phenomena from a perspective which does not coincide with the physical body. Often one will experience consciousness being transferred from the physical body to another "astral body," "second body," "etheric body," "double," or "doppelgänger." On other occasions, one may experience oneself as a mere point of awareness outside of the physical body. There seem to be several distinct, but related, types of experience which are sometimes lumped together under the general rubric of out-of-body experience. These include (1) lucid dreams where one seems to be conscious within a dreamworld, (2) clairvoyant awareness of distant locations, (3) the actual sensation of separation from one's physical body, floating above it, and looking down upon the physical form, (4) travelling outside of one's body to different locations in physical time and space, and (5) gliding and flying through the various supersensible "astral" and spiritual planes.

Thousands of OBE's have been reported by individuals of all ages and from all walks of life. As we have seen in the first chapter of this book, such experiences have played a major role in the shamanistic rites and esoteric schools of many previous cultures. Much occult literature abounds in unsubstantiated claims regarding the vast scientific and historical knowledge which can be imparted to visitors upon the "higher planes." Some of this literature is actually quite valuable because of the systematic explorations conducted by philosophically trained clairvoyants. This body of literature seems to put the OBE into a larger perspective. A typical description of astral travelling, from the "occult" viewpoint is provided by Yogi Ramacharaka:

It is possible for a person to project his astral body, or travel in his astral body, to any point within the limits of the earth's attraction,* and the trained occultist may do so at will, under the proper conditions. Others may occasionally take such trips (without knowing just how they do it, and having afterwards, the remembrance of a particular and very vivid dream); in fact many of us do take such trips, when the physical body is wrapped in sleep, and one often gains much information in this way, upon subjects in which he is interested, by holding astral communication with others interested in the same subject, all unconsciously of course. The conscious acquirement of knowledge in this way, is possible only to those who have progressed quite a way along the path of attainment. The trained occultist merely places himself in the proper mental condition, and then wishes himself at some particular place, and his astral travels there with the rapidity of light, or even more rapidly. The untrained occultist, of course, has no such degeee of control over his astral body and is more or less clumsy in his management of it. The Astral Body is always connected with the physical body (during the life of the latter) by a thin silk-like, astral thread, which maintains the communication between the two. Were this cord to be severed the physical body would die, as the connection of the soul with it would be terminated. . . .

---

*Apparently Ramacharaka is neglecting the extra-terrestrial possibilities here.

126

Perhaps the best way to make plain to you the general aspects and phenomena of the Astral World, would be to describe to you an imaginary trip made by yourself in that world, in the charge of an experienced occultist. We will send you, in imagination, on such a trip, in this lesson, in charge of a competent guide—it being presupposed that you have made considerable spiritual progress, as otherwise even the guide could not take you very far, except by adopting heroic and very unusual methods, which he probably would not see fit to do in your case. Are you ready for your trip? Well, here is your guide.

You have gone into the silence, and suddenly become aware of having passed out of your body, and to be now occupying only your astral body. You stand beside your physical body, and see it sleeping on the couch, but you realize that you are connected with it by a bright silvery thread, looking something like a large bit of bright spider-web. You feel the presence of your guide, who is to conduct you on your journey. He also has left his physical body, and is in his astral form, which reminds you of a vapory something, the shape of the human body, but which can be seen through, and which can move through solid objects at will. Your guide takes your hand in his and says, "Come," and in an instant you have left your room and are over the city in which you dwell, floating along like a summer cloud. You begin to fear lest you may fall, and as soon as the thought enters your mind you find yourself sinking. But your guide places a hand under you and sustains you, saying, "No just realize that you cannot sink unless you fear to—hold the thought that you are buoyant and you will be so." You do so, and are delighted to find that you may float at will, moving here and there in accordance to your wish or desire.

You see great volumes of thought-clouds arising from the city like great clouds of smoke, rolling along and settling here and there. You also see some finer vapory thought-clouds in certain quarters, which seem to have the property of scattering the dark clouds when they come in contact with them. Here and there you see bright thin lines of bright light, like an electric spark, traveling rapidly through space, which your guide tells you are telepathic messages passing from one person to another, the light being caused by the Prana with which the thought is charged. You see, as you descend toward the ground, that every person is surrounded by an egg-shaped body of color,—his aura —which reflects his thought and prevailing mental state, the character of the thought being represented by varying colors. Some are surrounded by beautiful auras, while others have around them a black, smoky aura, in which are seen flashes of red light. Some of these auras make you heart-sick to observe, as they give evidence of such base, gross, and animal thoughts, that they cause you pain, as you have become more sensitive now that you are out of your physical body. But you have not much time to spare here, as your trip is but a short one, and your guide bids you come on.

You do not seem to change your place in space, but a change seems to have come over everything—like the lifting of a gauzy curtain in the pantomime. You no longer see the physical world with its astral phenomena, but seem to be in a new world—a land of queer shapes. You see astral "shells" floating about—discarded astral bodies of those who have shed them as they passed on. These are not pleasant to look upon, and you hurry on with your guide, but before you leave this second ante-room to the real Astral World, your guide bids you relax your mental dependence upon your astral body, and much to your surprise you find yourself slipping out of it, leaving it in the world of shells, but being still connected with it by a silk-like cord, or thread, just as it, in turn, is connected with your physical body, which you have almost forgotten by this time, but to which you are still bound by these almost invisible ties. You pass on clothed in a new body, or rather an inner garment of ethereal matter, for it seems as if you have been merely shedding one cloak, and then another, the YOU part of yourself remains unchanged—you smile now at the recollection that once upon a time you thought that the body was "you." The plane of the "astral shells" fades away, and you seem to have entered a great room of sleeping forms, lying at rest and in peace, the only moving shapes being those from higher spheres who have descended to this plane in order to perform tasks for the good of their humbler brethren. Occasionally some sleeper will show signs of awakening, and at once some of these helpers will cluster around him, and seem to melt away into some other plane with him. But the most wonderful thing about this region seems to be that as the sleeper awakens slowly, his astral body slips away from him just as yours a little before, and passes out of that plane to the place of "shells," where it slowly disintegrates and is resolved into its original elements. This discarded shell is not connected with the physical body of the sleeping soul, which physical body has been buried or cremated, as it is "dead"; nor is the shell connected with the soul which has gone on, as it has finally discarded it and thrown it off. It is different in your case, for you have merely left it in the ante-room, and will return and resume its use, presently.

The scene again changes, and you find yourself in the regions of the awakened souls, through which you, with your guides, wander backward and forward. You notice that as the awakening souls pass along, they seem to rapidly drop sheath after sheath of their mental-bodies (for so these higher forms of ethereal coverings are called), and you notice that as you move toward the higher planes your substance becomes more and more etheralized, and that as you return to the lower planes it becomes coarser and grosser, although always far more etheralized than even the astral body, and infinitely finer than the material body. You also notice that each awakening soul is left to finally awaken on some particular plane. Your guide tells you that the particular plane is determined by the spiritual progress and attainment made by the soul in its past lives (for it has had many earthly visits or lives), and that it is practically impossible for a soul to go beyond the plane to which it belongs, although those on the upper planes may freely revisit the lower planes, this being the rule of the Astral World—not an arbitrary law, but a law of nature. . . .[61]

This description bears a fair resemblance to other accounts from such diverse sources as the *Egyptian Book of the Dead*, the *Tibetan Book of the Dead*, Plato's description of *Er*, Dante's *Divine Comedy*, and Swedenborg. Although the social climate in our culture is arriving at a point where it will soon be more prevalent, so far there have been few individuals with such genuine spiritual vision who felt that working with scientists would be a beneficial use of their time. Thus, science has currently little to say about higher spiritual experience.

Apparently not everyone who leaves their body is able to travel to the Empyrean heights (if they exist). Many individuals who have been spontaneously thrust outside of their bodies, or who have cultivated the ability to have OBEs at will, have sought a scientific confirmation and understanding of their experiences. These projections often result from hypnosis, anesthesia, drugs, stress, or accidents. The following case, a typical accidental projection, occurred to a seventy year old Wisconsin man:

He had hitched his team, one wintry day, and gone into the country after a load of firewood. On his return, he was sitting atop the loaded sleigh. A light snow was falling. Without warning, a hunter (who happened to be near the road) discharged his gun at a rabbit. The horses jumped, jerking the sleigh and throwing the driver to the ground head-first.

He said . . . that no sooner had he landed upon the ground than he was conscious of standing up and seeing another "himself" lying motionless near the road, face down in the snow. He saw the snow falling all about, saw the steam rising from the horses, saw the hunter running toward him. All this was very exact; but his great bemuddlement was that there were *two* of him, for he believed at the time that he was observing all that occurred from another physical body.

As the hunter came near, things seemed to grow dim. The next conscious impression he had was of finding himself upon the ground, with the hunter trying to revive him. What he had seen from his astral body was so real that he could not believe that there were not two physical bodies, and he even went so far as to look for tracks in the snow, in the place where he knew he had been standing.[62]

Projections most frequently occur in dreams. The following case, a classic example of a dream OBE, was reported in 1863 by Mr. Wilmot of Bridgeport, Connecticut:

I sailed from Liverpool for New York, on the steamer *City of Limerick.* . . . On the evening of the second day out, . . . a severe storm began which lasted for nine days. . . . Upon the night of the eighth day, . . . for the first time I enjoyed refreshing sleep. Toward morning I dreamed that I saw my wife, whom I had left in the U.S., come to the door of the stateroom, clad in her night dress. At the door she seemed to discover that I was not the only occupant in the room, hesitated a little, then advanced to my side, stooped down and kissed me, and quietly withdrew.

Upon waking I was surprised to see my fellow-passenger . . . leaning upon his elbow and looking fixedly at me. "You're a pretty fellow," he said at length, "to have a lady come and visit you this way." I pressed him for an explanation, . . . and he related what he had seen while wide awake, lying on his berth. It exactly corresponded with my dream. . . .

The day after landing I went to Watertown, Conn., where my children and my wife were . . . visiting her parents. Almost her first question when we were back alone was, "Did you receive a visit from me a week ago Tuesday?" . . . "It would be impossible," I said. "Tell me what makes you think so." My wife then told me that on account of the severity of the weather, . . . she had been extremely anxious about me. On the night mentioned above she had lain awake a long time thinking about me, and about four o'clock in the morning it seemed to her that she went out to seek me. . . . She came at length . . . to my stateroom. "Tell me," she said, "do they ever have staterooms like the one I saw, where the upper berth extends further back than the under one? A man was in the upper berth looking right at me, and for a moment I was afraid to go in, but soon I went up to the side of your berth, bent down and kissed you, and embraced you, and then went away." The description given by my wife of the steamship was correct in all particulars, though she had never seen it.[63]

Astral projection is so often associated with dreaming that many writers insist that the astral body normally separates from the physical during sleep. Most of us, this theory posits, are not sensitive to the separation and only maintain a vague memory of the experience as a dream. Many techniques for conscious astral projection involve regaining consciousness within the dream state. I would suggest however that you not engage in such practice if you often experience great discord within yourself. One technique offered by Sylvan Muldoon in his book *The Projection of The Astral Body* is as follows:

1. Develop yourself so that you are enabled to hold consciousness up to the very moment of 'rising to sleep.' The best way to do this is to hold some member of the physical body in such a position that it will not be at rest, but will be inclined to fall as you enter sleep. . . .

2. Construct a dream which will have the action of Self predominant. The dream must be of the aviation type, in which you move upward and outward, corresponding to the action of the astral body while projecting. It must be a dream of something which you enjoy doing.

3. Hold the dream clearly in mind; visualize it as you are rising to sleep; project yourself right into it and go on dreaming.[64]

Through the use of properly applied suggestion, prior to the dream, you will be able to remember yourself in your dream and bring your dream body—or astral body—to full waking consciousness. This technique may require months of gentle persistence.

Muldoon's book, first published in 1929, offers a wealth of information based on the hundreds of out-of-body experiences he had over a period of many years. However, Muldoon's experiences were seldom completely conscious, and never beyond the limits of the immediate earth environment. In one "superconscious" experience, after a lonely evening, he found himself in a strange house, watching a young lady, who happened to be sewing at the time. Six weeks later, he chanced to recognize this woman on the streets of the small Wisconsin town where he lived. Upon his approaching her, she was startled to discover that he was able to accurately describe the inside of her home. She eventually became a very close friend of his and participated with him in a number of projection experiments.

By systematically observing his own condition in the out-of-body state, Muldoon was able to derive some very interesting hypotheses. For example, he made numerous measurements of the "silver cord" connecting the astral and the physical bodies, stating that it varied in thickness from about 1½ inches to about the size of a sewing thread according to the proximity of the astral body to the physical. Muldoon doesn't tell us how these measurements were made. Presumably they are simply estimates of some sort. At a distance of from eight to fifteen feet, the cord reached its minimum width. It was only after this occurred that Muldoon was able to exercize complete control over his astral body. He also noticed that the impulses for the heartbeat and breath seemed to travel from the astral through the cord to the physical body.

I have tried the experiment many times of holding the breath, while consciously projected, and within cord-activity range. The instant that it is suspended the before-mentioned action of slight expansion and contraction ceases, in the psychic cable, as it likewise does in the physical body; but while the respiration ceases the regular pulsating action [the heartbeat] continues. A deep breath in the astral will produce an identical breath in the physical; a short one will produce a short one; a quick one will produce a quick one, etc.[65]

Muldoon also observed that physical debilities and morbid physical conditions seemed to provide an incentive for projection. He himself was quite frail and sickly during the years when his experiences were most pronounced. It was his hypothesis that the unconscious will—motivated by desires, necessities, or habits which would otherwise have resulted in somnambulism or sleep walking—led to astral projection for him because of the debility of his body. When he was thirsty at night, for instance, he might find his astral body travelling to the pump for water.

On one occasion it occurred to Muldoon that his heart was beating rather slowly. He went to a doctor who told him that his pulse was only 42 beats per minute and gave him a cardiac stimulant—strychnine—to correct the condition. For the next two months Muldoon took this stimulant, and during this period he was not able to induce a projection—although during the previous year he had been averaging at least one OBE each week. After he discontinued the medication, he was again able to astral project. He also noticed that if he experienced intense emotions while out of his body, it tended to cause his heart to beat faster. This resulted in his being suddenly "interiorized" again, often against his conscious will. Such sudden interiorization often resulted in painful, sometimes cataleptic, repercussions within the body.

As his health improved, Muldoon's abilities waned and practically disappeared. Eventually he lost all interest in astral projection—after having made the most significant contribution of his time. Since then several other individuals have contributed extensive reports of their own out-of-body experiences.[66,67]

Robert A. Monroe, the author of *Journeys Out of the Body*, describes how he visited several medical doctors looking for an explanation of his condition. They could find nothing wrong with him. In fact, Monroe is an excellent example of an individual whose reported experiences could not easily be attributed to defective mental or emotional functioning. A former vice-president of Mutual Broadcasting Corporation, Monroe is now president of two corporations active in cable-vision and electronics. He has produced over 600 television programs. During the years of his reported OBEs, Monroe has continued to lead an active business and a rewarding family life.

His book documents many dimensions of OBE activity. In what he termed "Locale I" and "Locale II" are found the common experiences of the occult literature—floating outside of one's body within the familiar physical environment and then travelling to the "astral" worlds of heaven and hell complete with spirits and thoughtforms. In "Locale III" Monroe describes his visits to a plane rather parallel to our own. Human beings there lived much as we do, with some rather odd exceptions. They had no electricity or internal combustion motors, yet a rather sophisticated technology was built around a sort of steam power. Their automobiles held a single bench seat large enough for five or six people abreast.[68]

Monroe is currently engaged in a very sophisticated program of training scientists and others to participate in out-of-body experiences.

While personal accounts of this sort are invaluable, they do little to satisfy the scientific need for information which has no possibility of subjective distortion or falsification. A small, but important, step in this direction has been made by the eminent British geologist, Dr. Robert Crookall. Struck by the many independent reports of OBE, Crookall attempted a critical analysis of the data from as many sources as he could possibly collect. By looking at this collection from different perspectives, he was able to discover a number of interesting, and previously undetected, patterns of out-of-body experience.

In his first analysis, Crookall revealed a basic OBE pattern which was scattered among hundreds of cases from many different cultures: The replica body is "born" from the physical body and takes a position above it. At the moment of separation, there is generally a blackout of consciousness—"much as the changing of gears in a car causes a momentary break in the transmission of power." Commonly the vacated physical body is seen from the released "double." Sometimes the "silver cord" would be noticed. The experience is generally not frightening. Many different phenomena are viewed after separation and the return of the double follows a reversal of the pattern just indicated. Rapid re-entry can cause shock to the physical body.[69]

In a second analysis, all cases were broken down into two large groupings. One group contained projections which were caused naturally and gradually—from illness, exhaustion or sleep. The other included forceable and sudden projections caused by accidents, anesthetics, suffocation, or willfull projection. Crookall reports that people who left their bodies in a natural manner enjoyed consciousness of a clear and extensive type—with telepathy. While the consciousness of the forcibly ejected was remarkably restricted and dim, with dreamlike elements. Those who left naturally tended to glimpse bright and peaceful conditions. The forcibly ejected, if not on earth, tended to be in the confused, and semi-dreamlike conditions that correspond to the "Hades" of the ancients. The former met many helpers (including dead friends and relatives), the latter sometimes encountered discarnate would-be hinderers.[70]

A third analysis compared the differences in experiences reported by ordinary people with those of individuals who claim to be psychics. By and large, the psychics reported experiences very much like enforced projections, whereas the non-psychics had experiences of natural projection. He also noted that the psychic and mediumistic people commonly observed a mist or vapor leaving their bodies and forming part of the double. Similar statements are often made by those who observe the permanent release of the double during the process of death.

This suggested to Crookall that the double actually comprised a semi-physical aspect called the vital or etheric body as well as an astral or super-physical Soul Body. If after the projection, the semi-physical body is still attached, the double will be able to move physical objects, cause rappings, etc. However, if the projection occurs in two stages, so that the Soul Body is separate from the vital body, then the Soul Body is free to travel to the higher "paradise" realms. This second stage would be equivalent to discarding the "astral shell" in Ramacharaka's account. In his most recent work, Crookall documents many cases in which the projection experience occurs in two stages.[71]

Other researchers have also surveyed hundreds of reported experiences. Dr. Charles Tart, of the University of California at Davis, notes that OBEs characteristically last from half a minute to half an hour. He is particularly interested in the externalized consciousness' apparent ability to defy gravity and to travel to a distant place or person merely by thinking about being there. Tart furthermore points out that almost all individuals who experience the out-of-body state develop a firm belief in a life after death. The typical reaction is, "I no longer *believe* in survival after death—I *know* my consciousness will survive death because I have *experienced* my consciousness existing outside of my physical body."[72]

Another extensive survey of OBE reports was conducted by Celia Green of the Institute for Psychophysical Research in Britain. Ms. Green notes that 80% of her respondents reported an *asomatic* experience—although their consciousness seemed independent from the physical body, there was no awareness of an astral body or double. Furthermore, very few of her respondents reported seeing the "silver cord." Some of her respondents felt themselves to be in two distinct places at once. Sometimes the physical body is also quite active during the OBE. There is the example of the preacher who listened to his own sermon from the opposite end of the church. From the out-of-body state, a dentist actually watched himself extract the tooth of a client! Thus in certain types of experience, the physical body is not the least impaired by the OBE. Hundreds of sane individuals have reported some variety of consciousness that carries them beyond the limitations the physical body imposes.[73]

None of these surveys, valuable as they are, actually prove that the out-of-body experience is more than a syndrome—perhaps symptomatic of some mental disorder. The fact that the experience occurs across different cultures could indicate organic brain damage.

The type of experiences reported by OBEers are difficult to evaluate. Within the medical tradition experiences of viewing one's image outside of the body are known as *autoscopic hallucinations*. Such phenomena are often associated with epilepsy, infectious fevers, cerebral lesions, brain tumors, alcoholism,

Dr. Charles Tart
(*Courtesy* Psychic Magazine.)

133

drug addiction and other recognized pathological conditions.[74] Many individuals who have OBEs do in fact suspect some sort of physical or mental disorder.

It is very tempting to regard these experiences as some form of subjective delusion, hallucination, or perhaps even a highly developed sense of ESP. Carl Jung has suggested, for example, that the OBE is a product of the "collective unconscious"—subjective, but also archetypal and deeply rooted in man's experience.[75] The challenges raised by these criticisms can only be met through controlled experimental studies.

In 1919, Hereward Carrington reported on the studies by the French researcher, Dr. Charles Lancelin, who claimed to have established objective proof for the physical reality of the OBE. Using techniques of hypnosis and self-hypnosis, Lancelin found subjects who were able to leave their bodies at will and appear to a hypnotized, or clairvoyant, observer in another room. Often the astral phantoms made themselves known by speaking, touching, rapping, causing images to appear on photographic plates, or by touching calcium sulphide screens and making them glow.[76] These are the only laboratory investigations reported in the parapsychological literature until the studies conducted by Dr. Charles Tart in the late 1960s.

Tart arranged for his first subject, Miss Z., to sleep in a physiological laboratory so that he might be able to monitor her brain waves, eye movements, blood pressure, and the electrical resistance of her skin while she was having an OBE. Then, he placed a randomly chosen five-digit number on a shelf above her bed in a position where it would only be visible to an observer near the ceiling. There was also a clock above the shelf. It was impossible for Miss Z. to get out of bed to look at the number without clearly disrupting the operation of the brain-wave recording machine. (However, some researchers have suggested that she could have used a small mirror on a telescope stick to see the number without juggling the EEG.)

Over the course of four nights, she had several OBEs which she reported to the experimenters. In all but one she did not feel that she had floated, in her astral body, to a position from which she was able to observe the target number. On the final night, however, she could see the number which she correctly stated to be 25132. This was a highly significant result, as the odds of guessing a five-digit number in one trial are 1 in 100,000;

Furthermore, Tart noted an unusual brain wave pattern which was associated only with her reported OBE experiences —alpha waves that were about 1½ cycles per second slower than her ordinary alpha rhythm (of 10 cycles per second) and of a slightly lower voltage. The significance of this "alphoid pattern" which is not found in other OBE subjects, is unclear.[77]

The results of Tart's experiment could still be explained as ESP accompanied by some physiological change. More conclusive studies, however, have been conducted at the Psychical Research Foundation in Durham, North Carolina. This research is unique in that the subject, or projector, Mr. Blue Harary, was also a member of the scientific team which designed the experiments. Harary was an undergraduate

Gerald Solvin monitoring EEG tracings from Blue Harary during OBE experiment. (Courtesy Psychical Research Foundation.)

psychology student at Duke University and was able to voluntarily induce out-of-body experiences.

The experimental design was similar to the Tart study, although a bit more complex. In addition to monitoring physiological changes and having target material in another location for Blue to observe while projecting, the PRF team sought to determine if any animal, human or mechanical devices could *detect* the presence of the "second body" near the target area.

The ESP results during these experiments did include some remarkable hits, but overall the scores were not significant. Blue, himself, felt that his vision was very hazy in the out-of-body state. However, the physiological indicators were very interesting. In these studies, each OBE was preceded by a "cool down" stage in which all of eight physiological indicators showed extreme relaxation. This generally lasted from two to fifteen minutes. When Blue felt he had entered a state he knew to be conducive for an OBE visit to the target area, he signalled the experimenters by uttering the syllable, "soon." The word "back" similarly denoted the end of the OBE. The actual OBE period was marked by a slight increase in respiration, heart rate, and blood pressure. The EEG tracings were similar to those of a normal, waking, eyes closed state.

The most significant results of these experiments were with the subject's pet kitten which was used in the target room as a detector. The cat was placed in a three-foot-deep "open field" container which was divided into 24 numbered ten-inch squares. During the non-OBE control period, the kitten was very active, meowing frequently, crossing a large number of squares, and attempting to get out of the container. However, during the times when Blue was allegedly out-of-his body visiting the target room, the cat became strikingly quiet and calm. This effect was repeated throughout four experimental sessions! Another experiment using a snake as a detector also produced a striking response—literally speaking that is. The snake was characteristically calm during the control periods, but began striking and gnawing against the glass front of his cage during the initial OBE test.

Unfortunately, the animals had a tendency to rapidly habituate to the experimental conditions and their use as detectors over extensive periods of time proved unreliable. So far, satisfactory results have not been consistently obtained with human or mechanical detectors. Further research is continuing.[78,79]

Other studies on the out-of-body state have been conducted in the New York laboratories of the American Society for Psychical Research. Initial studies were conducted with Mr. Ingo Swann, an artist whose illustrations often convey a psychic perception of auras and energy fields as well as distant parts of the cosmos. The research with him was very similar to the Miss Z. studies. While producing physiological changes somewhat similar to the alphoid pattern he was on many occasions able to describe target objects placed in another location. The computed probabilities that he could have done this by chance were in the neighborhood of one in forty thousand.[80,81]

Robert Morris, Ph.D., conducted OBE experiments with Blue Harary in Durham, N.C. Now he is a full-time instructor of parapsychology at U.C., Santa Barbara. (Courtesy Psychic Magazine*).*

In some OBE experiments Blue Harary was asked to project himself into this cage with his kitten. The meters in the background monitored the motions of the animal.

135

A second series of experiments were conducted with Ingo Swann and another psychic, Harold Sherman, in which they were asked to leave their bodies and travel to Jupiter and Mercury. The parapsychologists were hopeful that the psychics would return with data which could then be checked against information obtained from the NASA space probes. The results from the planet Jupiter were somewhat ambiguous, however very significant data was obtained about Mercury. This experiment was conducted several days before the arrival of Mariner 10.

Swann and Sherman predicted the presence of a very weak magnetic field on the planet. Before the space probe, this fact was not known about Mercury and was not even hypothesized to exist as Mercury has very little rotation. However, these OBE explorations correlated very highly with the NASA report. They also accurately described the surface characteristiscs of the planet. All of their results were signed, notarized, and sent to scientists before the new data from Mariner 10 was released.[82] Experiments such as this show the enormous potential which psychic development holds for future scientific exploration.

A third series of experiments at the ASPR used a very ingenious arrangement in order to distinguish an out-of-body perception from ESP. Several target devices which work on optical principles were developed. Only through a small viewing window could the full target arrangment be seen. From any other location, the target, if it were visible at all, would not appear in the optically transformed version. Thus an individual who was making a "clairvoyant sweep" of the area would not be expected to report the correct target information. Even the experimenter could not know the actual target until after the experiment as the random target is chosen by the instrument.

The ASPR issued invitations to any gifted subjects to *fly-in* and participate in these experiments. Over 100 subjects have been tested in this fashion with generally disappointing results. However, the subjects who did score well were quite certain that they had actually seen the target. When subjects were uncertain, their descriptions were usually inaccurate.

Ingo Swan
(*Courtesy* Psychic Magazine.)

Harold Sherman
(*Courtesy* Psychic Magazine.)

136

One subject, Dr. Alex Tanous, tried for weeks without success to learn to distinguish his actual out-of-body vision from his own fantasy experiences. Although he failed miserably in this effort for some time, he did not give up. Finally, one day he hit upon the correct criteria and now is a highly reliable scorer. Normally when he is out-of-body he experiences himself as a large, amorphous light. This gradually becomes more and more concentrated. He feels now that he will start to score well when it is about the size of a dime—and when the light is concentrated to a point, he is extremely accurate! Nevertheless it is difficult to distinguish this experiment from a simple test of ESP; rather it gives us clues to the possible OBE mechanism of ESP.

Another aspect of the ASPR research involved an attempt to measure a possible physical influence on the spot to which an astral traveler has projected. This study involves the use of a device called a "diving pool" which is an enclosed, electronically isolated space with an object suspended in it. Sensitive instrumentation registers the slightest movement of this object. So far, one psychic, Pat Price, has been able to cause enormous variations on the suspended object, at least in some of his experimental sessions.[83]

Similar observations were made at the Stanford Research Institute by physicists Puthoff and Targ, using a superconductor-shielded magnetometer which was at the time measuring a decaying magnetic field. Previous tests had shown that no signals had been induced in the shielded magnetometer from the outside. The scientists asked Ingo Swann if he could effect this instrument, and as Swann concentrated his attention inside the device, the recording chart output showed the frequency doubling for about thirty seconds. Several other unusual disturbances were also noted. Furthermore, Swann, who felt he was out-of-his body at the time, was able to provide an accurate description of the magnetometer, even though it was buried underneath the building. While the SRI scientists feel that this was a very significant observation, they do not regard it as a carefully controlled experiment.[84]

The scientific case for the out-of-body experience rests at this point. While I have been freely interchanging the term *astral projection* with OBE, many researchers would hesitate to have their work associated with the occult and theosophical traditions from which the notion of astral traveling stems. The current effort is rather to wipe the slate clean of prior ideologies and approach the topic with a fresh phenomenalism. This is a very tricky area. Since the experience seems so much to be affected by the thoughts of the projector, any prior theoretical expectations may become realized and confirmed. It seems that all individuals have their unspoken assumptions about the existence and nature of the out-of-body state. I personally feel that the associations implied by the term *astral projection* must be considered as valid as any other hypotheses—perhaps moreso, when one considers the depth of our visionary tradition. On the other hand, it seems that we will not even be able to distinguish an OBE from simple ESP and PK until scientists are able to gather more data from the inside of the experience.

From my perspective, it is clear that we are entering a period where OBE research is beginning to utilize the *state-specific science* approach. Scientists themselves are now learning to enter the out-of-body state—make observations and test their hypotheses from that perspective. We are entering an era when the traditional roles of scientist, priest, shaman, and artist are fusing into a new integrated person ready to delve into the great mystery of life beyond.

Gerald Solvin and Blue Harary during an OBE experiment. (Courtesy Psychical Research Foundation, Durham, N.C.)

Consciousness and Healing

The history of mental healing has an ancient tradition going back to prehistoric shamanism. It has survived in such modern social movements as hypnotism, Christian Science, shrines such as Lourdes in France, evangelistic faith healing, and psychic or spiritualistic healing. The most prominent twentieth century psychic healer was Edgar Cayce (pronounced Casey) who died in 1945. While in an unconscious trance state, Cayce made diagnoses and prescribed treatments for thousands of individuals.

Although Cayce tried to arrange for his patients to be treated by qualified physicians, like all unlicensed healers, he met with a deeply entrenched opposition from the medical profession. It was, however, a homeopathic doctor, Wesley Ketchum, M.D., who examined the records of Cayce's treatments and made a favorable report, in 1910, to the American Society of Clinical Research at Boston:

Edgar Cayce
(Courtesy Association for Research and
Enlightenment)

I have used him in about 100 cases and to date have never known of any errors in diagnosis, except in two cases where he described a child in each case by the same name and who resided in the same house as the one wanted. He simply described the wrong person. . . .

The cases I have used him in have, in the main, been the rounds before coming to my attention, and in six important cases which has been diagnosed as strictly surgical he stated that no such condition existed, and outlined treatment which was followed with gratifying results in every case.

Files of over 9,000 readings by Edgar Cayce are kept on record by the Association for Research and Enlightenment in Virginia Beach, Va. Since 1931, this organization has attempted to foster scientific investigation of Cayce's healings.

However, the state of our scientific understanding of healing is still at a very primitive level. It wasn't until 1959, for example, that the American Medical Association officially approved hypnosis as a therapeutic tool. In this context, it is somewhat understandable that an International Study Group on Unorthodox Healing sponsored by the Parapsychology Foundation in 1954 concluded that it would be premature to consider an alleged psychic influence in the multifarious types of mental healing before the whole field had been investigated in regard to its normal aspects. Since then a number of experimental studies have clarified things somewhat.

In 1955, the Institute for Border Areas of Psychology and Mental Hygiene, headed by Professor Hans Bender in Freiburg Germany, conducted a thorough study of a mental healer, Dr. (of political science) Kurt Trampler. This study, while not indicative of any paranormal healing, does give us a good picture of the role which psychological factors can play in the healing process. Trampler was seeking to exculpate himself legally as he had been tried and found guilty of violating the statutes governing medical practice. In light of hundreds of testimonials from his patients, the Board of Health ruled that a research study would be of sociological and medical interest.

Trampler's philosophy and methods are not untypical of psychic healers in general. He stresses the need for the patient

139

to establish a "reconnection with the fundamental source of life." In his view sickness is a "disturbance in man's contact with the higher interrelationships of life." Each treatment session begins with a philosophical discussion of this sort, eloquently delivered in a manner found appealing to an audience of varied backgrounds.

Trampler then "charges" the patient with his own raised hands, held at some distance. He claims that he can feel the streaming of "an impulse which is transmitted to the patient who then, by some so far unexplained process of a spiritual or energetic nature seems to bring about a change for the better." The patient describes his own sensations during this "atunement." He experiences feelings of warmth and cold, a prickling sensation or a sense of a powerful current. To sustain his therapy Trampler gives the patients sheets of aluminum foil which he has first "charged" in his hand and which upon returning home the patients are to lay on the afflicted spots or spread out under their pillows, or even carry constantly on their persons.

Every evening at a certain hour Trampler tunes in on all his patients. In his preliminary lecture, he gives notice of this "remote treatment" and cites examples of its success.[85]

During a six month period, 650 patients treated by Trampler were examined intensively by a research team before treatment. Follow up studies were conducted on 538 of these individuals. Two thirds of these patients were women.* As far as educational, occupational, or family background the patients were representative of the population of the area surrounding Freiburg.

A wide variety of maladies was found in this group. Almost 75% of the patients were chronic cases who had been suffering for more than five years from the conditions which prompted them to see the mental healer. Over half of them were simultaneously undergoing medical treatment—which is something that Dr. Trampler encouraged. They had come to the mental healer because other modes of treatment had failed.

Medical evaluation indicated unexpected, objective improvement in 9% of Dr. Trampler's patients. On the other hand, 61% of Trampler's patients had the subjective experience of permanent or temporary improvement in their condition. In fact, 50% of those patients whose condition had objectively worsened nevertheless declared that they were considerably better, at least temporarily. The subjective improvement of the malady seemed to depend very little on the diagnosis or seriousness of the disease. The results indicated that the subjective improvement was chiefly a function of the attitude which the patients had before treatment by Dr. Trampler. Patients with the highest expectations seemed to respond the most.

Oddly enough, the patients who responded the least to Dr. Trampler's methods were more intelligent, imaginative, and self-confident than those who seemed to benefit the most. The patients who experienced the greatest improvement were, however, more relaxed!

---

*Interestingly enough, another survey indicates that two-thirds of the psychic healers in Britain are men.[86]

In no case was Trampler's treatment found to be objectively harmful to the patient![87]

Essentially this study exemplifies what is now a well-known and important medical effect—patients with a relaxed and positive attitude show greater response to medical treatment. Studies have shown, for example, that trancendental meditators report fewer instances of allergies and also infectious diseases than before they began meditating regularly.[88] Other studies conducted at the University of Rochester over a 20 year period have shown that the presence or absence of cancer in a patient can be predicted on the basis of the feelings of "hopelessness" which the person has toward life in general.[89] Studies of this sort have led to the development of a recognized specialty in *psychosomatic medicine*. Doctors now realize that the attitudes of their patients are just as significant as the symptoms of their disease.

In Fort Worth, Texas, for example Dr. Carl Simonton, in addition to treating cancer patients with conventional radiation, chemotherapy, and surgery—also uses relaxation and visualization techniques.

Dr. Carl Simonton
(*Courtesy* Psychic Magazine.)

The patient is asked to meditate regularly three times a day for 15 minutes in the morning upon arising, around noon, and at night before going to bed. In the meditation exercise, the first couple of minutes are used to go into a state of relaxation, then once the body is completely relaxed, the patient visualizes a peaceful scene from nature. A minute later, the patient begins the main part of the work of mental imagery. First, he tunes in on the cancer, "sees" it in his mind's eye. Then as Simonton describes it, "he pictures his immune mechanism working the way it's supposed to work, picking up the dead and dying cells." Patients are asked to visualize the army of white blood cells coming in, swarming over the cancer, and carrying off the malignant cells which have been weakened or killed by the barrage of high energy particles of radiation therapy given off by the cobalt machine, the linear accelerator, or whatever the source is. These white cells then break down the malignant cells which are then flushed out of the body. Finally, just before the end of the meditation, the patient visualizes himself well.[90]

The patient is instructed in the general principles of the immune mechanism and is shown photographs of other patients whose visible cancers—such as on the skin and mouth— are actually responding to the treatment, getting smaller and disappearing. In a study of 152 patients, Simonton found the greatest success with those who were the most optimistic and committed to full participation in the entire therapeutic process. Furthermore, these patients also showed fewer distressing side-effects to the radiation therapy.[91] These results are very encouraging. However, further research and longer follow up studies are necessary before the medical establishment can form a conclusive judgement on the radical possibility of using psychological treatment to cure organic disease.

Meanwhile evidence is accumulating which points to types of psychic healing which go far beyond the possibilities of suggestion, relaxation, and attitude change.

In 1959, a Canadian researcher, Dr. Bernard Grad, was introduced to a Hungarian refugee named Oskar Estebany who claimed that some form of healing energy emanated from his

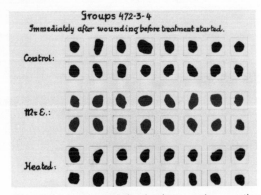

Wound size in mice immediately after removing a portion of the skin. The center group received psychic healing treatment. (Courtesy Dr. Bernard Grad.)

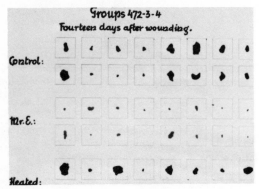

Wound size after 11 days.

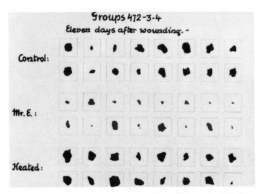

Wound size after 14 days.

hands. Estebany had been a cavalry officer in the Hungarian army before the 1956 uprising and originally discovered his healing abilities in treating the army horses. In a series of ingenious experiments with Estebany, Grad provided the scientific foundation for the existence of psychic healing.

His first experiments were with laboratory mice whose backs had been deliberately wounded by carefully removing an area of skin. The areas of these wounds were measured over an eighteen day healing period. The treatment consisted of Mr. Estebany's holding the caged mice between his hands for twenty minutes twice daily. One control group received similar handling from medical students who did not claim to have unusual healing ability, while the mice in another control group simply remained in their cages without handling at all. The experiment was carefully controlled so that the individuals who cared for the mice and measured their wounds did not know which of the test groups they were in. A total of 300 mice were used in one experiment, which was eventually published after several pilot studies. This experiment showed significantly faster wound healing in the mice treated by Mr. Estebany.[92] It was difficult to maintain that the mice were susceptible to the power of suggestion. Rather the experimenters felt that there was some sort of healing emanations coming from Estebany's hands.

In his next experiment, Grad used barley seeds which were treated with a saline solution. Sterile and sealed in bottles under vacuum the solution was normally used for intravenous infusion of humans. The healer merely held one sealed bottle in his hands for thirty minutes. A control bottle of solution was not "healed." The seeds were soaked in the solution and allowed to dry for 48 hours. Then they were baked in an oven just long enough to injure, but not kill them. Twenty seeds were planted in each of twenty-four pots—with identical soil, temperature, and humidity conditions. During the test period no person knew which seeds had been given the treated water. Estebany himself had no contact with the barley seeds. However, after the conclusion of the experiment it was found that those pots with seeds which had been watered from the bottles treated by the healer had more plants growing in them and the plants were also taller.[93]

In a third experiment, Grad attempted to determine if he could get effects from other subjects. In fact, he hypothesized that if a psychic healer could cause greater plant growth, perhaps treatment by psychiatric patients would inhibit growth. A similar experimental technique was used with three subjects. One of these was psychiatrically normal, the second was a hospitalized depressed neurotic, and the third a hospitalized depressed psychotic patient. A control group of plants received no treatment at all. The results of this experiment were very intriguing. The plants treated with the solution held by the normal subject showed greater growth than either the control or the depressed subjects. This effect was statistically significant and the "normal" subject also claimed to feel some sort of flow through his hands during the experiment. One of the depressed subjects was so amused with the experiment that her mood picked up as soon as she was asked to hold the bottle of saline solution. Her plants grew consistently, but not significantly larger than the control plants. The third subject stayed in an unhappy mood throughout the experiment. The seeds treated from the bottle of solution which she held showed less growth than the untreated control group.[94] This effect was small in Grad's experiment, but we will see that it has been confirmed by other studies.

For example, in 1966, Dr. Carroll B. Nash, who directed the Parapsychology Laboratory at St. Joseph's College in Philadelphia, performed an experiment with 19 psychotics in which each held a bottle of glucose solution. When poured on suspensions of yeast cells the solutions were found to have a slight inhibiting effect on the growth of this organism as compared with controls in which the glucose had not been subjected to treatment.[95]

Plant growth affected by psychic healing treatment. (Courtesy Dr. Bernard Grad.)

The demonstrated existence of effects caused by the laying on of hands still left unanswered many questions regarding the mechanisms of this phenomena. What is it about the hands of a healer that can effect wound healing or plant growth?

This question was on the mind of the biochemist, Sister Justa M. Smith, who, in 1970, invited Mr. Estebany to her laboratory at Rosary Hill College in Buffalo, New York. Sister Smith's research had focused on enzymes—large protein molecules which act as catalysts, speeding up biochemical reactions such as those associated with wound healing and growth of tissue. Her research had shown that the reactivity of enzymes, which were treated by a strong magnetic field, was increased;[96] and she wondered if Estebany's hands might imitate this effect.

In her laboratory, Estebany held sealed test tubes of enzymes in his hands while her assistants tested their reactivity every fifteen minutes, using an infrared spectrophotometer. They found that the enzymes behaved as if they had been exposed to a magnetic field of 13,000 gauss. This is a very strong field when one considers that the magnetic field of the earth is only about one-half of a gauss. Further testing with a magnetometer, however, revealed that there was no unusual magnetic field around Estebany's hands.[97]

In another experiment with Mr. Estebany, Dr. Dolores Krieger, a nursing instructor at New York University, measured the hemoglobin levels of 16 patients who were treated with laying-on-of-hands for fifteen minutes three times daily. Over a six day period, the patients showed an average increase of 1.2 gm. of hemoglobin per 100 cc. of blood. There was no increase in the level of patients who did not receive the healing treatment.[98]

Further testing of the water treated by Mr. Estebany showed distinct spectrophotometric differences from untreated water. This effect was confirmed independently in several laboratories. These differences according to Douglas Dean, indicate that the internuclear distance between the oxygen and hydrogen atoms in a molecule of water has been altered—

probably increased. Dean, an electrochemist from the Newark College of Engineering in New Jersey, also suggests that the water molecules treated by Estebany have been somewhat ionized.[99]

Dramatic healing effects were recently reported by Dr. Thelma Moss and her colleagues at U.C.L.A. in a study with eleven patients who had been treated by medical doctors and had been told that no further improvement in their conditions could be expected. In six of these patients, considerable improvements were noted which defied medical explanation. One of these cases was a young man with a leg which had been badly shattered from an automobile accident. Doctors felt that he would never be able to walk again and they urged that his leg be amputated. After two years of treatment with "magnetic passes," this individual is now able to walk without a cane or a brace with almost full control of his legs. Another case is that of a man who had several nerves in his neck severed by a bullet wound. His right arm and hand were completely paralyzed and the neurologist who had been treating him felt that there was absolutely no hope for improvement. This patient, after similar "magnetic" treatments from a hypnotherapist, has now regained movement, flexion, and sensation.[100]

It's valuable for the reader to understand that a good deal of the healing evidence, particularly in relationship to spontaneous effects, must be viewed with caution as research has sometimes been presented informally without an adequate report of the experimental controls. However, the strength of the evidence lies not so much in any individual study but rather from the coherent picture which emerges from the composite of all of the healing research.

For example, a number of striking phenomena have been reported with Dr. Olga Worrall and her late husband Ambrose Worrall. A typical example involving Ambrose is found in the Worrall's own book *Explore Your Psychic World:*

Julius Weinberger, an electronic scientist, devised the method used. A piece of dental X-ray film was placed in the palm of my hand with a lead bar across it; the whole apparatus was attached with adhesive tape. I asked, "What is that for?" Dr. Weinberger said, "You say you feel this force flowing down your arm and out of your hand, and we think it might build up against the lead bar and maybe it will show something on this film." There was an ill woman in the next room who had been brought in to participate in the experiment. Dr. Weinberger asked me to put my hand on her and tell him if I felt the power flowing. This I did. They took the X-ray film from my hand, developed it, and there appeared a line of light on the film where the bar had been. They made some checks which indicated that the line was not caused by X-ray. I don't know whether they pursued it enough to find out what energy was involved, but . . . it takes only a few electron volts to affect X-ray film.[101]

Another study is reported by Dr. Robert N. Miller, a chemical engineer from Atlanta, Georgia, who tested Olga Worrall with a sensitive instrument known as a cloud chamber, normally used to detect high-energy, sub-atomic particles. The cloud chamber is essentially a cylindrical glass container which is saturated inside with an alcohol vapor at a very low temperature. High energy particles which pass through the chamber cause an ionized path which can be observed and photographed. When Olga Worrall put her hands three inches above such an instrument in Georgia, a very unusual effect occurred. Pulsating waves—about one per second—were observed within the chamber moving parallel to her hands. When she shifted her hand ninety degrees, the pulsations also slowly shifted until they were again parallel to Dr. Worrall's hands. This is an effect which no one else has subsequently been able to reproduce within the chamber.[102]

Any possible attempt to explain this effect is further complicated by a second experiment which Dr. Miller conducted with Olga Worrall—this time from a distance of over 500 miles as she was at her home in Baltimore, Maryland, while he was still in Atlanta. Having set up the cloud chamber, he phoned her from the laboratory and asked her to try to effect the instrument from a distance. At the pre-arranged time, the same pulsation effect as previously noted began to form within the chamber, and persisted for about three minutes. Dr. Miller was quite excited; however a colleague of his, a physicist, Dr. Reinhart, remained somewhat skeptical and claimed that the effect would only be significant if it could be repeated. At this suggestion, Dr. Miller immediately phoned Mrs. Worrall again in Baltimore and asked her to try to effect the cloud chamber once again. For a second time the scientists observed the instrument, and after a minute the same pulsations once again appeared, and persisted for eight minutes. Dr. Reinhart was convinced.[103]

Dr. Worrall is actually well-known for her ability to heal at a distance. Every evening at 9:00 p.m. in Baltimore she engages in a silent meditation for the purpose of healing the many people in need who are unable to receive individual treatment during personal visits. In a fashion similar to that described by Dr. Trampler, individuals in need of healing can simply *tune in* psychically at that time. However, in the case of Dr. Worrall, we have evidence of the efficacy of her distant healing—at least if she is consciously concentrating on the person or object to which she is attempting to direct healing energy. In the cloud chamber experiment, for example, she visualized in her mind the idea of holding her hands over this instrument and sending energy to it.

Another experiment conducted by Dr. Miller involved measuring the growth rate of a rye plant in Atlanta while Mr. and Mrs. Worrall were attempting to send healing energy to it from Baltimore. Using a device developed in 1966 by Dr. H. H. Kleuter of the U.S. Department of Agriculture, Miller was able to measure the growth rate of this plant to an accuracy of a thousandth of an inch per hour. A number of preliminary studies indicated that the growth rates of rye plants would vary from 0.002 to 0.010 inch per hour. Under the constant conditions of lighting, temperature, and watering frequency which Dr. Miller used for his experiment the growth rate was approximately

Olga Worrall
(*Courtesy* Psychic Magazine.)

145

0.006 inch per hour. This rate was continually being monitored on a strip chart recorder. Miller describes his experiment as follows:

> Before the experiment began in January of 1967, the growth rate of a new blade of rye grass had been stabilized at 0.00625 inch per hour. During the night of January 3rd the trace on the strip chart recorder was a sloping straight line indicating a constant growth rate. The straight line continued with little or no deviation during the next day. At 8:00 p.m. on the evening of January 4th, I telephoned from Atlanta to Baltimore to ask the Worralls to hold the seedling in their thoughts at their usual 9:00 p.m. prayer time. One hour later they "prayed" for the plant by visualizing it as growing vigorously in a white light.
>
> The next morning I carefully examined the strip chart recorder trace. . . . All through the evening and until 9:00 p.m. the trace was a straight line with a slope which represented a growing rate of 0.00625 inch per hour. At exactly 9:00 p.m. the trace began to deviate upward and by 8:00 a.m. the next morning the grass was growing 0.0525 inch per hour, a growth rate increase of 840 percent.[104]

Dr. Miller claims that there was no known physical variable which could have caused such a large variation in the growth of his rye plant. His experiments imply that the interactions found in psychic healing can easily traverse great distances of space guided simply by the mental intentions of the healer. The mere notion of energy radiating from the hands of the healer is insufficient to account for the known phenomena. It may simply be that the hands form a psychological tool for the focusing of concentration.

The history of *radionics* provides an even more provocative illustration of this concept. This is the term applied to a social movement concerned with diagnosis and healing through the use of complicated devices or "black boxes," which (although no one understood how they worked) resulted in miraculous cures. The father of this movement was Dr. Albert Abrams, a professor of pathology at Stanford University's medical school. Basing his discoveries on the philosophy that all matter radiates information which can be detected by his instruments in conjunction with the unconscious reflexes of another human being, Abrams succeeded in attracting a large following and also arousing the unremitting ire of the medical and scientific establishment. Thousands of self-professed healers were effecting cures, making diagnoses, and even removing pests from gardens merely by twisting dials, swinging pendulums, or rubbing their fingers across strange devices.[105,106] The following passage describes the use of one such instrument known as the Delawarr machine:

> Suppose that it is required to find out the condition of a patient's liver. We place a bloodspot or saliva sample in one of the two containers at the top of the main panel, according to whether the patient is male or female, and start turning the tuning knob slowly, passing the fingers of the right hand over the rubber detector at the same time with a series of "brushing" strokes until a "stick" is obtained. The patient's bloodspot is then tuned into the set.[107]

The "stick" refers to a particular rubbing sensation in the finger. The location of the dials when the "stick" occurs, when

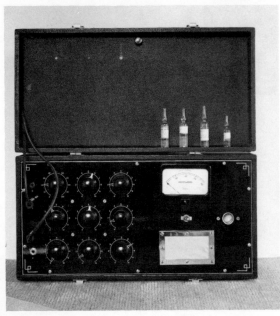

Radionics "Black Box"

146

properly translated is said to indicate the diagnosis of the disease. When the disease is tuned in to the instrument, the cure can be "broadcast" over any distance, to the patient.

Other radionic developments have been even more startling, such as the camera developed by the Los Angeles chiropractor, Dr. Ruth Drown. Using nothing but a drop of blood, this camera could take pictures of the organs and tissues of patients—sometimes at a distance of thousands of miles. She could also take pictures in "cross-section"—a feat which cannot be duplicated even with X-rays. While she received a British patent for her apparatus, Dr. Drown was persectued as a charlatan by the FDA.[108]

The following story about Drown's ability is told by the cosmologist Arthur M. Young, who invented the Bell helicopter:

Ruth Drown was truly an angelic sort of a person—if you can imagine an angel in the flesh. And she started reeling off these Pythagorean relationships that just made my mind spin. I had to go outside and cool down; I couldn't keep up with her.

It wasn't on the first occasion, but maybe on the second, that I wanted to put her to a test. I was at that time having a toothache. So I asked her if she would diagnose my condition and take a photograph. But I didn't tell her anything. And she took these photographs that were about eight by ten. It looked like a very detailed picture of teeth!

She put the film in this box, but there were no lenses or anything like that. Whatever this radiation was, it exposed the film. It was not done with light. And she got a photograph of the tooth.

Being scientific in nature, I said, "Now do it again." This was all in the dark. She couldn't see me. So I pressed the tooth hard with my finger to make it hurt more, to see what would happen. The next picture was an enlargement of this same tooth![109]

Today there are two important developments effecting the standing of radionics. On the one hand, psychotronic researchers are taking a serious interest in understanding the possible mechanisms which such instrumentation might have.[110,111] At the time of this writing, it is not clear however that a major breakthrough is at hand. On the other hand, a number of radionic practitioners and investigators have reported that after becoming proficient in the use of the "black boxes," they were able to obtain the same effects without them.[112,113]

One radionics expert, Francis Farrelly, demonstrated her ability to work without her instrument at the International Conference on Psychotronics in Prague in 1973:

. . . she was confronted by a professor from the Czechoslovak Academy of Sciences who gave her a chip of mineralized rock and asked her before a large audience if she could state its origin and age. Rubbing the table before her to get a radionic type "stick," Farrelly, after putting a dozen questions to herself, stated that the mineral in question came from a meteor and was about 3,200,000 years old, answers which exactly matched the most considered conclusions of expert Czech minerologists.[114]

It was her contention that she had learned to "run the instrument in [her] head." Perhaps, then, the "black box" is to

This picture shows the subject's view of the mice through one-way glass. Either the right or left side would be the target, the other mouse serving as a control. Funnels in the background were used to guide the mice onto the photocell platform without touching them. (Courtesy Graham Watkins.)

radionics what the "laying on of hands" is to psychic healing—a tool for focusing consciousness within the structure of one's belief system.

Further research into this phenomena is necessary, as not all the radionics effects—such as the Drown photographs—have been duplicated without instrumentation. The nature of radionic phenomena, subtle energy fields, and unconscious psychic mechanisms all point fruitful avenues for investigating mind-body interactions.

One of the most significant series of experiments in psychic healing was conducted by Graham and Anita Watkins at the Foundation for Research on the Nature of Man in Durham, North Carolina. They attempted to find out whether psychics would be able to cause mice to awaken more quickly from ether anesthesia than would normally be expected. Altogether thirteen different subjects were used for this experiment. Three of these subjects were members of the laboratory staff who claimed no special healing ability or significant psychokinetic ability in general. The remaining ten subjects had either claimed to have healing abilities or had performed well on a psychokinetic test under controlled laboratory conditions. In some of the experiments, the subjects were in the same room with the mice they were attempting to revive. In another experiment, the mice were in one room and the subject was in an adjoining room viewing them through a one way glass.

The results of this experiment were highly significant overall. Thirty-two runs were performed with twenty-four trials in each run. In each trial the subject was presented a mouse to revive, and a control mouse which was simultaneously anesthetized. The control mice averaged 30.43 seconds and the experimentals 25.36 seconds to revive from the ether. The probability that this result was due to chance is less than one in a million. Only one of the talented subjects scored at a chance level as did all three of the laboratory staff. The nine remaining talented subjects scored extremely well.[115]

One unusual finding of this experiment was that the subjects failed to produce a significant effect when they were assigned a random target series instead of using one target location (right or left) throughout a half run of twelve trials. This apparent failure could be explained, however, if the psychic effect which was causing the accelerated waking of the mice did not immediately dissipate when the subject ceased to concentrate, but rather lingered on for a certain period of time. This was suggested to the experimenters by the fact that when the subjects were asked to change target sides at the end of a half run, approximately thirty minutes was required between halves to insure a successful second half. This was seen in a number of preliminary runs in which this interval was varied between five minutes and an hour.

To test this hypothesis, the Watkins conducted another experiment in which the subject was asked to leave the building upon completing the first half run, and the second half began immediately with a pair of mice being placed on the table as though the healer were still present in the adjoining room. In this experiment, the mice which were on the side of the table which had previously been the target side continued to revive faster—even though no healer was concentrating on them! This "linger effect" was found to be at least as reliable as the main healing effect.[116]

In fact, this effect is quite useful in distinguishing genuine psychokinetic and healing phenomena from possible artifacts, experimenter error, and fraud.

Certainly the most controversial phenomena reported in relationship to healing are the alleged cases of *psychic surgery*. These cases which generally stem from Brazil or the Phillipines, although they have been known to occur in other parts of the world, center around the extraordinary talents of uneducated healers guided by the power of spirit. Operations are performed without the benefit of anesthesia or antisepsis, under unsterile conditions, often without even the benefit of a knife. Blood appears. Tissue is removed. And yet, when the procedure is completed there is often no trace of a wound or an opening! As Dr. Andrija Puharich has put it, these operations mimic, yet violate every principle of modern surgery.

During the period from 1963 to 1968, Puharich, then a senior medical researcher at New York University, conducted extensive studies in Brazil with the wonder-healer José Pedro de Freitas—known by his nickname Arigó. Born in 1918, Arigó received four years of education in primary school, worked as a mine laborer, and also owned his own small restaurant. At the age of 30 he entered into a period of severe depression, nightmares, sleep talking and sleep-walking. For two years neither a doctor nor a priest were of any benefit to him whatsoever. Finally a local spiritualist, Sr. Olivera, prayed for Arigó and told him that a spirit was trying to work through him. [117]

In 1950, Arigó first achieved his unsought fame as a healer, during a visit to the city of Belo Horizonte where he stayed at a hotel where state senator Bittencourt was also a guest. Bittencourt stated to Puharich that Arigó whom he knew, entered his room early in the morning, telling him to lie down on the bed. Then he produced a razor, proceeded to remove a tumor from Bittencourt's abdomen, and he left. Previous diagnosis had shown his colonic tumor to be inoperable. Subsequent diagnosis indicated that the tumor dissipated. Bittencourt's pajamas were torn and an orange-sized piece of tissue was found in the hotel room. While there was blood on his pajamas and body, no scar was found. Eventually Arigó went on to do surgery of a similar kind in public. [118]

Puharich himself claims to have observed over one thousand instances in which Arigó diagnosed and treated patients —with complete accuracy as far as he himself was able to determine.

We found we were able to verify 550 verdicts, because in those cases we ourselves were able to establish a pretty definite diagnosis of the problem. In the remaining 450 cases, for example in rare blood cases, we could not be certain of our own diagnosis because we lacked available on-the-spot resources to enable us to do so. But of those of which we were certain we did not find a single case in which Arigó was at fault. Every patient was helped and none had post operative complications.[119]

Puharich was further impressed with the accuracy and sophisticated terminology of the medical prescriptions which Arigó frequently gave. The medical team working with Puharich was never able to find a mistake in the medical or registered trade name of a drug prescribed. Thousands of surgical operations were conducted under conditions which Puharich described as resembling a train station at rush hour. In order to satisfy his own curiosity, Puharich even allowed himself to be operated on.

Arigó agreed to operate on a benign tumor on his elbow. The scene was a crowded room with some ninety people gathered around as spectators. With a flourish, Arigó asked that someone furnish him with a pocket knife; this was produced. Arigó asked Puharich not to watch the operation so Puharich turned his head toward his cameraman who was filming a motion picture. Within a matter of seconds, Arigó placed the tumor and the pocket knife in Puharich's hands.

In spite of being perfectly conscious, Puharich had not experienced any pain or even any sensation at the surgical site. Yet there was a bleeding incision and a tumor. Knowing that the knife was dirty, that his skin was not cleansed and that Arigó's hands were not clean, Puharich suspected that he might get an infection—perhaps even blood poisoning. Nevertheless, the wound healed clean without a drop of pus in three days, according to Puharich, half the time required under normal precautions. [120]

According to Arigó, however, all of this is very simple: "I simply listen to a voice in my right ear and repeat whatever it says. It is always right." Arigó claims that this voice belongs to a deceased German medical student, Adolphus Fritz. However, after five years of observation, Puharich still felt unable to arrive at any conclusion as to the reality of "Dr. Fritz" as an independent spirit.

Arigó has been twice put in jail for the illegal practice of medicine. In 1971, he died of an automobile crash. Nevertheless, other healers continue to be active in Brazil where the spiritualist movement has even established its own hospitals! [121]

The psychic surgeons of the Phillipines are renowned for their ability to operate without knives, removing tissue, yet leaving no wounds. This phenomena has proved extremely controversial and the healers have often been accused of fraud —even by those who have studied them sympathetically. This undoubtedly places the healers in a questionable legal and moral position; however it does not answer the scientific question. Unfortunately, sufficient scientific investigations have not yet been made into this phenomena. Yet, some of the evidence in their favor is very compelling. (See color Plate 9.)

Hundreds of home movies have been taken by Americans who went to the Phillipines with serious, sometimes incurable, ailments and returned fully cured. Medical doctors who have examined these patients before and after their treatment are often baffled. [122]

In 1971, a young American named Doug Voeks, with a B.A. in psychology from the University of Alaska, happened to view one of these movies in the living room of some friends in San Jose, California. What he saw was so inspiring to him that he left the United States to become a student of the Phillipino healers. During a period of several years he lived and studied with the healers, travelling with them on their missions through desert and jungle, evangelizing and preaching in the tiny *Espiritista* chapels. During the missions, Voeks received instruction from spirit voices speaking through mediums. At first he was shown magnetic healing or the "laying on the hands." He was asked to practice this simple form of healing extensively, and told he would become more adept through practice. The *espiritistas* believe that this form of healing is just as effective, although perhaps slower, than the more dramatic psychic surgery.

In fact, in their opinion, the surgical "gift" is simply a temporary tool which is being used by the spirit primarily in order to reach people who need to see phenomena. Often the psychic surgeons will materialize something like a piece of plastic or a tobacco leaf and claim that this was the embodiment of evil thoughts within the patient—which perhaps had been planted there as a result of a psychic attack. (See Plate 9, right-center photograph.) The object did not exist within the person before the operation, yet it often seems that it could not have been produced by sleight of hand either! Voeks who eventually received the gift of performing the surgical operations explains them in the following manner:

It is simply using the power of the source that you have prayed for and asked for, through your hands being a focal point.

When the hands are applied and I begin to knead the skin, I can say that the skin opens because I see it through my own visual process. However, I lose feeling in my hands up to about my elbows. They call this over there about a 10% trance. The hands do not actually go deeply into the body, but rather the afflicted area comes to the hand, as though the hand were a magnet. . . . Individual cells are separated and not severed, so you have no cell damage. The healers hand then acts as a maintaining force to hold the skin apart and bring it together.

In my first operations I was as startled as the people who were watching. . . . I cannot control this. It is something that happens.[123]

After Voeks had learned this skill, he operated on his own grandmother who visited the Phillipines. I have had the opportunity to interview her and she testified to the genuineness and effectiveness of Doug's uncanny powers. According to the custom of most of the Phillipine healers, Voeks charges no fee for his services as a healer. In my personal contact with him he has appeared very aware, alert, and articulate. There is certainly little indication in my mind that he is a fraud. It is his contention that the tools of psychic healing and psychic surgery are just one small part of the larger spiritualist movement in the Phillipines.

Interestingly enough, several Americans who have been to the Phillipines and travelled on missions have now organized a Christian spiritualist church in San Francisco based on the spirit contact which originated for them in the Phillipines. Although they are not allowed to practice psychic surgery in this country, they do engage in other forms of healing when

151

they feel they have the power and when there is a need for it. This group is one of thousands in this country now practicing spiritual healing with a firm belief that it really works.

If after having read this far, you are much more willing to explore the potential for healing which you may possess yourself, you will find the following passages, written more than seventy years ago by Yogi Ramacharaka, of great practical value. Remember that *prana* is the Hindu term for the life energy which permeates the atmosphere, enters the human being through the breath, and can be directed by thought:

Pranic Healing

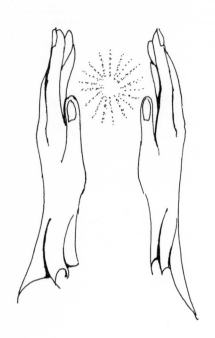

We will first take up a few experiments in Pranic Healing (or "Magnetic Healing," if you prefer the term):

(I)   Let the patient sit in a chair, you standing before him. Let your hands hang loosely by your sides, and then swing them loosely to and fro for a few seconds, until you feel a tingling sensation at the tips of your fingers. Then raise them to the level of the patient's head, and sweep them slowly toward his feet, with your palms toward him with fingers outstretched, as if you were pouring force from your finger tips upon him. Then step back a foot and bring up your hands to the level of his head, being sure that your palms face each other in the upward movement, as, if you bring them up in the same position as you swept them down, you would draw back the magnetism you send toward him. Then repeat several times. In sweeping downward, do not stiffen the muscles, but allow the arms and hands to be loose and relaxed. You may treat the affected parts of the body in a similar way, finishing the treatment by saturating the entire body with magnetism. After treating the affected parts, it will be better for you to flick the fingers away from your sides, as if you were throwing off drops of water which had adhered to your fingers. Otherwise you might absorb some of the patient's conditions. This treatment is very strengthening to the patient, and if frequently practiced will greatly benefit him.

In case of chronic or long seated troubles, the trouble may be "loosened up" by making "sideways" passes before the afflicted part, that is by standing before the patient with your hands together, palms touching, and then swinging the arms out sideways several times. This treatment should always be followed by the downward passes to equalize the circulation.

Self-Healing

(II)   Lying in a relaxed condition, breathe rhythmically, and command that a good supply of prana be inhaled. With the exhalation, send the prana to the affected part for the purpose of stimulating it. Vary this occasionally by exhaling, with the mental command that the diseased condition be forced out and disappear. Use the hands in this exercise, passing them down the body from the head to the affected part. In using the hands in healing yourself or others always hold the mental image that the prana is flowing down the arm and through the finger tips into the body, thus reaching the affected part and healing it. . . .

A little practice of the above exercise, varying it slightly to fit the conditions of the case, will produce wonderful results. Some Yogis follow the plan of placing both hands on the affected part, and then breathing rhythmically, holding the mental image that they are pumping prana into the diseased organ and part, stimulating it and driving out diseased conditions, as pumping into a pail of dirty water will drive out the latter and fill the bucket with fresh water. This last plan is very effective if the mental image of the pump is clearly held, the inhalation representing the lifting of the pump handle and the exhalation the actual pumping.

Healing Others

The main principle to remember is that by rhythmic breathing and controlled thought you are enabled to absorb a considerable amount of prana, and are also able to pass it into the body of another person, stimulating weakened parts and organs, imparting health and driving out diseased conditions. You must first learn to form such a clear mental image of the desired condition that you will be able to actually feel the influx of prana, and the force running down your arms and out of your finger tips into the body of the patient. Breathe rhythmically a few times until the rhythm is fairly established, then place your hands upon the affected part of the body of the patient, letting them rest lightly over the part. Then follow the "pumping" process described in the preceding exercise and fill the patient full of prana until the diseased condition is driven out. Every once in a while raise the hands and "flick" the fingers as if you were throwing off the diseased condition. It is well to do this occasionally and also to wash the hands after treatment, as otherwise you may take on a trace of the diseased condition of the patient. Also practice the Cleansing Breath several times after the treatment. During the treatment let the prana pour into the patient in one continuous stream, allowing yourself to be merely the pumping machinery connecting the patient with the universal supply of prana, and allowing it to flow freely through you. You need not work the hands vigorously, but simply enough that the prana freely reaches the affected parts. The rhythmic breathing must be practiced frequently during the treatment, so as to keep the rhythm normal and to afford the prana a free passage. It is better to place the hands on the bare skin, but where this is not advisable or possible place them over the clothing. Vary above methods occasionally during the treatment by stroking the body gently and softly with the finger tips, the fingers being kept slightly separated. This is very soothing to the patient. In cases of long standing you may find it helpful to give the mental command in words, such as "get out, get out," or "be strong, be strong," as the case may be, the words helping you to exercise the will more forcibly and to the point. Vary these instructions to suit the needs of the case, and use your own judgement and inventive faculty.

(III)   Headaches may be relieved by having the patient sit down in front of you, you standing back of his chair, and passing your hands, fingers down and spread open in double circles over the top of his head, not touching his head, however. After a few seconds you will actually feel the passage of the magnetism from your fingers, and the patient's pain will be soothed.

(IV)   Another good method of removing pain in the body is to stand before the patient, and present your palm to the affected part, at a distance of several inches from the body. Hold the palm steady for a few seconds and then begin a slow rotary motion, round and round, over the seat of the pain. This is quite stimulating and tends to restore normal conditions.

(V)   Point your forefinger toward the affected part a few inches away from the body, and keeping the finger steadily pointed move the hand around just as if you were boring a hole with the point of the finger. This will often start the circulation at the point affected, and bring about improved conditions.

(VI)   Placing the hands on the head of the patient, over the temples and holding them for a time, has a good effect, and is a favorite form of treatment of this kind.

(VII)   Stroking the patient's body (over the clothing) has a tendency to stimulate and equalize the circulation, and to relieve congestion.

(VIII)   Much of the value of Massage and similar forms of manipulative treatment, comes from the Prana which is projected from the healer into the patient, during the process of rubbing and manipulating. If the rubbing and manipulating is accompanied by the conscious desire of the healer to direct the flow of Prana into the patient a greatly increased flow is obtained. If the practice is accompanied with Rhythmic Breathing, the effect is much better.

(IX)   Breathing upon the affected part, is practiced by many races of people, and is often a potent means of conveying Prana to the affected part. This is often performed by placing a bit of cotton cloth between the flesh of the person and the healer, the breath heating up the cloth and adding the stimulation of warmth in addition to the other effects.

(X)   Magnetized water is often employed by "magnetic healers", and many good results are reported to have been obtained in this way. The simplest form of magnetizing water is to hold the glass by the bottom, in the left hand, and then, gathering together the fingers of the right hand, shake them gently over the glass of water just as if you were shaking drops of water into the glass from your fingertips. You may add to the effect afterwards making downward passes over the glass with the right hand, passing the Prana into the water. Rhythmic breathing will assist in the transferring of the Prana into the water. Water thus charged with Prana is stimulating to sick people, or those suffering from weakness, particularly if they sip it slowly holding their mind in a receptive attitude, and if possible forming a mental picture of the Prana from the water being taken up by the system and invigorating them.

Mental Healing

We will now take up a few experiments in the several forms of Mental Healing . . .:

(I)   Auto-suggestion consists in suggesting to oneself the physical conditions one wishes to bring about. The auto-suggestions should be spoken (audibly or silently) just as one would speak to another, earnestly and seriously, letting the mind form a mental picture of the conditions referred to in the words. For instance: *"My stomach is strong, strong, strong–able to digest the food given it–able to assimilate the nourishment from the food–able to give me the nourishment which means health and strength to me. My digestion is good, good, good, and I am enjoying and digesting and assimilating my food, converting it into rich red blood, which is carrying health and strength to all parts of my body, building it up and making me a strong man (or woman)."* Similar auto-suggestions, or affirmations, applied to other parts of the body, will work equally good results, the attention and mind being directed to the parts mentioned causing an increased supply of Prana to be sent there, and the pictured condition to be brought about. Enter into the spirit of the auto-suggestions, and get thoroughly in earnest over them, and so far as possible form the mental image of the healthy condition desired. See yourself as you wish yourself to be. You may help the cure along by treating yourself by the methods described in the experiments on Pranic Healing.

(II)   Suggestions for healing, given to others, operate on the same principle as do the auto-suggestions just described, except that the healer must impress upon the the patient's mind the desired conditions instead of the patient's doing it for himself. Much better results may be obtained where the healer and patient both co-operate in the mental image and when the patient follows the healer's suggestions in his mind, and forms the mental picture implied by the healer's words. The healer suggests that which he wishes to bring about and the patient allows the suggestions to sink into his Instinctive Mind, where they are taken up and afterwards manifested in physical results. . . .

In many cases all that is needed in suggestive treatment, is to relieve the patient's mind of Fear and Worry and depressing thoughts, which have interfered with the proper harmony of the body, and which have prevented the proper amount of Prana from being distributed to the parts. Removing these harmful thoughts is like removing the speck of dust which has caused our watch to run improperly, having disarranged the harmony of the delicate mechanism. . . .

154

(III) In what is called strictly Mental Healing, the patient sits relaxed and allows the mind to become receptive. The healer then projects to the patient thoughts of a strengthening and uplifting character which, reacting upon the mind of the patient, causes it to cast off its negative conditions and to assume its normal poise and power, the result being that as soon as the patient's mind recovers its equilibrium it asserts itself and starts into operation the recuperative power within the organism of the person, sending an increased supply of Prana to all parts of the body and taking the first step toward regaining health and strength.

. . . In treating a patient in this way, keep firmly in your mind the thought that physical harmony is being re-established in the patient, and that health is his normal condition and that all the negative thoughts are being expelled from his mind. Picture him as strong and healthy in mind and in body. Picture as existing all the conditions you wish to establish within him. Then concentrate the mind and fairly *dart* into his body, or into the affected part, a strong penetrating thought, the purpose of which is to work the desired physical change, casting out the abnormal conditions and re-establishing normal conditions and functioning. Form the mental image that the thought is fully and heavily charged with Prana and fairly drive it into the affected part by an effort of the will. Considerable practice is usually needed to accomplish this last result, but to some it appears to come without much effort.

(IV) Distant healing, or "absent treatment," is performed in precisely the same way as is the treatment when the patient is present. . . .

Prana colored by the thought of the sender may be projected to persons at a distance, who are willing to receive it, and healing work done in this way. This is the secret of the "absent healing," of which the Western world has heard so much of late years. The thought of the healer sends forth and colors the prana of the sender, and it flashes across space and finds lodgment in the psychic mechanism of the patient. It is unseen, and it passes through intervening obstacles and seeks the person attuned to receive it. In order to treat persons at a distance, you must form a mental image of them until you can feel yourself to be in rapport with them. This is a psychic process dependent upon the mental imagery of the healer. You can feel the sense of rapport when it is established, it manifesting in a sense of nearness. That is about as plain as we can describe it. It may be acquired by a little practice, and some will get it at the first trial. When rapport is established, say mentally to the distant patient, "I am sending you a supply of vital force or power, which will invigorate you and heal you." Then picture the prana as leaving your mind with each exhalation of rhythmic breath, and traveling across space instantaneously and reaching the patient and healing him. It is not necessary to fix certain hours for treatment, although you may do so if you wish. The respective condition of the patient, as he is expecting and opening himself up to your psychic force, attunes him to receive your vibrations whenever you may send them. If you agree upon hours, let him place himself in a relaxed attitude and receptive condition. . . .

Some healers form the picture of the patient sitting in front of them, and then proceed to give the treatment, just as if the patient were really present. Others form the mental image of projecting the thought, picturing it as leaving their mind, and then traversing space entering the mind of the patient. Others merely sit in a passive, contemplative attitude and intently *think* of the patient, without regard to intervening space. Others prefer to have a handkerchief, or some other article belonging to the patient, in order to render more perfect the *rapport* conditions. Any, or all, of these methods are good, the temperament and inclinations of the person causing him to prefer some particular method. But the same principle underlies them all.

A little practice along the lines of the several forms of healing just mentioned, will give the student confidence, and ease in operating the healing power, until he will often radiate healing power without being fully conscious of it. If much healing work is done, and the heart of the healer is in his work, he soon gets so that he heals almost automatically and involuntarily when he comes into the presence of one who is suffering. The healer must, however, guard against depleting himself of Prana, and thus injuring his own health. He should study . . . methods . . . of recharging himself, and protecting himself against undue drains upon his vitality. And he should make haste slowly in these matters, remembering that forced growth is not desirable.

This lesson has not been written to advise our students to become healers. They must use their own judgment and intuitions regarding that question. . . .

For ourselves, we cling to the principles of "Hatha Yoga," which teaches the doctrine of preserving health by right living and right thinking, and we regard all forms of healing as things made necessary only by Man's ignorance and disobedience of Natural laws. But so long as man will not live and think properly, some forms of healing are necessary, and therefore the importance of their study.[124,125]

Recharging Yourself

If you feel that your vital energy is at a low ebb, and that you need to store up a new supply quickly, the best plan is to place the feet close together (side by side, of course) and to lock the fingers of both hands in any way that seems the most comfortable. This closes the circuit, as it were, and prevents any escape of prana through the extremities. Then breathe rhythmically a few times, and you will feel the effect of the recharging.[126]

Firewalking

The photographs on plate ten were taken at firewalking rituals on the island of Taiwan. The upper two pictures show individuals walking in formation over a bed of red-hot coals (although you cannot see the glow in the sunlight) carrying shrines with images of the Taoist gods. The other three pictures come from a ceremony where the coals were piled over a foot high. Witnesses stated that at this event, the firewalkers were up to their ankles in hot coals! While I was unable to obtain photos of the firewalkers actually in the coals here, such pictures have been published in a Taiwan magazine, *Echo*.[127] Extensive chanting and ritual preparation preceeded the actual firewalking.

Without any such preparation, I myself had the opportunity to participate in a firewalking ritual with a group of Kailas Shugendo Buddhists in San Francisco under the direction of Dr. Ajari Warwick. The religious practices of these individuals include daily fire rituals of several kinds, maintaining an ambulance rescue service (pulling people out of plane wrecks and fires), as well as mountain climbing—and country-western music. Unlike many "spiritual groups," the Kailas Shugendo people make no effort to proselytize. In fact, they actually discourage would-be converts. They are extremely disciplined, yet they possess an overflowing humor. It was in one such peak of gaiety that Ajari invited me to come to a ritual with my camera and tape-recorder. I regarded the invitation as an honor because I knew that the group was very cautious about allowing the public to treat the practices as a circus sideshow. I didn't expect to attend, as I was without transportation at the time and the ceremony took place on a remote beach. I put the idea out of my head. However, by a *coincidence*, a friend with a car appeared at 7:30 a.m. on the appointed day—and off we went.

The ceremony was modest. Simply a six foot pit of flaming logs which we walked over dozens of times, quite briskly, generally stepping once with each foot. The flames rose up and singed the hair on my legs, although I felt no pain and suffered no burns. I had complete confidence in Ajari who asked that I follow him across the pit. Microphone in hand I recorded my impressions on tape as we went over the flames. I must admit that I actually felt protected in some way. It was a totally uplifting experience. Later on, some psychic readers mentioned that I was surrounded by a white light. Perhaps they noticed my silly smile.

Actually the phenomena of handling or footing hot coals provides a very tricky problem for logical analysis. The first experimental tests of firewalking were conducted by the University of London Council for Psychical Investigation in 1935 under the direction of Harry Price. In his initial report Price discussed several sessions which were held with the Indian fakir, Kuda Bux, who also performed acts of blindfolded clairvoyance of questionable authenticity. According to Price, the blindfolds always allowed a line of vision along the side of the nose. His firewalking was more impressive. In nearly a year of advertising for firewalkers with which to conduct experiments, Kuda Bux was the only individual to step forward.

Firewalk ritual with Ajari Warwick of Kailas Shugendo in San Francisco.

Microphone in hand, the author follows Ajari over the flames. "It doesn't hurt."

157

Kuda Bux firewalking.

Before a large audience of newsmen and scientists, he demonstrated that he could walk barefoot across a twelve foot pit of burning coals. During one demonstration, it was a windy day and the surface temperature of the fire was measured at 806° Fahrenheit, while the body of the fire was 2552° F.—hot enough to melt steel. Kuda Bux took four steps across the pit and suffered no burns. His feet were carefully inspected both before and after his performance. There was no possibility that he could have used chemicals of any sort to protect himself. The entire event was also recorded on film.

Kuda Bux claimed that he could convey an immunity to other individuals who followed him across the coals. Unfortunately, this was not the case during the first set of experiments. All other individuals who followed him over the coals suffered minor burns.

Human flesh scorches more easily than cotton fabric, and experiments with a wooden shoe covered with calico indicated scorching in less than a second when placed on the hot embers. However, the scientists noticed that no portion of the skin was in contact with the hot embers for as long as half a second. Perhaps, they thought, the art of firewalking merely involved the skill of stepping quickly and properly.[128]

A second series of experiments seemed to confirm this opinion. This time the firewalker was another fakir from India, Ahmed Hussain. He showed approximately the same ability as did Kuda Bux. Interestingly enough, the temperature of his feet was found to be 10° F. *lower* after the firewalk than before, indicating a certain amount of autonomic physiological regulation. However, when the length of the trench was increased to twenty feet, Hussain also suffered burns. Furthermore, several amateurs now found that they could walk across the twelve foot fire-trench without suffering burns. These tests led Price to conclude:

> . . . any person with the requisite determination, confidence, and steadiness, can walk unharmed over a fire as hot as 800° Centigrade. The experiments proved once and for all that no occult or psychic power, or a specially induced mental state, is necessary in a firewalker.[129]

Price's conclusion is supported by the measurements of feet movement. In normal walking, it was found that the time from the contact of the heel with the floor until the big toe left the floor was 0.65 second. For only 0.05 second was the entire sole of the foot in contact with the floor. During the brisk firewalk contact was even less. Price's argument entirely depends upon this brief contact time.

The literature on fire-handling is much more difficult to deal with. Careful measurements such as Price's have not been made, but the observations seem to mitigate against a simple physical interpretation. The following description of a fire-test with the nineteenth century medium, D. D. Home, was written by Lord Adare who later became the Earl of Dunraven:

> He went to the fire, poked up the coals, and putting his hand in, drew out a hot burning ember, about twice the size of an orange; this he carried about the room, as if to show it to the spirits, and then

158

brought it back to us; we all examined it. He then put it back in the fire and showed us his hands; they were not in the least blackened or scorched, neither did they smell of fire, but on the contrary of a sweet scent which he threw off from his fingers at us across the table. Having apparently spoken to some spirit, he went back to the fire, and with his hand stirred the embers into a flame; then kneeling down, he placed his face right among the burning coals, moving it about as though bathing it in water. Then, getting up, he held his finger for some time in the flame of a candle. Presently, he took the same lump of coal he had previously handled and came over to us, blowing upon it to make it brighter. He then walked slowly around the table, and said, "I want to see which of you will be the best subject. Ah! Adare will be the easiest . . ." Mr. Jencken held out his hand saying, "Put it in mine." Home said, "No, no, touch it and see." He touched it with the tip of his finger and burnt himself. Home then held it within four or five inches of Mr. Saal's and Mr. Hurt's hands, and they could not endure the heat. He came to me and said, "Now if you are not afraid, hold out your hand;" I did so, and having made two rapid passes over my hand, he placed the coal in it. I must have held it for half a minute, long enough to have burned my hands fearfully; the coal felt scarcely warm. Home then took it away, laughed, and seemed much pleased. As he was going back to the fireplace he suddenly turned round and said, "Why, just fancy, some of them think that only one side of the ember was hot." He told me to make a hollow of both of my hands; I did so, and he placed the coal in them, and then put both his on the top of the coal, so that it was completely covered by our four hands, and we held it there for some time. Upon this occasion scarcely any heat at all could be perceived.[130]

Sir William Crookes also describes a fire-handling incident with Home. Crookes states that he tested, in his laboratory, a fine cambric handkerchief that the medium had folded around a piece of red charcoal, then fanned to white heat with his breath without damaging the handkerchief. Crookes concluded that the cloth "had not undergone the slightest chemical preparation which could have rendered it fire-proof."[131]

More recently, a similar fire-test was performed by Jack Schwarz, of Selma, Oregon, before physicians of the Los Angeles County medical and hypnosis associations. After having been examined by the doctors, Schwarz put his hands into a large brazier of burning coals, picked some up, and carried them around the room. Subsequent examination showed no burns or other signs of heat on his hands.[132]

A number of observations of similar fire-handling among the "saints" of the Free Pentacostal Holiness Church are reported by Dr. Berthold E. Schwarz. Members of this church, in states of religious ecstacy are well-known for handling poisonous snakes, swallowing strychnine, and handling fire. Schwarz witnessed the following incident:

Once this saint, when in a relatively calm mood, turned to a coal fire of an hour's duration, picked up a flaming "stone-coal" the size of a hen's egg and held it in the palms of his hands for 65 seconds while he walked among the congregation. As a control, the author could not touch a piece of burning charcoal for less than one second without developing a painful blister.[133]

Apparently the saint's immunity is related to their trance state. Schwarz describes another incident in which a "brother" was applying a coal oil torch to the palm of his hand for several seconds with complete immunity. However, when he noticed that

159

a piece of the wick was breaking off, he woke up from his trance and subsequently suffered a blistering burn.

In so far as these reports cannot be explained on the basis of Price's theory of deft and speedy handling, science has yet to arrive at an adequate explanation of the fire-tests. One hint of a theory comes from the notion of Professor Clark Maxwell's Sorting Demons—tiny little beings who can stop, strike, push or pull atoms and molecules in such a fashion as to insure that there would always be a layer of cool, fresh molecules between the skin and the frenzied, spinning, energetic molecules at redheat. If the answer is to be found on the molecular of atomic levels, further investigation of the phenomena of fire-handling will certainly expand our knowledge of bio-physics.

Psychokinesis

In 1934, several months prior to publishing his famous paper on *Extra-Sensory Perception*, Dr. J. B. Rhine received a visit from a young student with a penchant for gambling. After comparing notes on conditions for success in psychic testing, he remarked that similar conditions seemed to favor his luck in gambling. Furthermore, he claimed that he himself was sometimes able to exercise a mind over matter effect on dice-throwing games. While belief in such an influence on dice was both common and ancient, until then it had not been deemed a serious problem for scientific study. Rhine discovered that preliminary experimentation would be quick, easy, and inexpensive. The results proved encouraging enough to warrant further research.

Experiments continued during the next decade using protocols that systematically eliminated bias from unbalanced dice. The dice were placed in special cups, so that subjects could not use special tricks to throw them. Still later, the dice were placed in electrically-driven rotating cages and were also photographed automatically in order to eliminate experimenter error. In general, the tests entailed asking the subjects to will the fall of the dice with selected target faces showing. Numerous throws were made in succession for each target before another target was chosen.

By the end of 1941, a total of 651,216 experimental die throws had been conducted. The combined results of these experiments pointed to a phenomena with 10^{115} to 1 odds against chance occurrence. Nevertheless, Rhine hesitated to publish his results. The scientific world was still reacting emotionally to his announced proof of ESP, and he felt no need then to raise eyebrows by announcing another unorthodox discovery.[134]

In 1942, with most of the staff at the Parapsychology Laboratory called away to war, continued experimentation in PK proved difficult. At this time, Rhine went over the records of the earlier experiments which had been so conducted that an analysis of position effects could be made, similar to the decline of high ESP scoring toward the end of experimental sessions, which had been detected a few months earlier. If the above chance results had been caused by probability, artifacts, or illegitimate means, one would expect that the distribution of hits would be consistent throughout the experiment and would not decline.

The results of this survey indicated that there were more hits near the beginning of each run of 24 die throws. There were also more hits during the earlier runs of each experimental session which would typically last for ten runs. These results were not expected or even considered by the experimenters and subjects at the time of the experiments. The odds against such distribution occurring by chance were about a hundred million to one. This evidence of a presumably psychological effect, similar to that noted with ESP, made a case for psychokinesis strong enough to warrant publication. The first of the papers appeared in the *Journal of Parapsychology* in 1943.[135] Many others followed.

Dr. J. B. Rhine conducting a PK experiment using dice in a mechanical dice tumbler. (Courtesy Foundation for Research on the Nature of man.)

Actual photograph of livery stable in Central City, Colorado.

Ted Serios thoughtograph of livery stable (Courtesy Dr. Jule Eisenbud.)

In 1946 a study was published which pitted the psychokinetic skills of veteran gamblers against those of divinity students.[136] In this contest atmosphere, both groups scored well above chance expectations. Other experiments began to use more sophisticated instruments such as delicate pendulum systems and measurements of plant growth rate, as well as polygraphs connected to living plant and animal tissues.

One interesting technique for measuring psychokinesis is thought-photography. Claims of spirit photographs, where extra faces appear on developed film go back as far as the history of photography itself. Some have even claimed to photograph actual human thoughtforms. Photography of this sort almost inevitably provoked accusations of fraud, which were difficult to disprove. In 1910, Dr. Tomokichi Fukurai, a professor of literature at the Imperial University of Tokyo conducted a series of experiments in thoughtography. The publication of his findings aroused such hostility among Japanese scientists that he was forced to resign his position. He then continued his work at a Buddhist university which was associated with a temple of the esoteric Shingon sect of Buddhism on top of Mt. Koya.[137] His works were translated into English in 1931 in a book titled *Spirit and Mysterious World*. Although it showed a carefully planned scientific investigation, even the parapsychologists of the time were not ready to deal with this type of data, embedded as it was in Buddhist philosophy.[138]

It was not until the late 1950's that a claim for psychic photography was taken seriously by researchers. The special gift for creating these photographs was discovered in Ted Serios, a Chicago bellhop who had little formal education. The phenomena began when Serios allowed a friend to hypnotize him just to pass away the time. Serios claimed to be able to describe the locations of buried treasure. The friend then suggested that he concentrate on making photographs of the locations when he pointed a camera at a blank wall and triggered the shutter. They did not find buried treasure, but to their amazement, actual images appeared on the Polaroid prints of things that were not visible in the room.

The phenomena came to the attention of members of the Illinois Society for Psychic Research who eventually persuaded a Denver psychiatrist, Dr. Jule Eisenbud, to observe one of Ted's demonstrations. After a long string of failures, Serios managed to produce a striking success for Eisenbud, who, although he had engaged in previous parapsychological research, was unprepared for phenomena of this sort. After a sleepless night, he invited Serios to Denver for further study. Eisenbud spent two years conducting well-controlled studies with Serios. He was quite aware of the history of fraud and gullibility in research of this sort and took every precaution to guard against it. His book, *The World of Ted Serios*, published in 1966, contains the results from his detailed examinations.

The way in which Ted's mind actually shapes the pictures is sometimes quite remarkable. In one session, in front of several witnesses, Ted first tried to reproduce images of the medieval town of Rothenburg. Then the experimenters asked him to try and reproduce an image of the old Opera House in Central City,

Colorado. Serios agreed, and then asked the experimenters if they would like a composite of both images. The results are extraordinary. The photograph shows a striking resemblance to the livery stable across from the old Opera House. However, instead of the brick masonry, the image shows a kind of imbedded rock characteristic of the buildings in the medieval town!

The photograph shown on color Plate 15 is an enlargement of a Polaroid "thoughtograph" of the Denver Hilton Hotel. Eisenbud held the camera, which was pointed at Serios' forehead. Ted, at the time, was trying to produce an image of the Chicago Hilton ("I missed, damn it.") Eisenbud points out that this image could only have been made with a lens different from that of the Polaroid 100, from an angle well up in the air, between the tree tops. This suggests that the thoughtographs are associated with out-of-body or traveling clairvoyance states.

That the range of such vision can extend great distances is implied in the photograph of a Russian Vostok rocket. A diligent search through the worldwide photographic literature failed to reveal any existing photographic counterpart.

Eisenbud's book is noted for detailed observation, but even more remarkable is the penetrating study of this anomalous phenomena and the reaction to it of scientists and educators. To Eisenbud, the photographic manifestations seemed to follow a pattern which pointed to the active operation of the animistic powers known to ancient man.

> As to building blocks for a theoretical structure that might bridge the gulf on other fronts between the mental and physical, . . . I can't think of a better place to begin than right where Ted is (and hopefully where others like him will be). For in a study of images and imagery of this sort-and in phenomenon like dreams, hallucinations, and apparitions, which prove no less remarkable and even more familiar than Ted's images—we are confronted by various organized entities with one leg in the world of reality and one leg in that extraordinary world we ordinarily term appearance.[139]

While truly adequate understanding of the Serios phenomena can only be obtained through detailed study of the experimental reports, the case presents general features which should be readily recognizable in the context other evidence in this book provides.

During the following years, studies were also conducted by researchers at the division of parapsychology of the University of Virginia Medical School. These researchers failed to detect any signs of fraud in their cooperative subject and they successfully obtained numerous striking photographs. While they were calling for further study of this puzzling phenomena, Serios' abilities began to fade and he has remained less active for the past six years.[140]

Meanwhile, in the Soviet Union, researchers claimed to have discovered a woman, Nina Kulagina, who could exert a psychokinetic influence upon static objects. In 1968, Western researchers attending a conference in Moscow were shown a film of her in action. This film, which has since been seen many times in the United States, shows Kulagina apparently moving

Nina Kulagina
(*Courtesy* Psychic Magazine.)

163

Genady Sergeyev
(Courtesy Dr. Milan Ryzl.)

small objects, without touching them, across a table top. The Soviets claimed that this woman also known as Nelya Mikhailova had been studied by some forty scientists, including two Nobel laureates. They also reported that, like Serios, Madame Kulagina was able to cause images to appear on photographic film.[141] The communist scientists, who were by no means inclined to take a spiritualistic world-view, felt that they had encountered a new force in nature.[142] Very thorough studies of the electrical fields around her body as well as the electrical potentials in her brain were conducted by Dr. Genady Sergeyev, a well-known physiologist working in a Leningrad military laboratory. Exceptionally strong voltages and other unusual effects were observed:

There is a large gradient between the electrical characterisitcs in the forward part of Mikhailova's brain versus the back part of the brain (fifty to one), whereas in the average person the gradient is four to one. The usual force field around Mikhailova's body is ten times weaker than the magnetic field of the earth.

During PK, her pulse rises to 240 per minute. There is activation of deeper levels of the occipital lobe and reticular formation. This enhances polarization in the brain between front and back, says Sergeyev. When the gradient between front and back of the brain reaches a certain level, and there is most intense activity in the occipital lobe, radiation of electrostatic and electromagnetic fields are detected by the force field detectors four yards from the body. . . . Heartbeat, brain waves, and force field fluctuations are in ratio. The fields around the PK medium are stronger further away than close to the head. Mikhailova appears to focus these force field waves in a specific area.[143]

Detailed physiological studies of this sort with outstanding psychics are so rare that they raise more questions than they answer. We can be fairly certain at this point, at least, that Kulagina's phenomena are genuine—although she has received a certain amount of adverse publicity. Since 1968, several groups of Western researchers have had opportunities to test her under differing circumstances. In every case, their reports attested to the authenticity of her psychokinetic abilities.[144,145,146,147]

Her mediumship has led to a strain on her health leading to a heart attack, and her doctors have suggested that she limit this type of activity. The Soviets, however, are reported to have found others who have developed talents for psychokinesis, and are also researching ways to train this ability in normal individuals. The training begins with long hours practicing to move the needle of a compass.[148]

A medical assistant named Felicia Perez at the Miamonides hospital in Brooklyn, N.Y. developed her psychokinetic abilities in this way after watching a film of Kulagina. Her talents were observed and photographed by Charles Honorton of the dream laboratory at Miamonides. She has since discontinued doing PK, finding it a great physical strain.[149,150]

Another psychic whose PK abilities were studied by Puthoff and Targ at the Stanford Research Institute is Ingo Swann. The effects which he produced on shielded magnetic instrumentation as well as photographic equipment also seem to have been accompanied by out-of-body experiences.[151,152]

164

The most unusual psychokinetic effects currently being reported by scientists are associated with a young Israeli psychic named Uri Geller. Dr. Andrija Puharich, a physician known for his theoretical efforts to grasp the physics and physiology of psychic phenomena,[153] as well as for his previously mentioned researches into psychic healing, in August of 1971, encountered Geller in Israel, where he arranged to conduct an extensive series of experiments with him. Eventually he brought Uri to the United States where his research continued and where he negotiated for further testing at the Stanford Research Institute in Menlo Park, California. It was at a symposium in Berkeley, sponsored by KPFA-FM at the University of California, that Andrija Puharich made the first public presentation of experimental research with Uri Geller.

Puharich carefully went over his investigations with Geller, indicating the conditions under which he had observed Geller bend and break metal objects, erase magnetic tape, make things disappear and reappear elsewhere, and cause the hands of a clock to change time. He also discussed how his sessions with Geller led him to believe that there was some other intelligent form of energy working through Geller, possibly from an extra-terrestrial or extra-dimensional source.

The following week, the controversy over Geller deepened as *Time* magazine published a story claiming that Geller was a fake. Physicists Harold Puthoff and Russell Targ of Stanford Research Institute also presented a paper about their research with Geller at a physics colloquium at Columbia University.

Always conservative in their approach, the S.R.I. scientists primarily emphasized the telepathic studies they had done with Geller. However, they did report on two significant psychokinetic experiments with Uri.

Andrija Puharich
(*Courtesy* Psychic Magazine)

A precision laboratory balance was placed under a Bell jar. The balance had a one-gram mass placed on its pan before it was covered. A chart recorder then continuously monitored the weight applied to

Uri Geller, a 26-year-old Israeli psychic, is creating considerable controversy with his demonstrations of telepathy, the bending and breaking of metallic objects, and repairing watches by mental energy. The subject of an in-depth interview and report in the July issue of Psychic Magazine.

the pan of the balance. On several occasions Uri caused the balance to respond as though a force were applied to the pan. The displacement represented forces from 1.0 to 1.5 grams. These effects were ten to 100 times larger than could be produced by striking the Bell jar or the table or jumping on the floor. In tests following the experimental run, attempts were made to replicate Geller's results using magnets and static electricity. Controlled runs of day-long operation were obtained. In no case did the researchers obtain artifacts which resembled the signals Geller had produced.[154]

Similarly successful results were obtained in an experiment in which Geller altered a magnetic field as measured by a magnetometer.

After Puharich made his original presentation in Berkeley, it was arranged, with the help of the California Society for Psychical Study, for Geller to come to Berkeley himself to give a public demonstration of his abilities and to be tested by scientists on campus. It was during the weekend of April 13 (Friday) and 14 in Berkeley that Geller began the first of his many brilliant public appearances in the United States. The scientific work with him has been very slow and tedious.

On several occasions, a group of nearly eighteen scientists, organized by myself and Dr. Joel Friedman of the philosophy department at U.C., Davis, met with Geller and observed a wide variety of unusual phenomena in his presence. However, none of them occurred under conditions of sufficient control for us to feel confident about publishing the results. One of our researchers, Saul-Paul Sirag, conducted an experiment with Geller in which Saul-Paul unexpectedly handed Geller a bean sprout and asked him to "make the movie run backwards." Uri closed his fist over the sprout and when he opened his hand some thirty seconds later there was no longer a sprout, but a whole solid mung bean. This effect, if verified by further replication, seems to indicate a psychokinetic influence involving time.

Another study that the Berkeley research group conducted was a follow-up survey of the reactions of individuals who witnessed Geller's performances. Many people reported experiencing unusual visual or telepathic phenomena and several reported that, after watching Geller's demonstrations, they also were able to produce various psychokinetic effects. On occasions when I have broadcast radio interviews with Uri, dozens of listeners have reported psychokinetic phenomena in their own homes.

In England, Geller's impact has been even more phenomenal. At Birkbeck College, physicists Jack Sarfatti, John Halstead and David Bohm observed a number of PK phenomena under well-controlled conditions. Particularly interesting was Geller's ability to alter the decay rate of radioactive isotopes.[155] Perhaps even more remarkable, thousands of individuals in England, France, Germany, Switzerland, Norway, Denmark, Holland and Japan are now reporting that they can also use PK to bend spoons after having only seen Geller on television. Some of these cases are now being studied by the noted mathematician John Taylor at King College, University of

A flower made withered and dry in a few seconds by Uri Geller is shown next to a fresh bloom of the same species. (Courtesy Psychic Magazine.)

Key bent psychokinetically by Geller while held in the hands of researcher Alan Vaughan. (Courtesy Psychic Magazine.)

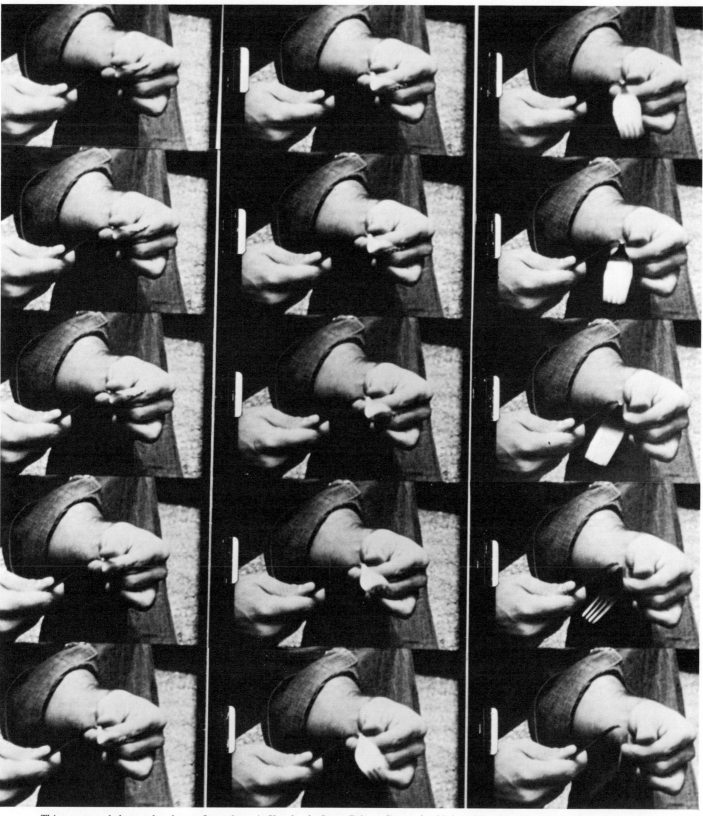

This sequence of photos taken from a Super 8 movie film shot by James Bolen, editor and publisher of Psychic *shows the bending and breaking of a fork in the hands of Uri Geller. The [167] fork, which Bolen personally verified as being intact before the demonstartion, gradually becomes pliable at its mid-section in Geller's hands as he rolls his thumb and index finger over it. The fork finally breaks apart, the prong part falling to the ground. Note how the prong section clings slightly to the handle just before it drops away, suggesting that the stainless steel metal momentarily became plastic-like. (Courtesy* Psychic *Magazine.)*

London, and by the Institute of Borderland Sciences in Freiburg, Germany.[156,157]

In a significant letter published in the April 10, 1975, issue of *Nature,* physicists J. B. Hasted, D. J. Bohm, E. W. Bastin, and B. O'Regan report on the apparent partial dematerialization of a single crystal of vanadium carbide, encapsulated in plastic. The authors claimed that "there is no known way of producing this effect within the closed capsule and no possibility of substitution." The letter stressed the need for scientists to remain open-minded toward paranormal phenomena and to pay attention to psychological variables which can effect experiments. The crystal disappearance was not regarded as conclusive evidence as the authors did not actually observe or measure the change as it occurred. Nevertheless, they claimed to have "significant work in progress."

At a recent conference on The Physics of Paranormal Phenomena held in Tarrytown, New York, it was estimated that psychokinetic metal-bending has been reliably witnessed in at least sixty different people.[158]

Metallurgic analyses have been made of several objects bent or fractured by Geller. In many instances, the results were no different than those of similar objects broken by the scientists as controls. In some instances, fatigue fractures were observed, even though the metal was new (i.e., key blanks) and was bent without the application of known physical stress.

Perhaps the most interesting finding relates to a platinum ring which spontaneously developed a fissure in Geller's presence—although he was not touching it. This ring was analyzed by physicist Wilbur Franklin with a scanning electron microscope. The remarkable finding was that adjacent areas of the ring indicated totally different conditions resembling (1) fracture at a very low temperature, such as with liquid nitrogen, (2) distortion as if by a mechanical shear, and (3) melting at a very high temperature. Although the ring was fractured at room temperature, conditions (1) and (3) were observed at locations only one hundredth of an inch apart. Franklin points out that there is no known method to duplicate such findings at room temperature—and extremely difficult to fabricate even by known laboratory techniques.[159]

An altogether different line of PK investigation has been poltergeist research. The word poltergeist is German and means a noisy and rattling spirit. Modern investigators however view the poltergeist as a spontaneous, unconscious, recurring psychokinetic phenomena centering around a person, usually an adolescent simmering with repressed feelings of anger. Unable to vent these feelings in a normal fashion, they manifest through psychic means.

W. G. Roll, of the Psychical Research Foundation in Durham, North Carolina, is the formost American researcher of poltergeist phenomena. The case of his which at this writing was most thoroughly investigated occurred in a warehouse in Miami which was full of glasses, ashtrays, plates and other novelties. The disturbance, which involved more than 200 incidences, took place in January 1967. Police officers,

Broken glass from Miami Poltergeist. (Courtesy Psychical Research Foundation.)

insurance agents, a magician and others were unable to explain the mystery. Roll describes his approach:

> It soon became clear that the incidents were concentrated around one employee, Julio, a nineteen-year-old shipping clerk. Certain areas of the large warehouse room where the disturbances took place were more frequently affected than others and these became the focus of the investigation. The investigators designated certain parts as target areas and placed objects in them hoping that the objects would be affected while Julio and the other employees were under observation.[160]

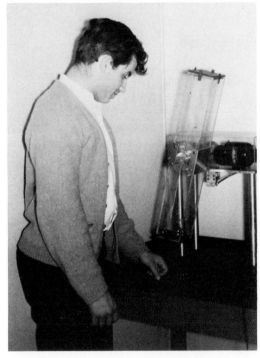

Julio being tested for PK. (Courtesy Psychical Research Foundation.)

In several cases this is precisely what did happen. Julio was brought to Durham, N.C. for further testing which revealed his strong feelings of hostility, especially towards parental figures, which he could not express openly and from which he felt personally detached. PK tests with a dice-throwing machine produced suggestive results with Julio. In addition there was a poltergeist disturbance of a vase in a hallway in the laboratory while Julio was standing with the parapsychologists several feet away. Within recent times there have been about thirty well-documented poltergeist cases.[161]

Perhaps the most intriguing "poltergeist person" to be studied so far is Matthew Manning, who since 1966, at the age of eleven, has been the center of various psychokinetic outbreaks. Dr. A. R. G. Owen, former Cambridge mathematician and geneticist, who authored perhaps the most comprehensive book on poltergeists, claims that Manning "is probably the most gifted psychic in the western world."[162]

In addition to typical psychokinetic outbreaks, Matthew has shown an apparent ability to communicate with spirits via automatic writing and drawing. Although his schoolmaster claims he has never shown any particular drawing talent, he is able to reproduce—without any apparent effort or concentration—detailed and precise works of art in the style of deceased masters such as Dürer, Picasso, Beardsley, and Matisse. Automatic writing has often been produced in many languages with which Manning is unfamiliar. Often verified information, and even psychic diagnoses, come through in this way. Thus the phenomena contain the kinds of evidence which we might really associate with spirit phenomena.[163,164]

Particularly since the public demonstrations of Uri Geller, Manning has exhibited intentional psychokinetic effects amenable to scientific testing. When tested by Nobel laureate physicist Brian Josephson in Cavandish Laboratory at Cambridge University, Matthew demonstrated an unusual spinning effect over a compass needle. Ironically, when further instrumentation was used to record magnetic changes in the vicinity of the compass, the needle of the compass would only remain stationary. Nevertheless, the instruments did detect magnetic changes. Josephson maintains that until further data is collected, his results will still have to be labelled "inconclusive."[165,166]

In other tests, conducted at the New Horizons Research Foundation in Toronto, Manning was able to demonstrate metal-bending, on demand, which was actually recorded on motion picture film. Several tests were conducted which recorded physiological measures such as muscle tension and brain waves during psychokinetic activity.[167]

No unusual muscular activity was noted. However, rather profound changes were seen in the electrical activity of the brain which have been described by Dr. Joel Whitton as a *ramp function* (actually a rather pictorial description of the chart printout). The ramp functions appeared similar to the EEG patterns in a patient suffering from an overdose of a hallucinatory drug and is suspected to stem from the older and deeper areas of the brain.[168]

These findings led the Toronto scientists to speculate on neurophysiological-parapsychological interrelationships. Dr. Whitten conducted a small-scale investigation with a number of known psychics to determine if they had any common childhood experiences. The answer was quite fascinating—for the one experience which all of the psychics had suffered in common was a severe electric shock before the age of ten. Although Matthew Manning did not recall such an incident, his mother informed the scientists that she had been so severely shocked three weeks before Matthew was born that she was afraid she would lose him.[165]

This line of research seems to have enormous implications for parapsychology. Perhaps the increasing number of children who can now demonstrate PK is associated with the greater number of electronic gadgets in modern homes—with the correspondingly increased probability of electric shocks. However, even if further inquiry in this direction proves revealing, it will still fail to account for another type of poltergeist case also documented by the Toronto group.

One most exciting PK case of the poltergeist variety actually did not involve a real ghost, or an individual, but rather an imaginary spirit named Phillip. This unusual situation developed in Toronto as a group of members of the local Society for Psychical Research decided to meet regularly in the effort to conjure an apparition they created. They invented the character of Phillip, an aristocratic Englishman who died of a tragic remorse during the seventeenth century. Every week for an entire year the group met for meditation, concentrating on Phillip's story, in an attempt to manifest an apparition.

There was no success, but in the summer of 1973 they learned about similar efforts which had been made in England since 1964 by Batcheldor, Brookes-Smith, and Hunt. The British approach had been directed toward producing the physical phenomena of the old type séances of the Victorian era. Instead of quiet meditation, they created an atmosphere of jollity, together with singing songs, telling jokes, and exhortations to the table to obey the sitter's commands. Consequently, the Toronto group decided to take this approach.

Extraordinary things began to happen: the table began to produce raps which became louder and more obvious as time went on. Using one rap for yes and two for no, the table was actually able to answer questions and recreate the personality of Phillip! Occasionally, however, the answers were out-of-character for Phillip.

The "Phillip" table tilting while everyone's hands are in light contact with the top. (Courtesy Robin E. Owen, New Horizons Foundation.)

These raps occurred in a fair amount of light, with all the participants' hands in view on the table. The thickly carpeted floor generally prevented foot-tapping. At least four members, of the original group of eight, were necessary to produce this phenomena. However no single person was found to be essential. Eventually the table began to move around the room at great speed with no one touching it. On one occasion, the table completely flipped over.

These phenomena are still continuing and are now being duplicated by other groups who are learning how to unlock their own hidden PK abilities. All efforts at investigation have so far been unable to detect fraud and a two-hour film has even been made documenting these occurrences.[169,170]

This imaginary communicator, created by a group consciousness, seems to suggest that other alleged spirits, ghosts, entities, and perhaps even flying saucers also originate from within us.

The "Phillip Group" from left to right Iris M. Owen, Sid Korman, Bernice Mandryk, Al Peacock, Margaret Sparrow, Dorothy O'Donnell, Andy Henwood, Lorne Henwood. (Courtesy Robin E. Owen, New Horizons Foundation.)

On several occasions the Philip group has been able to produce psychokinetic phenomena for live television audiences in Toronto. Indications were, in fact, that the large audience aided in the production of more dramatic phenomena. Recent reports state that there are now two other groups within the Toronto Society for Physical Research which are also able to produce spirit-like psychokinetic phenomena.

One of these, the "Lillith group" has concocted a fictitious ghost story as the focus of their concentration. Like the Philip story, it has all the proper dramatic elements of romance and tragedy. Learning from the Philip group, the Lillith group was able to enter into the jovial atmosphere conducive to phenomena without spending time on meditations or visualizations. The phenomena they produced have been quite striking, including table levitations said to be more impressive than those caused by the original group. The Lillith group is now attempting to produce voices on magnetic recording tape. Preliminary results are encouraging.

During the annual Christmas party of the Toronto SPR, a large group of individuals were able to spontaneously develop psychokinetic table-rapping. Somebody asked the "spirit" if it were Santa Claus and from then on the responses continued as if it were old Saint Nick himself rapping. Since then a third Toronto group has developed psychokinetic table-rapping, this time ostensibly coming from Dicken's Artful Dodger.[171]
Since the metal-bending demonstrations of Uri Geller and Matthew Manning in Toronto, the Philip group has also shown some success in this direction. In one instance, a metal medallion, which was partially bent during the group session, continued to bend after the group departed until it completely crumpled.

Perhaps the most significant development in the Philip story is the qualitative acoustic measurement of psychokinetic table-rapping. Normal raps on the table used in the Philip session produced a sound which typically lasted for about half a second. On the other hand, many of the raps produced by Philip were shown to last only 0.16 sec. This was true in spite of the similarities in loudness and frequency of the raps.[172]

Further research along these lines will provide a clearer notion of how the paranormal sounds are produced. Although, it would seem likely that once a clear understanding of the phenomena is gained—the quality of the raps themselves will change.

The most successful paradigm of PK experiments have used the high-speed random number generators designed by Helmut Schmidt. [These have already been mentioned in detail in the chapter on ESP.] One such series of experiments used an electronic generator which could produce binary numbers (+1 and −1). The generated numbers were displayed to the subjects acoustically by presenting clicks to the right and left ears through headphones. The subjects were instructed to obtain an increased frequency of clicks in the target ear. A visual display was also given by the ink pen of a paper chart recorder. At the beginning of the test, the pen was in the center of the chart. During the test run, the deflection of the pen to the right or left was controlled by the difference between the numbers of +1's and −1's generated thus far. The subjects tried mentally to deflect the pen in the target direction. Tests were run with both displays at speeds of 30 and 300 numbers generated per second. Under all four of those conditions, statistically significant results were obtained.[173] The following charts give the results of the experiment.

Test Results for the Individual Subjects Under the Four Different Test Conditions

Display Speed	Subject No.	Random Events	Deviation	Rate (%)
Visual Slow	1	12,000	199	51.7
	2	3,000	68	52.3
	3	5,000	106	52.1
Auditory Slow	4	10,000	89	50.9
	5	5,000	132	52.6
	6	5,000	55	51.1
Visual Fast	1	100,000	218	50.22
	2	60,000	381	50.64
	3	40,000	116	50.29
Auditory Fast	4	50,000	222	50.44
	7	50,000	191	50.38
	8	60,000	299	50.50
	9	30,000	97	50.32
	10	10,000	−35	49.65

Total Results Under Four Different Conditions

Display Speed	Random Events	Deviation	Rate (%)	Critical Ratio
Visual Slow	20,000	373	51.9	5.28
Auditory Slow	20,000	276	51.4	3.90
Slow Total	40,000	649	51.6	6.49
Visual Fast	200,000	715	50.36	3.20
Auditory Fast	200,000	774	50.39	3.46
Fast Total	400,000	1489	50.37	4.71

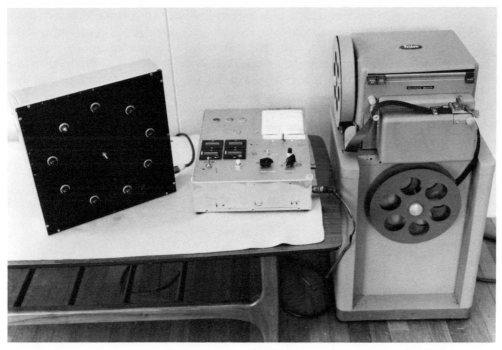

PK test equipment. (Courtesy Dr. Helmut Schmidt.)

The *critical ratio* is a term meaning the number of *standard deviations* the experimental results diverge from the expected statistical mean. The probability that a critical ratio will be greater than 3.00 is less than three times in a thousand. The CR value will only be greater than 4.00 in fewer than seven out of 100,000 trials. And the probability that a critical ratio will be greater than 5.00, as it is in this experiment, is less than .0000003.

This means that the results of Schmidt's experiment could have been obtained by chance less than three out of every ten million times. However, when the probability falls this low and the results are consistent, it is safe to assume that there may be another force involved. Furthermore, randomness tests in the absence of human subjects were conducted with the generator for ten successive nights before, during, and after the experiments. In these tests, the results accorded with chance expectation.

The subjects used in these experiments were not extraordinary individuals like Serios, Manning or Geller. They were selected for moderate PK ability in some informal pretests, and their momentary ability was frequently rechecked in warmup runs before the official experimental tests. In order to minimize the "decline effect" experimental runs were kept to a duration of three seconds each, with breaks of five to forty seconds between runs. A single experimental session would usually contain between ten and forty runs. An effort was made to use each subject only in test conditions which personally appealed to that person. This type of experiment has been replicated several times with both animal and human subjects.[174]

We are still a long way from understanding the actual mechanism through which PK operates. All present data indicates

173

the mind operates beyond what we normally consider the boundaries of the body to be—the skin. Rhine, and Myers before him, have suggested that the mechanism by which the mind is able to operate the body itself is psychokinetic in nature and that PK events outside the body comprise a natural extension of this process. A scientific theory of psychokinesis is developing from the current efforts of physicists to grapple with the influence consciousness exerts upon sub-atomic interactions—a quest similar in spirit to that of the creation hymn quoted in the introduction of this book.

Life Within Death—Death Within Life

Whether or not we come to any conclusion at all about ghosts, spirits, reincarnation, or any other form of survival after death is actually less important than our willingness to look closely at the evidence for these phenomena. For the great by-product of the search for the life beyond is an extraordinary enrichment of our understanding of the life within.

In my first draft of this chapter, as I was writing about this topic, I found it difficult in my excitement to keep from floating off into romantic speculation about the great beyond. The feeling was something like looking at a mountain peak in the distance, being stimulated by the excitement of its beauty and majesty, just by knowing it is there. What *The Roots of Consciousness* is about (I had to remind myself) is the existence of a continuous path between being here in my life and being there. It's something like the space between sleeping and waking. Moving from one to the other is really a gradual process. Each step takes us to the next. Living and dying, breathing, sleeping, dreaming, being, communicating—our consciousness touches all of these worlds.

The evidence for life beyond death comes from several sources. There are cases of hauntings and apparitions, mediumistic communications and automatic writings, possessions, incidences of child prodigies, and reincarnation data. A large amount of this evidence was gathered during the heyday of spiritualism in the nineteenth century, and is recorded in *The Human Personality and It's Survival of Bodily Death* by F. W. H. Myers. Modern research places a much greater emphasis on laboratory studies which implies a different approach to the evidence.

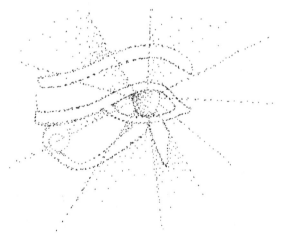

Apparitions and Hauntings

Apparitions and personal experiences of seeing the dead still occur and there is a great need for people to feel comfortable discussing them openly. The following article appeared with a front-page headline in the *Berkeley Gazette* on March 19, 1974. The reason for the headline was not that this experience with a phantom was unusual; but rather that it was uncommon—and commendable—for a person of professional standing in the community to speak so directly about his experiences.

A haunting at the faculty club

By RICHARD RAMELLA

I-G Staff Writer

Dr. Noriyuki Tokuda did not believe in ghosts until he encountered some recently in his room at the Faculty Club on the University of California campus here.

The visiting Japanese scholar, described by a local friend as "an intelligent, rational man," had no pat explanation to give for what he saw the evening of March 9.

In a half-somnolent state, he recalls, he saw a "very gentlemanly" looking Caucasian man, sitting on a chair and peering at him. As Dr. Tokuda shook out of his sleep, he next saw "something like two heads, floating, flying high across the room."

A moment later the apparitions had vanished.

LATER, WHEN Dr. Tokuda told club personnel about his unsettling experience, they told him the room in which he was staying had been occupied for 36 years by a University of California professor who died two years and a week before Tokuda checked into the room.

Officials described the professor. To Tokuda, there seemed to be a resemblance.

Tokuda says he, his wife and children lived in Berkeley from 1967 to 1969. "I love Berkeley very much." Given this feeling, he discounts any possibility of his vision being engendered by being in a strange place.

HE RECALLS what happened:

"On March 9 I flew to Berkeley from Boston. Prof. Chalmers Johnson of the political science department took me from the airport to the faculty club. He advised me to take a short nap because of the three hour gap in time. I was tired, so I took a nap."

"At 7 p.m., while sleeping, I had a funny impression—felt some kind of psychological pressure. I was almost awake. I saw something in my dream. I felt some old gentleman—Western, white—sitting on the chair by the bed, watching quietly. It was quite strange.

"I opened my eyes then and saw a funny picture—two heads with a body passing out of my sight and disappearing."

WITH THAT Dr Tokuda opened his eyes very wide and saw nothing strange. "I was surprised. Maybe it was a dream or a fantasy. I went out to dinner, came back and slept. I wasn't visited again."

After a trip to Stanford, Dr. Tokuda returned to the faculty club. By then he had told his strange story to his friends, Prof. Chalmers Johnson and his wife Sheila. They insured that he did not get Room 19 during the second stay.

When Tokuda checked out of the club yesterday, an official there told him his former room had for 36 years been the home of a solitary professor who died (not in the room) in March 1971.

"YOU'RE KIDDING me. Don't scare me," Tokuda responded.

"I cannot believe in ghosts," says Tokuda, a political scientist specializing in modern China.

But still, he smiled and said: "I think perhaps Prof. X still likes to live there and doesn't want to leave."

Tokuda, 42, is senior researcher and chairman of East Asian studies at the Institute of Developing Countries in Tokyo. He teaches at Keio University in Japan's capital.

"We have lots of ghost stories in Japan, too," the scholar says, "but I have never been so serious about it except when I was a child."

Professor Tokuda was quite clear about the fact that he was not in a normal state of consciousness during his experience. Yet one senses from his statements and the fact that he was motivated to mention the incident publicly that whatever he perceived was much more real to him than the hypnopompic imagery which typically precedes full awakening. The fact that the apparition seemed to resemble the deceased former resident is also interesting. Tokuda's apparition, however, is not typical in many respects. Most of the apparition sightings reported to psychical researchers are, in fact, much more vivid. Culling over hundreds of case studies, G. N. M. Tyrell provides us with a picture of the "perfect apparition."[175] If the "perfect apparition" were standing next to a normal individual, we would find the following points of resemblance:

(1) Both figures would stand out in space and be equally solid.
(2) We could walk around the apparition and view it from any perspective as vividly as the normal individual.
(3) The two figures would appear the same in any sort of lighting conditions, whether good or bad.

176

(4) On approaching the apparition, one could hear it breathing and making other normal noises, such as the rustling of its clothes.

(5) The apparition would behave as if aware of our presence. It might even touch us, in which case it would feel like an ordinary human touch.

(6) The apparition could be seen reflected in a mirror just as a real person.

(7) The apparition might speak and even answer a question, but we would not be able to engage it in any long conversation.

(8) If we closed our eyes, the apparition would disappear from view just as the ordinary person would.

(9) The apparition would appear clothed and with other normal accessories such as a stick or a package, perhaps even accompanied by a dog.

(10) Many times, when close to, or touched by, the apparition, we would feel an unusual sensation of coldness.

(11) If we tried to grab hold of the apparition, our hand would go through it without encountering any resistance. The apparition may disappear when cornered in this fashion.

(12) The apparition would generally not remain more than half an hour. It might vanish through the walls or floor. Or it might simply open the door and walk out.

(13) Apparitions differ in the extent to which they are able to actually effect physical objects, open doors, cast a shadow, be photographed. The "perfect apparition" cannot really cause any objectively measurable effects, although it may cause the subjective appearance of doing so.

When several individuals, independently or simultaneously, observe the same phantom under conditions which make deception or suggestion unlikely, the event can no longer be interpreted as a totally subjective experience. Some kind of parapsychological explanation is probably required.

Collective cases of this sort account for approximately eight percent of the total number of reported apparitions. Naturally, many times only one person is present to see the phantom. Collective cases are more common when several potential observers are present. In a group situation, if one person sees an apparition, there is about a forty percent likelihood that others will share his perception.[176]

However, even collective cases of apparitions of a person known to be dead do not provide certain evidence for survival. The research on out-of-body experiences has shown that it is possible for one to cause one's own apparition to appear to others. Likewise, there is evidence that an individual, through concentration, can create the apparitional appearance of a different person as well. Such experiments were documented in 1822 by H. M. Wesermann, who was the Government Assessor and Chief Inspector of Roads at Düsseldorf. The account of the appearance is recorded by one of the percipients, a Lieutenant S. He says that Herr n had come to spend the night at his lodgings.

After supper and when we had undressed, I was sitting on my bed and Herr n was standing by the door of the next room on the point also of going to bed. This about half-past ten. We were speaking partly about indifferent subjects and partly about the events of the French campaigne. Suddenly the door out of the kitchen opened without a sound, and a lady entered, very pale, taller than Herr n, about five foot four inches in height, strong and broad in figure, dressed in white, but with a large black kerchief which reached down to the waist. She entered with bare head, greeted me with the hand three times in a complimentary fashion, turned around to the left toward Herr n, and waved her hand to him three times; after which the figure quietly, and again without creaking the door, went out. We followed at once in order to discover whether there were any deception, but found nothing.[177]

Even though the woman had been dead for five years, Wesermann claims that he was the agent of her appearance. Furthermore, it appears as if he had expected Herr n to be asleep alone in his bedroom at the time instead of in the anteroom with Lieutenant S. Thus the observation of the phantom by two awake individuals went beyond even the intentions of the agent. By appearing in the anteroom, the phantom seemed to show a will independent of the agent, Wesermann; it was perhaps a product of the percipient's mind as well.

Wesermann's experiments were conducted at a time when many researchers, including the French government commission, were reporting unusual effects with Mesmerism. Wesermann himself acknowledges that the successful production of such a phantom was, indeed, a rare event. It's unfortunate that efforts have not been made among scientific researchers within recent years to replicate this important work.

The point of such evidence is that the human mind seems capable of generating apparitional appearances identical to those which are often attributed to "departed spirits." However, in nearly all apparitions, there is no living individual attempting to create the appearance. It's unlikely that most apparitions were consciously created although they may have been unconscious—but still "paranormal"—human productions.

Furthermore, even if an apparition results from efforts by a once-living person, the apparition itself is not yet evidence of a fully conscious disembodied spirit. Such phenomena may well be mere images or thought-forms hanging around in the psychic space. Very rarely do they show the characteristics of a well-developed personality, even though they exhibit some independent consciousness. The apparition evidence suggests that we are continually swimming in a sea of thoughts and images which exist independently of our own minds and which occasionally intrude dramatically into our conscious awareness.

Some interesting data relating apparitions to survival appears in a survey of physicians' and nurses' observations of dying patients. The 640 respondents to the survey, conducted by Dr. Karlis Osis, had witnessed over 35,000 incidents of human death. Of these, only about ten percent of the patients were conscious in their last hours. These dying individuals often experienced states of exultation or hallucination which

Karlis Osis, Ph.D.
(*Courtesy of* Psychic Magazine)

could not be attributed to the nature of their illness, or to drug usage. While many patients had visions of spiritual worlds opening up to them in accordance with their particular religious beliefs, most of the hallucinations were of individuals already dead. Half of the percipients stated that the apparitions were coming to help "enter the other world." The education, age or sex of the patients seemed to have nothing to do with the manifestation of such apparitions. However the apparitions seemed most likely when the dying patient was in a state of physiological and psychological peace and equilibrium.[178] Oddly enough a number of these apparitions were of individuals whose death was unknown to the dying patient.

W. G. Roll, Director of the Psychical Research Foundation in Durham, N.C., has suggested that "psi fields" exist around all beings and objects and are charged with the thoughts and emotions which have been associated with them. This accounts for the apparitions seen in haunted houses as well as the ability of some psychics to pick up images and emotional residues from objects in psychometry.[179] We have yet to understand the psi-field in any precise scientific way; however it clearly seems consistent with the astral and mental bodies spoken of by Theosophists. An examination of mediumship phenomenon demonstrates more vividly the relationship between the subjective world of mind and the objective world of mind inhabited by thoughtforms and perhaps also by spirits.

One of the classic cases of mediumship, that of Mrs. Piper, has already been discussed. Her "Pellew" guide offers some of the best mediumistic evidence for survival. This "spirit," speaking through Mrs. Piper, was able to correctly identify and interact with 30 former friends out of 150 individuals presented to him. Not a single mistake was made. But on other occasions, this personality did slip up to a considerable extent. Later in 1905, Richard Hodgson died of heart failure and his "spirit" became a communicator through Mrs. Piper.

In the presence of William James, America's foremost psychologist, the "Hodgson control" was able to describe incidents which Hodgson and James had intimately experienced together in life and were unknown to other individuals. The personality was quite clear and distinct. At other times this was not the case and the "spirit" seemed like an obvious personation from Mrs. Piper's mind. In analyzing this data, James suggested that several factors were at play:

W. G. Roll (courtesy of the Psychical Research Foundation.)

Extraneous "wills to communicate" may contribute to the results as well as a "will to personate," and the two kinds of will may be distinct in entity, though capable of helping each other out. The will to communicate, in our present instance, would be, on a *prima facie* view of it, the will of Hodgeson's surviving spirit; and a natural way of representing the process would be to suppose the spirit to have found that by pressing, so to speak, against "the light," it can make fragmentary gleams and flashes of what it wishes to say mix with the rubbish of the trance-talk on this side. The two wills might thus strike up a sort of partnership and reinforce each other. It might even be that the "will to personate" would be comparatively inert unless it were aroused to activity by the other will. We might imagine the relationship to be analogous to that of two physical bodies, from neither of which, when alone, mechanical, electrical or thermal activity can proceed. But, if the

179

other body be present, and show a difference of "potential," action starts up and goes on apace.

I myself feel as if an external will to communicate were probably there— that is, I find myself doubting, in consequence of my whole acquaintance with that sphere of phenomena, that Mrs. Piper's dream-life, even if equipped with telepathic powers, accounts for all the results found. But if asked whether the will to communicate be Hodgson's, or be some mere spirit counterfeit of Hodgson, I remain uncertain and await more facts, facts which may not point clearly to a conclusion for fifty or a hundred years.[180]

Sir Oliver Lodge

While James affirmed his belief in the reality of the Hodgson spirit, based on his sense of dramatic probabilities, he acknowledged that the case was not a good one because Hodgson had known Mrs. Piper so well in life. There was no way of proving that any of the evidential material did not simply come from her unconscious mind.

One of the more significant cases of mediumistic communication concerns the many messages received by Sir Oliver Lodge from his deceased son Raymond. An eminent physicist, Lodge pioneered in the development of radio technology which actually was as much his brainchild as it was Marconi's, although he did not pursue its commercial development to the same extent as his Italian colleague. Lodge (an SPR founder) was already satisfied with the evidence for survival which had been gathered by Myers and others before his son's death during a mortar attack on September 14, 1915.

Actually, the story of Raymond's "spirit communications" begins a few weeks before his death, on August 8, when a message allegedly came from the spirit of Myers through Mrs. Piper in America. Hodgson's "spirit" claimed to be in control of the medium at the time he delivered a message for Lodge which he claims to have received from Myers. The enigmatic message stated:

> Now Lodge, while we are not here as of old, i.e. not quite, we are here enough to take and give messages. Myers says you take the part of the poet and he will act as Faunus. Yes. Myers. *Protect*. He will understand. What have you to say, Lodge? Good work. Ask Verrall, she will also understand.[181]

In order to interpret this message, Lodge wrote to Mrs. Verrall—a medium, psychic researcher, and wife of a deceased Cambridge classical scholar—asking her to interpret the message. She replied at once referring to Horace (*Carm.* II. xvii. 27-30), saying that the reference was to an account of the poet's narrow escape from death, from a falling tree, Faunus, the guardian of poets, lightened the blow and saved him.

On September 25, Raymond's mother, Mrs. Lodge, attended a sitting with a reputable medium, Mrs. Osborne Leonard. The visit was anonymous, and there was no intention of contacting Raymond; the purpose being, rather, to accompany a grieving friend whose two sons had also been killed in the war. In fact, it seemed as if the spirits of those sons did communicate through Mrs. Leonard. However on that occasion, a message also came through purporting to be from Raymond:

R: Tell father I have met some friends of his.
ML: Can you give any name?
R: Yes. Myers.

Two days later, Sir Oliver himself attended anonymously a sitting with Mrs. Leonard. The voice speaking through Mrs. Leonard was that of her childlike "spirit control," Feda, who described Raymond's condition, saying that he was being taught by an old friend, M., and others. Feda also made an allusion to the Faunus message:

. . . Feda sees something which is only symbolic; she sees a cross falling back on you; very dark, falling on you; dark and heavy looking; and as it falls it gets twisted round and the other side seems all light, and the light is shining all over you. . . . The cross looked dark and then it suddenly twisted around and became a beautiful light. . . . Your son is the cross of light.[182]

This message seemed to be perceived symbolically as a thoughtform. One might complain that the allusion was too vague to be evidential; although it cannot be denied that it is remarkably consistent with the original Faunus message. In many respects this is typical of the complex series of over 3,000 cross-correspondence messages that were to develop between a number of mediums over the next several decades. Taken as a whole, they seem to weave a pattern indicative of a unifying intelligence.

That afternoon, after seeing Mrs. Leonard, Lady Lodge visited another medium, separately and strictly anonymously. The following is a transcript of Mrs. Lodge's sitting, with Sir Oliver's own annotations in brackets:

Was he not associated with chemistry? If not, someone associated with him was, because I see all the things in a chemical laboratory. That chemistry thing takes me away from him to a man in the flesh [O. J. L., presumably as my laboratory has been rather specially chemical of late]; and connected with him, a man, a writer of poetry, on our side, closely connected with spiritualism. He was very clever—he too passed away out of England.
[This is clearly meant for Myers, who died in Rome.]
He has communicated several times. This gentleman who wrote poetry—I see the letter M—he is helping your son to communicate. . . . If your son didn't know the man he knew of him.
[Yes, he could hardly have known him, as he was only about twelve at the time of Myers death.]
At the back of the gentleman beginning with M, and who wrote poetry, is a whole group of people. [The S.P.R. group, doubtless.] They are very interested. And don't be surprised if you get messages from them even if you don't know them.[183]

At this sitting the "spirit control" also made particular reference to a photograph of Raymond with a group of other men in which you could see his walking stick. This puzzled Lady Lodge as they knew of no such photograph. However several months later they received a letter from the mother of one of Raymond's fellow officers with an offer to send a copy of a group photo which she had.

Two days later, Sir Oliver also had a sitting, anonymously, with the same medium and received the following material from the "spirit control":

Your common-sense method of approaching the subject in the family has been the means of helping him to come back as he has been able to do; and had he not known what you had told him, then it would have been far more difficult for him to come back. He is very deliberate in what he says. He is a young man that knows what he is saying. Do you know F W M?
O. J. L.—Yes I do.
Because I see those three letters. Now, after them, do you know S T; yes, I get S T, then a dot, and then P? These are shown to me; I see them in light; your boy has shown these things to me.
O. J. L.—Yes, I understand. [Meaning that I recognised the allusion to F. W. H. Myer's poem *St. Paul*.]
Well he says to me: "He has helped me so much more than you think. That is F W M."
O. J. L.—Bless him!
No, your boy laughs, he has got an ulterior motive for it; don't think it was only for charity's sake, he has got an ulterior motive, and thinks that you will be able by the strength of your personality to do what you want to do now, to ride over the quibbles of the fools, and to make the Society, *the* Society, he says, of some use to the world.[184]

About five weeks later, Lodge again sat with Mrs. Leonard, who by this time grasped his identity. He asked Raymond, through the control Feda, to describe further the group photograph, which had not yet arrived. Further details were given in terms of the position Raymond took relative to the man behind him who was leaning on his shoulder. These details were confirmed when the picture finally arrived.

Communications from Raymond, filled with evidential material, continued for many years through Mrs. Leonard and also through other mediums. Lodge's entire family participated in these sittings and all became convinced of the reality of Raymond's departed spirit. On one occasion sittings were held simultaneously at two different locations and Raymond successfully managed to convey information from one group to the other. The complete account of these many sittings is recorded in Lodge's book *Raymond*, published in 1916, which did a great deal to further the cause of spiritualism.

Raymond clearly conveys the excitement which Lodge and his family felt at the time. However Raymond himself never actually seems to control a medium. He either speaks through a "spirit control" or through automatic writing or table-rapping. There was a consistency to his personality, but not with the vividness of the Hodgson or the Pellew controls experienced through Mrs. Piper.

Mrs. Leonard's integrity has never been called into question. For over forty years her mediumship was the subject of exhaustive study by members of the S.P.R.. Throughout this time, Feda was her only "control," although with a few sitters she would sometimes allow other "spirits" to speak directly through the medium. In these cases, the characterizations were

Douglas Johnson, perhaps the most thoroughly tested medium alive in the world today, lectures throughout the world and is based at the College of Psychic Science in London. (Courtesy Psychic Magazine, *February 1971.)*

brilliant and seemed to go much beyond mere reproduction of mannerisms. For years, one occasional communicator, a person Mrs. Leonard had never met in life, gave message after message to former loved ones without ever speaking out of character or using inappropriate emotional inferences.[185] If one refuses to accept the survival hypothesis to explain such cases, one must at least acknowledge extraordinary ESP capabilities on the part of the medium.

The super-telepathy theory is strained somewhat in dealing with the phenomena of cross-correspondences. The Faunus message which was received by Sir Oliver Lodge and then alluded to by another psychic is a minor example. The idea is that of creating a kind of jig-saw puzzle in the messages coming through different mediums. Any individual piece, when taken alone, seems to have no meaning. But when the separate pieces are put together, they form a coherent whole, and provide evidence for a constructive mind behind the entire design.

The major messages seem to have been directed by the spirit of F. W. H. Myers who died in 1901. Records show that the notion never occurred to him while he was alive. Other deceased members of the SPR also seem to have originated cross-correspondence messages. The mediums received these messages about the same time in places as distant from each other as London, New York, and India. Often the messages were filled with Greek and Latin allusions which were beyond the understanding of the different mediums. In fact, the messages seemed to contain the type of humor, style, and scholarship which was characteristic of the deceased researchers. The messages were often so complex that the puzzles could only be understood by classical language scholars.[186]

A baffling cross-correspondence series occurred in the United States, supposedly originating through "Walter," the deceased brother of Mina Crandon. Mrs. Crandon, the wife of a professor of surgery at Harvard University, has been one of the most controversial mediums of the twentieth century. Her psychokinetic manifestations were verified by many researchers throughout the world under strict conditions. Yet at other times she was accused of fraud.

The Crandons lived in Boston; however Walter also appeared through other mediums in New York, Niagara Falls, and Maine. On one occasion he announced a cross-correspondence in which "Margery" (as Mrs. Crandon was called) would make up a problem and two other mediums would each provide half of the answer. The problem written automatically by the medium was: "11 × 2—to kick a dead." The mediumistic circle in New York was rung by telephone and told by Judge Cannon that Walter had given the following message: "2—no one stops." The next morning a telegram was received from Niagara Falls announcing this fragment: "2 horse." When the fragments are put together, one can see that the problem which Walter worked out and communicated—assuming that there was no conspiracy to cheat—was this: "11 × 2 = 22. No one stops to kick a dead horse.[187]

One might argue that this case is an instance of group telepathy as the medium obviously knew the entire puzzle. Other

James A. and Diane Kennedy Pike whose books, The Other Side *and* Search *document their encounters with what they considered to be a life after death. (Courtesy* Psychic Magazine, *September 1969.)*

evidence, however, also strengthens the case for Walter's autonomous existence. At times he was able to speak with a "direct voice"—that is without using the vocal cords of either the medium or the sitters. His voice just appeared in the room. Furthermore, some cross-correspondences devised by Walter were in Chinese—a language which Margery did not know. Walter claimed that he was getting help from some Chinese spirits.[188] Even if telepathy were at play in the transmission of information, it is hard to explain the actual design of the puzzles with that hypothesis.

Another line of survival research focuses on reincarnation. The popular view of reincarnation is that after a person dies, the spirit of that person is reborn in another body. This process, of entering the womb, is vividly described in the *Tibetan Book of the Dead*. The concept is much more complex, however, when considered in the light of mystical philosophies which see one underlying reality beyond and within all time and individuality.

Some evidence for reincarnation comes from cases where individuals under hypnosis produce memories from what might be taken as a prior lifetime. These memories come through with a vividness of emotion and detail very much like early childhood memories. Often the reincarnation dramas seem to explain important characteristics in the subject's psychological makeup. This type of testimony is very interesting from a psychodynamic point of view. However, it cannot constitute acceptable evidence for reincarnation until it is shown that the descriptions match actual life-histories which are unknown to the subject—even then it could be merely *post*cognition. Still another explanation for so-called reincarnation evidence would be simple spirit possession.

Even if we were to conclude from other evidence that reincarnation was real, we need not assume that it always occurs. Some cultures maintain the belief, for example, that one only reincarnates if one dies prematurely by accident.

The cases which are coming under serious scientific scrutiny are typically those in which a small child, two to four years old, begins talking to the parents about another lifetime. Generally, the parents will dismiss such talk as nonsense—even in cultures where reincarnation is believed to occur. However, the child may persist and even insist upon visiting the community of his former residence. If the child supplies many details the parents may initiate an inquiry. Ideally at this stage, a scientific investigator is introduced to the scene. Careful records are made of all the child's statements. Verification can then begin by visiting the indicated community. If a family exists meeting the child's descriptions of his former household, the investigator can arrange for the two families to visit. Tests are then arranged to determine if the child can recognize places, objects, and people. Often it seems that these memories are lost as the child grows older.

Unfortunately, most investigations do not proceed so smoothly. Nevertheless over a thousand such cases have now been investigated and a very suggestive body of evidence is accumulating. As an example of an actual study, the case of Swarnlata Mishra is instructive.

On March 2, 1948, Swarnlata was born the daughter of the district school inspector in Chhatarpur, Madya Pradesh, India. At the age of three and a half, while on a trip with her father passing through the town of Katni, she made a number of strange remarks about her house in this village. The Mishra family had never lived closer than 100 miles from this town. Later she described to friends and family further details of a previous life. Her family name, she claimed, had been Pathak. She also performed unusual dances and songs which she had had no opportunity to learn.

At the age of ten Swarnlata recognized a new family acquaintance, the wife of a college professor, as a friend in her former lifetime. Several months later, this case was brought to the attention of Sri H. N. Banerjee, of the Department of Parapsychology, University of Rajasthan, Jaipur. He interviewed the Mishra family; then, guided by Swarnlata's statements, he located the house of the Pathak family in Katni. Banerjee found that Swarnlata's statements seemed to fit the life history of Biya, a daughter of the Pathak family and deceased wife of Sri Chintamini Panday. She had died in 1939.

In the summer of 1959, the Pathak family and Biya's married relatives visited the Mishra family in Chhatarpur. Swarnlata was able to recognize and identify them. She refused to identify strangers who had been brought along to confuse her. Later Swarnlata was taken to Katni and the neighboring towns. There she recognized additional people and places, commenting on changes which had been made since Biya's death. Unfortunately Sri Banerjee was not present during these reunions.

It wasn't until the summer of 1961 that Dr. Ian Stevenson, an eminent psychiatrist and psychical researcher from the University of Virginia, visited the two families and attempted to verify the authenticity of the case.

Stevenson determined that of 49 statements made by Swarnlata only two were found to be incorrect. She accurately described the details of Biya's house and neighborhood as they were before 1939. She described the details of Biya's disease and death as well as the doctor who treated her. She was able to recall intimate incidents known only to a few individuals. For example, she knew that Sri Ciantimini Prndey had taken 1200 ruples from a box in which Biya had kept money. He admitted this, when questioned, and stated that no one but Biya could have known of the incident. She accurately identified former friends, relatives, and servants in spite of the efforts of the witnesses to deny her statements or mislead her. Most of the recognitions were given in a way which obliged Swarnlata to provide a name or state a relationship. It was not a case of asking, "Am I your son?" but rather, "Tell me who I am."

Perhaps because of her family's tolerance, Swarnlata's impressions of Biya's life have not faded. In fact, Swarnlata continues to visit Biya's brothers and children and shows great affection for them. Remarkably she continues to act as an older sister to the Pathak brothers—men forty years older than her.

Arthur Ford, the medium noted for allegedly cracking the post-mortem code which Houdini left with his wife and also for contacting the deceased son of Bishop James A. Pike. (Courtesy Psychic Magazine, *October 1970.)*

Furthermore, the Pathak family was rather westernized and did not believe in reincarnation before their encounter with Swarnlata.

Swarnlata also talked about another intermediate life as a child named Kamlesh in Sylket, Bengal, where she died at the age of nine. While this claim has not been verified in detail, many of her statements were found to correlate with the local geography. Her songs and dances were also verified as Bengali, although she had lived all her life only among Hindi speaking people.[189]

If one rules out the possibility of fraud in such cases—and there are many which are as evidential as this one—one might assume that a child like Swarnlata was recalling the memories of stories which she had overheard during her very early childhood or infancy. However, such claims should not be made without a clear delineation of the possible sources of information. The other explanation—as with mediumship—involves ESP along with a remarkable skill for impersonation.

Perhaps the most extraordinary cases which challenge the super-ESP hypothesis are those which involve *xenoglossy* or the ability to speak a language one has never learned. The Bengali songs and dances which Swarnlata was able to recite offer a minor example of xenoglossy. Other cases are far more intriguing.

Dr. Ian Stevenson documents the case of a Russian-Jewish woman living in Philadelphia who, under hypnosis, claimed to be a Swedish peasant named Jensen Jacoby. Furthermore, she was able to carry on rather involved conversations in this state using a mixture of Swedish and Norwegian with proper grammar and inflectional intonations. Speaking in a gruff male voice, she vividly protrayed the personality of the illiterate peasant and was also able to accurately identify objects borrowed from the American Swedish historical museum in Philadelphia. Most of these hypnotic sessions were tape-recorded.

Stevenson spent over six years researching this case, interviewing witnesses and family members in order to determine if there was any possibility that the subject had been exposed to the Swedish language at any time in her life. The case was not merely a question of reciting memorized or remembered passages—but rather one of carrying on an active dialogue. After extensive and thorough research, Stevenson felt that there was no period in the subject's life when she would have been able to acquire the languages spoken in trance.

The lady and her husband, the medical doctor who hypnotized her, were both subjected to a battery of personality, language, aptitude, and lie detector tests. The indications from these tests further added to the authenticity of the case. Stevenson feels that while ESP might account for the informational aspects of a foreign language, it does not necessarily explain the skill of using the language conversationally in a meaningful way. Thus the case strongly points toward the survival hypothesis—even though the historical existence of the Swedish peasant has not been fully documented.[190]

It's difficult, if not impossible, to base an airtight argument for survival after death upon any one instance of apparitions,

186

mediumship, possession, reincarnation, or xenoglossy. Nevertheless as one investigates the extraordinary depths of the human personality which are illustrated in the range of well-documented survival material, it does become apparent that events and process do occur which seem to confirm our boldest conceptions.

Other Worlds

Andrija Puharich, the scientist who has done the most to bring Uri Geller's psychokinetic feats to the educated public's attention believes that Geller is being used as an agency of flying saucer occupants in order to prepare mankind for psychic adulthood within a larger cosmic community. The evidence to support this claim which has been presented in his book *Uri,* is actually rather scant.[191] Alleged tape recorded messages from the UFO occupants have disappeared. Essentially all that is left is the testimony of individuals who have seen UFOs in Geller's presence or in ways connected with him as well as a number of photos taken by Geller or Puharich. Although a new wave of psychokinetic phenomena seems to have been initiated by Geller, such experiences have been recorded for a long time and seem to rise from the supra-ordinary consciousness within us.

Puharich implies that we may soon experience a major contact between our civilization and the distant intelligent powers who work through Geller. In a sense, Geller is being sent as a barometer to test our reaction in the face of his mind-bending metal-bending. Such statements do not seem unreasonable. Some evidence, though it may be meager, does exist. Further studies are forthcoming. However, Puharich's claims have been ridiculed as unworthy of examination by some elements of the scientific community.[192]

We can understand this attitude even if we do not share it, since the status of research today on unidentified flying objects is in many ways comparable to nineteenth century psychical research. Spontaneous observations have been recorded. Documentary photographs have been taken. Researchers have certainly learned a great deal about what is not a UFO—weather balloons, sundogs, birds, aircraft, searchlights, reflections, satellites, and astronomical bodies. Numerous frauds have been also detected. At least five percent of the UFO sightings reported to the United States Air Force, during its period of investigations from 1948 until 1969, still remain unexplained in spite of reliable witnesses and adequate information.[193,194] Nevertheless, there has been no conclusive physical proof that UFOs are actually intelligently designed flying machines from a non-human source. No UFOs have been captured. None have even crashed and left parts. There have been no regularly acknowledged communication channels between scientists on earth and non-human intelligence. Nor have the ufologists provided us with any repeatable experiments.

It's hard for many individuals to accept the possibility fhat UFO occupants are interacting with the general public, when "officially" they have not been shown to even exist. The alleged parapsychological aspects of UFO reports add even more fuel to the skeptic's fire. In 1969, a government committee, headed by Dr. E. U. Condon at the University of Colorado, declared that UFO phenomena should no longer be considered of any scientific value.[195] The Air Force discontinued its Project Blue Book investigations the same year.

Nevertheless a number of dedicated scientists have continued to investigate UFO reports under the sponsorship of various civilian organizations. Dr. J. Allen Hynek, chairman of the department of astronomy at Northwestern University, and for twenty years a consultant to the Air Force Study, has recently published a book, *The UFO Experience*, which takes issue with the Condon report.[196] Dr. Hynek's book was favorably reviewed in *Science*, the weekly journal published by the American Academy for the Advancement of Science.[197] While there has been no great clamor for another government investigation, it's quite clear that the case against UFOs is no longer closed.

At the Aerial Phenomena Research Organization (APRO) with worldwide headquarters in Tucson, Arizona, over a thousand cases are on file of witnessed UFO landings and many more aerial sightings. Similar cases are investigated by two other major civilian research organizations—National Investigations Committee on Aerial Phenomena (NICAP) and the Mutual UFO Network (MUFON). Occupants have been seen on hundreds of occasions—although, ironically, never photographed.[198] Further examination of the data reveals patterns which lend support to parapsychological interpretations. For example, there is the case of Mrs. Stella Lansing of Palmer, Massachussetts, which has been studied for many years by the eminent psychiatrist, Dr. Berthold E. Schwarz.[199,200]

Since 1967, Mrs. Lansing has produced over fifty rolls of 8mm movie film depicting saucer-shaped UFOs and other unidentified objects, using a variety of cameras under many different conditions. It's become something of a hobby for her —almost a compulsion. Following her intuitive impressions, at all hours of the day or night, in all sorts of weather, often accompanied by researchers, she roams about the countryside with her camera. Many times the strange lights in the sky which she manages to photograph have been witnessed by friends, neighbors and independent observers. Some of her sightings have been verified by officials at the local airport. Sometimes other people accompanying Mrs. Lansing are also able to photograph the strange lights.[201]

On the other hand, many of her pictures are quite unlike the lights that have been witnessed. Objects and faces appear on the film very reminiscent of Ted Serios' psychic photographs. In fact, investigation indicates that Mrs. Lansing can exert a psychokinetic effect upon film, videotape, and even large static objects. Strange sounds and voices also appear on

Stella Lansing with Joseph Dunninger, master telepathist who has written over thirty books on telepathy, magic and the exposure of fraudulent mediums. (Courtesy Dr. Berthold E. Schwarz.)

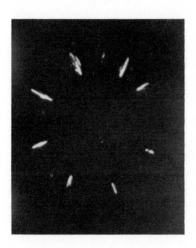

Clocklike UFO patterns photographed by Stella Lansing. Although the images appear similar to flying saucers, the photograph also bears elements of psychic photography. (Courtesy Berthold Schwarz.)

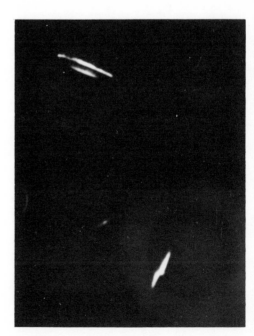

Enlargement of UFO image.

189

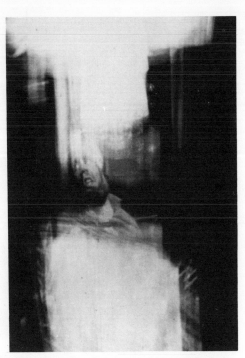

This apparently psychic image appeared on a series of photos taken by Stella Lansing.

audio tapes in her presence. Some of her apparent psychic photographs show images of flying saucers in a clocklike formation. Often Mrs. Lansing claims to see these strange images, which show up on the film, even though they are invisible tohbr observers. Other individuals standing next to Mrs. Lansing are unable to photograph these odd images.

She has always shown complete openness and willingness to cooperate with scientific investigators. Years of psychiatric observations have convinced Dr. Schwarz of her honesty. The famous mentalist, Dunninger, a friend of Dr. Schwarz, also has examined Mrs. Lansing, finding no signs of fraud nor any logical explanation for her phenomena. Her photographs point to the physical existence of possible UFOs and associated entities. However the psychic events which accompany this evidence strongly suggests other dimensions to this phenomena.[202]

One of the most unusual claims made by Puharich regarding the talents of Uri Geller involves Geller's alleged ability to teleport automobiles. (The topic is so mind-blowing that when I first appeared with Geller on the radio, in 1973, he asked me not to mention it for fear of ridicule.) Since Puharich's book, several other reports on auto teleportation have been filed.

Ray Stanford of Austin, Texas, discusses two instances, connected with Geller, in which his automobile was apparently teleported. One of these involved an automobile accident. Testimony from witnesses is recorded in the traffic-court transcripts. They observed Stanford's car suddenly appear in front of them, "like a light that had been switched on." The distance of this teleportation was about fifty feet. On the second occasion, the teleportation was even more dramatic. Driving with his wife along Interstate 10 in Texas, Ray suddenly noticed a silvery-metallic, blue glow around the car. Stuck in heavy traffic at the time, he actually mentioned to his wife that he hoped "Uri's intelligences . . . *would* teleport us!" Then, according to his testimony he felt a strange sensation in his brain and the scene instantly changed. They had travelled thirty-seven miles in no time and using no gas. Later, as the car was not functioning well, it was hauled to a garage. The alternator and voltage regulator were completely burned out and all the wiring was completely charred.[203]

More recently, in South Africa, a couple reported that after they had observed a UFO from within their car, they lost control of the vehicle which continued at a high speed across the African plain. Except for a few short intervals, they were unable to steer or brake the car for five hours. They also felt unusual coldness within the car. Under hypnosis, one of the couple stated that a humanoid from the UFO had entered their car and was with them, in the back seat, during the entire journey.

UFO investigators have files on at least five other cases of alleged automobile teleportation in South America. In three instances, individuals found themselves suddenly transported thousands of miles from Argentine or Brazil to Mexico. These cases are very difficult to carefully investigate. Many of the published reports simply lack significant details. Nevertheless the reports do suggest a pattern of events.[204]

190

Oddly enough, many reported UFO sightings and contacts involve incidences of what could be called paranormal healing. A prime example is "The Strange Case of Dr. X" which was reported by the French scientist Aime Michel in *Flying Saucer Review* in 1969.[205] "Dr. X" is the pseudonym for a well-known and respected physician who holds an important official position in southeast France.

Early one morning in November 1968, the doctor was awakened by the cries of his fourteen month old son. He got up painfully, due to an injury he had received a few days earlier while chopping wood, and found the baby pointing toward light flashes which were coming in through the shuttered window. Opening a large window, Dr. X observed two horizontal, disk-shaped objects that were silvery white on top and bright red underneath. The flashes were caused by a sudden burst of light between the two disks with a periodicity close to one second. As the doctor watched these disks they approached him and actually seemed to *merge* so that there was only one disk from which emanated a single beam of white light. Then the disk began to flip from a horizontal to a vertical position, so that it was seen as a circle standing on its edge. The beam of light came to illuminate the front of Dr. X's house and shone directly into his face. At that moment a loud sound was heard and the object vanished.

The doctor immediately woke up his wife to tell her what had occurred. It was at that time that she observed that the swelling and wound on his leg had disappeared. Furthermore Dr. X had suffered from a partial paralysis of his right side from a war wound received ten years previously in Algeria. In the days that followed the sighting, these symptoms also disappeared.

There are many unusual aspects of this case which are still being investigated by a competent team of researchers. One study, reported several years after the original sighting, noted that an odd red pigmentation has periodically appeared in a triangle shape around the naval of both Dr. X and his young child. It would stay visible for two or three days at a time. This had happened even when the child was staying with his grandmother who knew nothing of the UFO sighting. Other phenomena of a psychokinetic nature have been noted such as levitation and poltergeist-type phenomena. The sighting seems to have been a landmark event in Dr. X's life as he now faces life with a rather mystical acceptance, showing no fear of death or tragedy. This new attitude has been recognized by friends and relatives who also knew nothing of Dr. X's experience.[206]

Several other instances are known of unusual healings which have been triggered by a flash of light coming from an unidentified flying object. A case was reported in Damon, Texas, in 1965, in which the wound received by a deputy sheriff from his pet alligator healed after being exposed to a brilliant flash of light and heat coming from a UFO. This incident was witnessed by a fellow officer.[207]

On other occasions, however, the effects of such contact more clearly resemble the symptoms of disease. Sometimes the effects are mixed. For example, in December 1972, a 73 year old an Argentine watchman, Ventura Macieras, observed a glowing craft hovering over a nearby grove of eucalyptus trees. The object was near enough so that he was able to see figures staring at him through the windows in a round cabin. Then, as in the Dr. X case, the craft tilted toward him and he was momentarily blinded by a flash of light. Seconds later he had recovered and was able to watch the object move slowly away and disappear behind the trees on a low hill.

After his experience, Macieras developed swollen pustules on the back of his neck. He suffered from nausea, headaches, and diarrhea. His eyes watered constantly and he experienced difficulty in speaking. At the site where the object had been, the tops of the eucalyptus trees were scorched and burned. On the positive side, since his experience, Macieras has been growing a third set of new teeth.[208]

These incidences may represent a form of healing as yet unknown to us, perhaps involving electromagnetic waves or ionization of some sort. The technology required to duplicate such feats may already be within our grasp. The real challenge is developing the consciousness and psychic skill necessary to use such technology with responsibility.

Another unusual healing associated with a UFO was reported in October 1957 in the mountains west of Rio de Janeiro, Brazil, where the daughter of a well-to-do family was sick with stomach cancer. Seven members of the family were present, as the girl was in agony and a strange glow shone outside the bedroom window. What followed could have been part of the intercosmic Red Cross emergency squad!

As the astonished family watched, two beings, just under four feet tall, with orange hair and slanting green eyes, emerged from a landed "saucer" and entered the sickroom, laying out their instruments as if in preparation for surgery! One of them placed his hand on the forehead of the father who began to communicate telepathically, he felt, the details of his daughter's illness. The rest of the operation is described in comparatively normal terms. By shining a light on the girls's stomach, the small surgeons lit up the inside of her abdomen so that the cancerous growth became visible. The surgical removal took about half an hour. Before leaving, the beneficient visitors left some medicine for the girl with telepathic instructions for its use. Several weeks later, the girl's doctor verified that she had been cured of cancer.

If taken out of context, the Brazilian case seems completely unbelievable. However, it does contain elements similar to other UFO contact cases which researchers are inclined to take seriously. The following case, the most prominent of UFO contact stories, cannot easily be dismissed as fraud or delusion.

On September 19, 1961, returning late at night from a Canadian vacation along a lonely New Hampshire road, an interracial couple, Betty and Barney Hill, noticed a large glowing object in the sky above their car. It approached so close that Barney stopped the car, got out, and, taking his binoculars, actually saw humanoid occupants through what appeared to be portholes in a spacecraft. Terrified he ran back to the car and stepped on the gas. As the Hills sped down the highway, they heard a strange beeping sound.

Although Barney very much wanted to forget this incident, Betty persisted in discussing the matter. She initiated reports to both the Air Force and the National Investigations Committee on Aerial Phenomena, a civilian organization in Washington, D.C. Barney participated reluctantly in the interviews which followed. NICAP investigators were particularly interested in their experience; and after six hours of intense questioning a report was issued favoring the case's authenticity. Subsequent to this report, further questioning turned up the fact that there was a two hour period of time between the sighting of the UFO and their arrival home that they could not account for. Both Barney and Betty seemed to be in amnesia's grip regarding some part of their UFO contact. Furthermore, strange markings were found on the car trunk which Betty associated with the beeping noises.

Eventually the Hills sought psychiatric aid in removing the memory blocks regarding their UFO experience. They were referred to Dr. Benjamin Simon, a highly regarded Boston practicioner particularly known for his skill in treating amnesia. Under Dr. Simon's skillful hypnotic induction, Betty and Barney each separately revealed memories from the forgotten two hours. What emerged under hypnosis was a most engaging tale of their abduction and physical examination by alien beings aboard a space craft, after which they were safely released. Betty actually engaged in some pleasant conversation with one of her captors before she and Barney were allowed to return! She was shown a star map marked with principle trade and exploration routes. Later she was able to produce a sketch of this map from memory.

Dr. Simon himself was not particularly interested in whether or not their reported experiences actually occurred. The purpose of his therapy, which lasted over six months, was to alleviate the stress which had resulted from the experience and the amnesia. It was his theory that the UFO sighting was real enough, but that the abduction story was a dream of Betty's which was somehow communicated to Barney. This seemed

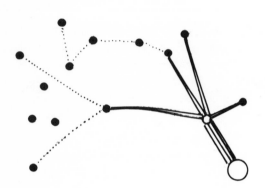

Star map reproduced from memory by Betty Hill.

probable since nearly all of the material revealed by Barney under hypnosis also appeared in Betty's account. There were, however, some notable exceptions. For example, Barney described how the UFO occupants placed a cold cup over his groin during the examination. Later he developed a circular ring of warts around the groin. Barney, who would rather have believed it was a dream, was never able to accept Dr. Simon's theory simply because his own memories, after hypnosis, were too vivid.

Neither the Hills nor Dr. Simon ever initially sought any publicity for this case. Against their wishes, however, the story eventually received press coverage based on the incomplete information uncovered by one reporter. After this happened, the Hills, taking the advice of a lawyer, decided to allow John Fuller, a professional writer, to publish the complete story in a book. Fuller was given full access to the audio tapes from the hypnotic sessions. His book, *The Interrupted Journey*, implies that the abduction actually did occur. He puts the case within the context of other UFO sightings in the New Hampshire area, as well as other possible UFO abduction cases. While Dr. Simon would not go so far as to accept Fuller's conclusions, he participated in the book to the extent of insuring that accurate psychiatric information was provided.[209]

Betty Hill's sketch of the star map was reproduced in Fuller's book.

This map inspired Marjorie Fish, an Ohio schoolteacher and amateur astronomer, to inquire whether Betty had been shown an actual pattern of celestial objects. Using beads dangling on threads suspended from the ceiling of her home, Ms. Fish constructed three dimensional models of the stars in the vicinity of our own solar system. What she discovered may actually be our first important clue to the location of intelligent life elsewhere in the galaxy. The view in Betty's map closely corresponds to the perspective one would see from the vicinity of a double-star system known as Zeta Reticuli, visible in the southern hemisphere, thirty-seven light years away.

A number of professional astronomers have carefully scrutinized Fish's data using sophisticated computer systems. Her hypothesis has been confirmed by scientists at Ohio State University, the University of Pittsburg, Northwestern University, and the University of Utah. In each case, the likelihood of Fish's hypothesis has been confirmed. David R. Saunders, a statistics expert at the Industrial Relations Center of the University of Chicago, concluded that the odds of such a perfect match happening on a chance basis are about 1,000 to 1.[210]

Because the Zeta Reticuli system is one of sixteen nearby stars, similar enough to our own sun to support life-bearing planets, we would be most likely to visit there if we were looking for life as we know it in the vicinity of our solar system.

Another intriguing aspect of this case is the implication of telepathic interaction between the Hills and the UFO occupants. From the different accounts, it appears that the "extra-terrestrials" used a combination of speech, gestures, and ESP in their communication. Betty reports, for example, that

194

although they spoke English, they asked her the meaning of several simple words, like "vegetable." In other similar abduction case which occurred in 1967, policeman Herbert Schirmer of Ashland, Nebraska, also reported alien beings communicating to him with both ESP and speech. Schirmer also suffered from amnesia which could only be reversed through hypnosis. His case was evaluated by psychologist Leo Sprinkle of the University of Wyoming, who felt the testimony was·authentic.[211,212]

Further light is shed on the parapsychological dimensions of such UFO encounters as a result of an experience reported by Robert Monroe, author of *Journeys Out of the Body*. Monroe's many out-of-body experiences, which have been previously mentioned, actually began with an encounter strangely reminiscent of some of the more believable UFO abduction cases.

Monroe himself wasn't aware of the connection until many years after the following event when he first read Fuller's book on the Betty and Barney Hill case, *The Interrupted Journey*. There were three facts presented in the book which astonished him. The first of these was the physical examination which is described as taking place within the saucer vehicle. Secondly, were the beeping noises that the Hills heard, and lastly the blemishes which appeared on the Hill's automobile. Fortunately, Monroe had kept careful records of his experiences and he was able to check his notes for 1958 when this experience occurred.

He was alone one evening, in a little ten-by-ten office, which he had built for himself back in the Virginia Blue Ridge mountains. The first strange thing he noticed was a repeating tone about 800 cycles per second. Then it felt to him as if a beam of *heat* penetrated the walls of his office and hit his body, from a position about thirty degrees above the horizon. From that point on he was aware of the presence of three or four entities. He was unable to see their forms in detail, although he had a sense that he was seeing some forms. He also had the experience of telepathic communication with them which lasted for about two and a half hours. Particularly striking for Monroe was the sensation of having a cup-like object placed over his groin—precisely as Barney Hill had described!

The examination and communication which followed was rather detailed. Monroe felt the most important sensation was as if his brain were being probed—as if everything he knew or thought was examined. Of course, he was rather awestruck by the situation and didn't make all of the observations which he later thought of. Today, he maintains that the examination took place while he was outside of his body, but still in the physical environment of his office. However, being inexperienced at the time, he didn't know how to interpret the event. Now he even hypothesizes that the incident may have changed his brain in some way which led to his subsequent out-of-body journeying.

Generally speaking Monroe does not associate the out-of-body state with other UFO encounters. He acknowledges the presence of many strange creatures and beings in the out-of-body state, but feels that there is no evidence that they are

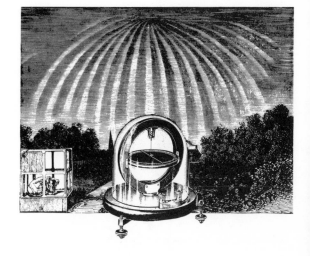

related to UFOs. Only on one other out-of-body trip did he experience anything like a UFO:

This happened in the early days of my out-of-body journeys, from the same office. I rolled out of the physical and thought I would go play for a while. It was a beautiful cumulus cloud day. So I went up and was doing power rolls through clouds and things like that. As I came out and circled round this one large cumulus, there was this disk shaped object sitting between two cloud towers. The cockpit was, I would assume, maybe ten or eleven feet in diameter. There were two snake-like heads coming out of it. They were long heads without any shoulders. They could have been mechanical devices. They appeared to be rotating, like rods with helmets on top. I perceived a peculiar sort of frequency coming out of them. I was within two hundred feet. Then I got nervous and just turned around and went home before I was discovered.[213]

These are the only UFO experiences which Monroe associates with the out-of-body state. However, he also describes peculiar visions which he gets which are preceeded by a hissing sound and a sensation like a valve opening in his brain. Monroe claims that these visions have produced accurate scenes of the future in so far as he has been able to verify them. One such vision, which has not yet manifested, describes what might sound like mass UFO landings:

Behind the first wave is row after row of the strange aircraft, literally hundreds of them. They are not like any airplanes I have seen before. No wings are visible, and each machine is gigantic, some three-thousand feet across. Each is shaped like the head of an arrow, V-shaped, but with no fuselage as in our swept-wing airplanes. The V shape is not a lifting surface, but houses the occupants in two or three decks. They sail majestically overhead, and I feel a tingle of awe at the mighty power they represent. I also feel fear, because I somehow know that these are not manmade.[214]

It would take a great deal of investigation to verify Monroe's claims in a strict parapsychological sense. This type of exploration is at the limits of what professional researchers have been willing to consider. I cannot present Monroe's claims with any authority behind them. However, I am clear that Monroe is a credible and worthy of serious consideration. Many other individuals are making similar claims; most, but not all, are easy to dismiss.

For example, members living in a Berkeley communal group called the *One World Family*, under the charismatic leadership of a "cosmic messiah," claim to be in regular telepathic communication with celestial beings who man flying saucers. In fact, according to these Bible-quoting utopians, the UFO occupants are nothing less than the angels of the Bible, sent to earth on a spiritual mission by galactic headquarters. Similar messages are echoed by dozens of small groups throughout the country. Generally important sounding, but vague, messages are "channelled" to these groups through mediums.

Another classic contactee is George Adamski, a trance medium, who received telepathic messages which led to his alleged encounters with numerous fair-haired and radiant Venusians, Martians and Saturnians. On one occasion several

individuals signed sworn affidavits saying that they had witnessed the landing of a small saucer-shaped craft as well as Adamski's conversation with the tall, radiant being, who stepped out and left foot prints in the middle of the desert. This landing had been predicted by Adamski and was said to be an effort to warn earthlings about nuclear misuse. The credibility of this particular incident has been overshadowed by the unmistakably deceptive character of Adamski's other reports. He claimed, for example, to have been taken to the far side of the moon aboard a spacecraft. There he discovered UFO bases along with cities, lakes, rivers, and even snow-capped mountains. Of course, subsequent space probes have proved this impossible.

We will probably never know the complete story behind Adamski's claims. All of the varied evidence tends to mitigate against any simplistic interpretations.

An interesting sequel to this case took place in England on April 24, 1965. A Mr. E. A. Bryant of Scoriton, South Devon, was out walking in the country when he was confronted by a large aerial object which appeared out of thin air and landed forty yards in front of him. An opening appeared in the side of the ''saucer'' and three figures dressed in ''diving gear'' stepped forward. One of them stated in English that his name was ''Yamski'' or something similar. He went on to say that it was a pity that ''Des'' or ''Les'' wasn't there, as he would understand the visitation. Metallic fragments were left at the spot and later analyzed by members of the Exeter Astronomical Society. The odd aspect of this story is that George Adamski, who collaborated with Desmond Leslie in the book *Flying Saucers Have Landed*, died on April 23, 1965.[215]

Evidentially this is not a strong case, as there was only one witness. However, such testimony does illustrate the complexity of the phenomena which we lump together in the UFO category. Perhaps the physical technology necessary for intersteller space travel necessitates a much greater understanding of psychic consciousness than that which our present day science possesses. Many UFO cases are intertwined with parapsychological phenomena. However, alleged psychic phenomena which imply extra-terrestrial contact can not be taken at face value.

In 1899, Professor Theodore Flournoy, a psychologist at the University of Geneva, published a book called *From India to the Planet Mars* which detailed the trance communications of Mlle. Catherine Muller (known under the pseudonym of Helen Smith). In this book he documented striking incidents of telepathy and even a good deal of evidence for a past reincarnation in India—complete with historical accuracy and a knowledge of Sanskrit. He further claimed to have observed incidences of psychokinesis. In spite of such accomplishments, Mlle. Muller's greatest claim was to have established mediumistic contact with people from the planet Mars. The medium actually furnished the investigators with a Martian language, complete with its own unique written characters. A number of other investigators defended the extra-terrestrial origin of the language.

Martian Landscape drawn by Catherine Muller while in a trance.

Flournoy, however, challenged this claim and produced evidence that the Martian language was actually a subconscious elaboration based on French grammar, inflections, and construction. Had it not been for Flournoy's careful analysis, Mlle. Muller might have been credited as the first human being to have established intelligent communication with Mars.

Actually the Swedish seer, Emmanual Swedenborg, also claimed to have engaged in extensive psychic communication with inhabitants of other planets. His descriptions certainly imply some sort of direct experience:

> The inhabitants of the Moon are small, like children of six or seven years old; at the same time, they have the strength of men like ourselves. Their voices roll like thunder, and the sound proceeds from the belly, because the Moon is in quite a different atmosphere from the other planets.

Carl Jung
(Courtesy Psychic Magazine.*)*

Carl Jung, the great Swiss psychiatrist, saw such descriptions as an archetypal mythmaking process within the collective unconscious, or subliminal mind of mankind.[216] He pointed out that, faced with decaying religious values and mythological structures, men attempt to create a new sense of cosmic unity and belonging. The round saucer shape itself has historically symbolized wholeness. When the traditional conceptions of religion are no longer potent, the mind's image-forming processes invest a great deal of psychic energy in forming new images and new unconscious links with the creator. Jung saw this process reflected in his patient's dreams as well as in modern art and fiction. This unconscious activity he felt, could account for many UFO experiences with religious or occult overtones.

However, it was not his intention to deny the reality of such experiences. After ten year's research into the UFO literature written by such respected scientists as Edward Ruppelt, former head of the Air Force Project Blue Book,[217] and Major Donald Keyhoe, director of NICAP,[218] Jung felt that there was no room for doubting that many UFOs sighted were physically real. He suggested that some religiously-oriented UFO experiences were simply occasioned by or projected upon actual sightings. He also hypothesized that certain psychic projections could throw back an echo upon a radar screen or result in other physical manifestations. Research in psychokinesis, particularly the story of Phillip the Imaginary Ghost, certainly suggests that this is possible.

The 1917 appearances of "the Virgin Mary" at Fatima, Portugal, seems to bear characteristics of a psychically triggered UFO manifestation.

Three young children, Lucia dos Santos, Francisco Marto and his sister Jacinta, figure in this series of extraordinary events. According to their testimony, they were first visited by an angel who asked them to pray. In May, 1917, they were visited by the figure of a lady who spoke to them and told them to return to the same field on the thirteenth of each month for more messages. Each month more and more people gathered with them to behold the appearances. Many witnesses noted strange lights and sounds, but only the children reported actual contact with the radiant Lady. The children claimed to recieve much information which was passed on to Roman Catholic Church officials, with instructions that it be released to the public in 1960.

In October, so many people were aware of the phenomena that over 50,000 had gathered at the Cova da Iria to witness the event. Much to the delight of freethinking skeptics, it was raining that day. The sky was completely overcast. Some spectators saw a column of blue smoke in the vicinity of the children which appeared and disappeared three times. Then suddenly the rain ceased and through the clouds was seen a radiant disk, not the sun, spinning, and throwing off fantastic streamers of light—a constantly changing montage of red, violet, blue, yellow, and white. This continued for about four minutes.

Then the disk advanced toward the earth until it was just over the crowd. The heat was enormous and many were terrified that the end of the world had come. When it finally retreated into the sky, the shaken masses realized that their clothes and the ground were completely dry—although they had been soaked to the skin a few minutes before.

On October 1930, after eight years of investigation, the Catholic Church announced that the apparitions seen had been genuine visitations of the Virgin Mary. However, for its own reasons, the Church has decided not to publish the prophecies which were given to the children.[219]

More recently, in 1968, a series of apparitions, seemingly of the Virgin Mary, appeared above the roof of a Coptic Orthodox Church in Zeitoun, Egypt, a suburb north of Cairo. For a period of several months, thousands of people observed and photographed these images. To this day, no rational explanations have been offered for the phenomena. Hundreds of spontaneous healings were reported at the site which were investigated by a commission of medical doctors headed by Dr. Shafik Abd El Malik of Ain Shams University. The apparitions ceased to appear only after the Egyptian government cordoned off the area and began selling tickets to the throngs who had come to observe the phenomena.[220]

The philosopher C. J. Ducasse mentions a case in which the Rev. Abraham Cummings, holder of a Master of Arts degree from Brown University, attempted to expose the apparition of a deceased woman which he had assumed was a hoax. Cummings writes as follows:

Some time in July 1806, in the evening, I was informed by two persons that they had just seen the Spectre in the field. About ten minutes after, I went out, not to see a miracle for I believed they had been mistaken. Looking toward an eminence twelve rods distance from the house, I saw there as I supposed, one of the white rocks. This confirmed my opinion of their spectre, and I paid no attention to it. Three minutes after, I accidentally looked in the same direction, and the white rock was in the air; its form a complete globe, with a tincture of red . . . and its diameter about two feet. Fully satisfied that this was nothing ordinary I went toward it for more accurate examination. While my eye was constantly upon it, I went on for four or five steps,

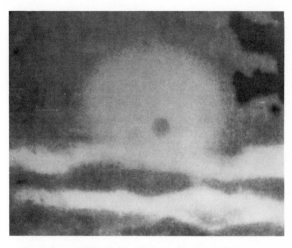

Rare photo of disk which miraculously appeared at Fatima, Portugal on Oct. 13, 1917. The disk is shown after it had descended, near the horizon. (Courtesy Association for the Understanding of Man, P.O. Box 5310, Austin, Texas 78763. Taken from the book Fatima Prophecy: Days of Darkness Promise of Light*)*

when it came to me from the distance of eleven rods, as quick as lightning, and instantly assumed a personal form with a female dress, but did not appear taller than a girl seven years old. While I looked upon her, I said in my mind 'you are not tall enough for the woman who has so frequently appeared among us!' Immediately she grew up as large and tall as I considered that woman to be. Now she appeared glorious. On her head was the representation of the sun diffusing the luminous, rectilinear rays every way to the ground. Through the rays I saw the personal form and the woman's dress.[221]

According to Cummings this apparition appeared many times, speaking and delivering discourses sometimes over an hour long. In his pamphlet on the subject, he produces some thirty affidavits from persons who had witnessed the spectre. Each time the manifestation began as a small luminous cloud which grew until it took the form of the deceased woman. Witnesses also observed the form vanish in a similar manner.

Sometimes events, which we might otherwise dismiss as uncanny coincidences, begin to take on a meaningful pattern. This has been the case regarding circumstances surrounding Uri Geller. In his account Dr. Andrija Puharich noted that at stressful times a white, hawklike bird often appeared and seemed to renew his faith in the intelligent powers working through Geller. The following description is typical:

At times one of the birds would glide in from the sea right up to within a few meters of the balcony; it would flutter there in one spot and stare at me directly in the eyes. It was a unique experience to look into the piercing "intelligent" eyes of a hawk. It was then that I knew I was not looking into the eyes of an earthly hawk. This was confirmed about 2 p.m. when Uri's eyes followed a feather, loosened from the hawk, that floated on an updraft toward the top of the Sharon Tower. As his eyes followed the feather to the sky, he was startled to see a dark spacecraft parked directly over the hotel. We all looked where he pointed, but we did not see what he saw. But I believed that he saw what he said he saw.[222]

Such a statement might well be taken as face-value evidence that Puharich has lost any claim to objectivity. However, within the context of Geller's extraordinary feats, there may be some reason to take Puharich seriously. Geller himself proposed a rather subtle interpretation of the hawk and spacecraft phenomena.

He felt that this was simply a form taken by IS [an abbreviated term for Intelligence in the Sky], just as they took the form of a spacecraft, because it suited their purposes.[223]

Other individuals besides Puharich have also noted the appearance of a white hawk in situations favorably connected with Geller. Ila Ziebel, a psychologist from Madison, Wisconsin, was with Geller and Puharich during some of the most dramatic sightings in Israel. Ray Stanford, the psychic from Austin, Texas, who works with the Association for the Understanding of Man has seen the hawk as a symbolic, yet real, form of the intelligence which works through Geller. Stanford also associates the Hawk with UFO phenomena.* Appropriately enough, Puharich himself still uses the term "Horus" when referring to this hawk.

Saul-Paul Sirag, a research associate at the Institute for the Study of Consciousness in Berkeley and author of the syndicated science column, *The New Alchemy*, has had a similar experience. While in a drug-induced altered state of consciousness, he had the opportunity to spend some time alone with Uri. At that time he asked Geller to reveal the source of his power to him. Geller agreed and asked Saul-Paul to stare into his eyes. Sirag, who at that time had never heard of the "Horus" experiences, exclaimed that he saw a very distinct eagle-like figure in Geller's eyes! Uri then confirmed that this was the source of his power.

These experiences are still quite subjective and easy to dismiss. However they fit into a larger pattern. On May 7, 1974, Uri Geller appeared in a most brilliant public demonstration before some 700 people at the St. Francis Hotel in San Francisco. The demonstration was sponsored by the Esalen Institute in connection with a larger symposium on psychic phenomena. The highlight of his performance was the bending of a spoon which was provided by a physicist from San Francisco State University. The stainless steel spoon was projected on to a large video screen so that the entire audience could clearly see Uri wiggle and bend it as though it were made of rubber. (By no means are all of his public appearances this successful—many are rather disappointing in terms of phenomena, although audiences are inevitably charmed by his boyish personality.) One striking thing, to me, was the white falcon engraving prominently on display in a showcase next to the hotel's main entrance!

Hoping to unearth more information about the mechanics of these archetypal coincidences, I managed to contact the man who had made the engravings. He was very disturbed by my mention of Uri Geller and psychic phenomena. He had learned to create drawings of these magnificent birds by watching them in their natural habitat. All he would tell me was this: "You have to be very careful. One false move and you've lost them."

Another falcon coincidence occurs on the cover of the October 18, 1974, issue of *Nature* magazine, which carried an article on the scientific research with Geller at the Stanford Research Institute. This illustration came from a century-old issue of *Nature* in which is mentioned the view of Alfred

Image of buzzard taken from the cover of Nature, *October 18, 1974.*

---

*An interesting coincidence further connecting Ray Stanford to the archetypal Horus intelligence, was evidenced in the January 1974 issue of *Analog* science fiction magazine. The magazine cover, illustrating a story called "The Horus Errand" depicted a hawk-shaped vehicle, and a "psychonaut" named Stanford whose duty was to guide the souls of departed citizens of a futuristic pyramid-shaped city safely into their next chosen incarnation. Further inquiry revealed the coincidence that the cover-artist, Kelly Freas (who also designed the official Skylab uniform patches) had known Ray Stanford and had a psychic reading from him some 15 years ago.

Russell Wallace, a spiritualist and co-author with Darwin of the theory of evolution, that man is more than a highly complex machine devoid of free will.

The outstanding twentieth century medium Eileen Garrett whose talents were examined by numerous researchers, including Puharich and Rhine, organized the Parapsychology Foundation. In a cogent passage relating the hawk symbol to consciousness she states:

Among all our psychological faculties, awareness is the capacity for cognizance. As such it transcends the limitations which time and space impose upon the senses, and is able to gather experience in areas of being which the senses can never reach. Its nature is to poise, like a hunting hawk, ready to be sent abroad in any direction, to impale the attractive face, idea, or event, to bring back to consciousness the trophy of its flight. It can move in any and all three of the dimensions of consciousness represented by memory, the senses, and the imagination; and when controlled by the will, its efficiency can become a creative force in the individual life.

If, briefly, we shut out all sensory intrusions, and focus awareness upon our inner selves, we shall acquire a sense of the dark and featureless vitality that moves in our bodies. And if then we ask ourselves, "What do I most want in this world and this life?" we shall experience the flight of the hawk—sensations created by awareness moving to find the answer. This movement may be in either of two directions but not in the third. If we have thought constructively of this idea before, awareness may move into memory to find the answer; but if the question is not repetitive, awareness will make its flight toward the open spaces of inspiration. It may not bring back the answer, for the question is deep and subtle; but if we continue to sustain our resistance to sensory intrusions, and keep perception centered on the hawk, we shall perceive at least the direction in which inspiration lies, and undoubtedly the first creative stirrings of response.[224]

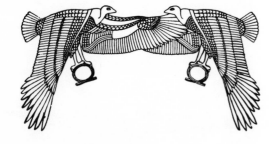

Egyptian buzzards, guiding the soul between worlds.

This interpretation is not purely a "flight of fantasy" as it is consistent with the esoteric teachings of many different cultures. In ancient India, Persia, Mexico, Babylon, and Egypt, the hawk was a symbol of the power which carried the soul of man from earth to heaven.[225]

The logic which attempts to relate these apparently disconnected events assumes a kind of connectivity which transcends mechanical causality and treats events symbolically in a meaningful way. It is similar to the reasoning which was used to infer the existence of discarnate personalities in the well-known cross-correspondence cases. One enters into a world where certain coincidences carry with them an intended message from some other intelligence in the cosmos or within us. This is the magical world view of the ancient Sumerians. It is also the type of logic commonly associated with psychotics in our culture. It is the logic of dreams, of art and poetry, and of modern depth psychology.*

I often approach interpreting the omens and dreams which occur in my life as if I were reading a good novel. At first the symbols may seem disconnected and irrelevant to me, but grad-

---

*In writing this passage, I am deeply struck with the interconnectedness of all of the ideas and traditions I am writing about. If my writing were to more closely approximate my actual thought processes, the result would be much less linear and more like looking at a picture.

ually they lead to the deeper mythological forces which are motivating me through the drama of my existence. In being particularly aware of the associations and puns in my mind, I have come to see that some symbols have a personal meaning for me while other patterns are indicative of the larger consciousness which guides the lives and fates of many people, even whole cultures. This seems to be the case with the hawk.

Like a hologram, the life of any one individual can reveal the archetypal processes which underly the dynamics of larger consciousness.

In November 1973 I had a lucid dream experience in which Uri was visiting me at the Institute for the Study of Consciousness in Berkeley where I then lived. In my dream, I witnessed him actually pass through a wall inside of the house; I was so shocked that I fainted. The next thing I remember, in the dream, is Uri holding me up, shaking me somewhat, and speaking to me. Then a UFO appeared in the sky and I felt a beam of tingling energy, like electricity, from the UFO, enter my body between my eyes. At the same time I sensed a telepathic message from the UFO intelligences that I should let them know how much energy, which was apparently vitalizing my body in some way, was tolerable for me. The energy permeated my entire body, through my forehead, until I began to feel uncomfortable. Then it stopped.

This was such a lucid dream that I told a number of people about it. I spoke to several people who were having comparable dreams involving the alteration of their bodies by "higher forces." Nearly six months later, I had the opportunity to discuss this dream with both Puharich and Geller. Immediately they asked me to tell them the exact date of the dream. I recalled that it had been several days before Thanksgiving. This excited both as they claimed that in November 1973, Geller had suddenly been teleported from his home in New York City to Ossinging, N.Y., fifty miles away where he came suddenly crashing into a room at Puharich's home. Puharich further stated that he and Uri had also experienced alterations of their bodies similar in feeling to my dream.

Another key to the mystery of Uri Geller is the implication that the intelligences which work through him are somehow very advanced *computers*. In his book *Uri*, Andrija Puharich quotes the following electronic transmission received by him and Uri from this intelligence:

> The real intelligence behind us is our innerselves. We have passed our souls, bodies and minds into computers and moved several millions of light-years backwards towards your time and dimension.*[226]

Several other passages in Puharich's book emphasize the computer-like quality of the powers which supposedly work through Geller. On some occasions, the voice which is heard speaking to them spontaneously over the tape recorder, telephone, or radio takes on an artificial, mechanical timbre.

---

*According to Puharich this message came from a tape recorder which began running by itself.

This aspect of the Geller phenomena has been corroborated in a strange way by the theoretical physicist Jack Sarfatti, the co-author of *Space-Time and Beyond: Toward an Explanation of the Unexplainable*.[227] Sarfatti—who has been on the physics faculty of San Diego State University, Birkbeck College of the University of London, and also the International Center for Theoretical Physics in Trieste, Italy—has published a number of papers, in major scientific journals, which attempt to provide a theoretical understanding of psychic phenomena and consciousness. His theories are presented in the following chapter. Generally speaking, Sarfatti's insights come to him in dreams and trance-like states of awareness. He has shown a particular interest in Uri Geller and tells one story about himself which tends to corroborate the most fantastic explanations of the Geller phenomena:

I'm probably about to destroy my credibility with most of the scientific establishment—but I don't think so. I'm trying to give all of the data that I know. I'm not going to evaluate the data. Anybody can form their own judgement as to the significance of what I'm about to report. I myself have not integrated it into my world view. I have no definite way of handling this experience.

In 1952 and 1953 when I was about twelve or thirteen years old, I received a phone call. In my memory at the moment I received a phone call in which a mechanical sounding voice at the other end said that it was a computer and gave some kind of name which I've forgotten. It was a computer on board a flying saucer. They wanted to teach me something and would I be willing? This was my free choice. Would I be willing to be taught—to communicate with them?

I remember a shiver going up my spine, because I said, "Hey man, this is real." Of course, I was a kid. I thought, well maybe it's some sexual pervert. A man trying to murder me or something like that. I went through a real paranoid trip. But I said, "yes."

My next memory of that is that I ran out of the house—ran out of my apartment in Brooklyn. My mother wasn't there. I ran down to my little buddies on the street and I said, "Hey, a flying saucer just called me up. Come on over to my house. They're coming and they're going to come through the window and take me away." I'm twelve years old.

We were sort of "dead end kids." This was a gang of kids right out of "The Lords of Flatbush." We went upstairs and, of course, nothing happened. This was a big joke. Okay.

But what's interesting is that my mother remembers this experience very well. It turns out that I had forgotten most of it. This was really something that occurred over several weeks. Apparently what happened, which is completely blanked from my memory, but not from hers, was that I continually received phone calls. Many phone calls from the same source. My mother says I was walking around really strange. She began to get worried about me. Finally one day she picked up the phone and she hears this computer. She remembers the voices very much the way Puharich talks about these things. But this is twenty years ago. It's not just me, it's my mother also remembering this. A Jewish mother; she said, "Leave my boy alone!"

The Jewish mother talking to the flying saucer or whatever the hell they were. My mother has a strong personality. And that was the end of it. We never got a phone call, apparently, after that.[228]

Sarfatti seems to feel that the origins of his scientific ideas regarding psychic phenomena are somehow related to this childhood experience.

Adding to the irony the name, Spectra, which Puharich associates with the powerful intelligence working through

204

Geller, also refers to the most advanced generation of computers yet designed. RCA Corporation (which, incidentally, owns Random House) was unable to match their brilliant engineering with a comparable marketing capability—and as a result Spectra computers are no longer on the market. These computers were actually designed by a previous generation of machines!

To push this exercise in the logic of synchronicity to its limit, I will mention a personal experience which could be thought of as another piece of the puzzle. One day several months ago I chanced to encounter an old friend of mine who I hadn't seen for about eighteen months. We were standing in front of a movie theatre where Andy Worhol's sensuous 3-d version of *Frankenstein* was playing. This story of the destruction resulting from the immature and misunderstood effort to master the mysteries of life and death has captured the imagination of western civilization since the early part of the industrial revolution. Upon seeing my friend, I recalled a striking and powerful dream I had had a few days previously involving her.

In my dream, which was embarrassing to talk about at first, I had been sucking on her breast and actually ended up biting off her nipple. When I said this she was astonished because a few days earlier she had experienced very strong emotions while watching another bizarre movie on television in which a godlike figure commanded that a woman's breasts be bitten off. The interesting thing about this movie, *The Steambath*, is that the omnipotent figure gave his instructions to a computer which then executed his commands.

This experience seemed to me to be a possible affirmation of the *notion* that computers could be used to execute the desires, positive and negative, of a higher intelligence. Whether or not actual computers are used, the image—like that of the flying saucer—is one which seems to have flourished in the imagination of modern man.

In the history chapter we discussed the image of the Invisible College, which was used by the early Rosicrucians to symbolize their internal contact with higher intelligence. Today this same term is used by scientists, such as Dr. J. Allen Hynek, to refer to the loosely connected network of scientists investigating the UFO data.[229]

An interesting perspective on the "invisible college" comes from a report from Dr. Shafica Karagula, director of the Higher Sense Perception Research Foundation in Los Angeles. Karagula specializes in clinical studies of individuals who are gifted with unusual perceptive talents. One of her subjects, whom she calls Vicky described a series of experiences she has in her sleep where she seems to be visiting a college and attending classes in many different subjects. Her vision is quite lucid, recalling the architecture of the buildings, and the subject matter of her lectures. The lectures follow an orderly sequence and Karagula claims to have carefully recorded a number of them from Vicky.

On one occasion, Vicky remembered that a friend of hers, who lived across the United States was in the classroom with

The Invisible College of The Rosicrucians

her. After some cautious questioning on the telephone, this person verified that he also remembered being present—although he didn't recall the details of the lecture as clearly as she did.[230]

Although similar experiences have been reported by many people, and are known to dream-researchers, they have yet to be more systematically probed. This phenomena is still at the very frontiers of parapsychological understanding.

The notion of hidden intelligences which influence the affairs of the human race has an old and venerable tradition and can be found in all religions. We have seen its operation in the Rosicrucian literature and it has been a particularly active notion in modern occultism. The founding of the Theosophical Society was based on phenomena very similar to that we have observed in the Geller situation—the crucial exception being that only the Geller phenomena were witnessed by scientists under controlled laboratory conditions.

The work of Ray Stanford in Austin, Texas, exemplifies a situation in which UFO phenomena of the type associated with Geller overlap with communications from the masters of the spiritual hierarchy. *Psychic Magazine* provides the following capsule description of Stanford's many activities:

During his teens, Ray Stanford had a fascination with rockets and their principles of operation. In 1955, he was awarded the Texas Academy of Science's top award for his report on "Experiments with

Lasar transmitting and recieving system for experimental communication attempts with unidentified flying objects. Components include an 8 inch Schmidt-Cassegrain telescope; video recorder-playback unit for modulating intermediate frequency lasar transmission; recording magnetometer; video monitor; video camera with built in microphone. Equipment not shown include a six-foot parabolic microphone for UFO sound studies and cameras used at other research sites for triangulation studies. (Courtesy Project Starlight International, P.O. Box 5310, Austin, Texas 78763.)

Multiple-Stage Principles of Rocketry.'' Some of his rockets weighed several hundred pounds each and challenged, if they did not break, amateur rocket altitude records.

From 1954 through 1959, he had a series of witnessed unidentified flying object (UFO) observations, including a landing on October 21, 1956, which he had predicted. One sighting in 1959 was simultaneously filmed by 8mm and 16mm movie cameras. The case is listed as ''unidentified'' in the U.S. Air Force files.

The turning point in his career, however, occurred in early 1960 during a group meditation, when he spontaneously passed into an ecstatic state which involved a sense of floating above his body experiencing ''. . . a unity with light and love from beyond my normal state.'' Lapsing into an unconscious state, he awoke some two hours later to learn that strange voices and personalities had manifested through him calling themselves ''Brothers.'' One of the voices announced that ''Stanford's unconscious being could, when given appropriate suggestion, give medical clairvoyance and describe former life personalities and activities for individuals.'' . . .

Final proof for him occurred in April of 1961 when he says that he along with four others in a lighted room in Austin, Texas, saw one of the Brothers, who had frequently spoken through him, suddenly materialize as a visible, glowing form over seven feet tall, complete with robe and metallic-like headpiece. That experience convinced him once and for all that the Brothers were something other than unconscious masquerades.[231]

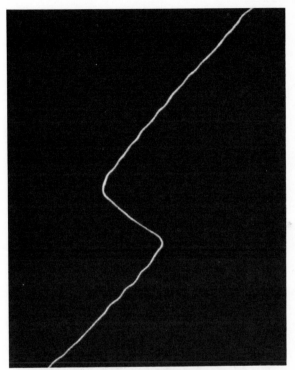

More recently in his trance readings, Ray has received instructions for designing a major laboratory for UFO research.[232] Now known as *Project Starlight International*, the laboratory's operation is in its initial stages. The project currently includes a large ring of flashing colored lights out in the Texas foothills (in order to attract UFOs) along with sophisticated monitoring and communication equipment. Photographs of UFOs which appear authentic have been taken and are currently being analyzed by scientists such as Dr. James Harder at the University of California, Berkeley.

One *Brother* who speaks through Ray is known as Kuthumi and appears to be—somewhat to Ray's embarrassment—a Mahatma as referred to by Madame Blavatsky. This entity bears all of the earmarks of an angelic, radiant, spiritual being. However Ray himself is quite careful to distinguish his own trance personalities from those of the UFO occupants—with whom he claims to have had no direct contact.[233] Ray does suggest that the UFO occupants are very skilled in psychic abilities as well as in forms of travel which alter space-time relationships as we understand them. In terms of our own relationship with the universe of UFO occupants, Stanford's readings suggest that:

UFO photographed over Texas, October, 1974 by Project Starlight International. Approximately three seconds exposure. (Courtesy Project Starlight International.)

Planets are to civilizations what rivers are to salmon—spawning places. When we become adult we will have to go out into the sea of space and accept our place in . . . the cosmological community.[234]

The Biological Vehicle of Consciousness

The Physical Body

In the introduction to *The Roots of Consciousness* we discussed the evolution of organized matter from the photon through particles, atoms and molecules to living cells that begin to differentiate in structure and function forming a wide variety of tissues and organs which play a specialized function in the human body. It is reasonable to assume that all these levels of organization including the whole human being play a role in shaping consciousness. Particularly important are the nervous system, comprising brain and spinal cord, and the endocrine system, comprising a number of ductless glands which secrete hormones into the bloodstream.

Neuron cells are the principle units of the nervous system. Their function is to conduct nerve impulses which transmit information. The twelve billion neurons in your body vary greatly in size and shape; however they all have two general parts: a *cell body* and *fibers*. The cell body contains structures that keep the neuron alive and properly functioning. The neural fibers are of two classes: *dendrites* which are stimulated by neighboring neurons or physical stimuli; and *axons*, which transmit impulses to other neurons or to an effector, such as a muscle or gland.

The process by which pulses transmit across the neural membrane is electrochemical. The pulses are caused by rapid and reversible changes in the permeability of the membrane to certain ions. The resulting flows of ions across the membrane give rise to electrical impulses which can be detected and recorded with various instruments. The size of the nerve impulses and the speed with which they travel characterize each particular neuron and do not relate to the strength of the stimuli which initiated them. Firing thresholds will vary with time from neuron to neuron depending on many factors; however once the threshold is reached, the electrochemical changes which cause the impulse proceed to completion. Therefore, information about any stimulus is carried by (1) the frequency of nerve firing and (2) by the number of particular fibers which carry impulses, and not by the strength of any single impulse. This, incidentally, is the same on/off principle by which information is coded in a digital computer. Some nerves transmit as many as 1000 impulses each second.

Neurons are stimulated to fire by either the sensory receptors or other neurons. Nerve impulses are transmitted from one neuron to another or from a neuron to a muscle or gland across an important gap known as a *synapse*. The whole region including the *bouton* on the end of the axon on one neuron, the gap, and the post-synaptic membrane of the adjoining cell, can be called the *synaptic region* (see illustration). Information is transmitted across the synaptic gap by enzymes which are delicately released from little spheres in the bouton called *vesicles*. The information is received at the postsynaptic membrane which is generally either excited or inhibited by these chemicals depending again on many factors, such as the particular

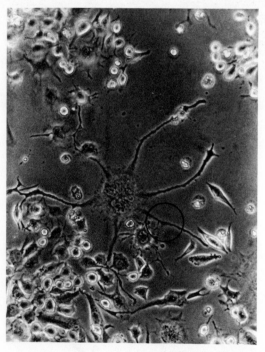

Multi-polar Neuron
(Courtesy Angela M. Longo)

208

combination of enzymes transmitted across the synapse or the interaction with the electro-magnetic environment around the body.

If the post-synaptic membrane is stimulated by an inhibiting neurotransmitter its firing threshold will become higher. An excitatory neurotransmitter will lower the firing threshold of a given neuron, causing it to fire more often. The actual firing threshold of a neuron is variable and is often determined by the combined influence of hundreds of synapses. Thus the synaptic aspect of neural transmission is not an all or none affair, and may be thought of as the analog or continuous aspect of the human bio-computer. Some nerves actually loop back upon themselves to form *reverbrating circuits* which may be the neural basis for memory storage.

The nervous system itself is quite complex and may be divided into several different structures.

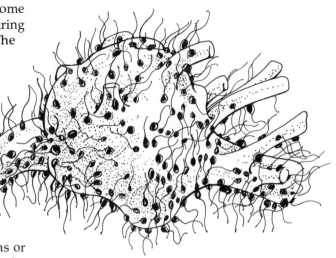

Neuron cell body with synapses from other neurons.

The peripheral nervous system comprises those neurons or parts of neurons which lie outside the bony case formed by the skull and the spine. The somatic nerves of this system mediate the sensory inputs and muscle movements which we are consciously aware of during waking hours.

The autonomic part of the peripheral system regulates many functions—such as the heart rate, blood pressure, endocrine and digestive processes of which we are not normally conscious, but which can be brought under conscious control through bio-feedback and yoga techniques. The *sympathetic* aspect of the autonomic system generally comes into play when we experience strong emotions, while the *parasympathetic* system tends to be active when we are calm and relaxed. The cell bodies of the autonomic nervous system, as well as of the sensory nerves of the somatic system, gather together in *ganglia* alongside the spinal column, and at other points in the body. The cell bodies of somatic motor-nerve fibers, however, are located inside the central nervous system.

The central nervous system is organized into two principle parts, the spinal cord and the brain. The spinal cord serves as a conduction path to and from the brain and also as an organ for effecting reflex action. The brain seems to play an important role in all the complex activities that constitute consciousness— thinking, perception, learning, memory, etc. The three main structures of the brain are known as the hindbrain, the midbrain, and the forebrain.

Within the hindbrain lie the *cerebellum*, the *pons*, and *medulla*. These neural centers regulate breathing, heartbeat, motor coordination, posture, and balance. They are also involved in mediating nerve impulses from the body to the higher brain centers. The midbrain contains numerous nerve fiber tracts and neural centers which regulate body changes in response to visual and auditory stimulation.

The forebrain has reached its greatest development in man and other highly evolved animals, such as porpoises. It comprises the *cerebrum* which is covered by the *cerebral cortex*, the

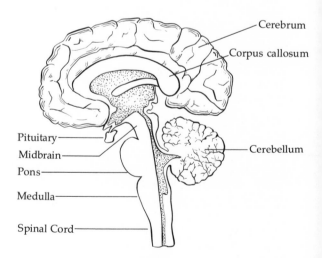

Cross-section of the human brain.

Cerebrum
Corpus callosum
Cerebellum
Pituitary
Midbrain
Pons
Medulla
Spinal Cord

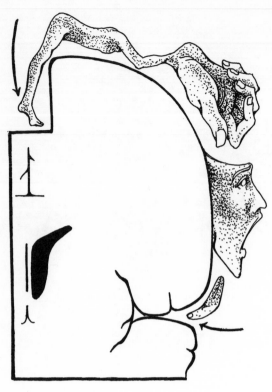

Sensory-motor mapping on human cortex.

thalamus, and a group of closely related structures forming the *limbic system.* These parts of the brain mediate our inner mental and emotional processes.

The perceptions of your own body are mapped out on the cerebral cortex of your brain, which mediates your conscious sensory and motor functions, as well as complex perceptual processes.

One method of researching cerebral functioning has been to electrically stimulate the exposed cortex of human subjects, under local anesthesia, who could then report on their experiences.* By stimulating certain areas various types of sensations, movements and thought patterns can be evoked. Another method of research is to observe the functioning of individuals who have had portions of their brain removed or damaged. Often, especially in the case of young children, removing a portion of the brain does *not* seem to impair the functioning of the mind.[235]

One important line of research has indicated that the two hemispheres of the cerebral cortex function differently. The speech areas of the human cortex are almost always located on the left hemisphere, regardless of whether the person is right or left handed. Several researchers have suggested that the mind's logical and linear functions are associated with the left hemisphere; while the more kinesthetic, pre-verbal, intuitive properties of consciousness derive from the right hemisphere.[236] Frederick Myers suggested such a relationship between a subliminal-right hemisphere and a supraliminal-left hemisphere.[237] The particular functions each hemisphere assumes may vary with different individuals. However, the capacity for two uniquely different modes of consciousness within each individual seems well-established. Important differences also seem to exist between the intellectual cortex and other deeper, emotional layers of the forebrain.[238]

Those parts of the brain which are most attuned to the body's needs and emotional states are the limbic system and the hypothalamus. The hypothalamus is a bundle of nerve bodies, about the size of a peanut, located just above the roof of the mouth. It contains several centers which mediate the excitement and inhibition of the hunger, thirst, and sexual drives, as well as emotional arousal. The activity of these centers is in turn regulated by such factors as hormones in the blood and signals from other parts of the brain, including the cortex. Certain areas in the hypothalamus and limbic system, when stimulated, can be a source of enormous pleasure for the body.

In conjunction with the reticular activating system, the hypothalamus is also involved in the mediation of sleep and arousal states.

By attaching electrodes to the skin of the head, psychologists are able to measure the electrical activity of the brain as a whole. Brain waves thus measured can generally be

---

*Since there are no pain receptors in the brain itself, only the scalp needs to be anesthized. While there are regions of the brain which seem to elicit pain when stimulated, these "pain centers" (i.e. in the limbic region) are simply the parts of the brain which are activated by the pain receptors of the body.

210

Bio-feedback Experimentation (Courtesy Dr. Elmer Green.)

correlated with different states of consciousness ranging from the alert waking state, to drowsiness, hypnagogic imagery, meditation, sleep, and dreaming. Individuals can learn to control their brain waves, and also their internal states of consciousness through techniques which provide them with immediate feedback on their physiological state. Researchers are now suggesting that there may be no biological functions which cannot be brought under conscious control in this fashion.[239] Many individuals are able to develop this control through simple techniques of yoga, hypnosis, and meditation.

The endocrine system, which comprises glands secreting powerful hormones into the bloodstream, is one of the most interesting areas of autonomic functioning. Our personality and character is profoundly effected by our hormone balance. The major endocrine glands are the pituitary and pineal glands in the brain, the thyroid and parathyroids in the throat, the thymus gland located near the heart, the adrenal glands, and the sexual glands. To a lesser degree, other parts of the body, including neurons, also secrete hormones into the bloodstream. The endocrine system is self-regulating in that hormone secretion from any gland is activated in part by other hormones in the bloodstream. The hypothalamus also plays an important role in stimulating certain hormone secretions from the pituitary gland.

The pituitary is often called the "master gland" because it secretes a number of hormones that stimulate or inhibit secretion in the other glands of the body. It also produces hormones which regulate the growth rate of children and which awaken the sexual glands at puberty.

211

Serotonin

Psilocybin

The pineal gland, (sometimes associated with the mystical *third eye* or *ajna chakra*) produces several substances including a hormone known as *5-hydroxytryptamine* or *serotonin*. Serotonin is of the same chemical series of indole alkaloids which also includes psychedelic drugs such as LSD-25, psilocybin, D.M.T. and *bufotenine*.*[240] The exact mechanism by which serotonin might effect consciousness or behavior is not well understood by scientists today. Research findings are paradoxical as serotonin is known to affect different parts of the body and brain in different ways, depending on the proportions and combinations of other hormones and enzymes present during the interaction. Generally speaking serotonin is recognized as a neural inhibitor in the brain. The stores of serotonin in the brain are depleted by reserpine, which is a tranquilizer, and augmented by iproniazid, a mood elevator.[241] Large amounts are present in the limbic system and the hypothalamus. Smaller concentrations occur in the cortex and the cerebellum. Ablation of the nerve network in the brain called the raphe system, which contains considerable amounts of serotonin, is known to produce permanent insomnia. The ingestion of serotonin is unlikely to effect the central nervous system as it does not cross the blood-brain barrier. If it did, its main result would be to put one to sleep. Most of the serotonin in the brain is in the reticular activating system where it plays an important role in the sleep-wake cycle. When serotonin levels in the r.a.s. rise, the brain goes into deep sleep.[242] Other studies have shown greatly increased amounts of serotonin in the brains of psychotic patients. According to biologist John Bleibtrau, "Bananas and plums abound in serotonin; so do figs, and among species of figs none is richer in serotonin than the *ficus religiosa*, known in India as the Bo tree, under which the Buddha reportedly sat when he became enlightened."[243] Thus the hormone produced by the pineal gland makes possible emotions, perception, sleep and wakefulness, and orientation to conventional reality.

The thyroid gland produces a hormone known as *thyroxin*, which controls the metabolic rate at which the body produces energy. Whether a person is slow and sluggish or extremely active is influenced by this hormone. (Occult systems often associate this gland with the throat chakra).

The hormones produced in the thymus gland regulate the process by which the body learns to differentiate its own proteins from foreign substances which may be harmful to it. By this process *antibodies* are manufactured which react only against invading *antigens* and not to the myriad similar substances which are a necessary part of the body.[237] One could think of the thymus gland as being closely related to the body's sense of organic identity. (This gland is sometimes likened to the heart chakra.)

The adrenal glands, located in the back of the body above the kidneys, secrete the hormones *epinephrine* and *norepinephrine* which are related to states of strong emotion.

---

*The last two drugs are derived in the body directly from serotonin—and bufotenine is also the active ingredient in the toads which are proverbally used in witches' brews.

The sympathetic nervous system can stimulate the adrenal glands and the action of the adrenal hormones produced generally intensifies the actions of the sympathetic system throughout the body. It helps mobilize sugar into the blood and makes more energy available to the brain and muscles. It stimulates the heart to beat faster and also constricts the peripheral blood vessels, thus raising blood pressure. (One can see the similarity in functions between this gland and the "power chakra" located at the navel.)

The sex glands or *gonads* are the testes in men and the ovaries in women. The hormones which they produce are responsible for the marked physical changes which take place during puberty—the beginning of menstruation, growth of the breasts, voice changes and beard and body hair growth.

It is important to recognize that the complex activity of manufacturing the hormones and enzymes which regulate both neural transmission and the endocrine system is guided by the subtle programming coded into the genetic structure of each cell in the body. One can view these three modes of physiological functioning as communication systems. Neural transmission provides rapid communication for the whole body—requiring fractions of a second for feedback. The endocrine system provides inter-organ, slow communication—requiring minutes to hours for feedback. While the genetic structure can be seen as an organism-environment communication system requiring many generations for feedback.[244]

It is recognized that manufacturing protein substances within the cells is guided by the DNA codes; however scientists have yet to find a satisfactory explanation for the development of tissues, organs, and whole organisms.[245] Consciousness, itself a function of the whole organism, is still unexplained in terms of biological functioning. Later we will discuss some of the more speculative ideas involving energy fields around the human body which may be related to consciousness.

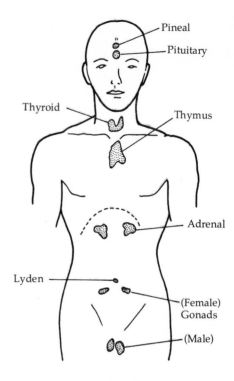

Location of the major endocrine glands in the physical body.

The Ecology of Consciousness

One of the most interesting new areas of science concerns electrostatic interactions between biological organisms and the environment. We've already indicated that the electro-chemical nature of neural transmission plays an important role in mediating information-transfer throughout the body. Now we will take a look at some of the more subtle extensions of our biological functioning:

Our bodies are influenced—in ways which are often overlooked—by the existence of small ions in the atmosphere. The research of scientists such as Dr. A. P. Krueger are sometimes dismissed as insignificant in the face of gross environmental pollution, however they seem to show important implications for consciousness:

Air ion formation begins when enough energy acts on a gaseous molecule to eject an electron. Most of this energy comes from radioactive substances in the Earth's crust, and some from cosmic rays. The displaced electron attaches itself to an adjacent molecule, which

213

becomes a negative ion, the original molecule then becoming a positive ion . . . natural gas or water molecules cluster about the ions to form small air ions of four types: $H+(H_2O)n$, $(H_3O)+(H_2O)n$, $O_2(H_2O)n$ and $OH-(H_2O)n$, where n is a small number.

In normal clean air over land, there are 1500 to 4000 ions/cubic centimeter. But negative ions are more mobile and the earth's surface has a negative charge, so negative ions are repelled from the earth's surface. Thus the normal ratio of negative to positive ions is 1.2 to 1.

Man often encounters very low concentrations of ions, and modern city life increases the ratio of positive to negative small air ions. A 14-day study in 1971 by B. Maczynski (Int. J. Biometeor, vol. 15, p 11) in an office containing four people showed that the small air ion concentration dropped as the day went on, falling on average to only 34 positive ions and 20 negative ions/cm³. And a test at a light industry area of San Francisco by J. C. Beckett (J. Amer. Soc. Heating, Refrig, and Air Cond, vol 1, p 47) showed a small ion count of less than 80 ions/cm³. In both cases the number of physiologically inert large ions rose considerably—apparently small ions react with dust and pollutants to form large ions.

People travelling to work in polluted air, spending eight hours a day in offices or factories, and living their leisure hours in urban dwellings, inescapably breathe ion-depleted air for substantial portions of their lives. There is increasing evidence that this ion depletion leads to discomfort, enervation and lassitude, and loss of mental and physical efficiency. This syndrome appears to develop quite apart from the direct toxic effects of the usual atmospheric pollutants. It occurs in the absence of such pollutants, in the "clean" air of rural schools or libraries which happen to be ion-depleted due to special factors which remove ions, such as stray electrical fields. On the other hand, evidence is accumulating that substantial increases in ions can have highly beneficial effects, from relieving the pain of burns to promoting plant growth.[246]

Experiments have shown that negative ions promote the healing rate of animals with severed peripheral nerves, skin lacerations, burns, and post-operative discomfort. They are known to greatly enhance cell proliferation, and under certain circumstances they are known to raise the critical fusion frequency threshold (the point at which a flickering light appears constant) in humans and decrease visual reaction time.[247]

In several instances both positive and negative ions are shown to have similar effects. High doses of either type of ion have been shown to be lethal to bacteria. High densities of negative or positive ions increase, on the other hand, the maze learning ability of rats. Low concentrations of positive and negative ions are known to produce fewer alpha frequency brain waves in human beings. High concentrations of ions tend to disrupt alpha frequencies in a more variable fashion. In rats, varying outputs of ions in either polarity will produce measurable changes in urine, defecation, sleeping period, respiration rate, and attacks on the aluminum foil ground plate used to generate the ions. In general, oddly enough, the lowest ion concentrations were the most effective in evoking (or provoking) such changes.[248]

Particularly interesting is Kreuger's demonstration of the effects small air ions have on the levels of serotonin in the blood and in the brain. He has shown that in mice positive ions raise blood levels of serotonin and that negative ions depress them.[249] In these rodents' brains, low dosages as well as high dosages of both negative and positive ions produced significant decreases in serotonin—as compared to normal atmospheric levels.[250] This disparity can be accounted for by the fact that serotonin does not cross the blood-brain barrier. (You will recall the important role that brain-serotonin plays in mediating many facets of consciousness.) Negative ions are also known to play a role in speeding up plant growth and in increasing resistance to influenza.[251]

Research from Israel dramatically illustrates the link between atmospheric ionization, physiological levels of serotonin, and consciousness. In many parts of the world, observers have noted that certain "winds of ill repute" have a discomforting effect upon individuals—the Santa Ana winds in Southern California, the Chinook winds in Canada, the Mistral winds of France, the Zonda winds of Argentina, Sirocco winds of Italy, and the Sharav or Chamsin winds of the Near East.[252] Symptoms such as sleeplessness, irritability, tension, migraines, nausea and vomiting, scotoma (diminished vision), amblyopia (dimness of vision), and edemata (swelling of tissue) have been noted. These symptoms resemble the effects of hyper-production of serotonin. In weather-sensitive people, urinary serotonin output showed a steep rise two days before the onset of the Sharav winds in Israel. They remained high the following day and dropped only after the winds began. In addition to increase in positive ionization, the salient meteorological features of these winds are a rapid rise in temperature and a decrease in humidity. These factors by themselves, however, fail to account for the physiological changes which have been noted. The negative psychological and physiological effects are attributed to the rise in the ratio of positively charged ions in the atmosphere which preceeds the onset of the winds.[253] It's interesting to note in this connection that the word *doldrums* has the following two dictionary meanings: (1) dullness; a state of listlessness and boredom, (2) a part of the ocean near the equator abounding in calms, light winds, and squalls. Dr. E. Stanton Maxey, a scientist, surgeon and flight instructor, feels that the ionic changes in such weather conditions can put pilots into a trance state, causing accidents which are otherwise unexplained. He suggests the installation of cockpit devices which will correct this condition.[254]

On the other hand, in locations where (−) air ion densities are relatively high, such as near water falls, the general effect of the local environment is tranquilizing and conducive to good health.[255] It's no wonder then that scientists in the know, such as Dr. Albert Krueger in Berkeley, use air filters and negative ion generators at all times to restore the environment around them to its natural unpolluted and electrostatically balanced state.[256]

Stepping into Krueger's laboratory in the Life Science Building at the University of California, Berkeley, and breathing deeply was like all of a sudden being out in the crisp, clean air of a mountain wilderness.*

Dr. Albert Krueger

*Equipment for adding negative ions to your own home environment is simple and easy to build. For instructions see *Radio-Electronics Magazine*, vol. 42, June 1971, p. 32. Or inexpensive generators can be purchased from Klycon, Inc., 7620 N.W. 36th Ave., Miami, Fla. 33120.

Closely related to the electrostatic and ionic phenomena of the biosphere, are electromagnetic phenomena which also play an important role in the ecology of consciousness.

The magnetic field of the earth extends around the planet like a large donut and is probably created by the flow of molten metals in the earth's core.[257] The average intensity of this field is about 0.5 gauss and it pulses at frequencies ranging from 0.1 to 100 cycles per second. The predominant frequency range of magnetic pulsations, known as the Schumann resonance, is around 7.5 cycles per second. Several researchers have suggested that this resonance in the geomagnetic and electrostatic field has an effect upon the human nervous system—and upon consciousness itself.[258]

The Schumann resonance is an effect due to the fact that an electromagnetic wave (which travels at the speed of light, 186,000 miles a second) goes around the earth's 25,000 mile circumference around 7.5 times a second. Perhaps it is useful to think of the 7.5 c.p.s. brain wave frequency as the boundary between alpha waves and theta waves. If that frequency predominates in your brain waves you are generally in the hypnogogic or hypnopompic state just on the border of waking up or falling asleep. The theta wave is frequently observed in the EEG patterns of experienced meditators, who must pass through the Schumann resonance portal without falling asleep!

The field of the earth is about 1000 times weaker than the field from a small horseshoe magnet. The reported effects of such weak magnetic fields include altered cellular reproduction, plant growth and germination, orientation to direction, amplitude of motor activity, and enzyme activity. Of particular interest is the work of Düll and Düll which showed a striking correlation between incidents of human illness and death during periods of sharp geomagnetic disturbances (such disturbances are often related to solar-storm activity).[259] Another study conducted by Robert Becker and his associates at the Veterans Administration Hospital in Syracuse, New York, showed a positive correlation between days of geomagnetic intensity and the number of persons admitted to a psychiatric hospital.[260]

Professor Michael Persinger, of the Psychophysiology Laboratory at Laurentian University, hypothesizes that the extremely low frequency (ELF) Schumann waves may serve as a carrier for psi information. He points out the near impossibility of shielding against such waves, requiring no less than "an underground bunker surrounded by several inches of steel."

Noting that ELF waves propagate more easily from midnight to 4:00 a.m., and that they are easier to transmit from west to east rather than east to west, Persinger surveyed the ESP literature for any correlations. His findings were as he predicted. Telepathy and clairvoyance do show a tendency to peak roughly between midnight and 4:00 a.m. There is also a slight tendency for the telepathic agent to be west of the percipient rather than to the east. To clinch his argument, Persinger observes that fewer psi experiences are reported during periods of geomagnetic disturbance. Such disturbances also impair the propagation of ELF waves. Persinger is now in the process of preparing experimental tests of his theory.[261,262]

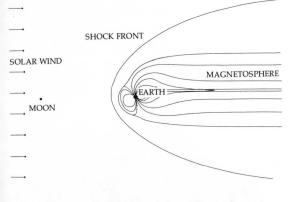

SHOCK FRONT

SOLAR WIND

MOON

EARTH

MAGNETOSPHERE

The magnetic field around the earth extending out beyond the earth, blown by the solar winds away from the sun.

216

Several investigators have shown that humans are sensitive to slight variations of magnetic intensity. Once accustomed to distinguish between the presence and absence of a weak magnetic field, subjects in several experiments were asked to walk back and forth over a given area without knowing whether an artificial magnetic field had been activitated. Under these conditions, the subjects were extremely accurate in guessing whether the current was in operation.[263,264] This sensitivity is offered as a partial explanation for the effectiveness of dowsers in finding water:

> Water filtering through porous media produces electric currents through electrofiltration potential and concentration batteries. If the medium is sufficiently conducting, and the current of the soil is sufficiently high, then there exists at the surface of the soil a small magnetic anomaly.[265]

The precise channels by which the human body detects magnetism are still a matter of speculation. However we know that most biological processes are based on chemical interactions, which can be accounted for, in the last resort, by the interactions of atomic nuclei and electrons. In one study with dowsers, using strict experimental controls and a double blind,* weak magnetic fields were shown to cause measurable changes in the electrical skin potential.[266]

Another study was conducted in which future astronauts spent up to ten days in a special chamber which was free of magnetic fields. During this time, no serious psychological or physiological deviations were reported—although some of the findings have remained classified. It was found, however, that the subjective perception of general brightness was lower under the non-magnetic condition—thus implying a magnetic effect upon the visual cortex. Soviet Studies, in addition, have determined that weak magnetic fields can effect the direction-finding orientation of birds, fish, and insects.[267,268,269] Research with honey bees shows that they are sensitive to fields of one gamma, i.e. several thousand times *weaker* than the earth's ½ gauss field. Homing pigeons may rival honey bees in sensitivity. Other studies have shown that germs and viruses are sensitive to the slightest departure of the earth's magnetic field from the average—this is reflected in reproduction rates and in genetic changes. For example, exposure to magnetic fields causes resistance to penicillin in certain strains.[270]

Sister M. Justa Smith, Ph.D., a biochemist associated with the Roswell Park Memorial Institute in Buffalo, New York, has shown that strong magnetic fields affect the reactivity of certain enzymes in the human body. These enzymes can act as a catalyst to speed up the body's natural healing processes; and, in fact, Sister Smith observed that psychic healers do exert a non-magnetic effect on the enzyme similar to the magnetic

Random motion in absence of electromagnetic field.

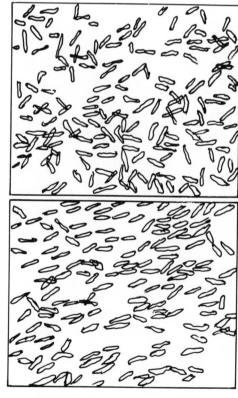

Oriented movement of unicellular organisms due to EmF of frequency 5-7 MHz. Motion is parallel to electric lines of force. (After Presman, p.163)

---

*A *double blind* is a basic experimental technique in which neither the subject nor the experimenter know whether a particular condition is part of the control or the test group, i.e. whether the magnetic field is on or off.

field.[271] Studies such as this have left scientists with a firm conviction that magnetic fields play an important role in the body's healing and immunological processes.[272]

The following map shows the variations in the intensity of the earth's geomagnetic field. Movement of high and low centers varies very slowly with time—the rate of this movement is measured in feet per year. The center of lowest magnetic intensity on the planet (.25 gauss) is in Brazil right over Rio de Janeiro.*[273]

The areas of greatest geomagnetic intensity center near the poles where readings are found in the .60–.70 gauss range. Spacecraft at the altitudes and latitudes of the usual near-earth orbits are generally not exposed to magnetic fields lower than those in Brazil. However, spaceflights more than about one-sixth the distance to the moon enter a magnetic environment near-zero in intensity.[275] It is still uncertain precisely how these variations of magnetic field will effect the consciousness of astronauts, as scientists are just beginning to explore the interactions of electromagnetism on the mind and body.

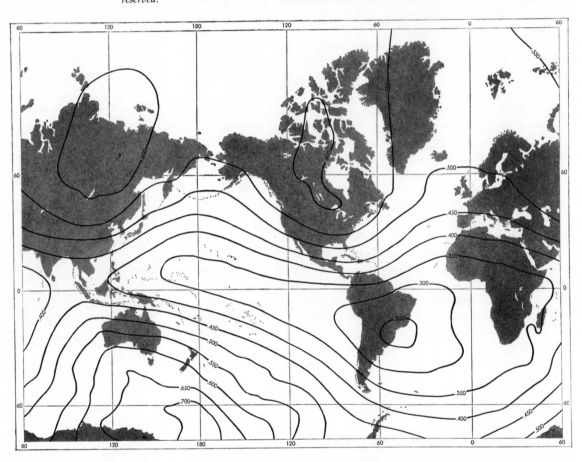

*In terms of psychic consciousness, it is interesting to note that Spiritism has flourished in Brazil, in spite of opposition from the Catholic Church, perhaps more than in any other nation. Brazilian spiritists, synthesizing modern European, native Indian, and African culture, number over a third of Brazil's population and comprise powerful interest groups with their own elected representatives in the national legislature. There are entire towns in Brazil composed solely of spiritists.[274]

For nearly thirty years doctors in Austria, West Germany and the Soviet Union have used a therapeutic technique known as *electrosleep* to cure a wide variety of psychological problems related to insomnia. A weak electric current (just enough to cause a tingling sensation) is passed through the head by attaching electrodes over the closed eyes and over the mastoid process (behind the ears). This induces an altered state of consciousness, and eventually sleep.

Over 500 articles about electrosleep have been published in the Russian literature and a number of sophisticated studies in Western Europe have produced evidence that the therapeutic process is effective. However, American clinicians have remained very skeptical about all electronic therapeutic processes, which have long been associated with medical quackery.[270] (The unfortunate exception to this assumption is *electroshock therapy* where powerful current—70 to 130 volts—jolts through a patient's brain causing convulsions, memory loss, temporary relief of depression and other symptoms. No one is sure how or why it works.)

In the last few years, American researchers have shown a new interest in electrosleep. A number of favorable research papers have been presented using electrosleep with humans and animals. Improvements have been shown in cases of insomnia as well as in removing neurotic and psychotic symptoms.[276] The exact mechanisms are still unknown; but it is quite clear, as we have already pointed out, that electromagnetic brain fluctuations are involved in the basic rest and activity cycle.

The problem of bio-electromagnetic interactions is much more intrinsic than the comparatively simple question of brain activity. The enormous role which light plays in our daily lives is so obvious that we ordinarily overlook it. The most dramatic responses to light can be observed in plants, upon which we are dependent for oxygen and nutrition. The Swedish naturalist Carolus Linnaeus (1707–1780) first noticed that various flowers opened at different hours and could actually be used as a clock.

Linnaeus Flower Clock:

    6 a.m. — Spotted Cat's Ear opens
    7 a.m. — African Marigold opens
    8 a.m. — Mouse Ear Hawkweed opens
    9 a.m. — Prickly Sowthistle closes
  10 a.m. — Common Nipple Wort closes
  11 a.m. — Star of Bethlehem opens
  12 noon — Passion Flower opens
    1 p.m. — Childing Pink closes
    2 p.m. — Scarlet Pimpernel closes
    3 p.m. — Hawkbit closes
    4 p.m. — Small Bindweed closes
    5 p.m. — White Water Lilly closes
    6 p.m. — Evening Primrose opens

"In nineteenth century Europe, formal gardens were sometimes planted to form a clockface, with the flowers in each bed blossoming at a different hour. On a sunny day one could tell the time to within a half hour by glancing at the garden."[277]

219

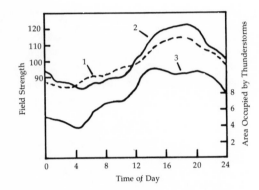

Durinal variations of electric field of atmosphere: 1) Over the ocean; 2) In polar regions; 3) Thunderstorm activity over whole earth's surface. (After Presman)

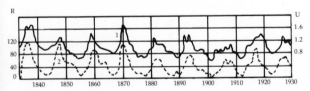

Relationship between mean annual magnetic activity (1) and number of sunspots (2). (After Presman)

We wake and sleep according to cycles of light and darkness. Furthermore, our adrenal hormones, pineal hormones (such as serotonin), and our sexual hormones all follow a twenty-four hour circadian production cycle which changes with the seasons according to the amount of available sunlight. Reflect for a moment yourself just how much your consciousness is effected by sunlight and artifical light in your environment . . . in a church or temple . . . in the forest . . . on a bright afternoon . . . in the moonlight . . . by the flickering firelight . . . a lamplit room . . . just after sunset . . . or in the dark.[278] One of the things I love to do is get up early in the morning, several hours before sunrise while it is still dark. From a hilltop, I can silently watch the gentle conquest of darkness as the earth turns and the birds, insects and the hormones flowing in my own blood are all part of the music— the planetary rotation raga. (The Hindu musicians understood this perfectly well when they composed different pieces of music to be played at different times of day.)

In Robert O. Becker's opinion, electromagnetic fields have enormous implications for understanding consciousness. He suggests that the analog-synaptic aspect of the central nervous system is regulated in part by electromagnetic interaction with the environment.[279] His research relating geomagnetic disturbances to psychiatric admission rates has already been cited. In other studies he has indicated that geomagnetic disturbances effect the behavior of patients on a psychiatric ward, [280] and that magnetic fields also have an effect on human reaction time.[281]

The earth's magnetic field changes slightly according to the solar day, the lunar day, and the lunar month. Geomagnetic disturbances are particularly correlated with solar storms which discharge large clouds of ionic plasma. These solar eddies generally impinge upon the earth's magnetosphere about two days after the solar flare causing polar lights, radio interference, and compression of the earth's magnetic lines of flux. Fluctuations in solar storm activity follow a cycle averaging 11.2 years and varying from about nine to thirteen years in length.

Scientists have correlated solar storm activity to rates of heart attacks, lung disease, eclampsias, and the activity of microbes. Epidemics of diptheria, typhus, cholera, and smallpox have also been correlated with solar activity. Much of this work was done between the two world wars by the Russian Scientist A. L. Tchijewski. In a huge study he drew up lists of wars, epidemics, revolutions, and population movements from 500 BC to 1900 and plotted them against curves of solar activity. He found that 78 percent of these outbreaks correlated with peaks of solar activity. He also found an amazing assortment of correlating phenomena ranging from locust hordes in Russia to succession of liberal and conservative governments in England from 1830 to 1930. Sturgeon in the Caspian Sea reproduce and then die in masses following cycles of 11 and 33 years which occur during periods of many sunspots (solar storms). The great financial crisis of 1929 coincided with a peak in solar activity. Other research has shown correlations between solar activity and the number of road accidents and mining disasters re-

220

ported. This may be due to delayed or inaccruate human reactions in conjunction with very violent solar activity.[282]

An Italian chemist, Giorgi Piccardi, was asked to figure out why "activated" water dissolves the calcium deposits from a water boiler at certain times and not at others. (Activated water is a vestige of alchemy. A sealed phial containing neon and mercury is moved around in the water until the neon lights up; there is no chemical change in the water; however the structure of the molecular bonds are altered somewhat.) After years of patient research measuring the rate at which bismuth sulfide becomes a colloid in activated and normal water, Piccardi showed that this colloid-forming rate varies with sunspot activity.[283] A colloid solution is one in which the dissolved particles have large enough molecular weight so that the surface tension of each molecule is of importance in determining the behavior of the solution. Common colloids are glue, gelatin, milk, egg white and blood. (The word colloid is derived from the Greek word *kolla,* meaning glue.) In general colloidal particles are too big to pass through membranes which will pass smaller dissolved molecules. The influence solar activity exerts upon the molecular structure of water is likely to be even more acute in human organisms as the human body temperature is fixed near the limit where changes in the structure of water normally occur.[284]

Not only are inorganic colloidal suspensions affected by solar activity, but so is at least one other organic colloid as well—blood. Research by Dr. M. Takata in Japan, since verified in Germany and the Soviet Union, indicates that blood samples showing flocculation (a cloud-like formation) as well as the leucocyte (white blood cell) content of the blood varies in accordance with solar storm activity.[285] This widespread solar influence upon all colloidal substances manifests itself in a wide variety of ways. Individual reaction times, pain felt by amputees, and the number of suicides all reveal a similar variation in response to sunspots. M. Guaquilin lists numerous ways in which the sunspot cycle effects weather conditions:

During violent solar eruptions, or at the time when important groups of sunspots move to the sun's central zone, a certain number of disturbances occur in our atmosphere, particularly the *aurorae boreales,* as a result of the greater ionization in the upper atmosphere, and magnetic storms, revealed by violent agitation of compass needles. . . .

The level of Lake Victoria-Nyanza changes in accordance with the rhythm of the sunspots, also the number of icebergs, and famines in India due to lack of rain. The *Bulletin Astronomique de France* brought out a very interesting article on the relation between the activity of sunspots and the quality of Burgundy wines: excellent vintages correspond with periods of maximum solar activity, and bad vintages with periods of minimum activity. Douglas, an American, and Schvedov, a Russian, have observed that the concentric rings formed in the growth of trees have a period of recurrence of eleven years as well. Finally, there is Lury's well-known statistical observation that the number of rabbit skins taken by the Hudson Bay Company follows a curve parallel to that of solar activity.

On this subject, perhaps the most interesting study is that carried out on varves. These say Piccardi, are many-layered deposits of sand or clay which are formed in calm waters, lakes, ponds, swamps, etc. in

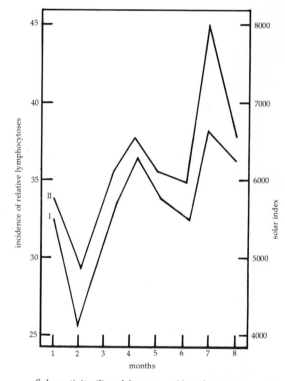

Solar activity (I) and frequency of lymphocytoses (II) during 1957 in Sochi. (After Presman, p.199)

glacial zones. A varve's thickness depends on the rainfall in a given year. Examination of these fossilized deposits in sedementary rock formed through the geological ages reveals the same inevitable eleven year cycle in the most distant past.[286]

The research of John H. Nelson, a technical director for RCA Communications, also indicates that the planets in the solar system can effect conditions on earth. When given the task of determining the variations in quality of radio reception, he learned that by adding the observation of the heliocentric positions of the planets to that of sunspots, he was able to bring about a significant improvement in the forecast of electromagnetic storms and days of poor reception. When planets were at right angles to each other (90°), in opposition (180°) or in conjunction (0°) with each other, in relationship to the sun, the radio interference was most intense.[287] Scientists still do not understand the mechanisms by which planetary arrangements cause radio interference.

F. A. Brown is an eminant biologist who has advanced the theory that the "biological clock" mechanisms observed in organisms can be explained by animals being sensitive to various subtle environmental factors. In addition to demonstrating the influence magnetic fields exert on a wide variety of living organisms, Brown has also demonstrated that several organisms including the potato, oyster, fiddler crab, and rat modify their behavior according to lunar rhythms. The experimental subjects were enclosed for long periods in hermetically-sealed rooms where the light, pressure temperature, and humidity were carefully kept constant.

He also notes that "fluctuations in intensity of primary cosmic rays entering the earth's atmosphere were dependent upon the strength of geomagnetism. The magnetic field steadily undergoes fluctuations in intensity. When the field is stronger, fewer primary cosmic rays come into the outer atmosphere; when it weakens, more get in."[288] Other researchers have shown influences on the circadian rhythm of electrostatic fields, gamma radiation,[289] x-rays, and weak radio waves.[290]

Recent years have shown an upsurge of interest in the ways in which human activity is effected by the remote environment. Scientists around the world who are doing research in this area have been meeting under the auspices of the International Society for Biometeorology. In 1969, the society created a special study group on the "biological effects of low and high energy particles and of extra-terrestrial factors." On this committee sit such scientists as F. A. Brown, Giorgi Piccardi and Michel Gauquilin. Many poorly understood phenomena, shrouded under the myths of mad poets and superstitious housewives, are now coming under the scrutiny of respectable members of the scientific community. Gradually the frontiers of science are being extended into territory which once belonged only to ecstatic mystics and secret psychic brotherhoods.

One can actually think of objects as complicated concatinations of interpenetrating electromagnetic fields dancing on a gravitational field of space-time curvature. As far as we know, all objects in our universe, with a temperature

222

above absolute zero, are emitting electromagnetic radiation. In this sense, the alchemical theories of Alkindi are perfectly true. Only recently have scientists appreciated this important fact.

The Physical Aura

In the 1920s and 30s, the Russian histologist Alexander Gurvitch proclaimed that all living cells produce an invisible radiation which he came to call *mitogenic radiation*. He observed increased cell division in plants and cultures that were exposed to these emanations. These results were obtained when the target cells were shielded from the transmitting cells by a quartz piece. However, no enhanced cell division was observed when a sheet of glass or gelatin was substituted for the quartz. Since glass and gelatin were known to block ultraviolet frequencies, Gurvitch believed that these mitogenic rays must be as short as ultraviolet or shorter. Other scientists replicated his experiments with only mixed results and eventually his theories were discarded—until recently.[291]

In 1967, a series of experimental studies were reported by Vlail Kaznacheyev, Simon Shchurin, and Ludmilla Mikhailova working in the Siberian science city of Novosibirsk. Conducting over 5,000 carefully controlled experiments, they were able to clearly replicate Gurvitch's early work. Different cell colonies were separated from each other by a quartz wall designed to allow only ultra-violet radiations to pass through them. Various means were used to kill one of the cell colonies: lethal radiation, chemical poisons, more viruses. Each time, the uncontaminated, shielded sister colony developed the same symptoms as the first. The problems of contamination are truly enormous in bacteria research; but if sufficient precautions were taken the inescapable conclusion is that the cells were radiating information—coded electromagnetic signals on the ultra-violet wavelength.[292]

Another Soviet researcher, Dr. Boris Tarusov, Chairman of Biophysics at Moscow University, began exploring electromagnetic luminescence using highly sensitive photo-electric multipliers. These devices are similar to the snooper-scopes used in military, espionage and police work to see in total darkness. They are also used in astronomy for tracking weak stars. Tarusov was able to discover extremely faint fluctuating rays of light coming from plant leaves and even from individual cells.[293] According to science journalists Ostrander and Schroeder, Tarusov made a significant research breakthrough in 1972. The light fluctuations he found were not random and were related to much more than plant metabolism. Specific light patterns were discovered which correlated with the onset of particular pathological conditions: too much water or salinity around the roots, lack or excess of fertilizer, the onset of a bacteria or a fungus attack. These light signals provided information long before the plants showed any sign of physical ill health.[294] American researchers haven't yet replicated these findings in detail. However William Joines and his colleagues at Duke Uni-

Professor William Joines (Courtesy of Psychical Research Foundation)

versity have found that some bacteria do produce ultra-violet radiation when destroyed by H_2SO_4 or from the pressure of a sterile, wooden rod.[295]

Soviet bio-energetic researcher, Dr. Victor Inyshin, and his colleagues at the State University of Kazakhstan in Alma-Ata, have also been exploring ultra-violet emanations—this time from the eyes of animals and humans. Inyushin is able to photograph this effect by using ultra-violet sensitive film with special filters and techniques for supressing all heat radiation. Very clear images were obtained, the significance of which is still uncertain.[296]

Two of the pioneers in the development of the electrodynamic theory of life were Harold S. Burr, professor of anatomy at Yale University, and Leonard J. Ravitz, a psychiatrist. Using sensitive instrumentation, they found that electromagnetic fields guided the growth and repair of living protoplasm. This discovery, which they termed the *life field* (or L-Field) is typified in an experiment conducted with frog's eggs. Using micro-pipettes filled with a salt solution and connected to a voltmeter, they found different voltage gradients along different axes of the eggs. The axis with the greatest voltage gradient was marked with a dye; and later, as the eggs developed it was found that *the frog's nervous system always grew along this axis.*[297] This finding, while it continues to stir great interest, has yet to be integrated into the mainstream of biological knowledge. If it withstands the test of further experimentation, Burr's theories will offer enormous potential for understanding human and animal developemnt. The L-fields suggest that an electro-magnetic matrix may play a crucial role in the development of tissues and organs.

Other studies conducted by Burr indicated a cyclic fluctuation in the L-fields, which included not only the daily circadian cycles, but also varied with the 28-29 day lunar cycle, as well as the 11.2 year cycle of solar storm activity. These long-range studies recorded the electrodynamic fields around a tree. Almost continuous records were kept from 1938 until 1968. Similar fluctuations were shown in the electrodynamic field around the earth itself, as well as the air.[298]

Further studies conducted by Dr. Ravitz involved over 50,000 measurements of some 500 different individuals at the Yale, Duke, and University of Pennsylvania medical schools. The same cyclical variations were found in human L-fields. Ravitz was also able to find differences in the L-fields of psychiatric patients which correlated with the extent of their psychoses. Other measurements seemed to correlate with emotional states and moods of the subjects. In a further study, done in 1948, measurements were made on individuals who were put into a hypnotic trance. Comparisons between L-field characteristics and the neuromuscular changes associated with trance states (by Dr. Milton Erickson) indicated to Ravitz a precise correlation between the L-field and the depth of trance. Particularly dramatic voltage shifts were recorded upon termination of the trance.[299]

It's tempting to suggest that these measurements are a result of skin resistance, or perhaps an electrical artifact. Burr

224

assures us, however, that as near as possible the measurements are pure voltage measurements. Every precaution is made not to disturb the living system being measured. Burr maintains that his microvoltmeters were unaffected by changes in the peripheral nerves, blood pressure, skin resistance, and sweating.[300] It is beyond the scope of this work to enter into the arguments over the adequacy of Burr's techniques. Technology has certainly advanced since Burr's original experiments, and the greatest strength of his claims lies in the ability of other researchers to reproduce his findings.

It's important to note that a number of studies conducted by Dr. Robert O. Becker at the Veterans Administration Hospital in Syracuse, New York, offer support for Burr's theories of an electrodynamic organizing matrix. Becker was interested in finding out why some amphibians were able to regenerate injured limbs, whereas other amphibians and all mammals lack this ability. Investigation showed him that in the regenerating type of amphibian a particular "current of injury" is produced by the fractured bone, which was related to tissue (blastema) formation which could regenerate a new organ. Becker found that he could induce partial limb regeneration—beyond the knee—by applying a delicately controlled current to the stumps of amputated limbs in non-regenerating amphibians and also in rats.[301] Becker has also found a similar process effective in healing fractured bones in humans.[302]

Dr. D. H. Wilson and his colleagues in Leeds, England were also interested in the role electromagnetic fields play in tissue regeneration and bone healing. In a recent experiment, the median ulnar nerve in the left forlimb of pairs of rats was divided and sutured under a general anesthetic. Then, one rat from each pair was treated each day to a pulsed electromagnetic field. Histological and nerve conduction studies showed that the nerve of the treated animals had progressed further toward recovery in thirty days than the nerve of the untreated animals at sixty days.[303]

In the Soviet Union, Dr. Alexander Studitsky at the Institute of Animal Morphology in Moscow minced up some skeletal muscle tissue and packed it into a wound in a rat's body. From this, the body was able to grow a new muscle, again as if there were some sort of organizing matrix.[304]

High voltage photography shows some promise as a means of graphically measuring the fields around the body. This is a technique for producing images on photographic film or paper using no light source except a luminous corona-discharge on the surface of an object which is placed in high-voltage, high-frequency electric field. Other names for this technique are Kirlian photography, electrography, radiation field photography, and corona discharge photography.

Vestiges of this curious phenomena were observed by Carsten in England as early as 1843. The technique was used in 1891 by Nikola Tesla, the electronic genius who invented alternating current. Soon thereafter a number of scientists were using the method to explore human "effluvia."

However, the most systematic and long-term studies appear to have been conducted in the Soviet Union by a husband

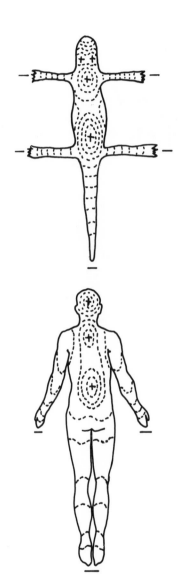

Distribution of surface electric potential over body of lizard and man. (After Presman, p.237)

and wife team, Semyon and Valentina Kirlian. Their basic technique involved a high-frequency spark generator, similar to an automobile coil, or an oscillator generating from 75,000 to 200,000 cycles per second. This is connected to one or two electrode plates, and the object to be photographed is inserted between the plates along with photographic film or paper. When the current is turned on, for a short time, the field created causes the corona discharge which is registered on the film. A camera isn't necessary for the photographic process.[305,306] The technique can be dangerous if not applied with care.[307,308] The image formed results from the ways in which the electric charge is conducted through and about the object being photographed.

For inanimate objects, this configuration, can generally be understood and predicted on the basis of the various physical parameters involved: film, developing process, exposure time, high-frequency waveform, electrical resistance, temperature, humidity, etc. However, with living organisms, the Kirlians report distortions of the image caused by conditions such as disease, aging, and dehydration. They also noticed that when photographing humans with multi-layer color film different parts of the skin were transposed into different colors—blue for the heart region, blue-green for the forearm, olive for the thigh. Furthermore, unexpected emotional experiences such as fear and illness also caused changes in the color of the image.[309]

Kirlian photography apparatus (Courtesy Dr. Thelma Moss.)

Scientists believe that what is being photographed is essentially a cold ion emission which is induced by the high energy field the object is placed in. Contrary to some popular misconceptions, no one knowledgably maintains that the method actually photographs the human aura. However, there is widespread controversy as to the different colors and patterns which the corona-discharge takes. One is very tempted to suggest that there is an organizing principle—related to the vitality of an object, the emotions, and even the thought processes of the mind—which does have an effect upon the photographed image. The data looks quite impressive; however there simply haven't been enough tightly controlled studies to discount other hypotheses. The most we can say with certainty is that the technique does seem to measure processes which correlate with mental states.

Using special light detectors for visual observation of the corona discharge, the Kirlians report observations of points, coronas, and flares of luminescent clusters:

They are of different colors: blue, lavender, and yellow. They may be bright or faded, constant or of varying intensity, periodically flaring up or constantly flaring, motionless or moving. All of these qualitative properties of discharge channels depend on the type and activity of the mechanisms contained in the skin.

The distribution of discharge channels is not uniform all over. For example, on the skin of the pads of the fingers, the channels are in flare form arranged only on the lines of the fingerprints. . . . On the forearm, the distribution of flares is irregularly shaped, apparently grouped as dictated by the structure of the skin. If the fingerprints are obliterated, they may be reconstructed according to the distribution of flares, seen through observation and photography.

On some sections of skin, points of blue and gold abruptly flare up. Their characteristic feature is a rhythm of flashes and mobility. Some clusters constantly splash out from one point of the skin to another where they are absorbed. It must be noted that until one cluster is absorbed, the next will not splash out. In some instances, luminous clusters are not oriented in their motion. They move slowly between flares and are finally extinguished with a flash or dissolve in space. The color of the clusters may be milky blue, pale lilac, gray, or orange. These faded clusters, possibly caused by some matter of undetermined origin, change from time to time to take on a spherical shape.

In our opinion, the different colors of adjacent parts of the discharge current indicates that each system of biomechanics of the skin has its own characteristic color.[310]

Similar visual observations have been made in the United States by Dr. Gary Poock at the Naval Postgraduate Research center in Monterey, California.[311]

There are even more dramatic research findings, yet to be substantially verified in this country, which have come out of the Soviet Union using the Kirlian photographic technique. Ostrander and Schroeder in *Psychic Discoveries Behind the Iron Curtain (PDBIC)* report that the Kirlians learned to detect the presence of pathological processes in plant leaves before any visible signs of disease were present. These writers also indicate a Soviet finding that Kirlian photography can be used for early diagnosis of human diseases, especially cancer.[312] Scientists in this country are attempting to replicate this important lead. So far, however, results are inconclusive.[313,314]

The Soviets have also reported that Kirlian photos are sensitive to changes in the emotions, thoughts and states of consciousness of human subjects. Support for this theory comes from data gathered by Dr. Thelma Moss and her colleagues at the UCLA Neuropsychiatric Institute. Studies with subjects in relaxed states produced by meditation, hypnosis, alcohol and drugs generally showed a wider and more brilliant corona discharge on the fingertips. In states of arousal, tension, or emotional excitement, the researchers observed the appearance of red blotches on the color film. (See Plate 11) Preliminary research seemed to indicate that these photographic indicators were independent of such physiological measurements as galvanic skin response, skin temperature, sweat, or constriction and dilation of the blood vessels. This is a difficult finding to accept, and not thoroughly documented in published reports. Other studies showed a brighter and wider corona in subjects who were in the presence of a close friend or someone of the opposite sex.[315]

In 1970, Lynn Schroeder and Shiela Ostrander published in PDBIC a rumor regarding research with the Soviet healer Colonel Alexei Krivorotov:

At the moment when he seemed to be causing a sensation of intense heat in a patient, the general overall brightness in Krivorotov's hands decreased and in one small area of his hands a narrow focused channel of intense brilliance developed. It was almost as if the energy pouring from his hands could focus like a lasar beam.[316]

Dr. Thelma Moss (Courtesy Psychic Magazine.*)*

These reports aroused the interest of western researchers who were determined to investigate this phenomena for themselves. E. Douglas Dean of the Newark College of Engineering in New Jersey, using Czechoslovakian designed equipment, had the opportunity to conduct similar experiments with a psychic healer by the name of Ethel E. De Loach. Dean took several sets of her fingers when she was at rest and when she was thinking of healing. In every case, Dean reported that the flares and emanations were much larger in the pictures when she was thinking of healing. (See Plate 13, lower-left and lower middle.)[317] Some of the effects with Mrs. De Loach were very striking:

> One time Ethel was doing a healing and she knew I was so happy about getting this big orange flare on the photograph. She asked me if I would like a green one. Well I said, "My goodness, yes! You mean you can make a green one to order?" She said, "yes." So we set up the equipment and we got a green flare, a small one.[318]

Further research along these lines has been conducted by Dr. Thelma Moss and her associates working at the UCLA Center for the Health Sciences. Using Kirlian photography, they have observed an apparent energy transfer from healer to patient. After the healer has finished a treatment, the corona around his fingertip is diminished. On the other hand, an increase in the brilliance and width of the corona of the patient is observed after treatment. Volunteers with no experience in healing were unable to replicate the same effect.[319] (See Plate 13, upper-left, center-left, upper-middle, and center-middle.)

In another series of experiments, the UCLA group explored the healing interactions between people and plants. In this study, the "healers" were people who claimed to have a "green thumb," in other words, people who had the ability to make plants flourish under their care. In each experiment there was both an experimental leaf and a control leaf. Both leaves were photographed after being freshly plucked from the same plant. Then each leaf was mutilated and photographed again. Typically this caused the leaf to become dimmer on film. Then the "healer" would hold his hand about an inch above the experimental leaf for as long as he felt was necessary, and the experimental leaf would be photographed again. Most of the twenty "green thumb" volunteers were able to cause an increased brightness in the leaves after treatment. *These leaves also remained brighter for many weeks longer than the control leaves!*[320]

In a similar vein to Grad's work with psychotic and neurotic healers, Moss and her co-workers found a number of subjects who claimed to have a "brown thumb" with plants—plants always seemed to get sick and die under their care. When these subjects attempted the leaf experiment, they were able to cause the corona around the leaf to disappear. This has been found to be a repeatable effect.[321] (See Plate 14, third-left and lower left.)

One of America's most famous healers, Dr. Olga Worrall, has exhibited a great deal of conscious control over the energy interactions being photographed. Oddly enough, the leaf had almost disappeared in the photograph of Dr. Worall's first test run:

> This was deeply disturbing to us: how could we tell Dr. Worrall, a lady for whom we had the deepest respect, what she had done to the leaf? But, obviously we had to tell her. She looked at the photographs with quiet dignity, and then asked if she might repeat the experiment. She believed she had given the leaf "too much power," and thought a more gentle treatment might have different results. The experiment was, of course, repeated. . . . the second, mutilated leaf . . . after a more gentle treatment . . . has become brilliant. This was the first time that someone had been able, deliberately, to reverse the direction of the bioenergy. Since then, we have had another subject who was able to predict the direction of the energy flow.[322]

There are methodological problems with all the Kirlian photographic research thus far reported which makes it almost impossible to achieve a precise understanding at this time. For example, the pressure the finger placed upon the film exerts is a variable that few experimenters have taken the trouble to carefully control. In a series of ingenious experiments, Manfred Clynes measured the vertical and horizontal pressure of people's fingers while they were fantasizing a number of different emotions. He discovered certain characteristic response patterns to emotions which seemed rather constant throughout time and also was consistent for subjects from different cultures.[323] (Clynes, incidentally, also discovered that fantasizing about different emotional states tends to lessen anxiety and increase one's mental energy.) These findings have led numerous people to question whether the Kirlian photography of fingertips was not merely another measure of finger pressure.

To test this hypothesis, William Tiller and David Boyers, at Stanford University, developed sensitive instrumentation utilyzing a special finger-holder with a micrometer-calibrated adjustment. A special air jet even forced dry air into the electrode compartment in order to prevent moisture buildup around the finder. Actual photographs were taken from a camera, loaded with special high speed film, located a few inches away from the transparent electrode on which the finger was placed. This was done to avoid the possibility of a chemical interaction between the film itself and the fingertip. These controls are probably the most rigorous ever used in Kirlian photography research. The experimental results with such a setup, however, show no effect on corona discharge of different emotional states or states of consciousness.[324] (See Plate 14, second-right.) Tiller and Boyers seemed to feel that all radiation emitted by the corona discharge was in the ultra-violet range. By exposing a piece of ektachrome film with *uv*, from both the front and back, they were able to produce red, white and blue images on the film. (See Plate 14, upper-right.) They hypothesized that the red colors which Moss associated with emotional arousal were actually an artifact due to film buckling, finger pressure, or the placement of electrodes in relationship to the film.[325] (See Plate 14, upper-center and second-center.)

Soviet "Phantom Leaf" (Courtesy Dr. Thelma Moss)

Kendall Johnson's "Phantom Leaf" (Courtesy Dr. Thelma Moss)

Burton, Joines and Stevens at the Electrical Engineering Department of Duke University confirmed Tiller's hypothesis that radiation entering the film from the back would produce an untrue color representation. However, using photomultiplier tubes with optical filters they determined that there is radiation in the red region of the spectrum, primarily near 660 nm., during Kirlian photography. In confirmation of Moss' reports, they discovered that the red radiation is virtually non-existent if the subject is relaxed. However, if the subject is aroused the radiation in the red region will gain over a fourfold increase.

This, they hypothesize, is due to an increase in skin conductivity during arousal as well as increased concentrations of sodium near the fingertips due to sweat. In no case did the Duke group discover any effects which were not explicable on the basis of existing knowledge of electrical corona effects. Apparently they did not look at effects relating to psychic healing.[326]

These studies clearly indicate a need for other researchers, those who claim to be getting dramatic effects, to institute more rigorous experimental procedures. One difficulty in sorting out such conflicting reports from different researchers arises from the fact that equipment has not yet been standardized. The enormous variations in the frequency and waveform of the high-voltage fields, as well as the use of various electrode designs may account for some of these apparent differences.

The most significant finding of Kirlian photography research is called the "phantom leaf" effect. Ostrander and Schroeder in *PDBIC* first reported that the Soviets were often able, after removing a portion of a plant leaf, to photograph a corona pattern around the leaf as if the whole leaf were still there. This suggested to researchers that radiation of energy around the leaf formed a holographic pattern acting as an organizing force field for physical matter.[327] The Soviets dubbed this hypothesized organizing field the *biological plasma body.*

For several years American experimenters tried unsuccessfully to duplicate this effect. While the relevant procedural variables were still unknown, scientists such as William Tiller maintained that this single observation was "of such vast importance to both physics and medical science that no stone should be left unturned in seeking the answer!"[328]

Finally, in late summer of 1973, Kendall Johnson, after more than 500 trials, succeeded in producing a "phantom leaf" with clear internal details. Immediately researchers suggested that the results were due to an artifact of some sort—possibly from an electrostatic charge which was left on electrode's surface before the leaf was cut.

John Hubacher, a graduate student working in Thelma Moss' laboratory has since produced about a dozen phantom leaves which show an internal structure—presumably belonging to the cut-off section of the leaf. Experimenting in the spring months (which is suggested as a relevant variable)

Hubacher has come to expect clear phantom images in about 5% of his attempts and partial images in another 20%. He is still unable to ascertain the variables which result in a perfect image. Perhaps a harmonic resonance must be established between the "biological plasma body" and the frequency of the high-voltage Kirlian field. He was especially careful to cut the leaf before it was placed on the electrode in order to avoid the possibility of an electrostatic artifact. In fact, he went further and attempted to deliberately creat a pseudo-phantom effect by pressing the leaf against the film emulsion before cutting a section off. The results of these efforts did not create any good looking phantoms.[329]

Perhaps the most encouraging efforts in this direction are the motion pictures taken of the fading phantom leaf through a special transparent electrode. The speed of the camera was slowed to about six frames a second. This work was in Dr. Moss' laboratory with the help of Clark Dugger, a graduate student in UCLA's noted cinema department. Both black and white and color Kirlian photographs show the "phantom" sparkling brilliantly and pulsing for several seconds before it disappears. In these experiments, the leaf was always cut before it was placed on the electrode; and the phantom leaves were obtained only during spring months.[330,331]

Working in Moss' laboratory, and also in the laboratory of Henry Dakin in San Francisco, I have been able to reproduce partial phantom effects with little difficulty. However, I can personally make no claims for the phenomena as it would take months of intensive research to control all of the possible sources of artifact. The leaf being photographed, for instance, must be grounded with an electrode; and the placement of this electrode, a possible source of additional corona discharge, seems crucial. Sometimes unaccountable images appear on Kirlian photographs of normal leaves, fingertips, and also inanimate objects. William Joines and his colleagues of the electrical engineering department at Duke University have been able to produce a "phantom leaf" effect, for example as a result of film buckling.[332] While only further well-controlled studies can resolve these tenous problems, my intuition is that the phantom effect will hold up and will point to something similar to the Soviet notion of a bioplasma body.

These findings, if true, carry such significance for science that it is essential that the experiments be replicated under tightly controlled conditions which can provide a secure foundation for theoretical models. Gary Poock, who is also doing motion picture Kirlian photography, has not reported observation of any phantom effects. I'm sure that most readers will agree that the astounding reports of some Kirlian photography researchers do point towards an understanding of those priceless experiences which we all sometimes enjoy—and which conventional science has sometimes thrown on the rubbish pile. Most of us can assume that the stairway to the heavenly city exists and that scientists are now also walking on that golden pathway. Thus, with a certain warm wonder at the excitement of our age and culture, we go about our business.

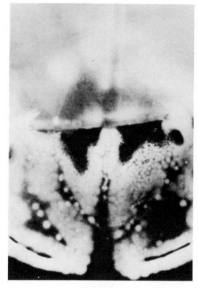

One of John Hubacher's "Phantom Leafs"
(Courtesy Dr. Thelma Moss.)

I don't doubt that there are many paths that go all through the seven heavens to the very highest throne and beyond. I also feel confident that what we now call science is capable of evolving to the point where it takes us all there. Yet, not every path leads to heaven. Just when you can hear that celestial music, and you're looking up at that golden light—you're often most likely to step off the edge of a cliff. The fool is so close to enlightenment, but watch out! One false step and that divine folly also evolves into a more human wisdom.

Science has not yet built adequate models for the existence of the aura, orgone energy, the chakras, the etheric body, the astral body, or astrology. With all due respect, in my opinion, anyone who speaks with dogmatic certainty about these alleged levels of being is either a charlatan, a madman, or a fool—although in any case, likely to be a fascinating individual—a Cagliostro. However one who speaks of these levels with familiarity, but also with a great humility and a desire to share experience and not simply dictate occult dogma or attract a clientelle or an audience is perhaps a genius, visionary, or saint. Science itself (although not scientists) makes no such pronouncements. Too many scientists have made daring speculations which were sincerely inaccurate. Phrenology is an excellent example. This was the recent, and well-received, attempt to diagnose personality traits by reading bumps on the head.

A lot of experimental work is required before scientists will accept the claim of the speculative adventurers who build bold maps and wait for other minds to follow in their wake and fill in the *essential details*. They can dance on air, but the rest of us may need an elevator to get up there—and also a good net to catch them if they fall—so they can tell us more. Then we can take turns playing fools for each other. It's fun. While, from a scientific standpoint, the concepts we will now explore are only speculations, they are—indeed—to be taken seriously.

A case in point here—and by no means the only one—is the Soviet concept of *biological plasma*. This is the latest version of what is essentially Mesmer's old notion of *animal magnetism*. The term plasma in physics refers to a gaseous collection of positive and negative ions—sometimes regarded as a fourth state of matter as it is not quite the same as a molecular solid, liquid or gas. The atmospheres of stars which extend out to interstellar space are composed of such plasma. The idea that a coherent plasma body might surround and interact with biological organisms was first proposed in 1944 by V. S. Grischenko, a physicist and engineer. Dr. Victor Inyushin, a biophysicist at Kirov State University in Alma-Ata, Kazakhstan, has been the leading theoretical spokesman for the biological plasma body.

In contrast to inorganic plasma, biological plasma is said to be a coherent, organized system. The entropic, chaotic motion of particles is reduced to a minimum. Like the visible human body, the bioplasmic body is relatively stable in varying environmental conditions—although it is particularly susceptable to electrical and magnetic perturbations.

All kinds of oscillations of bioplasma put together create the biological field of the organism. In the complex organism and its cerebral structures a complicated wave structure—a biologogram—is being created, characterized by its great stability as far as the maintenance of the wave characteristics is concerned.[333]

The euphonious term, biologogram, appears to be an application of the hologram idea—a three dimensional image formed by wave interference patterns. *The entire image can be reconstructed from any portion of the hologram.* This model appears very promising for consciousness researchers. Holographic analogies explain why brain functioning is not severely impaired when portions of that organ are removed. It also is consistent with the hermetic axion: As Above, So Below.—if we are willing to take the entire universe as a hologram. Perhaps the holographic concept of consciousness and biological fields will also account for psi phenomena. And telepathy can't be too unusual if it is theoretically possible to reconstruct the entire universe from any single portion of it.

The theory of the bioplasmic body is particularly valuable in a communist country where the official dogma is strictly materialist—and researchers must be careful to avoid heretical doctrines. However, the Soviets acknowledge that the biological plasma theory was originally conceived in the absence of any experimental proof.[334] The concept is now used as an umbrella explanation of all sorts of phenomena ranging from hypnosis to astrology, telepathy, psychokinesis, and Kirlian photography. The explanations I have seen in the translated literature seem like rather awkward efforts to fill in the gap in our knowledge left unfilled because of insufficient experimentation. Bioplasma is still, as far as I can tell, an entirely speculative concept. This is, however, understandable since sufficient financial resources needed to answer all of the experimental questions simply have not been available. Researchers have found it necessary to cut corners and rely on intuitive assumptions in order to build up the theory as much as they have. We still have no sound idea as to which Kirlian phenomena will someday be explained on the basis of current science and which phenomena will require a new understanding. Whether bioplasma will supply that new understanding is also somewhat in doubt. Perhaps bioplasm is little more than a euphemism for another more embarrassing term: consciousness.

That plasmic phenomena occur in connection with biological organisms is not doubted, but that such fields are organized into coherent and stable patterns requires even deeper explanation. However, if we face the truth, all our conceptions about consciousness are rather hazy. They all eventually point to the ultimate unknown, the void.

The research finding which lends support to the concept of bioplasma is the preliminary report that changes in the corona discharge of humans and certain animals can be shown to vary with the emotional state of the organism, or state of consciousness, in a way which is independent of other physiological variables which might effect the discharge. If

233

true, this finding is most unusual since we generally associate a number of physiological parameters with changes in emotional intensity. None of the reported experiments have been described in sufficient detail to be taken at face value.

A concept parallel to that of bioplasma is the notion of *orgone energy* developed by Wilhelm Reich, a Freudian psychiatrist noted for his analysis of character based on muscle tensions. The term *orgone* comes from "organism" and "orgasm" and refers to the orgasm reflex of repeated expansions and contractions as the basic formula of all living functioning. Reich made the bold assumption that he had discovered a new form of energy—underlying the pulsations of life—which was neither heat, nor electricity, magnetism, kinetic energy, chemical energy, nor an amalgam of any or all of these. Several different experimental procedures in support of this hypothesis were described.

Researches in the late 1930's in Norway led Reich to the discovery of *bions*, which he regarded as the basic units of orgone. Using high quality optical microscopes with magnification from 2000x to 4000x, Reich observed sterile solutions of organic compounds in water. He would, for example, take coal dust and heat it to incandescence in a gas flame and then, while aglow, put it into a sterile nutritive solution. Under the microscope, tiny vesicles were seen pulsating rhythmically in a soft, organic manner. Reich was able to clearly distinguish this motion from the random, angular Brownian movements also observed at that magnification. Eventually these vesicles, or *bions*, took on a blue glimmer, unlike the black carbon from which they seemed to originate. In fact, at a certain stage in their development they took on a positive blue stain reaction to a biological Gram stain, unlike the carbon particles. The bions were about one micron in diameter (or one millionth of a meter). In the same series of experiments Reich also discovered smaller elongated, red bodies, approximately 0.2 microns in length. He called these bodies T-bacilli and felt, through a series of experiments which are beyond the scope of the present book, that they were the cause of cancer. The essential point for now is that Reich felt he had observed the creation of life within his test tubes.[335]

Later experiments led Reich to postulate that the orgone energy permeated the entire universe and that it could be concentrated in a special device he called the *orgone accumulator*. Inside the accumulator he was able to observe, in addition to the small blue ion dots, a diffuse bluish-grey light and rapid straight yellowish rays—all manifestations of orgone. Reich began to observe these forms in dark rooms, and outdoors throughout nature. (Perhaps you also have had the experience of perceiving all of nature alive with scintillating light.) The accumulators themselves were simply boxes with walls made from alternating layers of an organic material, like wood, and an inorganic material, like iron. Sometimes as many as twenty layers have been used. The idea is something like a greenhouse effect such that orgone energy enters into the accumulator but cannot leave it.

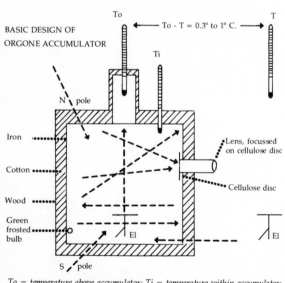

BASIC DESIGN OF ORGONE ACCUMULATOR

$To - T = 0.3°$ to $1°$ C.

To = temperature above accumulator; Ti = temperature within accumulator; T = control (temperature of air in room). El = electroscope. Size: 1 cubic foot. – – – – – – – → = direction of radiation.

Most significant, from the standpoint of experimental proof, was Reich's finding that the temperature inside the orgone "box" and also outside the walls was generally slightly higher than the temperature in the room or outside air about it. The difference averaged about one degree centigrade. Furthermore, this temperature difference was greater on dry days than in humid weather. This experiment, if verified, provides concrete evidence of some new and unknown form of energy generating heat.[336]

Reich took his findings directly to the most famous scientist in the world, Dr. Albert Einstein. After some correspondence, Reich visited Einstein in Princeton on January 13, 1941. For nearly five hours that day, Reich discussed his theories with Einstein. He actually demonstrated the visible radiation within the accumulator and explained the temperature difference effect. Einstein, realizing the importance of this work, offered to test the orgone accumulator himself for the temperature difference effect. He did so and arrived at the results predicted by Reich. However, in a letter to Reich, he added that his assistant had come up with an alternative explanation—that the temperature difference was due to air convection currents in the cellar of Einstein's home where the experiment took place. Reich retested the phenomena in the open air and with sufficient controls to rule out the possibility of air currents. His results were again positive; however Einstein refused to answer any of his further correspondence. Reich's letters at this time show reasonable arguments and thorough research.[337] Nevertheless, Einstein's rejection led him to turn away from all establishment science.

Eventually Reich's work with cancer and his rental of orgone accumulators brought him into conflict with the U.S. Food and Drug Administration. In 1954, Reich was brought to trial but refused to testify, claiming that his researches were a matter for scientific, and not legal, jurisdiction. He was sentenced to prison for two years for contempt of court. His books were actually burned by the government and withheld from the market! Nine months after sentencing he died in a federal prison. Careful examination of his writings shows, however, that, while they often lacked a scientific precision, they showed a scientific willingness to be led by the facts. For all his faults, Reich was a great genius and by no means a cancer quack. Reich's imprisonment and death were a great setback to those who were interested in pursuing his researches.[338] Only recently has his name become once more respectable.

While I am personally aware of several scientists (such as Dr. Bernard Grad at McGill University in Montreal) who claim to have observed the formation of bions under the microscope, there are—to my knowledge—no published replications of this crucial finding from independent laboratories.* Neither are there any published refutations. In *The Cancer Biopathy*, Reich does include a letter from Dr. Louis Lapique of the University

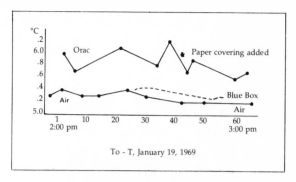

Temperature differences between the orgone accumulator and outside air.

---

*Grad does intend to publish several decades of his research finding, hopefully within the next year.

235

Experimental leaf after 15 days in Orgone Box.

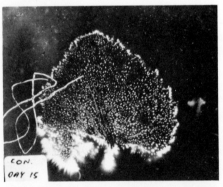

Control leaf after 15 days in identical wooden box. This experiment still requires further verification. (Courtesy Dr. Thelma Moss)

of Paris who had observed the pulsating bions and was prepared to offer a physical-chemical interpretation of this effect. Reich also states that his findings had been experimentally confirmed in 1937 by Professor Roger DuTeil in Nice.[339] However there is no independent report. Obviously something is happening here and why it has not been more thoroughly probed, I cannot explain.

The temperature difference experiment has been replicated and the results published in the orthodox Reichian *Journal of Orgonomy* (Nov. 1971). Clearly further verification from other laboratories is called for.

Other studies have pointed towards the unusual properties of orgone accumulators. For example, in Thelma Moss' laboratory at UCLA, experiments were conducted with an orgone accumulator and an identical-looking control box (built by an undergraduate student, Roger MacDonald) which was only made out of wood. Into each of these boxes was placed a tray containing ten leaves all plucked from the same plants. Kirlian photographs were then taken of the leaves every day for one week by an experimenter who did not know which leaves were in the orgone box and which were in the control. After seven days, eight of the ten experimental leaves were easily photographable and produced bright images, while only three of the control leaves produced pictures. Even after fifteen days, eight of the leaves placed in the orgone box were still producing Kirlian images, while all but two of the leaves in the control box were wilted and dying to the point that they were not photographable.[340]

This finding is important because it points to the possible therapeutic uses of Reich's orgone accumulators. Another important series of experiments with orgone accumulators was conducted by Dr. Bernard Grad of McGill University. Using careful experimental controls, Dr. Grad tested the effects of treatment in an orgone accumulator upon cancerous rats. The results of Grad's studies are complex. While the orgone treatment alleviated the symptoms of cancer, it did not really prolong the animal's lifespan.[341]

Another theory dealing with subtle physiological systems of the human body is the Chinese healing art of acupuncture, which unites ancient cosmology and astrology with a concept of life-energy, or Qi, flowing through channels in the body. One of the best ways to experience acupuncture is through a massage technique which focuses on the acupuncture points and meridians. This only requires a very gentle touch and is not difficult to learn or apply. Instructions can be found in several good books.[342,343] It's been my experience that such a massage, in addition to being healthful and sensual, provides an excellent way a person can actually feel the flow of something (call it Qi, or Chi, if you like) inside and around the body. For about twenty-four continuous hours after I've had acupuncture massage, I've clearly felt the awareness of my body flow extend about a foot out from my skin. This is something you really should try. The experience is extraordinary, but not scientifically evidential, unless one controls for expectations and suggestions.

236

There has been a lot of testimony regarding the successful use of acupuncture as a cure for all diseases and as an anesthetic. However many western doctors and researchers, unable to accept the "mystical" Chinese system, tend to ascribe these "miracles" to the power of suggestion.

Drs. Theodore Xenophone Barber and John Chaves of Medfield State Hospital in Massachusetts exemplify this view in an article recently published in *Psychoenergetic Systems*. They maintain that acupuncture can only be used successfully as an anesthetic when the patient is not fearful and has a strong belief in its efficacy. Furthermore, they add that additional sedatives, narcotics, and local anesthetics are generally used in combination with acupuncture. They also point out that the acupuncture needles can act as a counter-irritant, distracting the mind from the pain surgery occasions.[344]

This view is, in fact, consistent with the Gate Control Theory of pain. You have probably had the experience yourself, when you were in pain, of being able to alleviate your suffering by softly stroking or scratching some other part of your body. The suggested explanation for this phenomena is the "spinal gate" in the *substantia gelatinosa* through which pain signals must pass to be received in the brain. Fewer pain signals can get through this gate if there are other non-painful stimuli activating the nerves which must pass through. This theory is still problematic, but remains generally accepted among western scientists.[345]

Essentially, explanations of the sort Barber and Chaves have proposed are based on the assumption that there is simply no validity to the concepts of *chi* energy or acupuncture meridians. Dr. Felix Mann, a western researcher who at one time accepted the traditional theory, now argues differently:

> The Chinese have so many connections in their acupuncture theory that one can explain everything just as politicians do. . . . in reality I don't believe the meridians exist. . . . I think that the meridians of acupuncture are not very much more real than the meridians of geography.[346]

Mann points out the example of the meridians for the large and small intestines which are never used by the Chinese in treating intestinal problems. The only reason that the twelve meridians are there, he claims, is in order for acupuncture theory to be consistent with Chinese astrology. This argument is questionable as the S.I. meridians are used for treating a number of other problems. Nevertheless, experienced healers pragmatically avoid using any unnecessary points. Mann proposes that the effectiveness of acupuncture is actually due to stimulation of neural pathways which are mediated by spinal and ganglionic reflexes. In spite of his rejection of the Chinese theory, Mann still follows the traditional methods in his therapeutic practice.[347]

Perhaps the most ingenious theory of acupuncture functioning stems from the research of Professor Kim Bong Han in North Korea. This theory would place the acupuncture system within our anatomical knowledge of the physical body. By injecting radioactive phosphorus(P³²) into the acupuncture

● Bong Han corpuscle

X Surrounding tissue of Bong Han corpuscle

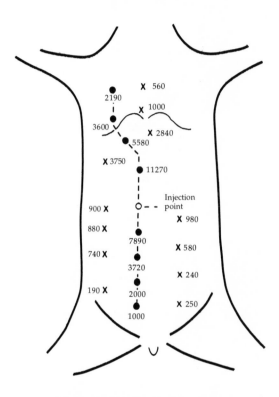

Distribution of P³² (100 μc) three hours after its injection into a Bong Han corpuscle (acupuncture point) located in the abdominal skin of a rabbit. (Courtesy Dr. William Tiller.)

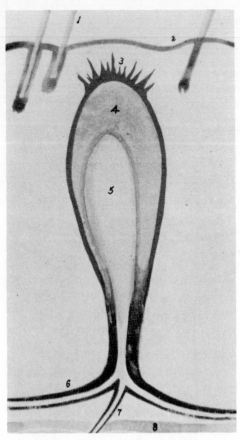

Model of the superficial Bong Han corpuscle (acupuncture point): (1) Hair, (2) Epidermis, (3) Radiating smooth muscle fiber, (4) Outer layer, (5) Inner substance, (6) Superficial Bong Han duct, (7) Profound Bong Han duct, (8) Skeletal muscle. (Courtesy Dr. William Tiller.)

points on the abdominal wall of a rabbit, he was able to trace the flow of radioactivity along the meridian to the neighboring acupuncture points. While the P^{32} concentrated at other acupuncture points, a small amount spread to the surrounding tissues. When the phosphorus was injected into a blood vessel, almost no difference was detected between the tissues of the alleged meridian system and those around it.

Further anatomical and histological studies revealed the existence of a system of ducts in animals and humans which seemed to correspond to the acupuncture meridians. Four systems of ducts were found: (1) ducts which were floating free inside of blood and lymph vessels, (2) ducts located on the surface of the internal organs, (3) ducts running along the outer surface of blood and lymph vessels (these seem to be the ones most familiar in acupuncture), and (4) ducts distributed in the central and peripheral nervous system.

Kim Bong Han and his colleagues have conducted hundreds of experiments on many species determining the electrical, mechanical, biochemical anatomical, and embryological characteristics of these ducts and the fluids which travel through them. Some of his findings have been confirmed by Japanese scientists. However, none of this research has been replicated in Western laboratories.[348] It is difficult to determine the likelihood that such a coherent and pervasive anatomical system, as is described, could remain so long undetected by Western scientists.

One of the most interesting investigations of acupuncture in support of the North Korean theory was conducted by Dr. Yoshio Nagahama at the medical school of Chiba University. Nagahama had been doing comparative studies, diagnosing patients with both acupuncture and western methods. One day he found a patient who had been struck by lightning and consequently had developed an extreme sensitivity in his skin. He was actually able to feel the "echo" of the acupuncture needle as the effect flowed through his body. Nagahama investigated this phenomena by inserting a needle at the Genketsu (fundamental point) of each meridian. By questioning his patient he discovered that the echo was slowly transmitted along the meridian to the other end. Using a stopwatch, he was even able to measure the speed of the needle "echo," which was considerably slower than the transmission of a nervous impulse. The effect of the acupuncture needle travelled through the meridian at speeds of from 15.2 centimeters/second to 48.1 cm/sec. This was slow enough for the patient to actually feel its progression. Nerve impulses often travel a hundred times faster than this.[349] It's uncertain, however, whether the experimenter's expectations had any influence on the subject's perceptions.

Another approach toward understanding acupuncture stems from the Soviet investigations of so-called bioplasm. Using a device called a tobiscope, which measures skin resistance, it was observed by Victor Adamenko that normal resistance between a subject's hand and points on the skin is about one million ohms. However when certain spots on the skin were tested—corresponding to Chinese maps of acupuncture points—the resistance dropped down to 50,000–100,000 ohms. During sleep, the resistance measured at the acupoints increased two to three times. During emotional excitation the low resistance spots increased in diameter and sometimes overlapped with each other. Unfortunately, we are given no statistical correlation between Adamenko's measurements and the 1000 odd acupuncture points on the body.[350]

At Thelma Moss' laboratory in UCLA, Kendall Johnson was able to build a device similar to the Soviet "tobiscope." Using two electrodes, one of silver and one of brass, the instrument utilizes the body as if it were an electrical battery. When the probe finds a place on the skin that has a concentration of electrolytes, the instrument is programmed to register a beeping sound. Like the Soviets, they were able to locate acupuncture points in this fashion. In addition, they found many points of which the traditional Chinese doctors were not aware. They were also able to detect acupuncture points by measuring slight temperature differences on the skin and also by stimulating the skin with either AC or DC current and observing when the subject felt a very strong sensation. However, when the skin was moist, they were unable to detect acupoints, because the entire area seemed to register. This led some of Moss' colleagues to surmise that the measurements were actually concentrations of sweat glands on the skin.

This hypothesis was tested by injecting a subject with the drug xylocaine, which blocks the sympathetic nervous system and stops sweating. Under this condition the acu-points were still detectable.[351]

Another Soviet study measured skin resistance at the acupoints during different stages of hypnotic trance. Subjects who were most hypnotizable showed the greatest variations of conductivity during the hypnotic process. The best hypnotic subjects, in the deepest hypnotic states, showed the greatest decrease in skin resistance.[352]

In further studies, Adamenko measured the resistance between symmetrical acupuncture points on each side of the body. It was found that if a person was ill relative to the organs associated with those particular points, then the resistance between these two points would be different in one direction than in the other. If the person was healthy, the resistance between points would be the same in either direction. This came to be known as the semiconductor effect. Stimulating the appropriate points in an ill person seemed to show a reduction of this imbalance.

William Tiller reports on various techniques of acupuncture stimulation, in order of effectiveness: (1) chemical stimulation, (2) manual massage, (3) acupuncture needles, (4) electrical stimulation, (5) lasar beam, and (6) psychic healing—the most effective.[353] These conclusions seem to be based on anecdotal reports.

Acupuncture, like many systems of wholistic healing, tends to base its diagnoses on the overall energy balance throughout the body. Whether one is measuring body temperature, electrical conductivity, blood pressure, or the flow of actual Qi en-

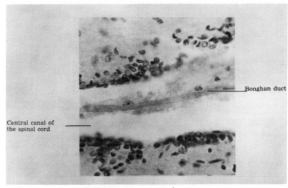

Neural Bong Han duct in the central canal of the spinal cord (Van Gieson stain, 400x). (Courtesy Dr. William Tiller.)

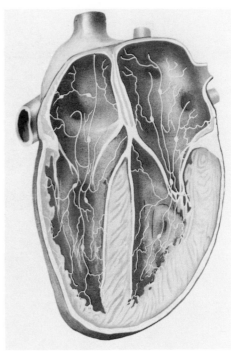

Artistic rendering of the Internal Bong Han duct system in the cardiac cavity. (Courtesy Dr. William Tiller.)

ergy (whatever that is) the principle of balance applies on all levels. Whether or not all specific acupuncture treatments turn out to produce the appropriate remedies, research thus far is upholding the general principle of balance within the body (although we shall notice some important exceptions as the picture becomes more complicated).

A series of studies illustrating this view were conducted by Dr. Hiroshi Motoyama at the Institute of Religious Psychology in Tokyo, Japan. Motoyama devised an apparatus which measured skin current at the tips of the fingers and toes where the acupuncture meridians end. A difference in value was calculated between the current in each digit and its corresponding member on the other side of the body. Using this method, Motayama discovered that whenever a patient came to him with specific complaints, the difference of current value between right and left points for the meridian corresponding to the organs in question would be quite large.

Sometimes patients would come to him with no specific complaint. However, an examination would reveal a difference in the current value of a particular meridian from the right to left side. Motayama discovered that in such cases, further medical examination would actually reveal illness in the corresponding internal organs. In a sample of 34 patients with an imbalanced current between the tips of the meridians relating to the heart (Shin-Kē and Shinpo-Kē), electrocardiograph studies indicated abnormal patterns in 29 individuals.[354]

Ostrander and Schroeder in *PDBIC* report on Soviet research which determined that the spots on the skin from which light flared most brilliantly in Kirlian photos matched the locations of the ancient Chinese points.[355] Some American researchers have observed this effect. (See Plate 13, lower-right.) In another very clever experiment, Victor Inyushin, the young Soviet researcher who is popularizing the term "bioplasma," measured, with Kirlian photography, the luminescence coming from specific acupuncture and control points on the skin. According to Chinese theory, the points he chose were connected to the teeth and inside of the mouth. Inyushin then irradiated the insides of the subject's mouths with a gas lasar and observed that the experimental acupoints increased in brightness. The control points remained the same. Inyushin has repeated this experiment many times.[356]

Further applications of Kirlian photography to an understanding of acupuncture have been reported by Dr. Thelma Moss' laboratory. Preliminary results look somewhat promising. For example, in one experiment it was decided to stimulate, by massage, the acupuncture point known as Large Intestine 10, located on the upper forearm about fiften inches above the tip of the index finger where the large intestine meridian ends. Through past experience, the experimenters had observed that when this point was stimulated subjects typically reported a pain sensation radiating down into the hand and index finger, sometimes even causing involuntary tremor. Two control groups were used in this study. One of these groups received a massage stimulation near L.I. 10, but not along the meridian. The second control group received no stimulation, but sat quietly for the one minute interval. There were ten subjects in the experimental group and in each control group. Kirlian photographs were taken just before the one minute stimulation (or rest period), immediately after, and again after three minutes. The results showed a red blotch, typically associated with arousal, on the fingerpads of the experimental subjects after stimulation. Neither control groups showed this change. The experimental report gives us no quantitative measurements.[357]

On the other hand, Moss reports the opposite effect when photographing fingertips after acupuncture treatment has been given for a specific complaint. The red blotch which is noticed before, or immediately after, insertion of needles, disappears and is replaced by a wide, bright corona.[358] More studies are necessary in order to resolve all contradictions within acupuncture. For the time being, it is safe to note that some effects of acupuncture treatment have been experimentally observed and verified. The Chinese explanation of Chi energy and meridians has been a useful tool for therapeutic applications. However the system is still inexplicable in western scientific terms.[359] Further research could well uncover new levels of our being.

While it's unfortunate that many of the experimental reports lack sufficient detail upon which an objective assessment of the experimental procedures might be founded, we have to realize that research into acupuncture is relatively new in this country. I am rather confident that the coming years will bring about scientific resolution of a multitude of tenacious problems in this area. The enigma of acupuncture is further heightened if it is seen as a link between the subtle mechanisms of the body's electromagnetic activity and the more subtle psychic systems such as *chakras* (centers of psychic focus) and *nadis* (channels which connect the chakras). (See Plates 1, 2, and 8.)

Dr. Hiroshi Motoyama's studies point toward this link. In addition to wearing the hats of medical researcher and psychiatrist, Motoyama is also a Shinto priest and a student of raja yoga. Using his intuitions, and those of several observers, Dr. Motoyama divided a yoga class of 100 members into three groups: (A) the "yogi" group in which the chakras had been clearly awakened; (B) those in whom the chakras had been slightly awakened; and (C) those in whom the chakras had not yet been awakened. The chakras are often visualized as lotus blossoms, which, when fully awakened, appear in full bloom. In this case, no controls seem to have distinguished between "awakened chakras" and skill in practicing yoga. A number of investigations were then made to determine if there were physiological differences between these three groups.

Examining the "disease tendency" of the different internal organs corresponding to chakras, such as the heart, the digestive system, the genitourinary system, and the nervous system, Motoyama found significantly greater instability of these systems in class A and B subjects. Acupuncture points associated with these organs were stimulated and measurement of skin current values were made on the palms of the hands before and after stimulation. Again the highest level of

response was found in the A group. Motoyama also measured differences in the current of the fingertips and toes on right and left sides. This time greater imbalances were found in the A group of "yogis" with awakened chakras. From these studies, he concluded that the nervous system and the autonomic functioning of individuals with awakened chakras shows a much wider range and flexibility of response than with ordinary individuals.[360] Certainly the study as reported could be criticized. One might even suggest that Motoyama was drawing inferences from random data in order to fulfill his own expectations. Nevertheless, the findings do seem cogent and consistent with other studies in which yoga and zen masters are able to dramatically vary heartbeat and brainwave measurements. Far from offering a panacea, these findings point to the need for great understanding and caution among those who teach or study yogic practices. Motoyama did not say how to distinguish between flexibility and instability of physiological response.

According to yogic tradition, the chakras themselves are not to be confused with any actual physical organs of the body. Dr. Rammurti S. Mishra—psychiatrist, endocrinologist, Sanskrit scholar, and yogi—in his translation of the *Yoga Sutras of Patanjali* states that the seven chakras are purely psychological classifications which have been adopted as *focuses of concentration* in yoga. He also adds that through the chakras mindstuff is able to operate upon the anatomical parts and physiological activities.[361] You might say that chakras are important parts of the software programmed into our biocomputers. As one becomes deeply involved in yogic meditation, one is taught practices which associate particular sounds or mantras, images, and mythological patterns to each chakra. Thus, to an extent the chakras are brought into awareness (or existence?) by a creative thought process, acting upon the unformed substance which we can loosely call the human aura, bioplasm, consciousness, or imagination. Lama Anagarika Govinda, an Indian National of European descent belonging to a Tibetan Buddhist Order, describes this process quite succinctly:

> 'Thinking is making,' this is the fundamental principle of all magic, especially of all mantric science. By the rhythmic repetition of a creative thought or idea, of a concept, a perception or a mental image, its effect is augmentized and fixed (like the action of a steadily falling drop) until it seizes upon all organs of activity and becomes a mental and material reality: a deed in the fullest sense of the word.[362]

The word chakra in Sanskrit means wheel; and according to the Theosophical tradition, the chakras are "a series of wheel-like vortices which exist in the surface of the etheric body of man."[363] The etheric body is that part of the human aura which is closest in proximity to the skin. It's sometimes referred to as the health aura, and I think can be equated to the electromagnetic field of the body or the bioplasma without doing injustice to the Theosophical system. The chakras actually extend out beyond the etheric body to the more subtle parts of the aura—such as the astral body. While normally invisible, some individuals perceive the etheric body as a faintly luminous mist extending slightly beyond the body.

In 1927, the Reverend Charles Leadbeater wrote a book on the chakras based largely on his own psychic perceptions. He describes them as follows:

> When quite undeveloped they appear as small circles about two inches in diameter, glowing dully in the ordinary man; but when awakened and vivified they are seen as blazing, coruscating whirlpools, much increased in size, and resembling miniature suns. . . . If we imagine ourselves to be looking straight down into the bell of a flower of the convolvulus type, we shall get some idea of the general appearance of a chakra. The stalk of the flower in each springs from a point in the spine. . . .
>
> All these wheels are perpetually rotating, and into the hub or open mouth of each a force from the higher world is always flowing. . . . Without this inrush of energy the physical body could not exist.[364]

Leadbeater also has uncovered descriptions of such vortices, similar to his own, in the works of the seventeenth century German mystic Johann Georg Gichtel, a pupil of Jacob Boehme. Gichtel assigned an astrological planetary influence to each of the seven centers in his system. It is uncertain to me whether he was influenced by the Sanskrit tradition. However, on the title page of his book, *Theosophia Practica* he claims to be presenting, ''A short exposition of the three principles of the three worlds in man, represented in clear pictures, showing how and where they have their respective Centres in the inner man; according to what the author has found in himself in divine contemplation, and what he has felt, tasted and perceived.''[365] (See Plate 8, upper-left.)

In Los Angeles at the Higher Sense Perception Research Foundation, Dr. Shafica Karagula, a neuropsychiatrist, has for many years made clinical observations of individuals gifted with extraordinary perception. One of her subjects, whom she calls ''Diane,'' reported the ability to visualize vortices of energy, like spiral cones, which seemed to be in remarkable agreement with Leadbeater's descriptions. She described the etheric body as a sparkling web of light beams in constant movement ''like the lines of a television screen when the picture is not in focus.'' There were eight major vortices of force and many smaller vortices. Seven of the vortices seemed to be directly related to the different glands of the body. Diane was able to successfully diagnose various diseases by noticing disturbances in the vortices. Karagula tested this ability by taking Diane to an endocrine clinic of a large New York hospital and having her read the auras of patients selected at random in the waiting room. Then Diane's observations were checked against the medical case records.

Karagula claims that she was amazed at the accuracy of Diane's diagnoses over a large number of cases. However she provides no exact figures in her book or in her published reports and we are not informed if independent judges and experimental controls were used.[366,367] It is difficult to ascertain the extent to which Dr. Karagula or her subjects may have had their perceptions colored by the Theosophical tradition. I'm

Dr. Shafica Karagula (Courtesy Psychic Magazine.)

hopeful that their research foundation will eventually release more thorough research reports. Many other psychic individuals I have been acquainted with report an ability to visualize chakras. However, I know of no tested psychics who have indicated the ability to percieve chakras prior to any occult training.

When it comes to making any physiological sense out of the chakras, the whole matter is filled with confusion. One widely quoted approach equates the first chakra with the reproductive system. Others associate the second chakra with sexuality and reproduction. Sometimes the sixth chakra or third eye is associated with the pineal gland, sometimes with the pituitary. The third chakra is sometimes associated with the solar plexus, sometimes with the spleen, and sometimes with the digestive system. Sometimes the second chakra is associated with the spleen. Sometimes all of the chakras are associated with nerve plexes, sometimes they are all associated with the endocrine glands. In the Tibetan system, the sixth and seventh chakras— the third eye and the "thousand petalled lotus" are thought of as one. The Qabalistic system divides the body into ten centers. Ironically, all these systems will go into great detail in specifying the circuitry—often called *nadis*–which connect the chakras together. I find it easiest to confront all of these paradoxical interpretations with a certain curiosity and humility (although I tend to think that some writers masked their lack of understanding with dogmatic assertion). Paradoxes of a comparable sort are not uncommon in the physical and natural sciences, and generally exist on the frontiers of knowledge. Most researchers tend to ignore these uncomfortable, and poorly substantiated, reports.

One ingenious hypothesis was developed by Dr. William Tiller at Stanford University. Tiller was impressed with the apparent relationship of location and function between the chakras and the endocrine glands. He wondered how these so-called "etheric" organs might interact with the glands. Drawing from concepts used by electrical engineers, he suggested that this interaction could be analogous to a process of *transduction*. Imagine great energy streams flowing through space and passing through our bodies, unabsorbed and unnoticed. Tiller suggests that perhaps the chakras can be tuned in to couple with this power source and transduce some of its energy from the astral or etheric levels into the glands. One can think of the chakras and glands as electrical transformer loads which will deliver maximum power if they are balanced with respect to each other.[368] These ideas are very speculative; however such imaginative thinking—especially when conjoined with a commitment for further systematic research—is a necessary and valuable part of the scientific method.

We still wonder, for example, whether chakras have some objective existence, or whether they are the creations of minds who claim to observe them. The same problem is actually encountered in all fields of human knowledge from politics to biology. For practical purposes, this is usually solved by consensus agreement. When enough individuals see approximately the same phenomena through a microscope, we safely

Transduction of etheric force through the chakra into the bodily force within an endocrine gland. (Courtesy Dr. William Tiller.)

244

assume that the phenomena exists independent of the observer's mind—even though none of their perceptions will be identical. This difficulty is enhanced in the introspective sciences because the phenomena being observed are even more dependent upon the state of consciousness and psychic development of the observer. We are like the chained slaves inside of Plato's cave listening to the reports from returned escapees, still partly blind, who have each felt part of an elephant.

The following material concerning the nature of the other bodies of man comes from the introspective investigation of various psychics. Max Heindel, founder of the Rosicrucian Fellowship, describes the etheric or vital body:

The vital body of plant, animal, and man, extends beyond the periphery of the dense body as the Etheric Region, which is the vital body of a planet, extends beyond its dense part, showing again the truth of the Hermetic axiom "As above, so below." The distance of this extension of the vital body of man is about an inch and a half. The part which is outside the dense body is very luminous and about the color of a new-blown peach-blossom. It is often seen by persons having very slight involuntary clairvoyance. The writer has found, when speaking with such persons, that they frequently are not aware they see anything unusual and do not know what they see.

The dense body is built into the matrix of this vital body during ante-natal life, and with one exception, it is an exact copy, molecule for molecule, of the vital body. As the lines of force in freezing water are the avenues of formation for ice crystals, so the lines of force in the vital body determine the shape of the dense body. All through life the vital body is the builder and restorer of the dense form. Were it not for the etheric heart the dense heart would break quickly under the constant strain we put upon it. All the abuses to which we subject the dense body are counteracted, so far as lies in its power, by the vital body, which is continually fighting against the death of the dense body.

The exception mentioned above is that the vital body of a man is female or negative, while that of a woman is male or positive. In that fact we have the key to numerous puzzling problems of life. That woman gives way to her emotions is due to the polarity noted, for her positive, vital body generates an excess of blood and causes her to labor under an enormous internal pressure that would break the physical casement were not a safety-valve provided in the periodical flow, and another in the tears which relieve the pressure on special occasions—for tears are "white bleeding."

Man may have and has as strong emotions as a woman, but he is usually able to suppress them without tears, because his negative vital body does not generate more blood than he can comfortably control.

Unlike the higher vehicles of humanity, the vital body (except under certain circumstances, to be explained when the subject of "Initiation" is dealt with) does not ordinarily leave the dense body until the death of the latter. Then the chemical forces of the dense body are no longer held in check by the evolving life. They proceed to restore the matter to its primordial condition by disintegration so that it may be available for the formation of other forms in the economy of nature. Disintegration is thus due to the activity of the planetary forces in the chemical ether.

There are certain cases where the vital body partly leaves the dense body, such as when a hand "goes to sleep." Then the etheric hand of the vital body may be seen hanging below the dense arm like a glove and the points cause the peculiar pricking sensation felt when the etheric hand re-enters the dense hand. Sometimes in hypnosis the head of the vital body divides and hangs outside the dense head, one half over each shoulder, or lies around the neck like the collar of a sweater. The absence of prickly sensation at awakening in cases like this is because during the hypnosis part of the hypnotist's vital body had been substituted for that of the victim.

When anesthetics are used the vital body is partially driven out, along with the higher vehicles, and if the application is too strong and the life ether is driven out, death ensues. This same phenomenon may also be observed in the case of materializing medium and an ordinary man or woman is just this: In the ordinary man or woman the vital body and the dense body are, at the present stage of evolution, quite firmly interlocked, while in the medium they are loosely connected. It has not always been so, and the time will again come when the vital body may normally leave the dense vehicle, but that is not normally accomplished at present. When a medium allows his or her vital body to be used by entities from the Desire World who wish to materialize, the vital body generally oozes from the left side—through the spleen, which is its particular "gate." Then the vital forces cannot flow into the body as they do normally, the medium becomes greatly exhausted, and some of them resort to stimulants to counteract the effects, in time becoming incurable drunkards.

The vital force from the sun, which surrounds us as a colorless fluid, is absorbed by the vital body through the etheric counterpart of the spleen, wherein it undergoes a curious transformation of color. It becomes pale rosehued and spreads along the nerves all over the dense body. It is to the nervous system what the force of electricity is to a telegraph system. Though there be wires, instruments, and telegraph operators all in order, if the electricity is lacking no message can be sent. The Ego, the brain, and the nervous system may be in seemingly perfect order, but if the vital force be lacking to carry the message of the Ego through the nerves to the muscles, the dense body will remain inert. This is exactly what happens when part of the dense body becomes paralyzed. The vital body has become diseased and the vital force can no longer flow. In such cases, as in most sickness, the trouble is with the finer invisible vehicles. In conscious or unconscious recognition of this fact, the most successful physicians use suggestion —which works upon the higher vehicles—as an aid to medicine. The more a physician can imbue his patient with faith and hope, the speedier disease will vanish and give place to perfect health.

During health the vital body specializes a superabundance of vital force, which after passing through a dense body, radiates in straight lines in every direction from the periphery thereof, as the radii of a circle do from the center; but during ill-health, when the vital body becomes attenuated, it is not able to draw to itself the same amount of force and in addition the dense body is feeding upon it. Then the lines of the vital fluid which pass out from the body are crumpled and bent, showing the lack of force behind them. In health the great force of these radiations carries with it germs and microbes which are inimical to the health of the dense body, but in sickness, when the vital force is weak, these emanations do not so readily eliminate disease germs. Therefore the danger of contracting disease is much greater when the vital forces are low than when one is in robust health.

In cases where parts of the dense body are amputated, only the planetary ether accompanies the separated part. The separate vital body and the dense body disintegrate synchronously after death. So with the etheric counterpart of the amputated limb. It will gradually disintegrate as the dense member decays, but in the meantime the fact that the man still possesses the etheric limb accounts for his assertion that he can feel his fingers or suffers pain in them. There is also a connection with a buried member, irrespective of distance. A case is on record where a man felt a severe pain, as if a nail had been driven into the flesh of an amputated limb, and he persisted until the limb was exhumed, when it was found that a nail had been driven into it at the time it was boxed for burial.* The nail was removed and the pain

---

*At first when I read this statement, I assumed that Heindel was merely drawing from an unsubstantiated occult tale. Later I was able to find the case recorded in a scientific manner.[369]

246

instantly stopped. It is also in accordance with these facts that people complain of pain in a limb for perhaps two or three years after the amputation. The pain will then cease. This is because the disease remains in the still undetached etheric limb, but as the amputated part disintegrates, the etheric limb follows suit and thus the pain ceases.[370]

Heindel's description is typical of the type of writing which can be found in the occult and mystical literature from many cultures and periods of time.

A word of caution here. There are a few effects of an optical or physiological nature which might easily be taken for an aura by a careless, or uninformed, observer. In a rather clever series of experiments, Dr. A. R. G. Owen determined that many people will see such "rim" auras, glowing about an inch or two from the edge of inanimate objects even more distinctly than around living plants, animals, and humans. Many people were unable to distinguish between the aura which appeared around a piece of cardboard shaped as a hand and that which they observed around a real human hand. Other observers, particularly those who saw a much larger and more vivid aura, were quite able to make the distinction. In any case, almost all of the subjects were able to see some aura-like visual phenomena. These perceptions are attributed to the active role which the retina and the visual cortex take in organizing and interpreting visual contours while the eye itself is constantly making tiny movements, scanning whatever is observed.[371]

You can easily experience this yourself simply by focusing on the contours of the word written in the margin. See what you notice. The power of suggestions also is active here. This effect is highlighted by the sharp black and white contrast.

On the other hand, Dr. Owen was able to repeatedly demonstrate a most unusual and vivid aura-like appearance on the end of a rod while it was the focus of concentration from two gifted psychics. A number of observers were able to independently verify this perception which was not normally seen around the rod.[372] However the exact conditions for replication of this effect are not known.

The Psychical Aura

Beyond the vital layer of the aura, is said to exist the astral or desire layer. It is here that the emotions of an individual distinguish themselves by their from and color. C. W. Leadbeater, one of the Theosophists who was responsible for popularizing the term "astral" plane, claims that it was inherited from the medieval alchemists. The term means starry and was applied to the plane above the physical because of its luminous appearance. Furthermore, the emotional currents were thought to be influenced by the planetary positions. The meaning of the different colors which appear in the astral body is recorded as follows by Yogi Ramacharaka:

Auric Colors and Their Meanings.

Black represents hatred, malice, revenge, and similar feelings.
Gray, of a bright shade, represents selfishness.

Gray, of a peculiar shade (almost that of a corpse), represents fear and terror.

Gray, of a dark shade, represents depression and melancholy.

Green, of a dirty shade, represents jealousy. If much anger is mingled with the jealousy, it will appear as red flashes on the green background.

Green, of almost a slate-color shade, represents low deceit.

Green, of a peculiar bright shade, represents tolerance to the opinions and beliefs of others, easy adjustment to changing conditions, adaptability, tact, politeness, worldly wisdom, etc., and qualities which some might possible consider "refined deceit."

Red, of a shade resembling the dull flame when it bursts out of a burning building, mingled with the smoke, represents sensuality and the animal passions.

Red, seen in the shape of bright-red flashes resembling the lightning flash in shape, indicated anger. These are usually shown on a black background in the case of anger arising from hatred or malice, but in cases of anger arising from jealousy they appear on a greenish background. Anger arising from indignation or defense of a supposed "right," lacks these backgrounds, and usually shows as red flashes independent of a background.

Crimson represents love, varying in shade according to the character of the passion. A gross sensual love will be dull and heavy crimson, while one mixed with higher feelings will appear in lighter and more pleasing shades. A very high form of love shows a color almost approaching a beautiful rose color.

Brown, of a reddish tinge, represents avarice and greed.

Orange, of a bright shade, represents pride and ambition.

Yellow, in its various shades, represents intellectual power. If the intellect contents itself with things of a low order, the shade is a dark, dull yellow; and as the field of the intellect rises to higher levels, the color grows brighter and clearer, a beautiful golden yellow betokening great intellectual attainment, broad and brilliant reasoning, etc.

Blue, of a dark shade, represents religious thought, emotion, and feeling. This color, however, varies in clearness according to the degree of unselfishness manifest in the religious conception. The shades and degrees of clarity vary from a dull indigo to a beautiful rich violet, the latter representing the highest religious feeling.

Light Blue, of a peculiarly clear and luminous shade, represents spirituality. Some of the higher degrees of spirituality observed in ordinary mankind show themselves in this shade of blue filled with luminous bright points, sparkling and twinkling like stars on a clear winter night.

The student will remember that these colors form endless combinations and blendings, and show themselves in greatly varying degrees of brightness and size, all of which have meanings to the developed occultist.

In addition to the colors mentioned above, there are several others for which we have no names, as they are outside of the colors visible in the spectrum, and consequently science, not being able to perceive them, has not thought it necessary to bestow definite names upon them, although they exist theoretically. Science tells us that there are also what are known as "ultra-violet" rays and "ultra-red" rays, neither of which can be followed by the human eyes, even with the aid of mechanical appliances, the vibrations being beyond our senses. These two "ultra" colors (and several others unknown to science) are known to occultists and may be seen by the person with certain psychic powers. The significance of this statement may be more fully grasped when we state that when seen in the Human Aura either of these "ultra" colors indicates psychic development, the degree of intensity depending upon the degree of development. Another remarkable fact, to those who have not thought of the matter, is that the "ultra-violet" color in the Aura indicates psychic development when used on a high and unselfish plane, while "the ultra-red" color, when seen in the Human Aura, indicates that the person has psychic development, but is using the same for selfish and unworthy purposes—"black magic," in

248

fact. The "ultra-violet" rays lie just outside of an extreme of the visible spectrum known to science, while the "ultra-red" rays lie just beyond the other extreme. The vibrations of the first are too high for the ordinary human eye to sense, while the second comprises vibrations as excessively low as the first is excessively high. And the real difference between the two forms of psychic power is as great as is indicated by the respective positions of these two "ultra" colors. In addition to the two "ultra" colors just alluded to, there is another which is invisible to the ordinary sight—the *true* primary yellow, which indicates of the Spiritual Illumination and which is faintly seen around the heads of the spiritually great. The color which we are taught characterizes the seventh principle, Spirit, is said to be of pure white light, of a peculiar brilliancy, the like of which has never been seen by human eyes—in fact, the very existence of *absolute* "white light" is denied by Western science.

The Aura emanating from the Instinctive Mind principally comprises heavier and duller shades. In sleep, when the mind is quiet, there appears chiefly a certain dull red, which indicates that the Instinctive Mind is merely performing the body's animal functions. This shade, of course, is always apparent, but during the waking hours it is often obscured by the brighter shades of the passing thoughts, emotions, or feelings.

Right here it would be well to state that even while the mind remains calm there hover in the Aura shades which indicate a man's predominant tendencies, so that his stage of advancement and development as well as his "tastes" and other features of his personality may be easily distinguished. When the mind is swept by a strong passion, feeling, or emotion, the entire Aura seems to be colored by the particular shade or shades representing it. For instance, a violent fit of anger causes the whole Aura to show bright red flashes upon a black background, almost eclipsing the other colors. This state lasts for a longer or shorter time, according to the strength of the passion. If people could but have a glimpse of the Human Aura when so colored, they would become so horrified at the dreadful sight that they would be far more hesitant about flying into rage—it resembles the flames and smoke of the devil's "pit" and, in fact, the human mind in such a condition becomes a veritable hell temporarily. A strong wave of love sweeping over the mind will cause the entire Aura to show crimson; the shade will depend upon the character of the passion. Likewise, a burst of religious feeling will bestow upon the entire Aura a blue tinge, as explained in the table of colors. In short, a strong emotion, feeling, or passion causes the entire Aura to take on its color while the feeling lasts. You will see from what we have said that there are two aspects to the color feature of the Aura; the first depending upon the predominant thoughts habitually manifesting in the mind of the person; the second depending upon the particular feeling, emotion, or passion (if any) is dominating him at that particular time.

The student . . . will realize readily that as the man develops and unfolds he becomes less and less prey to passing passions, emotions, or feelings emanating from the Instinctive Mind, and that Intellect, and then Spiritual Mind, manifest themselves instead of lying dormant in a latent condition. Remembering this, he will readily see how great a difference there must be between the Aura of an undeveloped man and that of the developed man. The one is a mass of dull, heavy, gross colors, the entire mass being frequently flooded by the color of some passing emotion, feeling, or passion. The other shows the higher colors and is very much clearer, being but little disturbed by feelings, emotion, and passions, all of which have been brought largely under the control of the will.

The man who has Intellect well developed shows an Aura flooded with the beautiful golden yellow betokening intellectuality. This color in such cases is particularly apparent in the upper part of the Aura, surrounding the head and shoulders of the man, the more animal colors sinking to the lower part of the Aura. Read the remarks under the head of "Yellow" in the color table in this lesson. When the man's Intellect has absorbed the idea of spirituality and devotes itself to the

Aura of sleeping cat.

Aura of aroused cat.

249

acquirement of spiritual power, development, and unfoldment, this yellow will show around its edges a light blue of a peculiarly clear and luminous shade. This peculiar light blue is indicative of what is generally called "spirituality," but which is simply "intellectual-spirituality," if you will pardon the use of the somewhat paradoxical term— it is not the same thing as Spiritual Mind, but is merely Intellect impregnated by Spiritual Mind, to use another troublesome term. In some cases when this intellect is in a highly developed state, the luminous light blue shows as a broad fringe or border often being larger than the center itself, and in addition, in special cases, the light blue is filled with brilliant luminous points, sparkling and twinkling like stars on a clear winter night. These bright points indicate that the color of the Aura of the Spiritual Mind is asserting itself, and shows that Spiritual Consciousness has either become momentarily evident to the man or is about to become so in the near future. This is a point upon which much confusion has arisen in the minds of students and even teachers of occultism. The next paragraph will also shed further light upon the matter.

The Aura emanating from the Spiritual Mind, or sixth principle, bears the color of the *true* primary yellow, which is invisible to ordinary sight and which cannot be reproduced artificially by man. It centers around the head of the spiritually illumined, and at times produces a peculiar glow which can even be seen by undeveloped people. This is particularly true when the spiritually developed person is engaged in earnest discourse or teaching, at these times his countenance seems fairly to glow and to possess a luminosity of a peculiar kind. The nimbus shown in pictures of mankind's great spiritual leaders results from a tradition based on a fact actually experienced by the early followers of such leaders. The "halo" or "glory" shown on pictures arises from the same fact.[373]

Interestingly enough most of Ramacharaka's descriptions accord with the teachings of Blavatsky, Leadbeater and other Theosophists. I am inclined to think that they may have all been influenced by the same source of teachings which Blavatsky quotes in her *Secret Doctrine*.

You might think that it would be relatively simple for scientists to test the objectivity of the aura, by comparing the independent observations of a number of psychics. In fact, the problem is difficult and there has been very little systematic research. For one thing, if the observations are being made at different moments of time, it's possible that the aura could change appearance. Also, a truly objective study would want to rule out any other sensory cues that could be confused with the aura. Charles Tart has suggested that the target person for such a study be hidden behind an opaque screen shaped so that only the aura should be visible beyond its perimeter and not the physical body at all.[374] To my knowledge there have been no experiments of this type.

In a study conducted by Dr. A. R. G. Owen of Torónto, fourteen different psychics made independent observations of the aura of a single subject. The reported descriptions show wide variation which, according to Owen, "seems to go beyond that degree of variability in the aura, which according to percipients of auras, is to be expected as a result of temporal variations in the physical, emotional or mental state of the possessor of the aura." However the study took place over a one year period. Going over the data, I myself was struck by the similarity of reports made by different observers on the same day. Owen maintains that there was no cogent evidence that the subject was in different physical or emotional states during the different days of experimentation. It doesn't appear that he was looking for subtle emotional changes. The fact that lighting conditions were different on the different days of experimentation further confuses the data. Furthermore, some subjects saw the aura with their eyes open, while at least one subject viewed the aura with his eyes closed.[375] Although Owen's study is the only one of its sort reported in the experimental literature, the anecdotal evidence is very strong. This area is certainly ripe for further research.

Another telling anecdote relating to the perception of the human aura on the "astral level" comes from the Texas psychic Ray Stanford. Ray, who seems to be very proficient at seeing auras, visited his twin brother Rex, a parapsychologist then at the University of Virginia; he gave a demonstration of his talents before a small group of researchers assembled by his brother. One of the guests was Dr. Robert Van de Castle, the director of the sleep and dream laboratory. Ray noticed a number of pink spots in the aura around Van de Castle's abdomen. This perception puzzled him since it is one which he normally associated with pregnant women; and he remarked to Dr. Van de Castle, "If I didn't know better, I'd say you were pregnant." This drew some laughter from the audience. However, Van de Castle then reflected that he had been analyzing the dreams of pregnant women all morning and had even remarked earlier that day that he was beginning to feel like a pregnant woman himself.[376] Perhaps Stanford Created this "aura" as a vehicle for allowing his psi impressions to become conscious.

Several related findings have been reported from the UCLA radiation field photography laboratory. One study attempted to observe the Kirlian fingertips of pairs of individuals, holding their fingers close together, but not touching, as they stared into each other's eyes. Frequently they found, for no apparent explanation, that one of the fingertips in each pair would practically disappear. (See Plate 14, third-right.) One of the subjects was a professional hypnotist, and it was repeatedly discovered that he could blank out the fingertips of any one of a number of partners. In a rather striking experiment, one subject was asked to visualize sticking a needle into her partner, who was known to be afraid of needles. The Kirlian photograph of their fingertips shows a sharp red line darting out of the agressor's finger toward that of her imagined victim whose emanations appear to be retreating! (See Plate 12, bottom). On the other hand, the photographed corona of two individuals taken while they have meditated together typically has shown a merging and uniting of the two individual coronas.[377]

Sometimes when two persons were able to generate feelings of hostility towards each other, the corona between their fingers would abruptly cut off, leaving a gap so sharp and clear that it became known as the "haircut effect." In some instances a bright bar, like a barrier, would appear between the two photographed fingerpads. (See Plate 14, lower-right.) Further studies with family groups engaged in family therapy were conducted. Group photographs were taken with the fingerpads of each member of the family. Typically one member of the

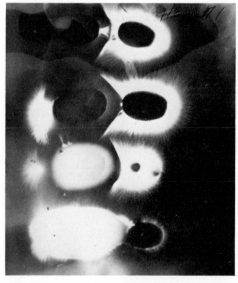

Kirlian fingerpads of two individuals meditating. The male on the left originally showed no corona, and eventually developed a tremendous pattern change through the onset of meditation. What was originally a barrier became a merging. (Courtesy Dr. Thelma Moss)

251

group, generally the son, would not photograph at all. Other photographs in this study strongly suggested to the researchers that Kirlian photography could provide valuable insights into the emotional reactions between people.[378,379]

In order to explain these uncanny phototgraphic events, researchers are drawing upon the efforts of Kurt Lewin (1890–1947) to apply the concepts of physical fields to the study of human personality. One of the unique characteristics of Lewin's theory was using of diagramatic representations of internal and external personality interactions. The following diagram is one Lewin used:

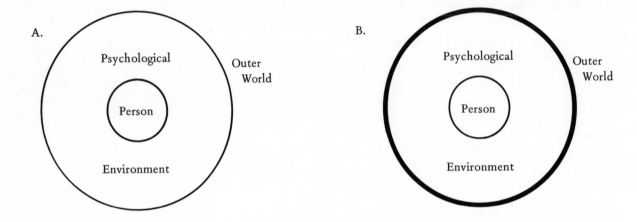

The individual is described graphically by the quality of psychological environment (or aura) around him. Person *b*, for example, is one with a thicker boundary. The outer world has little influence on the life-space and vice-versa. The life-space of person *a* is more open and expansive.[380]

Lewin has often been criticized for the unjustified application of physical concepts and terminology to the realm of personality where they did not belong. It was claimed that his diagrams were an attempt to appear scientific without using the requisite controls and measurements of science. Furthermore, it was difficult for these critics to see what these diagrams had to do with the "real world." Now however, Moss' studies and the work of other researchers suggest that Kirlian photographs can be read almost as if they were Lewin diagrams of personality fields![381] This finding, if it stands the test of further scrutiny, will provide an enormous theoretical breakthrough—far beyond what Lewin himself ever actually suggested.

This type of experience suggests that the psychic aura consists of precise conceptual images (theosophical mental body) as well as more nebulous emotional colorings (astral body). The astral body then relates to the instinctual levels of the Freudian unconscious—sex, aggression, love, and sublimation. These are the powerful emotions which motivate man's behavior. To pursue the analogy further, the mental body corresponds very nicely to the world of archetypes, and thoughtforms symbols described in the analytical psychology of Dr. Carl Gustav Jung. Jung himself stated many times that the archetypal world—although it exists within the mind—should be thought of as

252

objective reality. It resembles Plato's realm where ideas themselves exist as visible thought-forms. An example of the perception of thought-forms is provided by the famous medium Eileen Garrett:

One sees lines and colors and symbols. These move, and one is wholly concentrated on them and their movement. I say "symbols" here for want of a better word. I frequently see curving lines of light and color that flow forward in strata, and in these strips or ribbons of movement there will appear other sharply angled lines that form and change and fade like arrow heads aimed and passing in various directions. And in this flow of energy that is full of form and color, these arrow heads will presently indicate the letter H. Each line of the H will be an independent curve, and their combination will not remain identifiable for very long. But I shall have caught it; and holding it suspended in awareness, I continue to watch the process develop and unfold. Soon a rapidly drifting A appears in the field of concentration, and then, let us suppose, an R; and presently I have gathered the word HARRY out of the void, either as a proper name or as a verb temporarily without either subject or object. Whether it is actually a noun or a verb will depend upon the context of the perception as a whole.

This process is infinitely rapid. But I have achieved an alertness of attention, of awareness, of being, which is equal to this rapid flow of immaterial line and color and symbol, and out of this alertness, poised above the flowing stream of differentiated energy, I gather a message with a meaning—a message which has come to my consciousness out of the objective world as factually as the reflected light from the distant Moon may reach my consciousness by way of my sense of sight.[382]

The following descriptions of thought-forms and the mental body comes from Annie Besant and the Reverend Leadbeater:

The mental body is an object of great beauty, the delicacy and rapid motion of its particles giving it an aspect of living irridescent light, and this beauty becomes an extraordinarily radiant and entrancing loveliness and the intellect becomes more highly evolved and is employed chiefly on pure and sublime topics. Every thought gives rise to a set of correlated vibrations in the matter of this body, accompanied with a marvelous display of color, like that in the spray of a waterfall as the sunlight strikes it, raised to the nth degree of color and vivid delicacy. The body under this impulse throws off a vibrating portion of itself, shaped by the nature of the vibrations—as figures are made by sand on a disk vibrating to a musical note—and this gathers from the surrounding atmosphere matter like itself in fineness from the elemental essence of the mental world. We have then a thought-form pure and simple, and it is a living entity of intense activity animated by the one idea that generated it. If made of finer kinds of matter, it will be of great power and energy, and may be used as a most potent agent when directed by a strong and steady will. . . .

Each definite thought produces a double effect—a radiating vibration and a floating form. The thought itself appears first to clairvoyant sight as a vibration in the mental body, and this may be either simple or complex. . . .

If a man's thought or feeling is directly connected with someone else, the resultant thought-form moves toward that person and discharges itself upon his astral and mental bodies. If the man's thought is about himself, or is based upon a personal feeling, as the vast majority of thoughts are, it hovers round its creator and is always ready to react upon him whenever he is for a moment in a passive condition. . . .

Each man travels through space enclosed within a case of his own building, surrounded by a mass of the forms created by his habitual thought. Through this medium he looks out upon the world, and naturally he sees everything tinged with its predominant colors, and all

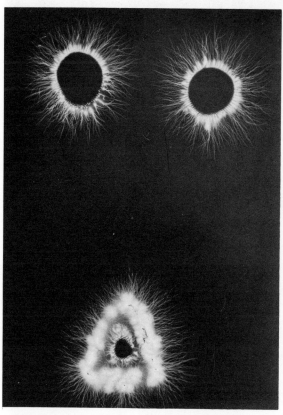

Some of the most significant evidence for the physical effects of thoughtforms comes from an experiment conducted by James L. Hickman with Uri Geller, using high-voltage photography. The experimental procedure was the following: The experimenter and the observers arbitrarily chose a geometric figure. With the lights off, the experimenter guided the subject's right forefingertip to the film surface while carefully feeling for any foreign material which might influence the photographic image. One or two control exposures were taken. Then the experimenter lowered the subject's fingertip to another portion of the film, again feeling for foreign material. The experimenter and observers concentrated on the target image and, on the subject's command, the high-voltage supply was activated. The exposed film was placed in a light-tight box and the lights were turned on. The lower image in the above figure indicates that the triangular target was correctly received by Geller and somehow made to appear on the photographic image. While successful results were obtained on several occasions and also with other researchers, the experimenters are cautious in interpreting their data without further investigation. (Courtesy Henry S. Dakin, High-Voltage Photography, 1975.)

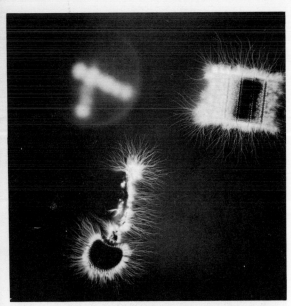

The above figure was taken using the same procedure as described on the previous page, except that the subject, Uri Geller, was asked to try to transfer mental energy from his finger to a wristwatch lying on the film surface. (Courtesy of Henry S. Dakin, High-Voltage Photography, *1975.)*

rates of vibration which reach him from without are more or less modified by its rate. Thus until the man learns complete control of thought and feeling, he sees nothing as it really is, since all his observations must be made through his medium, which distorts and colors everything like badly-made glass.

If the thought-form be neither definitely personal nor specially aimed at someone else, it simply floats detached in the atmosphere, all the time radiating vibrations similar to those originally sent forth by its creator. If it does not come into contact with any other mental body, this radiation gradually exhausts its store of energy, and in that case, the form falls to pieces; but if it succeeds in awakening sympathetic vibration in any mental body near at hand, an attraction is set up, and the thought-form is usually absorbed by that mental body.[383]

To this picture of the mental body, Yogi Ramacharaka adds a further description of the mental world as such:

Places and localities are often permeated by the thought of persons who formerly lived there, who have moved away or died many years ago. . . . The occultist knows that this thought-atmosphere of a village, town, city, or nation is the composite thought of those dwelling in it or whom have previously dwelt there. Strangers coming into the community feel the changed atmosphere about it, and, unless they find it in harmony with their own mental character, they feel uncomfortable and desire to leave the place. If one, not understanding the laws operating in the thought world, remains long in a place, he is most likely to be influenced by the prevailing thought-atmosphere, and in spite of himself a change begins to be manifest in him and he sinks or rises to the level of the prevailing thought. . . .

In the same way dwellings, business-places, buildings, etc., take on the predominant thought of those inhabiting them or who have dwelt in them.[384]

The existence of the mental world implies a view of nature which incorporates meaning as well as mechanism. We are no longer dealing with blind forces bouncing aimlessly throughout the universe. The substance of the mental world is embued with purpose. Minds, or monads, are constantly emitting radiation of an intelligent nature. Every thought may be thought of as an active spiritual force.

It is on this level that we need to consider some of the more extreme findings of astrology. Electromagnetic radiations and solar storm activity can certainly account for certain mass phenomena. But we cannot expect electromagnetic effects to bear much relationship to the individual horoscope. Nevertheless, data of this sort exists which must be considered. Most of the significant studies to which I am referring are the result of many years of experimentation by Michel Gauquelin in France. His findings do not support the type of astrology relating to sun signs which you normally read about in popular books, newspapers, and magazines. (In fact, there is really no good data I know of which offers evidence for the astrological value of sun signs, moon signs, or any signs at all.) What Gauquelin was able to discover was a weak relationship between the position of planets relative to the horizon and success in certain professions. While, with a few notable exceptions, Gauquelin did not predict his results in advance, his findings are consistent with the astrological interpretations of Ptolemy and Kepler. These results are independent of normal seasonal or circadian factors.

254

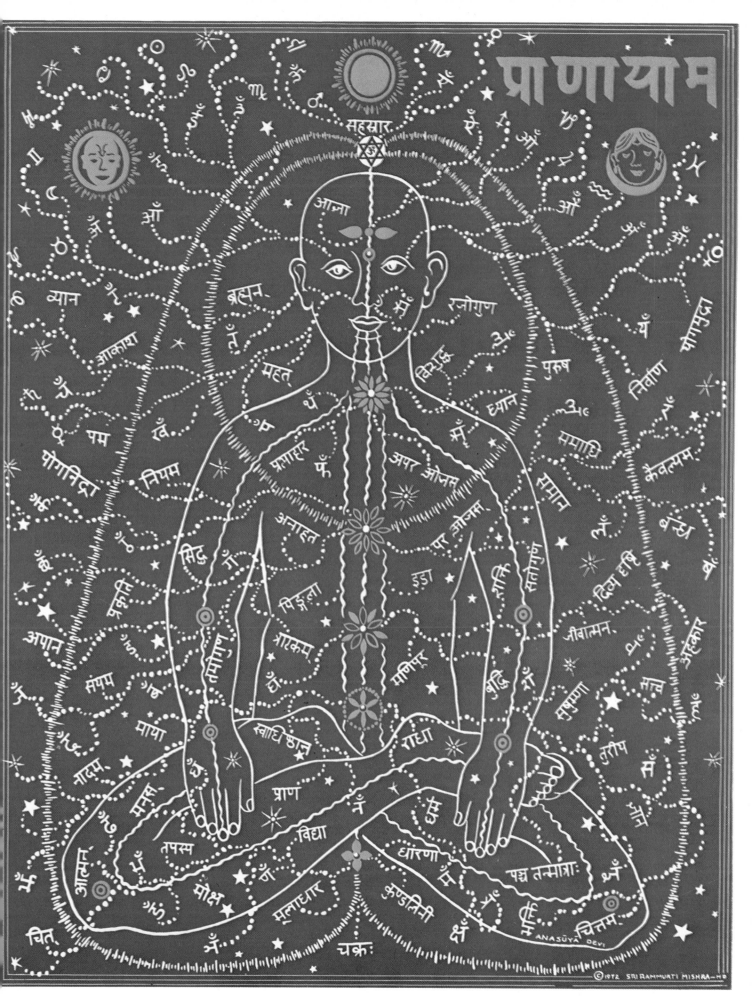

Plate 1

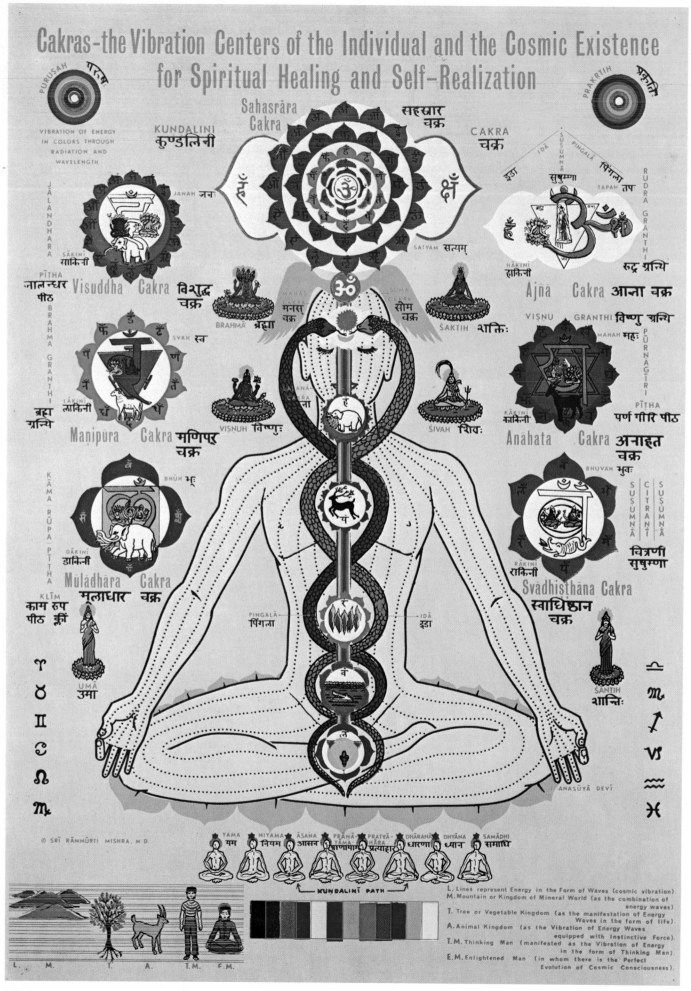

Plate 2

Plate 3

Plate 4

THE HUMAN AURA.

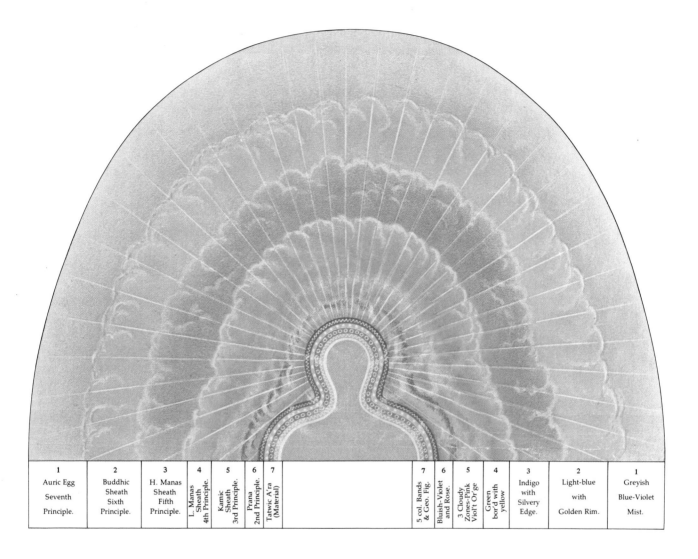

1	2	3	4	5	6	7		7	6	5	4	3	2	1
Auric Egg	Buddhic Sheath	H. Manas Sheath	L. Manas Sheath 4th Principle.	Kamic Sheath 3rd Principle.	Prana 2nd Principle.	Tatwic A'ra (Material)		5 col. Bands & Geo. Fig.	Bluish-Violet and Rose.	3 Cloudy Zones-Pink Viol't Or'ge	Green bor'd with yellow	Indigo with Silvery Edge.	Light-blue with Golden Rim.	Greyish Blue-Violet Mist.
Seventh Principle.	Sixth Principle.	Fifth Principle.												

☛ The **1st Principle,** Linga, Etheric Double or Shadow Body is not indicated on plate in order not to overcrowd it.

Of the material Emanations from the Body, only the Electric or Health Aura is indicated by the vertical lines, but the Magnetic and Caloric Emanations are not represented, as they crowd into the same space as the Pranic and Tatwic Auras, Columns 6 and 7.

The whole drawing is not in absolute proportion, the Tatwic colored and Geometrical Emanations having been kept nearly to their natural size, in order to make them apparent, while the others, going outward, have been greatly reduced, to fit in the page.

The natural colors are much more blended, ethereal, delicate and subdued than can possibly be reproduced.

General Perspective View of the Human Auras.

A. W. BUSH S.F., CAL.

Plate 5

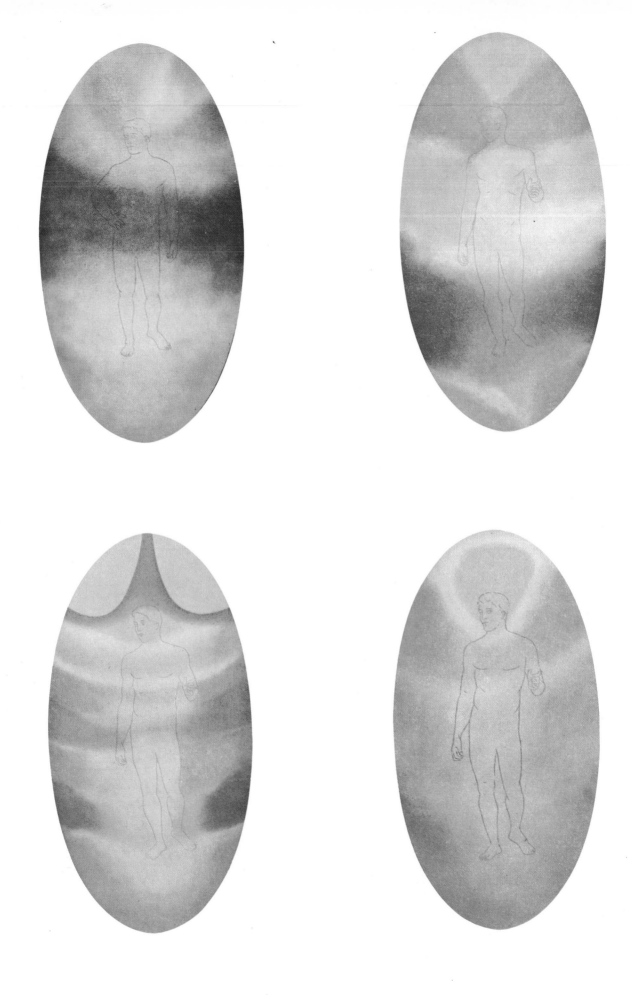

Plate 6

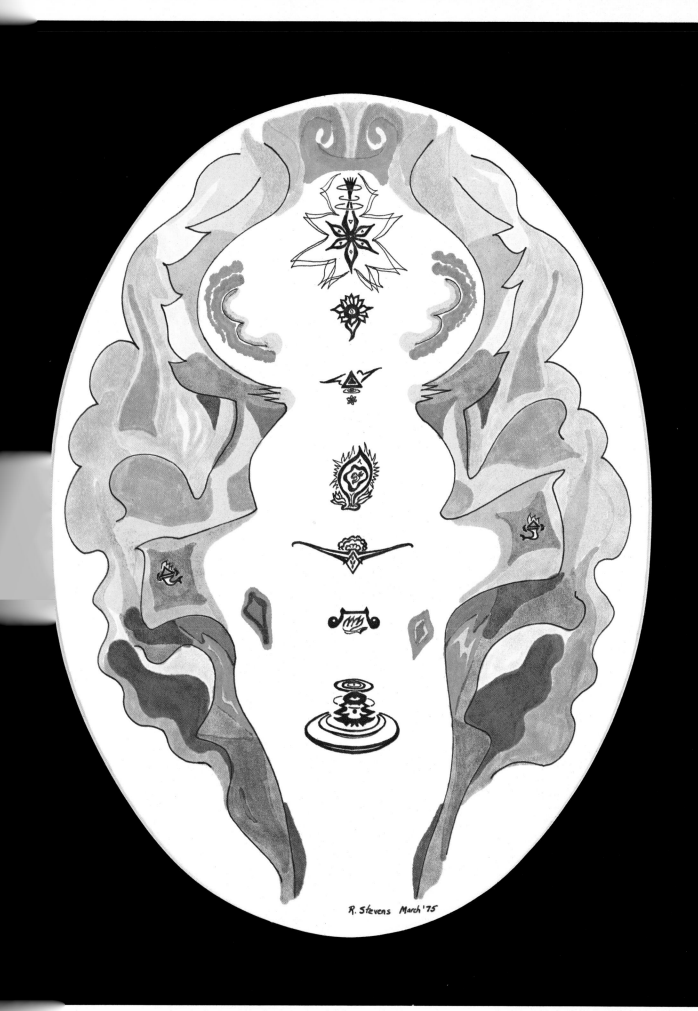

R. Stevens March '75

Plate 7

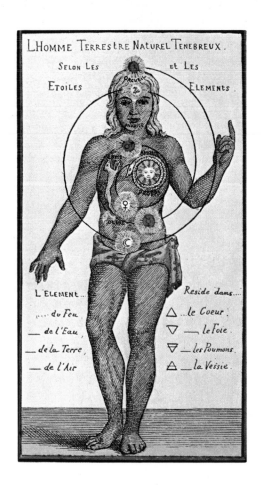

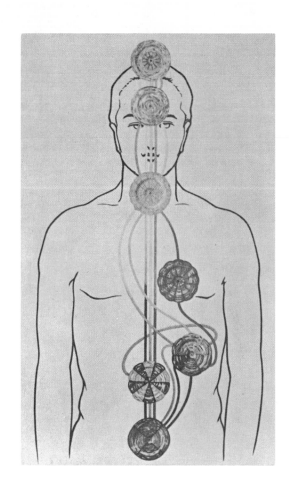

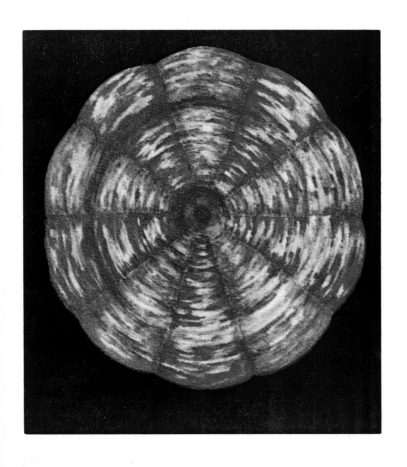

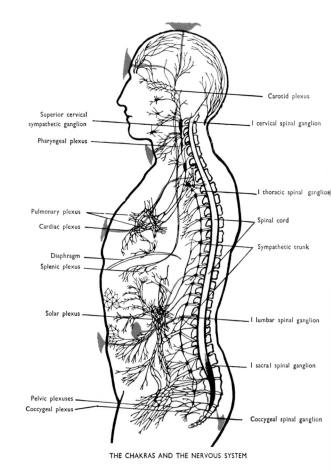

THE CHAKRAS AND THE NERVOUS SYSTEM

Plate 8

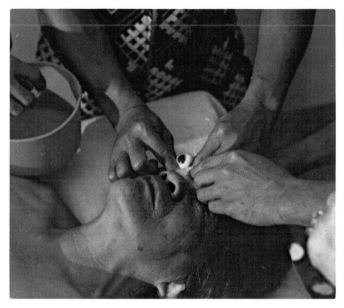

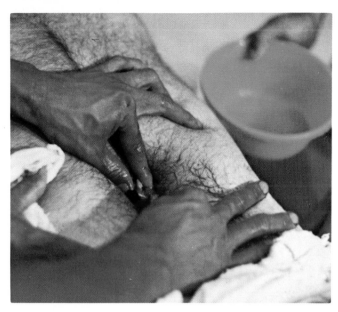

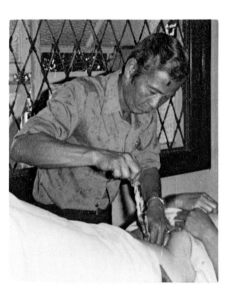

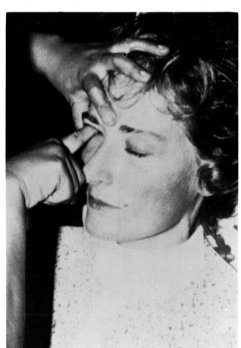

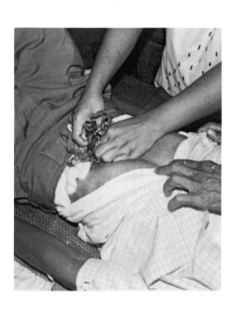

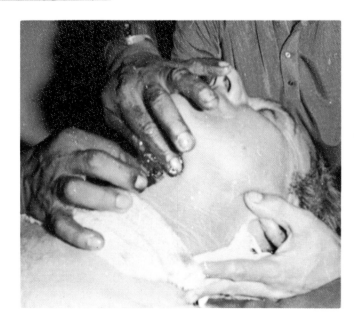

Plate 9

Plate 10

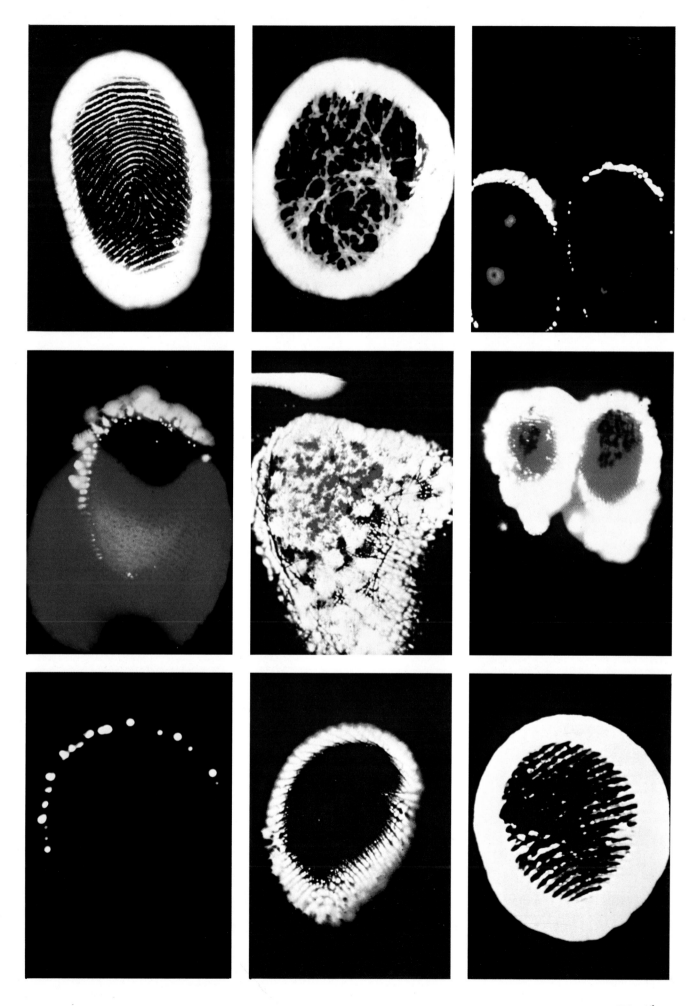

Plate 11

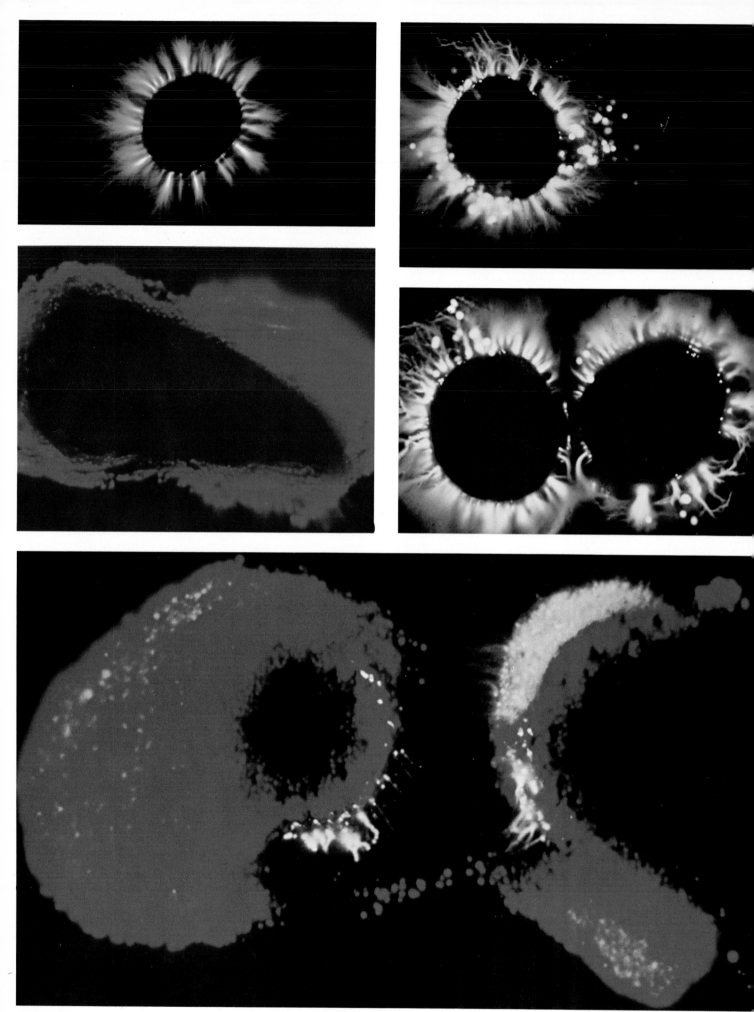

Plate 12

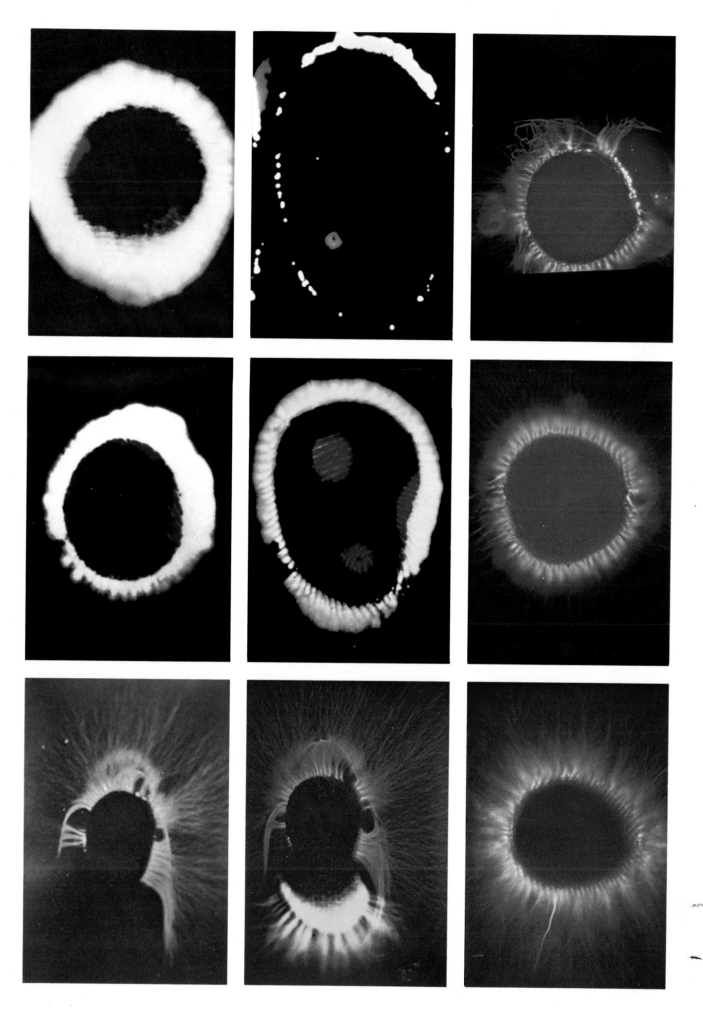

Plate 13

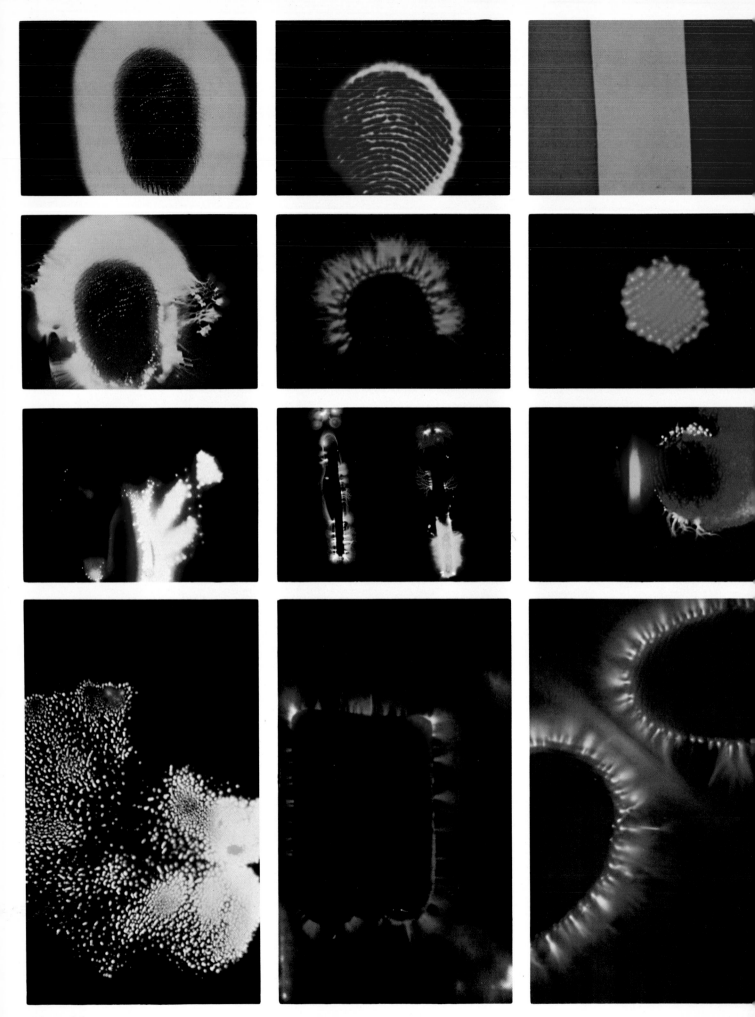

Plate 14

Plate 15

Plate 16

For example, of 3647 famous doctors and scientists he studied, 724 were born with Mars just above the eastern horizon or at the mid-heaven, directly overhead. Since you would only expect 626 men in this sample to have Mars rising or culminating, this effect has a probability of only 1 in 500,000 of having occurred by chance. In the same group of individuals, an unusually high number, statistically speaking, were born with Saturn rising or culminating.

In a group of 3438 famous soldiers, Jupiter or Mars were frequently found in the sectors following their rise or culmination.

In a group of 2088 sports champions, Mars dominates, being recorded 452 times rising or culminating instead of the expected 358. The probability that this effect could have happened by chance was only one in five million. Furthermore, this finding was repeated independently of Gauquelin by a Belgian committee of scientists studying so-called paranormal phenomena.

A number of other statistically significant findings were recorded with famous writers, politicians, journalists, and industrial managers. Interestingly, the data was significant only when dealing with prominent individuals. No correlations were found for individuals who did not achieve notable success in their professions. Furthermore, the correlations did not seem to apply for individuals whose birth was artificially induced at a certain time in order to conform with the schedule requirements of the attending physician. Only if the birth was allowed to occur at its own speed were the astrological correlates significant.[385]

It's hard to think that Gauquelin's findings have much relevance to the work of any given astrological interpreter of charts. Even the most significant correlations which he noted applied to less than one-fifth of the population in his sample. It's a big jump from a few weak, albeit significant, correlations to the interpretations of thousands of factors which appear on an individual chart. Astrologers have never been able to explain this process to my satisfaction and they often are in marked disagreement with each other. The strongest key to astrology seems to be meanings implicit in the mythological symbolism of the astronomical names. This is particularly evident when we think of soldiers being influenced by Mars and Jupiter.

Using an approach similar to that of Gauquelin, Carl Jung also conducted studies in astrology, In an analysis of 483 pairs of charts from married couples chosen at random, Jung found a preponderance of aspects which would signify such a relationship. Most notably the moon of the woman was found to be in conjunction with either the sun, the moon, or the ascendant of her husband. A control group of over 32,000 unmarried pairs of charts did not show these aspects. Statistical analysis indicated that the results obtained could have happened by chance only one time in ten thousand.[386]

Jung maintained that this amazing finding could be attributed to the role which ideas, thought-forms, and archetypes play in organizing events. He labelled this process *synchronicity*, an acausal connecting principle.

In 1959, the American psychologist Vernon Clark conducted a few simple experiments designed to test the accuracy of astrologers' claims. He collected horoscope charts showing planetary positions at birth, from people in ten different professions. Half were men and half were women. All were between forty-five and sixty years of age. The horoscopes were given to twenty different astrologers together with a separate list of professions; the astrologers were asked to match them up. The same information was given to another group of psychologists and social workers who knew little about astrology. Oddly enough, the astrologers were able to complete their task with a statistically significant accuracy—although they still made many mistakes. The psychiatrists and social workers scored no better than chance expectations.

In another experiment, Clark took ten pairs of horoscopes, matched for sex and year of birth. To each pair he attached a list of dates showing important events such as marriage, children, new jobs, and death. The astrologers were asked to state which of the two horoscopes in each pair predicted the pattern of events listed. Three of the astrologers got all ten right and the rest scored significantly above chance—with a probability of one in a hundred.

In a third test, the astrologers were given ten pairs of charts with no other data to work with. They were asked to determine which of the two charts indicated that the individual was a victim of cerebral palsy. Again the astrologers scored well above chance expectations![387]

One might attribute the astrologers' success to ESP. No matter. The findings will continue to remain a scientific anomaly until many of the speculations suggested in this section are grounded in a mass of incontrovertible data. Nevertheless, the experiences provided by the subtle levels of consciousness do not wait for science to legitimize them. And they're always so close at hand.

Experiencing the Deep and Subtle Rhythms of the Body

Consciousness of psychic and spiritual life is a natural extension of a deep knowing of one's self. This section of the *Roots of Consciousness* is a process which will gently guide you through the experience of various layers of your own being. You can read each paragraph to yourself and then close your eyes and allow yourself to float into the experiences suggested. Or, you may have a friend who will read this section to you so that you can explore the different levels without interruption. In either case, you will want to be in a comfortable, quiet room where you will not be disturbed for about half an hour.

Become aware of the position which you are in and the particular tensions which may exist in your limbs or torso as you are sitting. If you are feeling tense try and loosen the tension somewhat by tightening up that area of the body. Hold it tight for about five or ten seconds and then relax. Do this at least twice for every stiff area.

Be particularly conscious of your shoulders and neck. You can relax the neck by slowly rolling it around on the shoulders to the right in a full circle and then to the left.

Shake the tension out of your arms and legs and hands and feet. Become aware of how you hold your body. Now easily let yourself experience the lightness of your body. It's possible that you may have deeper tensions which you cannot so easily release. Simply be aware of these tensions and assume the most comfortable sitting (or lying down if someone is reading to you) position you can.

Slowly focus on your breathing. Feel the air enter your nostrils and throat. Become aware of the life-giving gases from the atmosphere—which touches all of us—entering into the tiny sacs within your lungs and becoming incorporated into your body through the bloodstream. Become aware of the rhythm of your breathing as your breath flows in and out of your body.

Take a deep breath and hold it for about five seconds. Release the air and let your breath return to normal. Recognize the breath as one of the doorways to higher consciousness. See how easily it passes between the conscious and the subliminal mind.

Tune into your digestive system, starting with your mouth, teeth, tongue and salivary glands. Be aware of your esophagus carrying food into your stomach.. Can you feel your stomach and intestines breaking down your last meal into the tiny particles which will be carried into the bloodstream? Feel the smooth muscles gently push the food through your digestive tract. Be aware of the tension, or lack of tension, in your stomach, intestines, and bowels. Let yourself remember the different emotions which you associate with eating, digesting and eliminating food. If there is any residual tightness or tension, just easily observe it for now. Are you feeling hungry or thirsty? Simply let awareness of these deeper levels of your being float through your stream of consciousness.

Become aware of the blood circulating the life-giving breath and food to every cell in your body, cleansing away impurities.

Feel the blood flowing from the tip of your feet to the top of your head. Feel it flow through your fingertips. Feel it flow inside your abdomen. Feel the blood flow through your face. Listen to the sound in your ears.

Easily feel your heartbeat, pumping the blood to every cell in your body. Just relax and tune into the rhythm of your own heart. Now feel the rhythms of your heart, lungs, and digestion working together.

As your blood removes the waste products and impurities from every cell in your body, the blood itself is cleansed through the functioning of your kidneys and bladder. Just as the heart and lungs follow a regular rhythm in your life, your urination has a pulse of its own. Become aware of the tension that may or may not exist in your bladder.

Some of your body's waste products are eliminated through the pores of your skin as sweat. Tune into your skin. Feel the touch of your clothing against your body. Feel the touch of the floor or the chair you are sitting in. How sensitive the skin is. Notice how your skin responds to the moisture or dryness of the room you are in, as well as to the temperature. Softly blow on your skin and feel the air currents. Feel the subtle touch of the sounds of the room you are in against your skin. Notice how different areas of your skin respond with different sensitivities.

Now relax and feel the many rhythms of your body all together. Your muscles. Your breathing. Your digestion. Your heartbeat. Your bladder. Your skin. Feel the billions of cells living and breathing, digesting and dying within your body.

Feel the emotions within your mind and body, the desires and anticipations, the residual feelings of frustration and anger. Feel your own relaxation. Be aware of the ebb and flow of the hormonal tides through your body and your mind. Notice the feelings in your chest area, through your guts, around your genitals, in your throat.

Watch the patterns within your own nervous system. Close your eyes and see the changing forms and colors in your visual field. Observe a train of thought as it emerges and delicately passes through your awareness.

Observe the dream-like forms always dancing in the deeper levels of your mind.

Now relax and feel the many rhythms of your mind and body together. Your breathing, your heartbeat, your digestion, your bowels and bladder, your muscles, your skin, your emotions, the dancing patterns of your nervous system. Allow yourself to breathe gently and be aware of all of these levels within you.

Imagine now the lifespace immediately around your body. Visualize your body's electromagnetic field which extends infinitely away in all directions.

Visualize the thought-forms which you generate in this lifespace as a result of your own personality and activities. Give your lifespace its own characteristic colors, shapes, sounds, and smells.

Recollect the rhythm of activity within your lifespace as you go through your day. Remember the states of awareness and the feelings with which you imbue your lifespace. Feel the different pulsebeats of your lifespace: From waking to sleeping and dreaming. From working to relaxing. From month to month. From season to season. From year to year. From birth to death. Feel the different qualities of living and dying within your lifespace.

Now let your awareness expand out beyond your immediate lifespace to fill up the room or area you are in. Feel the walls and corners and ceiling and floor of the room, and feel yourself within it as well. Be aware of the interaction between your presence and the qualities of the room you are now in.

Gradually imagine your awareness expanding out beyond the room you are in to encompass the entire building and even the surrounding neighborhood. Again feeling the quality of the fluctuation of life, be aware of the plants and animals and people within this space.

Now imagine yourself floating higher and higher above your neighborhood so that you can see for miles around you. Feel the children and the old people, the young lovers and the heartbroken, the wealthy and the needy, the sacred and the profane places. Feel the pulse of life in this space. Feel the earth touch the sky.

Still floating higher you can look down over lakes and rivers, over many towns and cities. Now you can see the great plains and the ocean and feel the slow rhythm of the entire planet turning. Imagine yourself, quite comfortably, floating even higher until you can see the continents beneath you. And there is both day and night. As you rise higher and higher, imagine the civilizations and the spirit of man on this planet.

Rising still higher, visualize the earth as a round turquoise set against the black starry sky. Now look out upon the moon circling the earth approximately every 28 days, changing its phases, exerting a gravitational pull upon the tides of the earth, influencing the minds of poets and lunatics.

Imagine yourself traveling farther out in space now, comfortable, and in the quiet company of others who are taking similar trips in their imagination. Feel the warmth and life-giving energy of the sun. Observe in your imagination solar-storm and solar flare activity, influenced by the electromagnetic and gravitational pull of the planets. Feel yourself bathed in the sun's ionic atmosphere which engulfs the earth and is responsible for the Northern Lights. Feel the life of the solar system interacting with your presence. Behold the planets, symbolic of the ancient gods of man, each following its own cyclical journey through time and space.

As you continue to travel farther and farther into space visualize the solar system growing smaller and smaller until it is just another star somewhat near the edge of the giant galaxy we call the *milky way*. Feel the great spiral of energy in which our own solar system, and many others, are nourished.

Now imagine yourself travelling farther, beyond the galaxy, beyond many other galaxies, farther into the blackness of space until you are at the very edge of the observable universe. Comfortably now moving even farther out into the vast abyss of space feel the absolute essence of the universe which inter-

259

penetrates all manifested life. Feel the unchanging calm which underlies all rhythm and fluctuation.

Become aware now of the quiet self within you, beyond all change, which has calmly observed yourself observing yourself, felt yourself feeling yourself, known yourself knowing yourself.

Feel the ultimate nourishment which this transcendental self provides for all of your other movements in life. Allow yourself to stay in this space for several more minutes.

Gradually, when you are ready, begin reentry into your body. As you begin to feel the minute vibrations of light and gravity, pulsing through the universe of your body, remember that the calmness of the transcendental space, beyond the edge of the universe, will always be there for you to return to.

Imagine the vibrations becoming more intense now forming cloudlike particles which dance and play like the images in your dreams. Gradually whirling atoms and chains of molecules are forming and you can feel the attractions and interactions which are the chemical basis of your very existence.

Now visualize the cells within your body and feel the billions of tiny, living monads, each with its own life-cycle, which constitute your being. Feel the desires and fulfillments of your body on the cellular level. Feel the cells actualizing themselves by forming into tissues and organs. Tune in to the wonderful intelligence within you which organizes this vast kingdom of life.

Now relax and feel the many rhythms of your being all together. Your breathing, your heartbeat, your digestion, the billions of cells living and dying within you, your skin, your emotions, the dancing patterns of your nervous system, your room, your community, nation, planet, feel the pulse of the solar system and of the galaxy. Allow yourself to breathe gently and be aware of all of these levels of your being.

When you are ready, easily get up and move about. Stretch yourself a bit, and with a new understanding of your beingness, continue the activities of your life, and the reading of this book.

PEOPLE, PLACES, AND THEORIES

III

PEOPLE, PLACES, AND THEORIES

The Reflexive Universe

One of my mentors in the field of consciousness has been Arthur M. Young, an inventor who developed Bell Aircraft's first helicopter and later became an iconoclastic philosopher of science. Many thousands of lives have been saved as a result of this revolutionary invention. Yet, the helicopter was only a tangible by-product of Young's deeper, lifelong search for a philosophy that could integrate human consciousness with the physical, biological, and social sciences.

In the following description, transcribed from a taped recording of an informal seminar, Arthur Young traces the events in his life that led to the development of his cosmology and also provides a window through which we can view a few pieces of the *consciousness movement* from 1945 to about 1955:

My first ambition was to have a philosophy of the universe. But once I recognized that it should incorporate *process* and not merely structure, I had no place to go. I didn't have any idea what process should consist of. In fact, I felt sort of out-of-breath, as though I'd climbed up a high mountain and didn't have any of the things that nourish the body. So I decided to take up the problem of designing a workable helicopter, more or less as an exercise in getting practical answers. I allowed myself fifteen years, but it actually took eighteen before I had the thing in production.

In 1945, just a few months before we had our first production model off the assembly line, they dropped the bomb. It was as though

Arthur M. Young

someone shot me! It hit me very hard. "If they're going to do that kind of thing," I said to myself, "I better quit fooling around with things like helicopters and get to the real question: What is the nature of man?" This was the only possible response to a violent thing like the bomb. In a sense we needed the "anti-bomb," which is to recognize the spiritual nature of man. Only that can survive this physical holocaust. The bomb reminded me of what I really wanted to do. But even if they don't use the bomb, we've got the problem from other ends now. What's going to happen to this world of ours with pollution, overpopulation, famine and all those things? So I began studying yoga and zen Buddhism.

I'd always been intrigued by zen. This time I had the advantage of a wonderful old lady next door who was over eighty. She stood on her head every day, and had spent a year in a zen monastery. She introduced me to D. T. Suzuki. We then concocted the idea of providing Suzuki with microfilm equipment so he could go back to Japan and take photographs of the zen manuscripts.

Being a Japanese he wanted a neat little case, with everything packed just so. So I was sort of buzzing around New York for quite a while getting all this equipment just right. Meanwhile I wanted to do what every zen student wants to do—ask the nature of the Buddha. But I knew perfectly well he'd hit me with a stick or do something like that. So I didn't ask.

I finally got the cassette all finished and left it with him at his quarters. That was to be goodbye, and I couldn't resist the temptation to ask him what was the nature of the Buddha.

He took a pad of paper and started writing what's called in mathematics an infinite series. He wrote down the terms of this thing on and on and on. It was an endless series that didn't converge or terminate. He kept on writing and I began . . . I said, "Well, I have to go now. I understand." He just kept on writing. I got more and more restive and said, "Well, I get it. I get it. Okay. Okay. Okay." But he didn't stop. He just kept on writing it. Finally I just walked out. I never saw him again!

I think he nailed my trouble, and fed it right to me. What do you do about infinity?

What really got me involved was Dunne's book, *An Experiment with Time.* Dunne found that sometimes he had. dreams that would predict the future. He was an Oxford don; so he devised an experiment to prove this kind of thing. He took his class off in the country for three or four days into an environment that was unfamiliar to them. Then he had them keep a record, both of the incidents that occurred and of the dreams that they had. Finally he took the dreams and incidents and mixed them all up in a box and had someone match the resemblances, to see which dream resembled which incident. They found that half of the dream resemblances were to future events!

After I read this, I began to have unmistakable precognitive dreams! Then I told some friends at a party about this; and they both told me that very night of dreams that they had had the previous night. I went home and wrote them down. I was always writing dreams down.

The next day I saw one of them. She had dreamt that she was washing her hands in a basin. There was blood on her arms and she looked over her shoulder and saw a person in white.

That night as she drove home from the party they saw someone who had been hit by a car, drunk; and they picked him up and took him to the hospital. In the hospital after they had had him attended to, she found blood on her arms. As she was washing it off, she looked around and saw the nurse. It wasn't until that moment that she remembered the dream.

A friend of mine knew Eileen Garrett quite well and arranged for us to meet. She was a prominent businesswoman who ran the Creative Age Press. But she was also a medium, one of the most talented in this period. She'd worked with McDougall and other scientists. Not only was she able to go into trance, but she could also do a certain amount of psychometry. Psychometry is reading the history of an object by just holding it in your hand. On one occasion we met at the Ritz for tea in New York. I gave her a pen that I had used all morning. From it she was able to tell me the conversations I'd had with my friend. She reeled it all off to me. Fantastic.

Somewhat later we'd had a severe helicopter accident in which the pilot and the assistant were both killed. I felt very badly about it. I thought the machine had been at fault. But we never could find what had broken. It was very curious, this feeling of tremendous responsibility. I remember wandering around in this swamp looking for pieces of the helicopter, thinking about what killed that pilot. Very emotional. We couldn't find the answer.

So I took a piece of the helicopter's broken blade to Eileen Garrett. She held it in her hand and said that the machine was all right, but that the pilot had been on the verge of a nervous breakdown and was about to enter a monastery when the crash had occurred.

I didn't want to go back and ask the pilot's bereaved parents these questions. So I just forgot the whole thing.

However about a year later I went to see the man who operated the helicopter company that hired the pilot—a company in Providence, Rhode Island. The conversation turned back to this pilot. He volunteered, saying, "that pilot was having a nervous breakdown at the time and was about to enter a monastery." This was a year after Eileen had told me the same thing! She couldn't have read my mind.

I was intrigued by Jungian analysis. For instance one of the concepts is the *shadow;* this is the part of yourself that you reject. I had one dream in which a pathetic old woman was trying to help me in the lab. In another dream, some black men took over the house. They were going to shoot my portrait; but they were not going to hurt anything else in the house.

It made a great impression on me that I could dream about events that I wouldn't ordinarily think about. The dream was revealing parts of myself that I didn't consciously acknowledge. For a while I just wallowed in this stuff. It was great. I think it did me a lot of good. But it didn't seem to go far enough.

I got interested in astrology, and I tried to have a contest between the astrologer and the analyst in order to see who could do the best diagnosis. But the analyst read the notes of the astrologer first, and that distorted her interpretation. So then I shifted over to astrology. I thought it was the more potent magic.

About the time that I realized there was a limit to analysis, I heard about a school and a teacher, M. B. M. She had been with Jung and also Freud. This was a school of self-development called the Source Teaching Society in New York. We went there first just for lectures.

In her first lecture she was talking about the Druids, and said that they used the mistletoe as a symbol of the soul—because as the mistletoe was a parasite on the tree, the soul was a parasite on the body. This remark immediately struck me as having the quality of high-caliber intelligence. It was not the goody-goody type Sunday school approach where the soul was so good. She said the soul was a parasite. This showed a type of thinking that went directly to the point.

In the school, we were required to report our dreams to her. The first dream which I had to present was a little bit embarrassing. Something about Groucho Marx. She said, "Well now, who is Groucho Marx?" I just had to tell her the truth, "Groucho Marx is you!" She asked, "Why?" I said, "Because he always goes directly to the point." "Remember how he walks across a room right through the furniture and steps right over the sofa?" She allowed that that was alright.

Among other things, she told us about alchemy. Of course, the purpose of alchemy was to transform lead into gold. But the question is what is lead and what is gold! Gold is value and lead, or any ore, is what you get from earthly experience.

M. B. M. said that the bees are born from the dead ox. It's the kind of statement Aristotle might have made. Of course, it's ridiculous from a scientific perspective. But that's not the point. What does it mean? What do bees do and what is the dead ox?

Alchemy takes the fruit of the earth, which is metal, and transforms it into gold, which is value. That's what we're all here for. The symbol of earth is the ox, the bull, the Taurus. The dead ox is the ox that has been conquered. From the ox is born this higher octave; the bees move through the air, and collect the nectar, the food for the gods. This is also our task here. To conquer the earthy part of our own nature which was holding us down, so we could ascend to the higher spheres.

We worked with M. B. M. for about two years. She was a very severe guru and didn't want me doing astrology. I had to stop astrology. But we finally became restive, and I was off on my own again.

After a number of remarkable dreams, it seemed that something was preparing me for a big step. It suddenly came into my head to go to California. So off we went to California.

Ruth remembered an old friend, Harwood White of Santa Barbara, and we all plunged into a terrific discussion about all these things which we'd been into. He had a very elaborate notebook which I immediately started reading.

The item that struck my attention was Oscar Brunler, the one who invented "brain radiation." Nothing would do but that we immediately go down and see Brunler and find out more about brain radiation. He and M. B. M. are hard to compare, but they were the two most remarkable people I've ever known. Brunler knew more about this whole field than anyone I've met before or since.

What he called "brain radiation" was actually a measure of the age of the monad—that is to say the amount of evolution or competence of each different person. For instance, Leonardo was the highest on his scale. It went on down to people who were not even capable of learning to read and write. His measurements went between 180 and 700. He had many followers. In fact, they're still going strong, though he died in 1952.

Brunler had a long mahogany box on which was a metal scale, graduated in biometric units. He would swing a pendulum at one end, and there was also a silk cord leading to the person's head who was being measured. The cord came to a little carriage that was moved by an assistant slowly along the scale, beginning at one end. All of a sudden the pendulum would start swinging to one side and Brunler would just say, *stop*. It wouldn't work if you suspended the pendulum from a tripod. It was an interaction between the person making the measurement and whatever the "brain radiation" was. It was related to divining.

We got very curious and wanted to learn how to do it. So we went back to California three times in one year to keep up with Brunler. We learned from Brunler to do it ourselves for quite a while until we finally decided it was too much responsibility. It was also very difficult. You had to really concentrate. In any case, it led to our looking up these high brain radiation people. That was the most interesting thing of all.

One of them was Ruth Drown. I had heard of her even when I was at Bell working on the helicopter. She could take photographs of a person's ailments from a bloodspot even when the person was 1000 miles away. This was one of those unbelievable things. In fact, I just wouldn't believe it at all until Brunler told me that she had a very high radiation. Of course we went to see her.

Most of the radionics people were in England so we dashed off to England. We went up and down England, visiting all of these far-out people. There was sort of an inner circle and they were tied in with other kinds of psychic people.

We met, for instance, Lord Dowding, who was head of the British Air Force. During the war when the pilots would be killed in battle, they would report to him in his office after they were killed. He had the problem of convincing them they were dead. It was a very real thing for him. He had written a book about it and was perfectly open. He was also a member of Parliament.

This was fantastic to us Americans. Anyone who'd confess to that kind of hocus-pocus, if he wasn't locked up in a lunatic bin, at least wouldn't be allowed to sit in the Senate. Yet here was Lord Dowding, deeply respected. We even asked people who knew Lord Dowding if they knew about the ghosts he saw. They just didn't know about that. That wasn't their affair anyway.

George De La Warr was an enterprising sort of businessman who assisted Drown when she came to England. He had instruments made and then went off on his own. He was running a business, making radionics equipment and training people to use it.

The radionic black box looked like a complicated radio with as many as ten dials that you adjusted for the tuning rates for different diseases. All these radionic people had the "rates book" that was laid down by Abrams, who was the originator of this idea. Once in a while they would invent a new rate of their own. And swap rates around. It was a sort of underground medical thing. There was a big split in England between the Drownites and the De La Warrites.

Heieronymus is one of the Americans. You may have seen an article about his work in *Analog,* it used to be called *Amazing Science Fiction.* About 1957, Campbell, the editor, got all enthusiastic about Heieronymus. I got hold of Campbell and warned him. I said, "This is not in the circuitry, it's symbolic." Campbell had the intelligence to go ahead on that basis and described it in the magazine, not as another kind of electronics gadget, but as symbolic wiring equipment.

This was already going through our heads in 1951 when I first met Heieronymus. I recall vividly waiting an extra week so that we could meet this great psychic inventor. Finally the day came when Heieronymus arrived. He kept talking for an hour and a half straight about how many ohms he put in this coil and how he wired it, and so forth. I finally got a word in edgewise and asked him, "Why do you bother with all that junk?" "You know perfectly well it doesn't matter how many ohms there are." And he said, "Well I thought you were a scientist!"

In a way I think it was right to prevent the proliferation of this kind of thing. The people who can really do it are sensitives. If everyone was trying to do it, it would result in an abuse. These devices were means of focusing the psychic power of those involved.

Another one that Brunler told us about was Frederick Marion. If you ever run across a book called, *Through My Mind's Eye,* grab it! It's out of print. He was a 575, which puts him up there with Sri Aurobindo and other highly developed people. He was a Czech and quite amusing. One time I remember there was nothing else going on and he took an electric lightbulb that was just loose on the table, rubbed it—and it began to glow!

He taught me things too. He thought he could teach everybody to do psychometry. His theory was that there was no ESP. It's all sensory; it's just *extended* sensory perception. The way to get ESP was to train and develop your normal senses. Then you would pass this threshold.

His method was to place objects on a table—in my case they were just playing cards with the face down. I was to shut my eyes and he would move one. Then I would open them and say which one he had moved. We did this for quite a while. He was moving them less and less. But each time I could always detect it. Then he suddenly said, "Well, which is the ace of spades?" And I picked it up and turned it over before I had time to realize that I just couldn't know that. You see, he was tricking me to go past my rational threshold. About that time we met Andrija Puharich, the professor who's been guiding Uri Geller. He found him in Israel and brought him over here. Andrija had The Roundtable Foundation in Maine which was dedicated to the study of psychic phenomena. Unfortunately, he was drafted during the Korean War. He asked me if I would run the foundation while he was away. So Ruth and I picked up our bags and went off to Maine.

We had a number of sensitives that we brought up to Maine for testing. The object was to put them in a copper Faraday cage to see how sensitive they were; and then put them outside the cage to test them again. The cage blocked out electromagnetic signals and was intended to improve their ESP performance.

This was difficult in most cases. I remember one reading in which my mother who had recently died came through along with the woman who was her arch-enemy in life—but now they were good friends.

267

That was fine. But now how could I say, "Well now please step in this cage and do it over again." It was difficult to experiment under these circumstances.

But with Marion, it was a cinch. We would take a shuffled deck of cards—and we would take new decks each time—and deal them off face down as indicated by Marion into red and black piles. He would make on the average of five or six mistakes. The odds of only five or six mistakes out of fifty-two cards are astronomical. But in the cage, he would only get three or four wrong! He could definitely show an improvement in the cage. This was replicated many times.

We kept on doing this and we got the whole area saturated with some kind of psychic charge. It got so that you couldn't tell the difference anyway. Everybody was being psychic all of the time.* That's even less credible. But the point is that this business of distinguishing, "turn it on—turn it off," t'ain't the way it is in psychic things!

I think there might have been a concentration factor. Marion himself said that he felt it work better in the cage. Whether it was due to the quietness, the ritualistic effect or to the electrical-magnetic effect I don't know.

I worked with Marion for several years. We found he could tell the history of an archeological object. One evening we invited Allen Priest, who was the curator of Chinese art at the Metropolitan Museum, to bring five objects of which he and no one else knew the history. Marion psychometrized them all, including one that had been robbed from a grave. He got the explosion and the robbers running off with it.

The thing that he didn't get to Allen's satisfaction was one object known to be a fake. Marion had described these sort of low people sneaking around and slipping this thing from one to another. But he didn't say the object was a fake. Well in a sense the object was perfectly real. The people misrepresenting it made it a fake. So I think Marion came out on top there.

Another friend of ours, who collected Inca gold, had a piece of Inca tapestry that Marion psychometrized. Marion said that this had hung over the box of the princess when she was watching a ball game being played. Our friend John Wise didn't seem very impressed by that. The evening eventually came to an end.

Another friend of ours, Walter, was quite psychic, and used to keep us up until three in the morning telling us about our spirit guides and so on. He was very good that way. He was fantastic on past lives! Of course, there was no way to verify them. At any rate, he kept us very much amused. He came when the party was just about over, and also gave a reading on the archeological pieces. He gave the same readings that Marion did! In fact, he even said that the cloth had been dry cleaned—which was a great mistake—and that it should be put on a piece of blotting paper, soaked in lanolin, so that it could reabsorb its natural oil, or it would rapidly deteriorate. This really puzzled me, because I had imported Marion from a long distance and he was a very gifted person. I knew that Walter wasn't that gifted.

Walter impressed John Wise more than did Marion. Then the party broke up; I grabbed Walter and said, "Come clean Walter, what's going on here?" "How did you get all this stuff?" And Walter said, "Well, it's very easy." "All these spooks around just told me what Marion had said." "In fact," he said, "one of them was an archeologist and told me about the lanolin deal." Well, Marion wasn't getting it from the spooks, you see Marion was getting it from the object. But the spooks were quite interested in what Marion had to say.

After we validated him by these objects and things like that, I tried to bring him to the attention of my friends. We took Marion around like Hurok. We had a show in Philadelphia, New York and Boston. We went trouping around with Marion the way Geller is doing demonstrations today. We thought we were going to get people to stop being so

---

*According to Dr. Harold Puthoff, a similar situation seems to have developed in the remote-viewing experiments at Stanford Research Institute.

stuffy. They generally were highly entertained but they would forget about it as soon as possible.

I did at one point get him to help me on buying paintings. He finally said, "Well, I don't want to do this, because whatever I do must be without any thought of gain or loss." "It doesn't work if I'm trying to help you buy paintings, if there's a financial factor involved."

After we had found all the ''gee-wizziest'' things we could find and grogged this whole area to our fill, then it became a question of *so what?* How are you going to fit this into modern culture? Science doesn't recognize it. Nobody's going to believe it. It will just remain a schism.[1]

Arthur Young's theory developed out of a desire to heal this schism.

As an anchor point for understanding Young's cosmology, we can begin with the formula for the volume of the Einstein-Eddington Universe, the boundary region of what physicists call the hypersphere, which is $2\pi^2r^3$. This is also the formula for the volume of a torus (donut) with an infinitely small hole. It is in the torus topology that Young sees a possible answer to the philosophical problem of the individual (or part, or microcosm) versus the collective (or whole, or macrocosm). In a toroidal universe, a part can be seemingly separate and yet connected with the rest.

If we think of the fence in the following diagram as separating the inner from the outer, the torus provides a paradigm that permits us to see a monad as both separate from the rest of the universe by the fence—and still connected to everything else through the core. The core of the torus, with its infinitely small hole, is for Young a representation of inner consciousness.

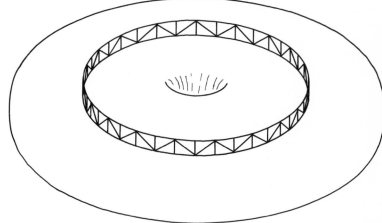

Young points out that magnetic fields, vortices and tornados all have the toroidal form. The vortex is, in fact, the only manner in which a fluid can move on itself. Thus it is a very suitable shape for the universe to have. We must, however, bear in mind that the volume of the torus is three dimensional and is kin to the surface of the four-dimensional hypersphere of Einstein and Eddington.

Suppose you had to draw a map on the surface of a torus so that all of the bordering countries would be distinguished by differences in color. On an ordinary surface, say a plane or sphere, such a map would require no more than four colors. The sphere $(4/3\pi r^3)$ to Young is analogous to structure in the universe. Later we shall show how a "cycle of action" divides the sphere from the torus—which is, in Young's scheme, analogous to universal process. It requires seven different colors to create a map on the surface of a torus. Therefore, Young reasoned, there might be seven stages to *process,* just as there is a fourfold division to *structure.*

This inspiration is affirmed somewhat by ancient myths and cosmogonies. The Hindu, Zoroastrian, Japanese and Genesis creation myths all describe a seven-stage process. There are also seven rows to the periodic table of elements. Taking these cues, Young divided all of nature into seven stages of process or evolution. The following diagram illustrates the seven kingdoms of Young's "reflexive universe" arranged in an arc, on four levels according to their relative degrees of uncertainty:

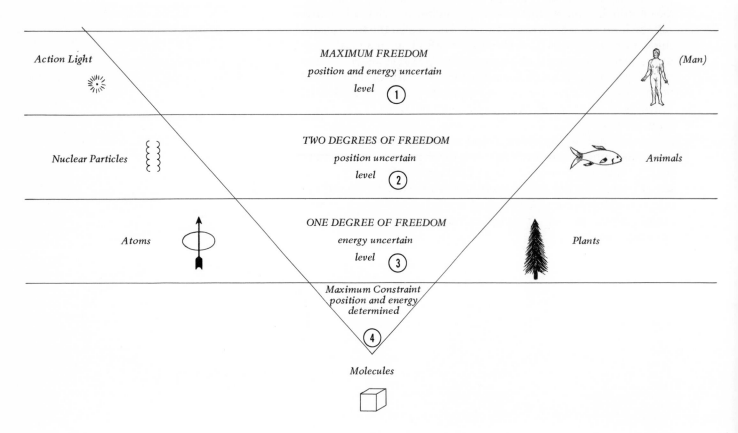

This chart symbolizes the mythological descent of spirit into matter and the corresponding ascent of matter into spirit. The greatest amount of constraint and symmetry occurs in the molecules' crystalline structure. This kingdom is most subject to science's deterministic laws, and thus is most predictable. Both atoms and plants possess radial or two dimensional symmetry. They have two degrees of constraint and one degree of freedom, which constitutes their ability to store and release energy, within certain boundaries, without any specified prompting from without. Animals have bilateral symmetry along one dimension. Young believes that electrons and protons also possess symmetry along one dimension.

270

The experiments of Lee and Yang, who discovered that chirality, or handedness, characterizes nuclear particle reactions, suggests this possibility. Young points out that only that which has bilateral symmetry can have handedness. Heisenberg's principle states that we are uncertain of the position and the momentum of the nuclear particle. Young states that this principle applies to the animal as well. Thus both nuclear particles and animals possess one degree of constraint and two degrees of freedom.

The first kingdom, which Young refers to as light (or action), and the seventh kingdom, of which man is a part, theoretically possess complete asymmetry and complete freedom. A photon released at a certain point could be anywhere within a radius of 186,000 miles a second later. Furthermore, since observation annihilates a photon, it cannot be predicted. Although light has no rest mass, when it is annihilated it can create electrons and protons which do have mass. It has no charge, yet the particles it creates do. In fact, for a pulse of light, time does not exist. Clocks stop at the speed of light. Thus mass, energy, and time are born when the photon condenses into a particle which is the first step in the process which engenders the universe.*

Young regards action as the primary constituent of the universe, and other measures such as force (including gravity), energy and even time as *derived* parts of a whole which manifests as action. He also introduces the notion of purpose or intention into his scheme. The *principle of least action* is the law that light always follows the precise path which gets it to its destination in the shortest possible time. Planck himself observed that this principle expresses, "an explicitly teleological character."

Thus the photons which constitute a ray of light behave like intelligent human beings: Out of all the possible curves they always select the one which will take them most quickly to their goal.

Leibnitz, who discovered this principle, believed himself "to have found evidence for an ubiquitous higher reason ruling all of nature. This characterization of light is the one exception to the exclusion of purpose from science. Purpose, associated with the quantum of action, becomes the keynote of Arthur Young's theory. He draws on a rich, although often discarded, tradition in science and philosophy.

. . . as Whitehead pointed out in his *Function of Reason:* "Scientists, animated by the purpose of proving they are purposeless, constitute an interesting subject for study."

Young points out that $2\pi h$ is the quantum of uncertainty. Thus we have a fundamental relationship between purpose and

---

*Action has the measure formula Mass × Length²/Time and is always an integral multiple of h, Planck's constant (in MKS units, 6.63×10^{-34} Joule-seconds). The smallest whole unit of action is equivalent to h, which is the quantum. While energy is proportional to frequency, action is a constant of the proportion between energy and frequency ($E = h\nu$) and comes in wholes. Gravity, the strong force, and the weak force can all be expressed in terms of action.

uncertainty, confirmed by the fact that h contains an angle, 2π, which according to Eddington (the physicist from whom Young derives the greatest inspiration), is a phase dimension. For Young, the 2π represents choice. Uncertainty then is not so much a limitation upon science as the positive introduction of purpose and choice and therefore free will.

Essentially then, a light pulse is a piece of uncertainty, and it is possible to account for the chain of effects which it can produce. If it is of a high frequency, it can become a nuclear particle, a proton, or an electron. Some uncertainty will become mass (or certainty). Another step combines nuclear particles into atoms with a further loss of uncertainty, followed by still more at the molecular stage. Nevertheless there still remains enough uncertainty and choice of timing (phase dimension 2π) in certain large molecules, within narrow temperature ranges, to extract energy from the environment and build organizations which emerge as life.

Referring to Young's "grid," one notices that each of the seven kingdoms is divided into seven substages. The turning point of the arc is the middle of the fourth substage of the molecular, or fourth, kingdom. The fifth substage of the molecular kingdom represents the non-functional (covalently bonded) polymers such as cellulose, celluloid, rayon, nylon, dacron, etc. Young maintains that the distinguishing properties of these polymers is that they grow, like cells, in chains or series of links. The growth of polymers reflects an ability to store order—to drain energy from the environment. This is an example of negative entropy and a prelude to the living kingdoms which follow the turn of the arc.

This turn marks the beginning of consciousness in Young's theory—although clearly not anthropomorphic consciousness. The amount of indeterminacy here is very small indeed, but it is such that it enables the molecule to *use the laws of determinism* to build more complex structures and processes with even greater freedom. The 90° turn in the arc is a change in direction which symbolizes this freedom. Thus the uncertainty which is unconscious on the left side of the arc achieves ever greater degrees of voluntary control on the right side of the arc. Self-control, as such, is generally not recognized in classical physics. But as will be shown in what follows Young assigns to it the measure formula T^3, the third derivative of position which is equivalent to the rate of change in acceleration.

A logically elegant feature in Young's scheme is the way basic characteristics of each of the seven kingdoms or stages (see the notated keywords on the grid) apply in an analogous fashion to the corresponding seven substages within each stage. Thus the chain polymers in the fifth substage of the molecular kingdom have the property of growth referred to above which is characteristic of the fifth or plant kingdom. Furthermore plants often consist of the polymers cellulose and lignin; so the fifth stage growth involves the fifth substage chemical. The ionic bonding in the second substage of the molecular kingdom is characterized by the binding potential of the sub-atomic particles of the second kingdom. And, in fact, these particles

This image is my sense of a symbolic representation of Young's sixth substage human being. Also see page 19 for a description of a state which is akin to the infinitely small hole in Young's torus.

272

THE GRID

© 1974 AM Young (7th version)

KINGDOMS / STAGES →	POTENTIAL	BINDING	IDENTITY	COMBINATION	GROWTH	MOBILITY	DOMINION
1. LIGHT	10^{25} / 10^{-15} / 10^{11} — Cosmic rays, Proton rest energy	10^{22} / 10^{-11} / 10^{7} — Gamma rays, Nuclear binding energy	10^{18} / 10^{-8} / 10^{4} — X rays, Atomic spectra	10^{15} / 10^{-4} / 10^{0} — UV, IR, Molecular spectra	10^{11} / 10^{-1} / 10^{-3} — Microwaves, Cellular rad.? $hv = kT$	10^{8} / 10^{3} / 10^{-7} — Radio waves, Animal radiations?	10^{4} CPS / 10^{6} CM / 10^{-10} EV — Low freq. waves
2. NUCLEAR	Work in progress						
3. ATOMIC	1 H — Hydrogen	2 He — Helium to Fluorine	10 Ne — Neon to Chlorine	18 Ar — Argon to Bromine	36 Kr — Krypton to Iodine	54 X3 — Xenon to Astatine	86 Ra — Radon to 117
4. MOLECULAR	Metals, Metallic bond	Salts, Ionic bond	Nonfunctional Compounds, Covalent bond	Functional Compounds	Nonfunctional Polymers	Functional Polymers (Proteins)	DNA & Viruses
5. VEGETABLE	Bacteria, Unicellular	Algae, Colonies	Embryophytes, Embryos	Psylophytes, Vascular stems	Pteridophytes, Segments	Gymnosperms, Seeds	Angiosperms, Flowers
6. ANIMAL	Paramecia, Unicellular	Sponges, Colonies	Coelenterates, One organ	Mollusks etc., Many organs	Annelids, Segmentation	Arthropods, Side Segments	Chordata, Integrated brain
7. DOMINION		TRIBAL SOCIETIES — Collective Unconscious	Self Consciousness	MODERN MAN — Objective Thought	Creative Genius	CHRIST BUDDHA — Cosmic Consciousness	

Kingdom descriptions

1. LIGHT — 3 deg. of freedom, no symetry.
POTENTIAL: No rest mass; No charge; Space-Time path has no length; Quanta of Action.

2. NUCLEAR — 2 deg. of freedom, bilateral sym.
BINDING: Substance; Force of Attraction & Repulsion. The spell aspect of image, hence Illusion.

3. ATOMIC — 1 deg. of freedom, radial sym.
IDENTITY: Acquires its own center. Order creates properties of the Elements by the Exclusion Principle.

4. MOLECULAR — 0 deg. of freedom, complete sym.
COMBINATION; Molar properties; Classical Physics; Determinism.

5. VEGETABLE — 1 deg. of freedom, radial sym.
GROWTH: Self multiplication; The Cell or organizing principle; Order building by negative Entropy.

6. ANIMAL — 2 deg. of freedom, bilateral sym.
MOBILITY: Action & Satisfaction; Eating & Sex; Force becomes volitional.

7. DOMINION — 3 deg. of freedom, no symmetry.
CONSCIOUSNESS: Memory of one's own acts leads to Knowledge & Control.

are actively involved in ionic bonding. A third example is the principle of mobility which manifests in the sixth substage of the molecular kingdom, via the stretching proteins—actin and myosin, as well as in the sixth kingdom of animals. Actin and myosin are involved in the muscular movements of animals. Numerous examples are evident throughout the grid.

One of the major characteristics of the fifth substage of the animal kingdom is a hierarchical series of organs from the head to the tail, through a segmented structure. The earthworm is a typical example. This segmented organization occurs in the fifth substage of the molecular and plant kingdoms as well. In the sixth substages of these kingdoms, the structural property involves side chains attached to the main segmented structure. This is evidenced in protein amino and side chains, the branches of gymnosperms, and the jointed feelers and antennae of arthropods.

While recognizing the importance of DNA genetic material in the organization of intercellular structure, Young shares the doubt previously expressed that the DNA code can account for the hierarchy and diversity of organs. Furthermore he thinks animal instinct cannot be explained by DNA. To account for this type of extra-cellular organization, he postulates an organizing field. Young suggests that the corresponding organizing principle in the fifth substage of human beings (genus) is related to the awakened kundalini concept of the yogis. Young implies that the awakened chakra system may be the equivalent in the fifth substage human kingdom (of great leaders) to the segmented hierarchy of organs in the fifth substage of the animal kingdom.[2]

Another important part of Young's theory is his derivation of a "geometry of meaning" from the angular relationships which exist between the measure formula of physics. He begins by plotting the motion of a pendulum (as a representative of simple harmonic motion—the basis of all wave motion) over time on a Cartesian coordinate system. The completion of the swing to the left and its return to A′ is referred to as a *cycle of action* whose halfway point is C.

The slope of the following curve represents the rate at which the position of the pendulum or its velocity changes.

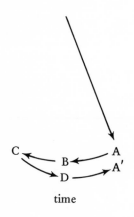

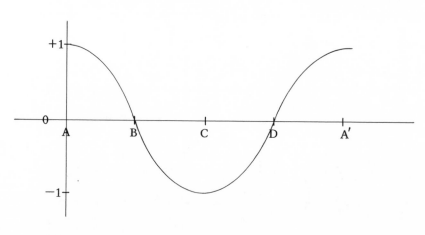

274

The rate at which the velocity changes is the acceleration, and the rate at which acceleration changes Young designates as *control*. These dimensions can be plotted in a likewise fashion.

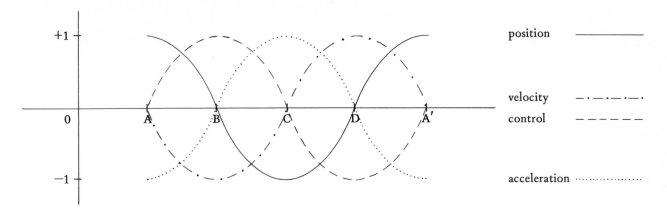

These curves are all the same shape, but the curve for velocity is displaced one-fourth of the cycle before the position curve. The velocity is at 0 when the position is either +1 or −1. The velocity is at a maximum (in a positive or negative direction) when the position of the pendulum is at 0. The curve for acceleration is displaced one-fourth of the cycle from the curve of velocity, and one half of a cycle from the curve of position. Thus when the pendulum's position is 0, and the velocity is at a maximum, the acceleration is 0. The control curve is displaced one-fourth of a cycle from the acceleration curve and one-half of a cycle from the velocity. This cycle of action can be represented as a full circle—with the designations of maximum position, velocity, acceleration, and control falling on four points 90° apart.

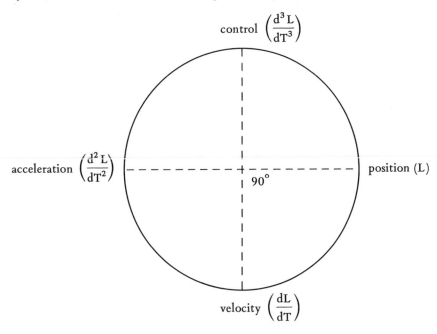

The fourth positional derivative repeats the cycle and becomes once more "position" in this scheme. Young maintains that "these four categories of the measure are necessary

control
(4)

spontaneous act (1)
feeling

observation
(3)

computation
reaction
(2)

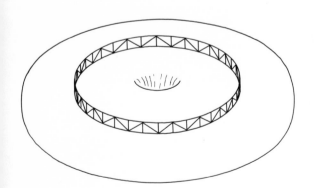

and sufficient for the analysis of motion of a moving body." He also states that there are fundamental qualitative differences between these measures.

In order to determine position, we make an observation—either visually or by some equally direct process. On the other hand, velocity cannot be observed directly. It must be computed. It can only be known intellectually. We must make two observations of position, determine their difference and divide by the time elapsed, obtaining a ratio. Acceleration can also be computed, but it can be directly and physically experienced by the knower, through feeling, in a way by which the other measures cannot be known. Control, or change in acceleration, must be initiated by an operator. This element is indeterminate and unknowable to an observer.

The four types of experience derived from the physical measure formulae now become the basis for another cycle of action called the learning cycle. This cycle begins with a spontaneous act, an impulse derived from feeling, and equivalent, Young believes, to acceleration. Unconscious reaction is the second element of this cycle. This reaction is based on habits, instincts, or "programming" in the language of bio-computer theory. It is equivalent to the computations involved in recognizing velocity. The third element of the cycle is observation and is equivalent to position, the observable physical factor. The fourth element of the learning cycle is control.

An example of the learning cycle would be a baby reaching out to touch something (spontaneous action). If a hot object like a flame is encountered, the hand is withdrawn (reaction). Then there follows observation upon the event. Further exploration consciously avoids fire until the learned behavior becomes automatically programmed and spontaneity is resumed. The cycle can be diagrammed as follows:

Young derives a formula for the cycle of action or learning which leads to consciousness. Note that the distance from spontaneous action to conscious control is 3/4 of 360° or 3/4 x 2π 3π/2. The common sense view of the universe is to consider it shaped like a sphere extending infinitely in all directions. However, if we multiply the formula for the volume of a sphere ($4\pi r^3/3$) by Young's formula for the cycle leading to consciousness, we obtain the formula for the volume of a a torus (donut) with an infinitely small hole ($2\pi^2 r^3$). This is significant for Young in that the formula for the volume of the Einstein-Eddington Universe, the boundary region of the so-called hypersphere is also $2\pi^2 r^3$.

Young sees in the torus topology a possible answer to the philosophical problem of the individual (or part, or microcosm) versus the collective (or whole, or macrocosm). In a toroidal universe, a part can be seemingly separate and yet connected with the rest. If we think of the fence as separating the inner from the outer, the torus provides a paradigm that permits us to see a monad as both separated from the rest of the universe by the fence and still connected with everything else through the core. The core of the torus with its infinitely small hole is for Young a representation of inner consciousness.

276

Young points out that magnetic fields, vortices, and tornados all have the toroidal form. The vortex is furthermore the only manner in which a fluid can move on itself. Thus it is a very suitable shape for the universe to have. However, we must bear in mind that the volume of the torus is three dimensional and is something akin to the surface of the four dimensional hypersphere of Eddington and Einstein.

If we expand upon the "geometry of meaning," we can add eight other measure formula of physics for a total of twelve.

Group I
L (position)
dL/T (velocity)
d²L/T² (acceleration)
d³L/T³ (control)

× M =

Group II
ML (moment)
dML/T (momentum)
d²ML/T² (force)
d³ML/T³ (mass control)

× L =

Group III
ML² (moment of inertia)
dML²/T (action)
d²ML²/T² (work)
d³ML²/T³ (power)

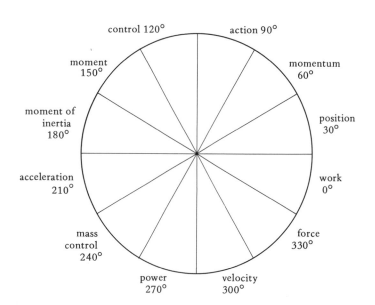

You will recall the logic by which Young determined that length (or position) and its three derivatives divided the circle into four quarters, thus giving the operation of T (time) an angular value of 90°. Through a process of trial and error, Young found that by assuming that M (mass) has the value of 120° and L the value 30°, the measure formula could equally spread around a circle in twelve positions. No proof is given for this assumption. However, when these values are applied to the measure formula and incorporated into the cycle of action we do get the above, symmetrically elegant, results.

Young then found he could assign the different astrological signs to the measure formula according to the appropriateness of the physical and astrological symbolism. Acceleration, at the starting point of our learning cycle, is equated with Aries, the first sign of the Zodiac. Mass control is translated into the sign of Taurus, the bull. Gemini, the sign of knowledge ruled by Mercury, is equated with the physical measure for power. ("After all," says Young, quoting Francis Bacon "Knowledge is Power.") The process continues in a way which is rather reasonable from the standpoint of astrology, if not outrageous to physicists. The results are as follows:

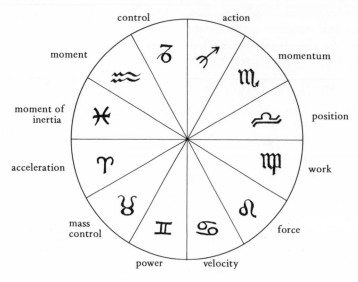

control   action

moment

momentum

moment of
inertia

position

acceleration

work

mass
control

force

power   velocity

The preceding diagram is Young's "Rosetta Stone," a diagram and subject treated at length in his book *The Geometry of Meaning*.[3] Its significance lies beyond the traditional realms of either astrology or physics. It may be a perfectly useless intellectual "bead game." On the other hand, it points toward the unification of symbolic meaning with mathematical manipulation. It provides a comprehensive metaphor with which to describe the processes of consciousness. It is also suggestive of a metasystem within which one can integrate the diverse disciplines of human endeavor. Such synergistic approaches are necessary in order to apply the vast resources of our *information explosion* to the social problems which confront us.

Young's theory fits within the context of historical cosmological speculations beginning with Pythagoras. In earlier cultures, psi phenomena were generally incorporated in the prevailing world view with a great deal of eloquence, if not rational lucidity. They were thought to stem from the heavenly hierarchies and celestial realms which were believed to interpenetrate or transcend all gross matter. However, in the attempt to be empirically grounded, modern cosmologists in rejecting supernatural elements have also unthinkingly rejected psi. Consciousness itself has been left out of the scientific picture. Something of an operational substitute has been provided by observable behavior.

Arthur Young has attempted to bridge this gap by developing a modern, scientific meta-theory within which one can account for human consciousness and process, including the data of parapsychology. What such a theory leads to is a wholistic view of the universe, oneself, and mankind.

Arthur Young is now the president of the Institute for the Study of Consciousness located in Berkeley, California. The focus of the institute is primarily intellectual or gnostic. It operates under Young's precept that a true understanding of the universe can only be grasped through the exercise of one's full human capacities.

The Physical Roots of Consciousness

by Jack Sarfatti, Ph.D.

> You're god in your universe.
> You caused it.
> You pretended not to cause it
> so that you could play in it,
> and you can remember you caused it
> any time you want to.
>
> Werner Erhard, EST.

Jack Sarfatti, Ph.D.

Introduction

The new physicists are forging deep and strong links between the foundations of physics and the psychology of consciousness. These links are not new in the history of physics. The great nineteenth century physicists Mach and Helmholtz were concerned with the relation of human perception to the notions of space, time and mass. One of the fathers of quantum theory, Niels Bohr, was influenced by the psychology of William James in his formulation of the quantum idea of complementarity between wave and particle. Observational data on the remote viewing of distant environments published by Harold Puthoff and Russell Targ at the Stanford Research Institute, and data on psychokinesis published by David Bohm and John Hasted from Birkbeck College and John Taylor from Kings College (University of London) are forcing physicists to explore the physical roots of consciousness.[4,5] Physicists at classified U.S. government laboratories are conducting experiments in psychic phenomena on an unofficial basis. An informal seminar with physicists from the Lawrence Radiation Laboratory of the University of California in Berkeley and the Physics/Consciousness Research Group (a tax-exempt non-profit California corporation) of San Francisco was created in the late spring of 1975 to reproduce, and possibly improve, the experiments at Stanford Research Institute and at the University of London. Recent theoretical discoveries in the quantum effect known as *EPR* (named for Einstein, Podolsky and Rosen for their 1935 paper on the quantum connection between spatially separated systems), now clearly formulated in a rigorous theorem by John S. Bell, allow for the transmission of information *instantly* between any two places in the physical universe.[6,7] There is no violation of Einstein's theory of relativity because the information transfer does *not* require the propagation of energetic signals. The quantum information utilizes energy already present at a particular place. If this hypothesis is confirmed, then psychokinesis, telepathy and precognition are likely to have a unified explanation within the presently known

*I would like to thank Saul-Paul Sirag, Professor Fred Wolf, and Werner Erhard for their contributions to this paper. I have benefited from conversations with Professor Henry Stapp and Professor Costa de Beauregard. I am indebted to Professor John Archibald Wheeler for sending me a recent account of his work.[9]

279

framework of modern theoretical physics.[8] Even more important than psychic phenomena is a proper understanding of man's normal consciousness! Physics and psychology are on the brink of a new unifying insight which will totally alter man's conception of who he is and why he is here.

Space-Time According to Einstein

The special theory of relativity, formulated by Albert Einstein in 1905, is based on the experimentally confirmed idea that the velocity of light is the same universal constant, $c = 3 \times 10^{10}$ cm./sec., for all inertial observers who move uniformly in straight lines relative to each other. Consequently, Einstein's genius deduced that events which are simultaneous to one observer are not simultaneous to a second observer. Furthermore, moving clocks run slow, moving measuring sticks contract in length along the direction of motion, energy is equivalent to mass, *i.e.* $E = mc^2$, and the mass of a particle increases to infinity as the velocity approaches that of light in vacuum. Einstein's results have been confirmed many times in physics laboratories. Like any scientific fact, these results presuppose that the observers are in a common state of consciousness whose legitimacy is determined by their agreement or social contract. The legitimacy of any scientific discipline is ultimately a political matter. According to modern physics, physical reality does not objectively exist independent of the participating observers. Kurt Gödel, of the Princeton Institute for Advanced Study, in a paper titled "A remark about the relationship between relativity theory and idealistic philosophy" [*Albert Einstein Philosopher-Scientist*, P.A. Schilpp, Harper, 1959] writes that relativity denies the objectivity of change and considers change to be an illusion caused by our "special mode of perception." In this same paper, Gödel points out that the *general* theory of relativity allows time travel to the past. Thus,

. . . it is possible in these worlds to travel into any region of the past, present, and future, and back again, exactly as it is possible in other worlds to travel to distant parts of space.

Gödel adds that a time traveller can meet up with himself "at some earlier period of his life." A way out of this kind of paradox is to invoke the *many-worlds interpretation of quantum mechanics,* due to Everett, Graham and Wheeler,[10,11] in which all possible measurement results are realized in an increasingly multiple branching of physical reality. One "branch world" exists for each possible sequence of possible measurement results. Psychic phenomena would result from communication between branch worlds. If you were to travel to the past and kill your father before you were born, then you would be automatically switched to a new branch world upon your return to the present. A world in which you were not born. the "truths" of modern physics are stranger than science-fiction!

Physicists use a simple geometric picture of the *flat* space-time of special relativity called a "Minkowski diagram." Relativity unites space and time into a unified "four dimensional space-time continuum" in which time appears as a mathematically imaginary space. Events are conceived of as *points* on the Minkowski diagram. The history of a sequence of events is described by a curve or path on the Minkowski diagram called a *world line.* Each event is the origin of a *future light cone* and a *past light cone.* World lines that are everywhere inside the light cones are called *time-like* and describe the history of particles moving at velocities less than the velocity of light. World lines that are everywhere on the light cones are called *light-like* and describe the histories of *real* photons, neutrinos and gravitons that move at exactly the velocity of light. World lines that are everywhere *outside* the light cones are called *space-like* and would correspond to *tachyonic* processes happening faster than the velocity of light. Such a process can be in two or more widely separated places at the same time! Furthermore, these space-like processes allow the effect to precede the cause for some observers and not for others. Space-like processes are not allowed in classical physics but are the essence of quantum physics according to my new interpretation. Quantum transitions or "quantum jumps" are space-like processes. This is why particles exhibit wave properties of interference. For example, in a double slit interference experiment, the electron passes through both slits at the same time in a space-like jump.

World lines have a length which is measured to be the same by all observers and which is called the *proper time,* s. Particles that are not acted upon by real forces follow *geodesic* world lines in classical physics. A geodesic is defined in the following way. Choose two points on the Minkowski diagram. Imagine all possible world lines that pass through the two points. Compute the value of the proper time, s, for all of these world lines. The geodesic world line has the property that the proper time of all its very close neighbor world lines have the *same* proper time that it has. This is called the *extremum* property. When real forces act, the particle no longer follows a geodesic world line. In quantum physics all possible world lines connecting two chosen points can occur with a *probability amplitude.* These probability amplitudes coherently interfere with each other. They reinforce each other along the actual world line that is predicted from the classical laws of physics. They destroy each other's effect for world lines that are very different from the classically predicted world line. Thus, classical physics is a limiting case of quantum physics.

General relativity applies to all observers, who are now allowed to accelerate relative to each other. This is a possibility not allowed for in special relativity. The basic new idea is that an observer inside a closed box that is uniformly accelerating in gravitation-free space cannot distinguish his situation from that of an observer at rest in a uniform gravitational field. This inability to distinguish two possibilities is called the "equivalence principle" and it allowed Einstein to formulate a purely *geometric* theory of gravitation. Non-uniformities in gravitation *curve* space-time. In Newton's physics, gravitation was a real force which would cause particles to follow non-geodesic world lines. In Einstein's physics, gravitation is a "fictitious" force. A particle moving in a gravitational field with no other kinds of

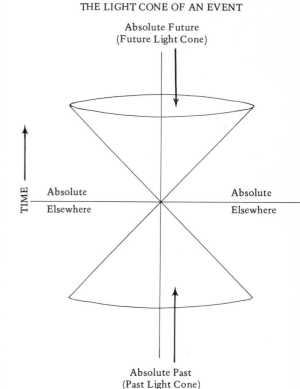

THE LIGHT CONE OF AN EVENT

Absolute Future
(Future Light Cone)

TIME

Absolute
Elsewhere

Absolute
Elsewhere

Absolute Past
(Past Light Cone)

SPACE

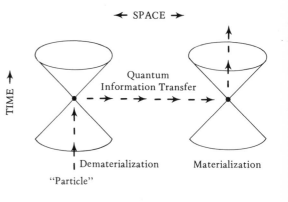

SPACE

TIME

Quantum
Information Transfer

Dematerialization

Materialization

"Particle"

forces acting is said to be "freely falling" and it follows a "straight line" or *geodesic* in a *curved* space-time. The earth in its motion around the sun follows such a geodesic world line. Gravitation, analogous to relative velocity in special relativity, distorts space and time. Clocks at rest in a gravitational field run slow relative to gravitation-free clocks that have geodesic world lines. Clocks that are at rest in a gravitational field require real forces to prevent their free fall. Thus, their world lines on the Minkowski diagram are not geodesic. The slowing down of clocks in the gravitational field is called the "Einstein red shift." For example, the sharp spectral lines of an atom on the surface of the sun will be very slightly shifted to lower frequencies compared to the spectral lines of the same kind of atom on the surface of the earth. This is because the gravitational field at the sun is stronger than that at the earth. This effect has actually been observed between two points on the earth using very sharp gamma ray photons coming from special kinds of nuclear quantum jumps in which the recoil of the nucleus is shared by the entire crystal in which the radioactive nucleus is situated. Recent experiments on the large particle accelerators at Stanford, Brookhaven and the National Accelerator Laboratory show the existence of unexpected "charmed" particles that are unstable and live at least a thousand times longer than they should.[12] I interpret this fact as evidence that the Einstein red shift is happening on the subnuclear scale in which gravitation can act very strongly. This interpretation connects with another fact; namely, that the strongly-interacting particles called "hadrons" rotate in proportion to the square of their mass. This is exactly what one expects if the elementary particles are tiny rotating black holes!

Euclidean geometry does not work in space that is curved by gravitation. A circle in Euclidean geometry has a circumference that is equal to 2π times the radius. In contrast, a circle in a gravitational field has a circumference that is *smaller* than 2π times the radius. This is because measuring sticks oriented along the gravitational field, and at rest in it, contract relative to freely-falling measuring sticks. Measuring sticks that are oriented perpendicular to the gravitational field, and at rest in it, do *not* contract relative to freely-falling measuring sticks. Therefore, the radius of a circle in a gravitational field contains an *excess* of contracted "unit" measuring sticks, while the circumference contains the "normal" number of uncontracted measuring sticks. I believe that this gravitational distortion of space has also been observed on the subnuclear scale in experiments at the National Accelerator Laboratory which show that hadrons increase their size when measured from close up in high energy collisons. This is a third fact that fits with the interpretation that elementary particles are tiny black holes in a super-strong gravitational field at short distances.

Gravitation tips the light cones on the Minkowski diagram and causes them to distort and their origins to fuzz out. Gravitation is closely related to the Heisenberg uncertainty principle of quantum mechanics. Professor John Archibald Wheeler of Princeton used to advocate the view of *geometrodynamics* which says that mass is an illusion of pure curvature, and electric charge is an illusion of chargeless electric lines trapped in the "wormhole" multiply-connected topology of three-dimensional space.[9] In this picture, an elementary particle can be conceived of as a *mini-black hole.* A mini-black hole is formed when gravitation gets so strong, that the light cone is tipped or tilted so much, that no light can escape to infinity along light-like world lines. Some light can actually leak out by quantum jumps along space-like world lines. The mini-black hole is actually unstable and explodes because of quantum jumps. The boundary between light cones that are tilted so much that the light cone cannot reach infinity and those light cones that do reach infinity is called an event horizon. Space-time collapses to a *singularity* inside the event horizon. The curvature of space is infinite at the singularity and the idea of space and time break down and are transcended to the level of *pregeometry.* A singularity hidden by an event horizon is called a mini-black hole. There is no real mass inside a mini-black hole. Real mass is only an illusion on the statistical level of large numbers of mini-black holes. When a star exhausts its nuclear fuel and gravitationally collapses to an *astrophysical* black hole, it simply turns back to its primordial state of mini-black holes. The protons, electrons, mesons and hyperons are crushed out of existence. Elementary particles are, at the deepest level, simply coherent organizations of the disordered quantum "zero point" fluctuations in the geometry of space-time. Elementary particles are formed by *information* which is a form of consciousness. Information quantum jumps to a different part of space in the gravitational collapse to a singularity. Gravitational collapse is the same kind of EPR information transfer that is found in psychic phenomena. As Sir James Jeans said, the universe is ultimately composed of a great thought. The universe is a cosmic computer on the pregeometric level of information in which space and time appear as secondary statistical constructs as suggested by Professor David Finkelstein of Yeshiva University. The pregeometry can be identified with the collective conscious from which we are unconscious except in enlightenment. This image is more than poetry it is physics as well, if we accept responsibility and create the facts of psychic phenomena. All scientific facts are created by those who participate.

Causality Overthrown

The prejudice of classical causality says that an event can only be influenced by other events that are in its past light cone. Events in the future light cone and outside the light cone in the "absolute elsewhere" are said not to influence the event of interest. Both general relativity and quantum theory in the form of Bell's theorem[6] show that classical causality is not correct in principle on the level of individual events. Causality does not work in your individual experience, which is part of a quantum reality, not a classical reality. Classical causality does work on the statistical level in which we average our observations over sets of events. This statistical average throws the baby out with the bathwater and is the source of man's alienation from himself. Psychic information is transmitted over space-like separated events and is not subject to the time delays of messages

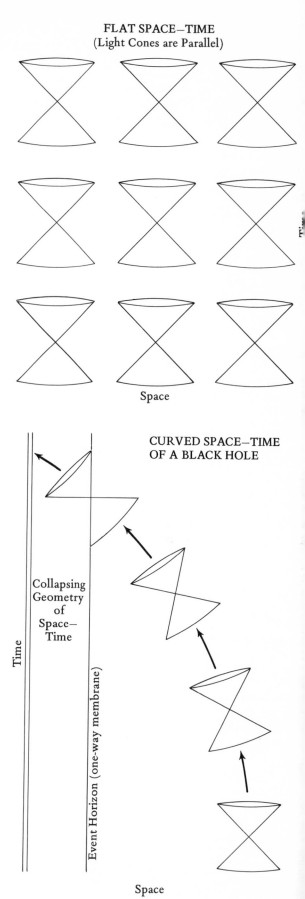

FLAT SPACE—TIME
(Light Cones are Parallel)

Space

CURVED SPACE—TIME
OF A BLACK HOLE

Collapsing Geometry of Space—Time

Time

Event Horizon (one-way membrane)

Space

283

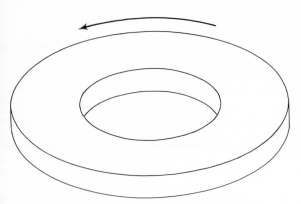

In Einstein's General Relativity, a rotating ring can act as a time machine to the past. Curved space-time of a rotating black hole gives causality-violating, closed time-like curve (i.e. a time machine).

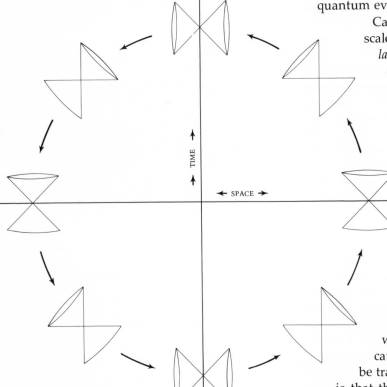

whose speed of propagation is limited to the speed of light. Information is more fundamental than space, time or energy. Psychic information is on the level of pregeometry. Psychic information creates space, time and matter. We can know the laws regulating psychic information.

Almost all of the measurements of atomic physics are adequately described by the statistical limit of the quantum principle. However, recent experiments by John Clauser at U.C. Berkeley show that classical causality is violated for individual atomic events. (Local causes operate within the velocity of light.) Clauser measures the simultaneous arrival of two photons at spatially separated detectors.[13,14] The two photons originate from the same atom. Bell's theorem enables one to calculate what the rate of simultaneous arrival should be if the statistical predictions of quantum theory are correct. It also enables one to calculate the rate of simultaneous arrival if physical reality is objective and locally causal for the individual photons. Clauser's measurements contradict the rate of photon coincidences predicted on the basis of an objective and locally causal reality. The measured rate agrees with the prediction of ordinary quantum theory. This means that physical reality either is not subject to the principle of *local* causation or does not objectively exist independent of the observers who participate in its creation. Bell's theorem and Clauser's experiment have great importance for the understanding of personal human experience. The human brain stores and processes its information at the level of single organic molecules and is a single macroscopic quantum system. Acts of consciousness are individual quantum events.

Causality also breaks down on the cosmological scale. The universe was created in an *initial singularity* which is the time reverse of the gravitational collapse to a black hole. We live in a white hole. The cosmic fireball in this "big bang" contained very hot electromagnetic radiation which has now cooled down to about three degrees above absolute zero temperature because of the expansion of the universe. Most of this remnant of the cosmic fireball is in the form of microwave radiation in thermal equilibrium. Observations of the sky in all directions show that the properties of the microwaves are the same to an accuracy of about a tenth of a percent. General relativity allows us to calculate the past light cones of those microwave events that we measure now. It is found that the past light cones of microwaves coming from different directions do not overlap. Thus the microwaves in different parts of the universe cannot causally influence each other if information cannot be transferred over space-like separations. Yet the fact is that the microwaves are the same all over which suggests that they have been in communication. The simplest way out of the dilemma is to suppose that information is

284

transmitted outside the light cone as it is in the quantum EPR effect. Furthermore, detailed mathematical study of Einstein's field equations for curved spacetime confirm that this is so in general relativity.[15]

The use of signals confined to the light cone is a very poor way to communicate in the universe. The proposed ten billion dollar Project Cyclops described by Carl Sagan and Frank Drake in the May 1975 *Scientific American* will give important information on the physics of the universe and should, perhaps, be built. However, it is a very inelegant way to communicate with advanced extra-terrestrial civilizations. Extra-terrestrials will use quantum EPR information transmission and will be able to communicate instantly to every place in the universe. These communications can be detected as "psychic" events by all human beings who agree to participate. You can directly communicate with all parts of the universe. The quantum physics of EPR is the physics of your personal and direct experience. You already are a physicist if you choose to know it.

The new physics is the physics of uniqueness. This kind of physics is closer to art than to the insurance tables of the actuary. The new physics transcends reproducibility and control as the final criterion for reality without rejecting its utility in order to survive as biological systems. The statistical average of the set of Beethoven sonatas is not music. The statistical average of your experiences is not your experience but a *non-experience* of experience. The non-experience reveals beautiful patterns of order and that is also a new experience! Your life will not work if you do not distinguish quantum reality from its statistical average which is classical reality.

Uncertainty, Self-Reference and Final Cause

The precise meaning of quantum uncertainty requires a bold and profound analysis of the nature of probability. Classical probability is concerned with the creation of an actuality from an ensemble of possibilities. The fundamental act is that of choice and is expressed by the technical idea of *information*. The fundamental unit of information is the "bit" which is the act of choice between two perceived alternatives. Quantum probability is more subtle than classical probability. Each alternative is assigned a pair of numbers called a *probability amplitude*. If we choose *not* to make measurements that can distinguish among a set of alternatives then we add the probability amplitudes for each alternative. The alternatives coherently interfere with each other. We must multiply the sum of probability amplitudes by itself in a special way in order to obtain the probability for a particular happening. Probability is by definition statistical and we hope to go beyond it to the unique event. Is probability objective or subjective? Is probability only measurable if we prepare an *ensemble* of copies of the system of interest and observe the fraction of times that a particular alternative occurs? Or can we simply use one system and make repeated observations on it in the course of time? Do all alternatives actually occur in different branch worlds? Can we speak of the probability of a unique individual event independently of an ensemble? These questions, and others equally important, are still in great debate. Probability is as elusive as consciousness. As soon as we think we have it, it mutates into something else like a mischievous elf!

The resolution of the puzzle of probability lies close to the roots of consciousness and provides an experiential distinction between the idealist and the materialist conceptions of the world. The materialist says that consciousness is a mere epiphenomenon of matter. In the materialist scenario, the atmosphere of the early earth is very different from what it is today. Nucleotides and amino acids are built up out of simpler molecules with high probability because of the non-equilibrium conditions and a plentiful supply of free energy. Life develops with the formation of biological membranes that concentrate certain kinds of molecules and not others. Blind accident gives the self-replicating DNA molecule with its genetic code that programs protein construction and eventually results in the ionic liquid biocomputer known as man. Consciousness is then simply the functioning of a very elaborate machine. The progress of science gives us more and more details in the scenario. The idealist position is *complementary* (in Bohr's sense) to that of the materialist. The idealist physicist points to the fact that even a very slight change in the fine structure constant e^2/hc $1/137$ that determines the strength of coupling of light to matter and the size of atoms (10^{-8} cm.); or a slight change in the age (10^{10} years) or mass (10^{56} gm.) or size (10^{28} cm.) of the visible universe would make life and consciousness impossible! In a strange sense this is "the best of all possible worlds" because cosmology, nuclear astrophysics, atomic physics and chemical kinetics conspire together to make sure we are here! Or is there a final cause? Does the universe exist because we are here? Gödel's tale of a time traveller meeting up with his earlier self is based upon the fact that general relativity permits closed world lines on the Minkowski diagram. Every segment of the world line is time-like lying inside the local light cone which is tipped by gravitation. Brandon Carter has shown how this phenomenon is associated with rotating black holes.[16] We now have a new teleological possibility. Imagine that a super-intelligence in the far future evolves because of its own conscious design of the DNA code and its own interference with its past evolution. The super-intelligence uses time travel to the past to create itself. The requirement is self-consistency. This is a requirement that can be met.

The most profound mathematical discovery of the twentieth century is Gödel's meta-mathematical theorem of 1931 on the formally *undecidable propositions* of Russell and Whitehead's *Principia Mathematica*.[17] Gödel showed that "no calculus can be devised in such a way that every arithmetical proposition is represented in it by a formula which is either 'provable' or 'disprovable' within the calculus." That is, arithmetic, in its very nature, is *incomplete* if it is to be *self-consistent* i.e. free from contradiction. Gödel's proof "talks" about itself and is a mathematical expression of *self-consciousness!* This feature of Gödel's 1931 theorem is called *self-reference*. The statements of the meta-

language are recursively mapped into the language by the technique of "Gödel numbers" in the course of the proof.

The super-intelligence extends self-reference to the principle of universal self-creation. Professor John Archibald Wheeler of Princeton writes[9] of a principle that "wires together past, present and future" and which does not even allow the universe to exist unless and until the "accidents" of evolution ensure the creation, in its future, of "consciousness, and consciousness of consciousness and communicating community" that provide final meaning to the universe from beginning to end. The closed time-like curves of Gödel and Carter "wire together past, present and future."

Wheeler's realization of the deeper implications of the quantum principle and gravitational collapse to a pregeometric singularity have caused him to renounce his magic of Einstein's vision of the world as geometry. Like Prospero Wheeler writes[9] of the "collapse for everything one has ever called a law, not least the concept of geometry itself. Farewell geometry." The prayer of self-referencing, self-creating "pregeometry" brings the idealist "new physics" inexorably close to the views of the Catholic theologian Pierre Teilhard de Chardin. Paranormal phenomena are part of normal consciousness in this view in which pregeometry appears as a "harmonized collectivity of consciousness equivalent to a sort of superconsciousness" connecting "both the internal and external films of the world."[18] According to Wheeler,[9] self-referencing quantum pregeometry is indescribable in terms of the "mathematical machinery of any formal axiomatic system." The source of indescribability is Gödel "undecidability." This is a modern form of Qabala, of the all-creating uncontained Aleph and the unpronouncible name of HYWY. The physics departments of the modern university are spawning grounds of the new cabalists.[19]

The New Physics of Consciousness

The illusion of the classical scientific paradigm that is shattered by the quantum principle is the assumption that there is an immutable objective reality "out there" that is totally independent of what happens in consciousness "in here." G. Spencer Brown in *Laws of Form* refers to R. D. Laing's "politics of experience" in which empirical data are not independently existing but are arbitrarily chosen by the hypothesis formed by a responsible act of choice. We actually have the power to create the physical world. The quantum theory is the child of classical "objective" science. Quantum theory forces a new kind of logic in science that is still mathematical and disciplined. Quantum reality is not an excuse for nihilism but demands even greater levels of personal responsibility. You do count in the universe! You are not simply a mite on a speck of dust in an alienated cosmos. That is bad physics!

Mathematics is the deep language of transcendent experience. The Nobel prize physicist Eugene Wigner of Princeton has repeatedly written[20] that consciousness is at the root of

the quantum principle. His colleague, John Wheeler agrees.[9] Another Nobel prize physicist, Brian Josephson of Cambridge, presents a case[21] that the laws of high-energy physics as revealed in the data from the large accelerators may be changing due to the *psychokinetic* action of the experimenters and theorists themselves! Farewell objective science! It now fades into a nostalgic memory of a simpler time. Science is dead. Long live Science!

Thermodynamic Order and Information

Josephson's suggestion[21] that "communication of knowledge" alters physical reality according to a psycho-energetic coupling is implicit in the well established field of physics called thermodynamics when interpreted in terms of information theory.[22] Information is equivalent to thermodynamic *free energy* that is available to do mechanical, electrical or chemical work in a coherent, orderly and directed way. Information, as measured in *bits*, i.e. binary choices between two alternatives, costs free energy. The number of bits of information in a given situation is defined to be equal to the logarithm to the base 2 of the total number of possibilities for that situation. One bit refers to two possibilities, two bits refer to four possibilities, three bits refer to eight possibilities, and so on. The number of possibilities increases much faster than the number of bits.

If knowledge in the form of ΔI bits of information is gained from a system, S, in any measurement or observation, then a minimum amount of free energy, ΔF is lost from S as given by the *psycho-energetic* formula

$$-\Delta F = kT\Delta I$$

where k is Boltzmann's constant of minimal *entropy*, $k = 1.38 \times 10^{-16}$ erg/degree, and T is the temperature at S. This is the passive sense of the psycho-energetic connection of information to free energy. Professor Costa de Beauregard, of the Henri Poincare Institute in Paris, in his Berkeley lecture of May 13, 1975, points out an active sense of this formula. Thus, according to Costa de Beauregard, since k is so small the yield of information out of free energy is high. That is, it is relatively easy for us to passively gain knowledge about the physical world. In contrast, for the reverse process, of actively upgrading the quality of energy, already present, by the transfer of information, the yield of free energy out of information is low. If k were larger psychokinesis would be easier, according to Costa de Beauregard! Your bit of information would be worth more free energy if k were larger. On the other hand, it would be harder to see quantum effects unless Planck's constant of action, h, were also increased. But then, according to previous arguments, we would have to change the charge on the electron, e, and the speed of light, c, as well in order to make the universe safe for consciousness! The universe is very finely balanced in a tight ecological order in the new physics.

In classical physics the information, ΔI, is tied to energy flow in the form of signals limited to the speed of light or less. In quantum physics, the information, ΔI, can jump along a

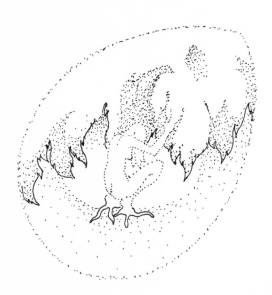

space-like path and show up at a place that is very far away from its point of origin. No energy is actually transferred in this quantum jump! The information, ΔI, simply refers to the quality or degree of coherent organization of energy already present in the zero-point motion of the geometry of space-time. Particles of matter are very low energy organizations of the very high unorganized zero-point energy. Imagine a Christmas tree with a chain of ornamental lights. The lights are synchronized to turn on, one right after another, along the chain. It appears as if something is moving along the chain. The motion is an illusion. Quantum jumps are like that! In quantum physics there is no necessary association of a quantity of information, ΔI, with the real flow of energy in the form of a signal. Information can be transferred by signals, but it can also be transferred instantly and directly by space-like quantum jumps. That is the essence of the EPR effect. Information transferred by signals is detected, sometimes with the help of instruments, by our normal senses. Information transferred by direct quantum jumps to our molecular information systems is called ESP. Relativity is not contradicted.

A gain in information in the consciousness of the observer is balanced by a loss in the free energy of the system that has been observed. Energy does not necessarily flow out of the system in this process. The total energy, E, in a system, according to thermodynamics, consists of two kinds, the free energy, F, and the bound energy, $T\Sigma$, where Σ is the entropy in the system. That is,

$$E = F \ T\Sigma \ .$$

A measurement on the system merely need change the partition of total energy E into its free and bound parts. Information makes use of the energy that it finds. Information is the ghost in the machine!

Psychokinesis is just the opposite of measurement. PK is anti-measurement. That is, information, ΔI, quantum jumps along a space-like path out of the participator. The physical energy of the participator is degraded in this act and must be replenished by the intake of free energy from the metabolism of food. One bit of transferred information degrades about 10^{-2} electron volts (ev.) of the participator's free energy. That same bit of information can end its quantum jump in a system of much higher temperature. It can then organize a much larger amount of energy than was lost from the participator! For example, if the bit shows up on the sub-nuclear level it will encounter a "Hagedorn temperature" of about 10^{13} degrees. That bit will be able to upgrade the quality of subnuclear energy by about 10^9 ev. which is enough to create pairs of hadrons out of the vacuum zero point energy. There is no violation of conservation of energy because total energy E is neither being created or destroyed, it is merely being reorganized. Furthermore, there is no violation of the second law of thermodynamics because the entropy loss from the participator is -k and the entropy gain is k, so that the net entropy change is zero. However, the net change in free energy is positive. That is, more free energy is gained in the high temperature system

than is lost from the low temperature participator. This net gain in free energy is used in *psychokinetic work*. In the example given, *thought actually creates matter* on the subnuclear scale. In classical thermodynamics, the second law of thermodynamics is formulated as the injunction against a spontaneous entropy decrease in a closed system. This form of the second law still holds in the new *quantum thermodynamics* that I have invented. The classical idea of a closed system is that energy and matter is not allowed to flow in or out of the system. The possibility that information can enter or leave without an energy or matter flow is not even conceived of in classical thermodynamics. Yet this is precisely what happens in EPR quantum jumps. The system may be classically closed yet open in the quantum sense. The second law is sometimes formulated as the impossibility of a spontaneous free energy increase in a closed system. This form of the law is transcended in quantum thermodynamics because communication, i.e. information flow, is no longer tied to energy and matter flow. One can have a "morphic ordering principle" in the sense of Lancelot Law White[23] without introducing a "vitalistic" violation of the second law of thermodynamics in its entropic formulation. A system closed to direct communication via space-like quantum jumps of information may be an impossibility in nature.

Since psychokinesis works by information quantum jumping out of the participators and reemerging as an ordering of random energy already existing at the site of the PK action, there is an *inherent confusion factor* or "Catch 22 Effect" attending these experiments. The source of this confusion is as fundamental as the uncertainty in Heisenberg's principle and the undecidability of self-reference in Gödel's theorem. Gregory Chaitin in his May, 1975 *Scientific American* article "Randomness and Mathematical Proof" says that Gödel's undecidability is a consequence of the constraints imposed by information theory. The quantum principle is information theory on the level of pregeometry where "thought" creates matter. Jean-Paul Sartre in *Being and Nothingness* says "one must be conscious in order to choose, and one must choose in order to be conscious. Choice and consciousness are one and the same thing." We have seen that the bit is the primitive choice. Undecidability, self-reference, uncertainty and the Catch 22 effect of psychokinesis all seem to have a common origin. Quantum systems do not have an independent existence but are brought into being by acts of choice of participators. There is nothing there if no one is looking at it! However, one looks and communicates not only by photons but also by direct EPR quantum jumps of disembodied information transfer which "stop the world."

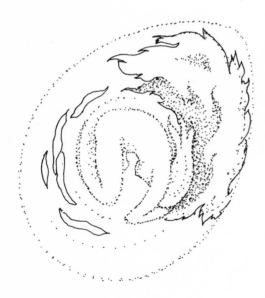

The Politics of Physics and Psychokinesis

In a lecture at the Toronto meeting of the New Horizons Research Foundation, Brian Josephson discussed the fact that the laws of high energy physics seem to keep on changing. He conjectures that consciousness can modify the Hamiltonian that controls the time evolution of the subnuclear particles. I have just given a mechanism for Josephson's suggestion. Another prime candidate for psychokinetic physics is Joe Weber's gravitational wave detector at the University of Maryland. Weber claims to have seen many gravitational wave events. However, several other groups, using even better equipment in some cases, see no evidence of gravitational waves. Still another candidate for psychokinetic physics, illustrating Josephson's suggestion, is the simultaneous discovery of the long-lived "charmed" particles seen at both Brookhaven and SLAC (Stanford Linear Accelerator).[12] These discoveries received great publicity in the popular press which was very convenient for the economic survival of these laboratories because the federal government has seriously cut back on their grants. High-energy physicists are working under the sword of Damocles and have been experiencing great emotional stress. These same conditions also obtain in poltergeist phenomena. The manifestation of psychokinesis increases with threats to survival. Professor Richard P. Feynman, also a Nobel prize physicist, in his speech before the 1974 Cal Tech graduating class spoke of "cargo cult science"[24] and accused high-energy physics of being such a pseudoscience. The new physicists are suggesting that all science is fundamentally pseudoscience in Feynman's strict moralistic sense of the word "cargo cult." Feyn-man's remarks are based on the classical idea that nature is objective. This is inconsistent with the nature of the quantum reality that Feynman has, in great measure, assisted in creating. Similarly, the vehement distrust of the data from the Stanford Research Institute and the University of London may come from an insufficient appreciation of the Catch 22 effect, rather than from actual fraud and incompetence on the part of psychic researchers. I have experienced suspicion of that data myself! However, I have no more reason to distrust the data from Stanford and London and other places, than I have to distrust the reports from SLAC, Brookhaven and Maryland!

Maxwell Demons and a New Kind of Measurement

I have been suggesting a new kind of mechanism for the transfer of form and order over space-like separations on the level of individual quantum events. All classical measurements, including classical measurements of quantum processes of the type considered by Heisenberg in his "microscope" that leads to the uncertainty principle, involve the actual flow of energy and momentum in order to convey information. For example, Heisenberg reasons that the position of an electron must be measured by means of a second particle, e.g. a photon, that must collide with the electron in order to get the information on the electron's position. The fact that action is quantized in units

of Planck's constant, h 10⁻²⁷ erg-sec., implies uncontrollable minimal energy and momentum transfers between photon and electron in the collision. The result of Heisenberg's thought experiment is that it is impossible to predict the simultaneous values of both the position and the momentum of the electron with complete certainty. The only way to gain knowledge of the uncertainties is to repeat the experiment many times under "identically prepared" conditions. These kinds of classical measurements of quantum processes are fundamentally statistical. Josephson intuits that there may be another level of measurement that transcends the limitations of Heisenberg's uncertainty principle.[21] He says that this limitation is perhaps only a "reflection of the kinds of observation we can make," and that "the physical description of the world would change radically if we could observe more things." Einstein was also firmly convinced that there was another way to knowledge, but his refusal to accept the "telepathic" implications that he saw so clearly in his EPR effect prevented him, like Moses, from seeing the promised land. Thus, Einstein's *Autobiographical Notes* contain the following remark about the EPR effect:

There is to be a system which at the time t of our observation consists of two partial systems S_1 and S_2, which at this time are spatially separated . . . If I make a complete measurement of S_1, I get from the results . . . an entirely definite Ψ-function Ψ_2 of the system S_2 The character of Ψ_2 then depends upon *what kind* of measurement I undertake on S_1. . . . One can escape from this conclusion only by either assuming that the measurement of S_1 (telepathically)* changes the real situation of S_2 or by denying independent real situations as such to things which are spatially separated from eath other. Both alternatives appear to me entirely unacceptable.[25]

I suggest that truly quantum measurements of quantum processes enable us to "observe more things." These new kinds of measurements are directly experienced as "psychic." The limits of the Heisenberg uncertainty principle and the limits of Leo Szilard's 1929 exorcism of the Maxwell Demon[26] only apply to classical measurements and not to quantum measurements of quantum processes. Classical measurements rely on actual energy flow to convey information and are therefore subject to the limit of Planck's quantum of action. Quantum measurements rely on the direct space-like quantum jumps of disembodied bits of information with no actual energy flows. Matter forms when bits of information coherently impose order on the substrate of chaotic zero-point motion. All motion and change is illusory being ultimately reducible to space-like quantum jumps of bits of consciousness. Think of the physical universe as the face of a vast color TV tube. Consciousness is like the stream of electrons hitting the inside face of the tube. Matter is like the colored spots seen on the outside face of the tube due to the electron impacts.

The new physics does not accept Niels Bohr's stipulation that all legitimate measurements of quantum processes must be couched ultimately in classical measuring apparatuses and

---

*"Telepathisch" in original German version.

described in classical language. The brain is not a classical measuring apparatus and consciousness does not follow classical laws. Bohr's stipulation is provincial to a particular state of consciousness which we might call the "observer mind set." It is not appropriate to that state of consciousness described by Wheeler as the state of *participation* in which the observer is not isolated from the world except "as he opens upon it one-way windows of perception." The participator is "coextensive" with the universe.[9]

The great nineteenth century physicist James Clerk Maxwell borrowed Laplace's demon[22] for a thought experiment that showed how to violate the second law of thermodynamics with consciousness. Imagine two compartments, A and B, filled with gas at the same temperature, and separated by a thin partition containing very small trap doors. An intelligent demon with sharp eyesight is put in charge of the trap doors. He is instructed to open the doors whenever a Particle in A comes toward it with more than a certain speed V and to keep the doors closed against all particles in A with speeds less than V. He is also to open the doors whenever particles in B approach it with speeds v that are smaller than V. Temperature is a measure of the random kinetic energy of the molecules. Therefore, the temperature of the gas in A will be lowered and the temperature of the gas in B will be raised in the closed system consisting of both A and B. The demon's consciousness has created free energy because the temperature difference created between A and B can drive a heat engine which can be used to do work. Space-like quantum jumps of information are equivalent to a Maxwell demon because they allow the nonlocal creation of net free energy out of chaos even though there can be a net increase in entropy. In 1929 Leo Szilard exorcised the demon.[22] Szilard argued that part of the heat energy inside the box, consisting of A and B, must be present as random electromagnetic "black body" radiation in thermal equilibrium with the gas and walls of the box. Therefore, the demon cannot see anything at all! He sees a uniform white mist of pure electromagnetic noise. The visual perception of objects requires a non-accidental inhomogeneity in the electromagnetic field which is not found in black body radiation. In order to see, the demon must have something like a radar beam which dissipates free energy. Szilard proved that the free energy gain made available by the trap doors, is, in principle, not larger than the free energy that must be lost in getting the information needed in order to decide whether to leave the trap doors open or shut! The demon exchanges free energy for information, and this information enables him to recover part of the free energy that he spent in getting the information. Information is proportional to free energy, and any ordering of things, including mental orderings, have thermodynamic consequences. This is how modern physics makes contact with Qabala. Szilard's analysis works for classical measurements in which information is conveyed by energy flow. It is not clear if Szilard's analysis will work if the demon uses EPR information. The thesis of this paper is that Szilard's analysis will not work for "psychic" EPR Maxwell Demons. We have met the demons. They are us![27]

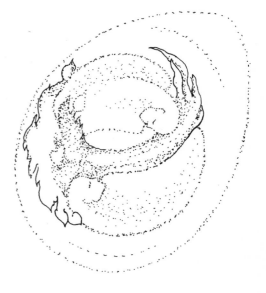

The Confusion Factor

According to Sarfatti's theory, psychic phenomena derive their necessary energy by creating confusion in the environment, particularly in immediate systems of measurement and observation. Parapsychologists are fond of criticizing the muddled viewpoints of emotional believers and hard-nosed skeptics; however it may be the case, ironically, that these elements of society are the actual thermodynamic consequence of psychic events. Thus we arrive at a sociological parapsychology which views all elements as part of the same dynamic system.

This is not to imply that the fervent believers or skeptics should be casually dismissed, but rather suggests that one may obtain a greater perspective, viewing these elements as part of the same system. For example, one of the foremost critics of reported psychic effects is Martin Gardner, the witty author of the "Mathematical Games" column in *Scientific American* as well as *Fads and Fallacies in the Name of Science,* a sarcastic attack on the pseudosciences.[28]

Gardner's involvement with the "occult" is something of an ironic passion. This fascination is often embodied in his literary alter-ego, Dr. Matrix, a numerologist whose clever theories provide the meat for Gardner's humor. Sometimes, however, much to a skeptic's embarrassment, his own sarcasm is the very vehicle of a psychic synchronicity.

In the July 1974 issue of *Scientific American,* which hit the newsstands on June 15, Gardner wrote a spoof titled, "Dr. Matrix Brings His Numerological Science to Bear on the Occult Powers of the Pyramid," in which he, with some justification, takes a good-natured poke at the current pyramid cultists. ("A booklet came with it, telling how the pyramid's 'psi-org energy' would keep razor blades sharp, preserve rosebuds and restore old typewriter ribbons.") At the height of his jesting, Gardner takes a swipe at the Stanford Research Institute physicist and psychic researcher Puthoff, who he styles as Dr. Harold Puton. Then aiming his barbs at the former U.S. President, Gardner suggests that Nixon should retire to Nixon, Nevada, (an actual town) and spend his days sitting on top of nearby Pyramid Rock in the middle of Pyramid Lake.

His humorous attack on "the occult" has an interesting twist here. For on the very day that Gardner's article reached the public, newspapers throughout the country carried pictures of President Nixon actually visiting the Great Pyramid in Egypt —a suddenly arranged visit presumably unknown to Gardner when he wrote his story! Such a synchronicity seems to embody the message that even the skeptical joker is part of the "cosmic puzzle."

Perhaps the foremost "official critic" of parapsychology is Professor C. E. M. Hansel of the University of Wales. His book, *ESP: A Scientific Evaluation*[29] was reviewed in over thirty scientific and literary publications, receiving more attention in the academic community than any other single book related to parapsychology.[30] The essential claim of Hansel's book is that

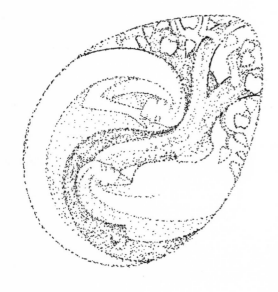

experiments which have "any defect such that their result may be due to a cause other than ESP cannot provide conclusive proof of ESP." This is scientifically correct. He then goes on to provide ingenious plots for non-parapsychological solutions to many classical ESP experiments, ultimately involving either experimenter or subject fraud. The situation is indeed tricky, for the only defense against experimenter fraud in any field of science is the independent repeatability of an experiment.

Actually parapsychological experiments have been successfully repeated. Between 1960 and 1970 the world's scientific psychological journals reported on thirteen experimental parapsychological investigations. Positive results were reported in eight cases, paranormal phenomena being unconfirmed in the other five. During the same period the parapsychological journals published reports on 143 experiments with positive results, and 19 with negative findings. (Positive results may include instances of negative psi.)[31]

However unlikely it might seem, some possibility of experimenter fraud exists in all of the reported experiments. Hansel, in his book, felt no obligation to provide evidence that fraud actually did occur. The careful weighing of evidence with regard to the several possible hypotheses—the meat of scientific analysis—was of no concern to him. He simply *assumed* that ESP was *a priori* so unlikely that any other possible alternative was more reasonable. The assumption that unsupported principles can determine or limit the possibilities of experience goes completely against the grain of the history and philosophy of science. Thus it's an ironic effect of the confusion factor that Hansel's criticisms prevailed and were lauded by such eminent historians of science as Professor E. G. Boring.[32]

To his credit, Hansel was able to unmask much confusion within the camp of experimental parapsychology. Of particular interest, he notes that the parapsychologists themselves published several contradictory versions of the highly touted Pearce-Pratt experiments. Hansel has suggested an experimental methodology for obtaining conclusive evidence for ESP involving the use of computer automated testing and scoring instruments. Such instruments came into widespread use the year following the publication of Hansel's book. Ironically, however, parapsychologists at the Foundation for Research on the Nature of Man in Durham, North Carolina, caught one of their own colleagues tampering with such a computer in order to falsify experimental results.[33] Logically speaking, there are no foolproof experiments in any science. After all, everyone may be in on the conspiracy—except us, whoever we are!

The confusion factor surrounding paranormal or alleged paranormal events is well-illustrated in the controversy surrounding Uri Geller. At the Stanford Research Institute, physicists Puthoff and Targ spent months trying to document Geller's alleged psychokinetic materializations and dematerializations, as well as metal-bending, under tightly controlled conditions. They were unsuccessful in producing publishable results. This is not to say that objects didn't actually bend right before their eyes. However, each time this occurred, uncanny coincidences prevented them from capturing the event on film or video tape and making the precise measurements they needed.[34]

Similarly, physicist David Bohm at Birkbeck College, the University of London, reports that Geller apparently dematerialized part of a vanadium carbide crystal in his laboratory under circumstances which cannot be explained by normal means and yet were insufficiently measured to provide solid scientific documentation.[35]

Magicians such as Charlie Reynolds and James Randi have further obfuscated issues by duplicating some of Geller's effects (or Ted Serios' effects) under informal conditions and claiming to be able to do the same in a scientific laboratory. Scientists in several institutions have challenged the magicians to make good on this claim. However, the magicians have either failed to perform as promised or the precise arrangements for such a contest were not agreed upon. Charles Honorton, of the Division of Parapsychology at Miamonides Hospital in Brooklyn, reports that Randi succeeded only in scratching his desk top when trying to bend a key for him.[36]

Perhaps the most quoted alleged exposé of Geller's talent was published in a *Popular Photography* article in June 1974 by Yale Joel with an accompanying piece by magician Charles Reynolds. Joel claims to have caught Geller cheating by removing the lens cap which had been taped on to a Pentax camera while attempting to take a psychic photograph of himself. The photograph which they offer as evidence does, indeed, look like it was faked as they describe. However, there is a discrepancy in this account. Joel claims to have been in the room with his son, Seth, and Geller while Geller snapped the first twelve or thirteen exposures. They then left the room to participate in another experiment, leaving the camera behind them. This is when they infer that Geller must have cheated. However, the photo which they produce as evidence is number seven on the roll, and must have been exposed in their presence! It's another confusing irony that some legitimate psychic photographs will resemble fakes.

Similar exposés of Ted Serios have been published.[37] In fact, one recent article claimed that in the presence of magician James Randi, Serios actually confessed to Dr. Jule Eisenbud that his fraudulent methods had been detected.[38] The article was published in several newspapers and Eisenbud was plagued by letters demanding an explanation. According to Eisenbud, however, the confession never occurred. This is substantiated in a series of letters between himself and Randi in which Randi backed down from his offer to duplicate the Serios phenomena before an independent panel of scientists, photographers and magicians.

Some of the confusion which skeptics create seems to be deliberate. An outstanding example of this is the notorious University of Colorado Report on Unidentified Flying Objects. Before the Air Force research funds, amounting to over half a

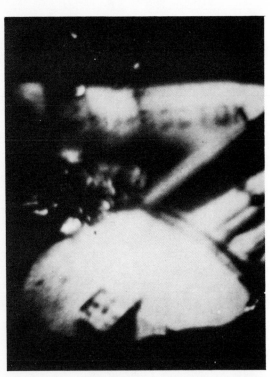

Thoughtograph of a Soviet Vostok rocket produced by Ted Serios. A diligent search of the world-wide photographic failed to produce a similar image (Courtesy Dr. Jule Eisenbud.)

million dollars, were accepted, Robert J. Low the project coordinator wrote the following memo to university administrators:*

Our study would be conducted almost exclusively by non-believers who, although they couldn't possibly *prove* a negative result, could and probably would add an impressive body of evidence that there is no reality to the observations. The trick would be, I think, to describe the project so that, to the public, it would appear a totally objective study but, to the scientific community, would present the image of a group of non-believers trying their best to be objective, but having an almost zero expectation of finding a saucer.[39]

Even though the Colorado report acknowledged that many sightings could not be explained by known physical or psychological phenomena, it concluded that UFOs were unworthy of further scientific investigation. Why anyone would suggest that science should turn its back on neglected and unexplained phenomena is a mystery. Perhaps it's because the investigation would open the Pandora's Box of magic. Perhaps it's simply another manifestation of the thermodynamic confusion factor.

Another hatchet job in the name of objective investigation is Dr. William A. Nolen's best-selling book, *Healing: A Doctor in Search of a Miracle*.[40] Nolen presents himself as an honest, open-minded surgeon who braves sleazy companions, steamy climates and ridicule from his colleagues in "the hope of finding a true healer." Nolen's quest is a story of fraud and delusion from cover to cover and ends in a smug tribute to the cooperative efforts of allopathic medicine and surgery combined with the body's natural, and still poorly understood, healing abilities.

Nolen's penetrating descriptions of what goes on behind the scenes with the superstar healer Kathryn Kuhlman and the flamboyant Norbu Chen are, in fact, quite impressive. However he managed to completely ignore all the scientific studies on psychic healing—although, in his eighteen month search he certainly could not have avoided them. Some would argue that this sort of omission is a form of professional dishonesty.

Nolen claims to have followed up a number of cases of individuals who had been treated by psychic healers in the U.S. or the Philippines. Some of his case histories are described in the book under fictitious names. Not one genuine healing was observed. In one instance, Nolen describes "Neal Cook," a wealthy businessman who had been treated for a brain tumor in the Philippines and remained there for many weeks observing the work of the healers. Nolen suggests that "Cook's" many public lectures in the U.S. (accompanied by movies) constituted a menace to the health of the community. Finally, his tumor, which had never really been removed by the Philippine

---

*The staff members who leaked this memo to the press, were, incidentally, fired.

psychics was surgically removed in the United States. Cook, having learned his lesson, now regrets his former propagandizing. A nice story, and one with a moral.

However, "Cook" is actually a pseudonym for a prominent Bay Area citizen who was interviewed by Nolen in preparation for his book. All of the details fit except for one: "Cook" (actually Don Westebeke) *never* had to have a surgical operation! While he admits that he lacks conclusive evidence that the tumor ever really existed, the tell-tale symptons which were the basis of a medical diagnosis did disappear after his treatment in the Philippines. He still tries to maintain an open mind and encourages medical researchers to explore the situation further. It appears then that Nolen's case histories are conveniently "doctored"—perhaps a little plastic surgery or grafts from other individuals—in order to create a suitable composite image.

Certainly, if the alleged psychic surgery is an actual phenomena—as many reports do suggest—the amount of confusion created in the environment from such extraordinary and frequently reported events must be considerable. Naturally this leads one to question whether the harm caused by the confusion does not, in some ways, offset the benefits of genuine psychic occurrences. Apparently what we need is some sort of "psychic lightening rod," so that the confusion created in the wake of paranormal events does not upset our efforts to carefully measure and observe them. Ideally, skepticism and belief should be carefully *grounded* in the observed facts in such a way as to become positive forces in the evolution of a truer vision of reality.

Such a balanced view is exemplified in the criticisms of Professor John Beloff at the University of Edinburgh, a parapsychologist whose careful experimental results have generally been at or below chance levels:

We naturally like to think of ourselves as somehow more imaginative, more finely attuned to nature's mysteries than other scientists and we look upon the skeptic as, by contrast, a dull dog, hidebound in his narrow and outdated materialism. Such an attitude, I submit, is a hangover from religion and has no place in science . . . If merit is anywhere involved it lies in following the implications of the evidence even when these run directly counter to one's fondest beliefs and expectations.[41]

Even though his own experiments provide very little evidence of psi, Beloff saw the need to look at all of the available data. Thus, in the midst of emotion and confusion, he retains an open mind.

Ever since the publication of *Psychic Discoveries Behind the Iron Curtain,* a book which did a great deal to expand interest in parapsychology among the American public, many have had the attitude that we are engaged in a race with the Soviets to conquer inner-space—and that the Russians are ahead! These notions are both true and false.

In 1973, leading Soviet psychologists examined the problem of parapsychology at a presidium meeting of the USSR Society of Psychologists. The results of their discussion, which may be taken as something of a policy statement from the psychology

Edward K. Naumov, a Soviet parapsychologist who has been in the forefront among those encouraging international cooperation among researchers.

298

establishment, were published in the Soviet Journal *Viprosy Filosofii* (Questions of Philosophy) and reprinted in English in the American journal *Soviet Psychology*.[42] The article, titled "Parapsychology: Fiction or Fact?" is quite revealing.

The authors include the following categories as legitimately falling within the field of parapsychology: telepathy, clairvoyance, precognition, dowsing, psychic diagnosis, psychic healing, psychokinesis, and psychic photography. While some psychical researchers are interested in yoga and astrology, the Soviet officials maintain that these topics are not legitimate concerns within parapsychology. (In fact, communist leaders now consider yoga as detrimental to a socialist society.)

It was interesting to observe that the Russian psychologists closely followed the western parapsychological literature. They observed that throughout the world, as well as in their own country, most of the commotion surrounding parapsychological phenomena is found in the popular press which generously exaggerates the achievements of psychics and researchers in an uncritical fashion. They were particularly wary of popular speculations regarding the use of parapsychology for defense, psychological warfare, or espionage. This, they felt, was a crude way of trying to obtain financial support. The state of research at the present time does not indicate that such uses are practical.

Unlike the United States, there is no parapsychological society in the Soviet Union. Enthusiastic researchers have had to form sections within other academic and scientific societies. This has naturally hampered communication among researchers. Nevertheless, Soviet researchers have been active since the pioneering studies of Professor L. L. Vasiliev, back in the 1920s, who demonstrated the ability to telepathically induce hypnotic trance states.

Perhaps the most impressive Soviet research concerns the phenomena of "dermal vision." For over a decade Professor A. S. Novomeysky and his co-workers in Sverdlovsk and adjacent Nishny Tagil have conducted meticulous investigations into this phenomena. Essentially they claim that individuals can distinguish colors through opaque screens by the sensitivity of the skin on the hands and fingers. The top Soviet academicians state that this phenomena "actually exists and deserves careful study." While they admit that they cannot determine the mechanisms of dermal vision, the tendency is to assume that it is an electrostatic sensitivity, rather than parapsychological.[43]

Many of the parapsychologists are individuals with a background in the exact sciences—physics, math, and engineering—and often have no psychological or biological training. The Soviet officials caution such people against trying to solve the most mysterious and interesting problems without adequate preparation. Many of the physical scientists seemed "childishly credulous and naive" regarding normal, as well as paranormal, psychological phenomena.

The Russians were particularly wary of individuals in the parapsychological arena who take the role of propagandists or impressarios for those who actually possess psychic abilities.

This random number generator was developed in 1967 by Milan Ryzl and his colleagues in Czechoslovakia at the same time Helmut Schmidt was designing similar devices in the United States. (Courtesy Dr. Milan Ryzl)

299

This is a large category and includes overly enthusiastic scholars as well as outright charlatans. In either case, such individuals are seen as detrimental insofar as their behavior discourages the interest of serious scientists who might otherwise make important contributions to the field. The Soviets are very clear that they wish all parapsychological findings to follow the usual protocol of publication and criticism in the standard scientific journals before presentation to the public in the popular press.

The positive effects of such a policy are considerable. Important scientific journals should be more inclined to present careful parapsychological research. The public will benefit from information which is likely to be accurate and reliable. Charlatans and profiteers will be prevented from distributing inaccurate information. However, the Soviet leaders seem to make no distinctions between the claims of mystics (whose world view may be puzzling to a bureaucratic administrator) and the fraudulent claims of pseudoscientists. Furthermore, little respect or toleration is shown for the serious scientist whose views happen to differ from the current social or scientific mores. In fact, there is a clear political interest in keeping Soviet parapsychologists from forming their own special discipline and organization, "since the only thing that unites parapsychologists is the mysterious, enigmatic nature of the phenomena they study."

Nevertheless, the Soviet leaders are urging all psychological institutes to mount programs of scientific research into these phenomena. They also suggest the organization of a laboratory to study individuals who possess unusual capacities—both parapsychological and otherwise.

Thus there is little doubt that significant research into measurable parapsychological phenomena will increase in the Soviet Union. It is also quite apparent that much of the research so far reported—including particularly the studies quoted in this book—whether American or Soviet—must be analyzed by the reader very thoughtfully. Whether or not a mutual interest in parapsychology and the development of consciousness will serve to unite communist and western peoples remains to be seen.

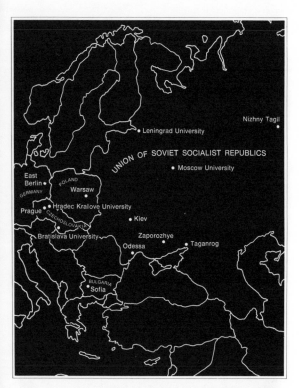

Consciousness Research centers in communist countries.
(Courtesy Psychic Magazine)

Practical Applications of PSI

Even for individuals who accept the reality of psychic abilities, the question of its practical applications remains controversial. Can these powers be used for detrimental purposes? What are the limits of psychic ability? Do psychic development courses really work? Can psychic abilities be brought under institutional or government control? Are we opening another *Pandora's Box?*

It's difficult to answer these questions based on the scant amount of solid, scientific evidence which we have so far accumulated. Certainly more inferences can be obtained by drawing upon the history, the literature, and the folk-wisdom of psi.

Many traditions teach that psychic abilities can only be used for good purposes, for instance healing. Other harmful applications are said either not to work or to rebound back upon the evil-wisher. Louisa E. Rhine takes such a stance in responding to the question of a seventh-grade enquirer:

No Nancy, ESP could not possibly be used to hurt anyone physically or mentally. It is true that sometimes people get the false idea that someone is influencing them by ESP. They think it is by telepathy, but this is very unlikely. Telepathy seldom, if ever, works that way, for no one can send his thought to another and *make him take it* . . .

The only way a person could be hurt would be by his belief that he could be so affected. It is possible sometimes for a person to "think himself sick" for other reasons and in the same way he could think himself sick by believing that someone was affecting him by telepathy. But, if so, his sickness would be caused by mistaken suggestion, not by telepathy.[44]

Mrs. Rhine has studied thousands of spontaneous ESP experiences over many decades. Her answer is reassuring and also reflects an understanding of the psychological mechanisms involved in mediating psi. It seems quite reasonable to think that individuals can reject telepathic suggestions as easily as you might reject any statement that you read in this book. For an aware and enlightened individual this would certainly be the case. It is also the case that much of what we think of as psychic phenomena is merely due to suggestion.

We might consider the reported instances of deaths, illness, and accidents from hexes, voodoo, spells, and curses to be the result of suggestion. Although, we must ask ourselves why, if psi can heal people independently of suggestion, it cannot also harm them. Isn't psi—whatever it is—likely to be a neutral force from a moral perspective? If we can use both electricity and atomic energy for good and evil, what not psi? In fact, there is some evidence that this is possible.

Ostrander and Schroeder in PDBIC report on several Soviet studies in which telepathic suggestions were used to put susceptible individuals, without their knowledge, into a hypnotic trance. Many of these experiments were carried out by Russia's pioneer parapsychologist Dr. Leonid Vasiliev and may be regarded as trustworthy accounts. Similar telepathic experiments have been used to awaken sleeping subjects, with slightly less success. However, few subjects are so susceptible and we have yet to understand the mechanisms which differentiate good and poor subjects. Research along these lines is, I would imagine, continuing in the Soviet Union.

While our understanding of such phenomena is still primitive, there is a tradition within occultism of techniques which can be used to protect oneself from "psychic attacks" of this sort.[45] Nevertheless, in spite of these real possibilities, our psychic potentials seem to offer much greater promise for effectiveness in other areas. Future psychic applications are likely to expand and ramify upon what now exists.

Dowsing, a poorly understood technique for finding underground water and minerals, is bound to become more important given our current needs for efficient development of resources. In the previous chapter, it was suggested that dowsing involved an extraordinary sensitivity to anomalies in weak magnetic fields. This is probably true, but still does not represent the entire picture.

Henry Gross, perhaps America's best known dowser, has in many instances been able to locate oil, water, minerals and even lost people by using only a map. Gross's abilities were confirmed somewhat in tests conducted by J. B. Rhine and published in 1950—however these laboratory studies were admittedly not related to dowsing as practiced by Gross in his everyday life.[46] Extensive documentation of Gross's actual work including the prevailing conditions, the people and areas involved have been published in a series of books by Kenneth Roberts.

In many instances Gross was successful in pinpointing wells when conventional geological techniques had failed or had indicated there was no water. He dowsed water for many industrial concerns including RCA Victor and Bristol-Myers pharmaceutical company. He map-dowsed from Maine fresh water in Bermuda where none had been found in 300 years. In Kansas he dowsed thirty-six wildcat oil wells and of the seventeen that were drilled he was correct in fifteen instances. Seismic predictions were wrong in nine out of seventeen cases. Although a strong advocate of Gross's abilities, Roberts also discusses a number of his failures[47,48,49]

Henry Gross's talents were investigated by the New Jersey psychiatrist and psychical researcher, Dr. Berthold E. Schwarz. His investigations included psychiatric interviews, physiological studies and field trips.[50] Schwarz found Gross—a modest, friendly game warden—to be a man of complete honesty. The physiological data, as well as direct observation, indicated that Gross expended a great deal of energy in the dowsing process. In the field studies, Schwarz was able to observe Gross successfully dowse seven oil wells in an area where oil was not geologically expected. He was also able to ascertain depth, flow and other quantitative measures that were presumably beyond the ability of normal sense perception.

In spite of his failures, Henry Gross was an unusual dowser. Few have been reported whose abilities have been so consistently demonstrated. However, with a greater social need, and more financial support, research into dowsing could be providing big payoffs. The evidence from Schwarz's report indicates that a genuine sensitivity to the psychodynamic and even the spiritual sides of life can provide rich rewards on the physical level.

In the Soviet Union, techniques of dowsing are applied to archeology. Chris Bird reports that the Russian anthropologist Pushnikov has successfully used psychic dowsers to probe the remains of the Borodino battlefield, seventy miles from Moscow, where the Russians battled Napoleon in 1812. Other Russian excavations utilized the talents of dowsers in probing the estate of the legendary Czar, Boris Gudenov.[51]

One of the most intruiging possible applications of psi are implied in the *psychotronic generators* invented in Prague by

An assortment of psychotronic generators
of various shapes and sizes developed by
Robert Pavlita of Czechoslovakia.
(Courtesy Psychic Magazine)

Robert Pavlita. These are devices which apparently have the capacity to store and utilyze "psychic energy." For example, Pavlita's daughter will "charge" a generator by concentrating on it, touching the side of her head and then touching the generator. The generators are used for an assortment of purposes such as rotating a small disc, purifying small amounts of polluted water, or acting as magnetizers. Pavlita claims that just about any material can be magnetized by one of his inventions. These generators are currently being manufactured and distributed in the United States by Mankind Research Unlimited (1143 New Hampshire Avenue, N.W., Washington, D.C. 20073).

Although Pavlita and his daughter have been able to successfully demonstrate these generators before western scientists on several occasions, other individuals have not been reported able to duplicate the effect. Like the radionics "black box," the psychotronic generator may simply be a logic-tool for breaking through one's belief barriers and focusing psychic concentration, similar to a magical amulet.

One of the most dramatic uses of psychic talent to recover treasure occurred here in the United States. The *National Enquirer* recently commissioned the Chicago psychic Olaf Jonsson to assist treasure hunters in the search for the sunken ruins of Spanish galleons loaded with gold and silver bullion. Jonsson seemed to sense the spot as the search vessel approached it and he asked the crew members to form a circle and concentrate with him. Going into trance, he actually relived the sinking of the ships. Under his directions the divers were able to recover part of the fortune, valued at $300,000.[53] Jonsson, incidently, is the same psychic who participated with astronaut Edgar Mitchell in an ESP experiment from outer-space.[54]

Some psychics have a difficult time, probably for psychological reasons, using their abilities for their own direct financial gain—although they perform satisfactorily when they charge others for "life readings," etc. Even Uri Geller fared very poorly in Las Vegas. (Although it would be interesting to test habitually successful gamblers for ESP.) The inabilities seem to be more a reflection of a person's personality, rather than a limitation upon psi itself.

A psychotronic generator designed by R. Pavlita for purification of water. Jar on the right shows murky water before treatment with psychotronically "energized" iron chips. Middle jar shows results—pollutants are attracted to the iron chips and together they precipitate to the bottom leaving clear, reportedly potable water.
(Courtesy Psychic Magazine, June 1974.)

There are things in life much more valuable than money, according to my psychic friend, Janus Moon Janus, who is clover rich. For years the clover spirits have spontaneously guided her hand to rare four-leaf clovers of which she has literally found hundreds.
(Courtesy Janus Moon Janus.)

Parapsychologists attempting to apply ESP to casino gambling have been able to use psi-missing to their advantage. In a series of studies reported by Robert Brier and Walter Tyminski several statistical techniques were used to apply ESP choices to gaming.[55] One of these was the *majority-vote technique.*

Suppose, for example, that we know a given subject can consistently score 52% on an ESP test where chance expectation is 50%. Although such scoring can be extremely significant over several thousand trials, there are many situations where one could not afford to be wrong 48% of the time. In this situation, scores can be strengthened, although the procedure is somewhat slower. Suppose we make ten guesses on each target instead of one—then we determine our final guess using the majority vote of those ten guesses. This is essentially the same repetition principle that a radio-communications engineer uses when a signal is obscured by noise. If we made a thousand guesses at the target, with 52% ESP chances are very high that a majority-vote would yield the correct answer—unless one's ESP were working in a negative direction.

Working with actual casino games as their targets, Brier and Tyminski utilized a majority-vote technique so that bets were determined by the vote of five different guesses. Furthermore, they divided the gambling situation into test-runs and play-runs. The guesses were made well in advance of the betting situation and were recorded carefully on scoring sheets. During the test-runs of twenty-five bets, the experimenters calculated whether the subject was psi-hitting or psi-missing. If the subject was showing positive psi, the play-run bets were predicted according to the regular majority vote. However, if negative-psi was indicated, the play-run bets were then predicted in the opposite direction of the majority vote. If scores in the test-run were close to chance, no attempt was made to predict the play-run bets.

This technique proved remarkably successful, from an experimental point of view, in the six test situations reported. Its promise of psi applications seems very encouraging. However, readers are not encouraged to rush out and try to apply this technique right away. The statistical procedures can be quite complex, particularly when one takes into account position effects and scoring declines. Attention must also be paid to creating a psychological atmosphere for the subject which is conducive to ESP testing. The point is simply that preliminary studies such as this clearly indicate the possible rewards of further research.

A number of case histories also testify to this possibility. For example, Dr. Georgi Lozanov, director of the Institute of Suggestology and Parapsychology in Sophia, Bulgaria, is said to have demonstrated a very impressive communications technique using the majority-vote technique. The telepathic receiver sits in front of two telegraph keys, one for each hand. Some distance away, the sender telepathically suggests that the receiver press either the right or left key, according to the beats of a metronome. Each telepathic suggestion is repeated ten times. The receiver must get six of these correct for the message

Dr. Georgi Lozanov with a subject.
(Courtesy Milan Ryzl.)

to be considered received. Lozanov reported at the 1966 Parapsychology Conference in Moscow that phrases and entire sentences have been sent this way with about 70% accuracy. Thousands of such tests are said to have now been demonstrated before many scientists.[56]

As the name of his institute implies, Lozanov is concerned with many of the psychological factors which effect ESP scores.

Using techniques derived from yoga, Lozanov combines suggestion and relaxation in a way which is different from hypnosis in that his subjects remain in the waking state. Used in education, these techniques show phenomenal promise to increase language learning, memory, artistic and musical ability.* Lozanov also is applying his techniques towards the development of mental healing and dermal vision.

One of Lozanov's many research activities involves the evaluation of the predictions made by the blind, peasant woman, Vanga Dimitrova, who may be the modern world's first government-supported prophetess. (In fact, the Institute of Suggestology and Parapsychology, with over thirty staff members, is supported by the Bulgarian government.) Studies are reported to have shown that Dimitrova's predictive abilities —particularly strong in terms of finding lost relatives and friends—are about eighty percent accurate.[56]

In Prague, Czechoslovakia, things were somewhat different. Dr. Milan Ryzl, a biochemist at the Czech Institute of Biology, had spent years trying to interest the government in supporting psychic research—all with very little success. Undaunted, Ryzl continued his own studies which, as indicated in the previous chapter, involved hypnotic techniques for developing ESP subjects. After practicing on some 500 individuals, Ryzl found fifty with very strong, testable psi abilities.

Ryzl used his psychic subjects to predict the winning numbers in the Czech public lottery. He was successful for weeks in a row, winning the equivalent of several thousand dollars. However, Ryzl's parapsychological success also proved to be detrimental to his safety. The Czechoslovakian regime became very interested in his work. He found himself constantly followed by secret agents. His manuscripts were stolen. Eventually he was asked, in rather forceful terms, to spy on his scientific colleagues in other countries. The authorities made it very clear that they were interested in the development of parapsychological techniques for espionage purposes. The government exercised such control over his life that Ryzl had no choice but to comply—or defect. His escape from Czechoslovakia was a masterpiece in precise timing. He actually contrived to leave the country with his entire family in three automobiles and many valuable possessions—including his prized library. Ironically, Ryzl recalls that the details of his defection had been predicted for him fifteen years earlier by a psychic who had been a friend of the family.[57]

Milan Ryzl with Jeffrey Mishlove

---

*In May of 1975, Lozanov spoke at several conferences of American educators who are interested in utilizing his techniques. Programs are currently being initiated through Manking Research Unlimited in Washington, D.C.

Communist researchers have continued the emphasis on the practical applications of ESP initiated by scientists such as Ryzl. Actually, since Ryzl's defection, western psychical research has become more oriented toward practical uses.

For instance, at the University of Toronto, Professor J. N. Emerson of the department of anthropology has reported on his use of psychic assistance in doing archeological field work. His friend, a psychic, George McMullen, has shown extraordinary ability to *psychometrize* artifacts and relate accurate details about the history and circumstances surrounding the object. George has also proven his usefulness in examining archeological sites before the digging begins. Just by walking over a site, he has been able to describe its age, the people who lived there, their dress, dwellings, economy and general behavior. He has also provided specific excavation guidance. Emerson estimates that George's clairvoyance is 80% accurate. Furthermore. Emerson has been able to achieve even greater degrees of accuracy by using teams of several psychics and evaluating their reports using a majority-vote technique.[58,59,60]

Other archeologists are also capitalizing on the insights of psychics. At the University of Arizona, Jeffrey Goodman has reported results as successful as Emerson's work with Canadian Indians. These studies were presented at a special meeting on parapsychology and anthropology held in Mexico City in 1974.

The use of psychics by police for solving crimes goes back many decades. As early as 1914, the Frenchman W. de Kerler, calling himself a psycho-criminologist, demonstrated on many occasions, without any reward or publicity, his ability to solve crimes which baffled police. Some of his many alleged exploits have been recorded.[61] In 1925, another case of clairvoyant detective work came to the attention of the German public. In this case, the psychic, August Drost, was on trial for fraud. The case resulted from an incident in which he had attempted, with little success, to help officials solve a burglary. During the trial, which lasted for several weeks, much of the testimony pointed toward Drost's successful ESP crime solving in other cases. He was acquitted and continued to practice his unorthodox detective work.[62]

Another psychic detective, Janos Kele, worked for years in Hungary and Germany without ever accepting fees or rewards. His abilities were tested by Professor Hans Dreisch at Leipzig University who pronounced him a "classic clairvoyant." He was also successfully tested by Dr. Karlis Osis, then at Duke University. According to Dr. Stephen Szimon, a deputy police chief in Hungary, Kele averaged 80 per cent accuracy in the clues he provided for tracing missing persons.[63]

Today in the United States, a number of police officials have publicly credited clairvoyants who have helped them with difficult investigations. One of the most prominent of these seers is Marinus B. Dykshorn, a Dutchman, whose recently published autobiography is titled, *My Passport Says Clairvoyant.*[64] Dykshorn's career spans three decades and three continents. He currently resides in the U.S. For his psychic detective work he has twice been made an associate member of the Sheriff's Association of North Carolina. In May, 1971, he received a commission from Louis B. Nunn, the governor of Kentucky as a Kentucky colonel, "in consideration of outstanding achievement." Dykshorn's book contains ten notarized affidavits from individuals who have received benefit from his clairvoyant abilities. It's particularly interesting to note in his book the difficulties which he had getting parapsychologists themselves interested in testing his abilities, well after his practical successes had been acclaimed.

Perhaps the psychic who has established the most lasting and effective relationship with police authorities is Irene F. Hughes of Chicago. Mrs. Hughes currently writes a weekly syndicated newspaper column for Community Publications. She is also the head of an organization called the Golden Path (30 W. Washington St., Chicago, Ill. 60602) where she teaches classes in psychic subjects and tests students interested in developing their own psychic abilities.[65] On the wall of her office, a plaque signed by three Chicago policemen expresses appreciation for the leads she has given in solving a number of cases. In one particular homicide case, Mrs. Hughes was able to provide police with the name and address of the murderer— adding that the case would take a long time to solve. It was, in fact, almost three years before the fugitive was found. According to crime reporter Paul Tabori, she is credited by police in Illinois with having helped to solve no less than fifteen murder cases.[66]

Irene Hughes
(*Courtesy* Psychic Magazine)

Other tested psychics who are known to have worked with police officials include Olaf Jonsson and Alex Tanous. Undoubtedly there are more who prefer to work quietly and without publicity. Police departments receive a regular stream of tips that allegedly come from psychic insights. Most of them simply don't prove useful. Nevertheless, this area deserves further exploration.

Paul Tabori writes of the Viennese Criminological Association meeting he attended in the early 1930s which was devoted to the question of "so-called occult phenomena" in police procedure and judicial investigation. Many learned academics voiced the opinion that clairvoyance, telepathy, and even hypnosis were too unreliable to be used with any advantage in police and judicial work. Equally insistent however were lawyers and police themselves who stated *practice* had proved the value of psi in certain investigations— and that it was foolish to reject it simply because of experimental and theoretical difficulties.[67]

In Berkeley, California, where the police department is respected throughout the nation as a model of professionalism and innovation, investigators often receive clairvoyant aid in solving difficult cases. Inspector Michael O'Keefe of the Berkeley Police Department informs us that whenever a significant case appears in the newspapers, calls come into the department and other agencies from individuals who feel they can help because of their "special abilities." Generally speaking, the police officials have been ill-prepared to handle this type of information. Often the psychics can only provide images and patterns which must then be interpreted. Even when solid data is given by clairvoyants, the interpretation is distorted. Police are

307

Peter Hurkos, world-famous psychic who has worked with police departments in England, France, Germany, Belgium, Holland and the United States. Research with Hurkos is described in The Sacred Mushroom by Andrija Puharich and Psychic by Peter Hurkos.

(Courtesy Psychic Magazine, April 1970.)

also uncertain just how much information to give a psychic who is working on a case.

O'Keefe admits that some psychics have been helpful in providing accurate and precise information relating to various investigations. However, he personally knew of no instances in which such information actually enabled the police to solve a crime or find a missing person. Nevertheless, members of the Berkeley Police Department, on a voluntary basis may take courses which will help them to work with psychics and also allegedly develop their own psi abilities.

One of the more ingenious uses to which psi has been put involves the use of psychokinetically triggered switches which can be hooked up to toy railroad trains, garage doors, burglar alarms, or most anything. These switches have been developed primarily by Paul Sauvin, a New Jersey engineer, who was largely inspired by the "primary perception" plant research of Cleve Backster. The switches are sensitive to very fine changes in the electrical resistance of plant leaves—changes which can be induced by psi signals sent to the plant.

For example, in one of Sauvin's early demonstrations, the switch was hooked up to an electric train like a Rube-Goldberg Machine. At a certain point along the track, the engine activated a device which sent an electric shock to Sauvin's body. This, in turn, created an emotional reaction in Sauvin which was picked up by a nearby philodendron. The electrical response of the plant then triggered the switch which would cause the train to reverse direction. Eventually, Sauvin learned that he could activate the switch simply by remembering the sensation of being shocked and projecting it mentally to the plant.[68] Currently, he believes that the plants are most responsive when positive and loving emotions are sent to them.[69]

Recently, a long-distance experiment was conducted with two psychics, Mary and Gene Condon, who were brought to San Francisco from Washington, D.C., to send psi messages to Sauvin's plants at his laboratory in New York. The experiment was arranged by Dr. Frank Lang, a Swiss film director, who carefully filmed both ends of the procedure. The Condon's had worked with Sauvin for some time and a good rapport had been maintained between them.

To further establish a psychic link with the plant, the Condon's went through a ritual of "charging" a sealed bottle of water with "psychic energy." The water was then fed to the plant. This experiment was unique in that several distinct kinds of signals were sent to the plant. First Gene concentrated on sending a sine-wave signal to the plant, then a saw-tooth wave, and then a square-wave. The plant's responses were monitered visually on an oscillograph which was filmed. Watches were synchronized on both sides of the continent to insure perfect timing. Condon's signals were received exactly as he had intended them. When Condon and his wife pictured all of the love that they felt for each other and projected that image to the plant, the recording instruments could not even keep up with the wildly fluctuating response of the plant. Then, for the grand finale, Gene Condon actually sent an SOS Morse code message (· · · --- · · ·) to the plant which was perfectly received.

308

This study is not yet published, and hasn't been sufficiently examined by other scientists. The entire experiment will be presented in Lang's film which is scheduled to be released in Europe. The practical applications of such communication abilities have not gone unnoticed by such concerns as Bell Telephone, the U.S. Army, Navy, and possibly also NASA.

The application of psi in medicine is a logical implication of the healing studies cited in the previous chapter. Dr. Bernard Grad, of McGill University, has suggested that medical schools screen prospective candidates for any natural healing talents. However, at the present time, I am aware of no instances in which the techniques of psychic healing and awareness are fully integrated into the teaching and philosophy of medical schools. There are, however, a number of situations where extra-curricular courses are taught on topics such as aura-reading and the laying-on-of-hands.*

Many psychics who feel that they have a gift for healing are reluctant to go through the training which would allow them to practice legally. In fact, a number have claimed that they would lose their abilities if they did. Naturally, this leads one to suspect fraud. However, it may be that current western medical practices do stifle the use of an intuitive, psychic, holistic, and preventive approach to healing. This need not be the case. While formal medical training is arduous and time-consuming, there seem to be many openings now in the para-medical field for psychic healers to work together with regular doctors.

Psychics can also provide useful diagnostic information. In a study recently conducted by Dr. Norman Shealy of the Pain Rehabilitation Center in LaCrosse, Wisconsin, the diagnostic talents of psychics were compared with medical doctors and with psychologists. The psychics and psychologists were shown photographs of patients, with their initials and city of residence, and were asked to fill out a complex diagnostic questionnaire. In this test, the psychologists actually scored lower than chance expectations. On over fifty items, the psychics also did not exceed chance expectations. Shealy now realizes that many of his questions were couched in medical language which would be difficult for the psychics to understand. Other questions, such as those relating to the patient's sex life seemed less relevant. However, in the two most important questions, the psychic subjects showed about 75½ accuracy. They were able to pinpoint quite accurately the location of the patient's pain as well as the etiology of the ailment.

Shealy contrasted this with medical doctors, working with actual patients, who he felt were about 80% accurate in their diagnoses. These results lead him to believe that psychic diagnosis could provide a useful adjunct to medicine—particularly in cases which have the doctors baffled.[70]

Although under few circumstances is it advisable to seek psychic diagnosis and treatment in lieu of available medical care, it's always wise to utilize all of one's resources in treating

---

*For many years now, for example, the University of California Medical Center in San Francisco has sponsored seminars on these topics with the noted psychic Jack Schwartz.

and caring for oneself. Two books, written by Mike Samuels, M.D. and Hal Bennett, deal, on a practical level, with self-care both physically and psychically. They are *The Well-Body Book* and *Be Well,* published by Random House-Bookworks.

It would be interesting to test very healthy individuals to see if they can exhibit more positive psi than normal people. Perhaps chronically ill people actually reject their own natural healing and ESP abilities and would show negative psi if tested. This hypothesis is not at all far-fetched when one considers that similar tests have been conducted with businessmen. The results were remarkable.

Professors Douglas Dean and John Mihalsky at the Newark College of Engineering PSI Communications Project have spent ten years testing the precognitive abilities of over 5,000 businessmen. They had heard numerous stories of how fortunes were made by men whose intuitive decisions seemed to defy all logical considerations. In one series of studies they looked at company presidents who had doubled their company's profits during the last five years. They found that these individuals scored much higher in the precognitive tests than other executives. In fact, the ESP test seemed to be a much better indicator of executive success than other personality measurements. A number of companies have shown an interest in using this technique to screen applicants for management positions.[71]

One of the interesting outcomes of the PSI Communications work with executives was the high percentage of subjects (about 80%) who openly acknowledged a belief in ESP. When questioned further, the businessmen admitted their belief was not based on either a familiarity with the scientific literature or an acquaintance with some psychics. These tough-minded individuals believed in ESP because they had seen it work in their own lives!

In developing your own psi abilities there will be times when you will need to throw all caution to the wind. Our own preconceptions and fears often inhibit the natural consciousness of psychic impulses. However, a note of caution at this point is appropriate.

There are hundreds of groups, churches, and organizations which claim that, for a fee, they will teach you the "secrets" of "psychic power," the "mastery of life," being "clear," or obtaining "cosmic consciousness." It's perfectly natural that a capitalistic society would foster such enterprises. Other occult traditions have generally insisted that there is little value in such mind-control type courses. Striving to attain psychic talents without first paying attention to personal growth seemed like putting the cart before the horse. "When the student is ready, the teacher will always appear," they claim. They generally stress the need to simply work on one's moral development, intellectual growth, emotional balance, and physical health.[72]

By no means are readers encouraged to try and develop their psi abilities. Such efforts often lead to delusion and imbalance. On the other hand, it would be a misuse of one's natural potential not to recognize the factual nature of psi in history and science, as well as in one's own experience. By paying attention to dreams and intuitions, you can become more familiar with the operation of psi as it already exists in your life. An awareness of subtle physiological rhythms also leads to an increased psi receptivity in a natural way. We are clearly living in a period when the options for such natural development, which used to be considered esoteric, are now open to everyone.

Most of the outstanding psychics have developed their psi rather spontaneously. Peter Hurkos' abilities appeared after an accident to his head. Uri Geller has had his abilities since childhood. Some abilities develop late in life. Some psychics learned to use their abilities through yoga or other disciplines. There are no clear rules regarding the development and use of psi.

We're not at all certain what psi even is. I can only suggest here that it is somehow related to fate. As Wittgenstein once suggested, the most wondrous fact concerning the universe is simply that it *exists.* Similarly, as suggested in the beginning of this book, for each individual the greatest mystery is his or her own existence. Everybody cannot be a great musician, artist, scientist, or psychic. But everybody can locate their own genius within. If this involves psychic development, so be it. But if one's life is truly deep and authentic, the appropriate circumstances for the enhancement of such a life can appear, as if by coincidence, with no deliberate efforts to develop or use psi!

Psychiatric studies have provided many examples of individuals who had yet to overcome their negative neurotic tendencies and whose psi abilities often worked to their own detriment.[73] Given the corruption of many social systems and beaurocracies, we seem to be fortunate in that we haven't developed greater psi abilities. Hitler, it should be noted, was a strong advocate of parapsychology and occultism.[74] Perhaps, as some mystics suggest, we will be unable to truly develop and use powerful psi abilities, without attaining the necessary spiritual growth as well. Or perhaps, focusing on personal and spiritual growth is actually the most efficient way to develop one's psi.

Tarthang Tulku, the Tibetan Lama associated with the Nyingma Institute in Berkeley, suggests that there are many arduous disciplines by which the Tibetans have been able to successfully develop a number of paranormal talents. However, the practice of simple forms of transcendental meditation, not aimed at any particular psychic achievements, generally produces equally impressive psi phenomena—which are then understood within a larger perspective.

Are psychic development courses effective? Even though the testimony of millions of individuals, who have paid for their weekend mind-control courses, would suggest so—this claim has not been confirmed through scientific studies. Admittedly scientists are somewhat hostile to the claims of charismatic figures who misuse basic terminology while maintaining that their systems are based on years of careful and expensive, albeit unpublished, research. As one psychologist stated, the published literature of mind-control organizations

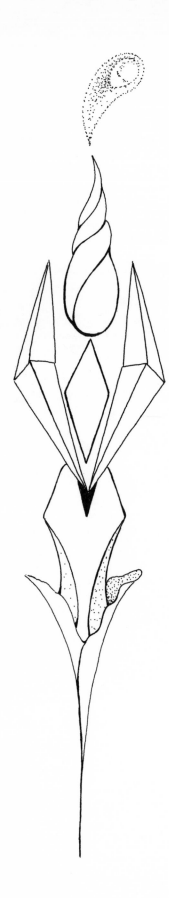

makes "suitable bed-time fairy-tale reading for the psychophysiologist."[75]

In two experimental studies conducted with mind-control graduates, procedures were set up which utilized the techniques of psychic reading already familiar to the subjects. Care was taken not to force the subjects into arbitrary or unaccustomed procedures. However, in both tests the subjects failed to demonstrate their supposed ability.[76,77]

This is not to suggest that such courses are useless, although they do tend to perpetrate certain delusions. Why have so many people been convinced that they had learned how to demonstrate ESP? This question certainly deserves further inquiry. The most likely hypothesis is that the mind-control courses give individuals an opportunity to use ESP in an optimism-inducing, highly supportive setting—which we know from laboratory studies is psi-conducive. Given the high-powered salesmanship, the morale-boosting atmosphere, and the financial investment the student has made in such a course, it is little wonder that many persons leave feeling it was a success.

The process of actually training an individual to beneficially use psi with complete accuracy is much lengthier and more difficult. Many who claim to have achieved this level are deluded. This type of training, which involves distinguishing genuine psi information from unconscious projections, demarcates the frontier of consciousness research today. Such development requires personal commitments which go beyond financial or professional obligations. When such procedures are clearly understood and developed, then the esoteric sciences will achieve maturity and full acceptance within our society.

Organizations

Out of the hundreds of organizations currently active in the area of consciousness and parapsychology, the following have particularly impressed me with their balanced perspective, their vision, and their potential social impact.

The Academy of Parapsychology and Medicine

Founded in 1970, the Academy of Parapsychology and Medicine is a non-profit educational organization established to increase man's understanding of the physical and biological sciences, metaphysics and religion as they relate to healing within a holistic world-view. It fosters scientific research within these fields and, through symposia and publications, brings the findings of such studies to the professional community and interested laymen. Dozens of significant events have been held which are summarized in several publications of the Academy.

Among the thousands of laymen and professionals who are now members of the Academy are over 600 medical doctors. The programs of the Academy have been well-received by establishment institutions.

Stemming from a conference which the Academy presented in 1974 jointly with the State of Florida Division of Retardation, a directive was initiated to develop a National Congress on Integrative Health, scheduled for the fall of 1975 at the University of Missouri. This event will explore new dimensions of diagnosis and treatment in areas of developmental dysfunction, chronic and degenerative disease, mental health and delivery systems. It has attracted the cooperative attention of a number of related agencies such as the National Association for Retarded Children and the United Cerebral Palsy Association of America. This, and the involvement of national leaders in the health care delivery system, private industry, and national media in the planning and implementation of this program, represent an unprecedented opportunity to focus top-level, broad based health establishment interest on alternative approaches to traditional Western medical practice.

Developing in parallel with the National Congress, the World Congress, planned for the fall of 1976, is designed to focus attention on alternative or nonallopathic medical practice, highlighting the distinction between medicine and health. Information about healing techniques nontraditional to Western medical practice will be gathered and communicated from major world clinical and research centers. To facilitate this, audio-visual documentation will be prepared at these centers and direct communication links via cable and satellite will be established to facilitate planning and provide flexible programming of documentary studies and interviews with world health authorities during the six-day conference.

The Academy is currently developing a computerized information center to provide up-to-date information about the progress of research in all fields relating to the healing arts and parapsychological phenomena. Through interconnecting computer data banks and a global communications network, it will eventually link definitive research throughout the world. Sophisticated natural language retrieval techniques will provide rapid access to the latest information. Now operational in part, the system links members of the Academy's National Congress Planning Committee who reside throughout the United States.

Under development, a demonstration diagnostic and treatment center is being established for the purpose of conducting trials and gaining documentation relating to the efficacy of non-traditional or alternative approaches to healing chronic and degenerative diseases, developmental dysfunction and mental illness. To be developed in a setting of unusual natural beauty, its location is uniquely suited to provide environmental conditions long considered most efficacious to a sense of well being and spiritual attunement.

The facility will be designed to provide for a small residence staff of medical professionals with additional accommodations for consulting research specialists and gifted sensitives who will participate in the exploratory program. Significant support will be provided by a resident program designed to serve as a backdrop and undergirding to the project by creating a "ground for transformation." Based in part on eurythmics and a technique of relaxation of body and mind, this proven program has been for many years associated with the site selected for the center.

A residence research facility is being proposed to create a center for ongoing dialogue among pioneering researchers and theoreticians and to establish a forum for the exchange and cross-fertilization of emerging conceptual theories underlying the psi field phenomena. Feasibility studies will be developed to explore scientist-sensitive interaction in psi field modeling, and resident inter-disciplinary colloquia utilizing advanced educational and display techniques and the communication facilities of the World Information Center will be employed. Facilitized within convenient range of Stanford and the Stanford Industrial Park complex, the Center will draw upon this outstanding scientific and technological resource in the design and implementation of its projects.

For information from the Academy regarding any of these projects as well as publications—which include a quarterly journal, a newsletter, and several symposia transcripts and tapes—contact The Academy of Parapsychology and Medicine, 314 Second Street, Los Altos, California 94022, (415) 941-0444.

The Anthroposophical Society

The Anthroposophical Society (from the Greek words *anthropos* and *sophia*, 'man' and 'wisdom') was founded in the early part of the century by Rudolf Steiner, an Austrian seer whose teachings extend throughout the range of human endeavor.

Steiner's early life was a combination of spiritual vision and prodigious scholarship. At the age of 23, he edited Goethe's scientific works for an edition of *Deutsche National-literatur*. (Steiner's view of Goethe is cited in the first chapter.) His eluci-

Rudolph Steiner

dation of Goethe's *Theory of Color* later was a deep influence on the Russian painter, Kandinsky. His early scholarship also embraced the works of Schopenhauer, Schiller, Kant and Nietzsche. Steiner's own philosophy was published in *Trust and Science* (for which he received a Ph.D. from the University of Rostock in 1891) and *The Philosophy of Freedom*. There he argued that *thought itself could become an organ of spiritual perception*.

During the course of his life, Steiner was to deliver over 6,000 different lectures, in addition to writing over sixty books as well as numerous articles and essays.[78] However, Steiner's personal accomplishments, and the activities fostered by the Anthroposophical Society, speak more eloquently than his erudite philosophy for the practical value of a "spiritual science."

As the General Secretary to the German branch of the Theosophical Society, Steiner travelled through Europe studying the art and architecture of the places he visited. In 1907, he produced Edward Schuré's *Drama of Eleusis*, at a Theosophical Congress in Munich. In the successive years, he himself wrote four mystery plays dealing with the karmic connections of a group of people through successive incarnations, with scenes in the spiritual worlds as well as on earth.

Around these dramas grew the Anthroposophical Society. To adequately portray his dramatic vision of the spiritual worlds, Steiner developed the art of *eurythmy*, a form of movement based upon speech—"speech made visible."

A western yoga, eurythmy allows the tendencies toward movement which activate the larynx to transpose themselves into the movements of the entire human body. The art of speech itself was also imbued by Steiner's emphasis on making spiritual impulses physically tangible. Few speakers have such eloquent presence as those trained in anthroposophy.

The watercolor painting on color Plate 4, "River of Light," was created by Maulsby Kimball, former director of the Anthroposophical Society in America, and is an example of the school of art founded by Steiner which attempts to portray the spiritual worlds through scintillating forms and colors.

This artistic activity required for Steiner a new form of architecture. This impulse led to the building of the first Goetheanum, at Dornach near Basle in Switzerland, as the headquarters of the Anthroposophical Society. The building also contained a massive sculpture portraying Steiner's vision of man. In 1922, the Goetheanum burnt down (sabotaged, some claim, by Steiner's enemies the Nazis). Not lacking energy, Steiner immediately designed a second structure, of a completely different and equally original style. This building remains one of the first, and finest, architectural examples of molded concrete. In addition to society headquarters, the current Goetheanum contains a theatre in which Steiner's plays, as well as Goethe's *Faust*, are performed. Performances are also held of Beethoven and Bruckner's symphonies arranged with special lights, colors and eurythmic movements. The premises also contain a scientific laboratory.

The Original Goetheanum

*The Existing Goetheanum
Dornach, Switzerland*

315

Perhaps the most significant anthroposophical "daughter movement" is the system of education instituted by Steiner and embodied in over 100 *Waldorf Schools* throughout the world. These schools, which stress the essential wholeness of man and the universe, do not attempt to serve as vehicles for indoctrinating anthroposophy or any other ideologies. Rather they serve to enhance the natural unfoldment of the genius within each child. The curriculum shows a sensitivity to the physiological rhythms of childhood development, as well as non-verbal forms of education. For instance, the alphabet is learned through body-movement and dance as well as recitation.

The anthroposophists have their own college in England, Emerson College, where Waldorf School teachers are trained. Educational programs also exist at Adelphi University in New York and Wayne State University in Michigan. The Waldorf system is actually the second-largest, non-sectarian, private school system in the world.

Steiner's thought has had an important influence on agriculture and has resulted in the bio-dynamic movement in farming which stresses the organic relationship between the soil, the plant and the animal. Also of interest are Steiner's techniques of curative education. These teachings are embodied in a rural community near Copake, New York, called Camphill Village, as well as several other small communities where the anthroposophists live communally with mentally retarded people.

In the area of medicine, hundreds of physicians are now practicing within the model outlined by Steiner. There are several organizations of anthroposophical physicians and therapists throughout the world.

All of these varied activities, and more, are said to stem from the concrete application of clairvoyant perceptions to the needs of everyday personal and community life. Yet the focus of anthroposophy, say as opposed to parapsychology, is not to measure or demonstrate *phenomena*, but rather the inner development and training of a conscious approach to the spiritual realities which penetrate all of life.

For further information about anthroposophical activities world-wide, contact:

The Rudolf Steiner Information Center
211 Madison Avenue
New York, New York 10016

International Meditation Society

According to a survey published recently in *Psychology Today*, nearly half of all individuals who have engaged in yogic or spiritual disciplines have been practicing transcendental meditation as taught by Maharishi Mahesh Yogi.[79] There are currently in America over a million meditators from all walks of life. The reason for TM's success is undoubtedly its effectiveness and simplicity.

Scientific studies now indicate that the regular practice of meditation for twenty minutes, twice a day, leads to greater relaxation, alertness, learning ability, and a reduced use of non-prescribed drugs. Some eager meditators tout TM as the perfect panacea for all personal and social ailments. Nearly a hundred scientific studies seem to support such claims,[80] and perhaps the only criticism of transcendental meditation is the enthusiasm of its proponents.

There are a multitude of growth techniques, for example autogenic training and bio-feedback, which according to the scientific research offer every bit as much promise as TM. However, none of these come complete with ancient Vedic philosophical underpinnings free of theological dogmatism, a charismatic and benevolent guru, hundreds of centers throughout the world, a television network, a host of dedicated instructors, and a genuine desire to eliminate social problems by guiding individuals to the cosmic field of pure creative intelligence.

Experimental studies, not using TM, have tended to show that meditation in general is effective in increasing ESP scores —positive and negative.[81] However, psi is not generally discussed in the lectures of the Maharishi—except in the general sense of referring to potential human resources. The essence of the Science of Creative Intelligence is that one can best utilize all of one's resources (including psi) after having achieved a state of enlightenment through meditative contact with the transcendental field of cosmic intelligence. Furthermore, although many of us have been conditioned to believe that the attainment of enlightenment is difficult and arduous, the Maharishi suggests that it is actually effortless, easy, and perfectly natural!

Of particular interest are the insights obtained from the transcendental state when applied to various fields of human knowledge. Courses of instruction, prepared by competent scientists and scholars, are now being produced on video tape and distributed throughout the world. The following fields are now included: astronomy, cosmology, physics, mathematics, chemistry, biology, psychology, medicine, literature, art, ecology, architecture, political science, history, music, philosophy and education. The Maharishi International University now offers a B.A. and other advanced degrees.[82]

For more information, contact:
International Meditation Society
1015 Gayley Avenue
Los Angeles, California 90024

Maharishi International University
Fairfield, Iowa 52556

Maharishi Mahesh Yogi

Organizations

The following organizations are listed so that interested readers may contact them for membership and information. This is by no means an exhaustive list of groups involved in promoting an understanding and expansion of consciousness; but does include the groups which have been impressive to me.

A.R.G. Owen

New Horizons Research Foundation
P. O. Box 427, Station F
Toronto, Ontario, Canada M4Y 2L8

This foundation is an almost ideal model of what a small, local research organization with a great deal of enthusiasm can accomplish. In cooperation with the Toronto Society for Psychical Research, NHRF publishes a journal called *New Horizons* which includes competent research papers on such diverse topics as dowsing, EEG studies, apparitions, auras, pyramids, strange lights, poltergeists, psychic photography, precognition, and psychokinesis. In June 1974, the foundations sponsored a very significant conference on psychokinesis, which attracted researchers throughout the world. Membership to the foundation is open and of particular interest are the psychokinetic phenomena of the *Philip* variety which have been produced by ordinary, non-psychic members of the group. Several significant books and films have resulted from the research of the NHRF.[83]

Parapsychology Foundation
29 W. 57th Street
New York, New York 10019

Founded by a medium, Eileen Garrett, this organization is active in funding research projects sponsoring scientific conferences for scholars in specific disciplines such as physics, anthropology, psychiatry, pharmacology; and publishing research monographs. For ten years it published the *International Journal of Parapsychology*. Its current publication, the bimonthly *Parapsychology Review* is perhaps the most informative periodical dealing with worldwide activity in the field. The library of the foundation contains about 8,000 volumes. The foundation also maintains a list of the hundreds of small parapsychological associations throughout the world.

Spiritual Frontiers Fellowship
800 Custer Avenue
Evanston, Illinois 60202

Parapsychological questions, particularly the issue of life beyond death, are explored within a religious or spiritual framework. The fellowship sponsors small study groups through the country and also works closely with the Academy of Religion and Psychical Research, which is located at the same address. SFF publishes a quarterly journal. *Spiritual Frontiers.*

Division of Parapsychology and Psychophysics
Miamonides Medical Center
Department of Psychiatry
4802 Tenth Avenue
Brooklyn, New York 11219

An active research center.

American Society for Psychical Research
5 West 73rd Street
New York, New York 10023

Publishes a quarterly journal and sponsors active research.

Foundation for ParaSensory Investigation
1 West 81st Street—Suite 5D
New York, New York 10024

Sponsors research as well as scientific gatherings.

Foundation for Mind Research, Inc.
315 East 86th Street
New York, New York 10028

The development of human potential by Drs. Jean Houston and R.E.L. Masters, is described in several fine books and articles.[84,85]

Association for Transpersonal Psychology
P.O. Box 595
Stanford, California 94305

Association for Humanistic Psychology
Humanistic Psychology Institute
325 Ninth Street
San Francisco, Ca. 94103

Human Dimensions Institute at Rosary Hill College
4380 Main Street
Buffalo, New York 14226

HDI is an almost ideal model of what a college-oriented organization can accomplish. Lectures and seminars are held with visiting scientists from throughout the world. Over 30 classes are held on topics ranging from yoga, creativity, the philosophy of Teilhard de Chardin, meditation, Senenca Indian wisdom, to handwriting analysis. Under the direction of Sister Justa Smith, the HDI sponsored significant research on the "Effect of the Laying on of Hands Upon Enzyme Activity." Other research continues. Weekend seminars are also held in a beautiful rural location. The Institute also publishes a quarterly journal. *Human Dimensions.*

F.R.N.M.

Foundation for Research on the Nature of Man
402 Buchanan
Durham, North Carolina 27708

FRNM was established by Dr. J. B. Rhine when he retired from Duke University in 1966. It is currently the most active parapsychological research center in the world, engaging in a variety of spontaneous case studies as well as experiments involving sophisticated computerized controls and analyses. Studies generally focus on the subtle psychological factors which effect psi scoring. The foundation publishes a quarterly *Journal of Parapsychology.* Research facilities are made available for serious students and professionals and the foundation also sponsors a summer study program to train researchers.

Psychical Research Foundation
Duke Station
Durham, North Carolina 27706

Specializes in research relating to life beyond death. Publishes a journal, *Theta.*

Association for the Understanding of Man
P. O. Box 5310
Austin, Texas 78763

Sponsors Project Starlight International. Publishes a quarterly journal.

American Society of Dowsers
Danville, Vermont 05828

New A.R.E. Library

Association for Research and Enlightenment
P. O. Box 595
Virginia Beach, Virginia 23451

Promotes inquiry into the life and work of Edgar Cayce.

Division of Parapsychology
Department of Psychiatry
School of Medicine
University of Virginia
Charlottesville, Virginia 22901

Specializes now in reincarnation cases, as well as in-depth studies of gifted psychics.

International Association for Psychotronic Research
Box 107
Cotati, California 94928

Institute of Mystical and Parapsychological Studies
John F. Kennedy University
Martinez, California 94553

Foreign Organizations

Telenoyology Group at Medical Academy
Atanas Smilov
Ivan Rilsky Street No. 55 V
Sofia 6, Bulgaria

Group for Psychotronic Investigations
Zdenek Rejdak
V Chaloupkach 59
Praha 9 — Hloubetin, Czechoslovakia

Institute of Suggestology and Parapsychology
9 Budapest St.
Sofia, Bulgaria

College of Psychic Studies
16 Queensberry Place
London SW7 2EB, England

Institute of Psychophysical Research
118 Banbury Road
Oxford OX2 8JP, England

Paraphysical Laboratory
Downton, Wiltshire, England

Religious Experience Research Unit
Manchester College
Oxford OX1 3TD, England

Society for Psychical Research
1 Adam and Eve Mews
London W8 6UQ, England

Institute Metapsychique International
1, Place Wagram
75017 Paris, France

Institut für Grenzgebeite der Psychologie und
Psychohygiene
Eichhalde 12
D78 Freiberg im Bresgau
West Germany

Department of Psychology and Parapsychology
Andhra University
Waltair
Visakhapatnam 3, India

International Society for Religion and Parapsychology
No. 121, 4 — 11 — 7 Inokashira, Mitaki-shi
Tokyo, Japan

Parapsychological Division
Psychologisch Laboratorium der Rijksuniversiteit
Varkenmarkt 2
Utrecht, Netherlands

Japanese Society for Parapsychology
26-14 Chou 4, Nakano
Tokyo 164, Japan

Theosophical Society in America
P. O. Box 270
Wheaton, Illinois 60187

R. M. Bucke Memorial Society
1266 Pine Avenue West
Montreal, Canada
    Focus is on the comparative study of mystical experience.

REFERENCES
ACKNOWLEDGMENTS
INDEX

If you didn't follow the numbered references when you read through *The Roots of Consciousness,* you may enjoy browsing through this section now. Hundreds of listings have been annotated to guide you to the most interesting and thoughtful literature in the field of consciousness.

References (Introduction)

1. *Rig Veda* 10.129, *Sources of Indian Tradition, Vol. I.,* ed. by William Theodore de Bary. New York: Columbia University Press, 1958. pp. 15–16. The two volumes of this set contain good translations for an introductory overview of religious development on the Indian subcontinent.

2. Arthur M. Young, *The Reflexive Universe.* New York: Delacorte, 1975. Young's theory, which is outlined in more detail in Chapter III, provides the link between science and mythology, and has been a great inspiration for this book.

3. Martin Gardner, "Mathematical Games," *Scientific American,* May 1974. It's ironic that Gardner, a professional skeptic, should be a spokesman for the scientific underpinnings of the paranormal. Further articles are cited by Gardner including the important paper of Hugh Everett, *Reviews of Modern Physics,* Vol. 29, July 1957, pp. 454–462.

References (Section I)

1. Heinz Werner, *Comparative Psychology of Mental Development.* New York: Science Editions, 1961. This is a classic text of cross-cultural psychological development.

2. Alexander Marshack, *The Roots of Civilization.* New York: McGraw-Hill, 1971. Scientific detective work of rare quality—well illustrated, quite technical, yet very readable.

3. Dr. Charles Musés, "A New Way of Altering Consciousness: Manual of Dynamic Resonance Meditation," *The Journal for the Study of Consciousness,* Vol. 5, No. 2, pp. 144–164. A great interdisciplinary scholar—linguist, historian, philosopher, mathematician, physicist—Musés brilliantly edited and contributed to the now defunct *J. S. C.*

4. Gerald S. Hawkins, *Stonehenge Decoded.* New York: Dell, 1965. This solution to an ancient mystery is now the basis for planetarium exhibits throughout the world.

5. Mircea Eliade, *Shamanism.* Princeton, New Jersey: Princeton University Press, 1972. The authoritative text.

6. Kilton Stewart, "Dream Theory in Malaya," *Altered States of Consciousness,* ed. by Charles T. Tart. New York: Doubleday, 1972. pp. 161–170. Stewart first introduced the amazing dream world of the Senoi to Western culture. His research has been the inspiration for several generations of scholars. Tart's anthology, incidently, remains the classic text in its field.

7. *Ibid.*

8. Michael J. Harner, ed., *Hallucinogens and Shamanism.* New York: Oxford University Press, 1973.

9. Sir Arthur Grimble, *We Chose the Islands.* New York: William Morrow, 1952.

10. Adrian K. Boshier, "African Apprenticeship," *Parapsychology Review,* Vol 5, No. 5, July-August 1974. Although Boshier's anthropological studies have received less acclaim than the similar explorations of Castaneda, they may well prove to be the most significant methodological, theoretical, and factual discoveries of the decade!

11. A. Leo Oppenheim, "Mantic Dreams in the Ancient Near East," *The Dream and Human Societies,* ed by G. E. Grunebaum and Roger Callois. Berkeley: University of California Press, 1966. An exciting and authoritative volume touching on the parapsychological as well as sociological nature of dreams.

12. Kurt Seligman, *Magic, Supernaturalism and Religion.* New York: Random House, 1948, pp. 1–11. This wonderful book is now available in paperback.

13. Roger Callois, "Logical and Philosophical Problems of the Dream," *The Dream and Human Societies.*

14. Kenneth Demarest, "The Winged Power," *Consciousness and Reality,* ed by Charles Musés and Arthur M. Young. New York: Avon, 1972. pp. 351. The accurate recording of the event referred to is quite veiled as the only preserved records come from Syncellus in Greek and Eusebius in Latin, both quoting the Greek chronicler Alexander Polyhistor, who is quoting from Berosus, who is in turn quoting from more ancient texts. This article tracing the esoteric symbology of the winged gods appears in an excellent anthology by the editors of *The Journal for the Study of Consciousness.*

15. E. A. Wallis Budge, *The Egyptian Book of the Dead.* New York: Dover, 1967. pp. lviii-lxx. Another classic.

16. *Ibid.*

17. E. A. Wallis Budge, *Osiris; the Egyptian Religion of Resurrection.* New Hyde Park, New York: University Books, 1961. First published in 1911.

18. Charles Musés, "Trance Induction Techniques in Ancient Egypt," *Consciousness and Reality,* pp. 9–17.

19. *Ibid.*

20. Manley Palmer Hall, *The Secret Teachings of All Ages.* Los Angeles: Philosophical Research Society, 1973. A magnificent, well-illustrated volume of uncertain accuracy.

21. A. L. Basham, *The Wonder That Was India.* New York: Grove Press, 1959. A fascinating document of ancient India.

22. Rammurti S. Mishra, *Yoga Sutras.* Garden City, New York: Doubleday, 1973. Linguist, yogi, psychiatrist—Mishra is one of the most articulate representatives of the Hindu tradition in the West.

23. W. Y. Evans-Wentz, *The Tibetan Book of the Dead.* London: Oxford University Press, 1960. Although the cumbersome translation is often difficult to follow, this book still remains a classic. The text contains commentaries by Carl Jung, Lama Anagarika Govinda, and Sir John Woodroffe.

24. *Ibid.,* p. 103.

25. *Ibid.,* p. 165–166.

26. W. Y. Evans-Wentz, *Tibet's Great Yogi, Milarepa.* New York: Oxford University Press, 1958.

27. *The Secret of the Golden Flower,* trans. by Richard Wilhelm. New York: Harcourt, Brace and World, 1962.

28. Richard Wilhelm, "Introduction," *The I Ching,* trans. by Richard Wilhelm. Princeton, New Jersey: Princeton University Press, 1970.

29. Michael Kahn, Theodore C. Kroeber and Sherman Kingsbury, "The *I Ching* as a Model for a Personal Growth Workshop, *Journal of Humanistic Psychology,* Vol. 14, No. 3, Summer 1974, pp. 39–51.

30. "Parapsychological Association, 14th Annual Convention (1971)," *Journal of Parapsychology,* December 1971, pp. 313–314. This paper refers to an experiment by Lawrence Rubin and Charles Honorton of the Miamonides Medical Center in Brooklyn. Forty subjects asked questions and threw coins for an *I Ching* reading. The experimenters then showed subjects the correct hexagram along with a control hexagram which was randomly chosen. Subjects who believed in the *I Ching* were able to identify the correct hexagram as being most appropriate to their questions. Non-believers generally could not differentiate the two hexagrams.

31. Ceasare de Vesme, *A History of Experimental Spiritualism,* Vol 1, trans. by Stanley de Brath. London: Rider and Co., 1931. This scholarly work quotes Herodotus (i, 47–48).

32. Manley Palmer Hall, *Secret Teachings,* p. LVII. While Hall claims that his ideas are derived from the great nineteenth century Greek translator Thomas Taylor, he does not provide specific source references.

33. William Godwin, *Lives of the Necromancers.* London: Frederick J. Mason, 1834. p. 82. While scholarly and skeptical,

this book contains some delightful excursions (such as the visit to a midieval magus who claims that *he* summoned *you)* and is well worth reading. For further reference on Pythagoras he cites Clemens Alexandrinus, Stromata, Lib. I, p. 302.

34. Walter Buckert, *Lore and Science in Ancient Pythagoreanism,* trans. by Edwin J. Minar, Jr. Cambridge, Mass.: Harvard University Press, 1972. p. 357. A most comprehensive modern volume on the Pythagorean tradition.

35. E. R. Dodds, "Supernormal Phenomena in Classical Antiquity," *Proceedings of the Society for Psychical Research,* March 1971. p. 194. Since its inception, the S. P. R. in Britian has been graced with gifted classical scholars, Dodds being among the most recent.

36. Plato, *The Republic, Book VII,* trans. by B. Jowett, New York: Vintage.

37. *Ibid., Book X*

38. Frank Thilly, *A History of Philosophy,* revised by Ledger Wood. New York: Henry Holt and Company, 1957.

39. *Iamblichus on The Mysteries of the Egyptians, Chaldeans and Assyrians,* translated from the Greek by Thomas Taylor. London: Bertram Dobell, 1895.

40. Tacitus, *Historia,* Lib. IV, p. 81. This passage was quoted in Ceasare de Vesme, *op cit.*

41. Lynn Thorndike, *A History of Magic and Experimental Science, Vol. 1.* New York: Columbia University Press, 1923. This magnificent treatise is *the* authoritative work in its field. The work is in eight volumes which were written over 35 years. If not otherwise noted, much of the material from this chapter through Newton, can be traced to Thorndike.

42. Violet MacDermot, *The Cult of the Seer in the Ancient Middle East.* Berkeley: University of California Press, 1971. An entertaining and most thorough scholarly examination.

43. Charles Poncé, *Kabbalah.* San Francisco: Straight Arrow, 1973, p. 35. This book is most valuable for its integration of many Hebrew and Christian systems.

44. Morton Smith, *Clement of Alexandria and a Secret Gospel of Mark.* Cambridge, Mass.: Harvard University Press, 1972. p. 357.

45. Violet MacDermot, *op. cit.*

46. D. D. Home, *Lights and Shadows of Spiritualism.* London: Virtue and Co., 1878. p. 77. Actually Home is quoting directly from Augustine, but neglected to acknowledge the specific source. It's interesting to note that the great nineteenth century medium placed himself in the same tradition as the venerable saint.

47. Evelyn Underhill, *Mysticism.* New York: E. P. Dutton, 1961, p. 331. Augustine here is quoted in a volume first published in 1911 which still remains the authoritative analysis of mysticism in western culture. The source is given as St. Augustine, Book vii, cap. xvii.

48. Aldous Huxley, *The Perennial Philosophy.* New York: Harper and Row, 1945.

49. Francis Yates, *Giordano Bruno and The Hermetic Tradition.* New York: Random House, 1969. p. 150. Yates is one of the most active and knowledgable new wave scholars exploring the occult roots in renaissance culture.

50. Wayne Shumaker, *The Occult Sciences in the Renaissance.* Berkeley: University of California Press, 1972. p. 225. A useful reference volume lacking both condescension and credulousness.

51. Charles Poncé, *op. cit.*

52. Carl Jung, *Alchemical Studies.* Princeton, New Jersey: Princeton University Press, 1967. Jung opened up a vast area of exploration by probing the psychological meanings within the enigmatic alchemical symbolism.

53. Kurt Seligman, *op. cit.* p. 120.

54. Lynn Thorndike, Vol. VIII. pp. 361–2, 470, 570.

55. Kurt Seligman, *op. cit.* pp. 123–4.

56. Lynn Thorndike, Vol. I. p. 643.

57. *Ibid.*

58. Idries Shah, *Oriental Magic.* New York: Philosophical Library, 1956. pp. 61–2. Hundreds of these delightful Sufi tales have been recorded and translated by Shah, who is now a spiritual father to story lovers throughout the world. It is said that one can develop inwardly by merely listening to these "teaching stories."

59. Francis Yates, *op. cit.*

60. Fulcanelli: Master Alchemist, *Le Mystère des Cathedrales,* trans. by Mary Sworder. London: Neville Spearman, 1971. Beautiful photography illustrates the alchemical symbolism built into the midieval cathedrals.

61. Lynn Thorndike, Vol. I. pp. 517–592.

62. *The Cloud of Unknowing,* ed. and trans. by Ira Progoff. New York: Julian Press, 1957. A classic guide to spiritual experience and the dynamics of the inner-life.

63. Dante Alighieri, *Purgatorio,* trans. by John D. Sinclair. New York: Oxford University Press, 1968. Canto ix.

64. Petirim A. Sorokin, *The Crisis of Our Age.* New York: E. P. Dutton and Co., 1957. p. 19. One of the greatest sociologists, Sorokin clearly placed himself within the mystic tradition. He was the only sociologist to predict the turmoil of our own period—which he did before W. W. II.

65. Thorston Sellin, "The House of Correction for Boys in the Hospice of Saint Michael in Rome," *Journal of the American Institute of Criminology and Law,* Vol. 20, No. 4, 1929, p. 550. This article written by one of America's great criminologists is a translation from the Italian research of Morichini who traced the forgotten origins of our penal systems to the Catholic Church. Only now are some innovative prison administrators realizing the potential of "ideational" growth techniques (i.e., yoga, meditation, psychodrama, EST) for genuine personal growth within the institutions.

66. Emory S. Borgadus, *The Development of Social Thought.* New York: Longmans, Green and Company, 1957. p. 169.

67. Thorston Sellin, "Dom Jean Mabillon—A Prison Reformer of the Seventeenth Century," *Journal of the American Institute of Criminology and Law,* Vol. 17, No. 4., 1926, p. 583. Sellin quotes from a treatise of this early reformer titled "Reflections on the Prisons of the Monastic Orders."

68. Johan Huizinga, *The Waning of the Middle Ages.* Garden City, New York: Doubleday, 1956, p. 17. This historical work, known for the beauty of its lyrical style, was written by a scholar with deep feeling for his subject.

69. *The Book of the Sacred Magic of Abra-Melin the Mage,* trans. by S. L. MacGregor-Mathers. Chicago: The deLaurence Co., 1948. There are scholarly disputes as to the actual authorship, date and origins of this grimoire. The magical operation itself seems to have captivated the imagination of British occultists in the Order of the Golden Dawn during the early part of the twentieth century. It's not known that anyone in recent times, however, has performed the invocations with success. Even the indomitable Aleister Crowley acknowledged failure.

70. Sayed Idries Shah, *The Secret Lore of Magic,* New York: The Citadel Press, 1970. pp. 226–229. Shah is quoting from Turner's eighteenth century translation of Agrippa.

71. Lynn Thorndike, Vol. V. pp. 617–651.

72. Paracelsus, *Selected Writings,* ed. by Jolande Jacobi. Princeton, New Jersey: Princeton University Press, 1951.

73. Peter J. French, *John Dee.* London: Routledge and Kegan Paul, 1972. This book has helped to establish Dee's forgotten importance as a renaissance figure.

74. Francis A. Yates, *The Rosicrucian Enlightenment.* London: Routledge and Kegan Paul, 1972. A fascinating, yet scholarly, history regarding the controversial origins of the famous Rosicrucians.

75. Lynn Thorndike, Vol. VII. pp. 11–32.

76. Wolfgang Pauli, "The Influence of Archetypal Ideas on The Scientific Theories of Kepler," *The Interpretation of Nature and The Psyche.* New York: Pantheon, 1955. Pauli, a Nobel prize physicist, was one of the first to inquire into the quantum physics of consciousness. He was known throughout Europe for the poltergeist-like effects which he seemed to have on laboratory equipment (the "Pauli effect"). Pauli studied with Carl Jung who contributed his important essay on *synchronicity* to this volume.

77. *A Christian Rosenkreutz Anthology*, ed. by Paul M. Allen. Blauvelt, New York: Rudolf Steiner Publications, 1974. p. 179. Deep within the mainstream of the western occult tradition, the anthroposophists have published the finest single anthology of Rosicrucian writings.

78. Francis Bacon, "Selections From *New Atlantis*," *On the Margin of the Visible*, ed. by Edward A. Tiryakian. New York: John Wiley and Sons, 1974. p. 143. This volume is the first product of another new wave of scholars who are attempting sociological analyses of esoteric movements, modern and historical.

79. Francis Yates, *The Rosicrucian Enlightenment*.

80. Thomas Vaughan, "The Holy Mountain, A Rosicrucian Allegory" *A Christian Rosenkreutz Anthology*. For a modern version of the same story see René Daumal, *Mt. Analogue*. San Francisco: City Lights Books, 1968.

81. Lynn Thorndike, Vol. VII. pp. 544–566.

82. Francis Yates, *The Art of Memory*. London: Penguin, 1969. p. 368. This interesting book shows the deep interconnections between mnemonics—the art of memory—the renaissance theatre, and the occult tradition.

83. Thilly, *op. cit.* p. 384–399.

84. Thorndike, Vol. VIII, p. 591. Thorndike here is quoting Lord Keynes.

85. *Ibid.*

86. *Ibid.*

87. Wilson Van Dusen, *The Natural Depth in Man*. New York: Harper and Row, 1972. Perhaps the most profound, yet simplist, study of the inner life of man.

88. Emmanuel Swedenborg, *The Heavenly Arcana*, Vol. II. New York: American Swedenborg Pub. Soc., 1873. pp. 114–121.

89. Wilson Van Dusen, *The Presence of Other Worlds*. New York: Harper and Row, 1974. A very sensitive biography of Swedenborg. Formerly the chief psychologist at a mental hospital in California, Van Dusen began to treat the hallucinations of his patients as if they were spirits. The experiment worked. In fact, he realized that he was encountering the very same world of spirits as described in the encyclopediac writings of Swedenborg.

90. C. D. Broad, *Religion, Philosophy and Psychical Research*. New York: Harcourt Brace, 1953. pp. 115–116. The case for Swdenborg is presented by the Emmanuel Kant in a letter sent to Fraulein von Knobloch. Later, in an anonymously published manifesto, Kant essentially retracted his support of the claims for Swedenborg. The evidence one way or another is actually quite shaky. Broad, an eminant philosopher of this century, demonstrates that Kant, undoubtedly a great thinker, was nevertheless, a very careless psychical researcher. This book is very valuable for its examination of the deep philosphical implications of psi.

91. Rudolf Steiner, *Goethe The Scientist*, trans. by Olin D. Wannamaker. New York: Anthroposophic Press, 1950. pp. 168–169. This book provides a beautiful example of the esoteric tradition within the very core of western cultural history——another anthroposophic classic.

92. Benjamin Franklyn, Lavoisier, Bailly, Guillotin, *et. al.*, "Secret Report on Mesmerism or Animal Magnetism," *The Nature of Hypnosis*, ed. by Ronald E. Shor and Martin T. Orne. New York: Holt, Rinehart and Winston, 1965. pp. 3–7.

93. Suzy Smith, *ESP and Hypnosis*. New York: Macmillan, 1972. p. 27.

94. Franz Anton Mesmer, *Mémoire sur la Découverte du Magnétisme*. Quoted in *ibid*.

95. J. P. F. Delevze, "Rules of Magnetising," *The Nature of Hypnosis*, pp. 24–29.

96. Charles Richet, *Thirty Years of Psychical Research*, trans. by Stanley de Brath. New York: Macmillan, 1923. p. 22. Richet is a French physiologist, also a Nobel Laureate, who figures prominently in the early years of psychical research.

97. Frank Podmore, *From Mesmer to Christian Science*. New Hyde Park, New York: University Books, 1965.

98. Karl von Reichenbach, *The Odic Force*, trans. and intro. by F. D. O'Byrne. New Hyde Park, New York: University Books, 1968.

99. G. Stanley Hall, *Founders of Modern Psychology*. New York: D. Appleton and Company, 1924. pp. 129–130. An innovative American psychologist, Hall actually studied with many of the German pioneers, such as Fechner, whom he writes about. This book touches on the human side of psychology's birth as a science.

100. *Ibid.* pp. 133–136.

101. *Ibid.* pp. 141–142.

102. *Ibid.* pp. 148–149.

103. *Ibid.* p. 151.

104. Alan Gauld, *The Founders of Psychical Research*. London: Routledge and Kegan Paul, 1968. This book is undoubtedly the best historical overview of the early years of the British S. P. R. If not otherwise noted, much of the material in this chapter relating to psychical research will be cited from Gauld.

105. Sir William Crookes, "Notes of an Inquiry into the Phenomena called Spiritual," *Crookes and the Spirit World*, ed. by R. G. Medhurst. New York: Taplinger, 1972. This volume contains descriptions of Crookes' experiments as well as his replies to his critics.

106. Nandor Fodor, *Encyclopedia of Psychic Science*. London: Arthur's Press, 1933. p. 95. Crookes is quoted by Fodor in what must be regarded as the most comprehensive single volume of paranormal peculiarities ever published. The book is now available in paperback edition through Citadel Publishers.

107. Charles Richet, *op. cit.*

108. Camille Flammarion, *Mysterious Psychic Forces*. Boston: Small, Maynard and Co. 1907. The famous French astronomer recounts his own personal experiences with Kardec.

109. Pedro McGregor, *The Moon and Two Mountains*. London: Souvenir Press, 1966. A fascinating first-hand account of spiritualism in Brazil.

110. Charles Richet, *op. cit.* pp. 407–408.

111. Sir William Crookes, "Experimental Investigation of a New Force," *Crookes and The Spirit World*. p. 24.

112. *Ibid.* p. 26.

113. D. D. Home, *op. cit.*

114. Sir William Crookes, "The Last of Katie King," *Crookes and the Spirit World*. p. 138. A poignant, yet comical story.

115. Sir William Crookes, "Spirit Forms," *Crookes and the Spirit World*. pp. 135–136.

116. Harry Price, *Fifty Years of Psychical Research*. London: Longmans, Green and Co., 1939.

117. *Proceedings of the Society for Psychical Research*, Vol. I, 1882, pp. 3–4.

118. Edmund Gurney, F. W. H. Myers and Frank Podmore, *Phantasms of the Living*. Gainesville, Florida: Scholars' Facsimiles and Reprints, 1970. pp. 163–164. This section is quoted in Gauld, *op. cit.* pp. 165–166.

119. "Notes on the Evidence Collected by the Society for Phantasms of the Dead," *Proceedings of the Society for Psychical Research*, Vol. III, 1885, pp. 69–150. This information is cited in Gauld, *op. cit.*

120. *Preliminary Report of the Commission Appointed by the University of Pennsylvania to Investigate Modern Spiritualism in Accordance with the Request of the Late Henry Seybert*. Philadelphia: 1887. pp. 150–151. This information is quoted in Gauld, *op. cit.*

121. Alan Gauld, *op. cit.* p. 208n. Gauld is citing a story mentioned in Julia Garrett, *Mediums Unmasked*. Los Angeles: 1892. p. 50.

122. Richard Hodgson, "Report of the Committee Appointed to Investigate Phenomena Connected with the Theosophical Society," *Proceedings of the Society for Psychical Research*, Part IX, December 1885.

123. Victor A. Endersby, *The Hall of Magic Mirrors*. New York: Carlton Press, 1969. Delightfully written with careful

scholarship (sometimes) and a consistent sense of humor, this book is now difficult to obtain. It is, however, available from the author c/o Box 427, Napa, California 94558.

124. Gertrude Marvin Williams, *Priestess of the Occult.* New York: Knopf, 1946. This biography, which depicts Blavatsky as a colorful charlatan, details various charges of plagiarism against her.

125. Alan Gauld, *op. cit.* pp. 226–228. Gauld is quoting here from the *Journal of The Society for Psychical Research,* Vol. VI, 1894, pp. 350–357.

126. Camille Flammarion, *Mysterious Psychic Forces.* pp. 75–76.

127. Charles Richet, *op. cit.* pp. 506–508.

128. *Ibid.* p. 543.

129. *Ibid.* p. 543–544.

130. Gauld, *op cit.* p. 253. Gauld here is quoting William James from *The Proceedings of the S. P. R.,* 1886.

131. Nandor Fodor, *Encyclopedia of Psychic Science,* p. 170.

132. F. W. H. Myers, *The Human Personality and It's Survival of Bodily Death.* New York: Longmans, Green and Co., 1954. p. xxix. This book remains *the* classic of psychical research!

133. *Ibid.* p. 333. Myers is quoting from Wordworth's "Prelude," Book VI.

134. *Ibid.* p. 360–366. Myers quotes the report published by Dr. E. W. Stevens in the *Religio-Philosophical Journal,* Chicago, 1879.

135. *Ibid.* pp. 367–368. Myers quotes Hodgson's report published in the *Religio-Philosophical Journal* for December 20, 1890.

136. William James, "What Psychical Research Has Accomplished," *William James on Psychical Research,* ed. by Gardner Murphy and Robert O. Ballou. London: Chatto and Windus, 1961. Originally published in *The Will to Believe and Other Essays,* 1897.

137. William James, "The Final Impressions of a Psychical Researcher," *William James on Psychical Research.* Originally published in *The American Magazine,* October 1909.

References (Section II)

1. Harry Price, *Fifty Years of Psychical Research.* London: Longmans, Green and Co., 1939. pp. 73–74. Price, who founded the National Laboratory of Psychical Research in London, was involved in exposing many fraudulent "psychics."

2. J. G. Pratt, J. B. Rhine, *et al., Extra Sensory Perception After Sixty Years.* New York: Henry Holt and Co., 1940. This book remains a classic document of ESP experimentation—the bible of card-guessing research.

3. J. B. Rhine, *Extra-Sensory Perception.* Boston: Society for Psychical Research, 1933. pp. 73–74.

4. Pratt and Rhine, *op. cit.*

5. Rhine, *Extra-Sensory Perception.*

6. Michael Scriven, "The Frontiers of Science: Psychoanalysis and Parapsychology," *Frontiers of Science and Philosophy,* ed. by Robert G. Colodny. Pittsburgh: University of Pittsburgh Press, 1962. pp. 79–130. A former president of the Oxford University Society for Psychical Research, Scriven is now highly respected as a philosopher of science and education. In this essay he dissects the relative scientific merits of psychoanalysis and parapsychology. Parapsychology, although less popular, proves more reasonable.

7. C. E. M. Hansel, *ESP: A Scientific Evaluation.* New York: Scribner's, 1966.

8. Ian Stevenson, "An Antagonist's View of Parapsychology. A Review of Professor Hansel's *ESP: A Scientific Evaluation,*" *Journal of the American Society for Psychical Research.* Vol. 61, July 1967, pp. 254–267. Stevenson points out that Hansel bases his conclusions on an inaccurate diagram of Pratt's office.

9. R. A. McConnell, R. J. Snowdon and K. F. Powell, "Wishing With Dice," *Journal of Experimental Psychology,* 50, 1955, pp. 269–275.

10. Helmut Schmidt, "Quantum Processes Predicted?" *New Scientist,* 44, 1969, pp. 114–115.

11. J. G. Pratt, *et. al.,* "Identification of Concealed Randomized Objects Through Acquired Response Habits of Stimulus and Word Association," *Nature,* Vol. 220, No. 5162, October 5, 1968, pp. 89–91.

12. Stanford Research Institute, news release, October 1974. This material was published by Puthoff and Tart in an article titled "Information Transmission Under Conditions of Sensory Shielding," in *Nature,* October 18, 1974.

13. J. C. Barker, "Premonitions of the Aberfan Disaster," *Journal of the Society for Psychical Research,* 44, 1967, pp. 169–180.

14. E. W. Cox, "Precognition: An Analysis, I," *Journal ASPR,* 50, 1956, pp. 47–58.

15. E. W. Cox, "Precognition: An Analysis, II," *Journal ASPR,* 50, 1956, 97–107.

16. Alan Vaughan, *Patterns of Prophecy.* New York: Hawthorne, 1973. pp. 37–55. Vaughan, one of the most success-

fully tested precognitive subjects, is also a researcher and theorist. His book provides a detailed discussion of the archetypal patterns of time.

17. *Ibid.* pp. 66–69, 101–102.

18. Helmut Schmidt, "A Quantum Process in Psi Testing," *Progress in Parapsychology,* ed. by J. B. Rhine. Durham, North Carolina: Parapsychology Press, 1973. pp. 28–35.

19. Helmut Schmidt, "A Quantum Mechanical Random Number Generator for Psi Tests," *Journal of Parapsychology,* 34, 1970, pp. 219–224.

20. Helmut Schmidt, "Precognition of a Quantum Process," *Journal of Parapsychology,* 33, 1969, pp. 99–108.

21. Helmut Schmidt, "PK Tests with a High-Speed Random Number Generator," *Journal of Parapsychology,* December 1973, pp. 105–118.

22. Carroll B. Nash, "Can Precognition Occur Diametrically?" *Journal of Parapsychology,* March 1960, pp. 26–32. Although the results of this study indicate significantly less than chance scores, it's major interest is the use of Dow-Jones averages eighteen months in the future as targets.

23. Rammurti S. Mishra, *Yoga Sutras.* New York: Anchor Press, 1973. pp. 131–176.

24. Jane Roberts, *The Seth Material.* Englewood Cliffs, N. J.: Prentice-Hall, 1970, p. 109.

25. Max Heindel, *The Rosicrucian Cosmo-Conception.* Oceanside, Ca.: The Rosicrucian Fellowship, 1969. p. 67.

26. D. Scott Rogo, *Parapsychology: A Century of Inquiry.* New York: Taplinger, 1975. This book appears to be the most thorough overall history of experimental parapsychology now available. Rogo points out that in the very early years of testing it was discovered that the best subjects were also the best experimenters.

27. E. Douglas Dean, "The Plethysmograph as an Indicator of ESP," *Journal SPR,* 41, 1962, pp. 351–353.

28. E. Douglas Dean and C. B. Nash, "Plethysmograph Results Under Strict Conditions," Sixth Annual Convention of the Parapsychological Association, New York, 1963.

29. Charles T. Tart, "Possible Physiological Correlates of Psi Cognition," *International Journal of Parapsychology,* 5, 1963, pp. 375–386.

30. Montague Ullman, Stanley Krippner, and Alan Vaughan, *Dream Telepathy.* New York: Macmillan, 1973. A valuable feature of this book is that, like *ESP After Sixty Years,* the authors invited contributions from known critics of their work.

31. Stanley Krippner, Charles Honorton and Montague Ullman, "An Experiment in Dream Telepathy with The Grateful Dead," *Journal Am. Soc. of Psychosomatic Dentistry and Medicine,* Vol. 20, No. 1, 1973.

32. Charles Honorton, "State of Awareness Factors In Psi Activation," *Journal ASPR,* 68, July 1974, pp. 246–256.

33. Stanley Krippner, James Hickman, *et. al.,* "Clairvoyant Perception of Target Material in Three States of Consciousness," *Perceptual and Motor Skills,* 35, 1972, pp. 439–446.

34. Charles Honorton, "Significant Factors in Hypnotically-Induced Clairvoyant Dreams," *Journal ASPR,* Vol. 66, No. 1, January 1972, pp. 86–102.

35. Edward A. Charlesworth, "Psi and the Imaginary Dream," Seventeenth Annual Convention of the Parapsychological Association, New York, 1974.

36. Gertrude R. Schmeidler, "High ESP Scores After a Swami's Brief Instruction in Meditation and Breathing," *Journal ASPR,* Vol. 64, No. 1, January 1970, pp. 101–103.

37. Karlis Osis and Edwin Bokert, "ESP and Changed States of Consciousness Induced by Meditation," *Journal ASPR,* Vol. 65, No. 1, January 1971, pp. 17–65.

38. Emille Boirac, *Our Hidden Forces,* London: Rider, 1918.

39. Rogo, *op. cit.* p. 238.

40. Boirac, *op. cit.*

41. *Ibid.*

42. Shiela Ostrander and Lynn Schroeder, *Psychic Discoveries Behind The Iron Curtain,* Englewood Cliffs, N. J.: Prentice-Hall, 1970. pp. 37–40.

43. Charles Honorton and Stanley Krippner, "Hypnosis and ESP: A Review of the Experimental Literature," *Journal ASPR,* 63, 1969, pp. 214–252.

44. H. Kanthamani and E. F. Kelly, "Awareness of Success in an Exceptional Subject," *Journal of Parapsychology,* Vol. 38, No. 4, December 1974, pp. 355–382.

45. Charles Honorton and James C. Terry, "Psi-mediated Imagery and Ideation in the Ganzfeld: A Confirmatory Study," Seventeenth Annual Convention of the Parapsychological Association, New York, 1974.

46. Lendell W. Braud and William G. Braud, "The Psi Conducive Syndrome: Free Response GESP Performance During an Experimental Hypnagogic State Induced by Visual and Acoustic Ganzfeld Techniques," Parapsychological Association Convention, New York, 1974.

47. John Palmer and Isabelle Aued, "An ESP Test with Psychometric Objects and the Ganzfeld: Negative Findings," Parapsychological Association Convention, New York, 1974.

48. J. G. Pratt and M. Price, "The Experimenter-Subject Relationship in Tests for ESP," *Journal of Parapsychology,* 1938, pp. 84–94.

49. Charles Honorton, "Experimenter Effects and ESP," Parapsychological Association Convention, Edinburgh, Scotland, 1972. Proceedings of the Parapsychological Association conventions are published by the Scarecrow Press, Metuchen, New Jersey.

50. Adrian Parker, "A Pilot Study of the Influence of Experimenter Expectancy on ESP Scores," Parapsychological Association Convention, New York, 1974.

51. H. C. Berendt, "Parapsychology in Israel," *Parapsychology Today: A Geographic View,* ed. by Allan Angoff and Betty Shapin. New York: Parapsychology Foundation, 1973. p. 68.

52. Gertrude R. Schmeidler and R. A. McConnell, *ESP and Personality Patterns.* New Haven: Yale University Press, 1958.

53. John Palmer, "Scoring in ESP Tests as a Function of Belief in ESP. Part I. The Sheep-Goat Effect," Journal ASPR, 65, 1971, pp. 373–408.

54. B. K. Kanthimani and K. R. Rao, "Personality Characteristics of ESP Subjects," *Journal of Parapsychology,* Vol. 36, 1972, pp. 56–70.

55. Milan Ryzl, "A Method of Training in ESP," *International Journal of Parapsychology,* Vol. 8, No. 4, Autumn 1966.

56. J. G. Pratt, *ESP Research Today,* Metuchen, N. J.: Scarecrow Press, 1973. pp. 84–100.

57. Milan Ryzl, *How To Develop ESP In Yourself and Others.* This is the training course recently developed by Dr. Ryzl. It includes a booklet and tape cassettes and is available from Ryzl c/o P.O. Box 9459, Westgate Station, San Jose, Ca. 95117.

58. Russell Targ and David B. Hurt, "Learning Clairvoyance and Perception With an Extrasensory Teaching Machine," *Parapsychology Review,* Vol. 3, No. 4, July-August 1972, pp. 9–11.

59. Russell Targ and Phyllis Cole, "Use of an Automatic Stimulus Generator to Teach Extrasensory Perception," Parapsychological Association Convention, New York, 1974.

60. Rex G. Stanford and Gary Thompson, "Unconscious Psi-mediated Instrumental Response and its Relation to Conscious ESP Performance," Parapsychological Association Convention, Charlottesville, Virginia, 1973.

61. Yogi Ramacharaka, *Yogi Philosophy and Oriental Occultism.* Chicago: Yogi Publication Society, 1931. pp. 192–199.

62. Sylvan Muldoon and Hereward Carrington, *The Projection of the Astral Body.* New York: Samuel Weiser, 1970. pp. 61–62. Originally published in 1929, as a collaborative effort between an excellent researcher and an unusual psychic, this book remains a standard reference in the OBE literature.

63. Frederick Myers, *Human Personality and Its Survival of Bodily Death,* Vol. I, New York: Longmans, Green, 1954, pp. 682 ff.

64. Muldoon and Carrington, *op. cit.,* p. 164.

65. *Ibid.,* p. 80.

66. Oliver Fox, *Astral Projection.* New Hyde Park, New York: University Books, 1962.

67. Roy Ald, *The Man Who Took Trips.* New York: Delacorte, 1971.

68. Robert Monroe, *Journeys Out of the Body.* New York: Doubleday, 1971. Monroe has written the clearest contemporary account of the out-of-body experience. The book contains a preface by Charles Tart describing research with Monroe.

69. Robert Crookall, *The Study and Practice of Astral Projection.* New York: University Books, 1966.

70. Robert Crookall, *Out-of-the-Body Experiences.* New York: University Books, 1970. pp. 14–15.

71. *Ibid.*

72. Charles Tart, "Out-of-the Body Experiences," *Psychic Exploration,* ed. by Edgar Mitchell and John White. *New York: G. P. Putnam's Sons,* 1974. pp. 349–357.

73. *Celia Green, Out-of-the-Body Experiences.* New York: Ballantine, 1973.

74. N. Lukianowicz, "Autoscopic Phenomena," *American Medical Association Archives of Neurological Psychiatry,* Vol. 80, 1958, pp. 199–220.

75. Dean Lucas, "Review of *The Jung-Jaffe View of Out-of-the-Body Experiences* by Robert Crookall," *Theta,* No. 38, Winter 1973. *Theta* is the Journal of the Psychical Research Foundation in Durham, North Carolina, one of the most active research centers exploring OBEs.

76. Hereward Carrington, *Modern Psychical Phenomena.* New York: Dodd, Mead and Co., 1919. pp. 146–154. Another of Carrington's many good books.

77. Charles Tart, *op. cit.*

78. J. Hartwell, J. Janis and Blue Harary, "A Study of the Physiological Variables Associated with Out-of-Body Experiences," Parapsychological Association Convention, New York, 1974.

79. Robert L. Morris, "PRF Research on Out-of-Body Experiences, 1973," *Theta,* No. 41, Summer 1974.

80. Janet Mitchell, "Out-of-Body Vision," *Psychic Magazine,* April 1973, pp. 44–47. *Psychic Magazine* is undoubtedly the finest popular publication dealing with psychic matters. Sometimes original research studies are reported before publication in scientific journals.

81. Ingo Swann, *To Kiss Earth Good-Bye,* New York: Hawthorne, 1975. This excellent book contains Swann's critical comments on scientific psychical research as well as his au-

tobiography. It is written in a very sensitive and erudite, yet lyrical style.

82. *Ibid.*

83. Karlis Osis, "Out-of-Body Research at the ASPR," *ASPR Newsletter,* No. 22, Summer 1974.

84. Harold Puthoff and Russell Targ, "Psychic Research and Modern Physics," *Psychic Explorations.* pp. 536–538.

85. Inge Strauch, "Medical Aspects of Mental Healing," *International Journal of Parapsychology,* Vol. 5, 1963, pp. 140–141.

86. Sally Hammond, "What the Healers Say," *Psychic Magazine,* August 1973.

87. Strauch, *op. cit.* This is definitely one of the most interesting studies of mental healing.

88. F. Papentin, "Self-purification of the Organism and Transcendental Meditation: A Pilot Study," *Scientific Research on Transcendental Meditation: Collected Papers, Vol. 1.* ed. by D. W. Orme-Johnson, L. Domash, and J. Farrow. Los Angeles: MIU Press, 1975.

89. A. H. Schmale Jr, M.D. and P. Iker, Ph.D., "The Affect of Hopelessness and the Development of Cancer," *Psychosomatic Medicine,* Vol. 28, 1966, pp. 714–721.

90. Jean Shinoda Bolen, M.D., "Meditation in the Treatment of Cancer," *Psychic Magazine,* August 1973, p. 20.

91. O. Carl Simonton, M.D., "Management of the Emotional Aspects of Malibnancy," Symposium of the State of Florida, Department of Health and Rehabilitative Service, June 1974. Simonton can be contacted through Oncology Associates, 1413 Eighth Avenue, Fort Worth, Texas.

92. Bernard Grad, R. J. Cadoret, and G. I. Paul, "The Influence of an Unorthodox Method of Treatment on Wound Healing of Mice," *International Journal of Parapsychology,* Vol. 3, 1961, pp. 5–24.

93. Bernard Grad, "A Telekinetic Effect on Plant Growth," *International Journal of Parapsychology,* Vol. 6, 1964, p. 473.

94. Bernard Grad, "The 'Laying on of Hands': Implications for Psychotherapy, Gentling, and the Placebo Effect," *Journal ASPR,* Vol. 61, No. 4, October 1967, pp. 286–305.

95. C. B. Nash and C. S. Nash, "The Effect of Paranormally Conditioned Solution on Yeast Fermentation," *Journal of Parapsychology,* Vol. 31, 1967, p. 314.

96. Sister M. Justa Smith, "Effect of Magnetic Fields on Enzyme Reactivity," *Biological Effects of Magnetic Fields,* ed. by Madeleine F. Barnothy. New York: Plenum Press, 1969.

97. Sister M. Justa Smith, "The Influence on Enzyme Growth By the 'Laying on of Hands,'" *Dimensions of Healing.* Los Altos, California: Academy of Parapsychology and Medicine, 1973.

98. Douglas Dean, "The Effects of Healers on Biologically Significant Molecules," *New Horizons,* Vol. 1, No. 5, January 1975, pp. 215–219. This exciting issue contains the Proceedings of the First Canadian Conference on Psychokinesis and Related Phenomena, June 1974.

99. *Ibid.*

100. John Hubacher, Jack Grey, Thelma Moss and Francis Saba, "A laboratory Study of Unorthodox Healing," Second International Psychotronics Conference, Monaco, 1975.

101. Ambrose and Olga Worrall, *Explore Your Psychic World.* New York: Harper and Row, 1970. pp. 99–100.

102. Robert N. Miller, Phillip B. Reinhart, Anita Kern, "Research Report: Ernest Holmes Research Foundation," *Science of Mind,* July 1974, pp. 12–16. This is a publication of the United Church of Religious Science.

103. *Ibid.*

104. Robert N. Miller, Ph. D., "The Positive Effect of Prayer on Plants," *Psychic Magazine,* April 1972, p. 25.

105. Peter Tompkins and Christopher Bird, *The Secret Life of Plants.* New York: Harper and Row, 1973. pp. 317–360.

106. A. R. G. Owen, *Psychic Mysteries of the North.* New York: Harper and Row, 1975. p. 125. Owen briefly describes his successful research with a radionics operator.

107. Vernon D. Wethered, *An Introduction to Medical Radiesthesia and Radionics.* Ashingdon, Rochford, Essex, England: C. W. Daniel Company, 1957, p. 75.

108. Tompkins and Bird, *op. cit.,* p. 333.

109. Arthur M. Young, "Reflections." Transcribed from a seminar at the Institute for the Study of Consciousness, Berkeley, California.

110. Francis K. Farrelly, "The Enigmatic Status of Radionics in the United States," *First International Conference on Psychotronics,* Prague, 1973.

111. William A. Tiller, "Radionics, Radiesthesia and Physics," *The Varieties of Healing Experience.* Los Altos, Ca.: Academy of Parapsychology and Medicine. 1971.

112. Tompkins and Bird, *op. cit.,* pp. 350–351.

113. Arthur M. Young, unpublished study.

114. Tompkins and Bird, *op. cit.,* p. 351.

115. Graham K. Watkins and Anita M. Watkins, "Possible PK Influence on the Resuscitation of Anesthetized Mice," *Journal of Parapsychology,* Vol. 35, No. 4, December 1971, pp. 257–272.

116. Graham K. Watkins and Roger Wells, "Linger Effects in Several PK Experiments," Parapsychological Association Convention, Charlottesville, Virginia, 1973.

117. Andrija Puharich, M. D., "Some Biophysical Aspects of Healing," *Dimensions of Healing,* Los Altos, Ca.: Academy of Parapsychology and Medicine, 1973.

118. *Ibid.*

119. Anne Dooley, *Every Wall a Door.* New York, E. P. Dutton, 1974. p. 144. Dooley here is quoting Puharich.

120. Puharich, *op. cit.*

121. Anne Dooley, *op. cit.*

122. Tom Valentine, *Psychic Surgery.* Chicago: Henry Regnery, 1973.

123. Doug Voeks and Jeffrey Mishlove, "Psychic Surgery," radio program broadcast on KPFA-FM in Berkeley, California, August 1973.

124. Yogi Ramacharaka, *Yogi Philosophy and Oriental Occultism.* Chicago, Yogi Publishing Co., 1931. pp. 154–163.

125. Yogi Ramacharaka, *The Hindu-Yogi Science of Breath.* Chicago: Yogi Publishing Co., 1905. pp. 68–72.

126. *Ibid.*

127. Ho Ku-li, "Firewalking in Hsinchuang," *Echo of Things Chinese,* January 1972, pp. 18–24. Available from ECHO Magazine Company, 5-2 Pa Teh Road, Section 4, Lane 72, Alley 16, Taipei, Taiwan, The Republic of China.

128. Harry Price, "A Report on Two Experimental Firewalks," *Bulletin II.* London: University of London Council for Psychical Investigation, 1936.

129. Harry Price, *Fifty Years of Psychical Research.* pp. 250–262.

130. Earl of Dunraven, *Experiences in Spiritualism with D. D. Home.* Glasgow: Robert Maclehose and Co., 1924. A great classic of psychical investigation. Introduction by Sir Oliver Lodge.

131. William Crookes, "Notes of Seances with D. D. Home," *Proceedings SPR,* Vol. 6, 1889–1890.

132. Elmer Green and Alyce Green, "The Ins and Outs of Mind-Body Energy," *Science Year 1974, World Book Science Annual.* Chicago: Field Enterprises Educational Co., 1973. p. 146.

133. Berthold E. Schwarz, M. D., "Ordeal By Serpents, Fire and Strychnine," *Psychiatric Quarterly,* Vol. 34, July 1960, pp. 405–429.

134. Louisa E. Rhine, *ESP in Life and Lab—Tracing Hidden Channels.* New York: Macmillan, 1967. pp. 166–168.

135. J. B. Rhine and L. E. Rhine, "The Psychokinetic Effect. I. The First Experiment," *Journal of Parapsychology,* 7, 1943, pp. 20–43.

136. Louisa E. Rhine, *op. cit.,* p. 175.

137. Soji Otani, "Past and Present Situation of Parapsychology in Japan," *Parapsychology Today: A Geographic View.* pp. 34–35.

138. J. Gaither Pratt, *ESP Research Today*. Metuchen, New Jersey: The Scarecrow Press, 1973. pp. 108–109. An insider's view of developments in parapsychology.

139. Jule Eisenbud, M. D., *The World of Ted Serios*. New York: William Morrow, 1967. p. 332. An outstanding example of careful and thorough psychical investigation—at once the best single study of psychic photography and the most brilliant psychodynamic analysis of a gifted subject.

140. Pratt, *op. cit.*, p. 114.

141. Ostrander and Schroeder, *PDBIC*. p. 84.

142. *Ibid.*, pp. 60–61.

143. *Ibid.*, p. 407.

144. J. G. Pratt, and H. H. J. Keil, "Firsthand Observations of Nina S. Kulagina Suggestive of PK Upon Static Objects," Parapsychological Association Convention, Charlottesville, Virginia, 1973.

145. H. H. J. Keil and Jarl Fahler, "Nina S. Kulagina: A Strong Case for PK Involving Directly Observable Movements of Objects Recorded on Cine Film," Parapsychological Association Convention, New York, 1974.

146. Montague Ullman, "Report on Nina Kulagina," Parapsychological Association Convention, 1973.

147. Benson Herbert, "Report on Nina Kulagina," *Journal of Paraphysics*, 1970, Nos. 1, 3, 5.

148. Lecture Presented by Stanley Krippner, U. C., Davis, 1973.

149. Charles Honorton, "Report on the Psychokinesis of Felicia Perez," Parapsychological Association Convention, 1973.

150. Graham Watkins, "Report on Felecia Perez," Parapsychological Association Convention, 1973. Testing in Durham, North Carolina, Watkins was able to obtain psychokinetic fogging of photographic film with Ms. Perez.

151. Harold Puthoff and Russell Targ, "Psychic Research and Modern Physics," *Psychic Exploration*. pp. 522–542.

152. Gertrude R. Schmeidler, "PK Effects Upon Continuously Recorded Temperatures," *Journal ASPR*, Vol. 67, No. 4, October 1973, pp. 325–340. In this experiment, Ingo Swann, repeatedly demonstrated his ability to induce temperature changes, both positive and negative according to instructions, in an insulated thermistor, from a distance of some 25 feet.

153. Andrija Puharich, *Beyond Telepathy*. New York: Doubleday, 1972.

154. Russell Targ and Harold Puthoff, "Experiments with Uri Geller," Parapsychological Association Convention, 1973.

155. Jack Sarfatti, "Geller Performs for Physicists," *Science News*, Vol. 106, No. 3, July 20, 1974, p. 46.

156. H. H. J. Keil and Scott Hill, "Mini-Geller PK Cases," Parapsychological Association Convention, 1974.

157. Uri Geller, *My Story*. New York: Praeger, 1975. Geller's own documentation of his worldwide spoonbending stir. This book should be read by anyone interested in the social ramifications of psi.

158. A. R. G. Owen, "Editorial," *New Horizons*, Vol. 2, No. 1, April 1975, p. 1.

159. Wilbur Franklyn, "Fracture Surface Physics indicating Teleneural Interaction," *New Horizons*, Vol. 2, No. 1, April 1975, pp. 8–13.

160. W. G. Roll, "Poltergeists," *Encyclopedia of the Unexplained*, ed. by Richard Cavandish. New York: McGraw-Hill, 1974. p. 200.

161. *Ibid.*

162. A. R. G. Owen, *Can We Explain the Poltergeist?* New York: Taplinger, 1964.

163. Matthew Manning, *The Link*. New York: Holt, Rinehart and Winston, 1975.

164. *Matthew Manning: Study of a Psychic*. This movie, made on location in England, shows how Matthew, an English schoolboy, developed the powers of clairvoyance and psychokinesis and brought them under voluntary control. The film may be hired or purchased from George Ritter Films Limited, 2264 Lakeshore Boulevard West, Toronto, Ontario M8V 1A9, Canada.

165. Peter Bander, "Introduction," *The Link*.

166. Brian Josephson, "Possible Relations Between Psychic Fields and Conventional Physics," and "Possible Connections Between Psychic Phenomena and Quantum Mechanics," *New Horizons*, Vol. 1, No. 5, January 1975.

167. A. R. G. Owen, "A Preliminary Report on Matthew Manning's Physical Phenomena," *New Horizons*, Vol. 1, No. 4, July 1974, pp. 172–173.

168. Joel L. Whitton, " 'Ramp Functions' in EEG Power Spectra during Actual or Attempted Paranormal Events," *New Horizons*, July 1974, pp. 173–186.

169. Iris M. Owen and Margaret H. Sparrow, "Generation of Paranormal Physical Phenomena in Connection with an Imaginary Communicator," *New Horizons*, Vol. 1, No. 3, January 1974, pp. 6–13.

The authors give us the following references for the British work:

K. J. Batcheldor, "Report on a Case of Table Levitation and Associated Phenomena," *Journal SPR*, Vol. 43, No. 729, September 1966; pp. 339–356.

C. Brookes-Smith and D. W. Hunt, "Some Experiments in Psychokinesis," *Journal SPR*, Vol. 45, No. 744, June 1970, pp. 265–281.

C. Brookes-Smith, "Data-tape Recorded Experimental PK Phenomena," *Journal SPR*, Vol. 47, No. 756, June 1973, pp. 68–89.

170. *Philip, The Imaginary Ghost*. This film may be hired or purchased from George Ritter Films Limited.

171. Iris M. Owen, " 'Philip's' Story Continued," *New Horizons*, Vol. 2, No. 1, April 1975.

172. Joel L. Whitten, "Qualitative Time-domain Analysis of Acoustic Envelopes of Psychokinetic Table Rappings," *New Horizons*, April 1975.

173. Helmut Schmidt, "PK Tests With a High Speed Random Number Generator."

174. Helmut Schmidt, "PK Experiments With Animals as Subjects," *Journal of Parapsychology*, Vol. 34, No. 4, December 1970, pp. 255–261.

175. G. N. M. Tyrrell, *Apparitions*. New Hyde Park, New York: University Books, 1961. pp. 69–70. Originally published in 1953, this book is valuable for its penetrating analysis of a difficult issue.

176. *Ibid.*, pp. 77–80.

177. *Ibid.*, pp. 132–133. The original material comes from H. M. Wesermann, *Der Magnetismus und die Allgemeine Weltsprache*, 1822.

178. Karlis Osis, *Deathbed Observations by Physicians and Nurses*. New York: Parapsychology Foundation, 1961.

179. William G. Roll, "Survival Research: Problems and Possibilities," *Psychic Exploration*. pp. 397–424.

180. G. N. M. Tyrrell, *Science and Psychical Phenomena*. New Hyde Park, New York: University Books, 1961. pp. 175–179. The actual quote is from William James in *Proceedings SPR*, Vol. 28, pp. 117–121.

181. Sir Oliver Lodge, *Raymond or Life and Death*. New York: George H. Doran, 1916. p. 90. Very popular in its day, this book still remains a classic in the literature of survival.

182. *Ibid.*, pp. 98–99.

183. *Ibid.*, p. 100.

184. *Ibid.*, p. 102.

185. Rosalind Heywood, *Beyond the Reach of Sense*. New York: E. P. Dutton, 1974. p. 118. A researcher as well as a sensitive, Heywood is one of the grand ladies of psychical research. This book provides an excellent general treatment of the early research.

186. Tyrrell, *op. cit.*, pp. 230–250.

187. Nandor Fodor, *Encyclopedia of Psychic Science*. London: Arthur's Press, 1933. pp. 71–72. Another classic work, very complete, full of odd facts. Now reprinted in paperback by Citadel.

188. *Ibid.*, 67–68.

329

189. Ian Stevenson, M.D., *Twenty Cases Suggestive of Reincarnation*. New York: American Society for Psychical Research, 1966.

190. Ian Stevenson, M.D., "Xenoglossy: A Review and Report of a Case," *Proceedings ASPR*, Vol. 31, February 1974.

191. Andrija Puharich, *Uri*. New York: Doubleday, 1974.

192. Martin Gardner, "What Hath Hoova Wrought?" *New York Review of Books*, May 16, 1974.

193. Jacques and Janine Vallee, *Challenge to Science: The UFO Enigma*. Chicago: Henry Regnery, 1966.

194. J. Allen Hynek, "Twenty-one Years of UFO Reports," *UFO's, A Scientific Debate*, ed. by Carl Sagan and Thornton Page. New York: W. W. Norton, 1972. This book contains the proceedings of a symposium on UFO's at the convention of the American Academy for the Advancement of Science in Boston, 1969.

195. E. U. Condon, *Scientific Study of Unidentified Flying Objects*. New York: Bantam, 1969.

196. J. Allen Hynek, *The UFO Experience: A Scientific Inquiry*. Chicago: Henry Regnery, 1972.

197. Bruce C. Murray, "Reopening the Question. Review of *The UFO Experience* by J. Allen Hynek," *Science*, Vol. 177, No. 4050, Aug. 25, 1972. pp. 688–689.

198. Charles Bowen, ed., *The Humanoids*. Chicago: Henry Regnery, 1969. This volume prepared by the editors of *Flying Saucer Review* contains accounts of encounters and observations from many different countries of probable UFO occupants.

199. B. E. Schwarz, "Stella Lansing's UFO Motion Pictures," *Flying Saucer Review*, Vol. 18, No. 1, Jan-Feb 1972, pp. 3–12. FSR generally provides the best international coverage of UFO sightings. Subscriptions can be obtained from FSR Publications Ltd., P.O. Box 25, Barnet, Herts. EN5 2NR, England.

200. B. E. Schwarz, "Stella Lansing's Movies of Four Entities and Possible UFO," *Flying Saucer Review*, Special Issue No. 5, *UFO Encounters*.

201. B. E. Schwarz, "Stella Lansing's Clocklike UFO Patterns," *Flying Saucer Review*, Vol. 20, No. 4, January 1975, pp. 3–9.

202. B. E. Schwarz, "Stella Lansing's Clocklike Patterns of UFO Shapes. Part II," *Flying Saucer Review*, Vol. 20, No. 5, March 1975, pp. 20–27.

203. Dwight Connelly and Joseph M. Brill, "Rhodesian Case Involves Occupants, Transportation of Auto," *Skylook*, No. 89, March 1975, pp. 3–9. This is the monthly publication of the Mutual UFO Network, 26 Edgewood Drive, Quincy, Illinois 62301.

204. Ray Stanford, "Uri: The 'Geller Effect'," and "The 'Geller Effect' Part Two," *Journal of the Association for the Understanding of Man*, 1974. This journal is available from A. U. M., P. O. Box 5310, Austin, Texas 78763.

205. Aimé Michel, "The Strange Case of Dr. X," *Flying Saucer Review*, Special issue No. 3, September 1969, pp. 3–16.

206. Jacques Vallee, "UFOs: The Psychic Component," *Psychic Magazine*, February 1974, pp. 12–17.

207. Ralph Blum and Judy Blum, *Beyond Earth: Man's Contact With UFOs*. New York: Bantam, 1974.

208. *Ibid.*, pp. 143–145.

209. Benjamin Simon, M. D., "Introduction," *The Interrupted Journey*, by John G. Fuller. New York: Dial Press, 1966.

210. Terrence Dickinson, "The Zeta Reticuli Incident," *Astronomy*, Vol. 2, No. 12, December 1974, pp. 4–19.

211. Ralph Blum, *op. cit.*, pp. 107–120. Blum's account contains transcripts of hypnotic sessions with Schirmer.

212. Jeffrey Mishlove, Leo Sprinkle, Herbert Schirmer, "Nebraska UFO Contact," radio interview broadcast on *Mindspace*, KSAN-FM in San Francisco, November 1974. This is one of my weekly radio programs.

213. Jeffrey Mishlove and Robert Monroe, "UFOs and Out-of-Body Experience," radio interview broadcast on *Mindspace*, March 1975.

214. Robert Monroe, *Journeys Out of The Body*. New York: Doubleday, 1971. p. 153.

215. Charles Bowen, "Few and Far Between," *The Humanoids*. pp. 20–22.

216. C. G. Jung, *Flying Saucers*. New York: Harcourt, Brace and Co., 1959.

217. Edward J. Ruppelt, *The Report on Unidentified Flying Objects*. New York: Doubleday, 1956. An inside story of the Air Force UFO Investigations.

218. Major Donald E. Keyhoe, *Aliens From Space*. New York: Doubleday, 1973. This is Keyhoe's most recent book on the UFO issue. His stance is generally quite critical of the Air Force investigations.

219. Ray Stanford, *Fatima Prophecy*. Austin, Texas: Association for the Understanding of Man, 1972. pp. 3–24.

220. *Ibid.*, pp. 43–50.

221. C. J. Ducasse, *Paranormal Phenomena, Science and Life After Death*. New York: Parapsychology Foundation, 1969. Ducasse is quoting from Abraham Cummings, *Immortality Proved by the Testimony of Sense*, Bath, Maine, 1826.

222. Andrija Puharich, *Uri*. pp. 151–152.

223. *Ibid.*, p. 152.

224. Eileen Garrett, *Awareness*. New York: Garrett Publications, 1943. pp. 29–30.

225. Kenneth Demarest, "The Winged Power," *Consciousness and Reality*, ed. by Charles Musès and Arthur M. Young, New York: Avon, 1972.

226. Andrija Puharich, *op. cit.*, p. 185.

227. Bob Tobin, Jack Sarfatti and Fred Wolf, *Space-Time and Beyond*. New York: E. P. Dutton, 1975. Funny, scientific, understandable, profound.

228. Jeffrey Mishlove and Jack Sarfatti, "Toward a Physics of Consciousness," *Mindspace* radio broadcast September 1974.

229. J. Allen Hynek, *The UFO Experience*.

230. Shafica Karagula, *Breakthrough to Creativity*. Santa Monica, Ca.: De Vorss, 1967. pp. 110–113. Dr. Karagula is a neuropsychiatrist with an excellent research background. However, her published reports rarely contain the detail and precision necessary for a scientific evaluation.

231. "Interview with Ray Stanford," *Psychic Magazine*, April 1974, p. 11.

232. *Ibid.*

233. Jeffrey Mishlove and Ray Stanford, "UFOs and Psychic Phenomena," *Mindspace* radio broadcast, December 1974.

234. "Interview with Ray Stanford," p. 10. While Stanford clearly distinguishes his psychic experiences from his UFO contact, he also maintains that the "visitation of UFOs to earth is archetypically a counterpart of the higher being coming down and contacting man through the traditional third eye and, perhaps through the pineal and pituatary glands." This applies to UFOs that are experienced in dreams.

235. Richard F. Thompson, *Foundations of Physiological Psychology*. New York: Harper and Row, 1967.

236. Joseph E. Bogen, "The Other Side of the Brain: An Appositional Mind," *The Nature of Human Consciousness*, ed. by Robert Ornstein. San Francisco: W. H. Freeman, 1973. pp. 101–125. An excellent anthology of scientific, philosophical and literary material.

237. Frederick Myers, *Proceedings SPR*, 1885, p. 63.

238. A. T. W. Simeons, M.D., *Man's Presumptuous Brain*. New York: E. P. Dutton, 1961. One of the most enjoyable and knowledgeable studies of brain science ever written. Even in an age of information-explosion, still worth reading.

239. Barbara Brown, *New Body, New Mind*. New York: Harper and Row, 1974. The story of biofeedback research seen through the eyes of one of the most colorful pioneer investigators.

240. Frank X. Barron, Murray Jarvik and Sterling Bunnell, Jr., "The Hallucinogenic Drugs," *Contemporary Psychology Readings From Scientific American*. San Francisco: W. H. Freeman, 1971. p. 305.

241. A. P. Krueger and S. Kotaka, "The Effects of Air Ions on Brain Levels of Serotonin in Mice," *International Journal of Biometeorology*, Vol. 13, No. 1, 1969, p. 27.

242. Angela Longo, " 'To Sleep; Perchance to Dream?' A Neurochemical Study of the States of Sleep." Unpublished paper, 1971.

243. John N. Bliebtrau, *The Parable of the Beast*. New York: Macmillan Company, 1968. p. 74.

244. Gunther Stent, *Scientific American*, September 1972.

245. Phillip Handler, ed., *Biology and the Future of Man*. New York: Oxford University Press, 1970. pp. 59–60. A survey of the life sciences sponsored by the National Academy of Sciences.

246. Dr. Albert Krueger, "Are Negative Ions Good for You?" *New Scientist*, June 14, 1973, p. 668.

247. A. P. Krueger, "Preliminary Consideration of the Biological Significance of Air Ions," *Scientia*, September 1969.

248. Krueger and Kotaka, "The Effects," p. 31–44.

249. A. P. Krueger, P. C. Andriese and S. Kotaka, "Small Air Ions: Their Effect on Blood Levels of Serotonin in Terms of Modern Physical Theory," *Int. J. Biometeor.*, Vol. 12, No. 3, pp. 225–239.

250. Krueger and Kotaka, The Effects, p. 33.

251. Krueger, "Are Negative Ions Good for You?"

252. N. Robinson and F. S. Dirnfield, "The Ionization of the Atmosphere As a Functioning of Meterological Elements and of Various Sources of Ions," *Int. J. Biometeor.*, Vol. 3, No. 2, March 1963.

253. A. Danon and F. G. Sulman, "Ionizing Effect of Winds of Ill Repute and Serotonin Metabolism," *Proceedings of the Fifth International Biometeorological Congress*, Sept. 1969.

254. E. Stanton Maxey, M.D., "Letter to the Editor: Electromagnetism," *Aviation Week and Space Technology*, May 29, 1972, p. 64.

255. A. P. Krueger, "Biological Effects of Ionization of the Air," *Progress in Biometerology*, ed. by S. W. Tromp. Amsterdam: Swets and Zeitlinger, 1974. p. 32.

256. A. P. Krueger, personal communication to the author.

257. Walter M. Elsasser, "The Earth as Dynamo," *Scientific American*, May 1958. This article provides a basic explanation of the earth's magnetic field.

258. James B. Beal, "The Emergence of Paraphysics: Research and Applications," *Psychic Explorations*. Beal is in the process of an intensive study of the electrostatic properties of the human body. His article is an excellent survey of this research as it relates to consciousness.

259. T. and B. Dŭll, "Über die abhängigkeit des Gesundheitszustandes von plötzlichen Eruptionen auf der Sonne und die Existenz einer 27 tägigen Periode in den Sterbefällen," *Virschows* Archiv, No. 293, 1934. This study is summarized in Michel Gauquelin, *The Scientific Basis of Astrology*. New York: Stein and Day, 1969.

260. Howard Friedman, Robert O. Becker and Charles Bachman, "Geomagnetic Parameters and Psychiatric Hospital Admissions," *Nature*, Vol. 200, November 16, 1963, pp. 626–628.

261. Michael Persinger, "ELF Waves and ESP," *New Horizons*, Vol. 1, No. 5, January 1975, pp. 232–235.

262. M. A. Persinger, *The Paranormal. Part II: Mechanisms and Models*. New York: M. S. S. Information Corp., 1974.

263. Selco Tromp, "Review of the Possible Physiological Causes of Dowsing," *International Journal of Parapsychology*, Vol. 10, No. 4, 1968. Tromp, a Dutch researcher, is currently the executive editor of the *International Journal of Biometeorology*.

264. Y. Rocard, "Actions of a Very Weak Magnetic Gradient: The Reflex of the Dowser," *Biological Effects of Magnetic Fields* ed. by Madeleine F. Barnothy. New York: Plenum Press, 1969.

265. *Ibid.*, p. 281.

266. Tromp, *op. cit.*

267. Yurij A. Kholodov, "Electromagnetic Fields and the Brain," *Impact: of Science on Society*, Vol. 24, No. 4, October 1974, pp. 291–297. Kholodov is one of the top Soviet researchers in the area of biomagnetic interactions. This entire issue of *Impact*, published by UNESCO, is devoted to the international developments in the "parasciences."

268. Yuri Kholodov, "The Brain and the Magnetic Field," *Journal of Paraphysics*, Vol. 6, No. 4, 1972, pp. 144–147. This article provides a more detailed description of Kholodov's experiments. Several other articles in this issue of the *Journal of Paraphysics*, published in England by Benson Herbert, deal with bio-magnetics.

269. A. S. Presman, *Electromagnetic Fields and Life*, trans. by F. L. Sinclair, ed. by F. A. Brown. New York: Plenum Press, 1970. This volume is a thorough compendium of the Soviet work in bio-magnetics. Presman is on the biophysics faculty at Moscow University.

270. Victor Yagodinsky, "The Magnetic Memory of the Virus," *Journal of Paraphysics*, Vol. 6, No. 4, 1972, p. 141. Translated from the Russian.

271. Sister M. Justa Smith, "The Influence on Enzyme Growth by the 'Laying on of Hands,' " *Dimensions of Healing*. Los Altos, Ca.: Academy of Parapsychology and Medicine, 1973.

272. Svetlana Vinokurava, "Life in a Magnetic Web," *Journal of Paraphysics*. Vol. 5, No. 4, 1971, p. 135.

273. Homer Jensen, "The Airborn Magnetometer," *Scientific American*, Vol. 202, No. 6, June 1961, p. 152. A graphic description of the process used for mapping the earth's magnetic smile.

274. Pedro McGregor, *The Moon and Two Mountains*. London: Souvenir Press, 1966. This book offers an unusual balance of emotional involvement and sociological objectivity. The author, an educated journalist, is also the founder of a spiritist church which is attempting to synthesize the many conflicting strains of Brazilian magic.

275. Charles C. Conley, "Effects of Near-Zero Magnetic Fields on Biological Systems," *Biological Effects of Magnetic Fields*, Vol. 2.

276. R. R. Koegler, S. M. Hicks, L. Rogers and J. H. Barger, "A Preliminary Study in the Use of Electrosleep Therapy in Clinical Psychiatry," *The Nervous System and Electric Currents*, ed. by Norman L. Wulfson. New York: Plenum Press, 1970. pp. 137–143. Not satisfied with the quality of the European work, these American researchers conducted their own study with encouraging results. This volume contains the Proceedings of the Third Annual National Conference of the Neuro-Electric Society.

277. Gay Gaer Luce, *Biological Rhythms in Human and Animal Physiology*. New York: Dover, 1971. pp. 120–132. This is an unabridged version of a report originally prepared for the National Institute of Mental Health. An excellent and lively summation of the research and thinking about bio-rhythms.

278. John N. Ott, *Health and Light*. Old Greenwich, Connecticut: Devin-Adair, 1973. Using the techniques of time-lapse photography, this fascinating volume demonstrates the effects of light variations on plants and points to similar responses in animals and people.

279. Robert O. Becker, "The Effect of Magnetic Fields Upon the Central Nervous System," *Biological Effects of Magnetic Fields*, Vol. 2, pp. 207–214.

280. Howard Friedman, Robert O. Becker and Charles H. Bachman, "Psychiatric Ward Behavior and Geophysical Parameters," *Nature*, Vol. 205, March 13, 1965, pp. 1050–1052.

281. Howard Friedman, Robert O. Becker and Charles H. Bachman, "Effect of Magnetic Fields on Reaction Time Performance," *Nature*, Vol. 213, March 4, 1967, pp. 949–950.

282. Michel Gauquelin, *The Scientific Basis of Astrology*. New York: Stein and Day, 1969. pp. 198–211. Gauquelin is the foremost scientific student of astrological correlations. He is presently doing research at the Psychophysiological Laboratory at Strasbourg University in France. Tchijewsky's work is not to my knowledge available, in English.

283. *Ibid.*, pp. 211–221. Further information is available in G. Piccardi, *The Chemical Basis of Medical Climatology*. Springfield, Ill.: Charles C. Thomas, 1963.

284. *Ibid.*

285. *Ibid.* pp. 222–231. For further reference Gauquelin cites Takata's article in *Helvetica Medica Acta*, 1950.

286. *Ibid.*, pp. 183–184.

287. J. H. Nelson, *Cosmic Patterns: Their Influence on Man and His Communication.* Washington, D. C.: American Federation of Astrologers, 1974. Nelson himself is not an astrologer and this pamphlet deals purely with the planetary influences on radio propagation—a subject which he has explored for nearly thirty years. The pamphlet is available from Amer. Fed. Astrol., 6 Library Court, S. E., Washington, D. C. 20003.

288. F. A. Brown, J. Woodland Hastings and John D. Palmer, *The Biological Clock—Two Views.* New York: Academic Press, 1970. In addition to discussing Brown's evidence of biological rhythms being tied to astronomical cycles, this book discusses the theory of an internally controlled timing mechanism. Both views are necessary for an overall understanding of bio-rhythms.

289. G. Edgar Folk, *Environmental Physiology.* Philadelphia: Lea and Febiger, 1966. p. 62.

290. Michel Gauquelin, *op. cit.*, p. 48. Gauquelin refers to the following article: J. H. Heller and A. A. Teixeira-Pinto, "A New Physical Method of Creating Chromosomal Abberations," *Nature*, No. 4645, 1959.

291. Peter Tompkins and Christopher Bird, *The Secret Life of Plants.* New York: Harper and Row, 1973. pp. 54–55. The authors have apparently read Gurvitch's work in the original Russian. This book is highly informative and a valuable source of references. However, it must be read with a critical eye as it delves into controversial areas with a predisposed theoretical orientation. (The same caution is warranted for nearly all texts—including the present one!)

292. V. P. Kaznecheyev, S. P. Shurin, L. P. Mikhailova and N. V. Ignatovich, "Apparent Information Transfer Between Two Groups of Cells," *Psychoenergetic Systems*, Vol. 1, December 1974, p. 37. This new and very worthwhile journal is published in New York and London by Gordon and Breach. Edited by Stanley Krippner and an international team of scholars, the publication focuses on "acupuncture, brain research, bioelectric fields, Kirlian photography, unorthodox healing, bio-communication, quasi-sensory communication, psi-process, subliminal perception. paraphysics and psychokinetic events."

293. Shiela Ostrander and Lynn Schroeder, *Handbook of PSI Discoveries.* New York: G. P. Putnam's Sons, 1974. p. 93. This is an excellent resource book. The authors cite the following reference: B. N. Tarusov, I. N. Ivanov, Yu. M. Petrusevich, *Superweak Luminescence of Biological Systems.* Moscow: Moscow State University, 1967.

294. Ostrander and Schroeder, *Handbook*, pp. 94–95.

295. W. Joines and L. Burton, "Electromagnetic Emission and Possible Cellular Communication," Parapsychological Association Convention, New York, 1974.

296. V. M. Inyushin, "Report No. 5," *Journal of Paraphysics*, Vol. 6, No. 5, 1972.

297. Harold Saxton Burr, *The Fields of Life.* New York: Ballantine, 1972. p. 62. This book, describing thirty years of Dr. Burr's research into Life Fields, contains a complete bibliography of his scientific publications. One ecstatic reviewer, Colin Wilson, suggests that Burr's book "could be just as important as *The Origin of Species.*"

298. *Ibid.* pp. 104–119.

299. Leonard J. Ravitz, "Electro-magnetic Field Monitering of Changing State-Function, Including Hypnotic States," *The Fields of Life*, pp. 173–185. This paper was also published in the *Journal of the American Society of Psychosomatic Dentistry and Medicine*, Vol. 17, No. 4, 1970.

300. Burr, *op. cit.*, pp. 85–103.

301. Robert O. Becker, "Stimulation of Partial Limb Regeneration in Rats," *Nature*, Vol. 235, January 14, 1972, pp. 109–111.

302. Robert O. Becker, "Electromagnetic Forces and The Life Process," *Technology Review*, Vol. 75, No. 2, Dec. 1972.

303. D. H. Wilson, *et. al.*, "The Effects of Pulsed Electromagnetic Energy on Peripheral Nerve Regeneration," *Annals of the New York Academy of Sciences*, 1974, pp. 575–585.

304. Becker, "Stimulation . . ." Becker cites the following reference: A. N. Studitsky, R. P. Zhenevskaya, and O. N. Rumyantseva, *Cesk. Morphol.*, 4, 331 (1956). Becker also claims that Studitsky's work has been confirmed and extended by B. M. Carlson, *Amer. J. Anat*, 128, 21, (1970).

305. S. D. Kirlian and V. Kh. Kirlian, "Photography by Means of High-Frequency Currents," *The Kirlian Aura*, ed. by Stanley Krippner and Daniel Rubin. New York: Doubleday, 1974. pp. 35–50. This book, incidently, seems to be the best anthology of Kirlian photography research and theory currently available. The article also appears in *Psychoenergetic Systems*, Vol. 1, December 1974, pp. 21–25.

306. William A. Tiller, "A Technical Report on Some Psychoenergetic Devices," *A. R. E. Journal*, March 1972, pp. 81–88. This report by a competent American physicist-engineer provides details of the Soviet equipment. It is available from the Association for Research and Enlightenment, P. O. Box 595, Virginia Beach, Va. (75¢)

307. H. S. Dakin, *High-Voltage Photography*. San Francisco, 1975. If you're thinking of building your own equipment, or otherwise engaging in Kirlian photography work, this book is essential. If you can't locate it in any bookstores, you can order it from the author for $5.00 plus shipping costs ($1.00 US, $2.00 foreign). Write to 3101 Washington St., San Francisco, Ca. 94118.

308. High-voltage photography equipment may be purchased from the Edmund Scientific Co., 800 Edscorp Building, Barrington, New Jersey 08007. Dakin's book is also available from this source.

309. Kirlian and Kirlian, *op. cit.*

310. *Ibid.* p. 45.

311. G. K. Poock and P. W. Sparks, *A Description of the Methodology used in the Poock-Sparks Technique of Motion-Picture Kirlian Photography*, G. K. Poock, 22374 Ortega Drive, Salinas, Ca. 93901, 1974.

312. Shiela Ostrander and Lynn Schroeder, *Psychic Discoveries Behind The Iron Curtain.* New York: Bantam, 1971. pp. 206–211. The use of Kirlian photography for human diagnosis comes from an unfootnoted quote by Dr. S. M. Pavlenko, Chairman of the Physiology-Pathology Department of the First Moscow Medical Institute. Some parapsychologists such as J. G. Pratt have criticized PDBIC for failing to distinguish between popular pseudoscientific notions and solid research findings. While their journalistic work is of enormous social and scientific value, the reader is urged to use a critical eye to sort the wheat from the chaff.

313. Thelma Moss and Kendall Johnson, "Bioplasma or Corona Discharge?" *The Kirlian Aura*, pp. 62–67.

314. Steve Aaronson, "Pictures of an Unknown Aura," *The Sciences*, Vol. 14, No. 1, January 1974.

315. Thelma Moss, John Hubacher and Francis Saba, "Visual Evidence of Bioenergetic Interactions Between People?" American Psychological Association Convention, New Orleans, May 1974. This paper can be ordered by sending a check for $1.00, payable to *Radiation Field Photography Research*, to Dr. Thelma Moss, Neuropsychiatric Institute, UCLA, Los Angeles 90024. A number of other interesting papers and slides are available from Dr. Moss's laboratory at a nominal cost.

316. Ostrander and Schroeder, *PDBIC*, p. 223.

317. E. Douglas Dean, "High-voltage Radiation Photography of a Healer's Fingers," *The Kirlian Aura*.

318. Jeffrey Mishlove and Douglas Dean, "From Parapsychology to Paraphysics," *Mind's Ear* radio program, broadcast on KPFA-FM in Berkeley, California, July 5, 1973. Available on tape from the Pacifica Tape Library, 5316 Venice Blvd., Los Angeles, Ca. 90019. Many other *Mind's Ear* programs are also available.

319. Thelma Moss, Kendall Johnson, Jack Grey, John Hubacher, Roger MacDonald and Francis Saba, "Bioenergetics

332

and Radiation Photography," First International Conference on Psychotronics, Prague, 1973.

320. *Ibid.*

321. *Ibid.*

322. *Ibid.*

323. Stanley Krippner, "Sentics, Kirlian Photography and Psychosomatic Illness," *Psychoenergetic Systems*, Vol. 1, Dec. 1974, pp. 31–34. For further details on finger pressure research, we are referred to the following articles: M. Clynes, "Biocybernetics of the Dynamic Communication of Emotions and Qualities," *Science*, 170, 1970, pp. 764–765. M. Clynes, "Sentic Cycles: The Seven Passions at Your Fingertips," *Psychology Today*, May 1972.

324. W. A. Tiller, D. G. Boyers and H. S. Dakin, *Towards a Kirlian Device for Monitering Physiological States—Part I*. Stanford University: Department of Materials Science, 1974. This paper can be ordered by sending a check for $4.00 to Dr. Tiller, Dept. of Materials Science, Stanford University, Palo Alto, Ca.

325. David G. Boyers and William Tiller, *The Colors in Kirlian Photography—Fact or Artifact?* Stanford University: Dept. of Materials Science, 1974. Available from the authors for $4.50.

326. Larry Burton, William Joines and Brad Stevens, "The Physical Mechanisms of Kirlian Photography," Duke University, Durham, North Carolina, Department of Electrical Engineering.

327. William A. Tiller, "Energy Fields and the Human Body: Part I," *ARE Medical Symposium on Mind Body Relationships in the Disease Process*, Phoenix, Arizona, January 1972. This paper is available from the author for $2.00.

328. William A. Tiller, "Some Energy Field Observations of Man and Nature," *The Kirlian Aura*, p. 122.

329. John Hubacher and Thelma Moss, *The "Phantom Leaf Effect" As Revealed Through Kirlian Photography*. UCLA Center for the Health Sciences, 1974. This paper can be ordered from the authors for $1.00.

330. Thelma Moss, Ph.D., *The Probability of the Impossible*. Los Angeles: J. P. Tarcher, 1974. pp. 54–58. This lively book documents the many research activities of Dr. Moss, a former broadway actress. It is particularly valuable for her firsthand accounts of her travels in the Soviet Union and Czechoslovakia as well as the inside story of her own laboratory activities.

331. Clark Dugger, John Hubacher, Thelma Moss and Francis Saba, "The 'Phantom Leaf,' Acupuncture, and Altered States of Consciousness," Second International Psychotronics Conference, Monaco, 1975.

332. Larry Burton, William Joines and Brad Stevens, "Kirlian Photography and its Relevance to Parapsychological Research," Parapsychological Association Convention, New York, 1974. Also presented before the Symposium of the Institute of Electronic and Electrical Engineers, November 1974.

333. V. M. Inyushin, "Biological Plasma of Human and Animal Organisms," Symposium of Psychotronics, Prague, September 1970. Published by the Paraphysical Laboratory, Downton, Wiltshire, England.

334. *Ibid.*

335. Wilhelm Reich, *The Cancer Biopathy, Vol. II of The Discovery of The Orgone*. New York: Farrar, Straus and Girous, 1973. pp. 15–21. This book, the major volume in which Reich describes his orgone research, contains over 70 microphotographs.

336. *Ibid.*, pp. 108–142.

337. Wilhelm Reich, *History of the Discovery of Life Energy—The Einstein Affair*. Rangeley, Maine: Orgone Institute Press, 1953. A documentation of the original correspondence between Reich and Einstein.

338. W. Edward Mann, *Orgone, Reich and Eros*. New York: Simon and Schuster, 1973. Mann is a professor of sociology at York University in Toronto, Ontario. His book is the major document tracing the scientific impact of Reich's work within a sociological framework which includes all research into life energies. In the summer of 1974, Mann organized the first conference of scientists working with neo-Reichian concepts.

339. Reich, *The Cancer Biopathy*. pp. 23–25.

340. Thelma Moss, *et al.*, "Bioenergetics and Radiation Photography."

341. Bernard Grad, "Orgone Treatment of Cancerous Rats," Esalen Institute Symposium on Reich and Orgone, San Francisco, August 1974.

342. John F. Thie and Mary Marks, *Touch for Health*. Santa Monica, Ca.: DeVorss, 1973.

343. Jacques de Langre, *The First Book of Do-In*. Hollywood: Happiness Press, 1971.

344. J. F. Chaves and T. X. Barber, "Acupuncture Analgesia: A Six-Factor Theory," *Psychoenergetic Systems*, Vol. 1, 1974, pp. 11–21.

345. Joan Steen Wilentz, *The Senses of Man*. New York: Thomas Crowell, 1968. pp. 89–109.

346. Felix Mann, "The Probable Neurophysiological Mechanism of Acupuncture," *Transcript of the Acupuncture Symposium*. Los Altos, Ca.: Academy of Parapsychology and Medicine, 1972. pp. 23–31.

347. *Ibid.*

348. William A. Tiller, "Some Physical Characteristics of Acupuncture Points and Meridians," *Transcript of the Acupuncture Symposium*. Tiller makes reference to the following papers: Kim J. Bong Han, *Democratic People's Republic of Korea Academy of Sciences*, 1963, No. 5; *Proceedings Academy of Kungrak of DPRK*, 1965, No. 2 (Medical Science Press, Pongyang, Korea); and S. Fujiwara, *Ido no Nippon*, Nos. 268–275, Japan, April 1967.

349. Dr. Hiroshi Motoyama, *Chakra, Nadi of Yoga and Meridian Points of Acupuncture*. Tokyo: Institute of Religious Psychology, 1972. pp. 15–17. Motoyama provides the following source: Yoshio Nagahama and Masaaki Maruyama, *Studies on Keiraku*. Kyorinshoin Co., Ltd.

350. Tiller, "Some Physical Characteristics . . ." Tiller refers to private communications received from Adamenko in 1971.

351. Kendall Johnson and Thelma Moss, "A Possible Technology of Acupuncture," Dimensions of Healing Symposium, UCLA Extension, 1972.

352. Victor Adamenko, "Electrodynamics of Living Systems," *Journal of Paraphysics*, Vol. 4, No. 4, 1970, pp. 113–121.

353. Tiller, "Some physical characteristics . . ."

354. Motayama, *op. cit.* This research, while innovative and interesting, will require further verification before it will find western acceptance. There is no indication, for example, of the use of experimental controls or blinds. Even under rigid conditions, it is difficult for scientists to accept research studies which confirm somebody's pre-existing religious beliefs.

355. Ostrander and Schroeder, *PDBIC*. pp. 226–227.

356. Ostrander and Schroder, *Handbook*. pp. 125–126. The authors refer us to *Bioenergetic Questions* (translations into English of Soviet papers presented in a 1969 conference in Alma-Ata) available from the Southern California Society for Psychical Research, 170 South Beverly Drive, Room 314, Beverly Hills, Ca. 90212. $15. Also see V. M. Inyushin, "The Problem of Bioplasm and Resonance Stimulation," *Problems of the Biodynamics and Bioenergetics of the Organism Under Normal Conditions and In Pathology*, materials of the Republic Conference, Alma-Ata, May 1971.

357. Thelma Moss and Kendall Johnson, "Biophysical Aspects of Acupuncture Points," *Advances in Neurology*, ed. by J. Bonica, M.D.

358. Thelma Moss, *et. al.*, "Photographic Evidence of Acupuncture Point Stimulation," UCLA, November 1973. Available from the author for $1.00.

359. Dr. John J. Bonica, "Summary Statement," *Proceedings NIH Acupuncture Research Conference*, ed. by Howard P. Jenerick, Ph.D. Bethseda, Maryland: USDHEW Publication No. (NIH) 74–165, 1973. This report contains nearly fifty experimental studies on acupuncture.

360. Motoyama, *op. cit.*

361. Dr. Rammurti S. Mishra, *Yoga Sutras*. New York: Doubleday, 1973. pp. 295–296.

362. Lama Anagarika Govinda, *Foundations of Tibetan Mysticism*. New York: Samuel Weiser, 1969. p. 135. An excellent

exposition of the esoteric teachings underlying the great mantra, OM MANI PADME HUM.

363. C. W. Leadbeater, *The Chakras*. Wheaton, Ill.: Theosophical Publishing House, 1972. p. 1. Originally published in India in 1927, this book contains a perplexing combination of allegedly first-hand clairvoyant reports and Theosophical dogma. There are a number of remarkable illustrations. (see Color Plate 8).

364. *Ibid.*, pp. 4–5.

365. *Ibid.*, pp. 19–20. According to Leadbeater, *Theosophica Practica* was originally issued in 1696. The illustrations to the book were apparently added about 1720. A French translation, used by Leadbeater, was published in 1897 in the Bibliothèque Rosicrucienne (No. 4) by the Bibliothèque Charcornac, Paris.

366. Dr. Shafica Karagula, *Breakthrough to Creativity*. Santa Monica, Ca.: De Vorss, 1967. A highly readable book describing the unusual talents of a number of Karagula's anonymous subjects. It has been used as a textbook in political science courses as exemplifying a significant challenge to socially accepted versions of reality. Karagula exerts care in making her clinical observations, however she chose not to include important experimental data which would have put her findings on more solid ground.

367. Shafica Karagula, M.D., "Higher Sense Perception and New Dimensions of Creativity," American Psychiatric Association Convention, May 1974.

368. William A. Tiller, Ph.D., "Radionics, Radiesthesia and Physics," *The Varieties of Healing Experience*, Academy of Parapsychology and Medicine, October 1971. pp. 72–78. Available from the author for $1.50.

369. E. N. Santini, *Photographie des Effluves Humains*. Paris, 1896.

370. Max Heindel, *The Rosicrucian Cosmo-Conception*. Oceanside, Ca.: The Rosicrucian Fellowship, 1969. pp. 59–64. Originally published in 1909.

371. A. R. G. Owen and G. A. V. Morgan, "The Rim" Aura: An Optical Illusion—A Genuine but Non-psychic Perception," *New Horizons* Vol. 1, No. 3, January 1974, pp. 19–31.

372. A. R. G. Owen, "Generation of an 'Aura': A New Parapsychological Phenomenon," *New Horizons*, Vol. 1, No. 1, Summer 1972, pp. 14–23.

373. Yogi Ramacharaka, *Yogi Philosophy and Oriental Occultism*. Chicago: The Yogi Publication Society, 1931. pp. 64–66. Originally published in 1903, this book offers an entertaining and often useful outline of occult beliefs.

374. Charles T. Tart, "Concerning the Scientific Study of the Human Aura," *Journal SPR*, Vol. 46, No. 751, March 1972.

375. A. R. G. Owen, "Generation . . ." pp. 11–13.

376. Ray Stanford, "On Viewing the Aura," KPFA-FM and the Interdisciplinary Parapsychology Program of U. C., Berkeley, Parapsychology Symposium, February 1974. Available on tape from the Pacifica Tape Library, 5316 Venice Blvd., Los Angeles, Ca. 90019.

377. Thelma Moss, John Hubacher and Francis Saba, "Visual Evidence of Bioenergetic Interactions Between People?"

378. Thelma Moss, John Hubacher, Francis Saba and Kendall Johnson, "Kirlian Photography: An Electrical Artifact?" American Psychological Association, August 1974.

379. Thelma Moss, John Hubacher, and Francis Saba, "Anomalies in Kirlian Photography: Interactions Between People Reveal Curious 'Disappearances' and 'Merging' Phenomena," Second International Psychotronics Conference, Monaco, 1975.

380. C. S. Hall and G. Lindzey, *Theories of Personality*. New York: John Wiley and Sons, 1957. pp. 296–335. This book provides excellent summaries of many important psychological theories. Of particular interest is the classification of each theory according to its emphasis along each of eighteen different parameters (p. 548).

381. Stanley Krippner and Sally Ann Drucker, "Field Theory and Kirlian Photography: An Old Map for a New Territory," *The Kirlian Aura*.

382. Eileen Garrett, *Awareness*. New York: Helix Press, 1943. pp. 99–100. An eloquent, lyrical testimony by the founder of the Parapsychology Foundation.

383. Annie Besant and C. W. Leadbeater, *Thought Forms*. Wheaton, Ill.: Theosophical Publishing House, 1971. pp. 8–17. Originally published in 1901, this book is an outstanding classic of occult literature. Besant, a former mistress of George Bernard Shaw, became head of the international theosophical movement after the death of Madame Blavatsky.

384. Yogi Ramacharaka, *Yogi Philosophy*. pp. 73–90.

385. Michel Gauquelin, *Cosmic Influences on Human Behavior*, trans. by Joyce E. Clemow. New York: Stein and Day, 1973. This book is essential for anyone with an interest in astrology, as it builds upon solid empirical evidence.

386. Carl Gustav Jung, *Synchronicity: An Acausal Connecting Principle*. New York: Pantheon, 1955. pp. 60–94. Jung's arduous discussion of an important philosophical concept is illustrated by his astrology experiment.

387. John A. West and Jan G. Toonder, *The Case for Astrology*. Baltimore: Penguin Books, 1973. pp. 204–209. A good introduction to the history and theoretical background of astrology.

References (Section III)

1. Arthur M. Young, "Recollections," transcript of a seminar at the Institute for the Study of Consciousness, Berkeley, Fall 1973.

2. Arthur M. Young, *The Reflexive Universe*. New York, Delacorte, 1975..

3. Arthur M. Young, *The Geometry of Meaning*. New York, Delacorte, 1975.

4. H. Puthoff, R. Targ, "Information transmission under conditions of sensory shielding," *Nature*, Vol. 251, Oct. 18, 1974. pp. 602–607.

5. J. B. Hasted, D. J. Bohm, E. W. Bastin, B. O'Regan, J. G. Taylor, *Nature*, Vol. 254, April 10, 1975, pp. 470–473.

6. J. S. Bell, "On the Einstein Podolsky Rosen Paradox," *Physics*, Vol. 1, No. 3, 1964, pp. 195–200.

7. N. Herbert, "Crytographic approach to hidden variables," *American Journal of Physics*, Vol. 43, No. 4, April 1975, pp. 315–316. This paper presents a proof of Bell's theorem by considering error rates in binary message sequences. It also speculates about the possibility of faster-than-light signalling.

8. George Weissman, in private communication, has pointed out that faster-than-light signalling is possible (by way of the Einstein Rosen Podolsky effect) only if the sender can psychokinetically control the spin state of one part of a quantum system.

9. J. A. Wheeler, C. M. Patton, "Is Physics Legislated by Cosmogony," Joseph Henry Laboratories preprint, Princeton Univ., February 25, 1975.

10. J. S. Bell, *Nature* Vol. 248, March 22, 1974, p. 297.

11. M. Gardner, "On the contradictions of time travel," *Scientific American*, May 1974, pp. 120–123.

12. S. D. Drell, "Electron-Positron Annihilation and the New Particles," *Scientific American*, June 1975.

13. J. F. Clauser, M. A. Horne, "Experimental consequences of objective local theories," *Physical Review D*, Vol. 10, No. 2, July 15, 1974.

14. H. P. Stapp, "Theory of Reality," Lawrence Berkeley Laboratory Report No. 3837, April 29, 1975.

15. F. J. Tipler, "Rotating cylinders and the possibility of global causality violation," *Physical Review D*, Vol. 9, No. 8, April 15, 1974.

16. B. Carter, "Global structure of the Kerr family of gravitational fields," *Physical Review*, 174, 1968, pp. 1559–1571.

17. E. Nagel, J. P. Newman, "Göedel's Proof," *Scientific American*, June 1956.

18. T. de Chardin, *The Phenomenon of Man*. New York: Harper and Row, 1959.

19. C. Suares, *The Cipher of Genesis*. Berkeley: Shamballa, 1970, and New York: Bantum Books, 1973.

20. E. Wigner, *Symmetries and Reflections*. Indiana University, 1967, and Cambridge, Mass.: M.I.T. Press paperback edition, 1970.

21. B. Josephson, "Possible connections between psychic phenomena and quantum mechanics," *New Horizons* January 1975, pp. 224–226.

22. L. Brillouin, *Science and Information Theory*. New York: Academic Press, 1956.

23. L. L. Whyte, *Aspects of Form*. Indiana University Press, 1971.

24. R. P. Feynman, "Cargo Cult Science," *Engineering and Science* (California Institute of Technology) June 1974, p. 10.

25. P. A. Schilpp, *Albert Einstein Philosopher Scientist*. New York: Harper Torchbook, 1959. p. 85.

26. D. Hawkins, *The Language of Nature*. San Francisco: Freeman, 1964. See especially the section, "Information, Order, and Free Energy" on pp. 207–216.

27. J. F. Clauser, A sign in his laboratory reads: "We have met the Hidden Variables, and they is us!"

28. Martin Gardner, *Fads and Fallacies in the Name of Science*. New York: Dover, 1957. Unfortunately, Gardner takes more pleasure in sarcastic pokes than in carefully reasoned discussion, thus detracting from his own purpose.

29. C. E. M. Hansel, *ESP: A Scientific Evaluation*. New York: Scribners, 1966.

30. Rhea A. White and Laura A. Dale, *Parapsychology: Sources of Information*. Metuchen, N. J.: The Scarecrow Press, 1973. Compiled under the auspices of the ASPR, this book is a thorough bibliography of important books in the field and includes references to book reviews.

31. M. Billig, "Positive and Negative Experimental Psi Results in Psychology and Parapsychology," *Journal SPR*, Vol. 46, No. 753, 1972, pp. 136–142.

32. E. G. Boring, "Introduction," *ESP: A Scientific Evaluation*.

33. J. B. Rhine, "A New Case of Experimenter Unreliability," *Journal of Parapsychology*, Vol. 38, No. 2, June 1974, pp. 215–225.

34. Personal communication with the researchers.

35. J. B. Hasted, D. J. Bohm, E. W. Bastin and B. O'Regan, "Letter," *Nature*, Vol. 254, April 10, 1975.

36. Personal communication with Honorton.

37. Charles Reynolds and David Eisendrath, *Popular Photography*, October 1967.

38. Dr. Jule Eisenbud, "Letter," *Journal ASPR*, Spring 1975.

39. David R. Saunders and Roger R. Harkins, *UFOs? Yes!*. New York: World Publishing, 1968. p. 243.

40. William A. Nolen, *Healing: A Doctor in Search of a Miracle*. New York: Random House, 1974.

41. John Beloff, "Belief and Doubt," *Research in Parapsychology 1972*. Metuchen, N. J.: The Scarecrow Press, 1973. pp. 189–200.

42. V. P. Zinchenko, A. N. Leontiev, B. F. Lomov, and A. R. Luria, "Parapsychology: Fiction or Fact?" *Soviet Psychology*, 1974, No. 4, pp. 3–20.

43. Milan Ryzl, "Parapsychology in Eastern Europe," *Parapsychology Today: A Geographic View*. New York: Parapsychology Foundation, 1973. pp. 88–100. This volume comprehensively treats global research.

44. Louisa E. Rhine, *PSI*. New York: Harper and Row, 1975.

45. Dion Fortune, *Psychic Self Defense*. London: The Aquarian Press, 1930.

46. J. B. Rhine, "Some Exploratory Tests in Dowsing," *Journal of Parapsychology*, Vol. 14, No. 4, December 1950, pp. 278–286.

47. K. Roberts, *Henry Gross and His Divining Rod*. New York: Doubleday, 1951.

48. K. Roberts, *The Seventh Sense*. New York: Doubleday, 1953.

49. K. Roberts, *Water Unlimited*. New York: Doubleday, 1957.

50. Berthold E. Schwarz, *A Psychiatrist Looks at ESP*. New York: New American Library, 1965. Originally published as *Psycho-Dynamics*, the book contains excellent in-depth studies of three different psychics.

51. Chris Bird and Jeffrey Mishlove, "Soviet Parapsychology," *Mindspace* radio broadcast, May 1975.

52. Stanley Krippner and James Hickman, "West Meets East," *Psychic Magazine*, June 1974.

53. "News Ambit," *Psychic Magazine*, December 1974.

54. Edgar D. Mitchell, "An ESP Test from Apollo 14," *Journal of Parapsychology*, Vol. 35, No. 2, 1971.

55. Robert Brier and Walter V. Tyminski, "Psi Application," *Progress in Parapsychology*, ed. by J. B. Rhine. Durham, N. C.: Parapsychology Press, 1973.

56. Ostrander and Schroeder, *PDBIC*.

57. Milan Ryzl, *ESP in the Modern World*. San Jose: Milan Ryzl, 1972. Available from the author, P.O. Box 9459, Westgate Station, San Jose, Ca. 95117. A fine firsthand account of Ryzl's adventure.

58. J. N. Emerson, "Intuitive Archeology: A Psychic Approach," *New Horizons*, Vol. 1, No. 3, January 1974.

59. J. N. Emerson, "Intuitive Archeology: The Argillite Carving," Department of Anthropology, University of Toronto, March 1974.

60. J. N. Emerson, "Intuitive Archeology: A Developing Approach," Department of Anthropology, University of Toronto, November 1974.

61. Paul Tabori, *Crime and the Occult*. New York: Taplinger, 1974.

62. *Ibid.*

63. *Ibid.*

64. M. B. Dykshorn and Russell H. Felton, *My Passport Says Clairvoyant*. New York: Hawthorne, 1974.

65. "Interview: Irene Hughes," *Psychic Magazine*, December 1971.

66. Tabori, *op. cit.*

67. *Ibid.*

68. Tompkins and Bird, *The Secret Life of Plants*.

69. Paul Sauvin and Jeff Mishlove, "ESP Communication with Plants," *Mindspace* radio broadcast, May 1975.

70. Normal Shealy and Jeffrey Mishlove, "Psychic Diagnosis," *Mindspace* radio broadcast, May 1975.

71. Douglas Dean, John Mihalsky, Shiela Ostrander and Lynn Schroeder, *Executive ESP*. Englewood Cliffs, New Jersey: Prentice-Hall, 1974.

72. Rudolf Steiner, *Knowledge of the Higher Worlds and Its Attainment*. New York: Anthroposophic Press, 1967.

73. George Devereux, ed., *Psychoanalysis and the Occult*. New York: International Universities Press, 1953. Thirty-one masterful essays by a number of well-known analyists.

74. Trevor Ravenscroft, *The Spear of Destiny*. New York: Bantam, 1973.

75. Rex Stanford, "Scientific, Ethical and Clinical Problems in the 'Training' of Psi Ability," American Association for the Advancement of Science annual meeting, New York, January 1975.

76. Bob Brier, Barry Savits and Gertrude Schmeidler, "Experimental Tests of Silva Mind Control Graduates," Parapsychological Association Convention, Charlottesville, Va., 1973.

77. Alan Vaughan, "Investigation of Silva Mind Control Claims," Parapsychological Association Convention, 1973.

335

78. Paul Marshall Allen, *The Writings and Lectures of Rudolf Steiner*. New York: Whittier Books, 1956. This bibliography runs 140 pages.

79. Robert Wuthnow and Charles Y. Glock, "God in the Gut," *Psychology Today*, November 1974.

80. *Fundamentals of Progress: Scientific Research on Transcendental Meditation*. Los Angeles: MIU Press, 1975. This pamphlet contains a number of well-documented and now classical studies as well as some questionable reports, still unpublished in the scientific literature.

81. Karlis Osis and E. Bokert, "ESP and Changed States of Consciousness Induced by Meditation," *Journal ASPR*, Vol. 65, 1971, pp. 17–65.

82. *Maharishi International University Catalogue, 1974–1975*. Los Angeles: MIU Press, 1974. Perhaps the most beautifully designed and written course catalogue I have ever seen.

83. A. R. G. Owen, *Psychic Mysteries of the North*. New York: Harper and Row, 1975. This book documents the remarkable discoveries made by Canadians in the last five years.

84. Robert Masters and Jean Houston, *Mind Games*. New York: Viking Press, 1972.

85. Robert Masters and Jean Houston, *Varieties of Psychedelic Experience*. New York: Holt, Rinehart and Winston, 1966.

Acknowledgments

The publisher wishes to thank the following for permission to reprint selections in this book. Any inadvertent omission will be corrected in future printings on notification to the publisher.

John Wiley and Sons for material from Kilton Stewart, "Dream Theory in Malaya," *Altered States of Consciousness* ed. by Charles Tart.

Parapsychology Review for material taken from Adrian Boshier, "African Apprenticeship," July 1974.

Columbia University Press for material from *Sources of Indian Tradition*, ed. by Wm. de Bary, 1958.

Princeton University Press for material from *The I Ching: Or Book of Changes*, trans. by Richard Wilhelm, rendered into English by Cary F. Baynes, Bollingen Series XIX (copyright © 1950 and 1967 by Bollingen Foundation).

Oxford University Press for material from W. Y. Evan Wentz, *The Tibetan Book of the Dead*.

The Regents of the University of California for material from Wayne Schumaker, *The Occult Sciences in the Renaissance* originally published by the University of California Press.

Manley Palmer Hall for material from *The Secret Teachings of All Ages*.

Idries Shah for material from *Oriental Magic*, published by E. P. Dutton and Co., Inc., New York, 1973 edition, pp. 61–2.

Harper and Row for material from Aldous Huxley, *The Perennial Philosophy*.

The *Journal of Parapsychology* for material from Helmut Schmidt, "PK Tests with a High Speed Random Number Generator," December 1973: "A Quantum Mechanical Random Number Generator for Psi Tests," 1970; and "A Quantum Process in Psi Testing," *Progress in Parapsychology*.

Parapsychology Foundation for material from H. C. Berendt, "Parapsychology in Israel," *Parapsychology Today: A Geographic View*, ed. by Allan Angoff and Betty Shapin, Copyright 1973; and Inge Strauch, "Medical Aspects of 'Mental Healing,'" *International Journal of Parapsychology*, Vol. V, 1963. Copyright parapsychology Foundation, 1963.

C. W. Daniel Co., Ltd, London, for material from Vernon Wethered, *Medical Radiesthesia and Radionics*.

Psychic Magazine, 680 Beach St., San Francisco, Ca. 94109, for material from Robert N. Miller, "The Positive Effect of Prayer on Plants," April 1972: "Interview with Ray Stanford," April 1974; and Jean Shinoda Bolen, M. D., "Meditation in the Treatment of Cancer," August 1973.

William Morrow and Company for material from Jule Eisenbud, M. D. *The World of Ted Serios*, Copyright 1966, 1967 by Jule Eisenbud.

E. P. Dutton and Co. for material from Anne Dooley, *Every Wall a Door*, Copyright © 1973 by Anne Dooley. Forst published in 1974 by E. P. Dutton.

Harper and Row for material from Peter Tompkins and Chris Bird, *The Secret Life of Plants*, Ambrose and Olga Worrall, *Explore Your Psychic World*; and Louisa E. Rhine, *Psi*, 1975.

The Estate of Eileen J. Barrett for material from Eileen Garrett, *Awareness*, Copyright 1943.

Doubleday and Company for material from Andrija Puharich, *Uri: A Journal of the Mystery of Uri Geller*, Copyright © 1974 by Lab Nine, Ltd.

Gordon and Breach for material from *Galaxies of Life*, ed. by Stanley Krippner and Danial Rubin, 1973.

Dr. Thelma Moss for material from "Bioenergetics and Radiation Photography," International Psychotronics Conference, Prague, 1973.

Theosophical Publishing House, Adyar, Madras, India for material from C. W. Leadbeater, *The Chakras*.

From the book, *Psychic Discoveries Behind the Iron Curtain* by Ostrander and Schroeder. © 1970 by Sheila Ostrander and Lynn Schroeder. Published by Prentice-Hall, Inc., Englewood Cliffs, New Jersey.

From the book, *The Seth Material* by Jane Roberts. © 1970 by Jane Roberts. Published by Prentice-Hall, Inc., Englewood Cliffs, New Jersey.

From William G. Roll, "Poltergeists," in *Encyclopedia of the Unexplained*, ed. by Richard Cavandish. Copyright 1974 by Rainbird Reference Books Ltd. Used with permission of McGraw-Hill Book Company.

Rudolf Steiner, *Goethe As Scientist*.

Julian Press for material from Rammurti S. Mishra, *The Textbook of Yoga Psychology*.

New Scientist for material from Dr. Albert Krueger, "Are Negative Ions Good for You?" June 14, 1973.

Samuel Weiser, Inc. for material from Muldoon and Carrington, *The Projection of the Astral Body*; and Lama Anagarika Govinda, *Foundations of Tibetan Mysticism*.

Regents of the University of California for material from *The Dream and Human Societies*, ed. by G. Grunebaum and Rober Callois.

ABOUT THE AUTHOR

Jeffrey Mishlove is the first student at the University of California, Berkeley, (or at any accredited university in the United States) to create an interdisciplinary, doctoral major in parapsychology. In fact, *The Roots of Consciousness* serves as partial fulfillment of his examination requirements. For over six years he has lead groups and taught courses in psychic exploration at a number of colleges and universities. He has also produced more than three hundred radio programs—approaching psychic consciousness from scientific, social, experiential, artistic, spiritual and humorous perspectives—for KPFA-FM, Pacifica listener-sponsored radio in Berkeley, California, and KSAN-FM, Metromedia radio in San Francisco. His current interests focus on development and application of psi abilities.

Index